THE PSYCHOLOGY OF WOMEN: FUTURE DIRECTIONS IN RESEARCH

THE PSYCHOLOGY
OF WOMEN:
Future Directions in Research

Edited By

Julia A. Sherman
Women's Research Institute of Wisconsin, Inc.

&

Florence L. Denmark
Hunter College & The Graduate School
City University of New York

Psychological Dimensions, Inc.
New York, N.Y.
A Wes-Den Property

©Copyright 1978 by Wes-Den, N.Y.

Printed in the United States of America

1987654321

Library of Congress Catalog Card Number 78-31824

ISBN 0-88437-009-7

Library of Congress Cataloging in Publication Data
Main entry under title:

The Psychology of women.

Sponsored by the Committee on Women of the American Psychological Association, the National Institute of Mental Health, and the Ford Foundation.
Bibliography: p.
Includes index.
1. Women--Social conditions--Congresses.
2. Women--Sexual behavior--Congresses. 3. Women--Psychology--Congresses. 4. Women--Employment--Congresses. I. Sherman, Julia Ann, 1934-
II. Denmark, Florence. III. American Psychological Association. Committee on Women. IV. United States.

Library of Congress Cataloging in Publication Data

National Institute of Mental Health. V. Ford Foundation.
HQ1106.1978.P78   301.41'2   78-31824
ISBN 0-88437-009-7

DEDICATION

To Leta Hollingsworth, pioneer in the nexus of psychological science and women.

PREFACE

In November of 1973 the American Psychological Association Committee on Women, chaired at that time by Martha Mednick, facilitated the formation of a Task Force for a Conference on Women's Research Needs in Psychology. Members of the Task Force were Martha Mednick, Judy Long Laws, Janet Spence, and Sandra Tangri, with Florence Denmark and Julia Sherman as co-chairs. The Task Force met to plan a small conference during which commissioned papers would be discussed. This conference was eventually funded by the National Institute of Mental Health and the Ford Foundation. We would particularly like to thank Betty Pickett and Joyce Lazar of NIMH, and Mariam Chamberlain of the Ford Foundation for their interest and assistance.

The conference, entitled "New Directions for Research on Women," was held in Madison, Wisconsin, on May 31 through June 2, 1975, at the Wisconsin Center of the University of Wisconsin under the auspices of the Department of Curriculum and Instruction of the School of Education. We would like to thank Norman Greenfield of the Wisconsin Psychiatric Institute and the Women's Research Institute of Wisconsin, Inc., particularly Corinne Koufacos and Jacque Macaulay, for their assistance in planning and for arranging local facilities. Our thanks are also offered to Wendy McKenna and Susan McCandless for serving as conference auditors, and to Susan McCandless for her work in editing the tapes.

Julia A. Sherman
Florence L. Denmark

LIST OF CONFERENCE PARTICIPANTS

Helen Astin
UCLA

Sandra L. Bem
Cornell University

Jessie Bernard
Honoris Causa
Pennsylvania State University

Maxine Bernstein
Empire State College, N.Y.

Jeanne H. Block
University of California @ Berkeley

Robert Brannon
Brooklyn College
City University of New York

E. Kitch Childs
Berkeley, California

Florence L. Denmark
Hunter College & The Graduate School
City University of New York

Irene H. Frieze
University of Pittsburgh

Janice Porter Gump
Silver Spring, MD.

Ravenna Helson
University of California @ Berkeley

E. Mavis Hetherington
University of Virginia

Judith Long Laws
Syracuse, N.Y.

Martha Mednick
Howard University

Wendy McKenna
Sarah Lawrence College

Karen Ericksen Paige
University of California @ Berkeley

Mary Brown Parlee
Graduate School
City University of New York

Morton Perlmutter
University of Wisconsin @ Madison

Joseph Pleck
Wellesley College

Eli Rubinstein
State University of New York @ Stony Brook

Nancy Felipe Russo
American Psychological Association

Pepper Schwartz
University of Washington @ Seattle

Julia A. Sherman
Women's Research Institute of Wisconsin, Inc.

Janet T. Spence
The University of Texas @ Austin

Sandra Tangri
U.S. Commission on Civil Rights

Rhoda K. Unger
Montclair State College

TABLE OF CONTENTS

Table of Contents (Cont.)

PUBLISHER'S STATEMENT

This book is experimental in two ways.

The first is that the editors, many of the authors, and the publisher feel that the almost exclusive use of male pronouns is a tremendous linguistic "put-down" for women, which results in the psychological internal and external barriers faced by most women. This harms both women and men, and prevents them from becoming truly androgenous persons. Clearly, this is not the only factor that keeps people from becoming androgenous, but it is an important one.

To overcome these linguistic barriers we tried to develop neuter pronouns, as explained by the Editorial Note on page viii.

The usage of tey, ter, and tem is only used when the sex of the individual is not known. The traditional use of his/her is used when gender is known. To me, however, this does not go far enough. In the opinion of the Publisher, and others associated with this book, the only effective way to begin to attempt to abolish the linguistic gender barrier is to completely abolish all sex referenced pronouns. Admittedly, there probably is a better system of pronouns that can be used, but as of this date, the tey, ter, and tem system seems to be a perfectly good one to use. It is not used in this book exclusively—the way I would like to see it used. This is unfortunate, but given a little time, maybe others besides PDI, will again utilize the system. Lets hope so.

The second experiment in this book lies in its design. The book was designed to accommodate all illustrative material (charts, graphs, tables, figures, etc.) but on the text pages a very large white space was allocated on the bottom of each page. This was done to provide note-making space for the reader. This still did not diminish the normal 400 word-count per page. The page was simply designed differently to give the user a space that can be utilized by ter. If you, the reader, likes this idea, then please let us know so we can use it in future publications.

Robert W. Wesner
President & Publisher
December, 1978

EDITOR'S NOTE

The new pronouns *tey, ter, tem,* have been substituted for the pronouns *he-she, his-her, her-him,* throughout this book. The editors feel that the practice of utilizing neutered pronouns is something we should all begin to strive for.

OVERVIEW

In the wake of the intense social change and questioning of the 1960s, social scientists have become increasingly aware that seemingly objective scientific areas need to be reevaluated in the light of recent social criticism. The need is probably nowhere more apparent than in the area of the psychology of women. Although conferences are commonly sponsored to evaluate the status of research in fast-moving areas, the New Directions conference was the first to be sponsored solely in the area of the psychology of women.

Psychology, as it relates to women, has been permeated with unexamined biases which have distorted scientific research and social progress. In addition to these implicit biases, the everyday practices of academic psychologists have further served to perpetuate the dearth of knowledge about women's psychology. For instance, many personality scales are standardized on male populations, and psychological theories are usually conceived by men with men in mind. Women are not even used as subjects as often as men. Whole areas of inquiry of importance to women are not researched at all—often they are not even considered of sufficient importance to warrant professional attention. Psychological theories are used to support particular views of the proper place of women: from Freud's "Kinder, Kirsche, and Kuche" to the more recent statement from a White House physician (Edgar Berman) that women are not suited for high-level positions of decision making and stress because of their "raging hormones."

Experimental results which fit stereotypic views are sometimes accepted and promulgated simply because they seem to "fit," when in fact the methodological weaknesses and errors of the study would result in its rejection in another area of research. The very delineation of findings, and the dissemination of research results are influenced by the value orientation of the writer, many times without ter awareness of underlying bias.

At this time there has been a sharp increase in interest in psychological questions which relate to women, and a number of trained women are scattered throughout the research institutions. One of the purposes of the conference was to bring these individuals together for an intensive exchange of ideas in areas of mutual concern. The conference participants were invited because of their areas of expertise and concern in selected topic areas. The conference also provided a unique opportunity to solidify the mutual identification and modeling of scholars across age cohorts.

The conference participants were 25 men and women, primarily from psychology, representing various kinds of professional experience, viewpoints, and geographical locations. The main purpose of the conference was to establish new research directions concerning the psychology of women, to increase the level of sophistication of problem delineation and problem solving as they relate to issues which affect women, and to establish a new high mark in the nexus of values, social progress, and intellectual inquiry in general. The Task Force delineated important areas of research on the psychology of women, and chose leading individuals to prepare papers synthesizing and critiquing existing research and pointing to new and necessary directions in research.

The contemporary version of the "psychology of women" is a field of inquiry in the process of birth and has not been formally defined, though it is generating its own definition by the *de facto* practices developing. From discussions at the conference, particularly with Nancy Russo, it would seem that the psychology of women might best be considered as the study of behavior as mediated by the variables female sex (XX persons) or gender (role associated with XX persons). Thus, the psychology of women includes not only female behavior, but also attitudes and behaviors of females and males toward females, and expectations about gender roles and their effects. This definition should make it clear that we are not supposing that there are laws of behavior that differ for females and males. Such an emphasis would be totally opposed to the tone of the conference discussions.

The first modern book-length treatment of the psychology of women can be found in the two-volume work of Helene Deutsch (1944). This work is psychoanalytical in orientation, but it is more reactionary than Freud's own essays on female psychology. A triumverate of traits—passivity, masochism, and narcissism—were said to characterize the female personality. The revisionist articles of Karen Horney and Clara Thompson were unfortunately largely ignored.

There were no major syntheses in this area until 1971 when two new books appeared (Bardwick, 1971; Sherman, 1971). The emphasis had shifted from the psychoanalytic to the empirical, and from the female to a consideration of the manifold variations of behavior possible to all humankind. In their own ways, each of these books has a strong biological emphasis. Bardwick (1971), for example, emphasized the biological basis of female behavior while Sherman (1971) spent a considerable proportion of her book either considering questions regarding "sex differences" and biological bases of behavior or discussing psychological events unique to the female life cycle. Since then, a variety of course bibliographies and books of readings have emerged with a more cultural emphasis, including some with an explicit feminist viewpoint.

The years since 1971 have seen a burgeoning of research and publication in the area of the psychology of women. A division (35) of the American Psychological Association has been formed bearing this name and now has over 1,200 members. A journal of that division, *Psychology of Women Quarterly,* has also been inaugurated. Many universities have established courses in the psychology of women; Women's Studies programs proliferate across the country, and the material is included in the greatly increased consideration given sex roles in the university curricula.

The amount of scientific material produced which related to the psychology of women in the period 1970-1976 probably equals or exceeds the amount produced up until that time during this century. Needless to say, the recent work is usually methodologically superior to the earlier research. The purpose of the present volumes is to provide a synthesis and critique of this research, and to offer some order and direction to what is obviously a very fast-moving field.

The conference papers were presented and discussed in four main areas of research: female development, women and their bodies, women and work, and personality theory related to women, particularly achievement and power. The papers dealt with questions of bias and methodology, presented a critical review of existing literature, and discussed indications for needed research. In addition to the formal paper sessions, a panel of male and female psychologists considered the question of male attitudes and the related issue of sexism in psychotherapy. The concluding session consisted of a general discussion and brainstorming about social trends and future goals for women, and how these might affect research needs and priorities.

The conference opened on the first day with a keynote address by Sandra Bem of Stanford University on androgyny and the role of sex-role adherence in the ideal and healthy human personality. Bem defined *androgyny* as the possession of both "masculine" and "feminine" characteristics used in behavior, depending on the situational appropriateness of these behaviors. Bem's research amply demonstrated that traditional sex roles restrict behavior in important ways, and that it is dysfunctional for both society and individuals to adhere rigidly to one or the other conception of "appropriate" sex-role behavior. Bem concluded with the speculation that as androgyny becomes reality and sex roles are abolished, the concept of androgyny will be transcended and become meaningless. At such a point, "behavior" will have no gender, and gender identity will refer merely to a healthy regard and acceptance of one's maleness or femaleness as a biological given, which "generates little more than a quiet background of experiential contentment."

The session on *female development* included papers focusing on sex-role prescriptions through the life-cycle, both as a focus for improving the understanding of female development and as an antidote to existing sex-typed beliefs. The papers looked at female development through the lens of the age-graded changes in sex norms for females, in comparison to male experience. While there has been considerable speculation about the different expectations accorded males and females, there has been a lack of systematic collation of this material, even in the early years where most of the work has been done. Looking at the material in this manner seemed to have several advantages: (1) discontinuities in developmental expectation could be more clearly spotted; (2) such material could provide a firmer basis for understanding the development of differences between the sexes; (3) emphasis on sex-caste prescriptions of this kind would provide a more precise conceptual tool for understanding female development; and (4) improved knowledge of changing sex norms could help females make more rational decisions about their lives and prevent "future shock."

Jeanne Block of the University of California at Berkeley reviewed the empirical evidence for the existence of sex-differentiated socialization processes in our society, and argued that parental "shaping" behaviors strongly influence the two sexes and indeed have implications above and beyond the behaviors being shaped. Block pointed to several theoretical and methodological inadequacies in the socialization literature which have served to limit our knowledge of the important processes involved in divergent sex-role socialization. She noted that new studies must be conducted on preschool children and older children, and stressed the necessity of including the father as a critical socialization agent in future research.

Nancy Russo of the American Psychological Association presented theory and research of some of the problems of traditional developmental psychology, and suggested some perspectives that would augment our understanding of the developmental processes which involve women throughout their life cycles. In particular, Russo called for theory and research that would embody an interactionistic perspective, one that would simultaneously consider the contribution of multiple factors.

The session on *women and their bodies* dealt with questions of female sexuality, menstruation, child bearing, and menopause. Papers in these areas evaluated research directed toward biobehavioral and psychosomatic topics. Many rationales for the differential and aversive treatment of women stem from opinions related to women and their bodies. However, research in these areas is very inadequate; therefore, not only are women deprived of helpful knowledge enabling them to be more healthy and to understand themselves better, but also the lack of such knowledge permits the proliferation of myths used to control them.

Pepper Schwartz, a sociologist from the University of Washington, presented a paper—co-authored by Deanna Strom—about the social psychological aspects of female sexuality. She noted that our beliefs and attitudes about gender and sexuality are constructed from our social realities, and that while we now have some understanding of the physiological processes involved, we are still a long way from an adequate conceptualization of the more psychological aspects. Whereas our physiology may dictate our sexual capacity, it tells us nothing about our appetites, desires, fantasies, or how we view our bodies. Schwartz speculated how socialization experiences during childhood and adolescence may contribute differentially for males and females to their respective "construction" of sexuality.

Mary Parlee of Barnard College reviewed the theory and empirical literature pertaining to the menstruation cycle, pregnancy, birth and menopause. She showed that the social contexts surrounding these life events have been ignored in the past. Traditional conceptual approaches to these topics, aside from being sexist, have tended to ignore what women have to say about their experiences, and empirical research has been methodologically unsound. Parlee also pointed to the growing evidence of many rhythmic cycles in both men and women, and suggested that future work should take this into account. Parlee stated that we still know almost nothing about the psychological processes involved in the birth cycle, and that we should be more aware that the experiences affect both parents.

The session on *women and work* focused on women's work motivation, labor-force participation, and internal and external barriers to women's career development.

Helen Astin of U.C.L.A. explored some of the developmental factors involved in the determination of career aspirations in females, and recounted some changes in attitudes which have occurred over the past 20-30 years. She suggested that employed mothers serve as role models for their children, and that parents' absence from the home during the day serves to create a situation where the children learn to be self-sufficient, competent, and view activities and work in special ways. Astin concluded by stating that there is a need for a theory of occupational development in women.

Judith Long Laws of Cornell University presented a paper which analyzed relevant existing theory and empirical research about women's motivation and performance in the labor force. Long Laws reviewed the premises of the major theories of occupational involvement. She noted that the extant theories are not generally supported by current data; that there exists a tendency to confuse motivation with behavior; that when, for example, women don't do something, it is assumed they don't want to. Long Laws argued that important unexplored determinants of women's achievement behavior in the labor force may be the attitudes and behavior of employers, co-workers, husbands, and children in their facilitative or inhibiting effects, and the sex ratio of employment cohorts.

Janice Porter Gump of Howard University spoke about sex-role norms and ideology for the black woman, and cautioned that trying to understand the black woman's experience by viewing sex role prescriptions for the traditional white middle-class woman would not lead to an adequate understanding of the black woman's milieu. Gump stated that black women are socialized to be independent and competent, and to expect and prepare for a life in the labor force, but are denied the possibility of being dependent and cherished. She speculated about the costs of such an upbringing for black women, and hoped that white women would not move in that direction without considering all the advantages and disadvantages involved.

The session on *achievement and power* focused on these attributes as being key male and sex-typed perogatives, concepts which are undeveloped in theory and research on the psychology of women. A paper presented by Florence Denmark (CUNY), Sandra Tangri (U.S. Commission on Civil Rights), and Susan McCandless (CUNY) reviewed the empirical literature on achievement, affiliation, and power—patterns of motives selected because of their centrality to sex-role stereotypes. Recent perspectives have yielded greater understanding of achievement in women, but have not yet significantly altered the state of knowledge regarding affiliation and power. Affiliation continues to be seen in stereotypic terms, and power is not seen in women at all. Denmark, Tangri, and McCandless found a need to examine the ways in which traditional occupations and other roles to which women are assigned may be used for the gratification of motives not traditionally attributed to women. A critical review of the current literature on these motives in women suggested that we still do not have enough information about these motives to integrate them into a comprehensive theory, and that it is important that we look to the interactions among all three patterns of motives in future empirical research.

Rhoda Unger of Montclair State College reviewed the empirical literature on status, power, and gender, and argued that power asymmetries between the sexes are all-pervasive and that such power differences are highly correlated with status differences. Unger concluded that women are treated in the same manner as that accorded low-status individuals, and that the behavior of males and females toward each other is based upon this difference in relative status.

Irene Frieze, Joan Fisher, Maureen McHugh (University of Pittsburgh), and Valerie Valle (Allegheny College) presented a paper on the topic of how women and others attribute the causes of women's success and failure, and the implications of such attributions to achievement behaviors.

Ravenna Helson of the Institute of Personality Assessment and Research of the University of California at Berkeley reviewed the theory and literature pertaining to that most prized achievement, creativity, and its expression in women. She noted that investigators have frequently been uninterested in women as subjects or in the creativity of women because of societal concerns which dictated questions about more traditionally "masculine" creative products and modes of creativity. Helson stated that the evidence suggests that women are just as creative as men, but that society imposes more barriers to their creative expression and to the ways their creative products are recognized by society. She concluded with a call for a theory about creativity motivation, and suggested that we might well begin with a conception of creativity as a search for wholeness. Such a theory would have particular relevance to women, as it reflects their search for validation, meaning, and identity.

A panel discussion of men's attitudes toward women dealt with such topics as male attitudes toward women's liberation, male attitudes as expressed in the psychotherapy of women and their treatment by the helping professions, and aspects of male psychology which interfere with constructive interaction with females.

Jospeh Pleck of the University of Michigan at Ann Arbor reviewed some of the major theoretical approaches to male attitudes toward women and concluded that no one approach offers conclusive theory or evidence that male attitudes reflect the operation of just one psychological process. Pleck suggested that male attitudes toward women are best understood as part of a more general sex-role attitudinal process that reflects women's and men's attitudes toward both sexes, rather than as a unique process that affects only males. His review of the literature of male and female attitudes suggests that it may not be true that men hold a more traditional view toward women than women do.

Robert Brannon of Brooklyn College reviewed the literature on racism and intergroup conflict, concentrating particularly on how present-day researchers could profit from the conceptual and methodological pitfalls of that body of knowledge. He discussed the lack of concern with behavioral validity and argued for structured multidimensional inventories with homogeneous scales.

Mort Perlmutter of the University of Wisconsin discussed some of his research into the existence and implications of sexism in the therapeutic relationship. Perlmutter felt that the power machinations which male therapists employ with their female patients reflect the conflicts and socialization effects within the therapists, both as males and as a function of their vocational training. Female patients are seen as convenient "victims" for the overt expression of male therapists' needs and conflicts because of shared beliefs about the female role and the nature of the therapeutic relationship.

Some of the conclusions generated by the conference, which reflect priorities for future research as well as critiques of past approaches, focus on the fact that there is neither a fund of empirical knowledge about women nor any useful contemporary theory to explain the behavior and motivations of women as a class or as individuals. This is true in some areas to a greater extent than in others; for example, women's physiology, and their beliefs and attitudes about their biological function. The dearth of data is particularly acute once one moves past adolescence into early and late adulthood. There is a great need for research and theory dealing with the effects of critical events within a developmental perspective—a need for focus on the on-going dynamics of change over time within an ever-changing social context. Too often, psychology has sought to capture "reality" by the postulation of universal invariant principles of behavior. This can be seen in the concern for isolating the experiences of early childhood and thinking of them as continuing to exert an unchanging impact throughout one's entire life. This perspective is also revealed in the tendency to overlook the situational constraints on behavior.

The papers and discussions mentioned above amply demonstrated the need for a great deal of research into the psychology of women. The recommendations generated by conference participants related to the direction and conduct of such future research, ideas for specific research, and research into more general topics. Some of the recommendations focused on improvement in methodology and research design, but all stressed an awareness of the urgency for solid information about women. Psychologists have a unique role to play in furthering our understanding of the experiences of women, but unless they are provided with supporting data, change may not occur at all. Otherwise, observations will proceed on the basis of the myths and stereotypes that have characterized our society in the past. The conference underscored this awareness. Many more conferences about women are needed to continue the process of separating fact from fiction and myth from reality.

Overall facilitators for the conference were Florence Denmark, Graduate School and University Center of the City University of New York, and Julia Sherman, of the Women's Research Institute of Wisconsin, Inc.

REFERENCES

Bardwick, J.M. *Psychology of women.* New York: Harper & Row, 1971.

Deutsch, H. *The psychology of women: A psychoanalytic interpretation.* New York: Grune & Stratton, 1944.

Sherman, J.A. *On the psychology of women.* Springfield, Illinois: Thomas, 1971.

SECTION I

PART I
KEYNOTE

CHAPTER *1*

BEYOND ANDROGYNY: Some Presumptuous Prescriptions For A Liberated Sexual Identity

SANDRA LIPSITZ BEM

Sandra Lipsitz Bem received her B.A. in psychology from Carnegie-Mellon University in Pittsburgh and her Ph.D. in developmental psychology from the University of Michigan. After getting her Ph.D., she returned to Carnegie-Mellon to teach for several years and then joined the faculty of Stanford University in 1970. Bem is a feminist, and her research on the psychology of sex roles represents a coming together of both her intellectual and political concerns. In addition to research on psychological androgyny, Bem has also done research on the effects of sex-biased job advertising, and has served as an expert witness in two major court cases involving this issue. She has also served as a member of a citizens' advisory committee to The Woman Traffic Officer project of the California Highway Patrol, and, together with her husband, has given literally hundreds of speeches across the country on the topics of sex-role stereotyping and equalitarian marriage.

This article attempts to develop a conception of mental health which is free from culturally imposed definitions of masculinity and femininity. Bem's recent research* on psychological androgyny is discussed in detail, and serious questions are raised about the traditional conception of sexual identity and its centrality in the definition of the healthy personality.

Traditionally, the ideal or healthy personality has included a concept of sexual identity with three basic components: (1) a sexual preference for members of the other sex; (2) a sex-role identity as either masculine or feminine, depending upon one's gender; and (3) a gender identity, a secure sense of one's maleness or femaleness. In this article, each of these components is discussed in turn, and particular emphasis is placed on the concept of sex-role identity. With respect to the first component, that of sexual orientation, it is argued that sexual preferences ought ultimately to be considered orthogonal to any concept of mental health or ideal personality. With respect to the second component, that of sex-role identity, it is argued that masculinity and femininity represent complementary domains of positive traits and behaviors, and that it is therefore possible, in principle, for an individual to be both masculine and feminine, both instrumental and expressive, both agentic and communal, depending upon the situational appropriateness of these various modalities. Moreover, it is argued that for fully effective and healthy human functioning, masculinity and femininity must each be tempered by the other, and the two must be integrated into a more balanced, a more fully human, a truly androgynous personality. Finally, with respect to the third component, that of gender identity, it is argued that a healthy sense of maleness or femaleness becomes possible precisely when the artificial constraints of gender are eliminated and when one is finally free to be one's own unique blend of temperament and behavior.

*The research described in this article was supported by a National Institute of Mental Health Grant 5 R01MH 21735 to Sandra L. Bem.

I consider myself an empirical scientist, and yet my interest in sex roles is and has always been frankly political. My hypotheses have derived from no formal theory, but rather from a set of strong intuitions about the debilitating effects of sex-role stereotyping, and my major purpose has always been a feminist one: to help free the human personality from the restricting prison of sex-role stereotyping and to develop a conception of mental health which is free from culturally imposed definitions of masculinity and femininity.

But political passion does not persuade and, unless one is a novelist or a poet, one's intuitions are not typically compelling to others. Thus, because I *am* an empirical scientist, I have chosen to utilize the only legitimated medium of persuasion which is available to me: the medium of empirical data. What I should like to do in this paper is to summarize the data on psychological androgyny that we have collected over the last four years, and, in addition, to utilize the congenial setting of this conference to raise even deeper questions about the traditional conception of sexual identity and its centrality in the definition of the healthy personality, questions which go well beyond my current data.

The ideal or healthy personality has traditionally included a concept of sexual identity with three basic components: (1) a sexual preference for members of the other sex; (2) a sex-role identity as either masculine or feminine, depending upon one's gender; and (3) a gender identity, i.e., a secure sense of one's maleness or femaleness (see Green, 1974). I should like to comment in this paper on each of these three components in turn.

SEXUAL PREFERENCE

With respect to the first component, that of sexual preference, my remarks can be brief. Let me simply assert, along with the proponents of gay liberation and the recently enlightened American Psychiatric Association, that one's sexual preferences ought ultimately to be considered orthogonal to any concept of mental health or ideal personality. Let us begin to use the terms "homosexual" and "heterosexual" to describe *acts* rather than persons and to entertain the possibility that compulsive exclusivity in one's sexual responsiveness, whether homosexual or heterosexual, may be the product of a repressive society which forces us to label ourselves as one or the other.

SEX-ROLE IDENTITY

I turn now to the concept of sex-role identity, a concept which has traditionally been conceptualized in terms of masculinity and femininity. Both historically and cross-culturally, masculinity and feminity have represented complementary domains of positive traits and behaviors. Different theorists have different labels for these domains. According to Parsons and Bales (1955), masculinity has been associated with an instrumental orientation, a cognitive focus on getting the job done or the problem solved, whereas femininity has been associated with an expressive orientation, an affective concern for the welfare of others and the harmony of the group. Similarly, Bakan (1966) suggested that masculinity is associated with an "agentic orientation, a concern for oneself as an individual, whereas femininity is associated with a "communal" orientation, a concern for the relationship between oneself and others. Finally, Erikson's (1964) anatomical distinction between "inner" (female) and "outer" (male) space represents an analogue to a quite similar psychological distinction between a masculine "fondness for what works and for what man can make, whether it helps to build or to destroy" and a more "ethical" feminine commitment to "resourcefulness in peacekeeping and devotion in healing."

My own research has focused on the concept of psychological androgyny. As such, it has been predicated on the assumption that it is possible, in principle, for an individual to be both masculine and feminine, both instrumental and expressive, both agentic and communal, depending upon the situational appropriateness of these various modalities; and even for an individual to blend these complementary modalities in a single act, being able, for example, to fire an employee if the circumstances warrant it, but to do so with sensitivity for the human emotion that such an act inevitably produces.

The possibility that a single individual can embody both masculinity and femininity has, of course, been expressed by others as well. Jung (1953) described the anima and animus which he believed to be present in us all, and more recently, Bakan (1966) argued that viability—both for the individual and for society—depends on the successful integration of both agency and communion. Moreover, the concept of androgyny itself can now be found not only in the psychological literature (e.g., Berzins & Welling, in press; Block, 1973; Pleck,

1975; Spence, Helmreich & Stapp, 1975), but also in the literature of other disciplines as well (e.g., Bazin & Freeman, 1974; Gelpi, 1974; Harris, 1974; Heilbrun, 1973; Secor, 1974; Stimpson, 1974).

And yet, although I believe that it is *possible* for people to be both masculine and feminine, I also believe that traditional sex roles prevent this possibility from ever becoming a reality for many individuals. Over the last few years, the Women's Liberation Movement has made us all aware of the many ways that we, both men and women, have become locked into our respective sex roles. As women, we have become aware of the fact that we are afraid to express our anger, to assert our preferences, to trust our own judgment, to take control of situations. As men, we have become aware of the fact that we are afraid to cry, to touch one another, to own up to our fears and weaknesses.[1]

But there has been very little data within psychology to give legitimacy to these experiential truths. In many ways, my goal over the last few years has been to gather some of that legitimizing data, to try to demonstrate that traditional sex roles do restrict behavior in important human ways.

Although there is no previous research which bears on this hypothesis directly, a review of the relevant literature nevertheless corroborates our underlying assumption that a high level of sex typing may not be desirable. For example, high femininity in females has consistently been correlated with high anxiety, low self-esteem, and low social acceptance (e.g., Cosentino & Heilbrun, 1964; Gall, 1969; Gray, 1957; Sears, 1970; Webb, 1963); and, although high masculinity in males has been correlated during adolescence with better psychological adjustment (Mussen, 1961), it has been correlated during adulthood with high anxiety, high neuroticism, and low self-acceptance (Harford et al., 1967; Mussen, 1962). In addition, greater intellectual development has been correlated quite consistently with cross sex typing, i.e., with masculinity in girls and with femininity in boys. Boys and girls who are more sex typed have been found to have lower overall intelligence, lower spatial ability, and lower creativity (Maccoby, 1966).

The point, of course, is that the two domains of masculinity and femininity are both fundamental. In a modern complex society like ours, an adult clearly has to be able to look out for himself and to get things done. But an adult also has to be able to relate to other human beings as people, to be sensitive to their needs and to be concerned about their welfare, as well as to be able to depend on them for emotional support. Limiting a person's ability to respond in one or the other of these two complementary domains thus seems tragically and unnecessarily destructive of human potential.

In addition, it would also seem to be the case that masculinity and femininity may each become negative and even destructive when they are represented in extreme and unadulterated form. Thus, extreme femininity, untempered by a sufficient concern for one's own needs as an individual, may produce dependency and self-denial, just as extreme masculinity, untempered by a sufficient concern for the needs of others, may produce arrogance and exploitation. As Bakan (1966) put it, the fundamental task of every organism is to "try to mitigate agency with communion." Thus, for fully effective and healthy human functioning, both masculinity and femininity must each be tempered by the other, and the two must be integrated into a more balanced, a more fully human, a truly androgynous personality. An androgynous personality would thus represent the very best of what masculinity and femininity have each come to represent, and the more negative exaggerations of masculinity and femininity would tend to be canceled out.

The Bem Sex-Role Inventory

With this model of perfection in mind, I then moved to the more mundane task of trying to bring the concept of androgyny down to empirical reality. I began by constructing the Bem Sex-Role Inventory (or BSRI), a paper-and-pencil instrument which permits us to distinguish androgynous individuals from those with more sex-typed self-concepts.

Unlike most previous masculinity-femininity scales, the BSRI treats masculinity and femininity as two orthogonal dimensions rather than as two ends of a single dimension (see Constantinople, 1974, for a critique of previous sex-role inventories). Moreover, masculinity and femininity each represent *positive* domains of behavior. Too often, femininity has been defined simply as the absence of masculinity rather than as a positive dimension in its own right, a practice which may itself be partially responsible for the negative picture of the feminine woman which emerges in the psychological literature. For once, I wanted to give the feminine woman an equal chance to be no "sicker" than anyone else.

Specifically, the BSRI consists of 20 masculine personality characteristics (e.g., ambitious, self-reliant, independent, assertive) and 20 feminine personality characteristics (e.g., affectionate, gentle, understanding, sensitive to the needs of others). I chose the particular characteristics that I did because they were all rated by both males and females as being significantly more desirable in American society for one sex than for the other. The BSRI also contains 20 neutral characteristics (e.g., truthful, happy, conceited, unsystematic), which serve as filler items. All 60 characteristics are shown in Table 1.1.[1]

When taking the BSRI, a person is asked to indicate on a scale from 1 (never or almost never true) to 7 (always or almost always true) how well each characteristic describes temself. The degree of sex-role stereotyping in the person's self-concept is then defined as Student's t-ratio for the difference between the total points assigned to the feminine and masculine attributes, respectively. We use the t-ratio rather than a simple difference score primarily because it allows us to ask whether a person's masculinity and femininity scores differ significantly from one another, and if they do ($t \geqslant 2.025$, $p \geqslant 0.05$), to characterize that person as significantly sex typed or sex reversed. Thus, if a person's masculinity score is significantly higher than her femininity score, that person is said to have a feminine sex role. In contrast, if a person's masculinity and femininity scores are approximately equal ($t \leqslant 1$, $ns.$), that person is said to have an androgynous sex role. An androgynous sex role thus represents the equal endorsement of both masculine and feminine personality characteristics—a balance, as it were, between masculinity and femininity. Normative data on a sample of over 2,000 undergraduates from both a university and a community college indicate that approximately one-third of both populations can be classified as significantly sex typed, and another third as androgynous. Fewer than 10% can be classified as sex reversed.[2]

---

[1]In attempting to balance the overall social desirability of the masculine and feminine adjectives, I was surprised to discover that many feminine adjectives were judged to be more socially desirable "for a woman" than were any masculine adjectives "for a man." This would seem to contradict the frequently reported finding in the literature that masculine attributes are more socially desirable than feminine ones. It should be noted, however, that my judges rated the social desirability of each adjective as it applied to a particular sex. In the absence of such specification, perhaps judges implicitly picture a male and make their judgments accordingly, thereby lowering the desirability of all feminine attributes. In order to equate the overall social desirability of the feminine and masculine adjectives, I was therefore forced to include a few feminine adjectives which were somewhat lower in social desirability (e.g., gullible), and thereby to increase somewhat the variance of the social desirability ratings within the set of feminine adjectives.

Psychometric analyses on the BSRI indicate that it is quite satisfactory as a measuring instrument (Bem, 1974). As anticipated, the Masculinity and Femininity scores turned out to be empirically as well as conceptually independent (average r = -.03), thereby vindicating our decision to design an inventory that would not treat masculinity and femininity as two ends of a single dimension. Moreover, the t-ratio itself is internally consistent (average α = .86), reliable over a four-week interval (average r = .93), and uncorrelated with the tendency to describe oneself in a socially desirable direction (average r = -.06).

The Avoidance of Cross-Sex Behavior

Once the BSRI was in hand, we were then in a position to ask whether traditional sex roles actually do lead some people to restrict their behavior in accordance with sex-role stereotypes. Specifically, do masculine men and feminine women actively avoid activities just because those activities happen to be stereotyped as more appropriate for the other sex? And, if they have to perform cross-sex activity for some reason, does it cause them discomfort to do so? In other words, is cross-sex behavior motivationally problematic for the sex-typed individual, or would tey be perfectly willing to engage in such behavior if the situation were structured to encourage it?

---

[2]As Spence, Helmreich, and Stapp (1975) and Strahan (1975) pointed out, this definition of androgyny serves to obscure what could be a potentially important distinction between those individuals who score high in both masculinity and femininity, and those individuals who score low in both. Accordingly, Spence, Helmreich, and Stapp (1975) recommend dividing subjects at the median on both the masculinity and the femininity scales, and then deriving a *fourfold* classification of subjects as either masculine (high masculine-low feminine), feminine (high feminine-low masculine), androgynous (high masculine-high feminine), or undifferentiated (low masculine-low feminine). In an attempt to clarify whether one or the other of these two definitions of psychological androgyny was likely to have greater utility for future research, we administered the BSRI along with a variety of other paper-and-pencil questionnaires, and we also reanalyzed the results of our laboratory studies with the low-low scorers separated out. On the basis of the available evidence, I now believe that a distinction between high-high and low-low scorers does seem to be warranted, that the term "androgynous" ought to be reserved only for those individuals who score high in both masculinity and femininity, and that the BSRI ought henceforth to be scored so as to yield four distinct groups of masculine, feminine, androgynous, and undifferentiated subjects. See the articles by Bem (1977) and Bem, Martyna, and Watson (1976) for a full discussion of this issue. It should be noted, however, that this change in scoring only serves to strengthen the findings reported in this article.

Table 1.1

The Masculine, Feminine, and Neutral Items on the BSRI

Masculine items	Feminine items	Neutral items
49. Acts as a leader	11. Affectionate	51. Adaptable
46. Aggressive	5. Cheerful	36. Conceited
58. Ambitious	50. Childlike	9. Conscientious
22. Analytical	32. Compassionate	60. Conventional
13. Assertive	53. Does not use harsh language	45. Friendly
10. Athletic	35. Eager to soothe hurt feelings	15. Happy
55. Competitive	20. Feminine	3. Helpful
4. Defends own beliefs	14. Flatterable	48. Inefficient
37. Dominant	59. Gentle	24. Jealous
19. Forceful	47. Gullible	39. Likable
25. Has leadership abilities	56. Loves children	6. Moody
7. Independent	17. Loyal	21. Reliable
52. Individualistic	26. Sensitive to the needs of others	30. Secretive
31. Makes decisions easily	8. Shy	33. Sincere
40. Masculine	38. Soft spoken	42. Solemn
1. Self-reliant	23. Sympathetic	57. Tactful
34. Self-sufficient	44. Tender	12. Theatrical
16. Strong personality	29. Understanding	27. Truthful
43. Willing to take a stand	41. Warm	18. Unpredictable
28. Willing to take risks	2. Yielding	54. Unsystematic

Note: The number preceding each item reflects the position of each adjective as it actually appears on the inventory. A subject indicates how well each item describes tem on the following scale: (1) never or almost never true; (2) usually not true; (3) sometimes but infrequently true (4) occasionally true; (5) often true; (6) usually true; (7) always or almost always true.

In order to find out, Ellen Lenney and I designed a study in which many of the more obvious external barriers to cross-sex behavior had been removed (Bem & Lenney, 1976). Thus, both masculine and feminine activities were explicitly available to all subjects; it was made clear that we did not care how well they could do each activity or, indeed, if they had ever done the activity before; and the less sex-appropriate activities were always the more highly rewarded.

Subjects were told that we were preparing to do a study to find out whether people make different personality judgments about an individual as a function of the particular activity that tey happens to be seen performing, and that we therefore needed pictures of the same person performing many different activities. The activities were arranged in pairs, and subjects were asked to select the one activity from each pair that they would prefer to perform during the photography session which was to follow. For example, one pair asked female subjects whether they would rather "prepare a baby bottle by mixing powdered formula with milk" for 2¢, or "oil squeaky hinges on a metal box" for 4¢. Although it was not made explicit, 20 of the activities were stereotypically masculine (e.g., "Nail two boards together"; "Attach artificial bait to a fishing hook"), 20 were stereotypically feminine (e.g., "Iron cloth napkins"; "Wind a package of yarn into a ball"), and 20 were stereotypically neutral (e.g., "Play with a yo-yo"; "Peel oranges").

Of the 30 pairs, 15 required the subject to choose between activities which differed in their sex-role connotations. Of these, five pitted neutral activities against masculine ones, five pitted neutral activities against feminine ones, and five pitted masculine and feminine activities against each other. In all sex-role conflict pairs, however, it was the less sex-appropriate activity which always paid more. In the remaining 15 pairs, both activities were either masculine, feminine, or neutral, and one activity was arbitrarily assigned to be the high-paying activity. These control pairs served primarily as a baseline measure of each subject's responsiveness to the differences in payment, and they also guaranteed that a minimum number of masculine, feminine, and neutral activities would be chosen by every subject.

In an attempt to get the purest possible measure of preference, unconfounded by the effects of competence at or familiarity with the various activities, great care was taken to assure the subjects that we were not at all interested in how well they could perform each activity or, indeed, if they had ever done the activity before. For example, they were explicitly told that they would be given only 1 or 2 minutes for each activity, not necessarily enough time for the activity to be completed, and that all we really wanted was for them to become sufficiently involved in each activity for a convincing photograph to be taken. They were also assured that simple written instructions would be available for each of the activities that they selected. In addition, in order to prevent subjects from becoming overly self-conscious about how their pictures would look, they were also assured that the later study would be done at a different university and that no one they knew would ever be likely to see their pictures. Finally, no emphasis whatever was placed on having the pictures reflect the "true" personality of the individual subject. If anything, what was implied was that we needed each subject to perform as wide a variety of different kinds of activities as possible.

As anticipated, the results indicated that sex-typed subjects were significantly more stereotyped in their choices than androgynous or sex-reversed subjects who did not differ significantly from one another. In other words, the masculine man and the feminine woman were significantly more likely to select their own sex's activities and to reject the other sex's activities, even though such choices cost them money and even though we tried to make it as easy as we could for the subject to select cross-sex activity.

In order to find out whether sex-typed subjects would also experience greater discomfort if they had no choice but to perform cross-sex activity, the subjects then proceeded to perform three masculine, three feminine, and three neutral activities while the experimenter pretended to photograph them, and they indicated how they felt after each activity on a series of rating scales. Specifically, subjects indicated on a seven-point scale how "masculine" (for males) or "feminine" (for females), how "attractive," how "likeable," how "nervous," and how "peculiar" they had felt while performing each activity. They also indicated how much they had enjoyed each activity.

The results indicated that sex-typed subjects felt significantly worse than androgynous or sex-reversed subjects who, again, did not differ significantly from one another. That is, it was the masculine men and the feminine women who experienced the most discomfort and who felt the worst about themselves after performing cross-sex activities. Thus, it would appear that cross-sex activity is problematic for sex-typed individuals, and that traditional sex roles do produce an unnecessary and perhaps even dysfunctional pattern of avoidance for many people.

Armed with this demonstration that sex-role stereotyping restricts simple everyday behaviors, we can now inquire into whether such stereotyping also constricts the individual in more profound domains as well. Is the masculine male low in expressiveness and communion? Is the feminine female low in instrumentality and agency? It is to these broader questions that the bulk of my research has been addressed, and it is to these that we now turn.

Independence and Nurturance

We began by designing a pair of studies on independence and nurturance (Bem, 1975). The first was designed to tap the "masculine" domain of independence. It utilized a standard conformity paradigm to test the hypothesis that masculine and androgynous subjects would both remain more independent from social pressure than would feminine subjects. The second study was designed to tap the "feminine" domain of nurturance. By offering subjects the opportunity to interact with a tiny kitten, this study tested the hypothesis that feminine and androgynous subjects would both be more nurturant or playful than masculine subjects. Taken together, these two studies offered one test of the hypothesis that nonandrogynous subjects would "do well" only when the situation calls for behavior that is congruent with their self-definition as masculine or feminine, whereas androgynous subjects would "do well" regardless of the sex-role stereo-type of the particular behavior in question. That is, they would perform as high as masculine subjects on the masculine task, and they would perform as high as feminine subjects on the feminine task.

In the study of independence, which Karen Rook and Robyn Stickney helped design, we brought four males or four females into the laboratory for what they thought was an experiment on humor. We placed the subjects into individual booths equipped with microphones and earphones, and showed them a series of cartoons, which we asked them to rate for funniness. The cartoons used in this study had been previously rated by a set of independent judges; half of the cartoons had been judged to be very funny and half judged to be very unfunny.

As each new cartoon appeared on the screen, the subjects heard the experimenter call on each person in turn for ter rating. Although the subjects believed that they were hearing each others' voices, they were in fact, actually hearing a tape recording. In order to induce conformity, the tape included 36 trials during which all three taped voices gave false responses, agreeing that a particular cartoon was funny when it wasn't, and vice versa. We gave subjects this somewhat subjective task of judging cartoons for funniness—rather than length of lines or the like—so that false norms might impose pressure to conform without appearing to be bizarre. As expected, the masculine and androgynous subjects did not

differ significantly from one another, and both were significantly more independent than the feminine subjects. This was true for both males and females.

In the study of nurturance, which Jenny Jacobs helped me to design, subjects
came to the laboratory individually for an experiment described as a study of
mood. The subjects were informed that we wanted to know how different
activities would affect their mood, and that we would therefore ask them to
perform a number of different activities and to rate their mood after each.

For one of the activities, we brought a kitten into the room and asked the
subjects to interact with it in any way that they wished. We placed the kitten in
a child's playpen, which had been completely enclosed by chicken wire, and we
showed the subjects how to open the playpen so that they could take the kitten
out if they wanted to. The room also contained various toys that a kitten might
enjoy; for example, a pencil or a ball of yarn. The subject was left alone in the
room with the kitten for 5 minutes while we observed from behind a one-way
mirror. The main behavior measured in this situation was how often the subject
touched the kitten. At the end of the 5-minute period, we also asked the subject
to indicate how much tey had enjoyed playing with the kitten.

Later in the experiment, we again placed the kitten in its playpen and gave
subjects 10 minutes to do anything in the room that they wished. They could
play with the kitten, or they could read magazines, work puzzles, play with a
three-dimensional tilting maze, or whatever. Once again, we observed them from
behind the one-way mirror to see how much they played with the kitten when
they didn't have to.

As expected, the feminine and androgynous men did not differ significantly
from one another, and both were significantly more responsive to the kitten
than were the masculine men. As expected, the male data confirmed our hypothesis. But the female data did not. The androgynous women, like the androgynous men, were quite responsive to the kitten, but the feminine women were
significantly less responsive, and the masculine women fell ambiguously in
between.

Considering these two studies together, we see that, as predicted, only the
androgynous subjects, both male and female, displayed a high level of masculine
independence when under pressure to conform, as well as a high level of feminine playfulness or nurturance when given the opportunity to interact with a
tiny kitten. Thus, only the androgynous subjects were *both* masculine and feminine.

In contrast, the nonandrogynous subjects all seemed to be low in one or the
other of these two behaviors. For example, nonandrogynous males "did well"

only when the behavior was congruent with their self-definition as masculine or feminine. Thus, the masculine males were low in feminine nurturance and the feminine males were low in masculine independence.

Interestingly, the results for the nonandrogynous females were more complex. As we had anticipated, the masculine women were quite independent, but they were not significantly less responsive to the kitten than were the androgynous women. Hence, we cannot conclude that the masculine woman is low in her expressive functioning. Rather, it is the feminine woman who, at this juncture, appears to be the most restricted. Thus, not only was she low in independence, but she was also low in her nurturance toward the kitten. Of course it is possible that feminine women might simply find animals unappealing for some reason, and that they could therefore be expected to display much greater nurturance if they were given the opportunity to interact with another human being rather than with a kitten. But the possibility must also be considered that feminine women may simply be more constricted than we had initially anticipated, and that their constriction may extend beyond the instrumental domain.

Further Explorations of the Expressive Domain

Why were the feminine women so unresponsive to the kitten? Do they simply find animals unappealing for some reason? Did some other feature of the situation inhibit them? Or, contrary to conventional wisdom, are they simply not competent in the expressive domain?

In order to give the feminine women a fairer test of their expressive functioning, we carried out two additional studies. Because we wished to clarify whether the feminine woman's low level of nurturance was unique to her interaction with animals, both studies were designed to be genuinely interpersonal situations in which the subject's nurturant sympathies would be more likely to be aroused. In addition, because it also seemed possible that feminine women might be insufficiently assertive to act out their nurturant feelings if the situation required that they take responsibility for initiating the interaction with their partner, the second study was designed not only to be genuinely interpersonal, but also to place the subject into a more passive role that would require very little initiative or improvisation and where there would be virtually no ambiguity about what a subject *ought* to do if tey wished to be nurturant. Accordingly, the first study gave the subject the opportunity to interact with a human baby, and the second required the subject to listen to a fellow student who openly shared some of ter unhappy emotions (Bem, Martyna, & Watson; 1976).

In the baby study, which Carol Watson and Bart Astor helped design, each subject was left alone with a five-month-old baby for a period of 10 minutes, with the understanding that we would be observing the infant's reactions to a stranger through the one-way mirror. In fact, we were measuring the subject's responsiveness to the baby. Using time-sampling procedures, we measured how much the subject smiled at the baby, how much the subject talked to the baby, how much the subject held the baby, how much the subject kissed or nuzzled the baby, and how much the subject played with the baby in a way that involved touching (e.g., tickling, patting, stretching). We then derived a global measure of the subject's overall responsiveness to the baby by adding together the measures of all these various behaviors.

Parenthetically, I would like to note that this study involved 14 different babies so that no baby was required to be "mauled" by more than six undergraduates. Most parents were eager to have their children participate, and they joined us behind the one-way mirror to watch the interaction. Naturally, great care was taken to protect the health and well-being of the babies who participated. For example, all subjects were urged to cancel their appointments if they felt the slightest bit ill; all toys and lab coats were thoroughly washed before every session; and each baby's mother or father was explicitly instructed to ask that the session be terminated if the child ever seemed to be particularly distressed. In addition, each baby was "interviewed" before the study began to make certain that tey was not yet afraid of strangers.

Happily, the results of the baby study supported our initial hypothesis. That is to say, feminine and androgynous subjects did not differ significantly from one another, and both were significantly more nurturant toward the baby than were masculine subjects. Moreover, the results did not differ significantly for men and women. Thus, the baby study conceptually replicated our earlier finding that masculine men were low in nurturance toward a kitten; and even more importantly, it indicated that the low nurturance of the feminine woman toward animals does not extend to ter interaction with humans.

As indicated earlier, however, we did still another study to clarify further whether the low nurturance of the feminine woman was situation specific. Because it seemed possible that feminine women might be most able to act out all their nurturant feelings in a situation where they did not have to take responsibility for initiating and sustaining the interaction, as they did to some degree with both the kitten and the baby, the situation in this study was designed not only to be genuinely interpersonal, but also to place the subject into a more passive or responsive role. More specifically, this study was designed to evoke sympathetic and supportive listening on the part of the subject, but without at the same time requiring the subject to play an active or initiating role in the interaction.

In this study, which Wendy Martyna and Dorothy Ginsberg helped design, two same-sex subjects (one of whom was actually an experimental assistant) participated in a study of "the acquaintance process." They appeared to draw lots to determine which of the two would take the role of "talker" and which the role of "listener," but in fact the experimental assistant always served as the talker and the subject always served as the listener.

The talker began with some relatively impersonal background information, (e.g., hometown, number of siblings), but tey soon became more personal. In general, the talker described temself as a recent and rather lonely transfer student to Stanford. Tey talked about missing old friends, about how difficult it was to make new friends now that cliques had already become established, and about spending much more time alone than tey really wanted to. In short, the talker described feelings common to many new transfer students. The talker did not seem neurotic, just somewhat isolated, and appeared rather pleased to have this opportunity to share some of ter feelings with another person. In contrast, the subject—as listener—was allowed to ask questions and to make comments, but was instructed never to shift the focus of conversation to temself.

We observed the conversation from behind a one-way mirror and recorded a number of the subjects' behaviors such as how much responsiveness tey showed in facial expressions, how many times tey nodded, how many comments tey made, and how positively tey reacted to the talker's implicit request for further contact. After the conversation, we also asked both the talker and the experimenter to rate how nurturant the subject had seemed to them. We then derived a global responsiveness score for each subject by averaging these various measures.

As in the baby study, the results confirmed our initial hypothesis once again. Thus, feminine and androgynous subjects did not differ significantly from one another, and both were significantly more nurturant toward the lonely student than were masculine subjects. Moreover, the results conceptually replicate the low nurturance of the masculine male for the third time, and they demonstrate for the second time that the low nurturance of the feminine woman was situation specific and does not generalize to her interaction with humans.

SUMMING UP

I believe that we are now in a position to state some of the things we have learned about androgyny and sex typing. I begin with the men because they're easy. Consider first the androgynous male. He performs spectacularly. He shuns no behavior just because our culture happens to label it as female, and his competence crosses both the instrumental and the expressive domains. Thus, he stands firm in his opinions, he cuddles kittens and bounces babies, and he has a sympathetic ear for someone in distress. Clearly, he is a liberated companion for the most feminist among us.

In contrast, the feminine male is low in the instrumental domain, and the masculine male is low in the expressive domain. Because at least one-third of college-age males would be classified as masculine under our definition, it is particularly distressing that the masculine males were less responsive in all of the diverse situations that we designed to evoke their more tender emotions—to tug, if only a little, on their heartstrings. I do not know, of course, whether the masculine men were simply unwilling to act out any tender emotions that they might have been experiencing, or whether their emotionality is sufficiently inhibited that they did not readily experience the emotions we sought to tap. But in either case, their partners in the interaction received less emotional sustenance than they would have otherwise.

We cannot conclude, of course, that masculinity inhibits all tender emotionality in the masculine male. Obviously, none of the laboratory situations that we devised was as powerful as, say, having a child who becomes ill or a friend who seems about to have a nervous breakdown. We can conclude, however, that their thresholds for tender emotionality are higher than all the other men and women we have observed. And that, I believe, is sufficient cause for concern.

Let us turn now to the somewhat more complex pattern of results shown by the women. Like their male counterparts, androgynous women also fare well in our studies. They, too, willingly perform behaviors that our culture has labeled as unsuitable for their sex, and they, too, function effectively in both the instrumental and the expressive domains.

In contrast, the masculine woman is low in the expressive domain, and the feminine woman is low in the instrumental domain. Thus, for both men and women, sex typing does function to restrict behavior. Masculine individuals of both sexes are high in independence but low in nurturance, and feminine individuals of both sexes are high in nurturance but low in independence.

In addition, however, it will be recalled that feminine women were not consistently high even in nurturance. That is to say, they were more nurturant toward the lonely student and the baby than they were toward the kitten, and there was even some evidence that they were more nurturant toward the lonely student than toward the baby (Bem, Martyna, & Watson, 1976).

What is the source of this variability? Although there is some evidence that the lonely student may have been especially able to arouse the nurturant sympathies of the feminine woman (Bem, Martyna, & Watson, 1976), it seems noteworthy that feminine women were the most nurturant in that one situation where the subject was required, as a listener, to play a relatively passive or responsive role with no need to take any responsibility whatever for initiating or even sustaining the interaction. In contrast, it seems noteworthy that feminine women were the least nurturant in that one situation where the subject was actually required to remove a kitten from its cage personally and spontaneously in order to be nurturant toward it. This leads me to speculate that femininity may be what produces nurturant feelings in women, but that at least a threshold level of masculinity is required to provide the initiative and perhaps even the daring to translate those nurturant feelings into action.

These speculations about the feminine woman conclude what I think I have learned up to this point about the evils of sex typing and the potential promise of androgyny. As I stated earlier, however, the major purpose of my research has always been a political one; to help free the human personality from the restricting prison of sex-role stereotyping and to develop a conception of mental health that is free from culturally imposed definitions of masculinity and femininity.

Certainly androgyny seems to represent the fulfillment of this goal. For if there is a moral to the concept of psychological androgyny, it is that *behavior* should have no gender. But there is an irony here, for the concept of androgyny contains an inner contradiction and hence the seeds of its own destruction. Thus, as the etymology of the word implies, the concept of androgyny necessarily presupposes that the concepts of masculinity and femininity themselves have distinct and substantive content. But to the extent that the androgynous message is absorbed by the culture, the concepts of masculinity and femininity will cease to have such content, and the distinctions to which they refer will blur into invisibility. Thus, when androgyny becomes a reality, the *concept* of androgyny will have been transcended. (See Rebecca, Hefner, & Oleshansky, 1976, and Hefner, Rebecca, & Oleshansky, 1975, for a discussion of the concept of sex-role transcendence.)

GENDER IDENTITY

As I noted in the introduction to this paper, the ideal or healthy personality has traditionally included a concept of sexual identity with three basic components: (1) a sexual preference for members of the opposite sex; (2) a sex-role identity as either masculine or feminine, depending upon one's gender; and (3) a gender identity, i.e., a secure sense of one's maleness or femaleness.

In discussing the first two of these components, it is clear that my contribution has been largely iconoclastic. Thus, I have proposed that we reject sexual preference as relevant to anything other than the individual's own love or pleasure. And I have all but said that the best sex-role identity is no sex-role identity. I think I am prepared to be somewhat less cavalier with the concept of gender identity.

For even if people were all to become psychologically androgynous, the world would continue to consist of two sexes; male and female would continue to be one of the first and most basic dichotomies that young children would learn, and no one would grow up ignorant of or even indifferent to ter gender. After all, even if one is psychologically androgynous, one's gender continues to have certain profound physical implications.

Thus, being a female typically means that one has a female body build; that one has female genitalia; that one has breasts; that one menstruates; that one can become pregnant and give birth; and that one can nurse a child. Similarly, being a male typically means that one has a male body build; that one has male genitalia; that one has beard growth; that one has erections; that one ejaculates; and that one can impregnate a woman and thereby father a child. No matter how psychologically androgynous one may be, one typically "inherits" one or the other of these two sets of biological givens, and one does not get to choose which of the two sets one would prefer.

Precisely because these are biological givens, which cannot be avoided or escaped except perhaps by means of very radical and mutilating surgery, it seems to me that psychological health must necessarily include having a healthy sense of one's maleness or femaleness—a "gender identity," if you like. But I would argue that a healthy sense of maleness or femaleness involves little more than being able to look into the mirror and to be perfectly comfortable with the body that one sees there. One's gender does dictate the nature of one's body after all, and hence one ought to be able to take one's body very much for granted, to feel comfortable with it, and perhaps even to like it.

But beyond being comfortable with one's body, one's gender need have no other influence on one's behavior or on one's life style. Thus, although I would suggest that a woman ought to feel comfortable about the fact that she can bear children if she wants to, this does not imply that she ought to want to bear children, nor that she ought to stay home with any children that she does bear. Similarly, although I would suggest that a man ought to feel perfectly comfortable about the fact that he has a penis which can become erect, this in no way implies that a man ought to take the more active role during sexual intercourse, nor even that his sexual partners ought all to be female.

Finally, I would argue that a healthy sense of one's maleness or femaleness becomes all the more possible precisely when the artificial constraints of gender are eliminated and when one is finally free to be one's own unique blend of temperament and behavior. When gender no longer functions as a prison, then and only then will we be able to accept as given the fact that we are male or female in exactly the same sense that we accept as given the fact that we are human. Then and only then will we be able to consider the fact of our maleness or femaleness to be so self-evident and nonproblematic that it rarely ever occurs to us to think about it, to assert that it is true, to fear that it might be in jeopardy, or to wish that it were otherwise.

* * *

Let me conclude, then, with my personal set of prescriptions for a liberated sexual identity:

Let sexual preference be ignored;
Let sex roles be abolished; and
Let gender move from figure to ground.

REFERENCES

Bakan, D. *The duality of human existence.* Chicago: Rand McNally, 1966.

Bazin, N.T., & Freeman, A. The androgynous vision. *Women's Studies,* 1974, *2,* 185-215.

Bem, S.L. The measurement of psychological androgyny. *Journal of Consulting and Clinical Psychology,* 1974, *42,* 155-162.

Sex-role adaptability: One consequence of psychological androgyny. *Journal of Personality and Social Psychology,* 1975, *31,* 634-643.

& Lenney, E. Sex-typing and the avoidance of cross-sex behavior. *Journal of Personality and Social Psychology,* 1976, *33,* 48-54.

On the utility of alternative procedures for assessing psychological androgyny. *Journal of Consulting and Clinical Psychology,* 1977, *45,* 196-205.

Martyna, W., & Watson, C. Sex-typing and androgyny: Further explorations of the expressive domain. *Journal of Personality and Social Psychology,* 1976, *34,* 1016-1023.

Berzins, J.I., & Welling, M.A. The PRF ANDRO Scale: A measure of psychological androgyny derived from the Personality Research Form. *Journal of Consulting and Clinical Psychology,* in press.

Block, J.H. Conceptions of sex role: Some cross-cultural and longitudinal perspectives. American Psychologist, 1973, *28,* 512-526.

Constantinople, A. Masculinity-femininity: An exception to a famous dictum. *Psychological Bulletin,* 1974, *80,* 389-407.

Cosentino, F., & Heilbrun, A.B. Anxiety correlates of sex-role identity in college students. *Psychological Reports,* 1964, *14,* 729-730.

Erikson, E. Inner and outer space: Reflections on womanhood. In R.J. Lifton (Ed.), *The woman in America.* New York: Houghton Mifflin, 1964.

Gall, M.D. The relationship between masculinity-femininity and manifest anxiety. *Journal of Clinical Psychology,* 1969, *25,* 294-295.

Gelpi, B.C. The politics of androgyny. *Women's Studies,* 1974, *2,* 151-160.

Gray, S.W. Masculinity-femininity in relation to anxiety and social acceptance. *Child Development,* 1957, *28,* 203-214.

Green, R. *Sexual identity conflict in children and adults.* New York: Basic Books, 1974.

Harford, T.C., Willis, C.H., & Deabler, H.L. Personality correlates of masculinity-femininity. *Psychological Reports,* 1967, *21,* 881-884.

Harris, D.A. Androgyny: The sexist myth in disguise. *Women's Studies,* 1974, *2,* 171-184.

Hefner, R., Rebecca, M., & Oleshansky, B. Development of sex role transcendence. *Human Development,* 1975, *18,* 143-158.

Heilbrun, C.G. *Toward a recognition of androgyny.* New York: Alfred A. Knopf, 1973.

Jung, C.G. Anima and animus. In *Two essays on analytical psychology: Collected works of C.G. Jung* (Vol.7). Bollinger Foundation, 1953, pp. 186-209.

Maccoby, E.E. Sex differences in intellectual functioning. In E.E. Maccoby (Ed.), *The development of sex differences.* Stanford, Calif.: Stanford University Press, 1966, pp. 25-55.

Mussen, P.H. Some antecedents and consequents of masculine sex-typing in adolescent boys. *Psychological Monographs,* 1961, *75,* No. 506.

PART II
FEMALE DEVELOPMENT

INTRODUCTION

JULIA A. SHERMAN & FLORENCE L. DENMARK

Female development has rarely been considered a topic in its own right. Development has generally been assumed to follow a male paradigm, and female development is frequently an addendum to a description of males. Not only was this the attitude of such historic figures as Freud, but it is commonly the position adopted in current textbooks and even in research publications. Inferences are frequently made about both sexes from data based only or mostly on males.

Another approach to female development tends to focus on "sex differences." Description of development of "sex differences" is a doubly difficult task because the psychological development of neither sex has in itself been well described. While the study of "sex differences" can be useful for monitoring discriminatory practices and to discern patterns of differences which might lead to useful hypotheses for further research, it shed little light on female development per se, particularly not on the dynamics of that development. On the one hand, a comparative frame is useful, but on the other hand, in many instances the female picture has been distorted beyond recognition.

The chapters by Jeanne Block and Nancy Russo each deal in its own way with these issues. In addition, one sees themes emerging which were to recur throughout the conference discussions: Early development has been over-stressed, little is known about development in older children and adults, and too often it is not recognized that important change can occur throughout the life span.

Block's article is particularly important because it focuses on parental behavior vis-a-vis boys and girls, and provides a cogent and convincing critique of the

51898

conclusion advanced by Maccoby and Jacklin (1974) that there are no important differences in the socialization of the two sexes. Block provides new data on this point, and shows how the confusion of data from different age levels and the overemphasis on the early years lead to faulty conclusions.

Russo concentrates on methodological problems, stressing the need for more dynamic and complex modes of thinking. The development time line is typically much more complicated for females than for males, as it involves more frequent and drastic bodily changes as well as more frequent and role changes. Women are typically expected to adapt to the social status, location, and job requirements of the husband. Marriage, divorce, and loss of spouse all involve more change for her than for the male. To what extent education could ease these many transitions is an interesting question in preventative mental health practices.

CHAPTER **2**

ANOTHER LOOK AT SEX DIFFEREN-TIATION IN THE SOCIALIZATION BEHAVIORS OF MOTHERS AND FATHERS

JEANNE H. BLOCK

Jeanne H. Block is a Research Psychologist at the Institute of Human Development, University of California, Berkeley, and holds an NIMH Research Scientist Development Award, which has supported her research activities for a number of years. Dr. Block received her Ph.D. from Stanford University and has taught at both Stanford and the University of California. She is currently engaged in a collaborative study with her husband and colleague, Jack Block, in which personality and cognitive development in young children is being studied longitudinally. In addition, Dr. Block has been involved in research on sex-role and ego development. She was the recipient of the 1974 Lester N. Heffheimer Award presented by the American Psychiatric Association for her research. "Conceptions of sex role: Some cross-cultural and longitudinal perspectives."

This chapter is an extended version of a paper presented at the Conference on New Directions for Research on Women in Madison, Wisconsin, May 1975, for which preparation and collection of portions of the data were supported by a National Institute of Mental Health Research Scientist Development Award to the author. The cross-cultural study was made possible by a National Institute of Mental Health Special Research Fellowship to the author at the Institute for Social Research in Oslo, Norway. During this period the Child-Rearing Practices Report (Block; Note 1 used in the several studies, was developed, and I wish to express my appreciation to several Norwegian colleagues who contributed substantially to its development: Professor Anni von der Lippe of the University of Oslo; Professor Bjorn Christiansen of the University of Bergen; Dagfinn As, Berit As, Per Olaf Tiller, and Kikkan Christiansen. The interest and generosity of other European colleagues made possible the collection of the cross-cultural data, and their help is gratefully acknowledged. The efforts of Professor Franz From, University of Copenhagen, Denmark; Professor Ingvar Johannesson, School of Education, Stockholm, Sweden; Professor Isto Ruoppila, Pedagogical University, Jyvaskyla, Finland; Professor Hilde Himmelweit, London School of Economics, London, England; and Professor R. Vuyk, University of Amsterdam, Amsterdam. I also wish to thank my colleagues Norma Haan of the Institute of Human Development and M. Brewster Smith of the University of California, Santa Cruz, for permitting me to use these jointly collected data. The final manuscript has profited from the thoughtful editing that I have come to expect over the years from my husband Jack Block.

The evidence surrounding the issue of differential socialization practices of parents of boys and parents of girls, summarized in Maccoby and Jacklin. The Psychology of Sex Differences, *is evaluated. It is suggested that conceptual, sampling, and methodological problems characterizing many studies forming the empirical data base about sex differences in parent behaviors have contributed to the inconsistency of results and have permitted them to conclude that their "survey of research on socialization of the two sexes revealed surprisingly little differentiation in parent behavior according to the sex of the child." (Maccoby & Jacklin, 1974, p. 338). Data on sex-differentiated socialization derived from self-reports of mothers and of fathers and from the perceptions of parental rearing practices by young adults, using the "Child Rearing Practices Report" are presented and discussed in relation to the Maccoby and Jacklin conclusions. The results of the several studies* [1] *presented suggest that sex-differentiated parental socialization occurs in many areas, and increases from early childhood to adolescence.*

---

[1] Reference to significant differences in the text indicates $p < .05$ by two-tailed test.

It has been prevalently believed, by professionals and lay persons alike, that boys and girls in our society are socialized differently and in ways that encourage behavior consistent with our cultural definitions of appropriate sex-role behaviors. Sex differences in the socialization emphases of parents (mostly mothers) have been described and discussed by many researchers over the years (e.g., Sears, Maccoby, & Levin, 1957; Barry, Bacon, & Childs, 1957; Hartley, 1959, 1964; Hetherington, 1965, 1967, 1972; Moss, 1967; Mussen, 1969; McCandless, 1969; Minton, Kagan & Levin, 1971; Biller, 1971; Block, 1973). However, after their recent comprehensive review of the literature with respect to the differential socialization hypothesis, Maccoby and Jacklin (1974) offered the following summary evaluation: "Our survey of the research on socialization of the two sexes has revealed surprisingly little differentiation in parent behavior according to the sex of the child. However, there are some areas where differential 'shaping' does appear to occur" (pp. 338-339).

These conclusions by Maccoby and Jacklin will be comforting to some, but are startling to many. Because of the reputation of these researchers, the large number of studies reviewed, and the expressed caution surrounding their conclusions, it may be expected that their evaluation of the empirical literature will come to be the prevalent view of this important psychological issue and will influence subsequent directions of research, theoretical conceptualizations, and even social policy. Because of the potential impact of the Maccoby and Jacklin conclusions, it is important to evaluate closely and carefully the empirical base from which their interpretations derived. Unfortunately, psychological research on socialization has been characterized by problems and deficiencies that permit the conclusions drawn by Maccoby and Jacklin. Some recognition of these deficiencies, therefore, is useful for keeping open inquiry on the existence and nature of socialization differences.

The first section of the present chapter develops additional perspectives on the studies bearing on differential socialization summarized by Maccoby and Jacklin. The quality and cogency of the evidence will be evaluated. The second section of the chapter presents data on sex-differentiated socialization derived from the self-reports of both mothers and fathers, as well as from the perceptions of parental rearing practices held by young adults. The results of these studies are compared to the Maccoby and Jacklin conclusions. Finally, some suggestions for new directions in research in the area of socialization are made—directions informed by our past failures and catalyzed by the provocative summary of Maccoby and Jacklin.

THE EVIDENCE AS EVALUATED BY MACCOBY AND JACKLIN

In collating the results of studies which bear on the differential socialization of boys and girls, Maccoby and Jacklin reviewed close to 200 published studies and evaluated parental behaviors in 11 different domains. Their conclusions about the empirical support or lack of support for the differential socialization hypothesis in each domain are now summarized.

1. No systematic differences are found (a) in the amount of total interaction parents have with girls and with boys, although they note a "consistent trend" for parents to stimulate gross motor activity more in their sons than in their daughters; and (b) in parental responses to the child's manifestations of sexuality (e.g., asking questions, engaging in sex play, masturbating). 2. Inconsistent findings are said to characterize (a) studies assessing the amount of verbal interaction when parent-son and parent-daughter dyads are compared, (b) studies of parental reactions to aggression, and (c) investigations of parental pressures for achievement in boys and in girls. 3. Little or no evidence of sex-differentiated parental behaviors is reported in relation to (a) parental warmth and nurturance, (b) parental restrictiveness, and (c) parental reactions to the child's dependent behaviors. 4. Significant differences in parental behaviors as a function of the child's sex were found in only three socialization areas: (a) parental encouragement of sex-typed activities in that greater pressure for appropriate sex-role behavior was found to be exerted on boys; (b) the use of negative reinforcements, both physical and nonphysical, which was found to be

significantly more characteristic of parents of boys; and (c) the use of praise and other positive reinforcements, which also was more characteristic of parents of boys.

On the basis of the review of the literature offered by Maccoby and Jacklin, few differences appear to characterize parental socialization emphases for the two sexes. Despite these negative conclusions, however, these authors do find evidence that parents tend to "shape" their male and female children in sex-appropriate ways by dressing them differently, by encouraging sex-typed interests, by providing sex-appropriate toys, and by assigning sex-differentiated chores. After searching the empirical data for evidence of sex-differentiated techniques used in the "shaping" process, the authors conclude, "We must summarize our analysis of this (shaping) hypothesis with the conclusion that we have been able to find very little evidence to support it, in relation to behaviors other than sex typing as very narrowly defined (e.g., toy preference). The reinforcement contingencies for the two sexes appear to be remarkably similar" (Maccoby & Jacklin, 1974, p. 342).

Parental sex-typing behaviors, however, even narrowly defined when viewed in the context of self- and sex-role development, may have important implications. For example, Whiting (1975) described one process by which sex-assigned chores may contribute to later behavioral differences noted between boys and girls. Citing data obtained from field studies in six cultures, Whiting noted that girls are more frequently assigned domestic and child-care chores than are boys (e.g., looking after younger children, cooking, cleaning, food preparation, grinding) and that girls are assigned responsibilities at an earlier age than boys. Boys, on the other hand, are assigned chores that take them from the immediate vicinity of the house and are given responsibility (albeit at a later age) for feeding, pasturing, and herding animals. For boys and girls these sex differences in assigned work are associated with different frequencies of interaction with various categories of people (e.g., adults, infants, peers). Girls interact more often both with adults and infants, whereas boys interact significantly more often with peers. Whiting suggested that the observed behavioral differences between boys and girls in their samples may be, to some extent, a function of sex distinctions in assigned chores. Younger girls in all cultures were found significantly more nurturant (e.g., offering help and giving support) and significantly more responsible than boys. In later childhood, girls remained more nurturant, but responsibility no longer differentiated girls from boys because boys showed a significant increase in initiative—an increase occurring after they began to take care of the pasturing and herding of animals. Although conjectural, Whiting's analysis is highly plausible and draws the attention to the possibility that a seemingly peripheral aspect of sex-typed socialization, chore assignments, may have broader implications.

Viewed from another, quite different perspective, these parental shaping behaviors urging the child toward sex-appropriate interests, activities, tasks, and the like may be seen as *labeling* behaviors. According to the cognitive-developmental theory of sex typing as explicated by Kohlberg (1966) and endorsed by Maccoby and Jacklin, sex typing is initiated by the very early *labeling* of the child with respect to gender. The gender label becomes an organizing rubric around which the child actively, selectively, and with increasing complexity constructs ter sex-role definition. Through experience with parents, siblings, and peers, with the outside world, with the media, and with books, the child learns—through a variety of techniques, including environmental manipulation, tutoring and reinforcement—those responses, interests, activities, clothes, play materials, and tasks that are deemed consistent with ter sex-role categorization. Viewed from this perspective, the process of parental sex-typing conveys information to the child which is essential for the cognitive construction of ter sex-role concept. The consequences of parental sex-role "shaping" behaviors— conjoined with other documented differences in the use of positive and negative reinforcement and parental pressures exerted on boys to avoid sex-inappropriate behaviors—constitute important evidence for sex-differentiated socialization emphases. It would be most unfortunate to conclude, because of the incoherence of the available research literature and the ephemeralness of the specific processes parents use in shaping their children, that differences in the way parents socialize their sons and daughters do not exist. Rather, the empirical inconsistencies characterizing studies of sex-differentiated parental socialization behaviors should stimulate close diagnostic evaluation of the adequacy of the literature in the socialization domain. The conceptualizations, operational indices, and the research designs employed must be scrutinized closely. It is to this task we turn.

A SECOND LOOK AT THE EVIDENCE

Several general problems—both theoretical and methodological—besetting the socialization literature have contributed to a premature embracing of the null hypothesis about divergence in child-rearing emphases as a function of sex. At a conceptual level, we have not yet developed a coherent formulation of the socialization process that permits specific and differentiated predictions about socialization practices as a function of the child's developmental level, the environmental context of the family, or parental role concepts. And, in our empirical efforts, research has tended to be of an ad hoc or after-the-fact nature rather than targeted toward areas where, conceptually, differences might be expected. Socialization studies frequently have depended upon globally-defined concepts, which may operate to obscure differences that might be revealed if more differentiated criteria had been used. Because these shortcomings have implications for the ways in which we may interpret the Maccoby and Jacklin compilation of the socialization literature, they will be discussed in some detail.

Theories of socialization (including sex-role socialization) make implicit assumptions about developmental shifts in socialization emphases, both as a function of age and sex; however, research efforts have only infrequently been concerned with documenting and articulating these developmental trends. Emmerich (1973) noted that the search for organizing processes in sex-role socialization calls for research studies designed to permit explicit age-related comparisons. Parental socialization emphases are dynamic and responsive to the changing environmental demands, to the emerging competence and responsibility of the child, and to reorganizing conceptions of the parental role over time. The particular circumstances in our society that contribute to different environmental contexts for boys and girls, as they progress from nursery school to elementary school, to high school, and to the threshold of adulthood, also create different situational "press" for parents that may be expected to contribute to sex-related divergence in their child-rearing patterns over time.

In one of the few longitudinal studies documenting changes in maternal behaviors as a function of the child's development between 9 and 18 months, Clark-Stewart (1973) reported significant changes. The child's increasing independence was accompanied by a decrease in maternal attention, as reflected by less physical contact, less care-taking, less social stimulation, and more leaving the child alone. Mothers were observed to institute more negative sanctions (punishment and scolding) with increasing age of the child. As the children approached 18 months of age, mothers became more directive, more effective in their interventions, and more responsive to their children's behavioral expressions, particularly in the social realm.

Reference to the Fels Institute longitudinal data, which assessed maternal behaviors at three time periods (0 to 3 years; 3 to 6 years; 6 to 10 years), provides additional evidence of changing socialization foci with the increasing age of the child (Kagan & Moss, 1962). Not only is there a shift in the salience of particular child-rearing practices associated with age-related demand characteristics of the child from birth to age 10, but with time, maternal behaviors become more stable and sex-differentiated patterns of maternal behavior are suggested. (Kagan & Moss, 1962, pp. 207-209).

Two recent studies extend the sparse literature related to developmental trends in socialization. In a cross-sectional study including 342 children in grades 1 through 4 who were administered the Child's Report of the Parental Behavior Inventory (PBI), (Schaeffer, 1965) changes in children's perceptions of parental child-rearing behavior as a function of age were found (Burger, Lamp, & Rogers, 1975). Perceptions of both maternal and paternal behaviors on the acceptance-rejection factor showed a significant decrease in acceptance with age (from grades 2 to 4 for fathers and from grades 3 to 4 for mothers); perceptions of parental behaviors on the autonomy versus control factor showed a significant decrease in psychological control with age, with scores at each level lower than those of the preceding grade level for both mothers and fathers; and on the firm-versus-lax control factor, a significant increase in the firmness of both parents was found from grades 2 through 4. The results of this study show significant developmental shifts in the children's perception of parental rearing practices on each of the three factors constituting the PBI.

Parental socialization values were assessed among parents of 44 preadolescent and adolescent boys by recording a discussion between parents and son about the meaning of the proverb, "A rolling stone gathers no moss" (Jacob, Fagin, Perry, & Van Dyke, 1975). A growth interpretation of the proverb emphasizing the value of development through mobility, exploration, and striving was more frequently endorsed by parents of preadolescent boys than was a stability interpretation emphasizing the attainment of security through maintaining close and long-lasting relationships. Among parents of adolescent boys, however, there was a shift, primarily among upper middle-class parents, toward the stability interpretation of the proverb. This shift is interpretable, according to the authors, as an expression of parental anxiety occasioned by challenges to their value systems on the part of questioning adolescent sons for whom it is feared the alternative life styles of the counterculture may be seductive. These results are intriguing, and therefore the study deserves replication with larger samples to include daughters as well. The findings suggest a shift in the focal anxieties and concerns of parents as they become older and as their children become older and are exposed to more, different, and less controllable (by parents) influences.

In commenting on the existing studies of differential socialization, Maccoby and Jacklin (1974) noted the predominance of studies in which parental socialization orientations are assessed while children are still quite young. They suggest that this age bias derives in part from an assumption of declining parental influence, once the child enters school where teachers and peers become salient socialization agents, and in part from an assumption that greater plasticity characterizes the young child. These assumptions imply that parental socialization is conceived by many researchers as a relatively static phenomenon, more readily observable during the child's early years. In Maccoby and Jacklin's comprehensive listing of studies, 77% of all investigations cited were based on the results of analyses comparing the socialization of boys and girls age 5 and younger.

But perhaps such young human offspring are treated more as children than as boys or girls. I suggest that it is simply unreasonable to expect that sex-related *differences* in socialization will be expressed by parents toward very young children in the areas of achievement emphasis, control of aggression, amount of parental interaction, parental supervision of the child's activities, tolerance for sexuality, or responses to dependency. Some areas (e.g., achievement emphasis, tolerance for sexuality) have not yet become salient for differential socialization, and in other areas (e.g., dependency, aggression), tolerances perhaps have not yet been stressed.

If we consider only the results issuing from the minority of studies (23%) assessing the socialization behaviors of parents of older children (age 6 or older), we may find a clear trend toward more frequent sex-differential parental behaviors. This trend becomes more robust when studies based on very small samples are excluded. However, with respect to certain psychological dimensions, age trends cannot be evaluated for two reasons: (1) no subjects older than age 5 have been included in research studies assessing total parental interaction with the child or stimulation of gross motor behavior; (2) no subjects older than age 6 have been included in studies assessing parental tolerance for dependency or parental response to aggression.

This age-range limitation in socialization research suggests that an important qualifier be appended to conclusions drawn from this body of data, to wit: *The differential socialization hypothesis has been examined primarily (and for some areas exclusively) in parent samples whose children are age 6 and under.* The Maccoby and Jacklin review starkly reveals the disproportionate research emphasis on socialization of young children and suggests the need for systematic studies of differential socialization among parents of older children, studies that would seek to identify the nature of the relationship between socialization emphases, the stimulus value of the child (of which sex and age are determinants), and the situational press (of which sex and age are determinants).

A second factor contributing to the essentially null conclusions drawn from studies evaluated by Maccoby and Jacklin is the tendency of most socialization research to focus on the mother as the critical socializing agent. These authors note the lack of information about fathers and recognize that this omission could be a source of bias because fathers may differentiate between the sexes in their child-rearing orientations to a greater extent than do mothers. Inferences drawn from studies of the effect of father-absence on sex-role typing in males (e.g., Tiller, 1958; McCord, McCord, & Thurber, 1962; Hetherington, 1966; Biller, 1971) and the impact of the father on personality and sex-role development in males (e.g., Payne & Mussen, 1956; Mussen & Distler, 1959; Nash, 1965) and in females (e.g., Heilbrun, Harrel, & Gillard, 1967; Hetherington, 1972; Block, Block, & von der Lippe, 1973) underscore the importance of the father and suggest that his socialization emphases for boys and for girls be studied more systematically.

In the studies contributing to the Maccoby and Jacklin evaluation of differential socialization for boys and girls, mothers-as-respondents account for 49% of the studies, fathers-as-respondents are the focus of inquiry in only 9% of the cited studies, and 30% of the studies, including those based on child-reports, have attempted to document the socialization orientations of both parents. (The remaining 12% of the studies summarized depend upon teacher or caretaker responses to the child.) Since fathers themselves were involved in only a small percentage of the total number of research studies reported, it could well be that evaluations of differential socialization effects are underestimated by virtue of the undersampling of paternal behaviors that is typical of socialization research. References to the data pertaining only to fathers' socialization emphases as reflected in the results of studies reviewed by Maccoby and Jacklin suggest that the father-daughter relationship is characterized by more warmth than is the father-son relationship; that fathers of boys are more firm, in contrast to fathers of girls; that fathers appear more concerned about the welfare of their daughters than of their sons; that fathers tend more to provide comfort when their daughters are upset than when their sons seek comfort; that fathers tend more to expect aggressiveness and competition in their sons than in their daughters; and that fathers are more accepting of verbal aggression directed toward themselves by their daughters than by their sons. By focusing explicitly and solely upon the socialization emphases of fathers, some trends obscured in the results of studies aggregating both parents become apparent, suggesting that fathers may be more sex-differentiating in their interpersonal and socialization behaviors than are mothers.

It is insufficient, however, only to conclude that fathers as well as mothers should be included in our socialization studies. It is required, as well, that our theories of socialization become more articulated with respect to the particular contribution of each parent to the socialization process. If parental socialization roles vary in their degree of sex differentiation with respect to specific areas, then our failure to sample the behaviors of the parent who primarily assumes responsibility for socialization in a particular area represents another source of potential bias. Investigations of differential socialization using a teaching strategy paradigm, for example, have only infrequently included fathers as well as mothers.

The results of a recent study by Block, Block, & Harrington (Note 2) suggest that the failure to find consistent differences in the socialization of boys and girls in the achievement domain may be a function of the failure to study fathers' behaviors in the achievement-relevant context. These investigators assessed the teaching behaviors of both mothers ($N = 117$) and fathers ($N = 96$) who each separately taught a battery of four cognitive tasks varying in their convergent-divergent demand characteristics to ter child. Two parallel test batteries were developed for use by parents, and a counterbalanced design was used to control for order of teaching and test battery. In all cases a minimum of five weeks separated the experimental teaching situations of the two parents, each of whom was always interviewed by different examiners.

The data of interest in the study are the Q-sort observations completed by the examiners to describe the parents' behaviors in the teaching situations. Summarizing the results of *t-test comparisons between mothers of girls and boys, the investigators reported that the teaching style of mothers did not differentiate between the sexes; only one of the 49 Q*-items significantly discriminated the sexes. Fathers, on the other hand, were found to manifest different teaching behaviors depending upon the child's sex, and 14% of the *t*-test comparisons between the fathers of boys and the fathers of girls were significant at or beyond the .05 level. Fathers of boys were more concerned with achievement and emphasized the cognitive aspects of the teaching situation, whereas the fathers of daughters appeared to be more attuned to the interpersonal aspects and were less concerned with performance per se. The latter attempted to make the situation more fun, were more protective, and were less pressuring of their daughters. The investigators concluded: "The items differentiating fathers of boys from fathers of girls clearly suggest that achievement emphasis (in the teaching strategy situation) is a more salient characteristic of the father-son than of the father-daughter relationship" (Block et al., 1974, Note 2, p. 8).

The results from the study by Block and associates concur with the data summarized by Maccoby and Jacklin with reference to achievement where mothers were found not to differentiate between the sexes in their pressures for achievement. Their results also agree with those of two of the three studies cited by Maccoby and Jacklin, in which fathers' pressures for *cognitive* achievement were evaluated. Together, these findings suggest an alternative interpretation of the data surrounding achievement emphasis, which recognizes (a) that *cognitive* achievement may be a less salient socialization domain for mothers relative to fathers, (b) that mothers are less sex-differentiating in their pressures for cognitive achievement, and (c) that fathers tend to be more pressuring of their sons than of their daughters for cognitive achievement. Generally, these results emphasize the importance of differentiating not only the sex of the child but also the differentiating parental roles with respect to particular areas of socialization.

Another source of potential bias in the accumulated findings bearing upon the differential socialization issue is concerned with construct definition and operationalization. In collating research findings derived from heterogeneous measures tapping different domains of child-rearing behaviors, a two-stage sequence of construct definition is involved. At the first stage, the operations of the investigator are crucial. Having decided to study a particular phenomenon or process, the investigator must define the construct, specify its expected behavioral manifestations, and select appropriate procedures of measurement. If a construct is too globally or equivocally defined, subsequent results may be blurred and inconclusive. Consider the concept of dependency, for example. This umbrella concept is not unidimensional, but as usually conceived it embodies components of the inability to sustain oneself without aid from others, the inability to cope with a problem, lack of psychological autonomy, subordination, and docility (Block & Christiansen, 1966). As operationalized, measures of dependency include proximity seeking, attention seeking, reassurance seeking, and help seeking; the resulting correlations among these various aspects of dependency are uniformly low (Martin, 1975). The low interrelations among these different behavioral expressions of dependency are hardly surprising if one considers that behaviors may be alternatively manifested. That is, the expression of dependent behaviors in one domain may render unnecessary (particularly in the case of a responsive environment) their expression in other ways, thus accounting for the low correlations typically observed. In the case of the low relationship among variables presumed to index different aspects of a concept, the use of differentiated measures becomes crucial if we are to find consistencies in our empirical data.

In a study cited by Maccoby and Jacklin, Hilton (1967) noted, in summarizing the findings derived from observing mothers' behaviors while their first- or later-born children were completing a puzzle task, that

> The sex differences which do arise do not lend themselves to parsimonious explanation. In some areas boys were more dependent and in others the girls were. It may be that parents tolerate dependency in boys in some areas (asking for help) but not in others (clinging). The dependency is present in both sexes but the form in which it is manifested varies (p. 228).

When parental behaviors in response to the child's request for help and in response to the child's clinging are *both* taken as indicators of dependency, cross-sex comparisons of mean scores will issue null findings as a function of the global nature of the concept definition. If, however, parental behaviors were studied *separately* with reference to help seeking and to clinging, significant differences previously obscured would have the opportunity to emerge.

At the second stage of construct definition, the classification scheme developed by the collators becomes crucial. When research results achieved with a variety of instruments, tapping different phenomena, are brought together in order to assess the empirical data base surrounding a particular construct, what criteria should be used for categorizing the existing studies with reference to the construct? In grouping studies under the rubric of "achievement" or "permissiveness for dependency," or "restrictiveness," how should we decide which studies properly relate to each construct? Should studies assessing parental pressures for developing competence be merged with those evaluating parental concerns for the achievement of long-range goals? As demonstrated in cognitive style studies of categorization behavior, the clarity and cohesiveness of a category is a function of the width of category boundaries. With broad category boundaries, cohesiveness is more difficult and even impossible to achieve.

In the present context, the category boundaries established for the inclusion of particular studies in a domain can powerfully affect subsequent interpretation. The task of sorting studies is not an easy one and, generally, Maccoby and Jacklin attempted to stay close to the data. However, the null conclusions they report for some areas of socialization may be a function of the heterogeneity of the dependent measures grouped together. For example, studies relating to parental pressures for achievement include the following dependent measures:

(a) amount of praise or criticism for intellectual performance; (b) parental standards for intellectual performance as expressed on a questionnaire item; (c) expectation that child will go to college; (d) pressure for competent task completion; (e) expectation of household help; (f) responses to an "achievement inducing" scale which reflects the ages at which parents feel it is appropriate to teach a child more mature behaviors; (g) amount of direct help and number of task-oriented suggestions offered by mother; (h) number of anxious intrusions into childs' task performance; (i) observed pressure for achievement (unspecified); (j) pressure for success on a memory task; (k) demands made upon the child during a joint problem-solving task and concern with the child's intellectual achievements.

Although many of these measures are obviously related to the achievement dimension, others are readily challengeable. A mother's expectations for household help, or anxious intrusions into the child's problem-solving attempts, or demands upon the child during a discussion in which a consensus must be reached, or pressures for competence in 2-year-olds observed in the home setting—all these are behaviors that lack both construct and discriminant validity with respect to achievement emphasis. Anxious intrusions, demands, and criticisms could as easily be construed as indicators of maternal anxiety, impatience, parental sense of inadequacy, intrusiveness, or other negative expressions. The posited interpretations of a particular measure must be supported by evidence of both convergent and discriminating relationships that exclude alternative interpretations. When one considers how infrequently the validity of psychological instruments is established rather than declared, it is little wonder that many of the findings in the socialization literature are inconsistent and even incoherent.

Finally, it is suggested that evidence for differential socialization can be obscured by aggregating and weighting equally studies widely divergent in statistical power. In reaching conclusions about sex-differentiated socialization pressures, Maccoby and Jacklin relied on a "box score" approach wherein both the positive and the null findings issuing from comparisons between parents of girls and parents of boys on dependent measures are grouped together without regard for the psychometric quality or statistical power of the respective studies.

The power of a statistical test is a function of three parameters: (a) the "effect size," which in this context means the size of the difference between the population of parents of boys and the population of the parents of girls with respect to a measured phenomenon: (b) the number of cases being evaluated; and (c) the significance criterion set for the rejection of the null hypothesis (Cohen, 1969). To the extent that measures of parental socialization attitudes and behaviors—whether indexed by interviews, questionnaires, or laboratory or home observations—are unreliable or irrelevant, the effect size will become small and therefore undetectable.

When this source of power reduction is compounded by the employment of small samples, the power of a statistical test is further reduced, increasing the likelihood of falsely accepting the null hypothesis of no difference. A false acceptance of the null hypothesis will lead us to conclude in the present context that no differences (have been proved to) exist between parents of boys and parents of girls in their socialization behaviors. However, improvement in the quality of the measures employed and the utilization of efficient research designs could well result in the discernment of relationships not presently observed, or noted only inconsistently.

When the studies listed by Maccoby and Jacklin as dealing with differential socialization are evaluated with respect to only one aspect of statistical power (sample size) wide differences in the power of the studies are noted. Of all studies contributing to the conclusion that there is little evidence for sex-related socialization, 43% are based on total sample sizes of 60 or less, yielding a maximum of 30 cases per subgroup. Coupled with the unreliability or irrelevance of many of the measures employed, these small sample sizes make it probable that many of the studies are so lacking in power that they are incapable of reflecting "true" population differences, thus leading us down the path of the Type II error.

In summary, it is suggested that—in the absence of socialization theories which articulate differences in child-rearing practices expectable as a function of age, sex, environmental context of the child, and parental role definitions—the critical research studies have not been completed. It is unrealistic to expect that similar socialization emphases will be characteristic of mothers and fathers across a variety of areas, across age levels, across contexts, and across sex of the child. A more complex model of socialization is required in order that we may develop differentiated hypotheses about differential socialization emphases. Methodological problems also have limited the implications of many of the studies cited. Small sample sizes, unreliability of instruments, and lack of construct validity have operated, both singly and conjointly, to reduce the power or cogency of many studies. Finally, it should be emphasized that the fact of *inconsistency* in research findings surrounding the differential socialization hypothesis does not imply that there are no differences in parental behavior. Rather, the inconsistency implies that we do not understand the reasons for this inconsistency.

With more differentiated hypotheses, with more reliable and construct valid measures, with more appropriate sampling, with better statistical design, we can reasonably expect that the findings on differential socialization will become more coherent. If well-executed comparisons of the socialization emphases of parents of boys and of girls uniformly yielded null (in contrast to inconsistent) findings, then the null hypothesis could be accepted more comfortably as a reasonable summary position. But, on the basis of the research evidence now available, as reported in the Maccoby and Jacklin (1974) review volume, I suggest that the question remains moot.

SOME DATA TO ENCOURAGE EXPLORATION
OF NEW DIRECTIONS

Having presented some conceptual and methodological problems that have operated to attenuate effects and to obscure the clarity of findings in the literature bearing upon the differential socialization hypothesis, I turn now to consider some data comparing the child-rearing orientations, values, and techniques of both mothers and fathers from two different perspectives: (a) parental self-report, and (b) perceptions of parental rearing practices by young adults. A standard instrument, the Block Child-Rearing Practices Report (CRPR; Note 1) was administered to samples varying with respect to cultural and subcultural origins, age, sex, and health status of the child. In all, data from 17 independent samples comprising 696 mothers, 548 fathers, and 1,227 young adults have been brought together for the present analyses and evaluation.

The CRPR consists of 91 socialization-relevant items to be evaluated by the respondent with reference to a specific, designated child in the case of the First-Person Parent form and with reference to a designated parent in the case of the Third-Person Parent form of the test. The CRPR is administered using a Q-sort format in order to minimize the operation of response sets. Each of the 91 items is assigned to one of seven categories, depending upon its salience to the respondent.

The CRPR was administered to six different samples of mothers and to five samples of fathers whose children ranged in age from 3 to 20 years, and who were heterogeneous with respect to ethnic and socio-economic backgrounds. Additionally, the CRPR was administered to six samples of young adults attending universities and technical colleges in each of six countries (United States, England, Finland, Norway, Sweden, and Denmark). These young people described the child-rearing emphases of their mothers, using the third-person form, and in the case of the United States sample only, they described the child-rearing emphases of their fathers as well.

The kind of information generated by the CRPR is heavily represented in the research on differential socialization reviewed by Maccoby and Jacklin, where 40% of the studies cited depend upon either questionnaire or interview responses by parents or children. In the present context, the use of a standard instrument for evaluating child-rearing orientations has a distinct advantage. Maccoby and Jacklin were faced with the problem of interpreting data derived from non-comparable procedures varying in domain coverage, format, vulnerability to response sets, and psychometric quality. It may be instructive, therefore, to look again at the differential socialization hypothesis, using an instrument that has extensive domain coverage and good reliability, which minimizes response sets and has been applied widely.

My purposes in presenting these data are three: (a) to examine sex-related socialization behaviors from the differing perspectives of mothers, fathers, and children; (b) to present a data base that may suggest some more differentiated hypotheses about the socialization of boys and girls, hypotheses differentiated with respect to developmental trends, construct definition, and parental roles; and (c) to keep open and to stimulate further inquiry into the question of differential socialization until the more inclusive and systematic studies required in this field have been completed.

The CRPR data were analyzed within each of the six samples of mothers by comparing via *t*-tests, the responses of the mothers of sons and the mothers of daughters for each of the 91 items. Similarly, within each sample of fathers, *t*-test comparisons of the responses of the fathers of sons and the fathers of daughters were completed. The results of these comparisons within each of the 11 parent samples as well as the combined probabilities calculated across the 6 independent samples of mothers and the 5 independent samples of fathers (Winer, 1971, p. 50) are presented in Table 2.1.

To guide the reader through Table 2.1, some explanation is in order. The column entries in the table indicate the direction of the mean difference between parents of sons (S) and parents of daughters (D); trends toward significance, indicated by S+ or D+, designate *t*-rations in excess of 1.0 but less than the 1.67 required for $p < .10$; when appropriate, the probability levels of the *t*-test comparisons (.01, .05, and .10) are given as cell entries. This method of data presentation was adopted in order to reveal cross-sample consistencies that might otherwise be neglected by the usual dichotomous practice of reporting only those results wherein the null hypothesis is rejected.

In order to facilitate the detection of age trends that might characterize the data, Samples 1 through 5 are ordered according to the increasing mean ages of the children. Sample 6 includes mothers and fathers from the Netherlands; the mean age of children in these samples is between those of Samples 3 and 4. The numerical designations of the samples of parents denote mother-father dyads; that is, the mothers and fathers in Samples 1, 2, 4, 5, and 6 are, for the most part, spouses, but some single parents are represented as well. Sample 3 includes only mothers. Sample 2 comprises parents of children with chronic illnesses. Sample 5 has the highest socioeconomic level and is composed of parents of college and university students.

Before abstracting the results based on parents' self-described child-rearing orientations, I shall present the data derived from the study of college and university students in six countries, who described their perceptions of their mothers' child-rearing values and practices and (for the United States sample only) their perceptions of paternal child-rearing orientations. These data are presented in Table 2.2, and the same conventions used in Table 2.1 for reporting results are applied. Combined probabilities are reported only for the descriptions of maternal rearing practices, since father descriptions were obtained from one student sample only.

In order to bring together the data from the four different perspectives (mothers' self-descriptions, fathers' self-descriptions, young adults' perceptions of mothers, and young adults' perceptions of fathers) in a form that permits an overall comparison of sex-related socialization emphases—their consistencies and their inconsistencies—a summary of the significant results is presented in Table 2.3. In reviewing this table and in evaluating the results of the several analyses, it is critical to recall that the young adults sampled are *not* the children of the parents participating in the study. Therefore, consistencies across data sources—because of the lack of correspondence between the parent and young adult samples, and because of the cultural and subcultural heterogeneities character-izing the samples—are underestimated in the present analyses. Obviously, a more desirable research paradigm would examine consistencies in socialization viewed from the different perspectives of parent and their *own* children. Although cross-data source (parents and students) consistencies are more difficult to dis-cern in the present analyses because of the differences and unrelatedness of the samples, the results (if achieved) are probably rather robust and permit broader generalizations.

Inspection of the results of these several analyses (*within* the several inde-pendent samples of parents presented in Table 2.1, *within* the several independ-

Table 2.1

Differential socialization emphases as reflected in t-test comparisons of parents of sons and parents of daughters

CRPR (Abridged)	Self-descriptions												Mothers		Fathers	
	1	2	3	4	5	6	1	2	3	4	5	6	Direction	p	Direction	p
	62M 65F	43M 32F	31M 32F	75M 46F	100M 83F	73M 54F	46M 55F	26M 18F	58M 61F	90M 66F	73M 55F					
Respected C's opinions	D	D	D	.05D	S	S	D	D	D+	D+	D+	S	D		D	
Encouraged C to do well	S	S	.05D	S+	.05S	S	S	S	S+	S+	S+	S	S	.10	S	.002
Put spouse's wishes first	.10D	S+	S	S	S	S	S+	D	S+	D	D	D	S		S	
Helped C when teased	D	S+	D	S	D+	D+	D	D	D+	D+	D+	S	D		D	
Felt angry with C	S	S+	S	S	D+	D	D	D+	S	S	S	D+	S		D	
Wanted C to handle own problems	S+	S	S	S	S	S	S	S	S	S	S	S+	S		S	.05
Punished by isolating C	D	S	S	S	D	.05S	S	D	D	.05S	S+	S+	S		S	
Watched C's eating habits	D+	D	D	S	D+	S	D	S	D	S+	S+	D	D		S	
Didn't think young C should be naked when with other children	S+	S+	D	S	S	D	S+	D	D	D	S	D	S		D	
Wished spouse to be more interested in C	D	S	S+	.01S	D	S	D	D	.10D	S	S	D+	S	.02	D	.08

Table 2.1 (continued)

Gave C comfort when upset	S	.10S	.05D	D	S	.05S	D+	D+	.05D	D+	D	S	D	.008
Kept C away from families with different ideas	S+	D	S	D	S+	S+.	D	S	S	S+	S		S	
Didn't allow rough games	D	D+	.05D	D+	D	S	D	D+	D	D+	D	.003	D	.10
Believed physical punishment best	D	D	.10S	D	S	S	.05S	S	.10S	S		S	S	.01
Thought C should be seen, not heard	S+	D	S+	S	S	S	S	S		S			S	
Sometimes forgot to fulfill promises to C	D+	D	D	D	.05D	D	D	S		D	S		D	.08
Thought it good for C to perform	.10S	D+	.05D	D	S	D+	S	D		S	D		S	
Expressed affection physically	S	.10D	D	.10D	D+	D+	.05D	.05D	.10D	D		.005	D	.0003
Obtained great satisfactions from C	S	D	S	D	S+	S+	D	.10S	D	D		S	D	
Protected C against failure	S	S	D	S	S	D+	D	D	D	D+		S	D	
Encouraged C to wonder about life	D	D	.01D	D	D	.05D	D+	D	D	D		D	D	.04
Included C in making plans	.05D	S	.05S	.05D	S	.10S	D+	.10D	D	D		S	D	.02
Was sorry to see C grow up	S	S	S	D	D+	S	D+	D	D+	D		S	D	.04

Table 2.1 (continued)

Allowed C to daydream and loaf	D	S	D	D	S	D	D	D	S	D+	D		D		D	
Found it difficult to punish C	D+	D	D+	D+	D	D	D	D	D	D	.05D	.10D	D	.03	D	.02
Let C make decision	S	.10S	.10S	S	S	D	D+	D+	D+	D	D	D	S	.03	D	.04
Didn't allow C to say bad things about teachers	S+	.10S	D+	D	D	S	.05S	S+	D	D	D	D	S		S	
Worried about C	S	D+	S	S	D	.05S	D	S	.01S	D	.01D	D	D		D	
Taught C punishment would come if bad	.10S	S	S	S	S	S	D	S	D	S	D	S	.02		S	
Didn't blame C if others provoked trouble	D	D+	D+	D	D+	D+	S+	S+	S	.10D	D	D	D		D	
Felt C to be a disappointment to me	S	D	S	D+	S	S	S+	S+	S	S	S	D	D		S	
Expected a great deal of C	S	D	S	S	S	S+	S+	S	S+	S+	S	S	S		S	.01
Was relaxed with C	S	S	.05D	S	D+	S+	D	.10D	D	S+	D	D	D		D	
Gave up my interests for C	.10D	D	S	D	D	D	D	D	S	S	D	S	D		S	
Spoiled C	.10S	S	S	D	D	S	S	S	.05D	S	S	D	S		D	
Believed C always truthful	D+	D+	D	D+	S	S	S	D	D	D+	D	D	D	.03	D	.05
Reasoned with C	S	S	.10D	D	D	S	D+	D+	D	D	D	D	D		D	
Didn't allow C to be angry with me	S	S	S	D	D	.10S	S+	S+	S	S	S	S	S	.03	S	.03

Table 2.1 (continued)

Didn't want C to have secrets from parents	S+	D+	D	D	S+	D	D	S	S	D	S	D	D	S	.05D	D
Encouraged C to control feelings	S+	.05S	S	D	.05S	S	S	S+	S+	S+	S+	.05S	.005		S .004	
Tried to keep C from fighting	D	.10S	D	D	D	S	D+	D	.01D	D	S	D	S		D .007	
Dreaded answering sex questions	S+	D	D+	S	S	S	S	D+	S	S	S	D	S		D	
Let C know when I felt angry	S	D+	S	S+	D+	S	D	S	S	S	S	D	D		S	
Encouraged competition	S	.05S	S+	S+	.05S	S	S	D	S+	S+	S	S	.0002		S .08	
Punished by taking away privileges	S	S+	S	S	.10S	S+	S+	S+	S	S+	.10S	S	.01		S .02	
Gave extra privileges for reward	S+	D+	.05D	S	S	S+	D	D	D	D	S+	D	S		S	
Enjoyed a houseful of children	D	S	S	S+	D+	D	D	D	.10D	D	D	D	S		D .08	
Felt affection can weaken C	S	S	D	S	S	S	S	S	S	D	S	S	S		S	
Thought scolding improved C	S	S+	D+	.05S	D	S	S	S	.01D	.05S	.10S	S	.02		S	

Table 2.1 (continued)

Sacrificed a lot for C	S	S	S+	D	D	.10D	D	.05S	D+	S	D	D	S
Teased C	D	D+	D	D+	D	D	S	D+	.05S	D	.10S	D	S .02
Taught C to be responsible for self	S	D	D	D	D	D	S	S	S	S	S	D	S
Worried about C's health	S+	S+	S+	.05D	S	D+	D+	S	.10S	S	.10D	D	D
Was conflict between us	D	D	D	D	.05D	S	S	D+	.05S	D	S	D	S
Didn't allow C to question decisions	S	D	D	D	D+	.10S	.10S	.05S	.01S	.05S	S	D	S .0003
Believed competitive games good for C	S	S	S+	S+	S+	.01S	S+	S	S+	S+	S	S .000	S .006
Liked time away from children	D+	D	D	D	D+	.10S	D+	S	S	D	S+	D	S
Shamed C for misbehavior	D	D	S+	S	D	S+	S	S+	S	S+	D	S	S
Concerned with impression C makes on others	S	S	S	S	S	S	S	S	D	.05S	S	S .05	S
Encouraged C to be dependent of me	S	D	D	D	D+	S	D	S	S	.01D	D	S .05	D
Kept close track of C	D	D	D	D	D	.05D	D	S	.05D	S	D	D .03	D

Table 2.1 (continued)

Variable																
Found children Interesting	S	D	D	D	D	D	.10D	D	D+	S	S	D	D	—	D	—
Believed in early weaning	D	S+	S+	.10S	S	S	D	.10S	D	D	S	S	S	.03	S	—
Expected C to stay clean	D+	D	D	D	D+	D	S	D+	D+	D	S+	D	D	.03	D	—
Didn't like leaving C with stranger	S	.10D	D	S	S	.01D	D	D	D	.10D	D	D	D	.01	D	.007
Punished sibling rivalry	D	D	D	S	D	D+	.05D	.10S	S+	S	S	D	S	—	S	—
Taught C early not to cry	S+	S	.10S	S+	S	D	S+	S	S+	S	S	S	S	.05	S	.07
Controlled C by warning of bad things	D	S	S	D+	S+	D	D	S+	S+	D	S	D	D	—	D	—
Mother had most authority in family	S	S	.01D	D+	D	S+	S+	.05D	D	.10S	.01D	D	D	.02	D	—
Wanted C to be same as others	S+	D	S	S	S+	S+	S+	S	S	S	S+	S	S	.008	S	.08
Believed sex information should wait until C is older	S	.10S	S	S	S	S	S	S	S	D	D	S	S	.04	S	—
Felt it important for C to play outside	S+	S	S+	D	.10S	S	S	S	S	D	D	S	S	.01	S	—
Liked seeing C eat well	D	S	S	D	S+	S	S	S	S	D	D	S	S	—	S	—

Table 2.1 (continued)

Did not allow C to tease others	D	S	S	S	D	.010	S	S	.10D	D+	D	D
Wrong to insist on different toys for boys and girls	D+	S	S	D	.10S	S	D	D+			D	D
Believed children need close supervision	D	D	D	D	S	D	S	D+	D		.03	D
Total number of comparisons yielding p values > .10	6	10	13	16	7	14	12	10	20	16	13 (p < .05) N = 26	(P < .05) N = 23

Note. Entries represent the results of t-test comparisons between parents of sons and parents of daughters. S and D indicate the direction of the mean difference (sons or daughters). S+ or D+ indicates T-test values in excess of 1.00 but less than the 1.67 required for **p** < .10. For significant comparisons, **p** levels based upon two-tailed tests of significance are given in cell entries. Combined probabilities are calculated across the independent samples of mothers and (separately) the independent samples of fathers according to Winter (1971, p. 50).

Table 2.1 (continued)

aSamples are described as follows:

Sample 1. Mothers and fathers of nursery school children participating in a longitudinal study. Age range of children 3 to 4 years. (Data from a study by Block and Block, NIMH Research Grant MN-16080.)

Sample 2. Mothers and fathers of children with chronic illness varying in degrees of severity (asthma, diabetes, congenital heart disease, hay fever). Age range of children 3 to 11 years (mean 7.2 years). (Data from a study by Block & Block, NIMH Research Grants M-2521 and MH-0777.)

Sample 3. Mothers of sixth-grade children. Age range of children 11.5 to 12.5 years. (Data obtained through the courtesy of Paul Messen, University of California, Berkeley.)

Sample 4. Mothers and fathers of urban high school students. (Data provided by Berkeley Board of Education and staff members of Berkeley High School.)

Sample 5. Mothers and fathers of university students. (Data from study by Institute of Human Development, sponsored by the Rosenberg Foundation Fund for Research in Psychology.)

Sample 6. The Netherlands. Mothers and fathers of children living in Amsterdam. Age range of children 7 to 13 years. (Data available through courtesy of Professor R. Vuyk, University of Amsterdam.)

Table 2.2

Differential socialization emphases as reflected in t-test comparisons of young adult sons' and daughters' descriptions of parental child-rearing practices

CRPR items	U.S.	England	Finland	Norway	Sweden	Denmark	Analyses of combined probabilities for mothers		Descriptions of fathers, U.S.
(Abridged)	238M 256F	95M 57F	58M 133F	84M 108F	40M 92F	30M 36F	Direction	P	234M 236F
Respected C's opinions	D	.10D	D	.10D	S+	D	D	.04	S
Encouraged C to do well	S	S	.05D	D	S	S	S		D+
Put spouse's wishes first	.05D	.01D	S	D+	D+	S	D	.004	D+
Helped C when teased	D	D	D	D	.10D	D	D	.03	S
Felt angry with C	.01D	D	S	D+	.10D	S+	D	.03	S
Wanted C to handle own problems	D	.01D	S	.05D	D	S+	D	.07	S
Punished by isolating C	D	D+	D	S	.10D	S	D		S
Watched C's eating habits	.01S	S	S	S	S	D	S	.04	.05S
Didn't think young C should be naked when with other children	.10S	.05S	.10S	S	D	D	S	.008	D
Wished spouse more interested in C	D	S	D	S	D	S	S		S
Gave C comfort when upset	D	D+	.10D	D+	D	S	D	.04	.05D

Table 2.2 (continued)

	1	2	3	4	5	6	7	8	9
Kept C away from families with different ideas	D	.10S	D	.05S	D	S	S	.05	D
Didn't allow rough games	S+	S+	S+	.01S	S	.05S	S	.0002	.001D
Believed physical punishment best	D	D+	S	S	.10D	S+	D		S+
Thought C should be seen, not heard	D	D	S	=	.05D	D	D		D
Sometimes forgot to fulfill promises to C	.05D	D+	D	S	D	D+	D	.006	S
Thought it good for C to perform	D+	D	D+	D	S	D	D	.07	S
Expressed affection physically	D	S	D	D	S	D+	D	.09	.001D
Obtained great satisfactions from C	S+	S+	S	D	.10S	S	S	.02	.10S
Protected C against failure	.10D	S	S	S	S	S	S		S
Encouraged C to wonder about life	D	.10D	D+	D	S	D+	D	.05	.01D
Included C in making plans	D	D+	D+	S	S+	D+	D		D+
Was sorry to see C grow up	S	D+	D	D	S	D	D		.001D
Allowed C to daydream and loaf	.05D	.01D	.10D	D	.05D	D+	D	.0000	.01D

Table 2.2 (continued)

Found it difficult to punish C	.10S	D	D+	S	S+	D+	S		.05D
Let C make decisions	D+	.05D	.10D	.10D	S	S	D	.004	D
Didn't allow C to say bad things about teachers	S+	D	S	S+	.05S	.05S	S	.005	S
Worried about C	D+	S	D	S	S	D+	D		.01D
Taught C punishment would come if bad	.05S	.01S	S	.01S	S	D	S	.0005	.05S
Didn't blame C if others provoked trouble	S	S	D+	D	D+	D	D		.05S
Felt C a disappointment to me	.05D	.10D	S+	S	.05D	D	D	.03	D
Expected a great deal of C	S	.01S	D	S	S	D	S	.04	D
Was relaxed with C	S	D	D	D	S+	D+	D		D+
Gave up my interests for C	.01S	S	D+	S	D	D	S		.01S
Spoiled C	S	S+	D	.10D	S	.10D	D	.10	.001D
Believed C always truthful	.05D	D	D+	.01D	D	.05D	D	.0000	.01D
Reasoned with C	D	.05D	D	S+	.10S	S	S		S
Didn't allow C to be angry with me	.01S	S+	S	S	D	S	S	.009	S+
Trusted C for proper behavior	.05D	.10D	.05D	D	S+	D	D	.001	D+

Table 2.2 (continued)

									p	
Joked and played with C	D	D	D	D	S	.10D	D		.009	.05D
Gave C responsibilities	.05D	D+	S	S	D+	S	S+	D		.05S
C and I shared warm times together	.05D	.05D	D	.01D	D	D+	D+	D	.0000	D+
Had firm rules for C	.05D	D+	.05S	.01D	S	D+	S+	D	.0000	S
Let C take chances	.10D	.01D	D+	.05D	.01D	D	D	D	.0000	S+
Encouraged curiosity	S	.10D	D	S	S+	S+	S+	S		D
Explained by using the supernatural	S	S	.10S	S	D+	D+	D+	S		S
Expected gratitude from C	D+	S+	D	.10S	D	D	.10S	S	.08	.05D
Was too involved with C	S	.10S	D	D	S	S	S	S		S+
Believed in early toilet training	D	S+	S	.01D	D	D	D	D	.03	.10S
Threatened more than punished	S+	.01S	S	S	S+	S+	S	S	.0005	S+
Praised more than criticized	S+	=	D	S	S·	D+	S+	S		D
Appreciated C's efforts	S+	D	D	.10D	S	D	D	D		.10D
Encouraged C to talk of troubles	S	D+	D+	D+	S+	D+	D+	D	.05	S
Didn't want C to have secrets from parents	.10S	.05S	S+	S	S	D	S	S	.01	.01S
Encouraged C to control feelings	.05S	S	.05S	S	S+	S	S	S	.001	.05S

Table 2.2 (continued)

Tried to keep C from fighting	S+	.05S	.05S	.01S	.01S	.01S	S	.0000	.05D
Dreaded answering questions about sex	.05D	S	S+	S	.10D	D	D		D+
Let C know when I felt angry	.01D	D	D	S	D	S	D	.06	D
Encouraged competition	.01S	.01S	D	.01S	S+	D	S	.0000	.01S
Punished by taking away privileges	S	S+	S	D	D	S	S		S+
Gave extra privileges for reward	.10S	S	S	D+	10S	S+	S	.04	S
Enjoyed a houseful of children	S	D	S	.01D	D	D	D	.06	D
Felt affection can weaken C	.01S	.01S	.05S	S+	D+	.05S	S	.0000	.001S
Thought scolding improved C	.10D	S	S+	S	D	S	S		S
Sacrificed a lot for C	D	S+	S	.10S	D	.10S	S	.01	S+
Teased C	.05D	.05D	D	.01D	.01D	.10D	D	.0000	.001D
Taught C to be responsible for self	S	S	S	.01D	D	D	D	.10	.10S
Worried about C's health	.01S	.10S	.10S	S	S	D	S	.0000	.10S
Was conflict between us	.05D	.10D	D	.05D	D+	D	D	.0002	S+
Didn't allow C to question decisions	.10S	S+	D	S	.05D	S	S		D

Table 2.2 (continued)

Believed competitive games good for C	.05S	S	.01S	.05S	.01S	.05D	S	.0001	.001S
Liked time away from children	.01D	D	S	S+	S	S	D		.10D
Shamed C for misbehavior	S+	.10S	S	.10S	S	S	S	.02	.05S
Concerned with impression C makes on others	.05S	.01S	S	.01S	S+	S+	S	.0000	S+
Encouraged C to be independent of me	.01D	.01D	D	.01D	D+	D	D	.0000	S
Kept close track of C	.05D	D+	D+	.01D	D	D	D	.0000	.01D
Found children interesting	D	.01D	D	D+	S	S	D	.01	S
Believed in early weaning	S+	S+	.01S	D	S+	S+	S	.001	S+
Expected C to stay clean	.05S	S	.10S	.01S	S	.10S	S	.0000	D
Didn't like leaving C with stranger	D+	.10D	D+	D	D+	S	D	.003	D
Punished sibling rivalry	S	.10S	D+	D	D	D+	D		.01S
Taught C early not to cry	.01S	.05S	.01S	S+	S	S	S	.0000	.001S
Controlled C by warning of bad things	S	.10S	D	S+	D	S	S	.06	S
Mother had most authority in family	D+	S	S	.01S	=	D	S		S+
Wanted C to be same as others	S	.10S	D	S	S	D+	S		S+

Table 2.2 (continued)

Believed sex information should wait until C older	S+	S	S	S+	D	S	.04	.05S
Felt important for C to play outside	S+	D	S	S+	.10S	S+	.02	.001S
Liked seeing C eat well	.01S	.01S	S	.05S	.01S	S+	.0000	.05S
Did not allow C to tease others	S+	S+	S	D	S	S+	.001	.05S
Wrong to insist on different toys for boys and girls	.01D	.01D	D+	S+	D	S	.0000	.001D
Believed children need close supervision	S	D	S+	D	D	D		S
Total number of significant differences (p V.05)	31	22	9	23	10	6	52	33

Note. Entries represent the results of *t*-test comparisons of sons' and daughters' descriptions of the child-rearing orientations of their mothers and FOR THE U.S. sample only their fathers. S and D indicate the direction of the mean differences (sons or daughters). S+ or D+ indicates *t*-test values in excess of 1.00 but less than 1.67 required for *pv* 10. For significant comparisons, *p* levels based upon two-tailed tests of significance are given in cell entries. Combined probabilities are calculated across the six independent samples of students (Winer, 1971, p. 50).

a. Samples are college and university students in each of the six countries who completed the 3rd person form of the CRPR in which the stems were "My mother. . ." or "My father. . .".

Table 2.3

Summary of results suggesting consistencies in sex-differentiated socialization

CRPR items	Parental CRPR Responses				Students' Descriptions			
	Mothers' direction	p	Fathers' direction	p	Mothers' direction	p	Fathers' direction	p
Items consistent in direction across all analyses								
Believed competitive games good	Sons	.000b	Sons	.006	Sons	.000	Sons	.001
Encouraged competition	Sons	.000	Sons	.08	Sons	.000	Sons	.01
Encouraged C to control feelings	Sons	.005	Sons	.004	Sons	.001	Sons	.05
Taught C early not to cry	Sons	.05	Sons	.07	Sons	.000	Sons	.001
Punished by revoking privileges	Sons	.01	Sons	.02	Sons	ns	Sons	ns
Taught punishment would come if bad	Sons	.02	Sons	ns	Sons	.001	Sons	.05
Thought scolding would improve C	Sons	.02	Sons	ns	Sons	ns	Sons	ns

Table 2.3 (continued)

Threatened more than punished	Sons .03	Sons ns	Sons .001	Sons ns
Believed no sex information given until older	Sons .04	Sons ns	Sons .04	Sons .05
Wanted C to be same as others	Sons .008	Sons .08	Sons ns	Sons ns
Concerned with impression C makes	Sons .05	Sons ns	Sons .000	Sons ns
Believed in early weaning	Sons .03	Sons ns	Sons .001	Sons ns
Did not allow anger at parents	Sons ns	Sons .03	Sons .009	Sons ns
Did not allow C to say bad things about teachers	Sons ns	Sons ns	Sons .005	Sons ns
Felt affection can weaken C	Sons ns	Sons ns	Sons .000	Sons .001
Shamed C for misbehavior	Sons ns	Sons ns	Sons .02	Sons .05
Gave extra privileges as reward	Sons ns	Sons ns	Sons .04	Sons ns
Liked seeing C eat well	Sons ns	Sons ns	Sons .000	Sons .05
Expressed affection physically	Daughters .005	Daughters .000	Daughters .09	Daughters .001
Child and I shared warm times	Daughters .001	Daughters .05	Daughters .000	Daughters ns

Table 2.3 (continued)

Believed C is truthful	Daughters .03	Daughters .05	Daughters .000	Daughters .01
Believed C is to be trusted	Daughters .009	Daughters .10	Daughters .001	Daughters ns
Encouraged C to wonder	Daughters .02	Daughters .04	Daughters .05	Daughters .01
Didn't like to leave C with a stranger	Daughters .01	Daughters .007	Daughters .003	Daughters ns
Kept close track of child	Daughters .03	Daughters ns	Daughters .000	Daughters .01
Allowed C to daydream	Daughters ns	Daughters ns	Daughters .000	Daughters .01
Wrong to insist on different toys for boys and girls	Daughters ns	Daughters ns	Daughters .000	Daughters .001
Worried about child	Daughters ns	Daughters ns	Daughters ns	Daughters .01
Sorry to see C grow up	Daughters ns	Daughters ns	Daughters ns	Daughters .001
Items suggesting cross-sex effects				
Tried to keep C from fighting	Sons ns	Daughters .007	Sons .000	Daughters .05
Didn't think young children should see each other naked	Sons ns	Daughters ns	Sons .008	Daughters ns
Items suggesting same-sex effects				
Had firm rules for child	Daughters ns	Sons .000	Daughters ns	Sons ns
Punished sibling rivalry	Daughters ns	Sons ns	Daughters ns	Sons .01

Table 2.3 (continued)

Items suggesting same-sex effects				
Had firm rules for child	ns	.000	ns	ns
Punished sibling rivalry	ns	ns	ns	.01
Was conflict between parent and C	Daughters ns	Sons ns	Daughters .000	Sons ns
Taught C was responsible for self	Daughters ns	Sons ns	Daughters .10	Sons .10
Thought it good for C to perform	Daughters ns	Sons ns	Daughters .07	Sons ns
Additional items suggesting mother-son agreement				
Important for C to play outside	Sons .01	Daughters ns	Sons .02	Sons .001
Did not want C to have secrets	Sons ns	Daughters ns	Sons .01	Sons .01
Obtained great satisfaction from C	Sons ns	Daughters ns	Sons .02	Sons .10
Wish spouse more interested in C	Sons .02	Daughters .08	Sons ns	Sons ns
Expected a great deal of C	Sons ns	Sons .01	Sons .04	Daughters ns
Encouraged C to do well	Sons .10	Sons .002	Sons ns	Daughters ns

Table 2.3 (continued)

Kept C away from families with different ideas	Daughters ns	Sons .05	Sons ns	Sons ns
Expected to be grateful	Daughters .05	Sons .08	Sons ns	Sons ns
Additional items suggesting father-son agreement				
Let C take chances	Sons ns	Daughters .000	Sons .006	Sons .08
Believed physical punishment best	Sons ns	Daughters ns	Sons .01	Sons ns
Wanted C to handle problems	Sons ns	Daughters .07	Sons .05	Sons ns
Gave C responsibilities	Sons .05	Daughters ns	Sons ns	Sons ns
Believed in early toilet training	Sons .10	Daughters .03	Sons ns	Sons ns
Gave up own interests for C	Sons .01	Sons ns	Sons ns	Daughters ns
Watched C's eating habits	Sons .05	Sons .04	Sons ns	Daughters ns
Additional items suggesting mother-daughter agreement				
Teased child	Daughters .001	Daughters .000	Sons .02	Daughters ns

Table 2.3 (continued)

Felt C a disappointment	Daughters ns	Sons ns	Daughters .03	Daughters ns
Let C know when angry	Daughters ns	Sons ns	Daughters .06	Daughters ns
Sometimes forgot promises to C	Daughters ns	Daughters .08	Daughters .006	Sons ns
Encouraged C to talk of troubles	Daughters ns	Daughters .009	Daughters .05	Sons ns
Respected C's opinions	Daughters ns	Daughters ns	Daughters .04	Sons ns
Found children interesting	Daughters ns	Daughters ns	Daughters .01	Sons ns
Helped C when teased	Daughters ns	Daughters ns	Daughters .03	Sons ns
Encouraged C to be independent of parent	Daughters ns	Daughters ns	Daughters .000	Sons ns
Additional items suggesting father-daughter agreement				
Did not allow rough games	Daughters .003	Daughters .10	Sons .000	Daughters .001
Found it difficult to punish C	Daughters .03	Daughters .02	Sons ns	Daughters .05
Gave comfort when C upset	Sons ns	Daughters .008	Daughters .04	Daughters .05

Table 2.3 (continued)

	Sons	Daughters	Daughters	Daughters
Joked and played with C	ns	ns	.009	.05
Spoiled C	ns	ns	.10	.001
Included child in planning	ns	.04	ns	ns
Let C make many decisions	.10	.04	.004	ns
Enjoyed a houseful of children	ns	.08	.06	ns
Appreciated C's efforts	ns	ns	ns	.10

aCRPR items are in abbreviated form

bThe p values are based upon two-tailed tests of significance and represent combined probabilities across the several independent samples (mothers, fathers, and students describing their mothers' child-rearing values). p values for student perceptions of fathers' child-rearing orientations are based on t-test comparisons for the U.S. sample only.

Table 2.4

Summary of results of statistical comparisons a cross parents'
self-reported and unrelated student-perceived child-rearing practices

Comparisons of parents' self-reports and student perceptions

Criteria used to evaluate agreements and disagreements	Mothers				Fathers			
	Agreements		Disagreements		Agreements		Disagreements	
	No. of items	%	No. of items	%	No. of items	%	No. of items	%
Direction of response only	10	11	12	13	16	18	17	19
Direction *and* results significant in one comparison ($p < .10$)	5	5	4	4	6	7	5	5
Direction *and* results significant in one comparison ($p < .05$)	27	30	12	13	26	29	9	11
Direction *and* results significant in *both* comparisons	17	19	4	4	11	12	1	1
TOTAL	59	64.8	32	35.2	59	64.8	32	35.2

Table 2.5

CRPR items significantly deviating in direction
of response when parent self-reports and student perceptions
of socialization emphases for sons and daughters are compared

Mother-student comparisons

CRPR items	Direction of response		Level of significance	
	Parent	Student	Parent	Student
Watched C's eating habits	D	S	ns	.04
Didn't allow rough game	D	S	.003	.000
Found it difficult to punish C	D	S	.03	ns
Sacrificed a lot for C	D	S	ns	.01
Worried about C's health	D	S	ns	.000
Expected C to stay clean	D	S	.03	.000
Believed children need supervision	D	S	.03	ns
Best if mother has most authority	D	S	.02	ns
Did not allow teasing	D	S	ns	.001
Put spouse's wishes first	S	D	ns	.004
Felt angry with C	S	D	ns	.03
Gave comfort when upset	S	D	ns	.04
Let C make decisions	S	D	.10	.004
Joked and played with C	S	D	ns	.009
Let C take chances	S	D	.08	.000
Believed in early toilet training	S	D	ns	.03

Father-student comparisons

CRPR items	Direction of response		Level of significance	
	Parent	Student	Parent	Student
Didn't blame C when others provoked	D	S	ns	.05
Encouraged C to talk of troubles	D	S	.009	ns
Didn't want C to have secrets from parents	D	S	ns	.01
Felt it important for C to play outdoors	D	S	ns	.001
Did not allow C to tease others	D	S	ns	.05
Encouraged C to do well	S	D	.002	ns
Expected a great deal of C	S	D	.01	ns
Expected C to be grateful	S	D	ns	.05
Teased C	S	D	.02	.001
Didn't allow C to question	S	D	.000	ns

ent samples of students presented in Table 2.2, and the combined results summarized in Table 2.3) suggests the following generalizations, which will be discussed later in greater detail.

1. *There is evidence for differential socialization of males and females.* Based upon the results of the combined probabilities analyses across the samples of mothers presented in Table 2.1, 26 (29%) of the CRPR responses are significantly sex-differentiated ($p < .05$).[1] For fathers, 23 (25%) of the CRPR items reveal significant differences in the socialization emphases of fathers of sons and fathers of daughters. For the samples of young adults describing the child-rearing practices and attitudes of their mothers, 52 (57%) of the items reflect significant sex-differentiated perceptions of maternal socialization behaviors, as shown in the analyses of combined probabilities presented in Table 2.2. The comparable figure based only on the sample of American students describing their mothers is 31 significant items (34%). For the American students only, who described their fathers' child-rearing practices and values, 33 (36%) of the items were significantly sex-differentiated.

2. *There is evidence that sex-related socialization emphases are appreciably consistent when viewed from the differing perspectives of mothers, fathers, sons, and daughters.* As shown in Table 2.3, 31 (34%) of the CRPR items are consistent in the direction of response across all four subject groups, while 29 of these items are both consistent in direction across all samples *and* are significantly differentiating in at least one of those analyses. Were we to consider *only* the directional effects, the probability of four independent events occurring in the same direction, as calculated according to the binomial expansion, is $p < .07$, a minimal estimate of the probability in this case because 29 items are also significantly different (5 items discriminate between sons and daughters in one analysis; 11 items significantly discriminate in two independent comparison; 6 significantly differentiate in three independent comparisons; and 7 CRPR items significantly differentiate between sons and daughters in all four independent comparisons).

3. *There is evidence of specific, consistent, sex-of-parent and sex-of-child effects.* In Table 2.3, the items reflecting specific sex effects are grouped under headings of cross-sex influences, same-sex influences, and specific mother-son, mother-daughter, father-son, and father-daughter influences. An overall summary of the degree of consistency characterizing the data with respect to parental self-reports and the perceptions of independent unrelated samples of students is presented in Table 2.4. Based upon all 91 CRPR items, we find strong evidence of consistency across independent data sources for both mothers and fathers. For mothers, 49% of the items are consistent in direction and significantly differentiating in at least one comparison when their self-reports are compared with the perceptions of maternal practices offered by the samples of unrelated students. The comparable data for fathers reveals that 41% of the items are consistent in direction and significant in at least one analysis. Looking at the discrepancies between parental self-reports and the perceptions of students using similar evaluative criteria, only 17% of the items for mothers and 12% of the items for fathers diverge significantly in direction of response in at least one analysis. These figures represent minimal estimates of agreement, as pointed out earlier, because the parent and student samples are not correspondent.

4. *There is some evidence suggesting that sex differentiation in socialization emphases appears to increase with the age of the child, reaching a maximum during the high school years.* Evidence for this assertion is found in Table 2.1, where the trend toward greater sex differentiation is shown to be consistent in the data for both mothers and fathers.[2] Only in Sample 2 for fathers, where the power of the statistical test is weak because of small sample size, is there a small departure from the monotonic trend.

5. *There is evidence of consistency in sex-related socialization emphases among samples of mothers and samples of fathers heterogeneous with respect to socioeconomic level, education level, cultural origins and the health status and age levels of their children.* Across the six samples of mothers representing the rather diverse backgrounds shown in Table 2.1 16 (18%) of the CRPR items were answered in the same direction by all six samples. The probability of an item showing a consistent directional effect across six samples is less than .02. Comparable consistency in response among the five samples of fathers was found on 27 (29%) of the CRPR items, yielding a probability with respect to directional effects alone of $p < .03$ for each of these 27 items.

6. *There is evidence of cross-cultural similarities in the sex-differentiated socialization patterns as reflected in students' perceptions of maternal rearing practices.* The relationships observed in student samples—which are relatively homogeneous within each country and comparable across countries (all college students)—are, despite the differences among the participating countries, relatively consistent and coherent. As shown in Table 2.2, 19 (21%) of the items are consistent in direction across all six countries, yielding a probability for the directional effects alone of $p < .02$. When it is also considered that 15 of the 19 items yield sex-differences in perceptions of maternal practices that are significant in two or more of the six countries, the cross-cultural consistencies are even more impressive. It is difficult to attribute these consistencies across nations to cultural similarity, since the countries represented vary widely on many demographic indices—such as the number of employed women (Holter, 1970), suicide and homicide rates (Hendin, 1965; Block & Christiansen, 1966), degree of industrialization and urbanization (Hendin, 1965)—as well as differences in sociopolitical and human values.

7. *There is an indication that the countries represented in the study differ in the extent of emphasis on sex-role differentiation.* If we take as a guide the number of significant differences between sons and daughters in the CRPR descriptions of their mothers, as presented in Table 2.2, the Danish, Swedish, and Finnish students see fewer distinctions in the socialization emphases of mothers of sons and mothers of daughters. American, English, and Norwegian students, on the other hand, perceive their mothers as engaging more distinctively in sex-related socialization behaviors.

The thrust of these several generalizations underscores the importance of taking a more differentiated view of sex-determined socialization practices. Although there are impressive consistencies in these data, there are differences as well, differences that ultimately may prove lawful.

Having outlined the results from the various comparisons of parental socialization orientations, the substantive findings are now discussed and related to the conclusions of Maccoby and Jacklin as summarized earlier.

DIFFERENTIAL SOCIALIZATION OF SONS

The CRPR data from several independent samples demonstrate first that both mothers and fathers appear to emphasize *achievement and competition* more for their sons than for their daughters. Second, there is strong evidence that both parents encourage their sons, more than their daughters, to *control the expression of affect*. Third, *punishment orientation* is a more salient concern of parents of males than parents of females. Fourth, the differentiating CRPR items suggest a greater emphasis on *independence* or the *assumption of personal responsibility* by parents of males than of females, an emphasis, however, that is more apparent in the responses of fathers than of mothers. Fifth, fathers appear more authoritarian in their rearing of their sons than of their daughters; They are *strict and firm,* believe in physical punishment, and are *less tolerant of aggression directed toward themselves by their sons.* Sixth, mothers encourage their sons, more than their daughters, to *conform to external standards,* wanting their sons to make a good impression on others and to be conforming. Although the particular standards are not elaborated, it may be that these items are manifestations of the generally observed greater parental concern for sex-appropriate behavior in males than in females.

Together, these data support the Maccoby and Jacklin conclusions that punishment orientation, negative sanctions, and conformity emphasis (at least in the area of sex appropriateness) is emphasized in child rearing by the parents of males more than by the parents of females. The present findings with respect to achievement and competition, independence in the sense of the assumption of personal responsibility, and parent-directed aggression appear stronger, more coherent, and more consistent than in the summary results offered by Maccoby and Jacklin. Control of affect expression, an important area of sex-differentiated socialization not addressed in the researches included in the Maccoby and Jacklin volumen, emerges strongly from the results of the analyses presented here. Despite the widely held assumptions that males in our society are less able to express deeply felt affects, it is surprising that so little empirical attention has been directed to the study of sex-differentiated socialization influences on affect expression.

DIFFERENTIAL SOCIALIZATION OF DAUGHTERS

The parent-daughter relationship is characterized first by greater *warmth and physical closeness,* according to the CRPR items significantly differentiating across the several independent samples of the parents of daughters and the parents of sons. Second, both mothers and fathers appear to have greater confidence in the *trustworthiness and truthfulness* of their daughters than of their sons. Third, there is greater expectation by mothers and fathers alike of *"lady-like" behavior* on the part of their daughters. They discourage rough and tumble games, mothers particularly expect their daughters to stay clean while playing, and fathers discourage fighting in their daughters more than in their sons. Fourth, there is expressed on the part of both parents a *greater reluctance to punish* their daughters, in contrast to their sons. Fifth, mothers' child-rearing practices are more sex differentiated with respect to *restrictiveness and supervision* of their daughters than of their sons. Sixth, daughters, more than sons, are encouraged by both parents to *wonder and think about life.* Interpretation of this isolated finding is a bit hazardous but when considered in combination with fathers' expressed attempts to include their daughters, more than their sons, in discussions of family plans, the greater perception of tolerance for daydreaming by women students, and parental encouragement to discuss their problems, a focus on communal familial concerns in the socialization of females may be being expressed, a focus that has been described by other investigators (e.g., Bakan, 1966; Carlson, 1971).

The findings with respect to differential socialization emphases of parents of daughters and parents of sons accord with the results of Barry, Bacon, and Child (1957), who reported significant and consistent sex-related socialization emphases in a variety of cultures, with girls receiving more pressure to be nurturant, obedient, and responsible while boys receive more pressure to achieve and be self-reliant. However, the present findings diverge from the summary conclusions about differential socialization offered by Maccoby and Jacklin. Parental warmth, a salient characteristic of the mother-daughter relationship as assessed by the CRPR, was not found to differentiate the sexes in the studies forming the data base for the Maccoby and Jacklin conclusions. The present findings of restriction and supervision of daughters are both more clear and more implicative than is apparent in the results and discussion of chaperonage provided by Maccoby and Jacklin. Restrictive parental behaviors are associated with, especially in the perceptions of daughters, parental anxiety, worry, and concern about the misfortunes that can befall young women as they grow up. The affective implications of restrictiveness-in-the-context-of-anxiety might be expected to have pervasive and persistent consequences, urging caution as women seek self-definition and project long-term goals. Finally, the greater discouragement of aggression in girls relative to boys represents another area in which the present findings diverge from the summary conclusions of Maccoby and Jacklin.

PERCEPTIONS OF PARENTAL REARING PRACTICES

Comparing the child-rearing orientations of mothers as they are perceived by male and female students in several countries has provided evidence of both cross-cultural and cross-perspective (parental self-descriptions and student perceptions) continuities. According to the perceptions of students, sons more than daughters described *both parents* as emphasizing *competition,* encouraging *control of affect expression,* demonstrating more concern about *punishment,* emphasizing *control of impulse* with respect to sex, being uneasy about the *consequences of affection on the development of masculinity,* concerned about *health issues,* emphasizing *early achievement of particular developmental landmarks* (weaning in the case of mothers, toilet training in the case of fathers), and *obtaining satisfactions* from the parent-son relationship. Additionally, mothers were described by their sons, more than by their daughters, as being more proscriptive, as exerting more *control on the expression of aggression,* as being concerned about *others' impressions of their sons,* and as attempting to *isolate their sons from values diverging from their own.* Fathers were perceived also by their sons, more than their daughters, as *emphasizing responsibilities* and as *sacrificing some of their own interests* for their children. Overall, the relationship between parents and sons, viewed from the vantage point of the son, is characterized by a variety of expectations, insistence on the control of both impulse and affect expression, salience of punishment-related concerns, and anxiety about health-related issues.

Looking now at the depictions of the parent-daughter relationship through the perceptions of young women students, we find that daughters, more than sons, describe *both parents* as *emphasizing affection and physical closeness, believing in* the *truthfulness* of their daughters, *encouraging introspection* (wonder and daydreaming), *keeping close track of* their daughters, *relaxed about sex typing,* having a more *playful relationship* characterized by both joking and teasing, and being more *indulging.* The mother-daughter relationship is described as somewhat *ambivalent.* Mothers are seen as warm, trusting, interested in and respecting of their daughters, encouraging discussion of problems at the same time that they are perceived as forgetting promises, expressing anger, feeling conflicted, and being somewhat disappointed in their daughters. Mothers are also seen as *encouraging independence,* both in terms of differentiation from parent and in making of decisions. Fathers were characterized by their daughters, more than their sons, as encouraging the *development of "ladylike" behaviors,* as *being anxious* about their daughters, as *sorry to see them grow up,* and as finding the *administration of punishment difficult.* Overall, the relationship between parents and daughters, viewed from the perspective of the daughter, is characterized by an emphasis on interaction physical closeness, encouragement of introspection, and less concern with prohibitions and punishments. In the mother-daughter relationship, the mothers are also perceived both as ambivalent and as encouraging differentiation. In the father-daughter relationship, the fathers are described additionally as encouraging femininity, as regretful of seeing their daughters grow up, as reluctant to punish them, and as being anxious about their daughters.

Many of the socialization themes characterizing the students' perceptions of the parent-son and parent-daughter relationships, as the reader undoubtedly has recognized, have much in common with the self-reported child-rearing emphases of parents. Vis-a-vis sons, parents encourage competition, foster control of affect and impulse expression, urge the assumption of responsibility, are oriented toward punishment, and are concerned about the impression created by their sons. These parental qualities are also to be discerned in the descriptions by independent and unrelated samples of sons characterizing the socialization emphases of their parents. Vis-a-vis daughters, parents emphasize closeness, are trusting, display a vigilant interest in their activities, encourage "ladylike" behaviors, encourage introspections, and are reluctant to punish. These qualities are also to be found in the descriptions of parental socialization practices offered by the independent and unrelated samples of daughters.

Discrepancies Between Parental Self-Reports and Student Perceptions

Because few researches have explored the congruence between parental self-reports and perceptions of parental child-rearing values held by offspring, it may be instructive to look explicitly at the items on which significant disagreements between the two data sources exist.

In the present study, as shown in Table 2.4, there are rather few significant deviations in direction of response when parent self-reports are compared with student perceptions of parental child-rearing orientations. The items on which statistically significant discrepancies between the two data sources exist are collected in Table 2.5.

Looking at Table 2.5, it appears that when parental responses are significantly sex-differentiated and also deviate from the perceptions of students, the like-sex parent-child relationship is involved. Thus, mothers describe themselves as encouraging feminine behaviors in their daughters, as exerting authority and close supervision, and as being reluctant to administer punishment. These items suggest a more authoritarian mother-daughter relationship, when viewed from the mother's perspective, than is described by female students. Viewed from the vantage point of the diverging and sex-differentiated items characteristic of female students, perceptions of the mother-daughter relationship reflect more interaction (both positive and negative) than is expressed in the mothers' self-reports. Although some degree of ambivalence was ascribed to the mother-daughter relationship by mothers' and daughters alike, these discrepant items suggest that ambivalent feelings are stronger in the perceptions of daughters than in the reports of mothers. Female students also perceive that they were granted somewhat greater freedom than is implied by mothers' self-characterizations of their child-rearing practices.

With reference to daughters' perceptions of fathers, paternal teasing and expectations of gratitude appear more salient than is suggested in the fathers' self-reported data.

For the father-son relationship, the significant sex-differentiating and deviating items characteristic of the fathers' self-descriptions stress the importance of achievement, acceptance of paternal authority, and admission of teasing. Again, these items suggest a more pressuring and authoritarian father-son relationship when viewed from the father's perspective than is perceived by male students. The significant sex-differentiating and diverging items characteristic of male students' perceptions of fathers extend the list of behavioral prohibitions (discouraging secrets from parents, forbidding teasing), reflect fathers as encouragers of outdoor play, and as defenders of their sons when others provoke trouble.

Attributions to mothers' socialization practices by male students, and which are not reflected in maternal self-reports, indicate maternal emphasis on the importance of cleanliness, maternal discouragement of participation in rough games, maternal anxiety about the health and eating habits of their sons, and maternal feelings of self-sacrifice.

When the inconsistently answered CRPR items are compared with the sex-differentiated socialization emphases where there is some degree of agreement between parents and students, the overall thrust of the findings seem not too discrepant. Differences both in emphasis and in specific item content exist, but they seem relatively few, particularly when it is recognized that three factors have operated to attenuate agreement. First, because the young adults represented in the student sample are *not* the actual children of the parents represented, the extent of agreement is underestimated. Second, the comparison of results derived from the student samples representing predominantly countries other than the United States, with parental self-reports obtained primarily from parents in the United States, would be expected to result in lower agreement between the two data sources, but inclusion of samples from other countries indicates that sex-differentiated socialization is a more general phenomenon characterized both by themes common across cultures and emphases that appear culturally specific. The third source of attenuation with respect to agreement across data sources resides in age differences. Parents completed the CRPR when their children were, on the average, approximately 12 years old, whereas perceptions of parental child-rearing approaches were obtained from students who were, on the average, 21 years old. If parental socialization practices and emphases do, in fact, change as a function of the different competencies, circumstances, and needs of children at different age levels, this age difference represents another important limitation on the agreement across data sources. Further, it must be remembered that these young people were describing their parents' rearing of them at a time when many of them were involved in defining their own identities and in differentiating themselves from their parents. Thus, their perceptions of parents during this period of flux and self-conscious examination might be expected to differ from those obtained when identity issues were less compelling. From the perspective of parents, the themes that were more salient in their self-reports, but not reciprocated in the students' perceptions of parents, appear to be appropriate socialization emphases when the average age of the child is considered. Parental authority and control undoubtedly are more salient child-rearing concerns for parents of 12-year-olds than for students of college age. Future research comparing self-reported and perceived child-rearing data will have to control for, or at least allow for, the age of the children being studied.

These analyses of agreements and disagreements across sources underscore the need for more studies in which socialization is viewed from multiple perspectives. In 1963, Yarrow called for studies of child-rearing practices that include systematically the mother, father, child, and observer as sources of information. Twelve years later, her recommendations are as cogent but have been largely ignored. However, in one of the research studies reported here (Sample 1 in Table 2.1), observer-based data describing mothers and fathers interacting individually with their children in a teaching-learning situation (Block, Block, & Harrington; Note 2) were available, along with the CRPR data. Because the observer-based ratings of the mother's and the father's interactions with the child in the teaching situation are not directly comparable to the CRPR data, it is difficult to quantify the extent of agreement between these two data groups. However, it will be recalled that mothers were less sex-discriminating in the teaching situation; the same trend characterizes the CRPR results for mothers in Sample 1.

Fathers of sons were found in the teaching situation to be more active, more pressuring, and more attuned to the cognitive demands of the situation than were fathers of girls who were described by observers as more attentive to the interactional elements of the teaching situation. Fathers were seen as protecting their daughters from failure experiences, making the situation fun, developing a comfortable working relationship, and both they and their daughters were described as enjoying the interaction. The sex-discriminating behaviors of fathers observed in the standardized teaching situation are consistent with the sex-differentiated socialization emphases expressed by Sample 1 fathers on the CRPR: Achievement pressures and firmness significantly differentiated fathers of sons, while fathers of daughters encouraged wonder, worried, wanted their daughters to be independent of them, and found their daughters interesting.

Despite these indications of correspondence, however, these data do not speak adequately to the question of validity of parental reports. Specifically designed studies are required in which self-reported behaviors of parents can be directly compared with observer-reports of parental behaviors in situations designed to permit the self-described behaviors to become manifest.

AGE-RELATED SOCIALIZATION EMPHASES

One of the fundamental tasks of the developing individual is the mediation between internal impulses, desires, wishes—both biological and physiological—and the external socialization forces of the society. This developmental requirement implies different socialization emphases at different stages, depending upon the developmental level of the child and the tolerance of society and its socializing agents for impulse expression in particular areas (Block, 1973). In the present study, there is the suggestion that socialization becomes more sex-differentiated with the increasing age of the child, reaching a maximum during the high school years. The observation is consistent with results obtained in England by Newson and Newson (1968), who found relatively little sex differentiation in the socialization practices of parents of 4-year-olds but did find more evidence of sex-related socialization at age 7, particularly with respect to greater restrictiveness of girls (Maccoby, Note 3). Both the findings reported here and the observations of the Newsons are consistent with the results of studies cited by Maccoby and Jacklin, who found sex-differentiation to be more characteristic of older-aged children than of younger children. These age-specific socialization emphases must be specified and understood, and for this task longitudinal studies are required. It is sufficient here simply to underscore the importance of age as a determiner of parental socialization emphases. Perhaps the data presented in Table 2.1 can provide a source of hypotheses for this needed research.

SUMMARY AND OVERVIEW

We find considerably more evidence of differentiation in parental rearing practices as a function of the sex of the child than is reported or summarized by Maccoby and Jacklin. Our results are consistent with those of Maccoby and Jacklin in finding that punishment orientation, negative sanctions, and sex typing are more characteristic socialization concerns of parents of sons than of parents of daughters. Further, the results presented here agree with the studies focusing explicitly on fathers in the Maccoby and Jacklin volume when these are disembedded and examined separately. Thus, fathers are more accepting of aggression directed toward themselves by their daughters than by their sons, provide comfort to their daughters more than to their sons, and characterize their relationship with their daughters as warmer than the relationship with their sons. Fathers of sons, on the other hand, tend to accept aggressiveness and competition more than fathers of daughters.

There appear to be several reasons for the discrepancies between the results of the present series of studies and the research findings reviewed by Maccoby and Jacklin. First, the discrepancies appear greater in those areas where they have employed concepts defined globally. With respect to the large concept, restrictiveness, for example, the *area* of restrictiveness is all important. Parents tend to be restrictive of their daughters in the sense of maintaining closer supervision of their activities; however, parental restrictiveness of sons appears to be focused on assertiveness toward parents and expression of feelings. With respect to the globally defined concept of independence, the relationships issuing from the present study suggest that parental encouragement of independence may have somewhat different meanings for sons than for daughters. Parents appear to encourage their sons to be independent in the sense of taking chances and assuming responsibility; for daughters, however, it appears that parental encouragement of independence may be in the service of encouraging differentiation from the parents. With respect to aggression, parents again appear to make more distinctions than are typically reflected in our measures. For sons, aggression in the sense of competition is encouraged, and participation in rough games is tolerated by both parents; fathers are more accepting of fighting in their sons than in their daughters. Teasing and expressions of sibling rivalry in sons do not elicit significant parental reactions, despite their aggressive implications. On the other hand, fathers of sons discourage expressions of anger toward themselves.

Obviously, the classification of conceptually distinct behaviors into one large category tends to suggest inconsistencies or to level differences that would otherwise be seen. Greater articulation of the global concepts on which much socialization research has depended in the past is essential if we are to discern clear and reproducible evidence of sex differentiation in parental socialization.

A second source of the discrepancy between the present findings and the conclusions summarized by Maccoby and Jacklin concerns the role of the father. The systematic information obtained about the child-rearing attitudes of fathers have revealed sex-differentiated socialization emphases obscured in the Maccoby and Jacklin conclusions as a function (a) of the paucity of information about fathers, (b) the secondary informational sources about fathers on which many researchers have depended, and (c) the aggregation of results derived from mothers, fathers, and perceptions of parents. The opportunity to compare directly the child-rearing orientations of mothers and of fathers has provided clear evidence in some socialization areas of parental role specialization, while in other areas both parents appear to have similar reinforcement emphases.

Thirdly, the appreciable sex-related socialization differences observed in the research reported here, as compared to the rather limited evidence reported by Maccoby and Jacklin, may be viewed as a function of differences in domain coverage. The socialization literature has tended to concentrate on relatively few child-rearing dimensions (e.g., warmth, dependency, aggression, achievement, positive and negative reinforcements). Some of the significant and consistent differences emerging in the present study have been found on dimensions only infrequently studied. Specifically, these are the emphasis on control of affect expression in sons, the encouragement of introspection (wonder, daydreaming, pursuing personal problems) in daughters, the sense of trustworthiness conveyed to daughters, the explicit valuing of competition separate from achievement in sons, and the greater parental concern about the impression made on others by sons. All these represent socialization emphases of parents that have been given relatively little attention in previous studies of parental influences on children.

Finally, the differing conclusions about the extent of sex-differentiation in parental socialization practices reported by Maccoby and Jacklin and those suggested by the present series of studies are a function also of age differences in children at the time parental child-rearing orientations are assessed. It will be recalled that more than 75% of the studies cited by Maccoby and Jacklin compared the socialization emphases of parents of sons and parents of daughters when the children were age 5 or younger. In the assessments of parental rearing practices reported here, only two samples included children as young as 5 years, and the average age of the children at the time parents described their socialization emphases was 12 years. If sex differentiation in socialization practices becomes more marked with the increasing age of the child, as suggested by our analyses and the observations of Newson and Newson (1968), then the generally young age of the children in the studies forming the data base for the Maccoby and Jacklin conclusions is responsible for the sparseness of their findings.

By attending to child-rearing behaviors frequently ignored, by using more differentiated concepts, by assessing the socialization emphases of parents when children are older, and by including fathers uniformly in our studies of child-rearing practices, it may be anticipated that we will establish more precisely the ways in which sons and daughters are differently socialized by their fathers and mothers.

Our discussion of the leveling conclusions drawn by Maccoby and Jacklin and the sharpening ones emerging from the present series of analyses requires, finally, that we consider the educational and social implications of these diverging views of the empirical situation.

Currently, there is a strong movement, deriving from various considerations of the connections between character and society, toward changing the traditional, culturally prescribed definitions of sex roles. In this context, the summary view of Maccoby and Jacklin that there are few differences in parenting as a function of the sex of the child can readily lead to the inference that there are few points of entry for change in the socialization process. On the other hand, the appreciable differential parenting as a function of the sex of the child found in the present analyses lends encouragement to current concerns and suggests specific directions and the ways in which socialization emphases might be modified.

With regard to the rearing of sons, agentic interests (e.g., competition, aggression, egocentrism) would be leavened by the encouragement of a more communal orientation (e.g., expression of deeply felt affects, sociocentrism). With regard to the rearing of daughters, the interlacing of a communal focus (e.g., interpersonal orientation, compromise, and sacrifice for the general welfare) with a greater sense of agency (e.g., self-assertion, self-valuation) can be expected to benefit ego development. Machismo dissimulates manhood; hyperfemininity feigns womanhood. In our view, the socialization changes now feasible within our civilization can permit self- and sex-role definitions that can transcend the stark and limiting conceptions of masculinity and femininity imposed in the past (Block, 1973).

REFERENCE NOTES

1. Block, J.H. *The Child-Rearing Practices Report.* Berkeley, Calif.: Institute of Human Development, University of California, 1965.
2. Block, J., & Harrington, D.M. *The relationship of parental teaching strategies to ego-resiliency in preschool children.* Paper presented at the Western Psychological Association, San Francisco, April 1974.
3. Maccoby, E. Personal communication, August 4, 1975.

REFERENCES

Bakan, D. *The duality of human existence.* Chicago: Rand McNally, 1966.

Barry, H., Bacon, M.K., & Child, I.L. A cross cultural survey of some sex differences in socialization. *Journal of Abnormal and Social Psychology,* 1957, *55,* 327-332.

Biller, N.B. *Father, child and sex role: Paternal determinants of personality development.* Lexington, Mass.: D.C. Heath, 1971.

Block, J.H. Conceptions of sex role: Some cross-cultural and longitudinal perspectives. *American Psychologist,* 1973, *28,* 512-526.

Block, J.H., & Christiansen, B. A test of Hendin's hypothesis relating suicide in Scandinavia to child-rearing orientations. *Scandinavian Journal of Psychology,* 1966, *7,* 267-288.

Block, J., Block, J.H., & von der Lippe, A. Sex-role and socialization patterns: Some personality concomitants and environmental antecedents. *Journal of Consulting and Clinical Psychology,* 1973, *41,* 321-341.

Burger, G.K., Lamp, R.E., & Rogers, D. Developmental trends in children's perceptions of parental child-rearing behavior. *Developmental Psychology,* 1975, *11,* 391.

Carlson, R. Sex differences in ego functioning: Exploratory studies in agency and communion. *Journal of Consulting and Clinical Psychology,* 1971, *37,* 267-277.

Clarke-Stewart, A. Interactions between mothers and their young children: Characteristics and consequences. *Monographs of the Society for Research in Child Development,* 1973, *38,* Whole No. 153.

Cohen, J. *Statistical power analysis for the behavioral sciences.* New York: Academic Press, 1969.

Emmerich, W. Socialization and sex-role development. In P.B. Baltes and K.W. Schaie (Eds.). *Life-span developmental psychology.* New York: Academic Press, 1973.

Hartley, R.E. Sex role pressures and the socialization of the male child. *Psychological Reports,* 1959, *5,* 457-463.

Hartley, R.E. A developmental view of female sex-role definition and identification. *Merrill-Palmer Quarterly,* 1964, *10,* 3-16.

Heilbrun, A.B., Harrel, S., & Gillard, B. Perceived child-rearing attitudes of fathers and cognitive control of daughters. *Journal of Genetic Psychology,* 1967, *111,* 29-40.

Hendin, H. *Suicide and Scandinavia.* New York: Doubleday, 1965.

Hetherington, E.M. A developmental study of the effects of sex of the dominant parent on sex-role preference, identification, and imitation in children. *Journal of Personality and Social Psychology,* 1965, *2,* 188-194.

Hetherington, E.M. Effects of paternal absence on sex-typing behaviors in Negro and white preadolescent males. *Journal of Personality and Social Psychology,* 1966, *4,* 87-91.

Hetherington, E.M. The effects of familial variables on sex typing, on parent-child similarity and on imitation in children. In J.P. Hill (Ed.), *Minnesota symposia on child psychology.* Minneapolis: Lund Press, 1967.

Hetherington, E.M. Effects of father absence on personality development in adolescent daughters. *Developmental Psychology,* 1972, *7,* 313-326.

Hilton, I. Differences in the behavior of mothers toward first- and later-born children. *Journal of Personality and Social Psychology,* 1967, *7,* 282-290.

Holter, H. *Sex roles and social structure.* 1970.

Jacob, T., Fagin, R., Perry, J., & Van Dyke, R.A. Social class, child age, and parental socialization values. *Developmental Psychology,* 1975, *11,* 393.

Kagan, J., & Moss, H.A. *Birth to maturity.* New York: John Wiley, 1962.

Kohlberg, L. A cognitive-developmental analysis of children's sex-role concepts and attitudes. In Eleanor E. Maccoby (Ed.), *The development of sex differences.* Stanford, Calif., Stanford University Press, 1966.

Maccoby, E.E., & Jacklin, C.N. *The psychology of sex differences.* Stanford, Calif.: Stanford University Press, 1974.

Martin, B. Parent-child relations. In F.D. Horowitz (Ed.), *Review of child development research*. Chicago: University of Chicago Press, 1975.

McCandless, B.R. Childhood socialization. In D.A. Goslin (Ed.), *Handbook of socialization theory and research*. Chicago: Rand McNally, 1969.

McCord, J., McCord, W., & Thurber, E. Some effects of paternal absence on male children. *Journal of Abnormal and Social Psychology*, 1962, *64*, 361-369.

Minton, C., Kagan, J., & Levine, J.A. Maternal control and obedience in the two-year old. *Child Development*, 1971, *42*, 1873-1894.

Moss, H.A. Sex, age, and state as determinants of mother-infant interaction. *Merrill-Palmer Quarterly*, 1967, *13*, 19-36.

Mussen, P.H. Early sex-role development. In D.A. Goslin (Ed.), *Handbook of socialization theory and research*. Chicago: Rand McNally, 1969.

Mussen, P.H. & Distler, L. Masculinity, identification, and father-son relationships. *Journal of Abnormal and Social Psychology*, 1959, *59*, 350-356.

Nash, J. The father in contemporary culture and current psychological literature. *Child Development*, 1965, *36*, 261-197.

Newson, J. & Newson, E. *Four years old in an urban community*. Harmondworth, England: Pelican Books, 1968.

Payne, D.E. Parent-child relations and father identification among adolescent boys. *Journal of Abnormal and Social Psychology*, 1956, *52*, 358-362.

Schaeffer, E.S. Children's reports of parental behavior are necessary. *Child Development*, 1965, *36*, 413-424.

Sears, R.R., Maccoby, E.E., & Levin, H. *Patterns of child rearing*. Evanston, Ill.: Row, Peterson, 1957.

Tiller, P.O. Father absence and personality development in sailor families. *Nordic Psychology Monograph*, 1958, Whole No. 9.

Whiting, B. & Edward, C.P. A cross-cultural analysis of sex differences in the behavior of children age three through 11. In S. Chess and Alexander Thomas (Eds.), *Annual progress in child psychiatry and child development, 1974*. New York: Brunner/Mazel, 1975.

Winer, B.J. *Statistical principles in experimental design*. New York: McGraw-Hill, 1971.

Yarrow, M.R. Problems of methods in parent-child research. *Child Development*, 1963, *34*, 215-226.

CHAPTER *3*

BEYOND ADOLESCENCE: Some Suggested New Directions For Studying Female Development In The Middle And Later Years

NANCY FELIPE RUSSO

Nancy Felipe Russo received her Ph.D. in social psychology from Cornell University. She currently holds the position of Health Scientist Administrator in the Center for Research for Mothers and Children in the National Institute of Child Health and Human Development, National Institutes of Health. Formerly, she served as Staff Associate in the Office of the Executive Officer of the American Psychological Association, where her duties included staff liaison in the Committee on Women in Psychology. She has published research in the areas of personal space and population psychology, and has a special interest in the relationship between sex roles and fertility. Her publications include "Youth and Population" (coauthored with Yvonne Brackbill) in Psychological Perspectives on Population, *J.T. Fawcett, editor. She currently holds the position of President-elect of Division 34 (Population and Environmental Psychology) of the American Psychological Association, and edits the* Population and Environmental Psychology Newsletter *of that division. A strong believer in an interdisciplinary approach, she is also a member of the American Sociological Association, the Population Association of America, and the Groves Conference on Marriage and the Family.*

I would like to thank Jessie Bernard, Florence Denmark, Margo Johnson, Martha Mednick, Julia Sherman, Serena Stier, Carolyn Suber, Sandra Tangri, and Raymond Yang for their suggestions. Natalya Krawczuk-Ayers and Leslie Wineland assisted in the preparation of the manuscript. Special thanks go to Allen Meyer for his suggestions and encouragement.

This chapter focuses on the need for new directions in theory and method, as well as in content, in research on the developmental psychology of women. It provides an overview of some of the methodological and conceptual biases in the current literature on the female experience in the middle and later years. After introducing the life-span developmental approach, the author highlights persistent issues of special significance for research on women: the importance of the distinction between age versus developmental psychology, the continued neglect of the interactionist perspective in theory and research design, and the influence of cohort and time-of-measurement effects. The marriage and family literature is selected to illustrate the pervasiveness of sexism in models and method in studies of developmental events in the life of the adult female. Selected empirical studies dealing with sex-role socialization beyond adolescence are discussed, with the interrelationships among roles related to marriage, pregnancy, work, and child-bearing and child-rearing receiving major attention. The need to focus on the process rather than the content of sex-role socialization is continually underscored. The chapter ends with 15 recommendations for actions to stimulate new directions in research on women.

This article is not a traditional review of the literature. After an initial literature search turned up over 2,500 references to research on important developmental events in the life of the adult female, it became apparent that to attempt an exhaustive review of such work would be pointless. The combination of (a) a *life-span* developmental focus, (b) on the *female sex,* (c) during the *middle and later years,* combines three recent frontiers in psychology. This combination means that, except for a few notable exceptions (for summaries see Havighurst, 1973; Kimmel, 1974), the literature is bereft of developmental theory applicable beyond adolescence, and is replete with nondevelopmental, fragmented, and methodologically questionable studies. It also became clear that the majority of such studies suffer from common methodological biases. These biases are not limited to research on women, but they have a particularly detrimental impact on such research.

The developmental psychology of women can provide new directions for all areas of psychology. In studying the formerly neglected female experience, we are developing a new subject area for psychology. This effort is long overdue. However, without the adoption of new methodological and conceptual perspectives, researchers will continue to amass data that are of limited generalizability and that quickly become obsolete. Since research on women has a complex substantive content, a relatively recent experimental history, and strong political implications, it seemed that a review of the common methodological and theoretical problems in the current literature would provide a more substantial contribution to new directions in research than would a traditional review at this time.

I begin with a description of the life-span developmental approach. I then highlight persistent issues of special concern to researchers on women, and discuss methodological problems in interpreting data obtained from earlier generations of women. I then move on to discuss selected empirical studies of women's life cycles, emphasizing developmental events in the family and work realms. Finally, I consider priorities for the study of female development in the middle and later years, and make recommendations for new research directions.

LIFE-SPAN DEVELOPMENTAL PSYCHOLOGY: SELECTED CONCEPTS AND METHODS

Human life-span developmental psychology is concerned with the description, understanding, and prediction of ontogenetic (age-related) behavioral changes from birth to death. Research attention has not been evenly distributed over the life span. Although much is known about the preadolescent and some is known about the adolescent, very little is understood about development in the so-called middle years, and development of the aged has received only slightly more attention.

Where does one find developmental research on women? Not until 1975 did topics directly related to the psychology of women receive separate treatment in the *Annual Review of Psychology* (Mednick & Weissman, 1975). A scan of the issues of the *Annual Review* from 1970 to 1975 reveals that developmental research on women will not appear under "developmental psychology." In fact, not until 1975 did the "developmental psychology" chapter of the *Annual Review* mention that there might be continued development over the life span (Hetherington & McIntyre, 1975, p. 111). The major source of information on the development of the adult female is to be found in chapters devoted to personality (Carlson, 1975; Holzman, 1974; Sarason & Smith, 1971; Singer & Singer, 1972). There are also chapters on "Geropsychology" (Botwinick, 1970) and adult development and aging (Schaie and Gribbin, 1975), which contain some information on sex-related differences in the aged. This situation reflects the historical evolution of theories concerned with adult development which have generally emerged from either the personality or the gerontological literature.

Summarizing the brief history of the development of a life-span perspective, Havighurst (1973) noted that the "psychology of personality development hardly moved beyond Shakespeare before 1930 (p. 6)". It was not until the period from 1930 to 1960 that psychologists such as Charlotte Bühler, Else Frenkel-Brunswick, Erik Erikson, and Carl Jung first attempted to generate a life-span approach to personality development. More recently, Loevinger's (1966; Loevinger and Wessier, 1970) theory of ego development has been specifically applied to sex-role socialization by Jeanne Block (1973; see Block, this volume).

Proportionately little of the empirical literature is devoted to developmental theories of adulthood, partially because few researchers have had access to longitudinal empirical data. I will thus devote little space to discussing such theories individually. One of their common properties is the incorporation of social or sociocultural (e.g., child-bearing events) into their analyses. This characteristic is at once a theory's greatest asset as well as a major liability. Sociocultural events *ipso facto* occur in a given society at a specific time. Unless theories also specify the mechanisms by which developmental events in a social context effect changes in people, the theories remain time-and-place bound.

An example of this problem is found in the widely cited but little researched theory of Erikson (1963). His assertion that "generativity" (concern for establishing and guiding the next generation) defines a major developmental crisis or turning point in the lives of individuals is probably appropriate in pronatalist Western society. However, to characterize individuals who do not have children, "through misfortune or genuine gifts in other directions," as pursuing altruistic or creative activities in order "to absorb their kind of parental drive" (Erikson, 1970, p. 78) reflects the attitudes of the society that Erikson resides in as much as an empirically determined hierarchy of drives within human beings.

The tasks of empirically researching and criticizing these theories as well as developing new ones will require recognition and resolution of several conceptual and methodological problems in the current literature. I have selected for special attention several problems which are of particular importance for evaluating and conducting research on women. They are: (a) understanding the difference between *age* psychology and *developmental* psychology; (b) clearly grasping the importance of the *interactionist approach* for new directions in research on the developmental psychology of women; and (c) appreciating special *methodological problems* resulting from the confounding of age of subject, birth cohort of subject, and the time of measurement of the study.

Age Psychology versus Developmental Psychology

One learns early in undergraduate courses in child development that there is a distinction between the study of child psychology and child development. In the study of child psychology, one asks the question, "What do children do at different ages?" Gesell exemplified a child psychology approach in describing various "stages" of development. The study of child development, however, involves the study of *process;* that is, asking the question, "How does one go from one 'stage' to another?" Piaget's theory provides an example of a developmental approach. The same kind of distinction must be made in the study of adults. By studying age differences among adults, we can speculate on how people change from one behavior pattern to another, but we do not really begin to understand adult development until we study the processes by which change occurs.

The feminist implications of this elementary point are not generally appreciated. When one studies development, one studies processes or mechanisms of development. It is the process, or mechanism, that is the key to growth and change, that makes us "liberated," "oppressed," or (more accurately) a jumbled, mixed-up combination of the two. A research strategy of cataloguing sex, age, or race differences over the life cycle may provide a useful description of past or current events, but the effort is relatively meaningless, scientifically and practically, unless we go further. The next step is to take a developmental approach.

Piaget: An illustration of a developmental approach

Piaget and his colleagues (1950) provide an example of a developmental theory which takes into account environmental factors without binding the factors to events in society. In addition, the theory has direct applicability to research on conceptions of sex roles and sex-role expectations in the adult years.

Piaget and his colleagues developed a theoretical structure to explain how a child passes through a series of developmental stages. That theory maintains that the child, in interacting with the environment, is continually called upon to deal with information that is inconsistent with ter views of the world. The child needs to maintain a state of cognitive "equilibrium" with respect to the information received from the environment. One of the mechanisms used to deal with the information is termed "accommodation," which is a restructuring of one's cognitive organization. A prime source of inconsistent, or discrepant, information for a child is social interaction with peers. Peer interaction that requires taking the role of others is particularly effective in requiring a child to confront discrepant information. A result of this confrontation is "decentration," an increased ability to "put oneself in another's place" or to see the same thing from different points of view. It is basic to the ability to consider multiple variables simultaneously.

As individuals develop, they begin to acquire the concept of reversibility of various transformations, and can think symbolically using "formal operations." The development of these capabilities enables a child to go from a preconservation stage to one of being able to conserve, that is, to extract invariances in the environment despite perceptual transformations. A child first starts conserving on tasks that are concrete and familiar, and eventually extends this ability to abstract tasks. Children have been found to acquire conservation of substance, weight, volume, and number in that order. The phenomenon of being able to conserve on one type of task and not another is called "horizontal décalage." For an introduction to this area, see Ginsburg and Opper (1969).

Although Piaget and his colleagues focused on the years of childhood, the mechanisms of cognitive growth, the principle of decentration and the concept of horizontal décalage are also applicable to adult development. Recently, the concept of decentration has been used in the study of egocentrism in "the later years" with some success (Looft, 1972; 1973). A related theoretical treatment is

Kohlberg's analysis of moral judgment, which is also currently being extended into the middle years (Kramer & Kohlberg, 1969).

The principle of decentration and the concept of horizontal décalage are particularly relevant to the psychology of women. Decentration plays a role in cognitive-developmental theories that address the development of sex typing and gender identity. During the years of childhood below approximately 10 years of age, children appear to have a preconservation concept of gender identity, believing that sex itself is changed when external characteristics such as dress or hair styles are transformed. As children grow older and acquire formal operations of adult logical thinking, their concept of gender identity changes, reflecting their increased cognitive ability. The concept of horizontal décalage suggests that, without appropriate experiences, adults who are able to use formal operational thought with respect to diverse areas may still retain a preconservation mentality regarding gender identities and sex-role concepts. This would explain, for example, why some persons define masculinity and femininity in terms of concrete behaviors and why these concepts take on an either/or, mutually exclusive nature.

This illustration serves to make several points. First, Piaget and his colleagues provide an important developmental theory with direct applicability to research on conceptions of sex roles and sex-role expectations in the adult years. Second, and even more important, they demonstrate the potential of a theory which takes into account environmental factors without binding the factors to events in society.

A continuing issue for developmental psychologists involves the questions: "Are the changes that occur after major developmental events of the social-learning variety, merely involving acquisition of new behaviors and reclassifying old behaviors?" or "Do events precipitate a restructuring of the individual's cognitions and perceptions so that one can point to qualitative, structural changes in a person's world view?" This continuing issue has barely begun to be addressed for adult behavior in general, let alone in terms of how being female mediates such experiences. The issue cannot be examined, however, unless studies focused on processes of change rather than on descriptions of sex and age differences become widespread.

The Interactionist Perspective, or Beyond the Question of "How Much"

An interactionist perspective does appear to be on the crest of today's *Zeitgeist,* but although it is receiving verbal attention, it has yet to be widely translated into research strategy (Vale, 1973). An interactionist approach entails the development of a theoretical formulation that takes multiple variables—organismic and situational—and attempts to explain how they work together to produce behavior. A one-way direction of effects is not necessarily assumed, nor are linear associations among variables.

When one begins to focus on principles and processes, it becomes clear in general that there is a need to deal with more than one variable at a time. Simultaneously looking at multiple variables makes it necessary to deal with interaction effects. The computer has given scientists the technology to analyze data for interaction effects. Unfortunately, the ability of scientists to comprehend and deal with interactions in their theoretical formulations and research designs has not progressed as far as computer technology.

The persistence of two kinds of old, familiar questions of great importance to women underscores the need for a widespread interactionist perspective on the part of researchers. These two questions are: (a) "Which is more important, heredity or environment, in determining behavior?", and (b) "Which is more important, personality or situation, in determining behavior?" To a researcher with an interactionist perspective, both (a) and (b) are the wrong questions. The relevant questions are: "How do heredity and environment interact to produce a specific behavior?" and "How do personality and situation interact to produce a specific behavior?" If developmental research on women is to progress, researchers must themselves decenter and discard the unidimensional either/or mentality that posing questions (a) and (b) reflects. We cannot afford to ask scientifically regressive questions like "What is more important with respect to the influence of menstruation on work performance, biological or social variables?" (see the literature summarized by Parlee in Part III of this volume). Schachter's work (1971), which demonstrated the interaction of physiological and cognitive variables in the determination of internal states such as hunger, reflects a more sophisticated, interactionist approach and provides an example of the kind of innovation needed in theory and method.

Given the immense importance of developing a research strategy that deals with questions of "how" behavior is produced, it is useful to speculate on the conditions that seem to prevent investigators from doing so. Unfortunately, both asking and answering the question of "how" takes a more sophisticated cognitive structure on the part of researchers themselves than does approaching the issue with a unidimensional either/or perspective. The concepts within these two controversies (heredity versus environment, person versus situation), as well as the two controversies themselves, are often confused (see Ekehammer, 1974). Genetic potential gets confused with biology, and biology gets confused with personality. It is obvious that the status of our biology *and* our personality at any moment in time is a product of the past interactions that we have had with our environment. The question "Is biology destiny?" becomes meaningless in a scientific context. This point is so self-evident that one might be tempted to dismiss it. However, one cannot dismiss it as long as the controversies persist and the question is still addressed (see Maccoby and Jacklin, 1974, p. 373).

The quantity of research and writing on such notions as the "maternal instinct" and "menopausal woman" (see Parlee, this volume) reflects the importance of the resolution of the heredity versus environment controversy to researchers interested in women. Women have been told to stay at home because of their biologically different nature, and it has been assumed that this nature is solely due to genetic differences. As noted by Mednick and Tangri (1972), a recent book on the psychology of women itself emphasizes the role of female physiology and biologically-based needs in the development of diverse behaviors (Bardwick, 1971). A vast and contradictory literature on men and women catalogues alleged differences between them, but there is comparatively little research on *how* such differences develop, especially in the adult years (Maccoby & Jacklin, 1974). Yet, as long ago as 1959, Anastasi (1970) pointed out that "how" was indeed the relevant question.

The approach of some researchers involved in this controversy has evolved from the either/or to the "how much" level (e.g., how much variance in a trait is due to genetics and how much is due to environment?). Researchers debate such questions as "Is 80% of intelligence genetically determined?" (Bronfenbrenner, 1972), and even a recent monograph entitled *A survey of research concerns on women's issues* (Daniel, 1975) asks: "If a differential pattern (of sex differences over the life cycle) emerges, how *great* a role does biology play?" (p. 28; italics added).

But "how much" is still a preliminary question, and answers to it are often misused. For example, in the debate over the relationship between heredity and environment, heritability statistics are often bandied about as if they were immutable. "Heritability" is defined as the percentage of variance of a trait attributable to heredity for a specified population under specified conditions. When researchers ask questions about the heritability of a trait, they are basically asking the question of "how much." It must be understood that such statistics are only relevant when presented in relation to a *specified population* of individuals *under a specified set of conditions.* A trait with high heritability under one set of conditions may have low heritability under another. To take a concrete and therefore more readily understandable case, consider the heritability of blindness. The heritability of blindness has increased markedly in the past 170 years because of the elimination of many environmental causes of blindness, such as smallpox. Should the situation change in the next 100 years (e.g., if there should be major smallpox outbreaks), the heritability of blindness could easily be decreased. Similarily, the "heritability" of so-called sex differences in development would be expected to increase as environmental conditions of the sexes are equalized.

The point is that such a variance prediction cannot be made in "absolute" terms. It can be made only on the basis of specified conditions. With respect to the heredity versus environment controversy, once the limitation of a variance prediction is recognized, researchers can develop the mental set necessary to pursue understanding of the mechanisms by which heredity interacts with environment to produce both biology and behavior. The salient biological aspects of pregnancy, childbirth, and menopause increase the importance of the quest for determining the relevant mechanisms. Researchers must take the needed leap beyond the question of "how much" to pursue understanding of such mechanisms.

The need to appreciate the limitation of a variance prediction also applies to the debate revolving around the importance of personality versus situation. That debate has generally evolved to an interactionist approach on the "how much" level (Bowers, 1973; Endler, 1973; Sarason, Smith & Diener, 1975). There are even investigators who have articulated an interactionist position in both theory and research strategy (e.g., Mischel, 1973). Yet the leap to the question of "how" on the level of research strategy has not been made on a widespread scale in the literature (an effect of publication lag, perhaps?).

Mischel (1973) concretely demonstrated the inadequacy of the "how much" approach in looking at personality-situation variables when he pointed out that a selective sampling of persons and situations can be manipulated so that the stronger of the main effects can be arbitrarily attributed to either the personality or the situation. Sarason, Smith, and Diener (1975) asserted that "personality x situation interactions may contribute greatly to specifying the processes that mediate situation-behavior relationships" (p. 204). With these developments in the literature, can the great leap forward to "how" be far behind?

One hindrance has been a lack of appropriate language. As an initial step, and in order to facilitate thinking beyond the "how much" level with respect to the personality versus situation controversy, I propose that psychologists should talk about the "homofacience" of behavior (*homo* from the Latin for the genus to which humans belong, and "facience" from the Latin word *facere,* meaning "to make, to do"). The homofacience of a behavior is thus the proportion of variance attributable to personality in a specified population under specified conditions. The concept of homofacience with respect to the personality versus situation issue can be considered analogous to the concept of heritability when discussing the heredity versus environment issue. (If anyone can think of a better word, tey is welcome to do so; the point is, we need some applicable word.)

Whereas the question of "how much" can be seen as a question of heritability or homofacience, an approach to the question of "how" can be seen as one of "metavariance." Researchers must ask how one can manipulate the variance of heritability or homofacience; that is, how one can manipulate the variables that influence the proportion of variance attributable to a particular causal origin such as heredity or personality. By focusing on the explanation of metavariance, rather than heritability or homofacience, as the goal of research and theory, the cognitive foundation is laid for one approach to pursuing the question of "how".

S. Bem's (1975) study of adaptability and androgyny is an example of research with implications for the study of metavariance in sex-role behavior. This study demonstrated that adherence to a sex-typed, sex-role identity influenced personality versus situation interaction effects. Whether or not the experimental situation was sex-role appropriate did not affect the behavior of androgynous subjects, though it did influence the behavior of sex-typed subjects. This finding suggests that labeling situations as sex-role appropriate would not be useful in an attempt to effect change in an androgynous person's behavior. However, for a person with a stereotyped sex-role identity, it may be a very effective mechanism. Studying how the labeling process affects the proportion of variance in a behavior attributable to androgynous characteristics over diverse situations is moving to a question of metavariance.

That an interactionist perspective can provide a resolution to both the heredity versus environment and personality versus situation controversies is almost a truism. Yet, there is continuing difficulty in translating this perspective into metavariance research strategies. Limitation of language is only one problem. Ekehammer (1974) discussed several reasons why the interactionist approach is not used on a more widespread basis. One difficulty has been the problem of conceptualizing the environment. As a start, Ekehammer (1974) described five major ways to approach situation classification—description of situation based on "(a) *a priori* defined variables of *physical* and *social* character, (b) *need* concepts, (c) some *single reaction* elicited by situation, (d) individuals' *reaction patterns* elicited by the situations, and (e) individuals' *perceptions (cognitions)* of situations" (pp. 1041-1042).

A systematic review of the literature on women that would classify studies in terms of these categories may be a fruitful next step. S. Bem's (1975) work, described earlier, suggests that the dynamics of how sex-role labels get attached and attended to in particular situations is an important avenue of research. But the task of delineating situational dimensions relevant to sex-role behavior has barely begun, and investigating how such situational dimensions change over the life-span has not even been suggested until now. Articulating the relevant situational dimensions in the life of the female and charting them over the life-span is another priority for future researchers interested in female development.

Another handicap is that only relatively recently have statistical methods been developed to handle interactions in data. Researchers have generally used those methods with which they have longer acquaintance (e.g., analysis of variance). Analysis of variance (ANOVA) has been one of the chief methods used to assess interaction effects. Indeed, one of the major pieces in the research literature advocating the interactionist position (Bowers, 1973) used ANOVA interactions to demonstrate that the largest proportion of predicted variance in a number of studies was that predicted by personality/situation interaction effects. Unfortunately, ANOVA provides a highly limited definition of interaction.

Ekehammer (1974) summarized problems with the ANOVA method: Its dependence on the persons and situations involved in the study; its limitation to unidimensional, rather than reciprocal, interaction data; its usual limitation to univariate analysis; and finally, its limitation to describing "how much" and concomitant failure to answer "how." Unfortunately, many of the new multivariate techniques have been developed long after most psychologists left graduate school. Access to continuing education is needed if researchers are to develop the advanced techniques that will enable them to handle multivariate procedures.

As long as researchers are fixated on the use of correlation and analysis of variance, research will continue to rely on the assumption of linear association. Researchers will continue to catalogue personality/behavioral relationships (all the while bemoaning the low correlations that they obtain with such an approach) rather than developing theoretical models that could specify the mechanisms guiding the expression of personality in particular contexts. But even having improved statistical procedures, however, is not a sufficient condition for implementation of an interactionist approach. Research design and theory must change.

A plea for more researchers to take a multivariate approach that considers multiple personality and situational variables may be unrealistic, considering that many studies currently neglect the interactions among personality variables themselves. The neglect of co-variance effects in personality research was underscored in Carlson's (1971) survey of 226 articles published in the 1968 volumes of *The Journal of Personality* and *The Journal of Personality and Social Psychology*. Carlson found that "not a single published study attempted even minimal inquiry into the organization of personality variables within the individual" (p. 209). The situation has improved somewhat since 1968, but is still far from acceptable. Jack Block (1971) provided a notable exception that demonstrates the potential richness of an interactionist approach. Using longitudinal data from the Berkeley Guidance and Oakland Growth Studies, Block identified five male and six female personality types for those adult subjects who were in their mid-thirties. In addition to developing typologies based on multiple characteristics, Block traced developmental sequences for the individuals, discovering that, among other things, persons may become similar through dissimilar routes.

In addition to work on typologies of personality, there are many studies focusing on aspects of development over the life span which could provide input into the development of a situational taxonomy as a foundation for the search for mechanisms. Before they can be interpreted, however, an appreciation of their limitations—due to confounding age of subjects, cohort of subject, and time of measurement—must be developed.

Two Neglected Variables: Cohort and Time of Measurement

Cohort. Given an interactionist perspective, and assuming the capacity for decentering on the part of the researcher, the importance of including the variable of cohort in developmental studies can be appreciated. Basically, a cohort is the collection of individuals who experience a specified event during a designated period of time, usually a particular year. A birth cohort comprises a number of individuals who are born in a particular year. (Usually, the word "birth" is understood and not used, and that convention will be followed in this chapter.) It does not take much imagination to appreciate that the significant factors in the lives of 20-year-old females are quite different for females born in 1930 compared with those of females born in 1950. Many of the inconsistencies in the literature on women can be explained by the fact that different cohorts were used, but cohort has not been widely recognized as an important confounding effect. Given the great changes that are taking place in society, recognizing the concept of cohort in studying females in the later years has become essential, and the older the subjects one is studying, the more essential it becomes.

Longitudinal studies of sex-related differences in the development of intellectual functioning illustrate problems of cohort effects. For example, Bayley (1971) reported on the relationship between achievement status and intelligence in subjects participating in the longitudinal Berkeley Growth Study, observing that education and occupation were related for males, and that males were "achieving pretty much in accord with their mental abilities. The female's achievements, however, as measured by these conventional criteria, are very little related to their capacities" (p. 140). Interestingly, although such women expressed feelings of inadequacy in taking the IQ test and often apologized for being "only housewives," being a housewife was not associated with a decline in IQ. In fact, housewives on the average had consistently higher IQs than working women in these cohorts.

How does one explain this latter result, given that "housewife" is a traditional feminine role and femininity, in girls of earlier cohorts at least, has been associated with IQ deceleration (Sontag, Baker & Nelson, 1958)? There are many alternative explanations, but in answering that question it helps to know that the women in the study were 36 years old *in 1965*. They were housewives during a period when the educated, middle-class woman stayed home, and women generally worked only "because they had to."

The extent to which the expectation that women, even gifted women, should stay at home has constricted women's lives in earlier cohorts is dramatically illustrated by Terman (1954) in a summary of case histories of the achievements of individuals identified as geniuses in his famous longitudinal study of the gifted. That summary reported only on the 800 *men* of the sample, since only a minority of women went on to professional careers. Insofar as this situation has changed, the relationships among IQ, achievement, and job status used in Terman's study can not be appropriately generalized to contemporary females.

I have chosen a longitudinal study to illustrate the problems of cohort effects because the limitations of findings obtained by cross-sectional studies are generally appreciated. In fact, the typical conclusion of a critique of research using cross-sectional designs is a plea for longitudinal research. But when it comes to studying the development of females in the later years, longitudinal research, as we have seen, will not necessarily provide the answers. Longitudinal studies, like cross-sectional studies, still confound aging with cultural change occurring over a particular individual's life span. Although some excellent longitudinal studies continue to contribute important findings from increasingly older subjects (for a summary and bibliography of such longitudinal studies, see Jones, Bayley, MacFarlane, & Honzik, 1971), their findings must be interpreted in the context of the time they were obtained.

A combination of cross-sectional and longitudinal research strategies focused on important developmental events in the lives of the adult female is needed to obtain the kinds of data that permit meaningful interpretation of developmental effects. Schaie (1973) articulated life-span developmental research strategies that attempt to separate the confounding of effects of age, birth cohort, and a third variable of importance—*time of measurement.*

Time of Measurement.   Schaie (1973) discussed the importance of time of measurement effects in analysis and interpretation of data. In looking at the effects of time of measurement, there are two factors to consider. First, the same experimental condition is very different from the subject's point of view, given the historical context of the times. For example, studying the abortion experience could mean something different to a subject if the study were to occur before rather than after the legality of abortion was established by the 1973 Supreme Court decision.

In addition, time of measurement is important from the point of view of experimenter bias. Helson's (1972) discussion of the changing image of the career woman provides a clear illustration of the effects of time of measurement. In reviewing the stereotypes of career women in the older studies in the literature, she makes the "old disquieting point that the design, visibility, and interpretation of the research relevant to social issues depend very much on the current purposes of the social organism and on entrenched opinions and values" (p. 40). Time of measurement is therefore important as an index of cultural change in both the experience of subjects and the experience of scientists.

How have cultural blinders based on assumptions about normal and proper roles for women limited past cohorts of scientists? How can such sexism influence our models and methods? These are the questions to which we now turn.

SEXISM IN MODELS AND METHOD

A developmental approach has much to offer, but not until sexist bias in research and theory is confronted and eradicated. Many articles in this volume, including this one, describe examples of sexism on the part of the scientist or clinician. For the female in her middle and later years, the problem of bias against women is compounded by problems of bias against old people. In addition, if researchers are white and middle-class, the life of the adult woman is studied in reference to a male, white, middle-class, nuclear-family norm.

Because the family has been the primary source of women's definition and self-fulfillment, it is appropriate to select the marriage and family literature to provide a case in point. Heiskenan (1971) performed a content analysis on the leading journal in the field *(Journal of Marriage and the Family)* between 1959 and 1968. Of 289 studies that involved empirical work, the percentage that focused on single persons other than college students, unwed mothers, members of ethnic groups, young children, or rural families (i.e., "deviant" groups) ranged from 1% to 5%. One-fourth of the studies were based on samples of college males and females. Middle-class groups outrepresented lower-class groups by 6 to 1. Of 90 studies that were considered "off strata," nearly 1 of every 5 still did not employ class variables in its analysis.

White middle-class sexist bias limits the advancement of knowledge at every level, from sampling strategy to theory construction, in both the sociological and psychological literatures (Carlson, 1971; Laws, 1971) concerned with adult development. A particularly pervasive bias is found in the literature on the maternal role, which continues to assume that the biological mother somehow must function as the primary childraiser if children are to develop normally (Wortis, 1971).

This combination of sex and class bias is especially limiting for contemporary researchers. Increasing numbers of women are remaining single for a longer period of time, and increasing numbers of couples are indicating a preference for a life-style without children (Bureau of the Census, 1975). In the past 10 years, the number of female-headed households has increased by 24%, as compared with an increase of 14% for all families. In 1962 the divorce rate was 2.2%. In 1974 the rate was 4.6%. Increasing numbers of women are working, and the working mother is a common event. In 1970, 30% of women who had children under 6 years of age were in the labor force. Of women who had children ages 6-17, 50% were in the labor force (Bureau of the Census, 1972). Unfortunately, sexist bias influences what researchers define as a "problem" when studying such changing life-styles. For example, the "problem" of the working mother has been studied; the "problem" of the working father has not. Changes in life-styles are but some of the new directions that need to be reflected in future research, but scientific advance will not occur if such changes are defined as "problems" before they have even been studied.

Gurion (1974) observed that psychologists "draw lovely pictures or diagrams and call them models, fill the models with terms they cannot operationalize, and give never a thought to the validities of the operational definitions they *do* use" (p. 292). Gurion's remarks are apt. Laws' (1971) feminist review of the marital adjustment literature contains numerous illustrations of errors of omission and commission in theory and method created by the sexist shortsightedness of researchers. Laws described how marital success is defined as marital stability, marriage is viewed as a closed system, and a typical model for the marital dyad is "institutional"—one of husband-instrumental, wife-expressive task specialization, á la Parsons (1955).

The dichotomous mentality advanced by the Parsonian institutional model of marriage can create such a strong mental set in researchers that they ignore data inconsistent with their hypotheses. Rossi (1968) underscores the limitations of this set when she points out that the typical wife's role in fact has involved a large component of instrumental function. Laws' (1971) description of a study by Kotlar (1965) provides another demonstration of the limiting effects of an "institutional model set." Kotlar's study was designed to test the hypothesis that marital satisfaction is associated with role specialization of husband and wife along task-expressive lines. Role "reversal" on the part of husband and wife was expected to reflect marital "maladjustment." Kotlar found that high marital adjustment was associated with having *both* spouses relatively high on expressive characteristics, while low adjustment couples were more likely to have both spouses lower on that characteristic. Yet, because of sex stereotyping in rating of "ideal husband" and "ideal wife" (which showed no relationship to marital adjustment), Kotlar did not reject the role-reversal hypothesis. Laws concluded that Kotlar's study is "an example of the way in which theoretical brainwashing can divorce the researcher from the accurate interpretation of data" (p. 490).

The institutional model's assumption that having an ability in an expressive function precludes or somehow devalues traits associated with an instrumental function is not credible (Rossi, 1968; Laws, 1971). Yet the research literature has been dominated by this approach, leaving other possibilities relatively unexplored. One problem is that researchers idealize the concept of role, failing to recognize that individuals have the power to adapt roles to their own needs and situations (and do). D. Bem and Allen (1975) underscored the need to look at situations from the point of view of the persons in them. Roles, too, should be studied in terms of the perspective of the individuals who enact them (see Goffman, 1959).

Over 20 years ago Burgess (1956) advanced a more democratic and permissive model of marriage, which he termed "companionship," but the model of the traditional, or institutional, marriage has remained "the model of choice" by marriage and family researchers (Laws, 1971, p. 489). How does this model fare in the attitudes of the "real world" of today? The most recent national data come from the 1974 Virginia Slims American Women's Opinion Poll. Virginia Slims commissioned the Roper Organization to interview a sample of over 3,000 women and 1,000 men, ages 18 and over, on attitudes toward marriage, divorce, the family, and sexual morality. Interpretation of poll data is subject to all the pitfalls of any research that relies on verbal report and cross-sectional sampling, but such findings can be suggestive. One item presented seven alternatives and asked, "What would be the most satisfying and interesting way of life . . .?" Ninety-six percent of the women and 92% of the men preferred an alternative that described either a traditional or a companionship marriage. The traditional-marriage item sounded very much like the institutional model of the family researcher, "with the husband assuming the responsibility for providing for the family and the wife running the house and taking care of the children" (p. 31). The companionship-marriage item, on the other hand, was more like the Burgess model, "where husband and wife share responsibilities more—both work, both share homemaking and child responsibilities" (p. 31). Figure 3.1 plots the percentages of men and women reporting a preference for traditional or companionship marriages by age and sex. The other alternatives—"living with someone of the opposite sex, but not marrying"; "remaining single and living alone"; "remaining single and living with others of the same sex"; "living in a big family of people with similar interests, in which some of the people are married and some are not"; and "none, don't know"—were all grouped under "other" because the proportions of responses to them were so small.

Age groups under 39 contained more persons who said that they preferred a companionship marriage arrangement, whereas for cohorts aged 40 and over, more preferred a traditional marriage. The cohort of women from ages 18-29 showed the largest percentage in favor of a companionship marriage (61%). Men in that age group did not differ greatly from their brothers in the 30-39 age bracket in choosing a companionship marriage (51% of both age groups preferred that alternative). Rather, a larger number of them chose alternatives to marriage, such as "living together" (15% of younger men versus 8% of men 30 to 39 years choosing such alternatives).

So, on the verbal level at least, both models were most frequently chosen as "satisfying and interesting" ways of life, with younger cohorts (especially women) preferring a companionship orientation. It is up to future research to discover if and how these preferences are translated into life-styles and what impact a particular family style has on the development of women and other family members over their life cycles. To do so requires discarding a dichotomous view of the world, whether that view be heredity versus environment; personality versus situation, male versus female, instrumental versus expressive function, or whatever. Research models and research strategies must begin to reflect the complexities of the phenomena that they are purporting to address, and the values that they serve must at least be honestly presented rather than cloaked behind theoretical jargon in the guise of scientific objectivity.

The Virginia Slims data have been presented here to support a relatively limited point—that both traditional marriage and companionship marriage have ample numbers of individuals who report viewing them as satisfying and interesting ways of life. To take traditional marriage as the "ideal" and study alternatives in terms of the problems they create is to deny reality.

The Virginia Slims data help illustrate another point, however. Consider some alternative interpretations that dramatize how such cross-sectional data can be taken out of the context of cohort and time of measurement to buttress divergent points of view. A person with a bias for the traditional marriage might argue something like this:

"The increase in preference for the traditional marriage with age suggests that women, as they grow older, develop a greater need to be cared for. These data suggest that a young woman who enters into a companionship marriage may develop problems of marital adjustment in later life as her increased need to be cared for goes unmet. Premarital counselors could perhaps be trained to alert young people to the dangers of organizing their marriage along companionship lines too early in their relationship in order to avoid marital stress that will occur later. Viewed in the context of increased divorce rates, this problem should have high priority for research and social-action programs."

Anyone who has read Laws' (1971) critique of the marital-adjustment literature will not view the preceding argument as ludicrous.

To present another point of view, a person biased toward the companionship marriage might offer an alternative interpretation, observing that:

"Younger people can be more honest in terms of their preferences for a companionship marriage because they are less likely to have already closed off their options. Therefore, because the companionship model is the preferred choice of individuals who have their options open, it is indeed a better choice. Social-action programs should be designed to help all those individuals locked into traditional marriages and who must deny their feelings and characterize their entrapment as a satisfying and interesting way of life."

I hope that these two alternative futures can be seen as extremes and that researchers will address their questions to the benefits and costs of both kinds of life-styles for different kinds of people in different kinds of situations. Meanwhile, we must remain alert to counter unjustified sexist statements supported by data based on older cohorts without regard to the effects of cohort and time of measurement.

With these methodological and conceptual observations in mind, let us turn to some existing research findings that help us understand a woman's development beyond adolescence in the context of our society.

SEX-ROLE SOCIALIZATION BEYOND ADOLESCENCE

In the interest of manageability, this section is organized around the sex-role socialization of women beyond adolescence. The inter-relationships among roles related to marriage, pregnancy, work, child-bearing and child-rearing will receive attention because they currently play such a direct and major part in defining a woman's identity and activity.

To look at sex-role norms and the impact that developmental events have on sex-role expectations requires some analysis of the dynamics of sex-role expectations themselves. As Angrist (1969) noted, "sex role may be seen as involving four elements: 'label, behavior, expectations, and locations' " (p. 218). The label can be used to elicit organized patterns of behavior considered appropriate for persons with that label. Expectations may be generically normative (what each sex as a group should be or do) or concretely normative (what you, a particular person with particular characteristics in this particular situation, should be or do). A label can elicit both expectations and behaviors on the part of oneself or on the part of others, but always in relation to context or "location" (Angrist, 1969, p. 219).

The organizing power of the label "female sex" should not be underestimated. Like black persons vis-à-vis whites, females cannot easily "pass" as members of a male group. The classification cues for the female membership group are multiple and usually obvious. Even more important, there are data suggesting that such cues are difficult to disregard.

Wolman and Frank's (1975) study of the role of the solo woman in six small professional groups provides a disquieting illustration of the organizing power of the label "female sex." Although their sample was small, their analyses of the processes by which their women subjects became isolates, deviates, or low-status members of the groups are suggestive for further research. Their report described how sex-role labels were attached to a female's coping strategies when an otherwise all-male group attempted to exclude her. Attribution of a "feminine" coping mechanism increased her perceived difference: Acting friendly was defined as flirting; acting weak elicited a "little sister" approach rather than peer treatment; apologizing for alienating the group fit the "submissive woman in her place" stereotype; and when she asked for help, she got the "needy female" label. "Masculine" coping mechanisms, on the other hand, threatened the men so that they isolated her more. When her response was to become angry or to point out rationally what the group process was doing to her, she was seen as competitive, bitchy, and unfeminine. Although the women in the groups did resist being defined as deviant, the men usually found a way to minimize their impact, ignore them, and continue in effect to maintain a male group. It is not surprising that after a while the women tended to give up, becoming depressed. Wolman and Frank concluded that gender is more powerful than any other cue for determining people's expectations of each other's behavior. A researcher using a metavariance approach, however, would maintain that the proportionate power of the sex-role label should vary with the persons and situations involved, and set out to study what variables influence the relative strength of this power.

It is important to recognize that sex roles and labels involve a whole complex of subroles and sublabels that also have organizing power. The content of those roles varies with age, race, and social status. "Mother" and "wife" are just two developmental role labels that women are assigned because of their sex. Angrist (1969) underscored the multiplicity of sex-role components. Exploration of the relationships among components—that is, asking such questions as when does a particular constellation of components assume primacy, and when do the expectations of different adult roles (e.g., mother, worker) supplement, complement, or conflict with each other—has yet to be undertaken. In asking questions regarding the development of sex-roles and in assessing the impact of sex-role labels, it is particularly important to ask: How does a woman *actively* participate in determining the content that a sex-role label implies? Researchers must not repeat the error of the studies of deviance that focused on the *reaction* of persons labeled deviant while neglecting such persons' active participation in determining the imposition and content of the label and role (Levitan, 1975).

Family research has overemphasized marital roles, and researchers must discard the unwritten assumptions that underlie much of the earlier research on family structure and process. There is an obvious need to eschew an overfocus on the nuclear family structure and to include traditional relatives such as grandparents, uncles, and aunts in studying family interaction. But, in addition, contemporary life-styles necessitate that spouses, children, and in-laws of earlier marriages also be included in such studies. While the effects of adults, especially parents, on the development of children in families has been studied extensively, comparatively little work has been done on the effects of children on the development of adults, especially parents (Harper, 1975). This neglect is a reflection of a larger mind-set, which assumes unilateral influence of the old on the young. That assumption not only precludes creative studies of the process of reciprocal family interaction, but also limits research on other kinds of intergenerational contact as well (e.g., as in studies of teacher-student interaction).

The study of reciprocal influences among generations is an area of special promise for the understanding of the development of sex roles. Today's young women are trying out new roles and experimenting with new life-styles. How does this situation affect the sex roles of their parents and grandparents? I know of several cases when a college-age daughter has been instrumental in channeling her mother toward feminist therapy during times of mid-life stress, but I know of no empirical studies of the roles of contemporary daughters in assisting mothers during times of role-related developmental crises. The attitudes of persons in the middle and later years toward sex roles are changing (Virginia Slims, 1974), and it seems logical that the woman's movement, stimulated by the actions of these older women's daughters, has had something to do with this change. How does it happen? To design research to answer such questions, the interactions among the age and status systems of American society must be appreciated.

Age Grading and Sex-Role Norms

The age-grading system of society reflects institutionalized cultural values, and these constitute a social system that shapes the life cycle (Neugarten & Datan, 1973). Age grading may be formally enforced by society (e.g., through legally specified ages for entering school, driving, leaving school, marriage, and voting, some of which may or may not differ for females, depending on the state of residence). Age grading may also be enforced informally (as when neighbors ask you why you have reached 30 and have not yet married).

In looking at the process of adult female development, the first point to remember is that enough contingencies between sex- and age-role classifications have been found at both earlier and later periods of the life cycle so that any generalization about sex-role norms over the life span must be made with caution (Emmerich, 1973; Kimmel, 1974; Neugarten & Gutmann, 1968). As Emmerich (1973) so aptly stated:

> Sex-roles may not be primary definers of socialization sequences. For example, formation of a firm sexual identity is an important phenomenon of childhood, and yet this milestone's significance could arise from its placement in an ontogenetic series in which sex-role contents are secondary. A firm sex-role identity may be just one of many manifestations of a general cognitive stage (concrete operations) and/or simply one phase in a life-long series of identity transformations, in which categories other than sex status typically are more salient. A life-span framework thus alerts investigators to the likelihood that sex-role phenomena are subordered into more fundamental organizing processes in personality development (pp. 143-144).

Sex-role norms interact with other kinds of norms in diverse ways. For example, sex-role norms may be overruled by age-role norms (a boy in middle childhood may be "supposed" to like boys better than he does girls, but he is also "supposed" to like his parents, including his mother, better than both (Emmerich, Goldman, & Shore, 1971)). Norms specific to class and occupational status may also overrule sex-role norms. Emmerich (1973) points out that "there is evidence that children attribute sex-role norms to various reference figures, that these attributions differ for the sexes, and that they are subject to developmental changes between childhood and adolescence" (p. 142).

Neugarten, Moore, and Lowe (1968) found age norms to differ for men and women. Earlier cohorts of middle-aged and older individuals appear to pay more attention to age norms than do younger individuals, perhaps because they have learned that to be "off time with regard to life events or to show other age-deviant behavior brings with it social and psychological sequelae that cannot be disregarded" (p. 28). The difference between middle-aged and older individuals may reflect that earlier cohorts held more respect for societal norms in general, however. In any case, consensus on age norms by subjects of all ages was quite high.

Many of the changes that women are making in their lives involve violations of both age- and sex-role norms. What happens when a woman over 35 decides to return to school (as 475,000 such women chose to do in 1972)? Studies of earlier cohorts will not be of much help in understanding these women because women students 25 years and over were so scarce in earlier years that they were not even counted until 1972. There has been more than a threefold gain in older women students from 1960 to 1972 (Women's Bureau, 1974). The decision-making process by which a woman decides to return to school, and thereby violate age- and sex-role norms (college students are young and women should be at home with their families), and the resulting reorganization of her family regime and social life are just two research topics of interest generated by this mid-life change. Though violation of age- and sex-role norms will be an important direction for future study, such research must reflect a feminist perspective. The traditional researcher would ask: "What problems does the woman's return to school create for the family?" A feminist researcher would ask, among other questions: "What benefits and costs will there be and from whose point of view?"

Changes in how sex-role norms interact with other kinds of norms, particularly in adulthood, and how norms are attributed to whom and under what conditions are unknown quantities at this stage of research. The delineation of the content of both age- and sex-role norms for current cohorts is necessary, but the important new direction for research is the discovery of *how* such norms are created and enforced.

Life Events, Periods, and Dimensions

The idea that one can teach "little girls" specific behaviors that will be functional for their adult roles as wives and mothers has always been spurious. This is particularly true for the traditional female, who is expected to structure her life around many contingencies (Angrist, 1969): the need to fit the expectations of an unknown spouse; the uncertainty about whether she will marry, and the necessity to provide backup education and training "just in case" she does not; the possibility of childlessness, with the concomitant need to develop alternative activities; the disruption of routine when children leave home, with the concomitant need to develop other options; and the possibility of divorce or widowhood, with the resulting necessity to prepare for some sort of occupation, again "just in case." For a traditional woman, the most appropriate training would seem to be in the preparation of decision trees.

The contingencies are real, and a woman's need to design her life on a contingency basis has its psychological costs. As Dohrenwend (1973) observed in a study of stressful life events and symptoms of psychological distress, "women's symptom levels were more affected by events they did not control than by all events, suggesting that this psychological distress tended to be associated with a lack of power to control their lives" (p. 332).

In addition to psychological distress, contingency planning may also have some effect on consistency of mental abilities. Bayley (1971) reported males showing greater consistency than females in six intellectual measures, especially between ages 18-26. Her interpretation was that this "may very well be a period when there are larger shifts in the women's motivations and attitudes toward intellectual goals" (p. 137).

A traditional approach toward describing the course of life events is to chart the milestones of development for the typical person in our society. Figure 3.2 contains a "lifeline" designed for females, a schematic representation of the developmental milestones of the female from birth to death. Charting such events serves only to present a very rough approximation of the timing of selected significant events in the lives of most females in our society. In picturing the "average" female, the lifeline approach has a white middle-class bias. For example, consider the timing for the developmental events of pregnancy and marriage. Women's average age at first marriage in the United States has ranged between 21 and 22 years of age for many years. On the average, people have children after 1 or 2 years of marriage; hence, pregnancy is placed approximately 2 years after marriage on the lifeline. However, the modal age for first births in our society is 19 years, and it has been estimated in earlier cohorts that at least as many as one-half to three-quarters of teenage brides are pregnant (Christensen, 1963). Schematic representations such as lifelines may be useful insofar as they provide a point of departure for discussion, but feminist researchers must not become engrossed in studying averages and so repeat the mistake of the 6-foot psychologist who could not swim and therefore drowned when crossing a stream that had an average depth of 4 feet.

Figure 3.2 contains several typical developmental events unique to the female. Menstruation, pregnancy, child-bearing, and menopause by definition necessitate a female biology. Parlee's article in this volume (Chapter 6), however, underscores the overemphasis on biology and the neglect of sociocultural variables in the effort to understand such experiences. Figure 3.2 differs from the typical lifeline in that it includes events such as abortion, nursing, mastectomy, and hysterectomy. Although these are not developmental events in the usual sense, they are additional experiences that can have a long-lasting impact on the female in some social contexts. They, too, require an analysis of the biological, psychological, social, and cultural variables in interaction.

Initial sexual experience, beginning of a career, marriage, parenthood, children going to school, children leaving home, retirement, and death are all events that both sexes experience, as are divorce, illness (of self and spouse), and death of spouse. But as Bernard (1974) observed, "men and women march to different drummers. They are not even in the same parade" (p. 82). If one takes an interactionist perspective that recognizes the importance of considering both personality and situational dimensions simultaneously, it is easy to appreciate that being present at the same time and place is not the same as having the same experience. Indeed, the study of the psychology of women can be seen as the study of how being female mediates human experiences.

There are some summaries of the literature on sex differences in roles over the life cycle (Baltes & Schaie, 1973; Eisdorfer & Lawton, 1973). These summaries suggest that sex-role perceptions change with age (Kimmel, 1974; Neugarten, 1968) and that interactions with other variables do not always turn out as would be predicted on the basis of sex-role research with younger subjects.

In earlier cohorts, there has been greater agreement regarding age expectations for both sexes during the period of young adulthood, and also a greater agreement on what is age-appropriate behavior for women than for men. This pattern of normative expectation may be one reason that (a) with age, both sexes seem to become more tolerant of what would have been considered cross-sex tendencies in themselves in earlier years (Neugarten & Gutmann, 1968); and (b) such increased tolerance has seemed greater for men than for women (Terman & Miles, 1936).

An evaluation of what is meant by "cross-sex" behavior is in order. What is "sex-appropriate" differs with age, cohort, and situational context. It is difficult to make absolute judgments about the sex-appropriateness of specific behaviors (e.g., a researcher may think it is sex-appropriate for a woman to cook, but ask a French chef which sex should prepare the *sauce bèarnaise*). Cataloguing *what* is or is not sex-appropriate should only be seen as the first step to asking *how* a specific behavior comes to be judged as sex-appropriate. Is it through a statistical approach (*most* women do X; therefore it is sex-appropriate)? Is it through a "significant other" influence (my mother did X, so therefore it is sex-appropriate)? Is it through a reinforcement process (I get smiled at when I do X; therefore it is sex-appropriate)? Or, more likely, do different people come to a similar judgment of the sex-appropriateness of a behavior by way of different processes (see Jack Block, 1971)? Future researchers must view the sex-appropriateness of a specific behavior as a relative concept. It is "in the eye of the beholder," and should be studied as such.

Middle-aged people of earlier cohorts perceived adulthood as divided into the following periods: young adulthood, maturity, middle age, and old age. Life was perceived to change over these periods along five dimensions: career health and physical figure, family cycle, psychological attributes, and social responsibility. Consensus on timing and patterning of these dimensions has been the rule, although sex and social class differences do exist in some areas. Middle-aged people have not necessarily defined their age in terms of chronological time, but rather have used their progress along these five life dimensions to "clock" themselves. The inconsistency in progress between one dimension and another can become a source of conflict and stress (Neugarten, 1968). Women have been seen as moving faster through the life cycle than men (Jackson, 1974; Neugarten, Moore, & Lowe, 1968), and historical changes in the relationships among timing of developmental events within the five dimensions have been observed.

Because the interrelationships of the life-cycle dimensions of family and career reflect what have traditionally been the primary definers of roles for females and males respectively, it is instructive to focus on developmental events related to marriage, pregnancy, child-bearing, and child-rearing as those events have influenced female development along these two dimensions.

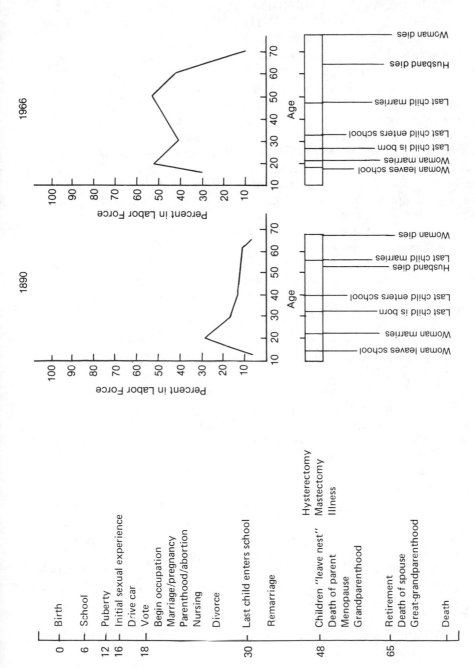

Figure 3.2 Women's Lifeline. Ages and order are approximate.

Table 3.2   Timing Relationships (Modified from Neuman & Moore, 1968, p. 12.)

A LOOK AT THE CHANGING SOCIAL CONTEXT OF
FAMILY AND CAREER

Neugarten and Datan (1973) described the changes in the timing relationships of main life events for men and women along the family and career dimensions of the life cycle. The statistics in Figure 3.3 (from Neugarten & Moore, 1968), indicating the timing of major life events in 1890 and 1966 for women generally, show a trend toward constriction; at the same time, the life span has increased. This trend has continued into the 1970s. These changes in family-cycle timing have been correlated with changes in work pattern. The interesting finding is not that more women work; it is the change in the pattern of the curve. The changing patterns of men's versus women's economic lives also deserve comment. As man's work life has become constricted (with age of beginning occupation increasing and age of retirement decreasing), woman's work has gone in the opposite direction. More women work at younger ages for longer periods without a break, and for longer periods over time.

Neugarten and Datan (1973) pointed out that the age of economic maturity has been postponed for many middle-class males because such men have delayed initiating their work roles in order to complete their education. In 1966, one of every four men in college or graduate school was married. That figure holds for 1970 as well. Women have typically worked to supplement family income, and many women are the sole providers of what have been termed "female-headed households." However, when the wife works while her husband is in school, she combines the role of sole provider with the wife's role under these specified conditions. As temporary as this situation might be considered by the couples, it is still precedent-setting (for society as well as for the couples themselves). The impact of these arrangements on the evolution of a particular couple's life-style, as well as on the image of the working woman, is yet to be determined. The women who put their husbands through school in the 1960s are the women "in their middle years" in the 1970s. Their position in the social structure suggests that their impact may be wider than their numbers.

Today's young women are setting their own precedents. They are increasingly going to college themselves instead of dropping out, and are choosing cohabitation rather than marriage as a life-style alternative—at least for the college years (Macklin, 1972). A recent survey of a random sample of students attending Arizona State University disclosed that 29% of the males and 21% of the females were currently cohabiting or had cohabited (Henze & Hudson, 1974). Thus, it is untenable to assume that the students who opt for this type of living arrangement are somehow a "fringe element." Studies of earlier cohorts may not help us in understanding the adult women of today, and neither group may be of great help in predicting the development of the cohorts of the women of tomorrow.

Cohabitation statistics aside, for the contemporary female the state of marriage is very much in style. The National Center for Vital Statistics reports that in 1960 the marriage rate was 8.5 per 1.000 of the eligible population. In 1974 the rate was 10.4. In our society, over 90% of women marry, and over 90% of that group bear children. Recent surveys have indicated that women still see marriage as the most desirable state for self-fulfillment (Campbell, 1975; Virginia Slims, 1974), and studies of youth have suggested that they agree with the parental generation's attitudes. For example, in a 1972 survey of entering first-year college students by the American Council on Education (ACE, 1972), 62% of males and 68% of females considered raising a family "essential or very important" in their life objectives. Because a desire for a child-free marriage has been an anomaly laden with stigma (Veevers, 1973), traditional marriage can be seen as a means to an end, that is, child-bearing and child-rearing. There are small changes in attitudes toward childlessness, but that state remains an atypical choice for married couples, with less than 8% of wives expecting no children in their married life (Bureau of the Census, 1975). The 1974 Virginia Slims poll found only 1% of women and men to consider no children as an ideal family size—replicating the 1941 findings of the American Institute of Public Opinion (Virginia Slims, 1974).

In a recent survey of over 2,000 adults, Campbell, Converse and Rodgers (reported in Campbell, 1975) concluded that men and women are "out of sync" when it comes to stages of satisfaction and stress over the life cycle. They found that marriage is still considered the most desirable state for individual self-fulfillment, with both men and women reporting themselves as "happiest" when they were newly married and without children. Young wives without children appeared to be the "happiest" of individuals, although young husbands also reported being "happier" than did young single men. The developmental event of marriage had an opposite effect on the sexes with respect to stress, however; women reported much less stress after marriage than previously and men reported more stress. Even though three of every four young wives in the sample were employed, the young husbands still reported themselves more burdened by the responsibilities of marriage. The reports of happiness dropped to average for couples with children, however. The young mothers reported pressure, and both husbands and wives (with children present in the home) described themselves as being restricted and more dissatisfied. "Satisfaction with life" appeared to return when the children left the nest. As Campbell (1975) put it, "raising a family seems to be one of those tasks, like losing weight or waxing the car, that is less fun to be doing than to have done" (p. 39).

Although effects of cohort and time of measurement make interpretation of such differences among age groups difficult, this U-shaped function of marital satisfaction over the family life cycle has been obtained in other studies (Rollins & Cannon, 1974; Rollins & Feldman, 1970). Whether this U-shaped curve is a reliable one has been a matter of dispute, and because the operational definition of marital satisfaction has varied in many studies, comparisons are difficult (Rollins & Cannon, 1974). One of the problems has been the use of instruments that lack validity (Laws, 1971; Rollings & Cannon, 1974). Campbell (1975) and ter colleagues devised their own measure of marital satisfaction, and comparison has thus not been facilitated.

Rollins and Cannon (1974) suggested that a mediating variable between family cycle and marital satisfaction may be role strain in the family, and the weak relationship found between marital satisfaction and the family life cycle thus may reflect the imprecision of the approach. Laws (1971) observed that the relationship between marital life-style (e.g., traditional or companionship) and marital satisfaction is affected by the degree of congruency in attitude of husband and wife toward the particular life-style.

Focusing on the roles and role strains of family members in terms of the divergence of individual members' role expectations and role behaviors should be an important direction for future research. However, without controlling for age and cohort effects, researchers will not be able to ascertain whether or not increased satisfaction over the marital life cycle reflects changes in the marriage relationship, differences in cohorts, or differences in age-correlated response sets. For example, older cohorts comprise only marriages that survive. Also, older persons may be subject to acquiescence and social desirability response sets (Ahammer, 1971; Ahammer and Baltes, 1972; Spanier, Lewis & Cole, 1975).

Conflict and role strain between the roles of mother and worker have received a largess of attention from marriage and family researchers. Bernard (1974) summarized and integrated a diverse literature on motherhood, including work focused on the conflicts between career and family. Hoffman and Nye (1974) also summarized much of the literature dealing with this conflict and its possible implications for the development of children in the families of mothers who work. These two summaries pointed out the inadequacy and bias in the current literature on the working mother, and also debunked myths with respect to negative impact that working mothers have on the development of their children. The latter conclusion is reassuring in light of the Virginia Slims poll finding that 61% of their sample of women ages 18-29 felt that the combination of marriage, career, and children would "offer the most satisfying and interesting life."

Transition to Parenthood: The Context, The Process

Parenthood may be considered important to self-fulfillment, but it is not without costs. Transition to parenthood, especially early parenthood, has been found to have devastating effects on the educational development of the female. Dixon (1975), for example, reported the findings of a survey made of high school seniors in 1965 who were reinterviewed in 1971. At the time of the second interview, 75% of the married women with children who had started college had dropped out of school, compared with 52% of married men with children, 22% of single women, and 27% of single men. Besides truncating a woman's education, early motherhood in the context of our society is also associated with subsequent divorce and poverty (Bacon, 1974). Transition into parenthood may be seen as a crisis for women at all ages, but it is particularly disruptive to the development of younger women (Bacon, 1974; Presser, 1974).

For current cohorts at least, the norms with respect to motherhood are as follows: Once a man and woman are married, the expectation is that they will have children, and the woman feels the expectation more than the man (Griffith, 1973). Some couples, of course, do opt for a child-free life-style. Once a woman has a child, the expectation is that she will have another. This expectation is almost more inviolate than the expectation to have children itself. Having an "only" child means that, by definition, the woman will be a "bad" mother because an only child is still stigmatized in our society. Prevalence of this position is evident in continued avoidance of the one-child family, despite the fact that the only child is in many respects more advantaged than a child with siblings (Terhune, 1974).

Traditionally, having children has meant that women withdraw from the work force until their children are at least old enough for school. However, the trend is toward more and more working mothers, even when mothers have preschool children. As a result, the developmental events of children entering and leaving school may not have the same kind of impact on their mothers' life cycles as did such events on earlier cohorts. As alternative-care institutions become more wide-spread in our society, the developmental events of children's lives will change, and thus the developmental events of mothers will also change to some extent. It is clear that in charting the events of a woman's life, one can only understand a woman's behaviors when they are placed in a larger context.

Given the impact of the developmental event of parenthood on women, it is not surprising to find a number of studies on pregnancy and childbirth with respect to the woman's experience (see Parlee, Chapter 6). However, the experience of becoming a father has been neglected. A study by Greenberg and Morris (1974) suggests that this neglect has had very high costs for the understanding of the development of parenting behavior.

Illustrations of A Focus on Process: Two Studies

Rather than attempt to review the vast literature on pregnancy and parenthood, I have chosen to discuss the work of Greenberg and Morris (1974), and Greenberg, Rosenberg, and Lind (1973) in detail. Their work provides an illustration of research that focuses on the *processes* by which one assumes the role of parent. Although their methods of observation and reporting were crude, and they relied on questionnaire and clinical interview techniques, their approach to their subject matter can provide a valuable conceptual lesson to future researchers.

Greenberg and Morris (1974) studied the impact of the newborn child on the behavior of the father. The fathers in their study were found to develop such a sense of preoccupation, interest, and absorption in the infant that the authors termed the phenomenon "engrossment." Their sample consisted of one group of fathers who had initial contact with their newborn at birth in the delivery room and another group who had initial contact after birth when their newborn was shown to them by nursing personnel. Both groups showed evidence of strong paternal feelings and involvement. Engrossment included a desire to watch and touch the newborn. The fathers reported an experience of extreme elation, often described as a "high." The infants' movements were reported to have a strong impact on the fathers and served as a source of "wonder and amazement," increasing the fathers' level of engrossment.

In studying behaviors—on the part of males or females—that are counter to the expectation of society, it is important to ask, "How do others react to this unexpected behavior?" That is, what happens when fathers violate the sex-role norm of not being too interested in babies? How do our settings discourage the development of behaviors counter to sex-role expectations?

With respect to the first question, Greenberg and Morris (1974) suggested that the wife's response to her husband's engrossment with the newborn may sometimes be negative because the man's feeling of involvement may be so intense that the "normal amenities" extended to the wife are "neglected." What "normal amenities" entail is not specified. Perhaps one mechanism for inhibiting fathers' involvement with raising their children is the mothers' attitude to their initial engrossment. The response of physicians and other hospital personnel to the fathers' engrossment may be another factor.

Barriers to the father's accessibility to the newborn provide an example of how settings can discourage the development of his parenting behavior. Greenberg and Morris suggested that the first hour after birth may be a significant period for the father to have contact with the newborn, because the influence that the newborn's activity has on the father (a newborn is more active in the first hour after birth than in subsequent hours). They also suggested that early contact with the newborn may result in a release of engrossment on the part of fathers who appear to be ambivalent in their attitudes. This "releasing phenomenon" was reported for several fathers in their sample. But, typically, fathers are not offered the chance to hold the newborn, so that they do not ordinarily share the immediate contact that the fathers in the Greenberg and Morris study reported as so very enjoyable. Whether or not engrossment has a long-term impact on a father's behavior toward his children has yet to be seen. However, this kind of study, focusing on the effects of reciprocal interaction among father, mother and infant over time in the development of parenting behavior, is an example of a needed approach.

Many of the recent changes in medical procedures with respect to pregnancy and childbirth, and the participation of the fathers in the childbirth experience create a new context for the study of child-bearing. Parlee's article, Chapter 6, (which has summarized much of the literature on pregnancy and childbirth) makes it clear that research on the socialization processes for women and men who are about to become parents has been much neglected. A study by Greenberg, Rosenberg, and Lind (1973) provides another illustration of the usefulness of focusing on processes in the study of socialization into the parenthood role.

Greenberg and colleagues studied the effects in a Swedish hospital of allowing first mothers to "room in" with their newborn. Their design was unusual in that they were able to obtain complete randomization in the selection procedure when they developed two groups, one of rooming-in mothers and one of nonrooming-in mothers. The rooming-in practice appeared to provide the mother with an opportunity to interact with peers on her ward and develop information-gathering strategies to aid her in coping with her newborn. Compared with nonrooming-in mothers, rooming-in mothers reported themselves as more self-confident with their infant and more confident in being able to care for the infant; and they also felt that they could understand one or more attributes of the cry of their infant. Interestingly, rooming-in mothers were unaffected by the crying of other infants in their hospital room, but were uneasy when their own infants cried. They also reported developing "maternal feelings" faster than did mothers who were placed in the conventional hospital setting. Although this study was done in Sweden, the changes occurring here in the United States offer an opportunity to perform similar kinds of needed research on the processes of transition to parenthood.

A Final Observation

I have focused on the marriage and family literature because of the importance given to it in the study of traditional women's lives, and I have used it as a source of studies to set a context for research and to illustrate the methodological rethinking that research on development of the female in the later years needs in order to progress. The changing times we live in require new models and methods that will reflect the complexity and activity of the women who are the subjects of study.

Attention to changes in society while studying the development of women means that we must not be cohort bound in our selection of problems. For example, lack of access to child care may be an important factor in the development of contemporary women. But we are in a time of declining fertility rates, increased longevity, and increasing accessibility to day care. This combination of factors has meant that women spend proportionately fewer years of their lives devoted to rearing children. Also, the factor of increased longevity may mean that "parent care," or care for the aged, may become a major issue. Not only is the aged parent more likely to be a woman, but her care is also (given current norms) more likely to fall on a woman. In seeking new directions in research, we must be alert to potential issues and develop alternatives before they become widespread problems.

RECOMMENDATIONS

This paper has focused on the need for new directions in theory and method as well as in content in research on the developmental psychology of women. The body of the paper contains numerous specific recommendations, and this section will highlight the major ones.

1. *Assemble and critique manageable units of the literature on women's development.* Such units could be organized in several ways, including (a) by content area (e.g., intellectual development, ego development); (b) by developmental event (e.g., literature on pregnancy, menopause, widowhood); (c) by life period (young adulthood, maturity, middle age, old age); and (d) by life dimension (career cycle, family cycle, etc.). Subject area critiques should incorporate age, cohort, and time of measurement effects in evaluating the conclusions in the literature, and special attention should be paid to the impact of sexist bias on research.

2. *Develop research strategies for future research which consider influences of age, cohort, and time of measurement effects.* Results from both cross-sectional and longitudinal designs must be viewed with caution. New research strategies must be developed and implemented.

3. *Develop and apply interactionist theories, models, and methods in studying female development.* This recommendation means more than using more than one variable at a time, although multivariate approaches are important. It means discarding bipolar dimensions and linear assumptions, and studying metavariance and reciprocal effects. It also means a reconceptualization of the role of biology in behavior, with a renewed focus on asking how diverse variables—biological, psychological, social, and cultural—interact to "determine" specific behaviors in specified contexts.

4. *Develop new scientific language to reflect our new research directions.* The need for new language in research on women goes beyond the development of nonsexist terminology. In developing increasingly complex designs and theories, a new research language may be needed to group our new ideas into manageable units. The terms "homofacience" and "metavariance" have been advanced as suggestions for new research concepts.

5. *Delineate the processes by which sex roles come to influence behaviors in various contexts.* A first step toward delineating such processes is to develop situational and personality taxonomies vis-à-vis sex-role behaviors. Labeling has been identified as a "cognitive organizer" with a powerful

influence on behavior in this area. Studying how labels influence behavior is one research direction, but identifying other mechanisms is also in order.

6. *Recognize the diversity of women and reflect this diversity in research theories and methods.*   Young women, old women, women of different races and different classes—all get lumped together and discussed as a whole (e.g., the lifeline approach). This paper is guilty of that oversimplification, but future research cannot afford the inability to tell women apart. Hopefully, a recognition of women's diversity will result from emphasizing the processes of development. Recognizing diversity will mean getting away from the overfocus on averages and turning to studies of ranges and variances in behaviors.

7. *As long as theories remain time-and-place bound, we must constantly question our conceptualization of what variables are relevant to our problems.*   Changing life-styles and changing technologies mean a constantly shifting context. Conceptualizing relevant influences in the family as including former spouses and in-laws in family studies is only one example of how we must constantly rethink our world views when developing our models and methods.

8. *Study women as* active *as well as* reactive *individuals.*   There is much research on the impact that roles have on individuals, but little on how individuals enact their roles. Norm violation is an area that is in special need of research to delineate this dual focus. Research on women who have developed strategies to overcome barriers to their development is particularly needed. Women's strengths and successes must be given research time equal to that for their barriers and failures.

9. *Expose and eliminate assumptions about the "normal and expected" life-styles of our research participants.*   The changing life-styles of contemporary women increase the importance of exposing experimenter bias due to assumptions of what is expected female behavior.

10. *Monitor the continuing changes in the timing and contexts of the developmental milestones of women's lives.*   Great changes have occurred and will continue to occur in the patterns of women's lives. We should not be bound by past assumptions of what constitutes an important event, and we must be on the alert for new events of significance.

11. *Develop relative, as opposed to absolute, conceptions of what is considered sex-appropriate.*   The judgment "sex appropriate" (as long as

people continue to make it) is in the eye of the beholder. Studying what is considered sex-appropriate should only be a preliminary step to asking how it gets to be defined in those terms.

12. *Develop more unbiased approaches to the study of groups that violate white, middle-class expectations about normal and proper adult life.* Research on maternal deprivation, childless couples, only children, working mothers, "broken" homes, and "illegitimate" children—all provide examples of areas riddled with value-laden bias. The articles in this volume can be viewed as an initial beginning to what must be a continuing effort to confront assumptions on the part of researchers, thus helping them to further decenter and to see the female experience from increasingly diverse viewpoints.

13. *Develop programs for the training and continuing education of psychologists to equip them to pursue new directions in research on women.* The studies reported in this chapter demonstrate the need for changes in both training and continuing education of psychologists as well as of other social scientists in order to equip them to pursue more complex research directions. Without opportunities to be exposed to new techniques and to learn about this burgeoning content area, research progress will be sluggish.

14. *Develop facilitative research environments for research on women.* Such research environments are needed to legitimize this new research area. More importantly, even though research on women requires an interdisciplinary approach, typical university settings are not congenial to interdisciplinary cooperation. Interdisciplinary research centers dedicated to research on the developmental psychology of women would not only facilitate research in this content area, but would also provide models and methods that would advance the entire scope of psychology.

CONCLUSION AND A FINAL PLEA

The changing times we live in require new models and methods that will reflect the complexity and activity of the female experience. I have attempted to underscore some of the problems in the literature which demonstrate the need for methodological and theoretical rethinking if research progress is to be made.

In seeking new directions for research and studying development over the life span, one could seek understanding on the macro level—in terms of effects resulting from a changing demographic situation, historical context, economic instability, increased urbanization, technological innovation, and so forth. Or understanding could be addressed in micro terms—changing socialization agents, new information inputs, differing accessibility to role models, changing patterns of reinforcements for various behaviors, and so on. Sociologists and psychologists have traditionally developed "camps" and macro and micro "turfs," respectively. Investigators are now beginning to appreciate the limitation that such a division of labor and conceptualization produces. Communication among fields has increased as *problems* rather than *disciplines* have begun to guide research. The use of the concept of cohort is an example of the result of this kind of needed communication. It is an old concept to those with an acquaintance with sociology, but a relatively new concept to most psychologists.

Each discipline's level of perspective gives a little different view of "truth." Future psychologists, be they male or female, must be able to comprehend such varied approaches and to integrate them into a larger perspective. We must increase communication among disciplines and develop more eclectic strategies. This chapter has attempted to draw upon both sociological and psychological literature dealing with marriage and the family as an initial step toward the integration of disciplinary perspectives. Most important of all, we must go further and recognize that future directions must be charted, not in terms of content but rather in terms of process.

REFERENCES

Ahammer, I.M. Desirability judgments as a function of item content, instructional set, and sex: a life-span developmental study. *Human Development,* 1971, *14,* 195-207.

Ahammer, I.M., & Baltes, P.B. Objective versus perceived age differences in personality: How do adolescents, adults, and older people view themselves and each other? *Journal of Gerontology,* 1972, *27,* 46-51.

American Council on Education (ACE). National norms for entering college freshmen—Fall 1972. Washington, D.C.: ACE Research Reports, Vol. 6, 1972.

Anastasi, A. Heredity, environment, and the question "how?". In H.E. Fitzgerald, & J.P. McKinney, *Developmental psychology: Studies in human development.* Homewood, Ill.: The Dorsey Press, 1970.

Angrist, S.S. The study of sex roles. *Journal of Social Issues,* 1969, *25,* 215-232.

Bacon, L. Early motherhood, accelerated role transition, and social pathologies, *Social Forces,* 1974, *52(3),* 333-341.

Baltes, P.B., & Schaie, K.W. (Eds.). *Life-span developmental psychology: Personality and socialization.* New York: Academic Press, 1973.

Bardwick, J.M. *Psychology of women.* New York: Harper & Row, 1971.

Bayley, N. Learning in adulthood: The role of intelligence. In M.C. Jones, N. Bayley, J.W. Macfarlane, & M.P. Honzik (Eds.), *The course of human development.* Waltham, Mass.: Xerox College Publications, 1971, 132-140.

Bem, D.J., & Allen, D. On predicting some of the people some of the time: The search for cross-situational consistencies in behavior. *Psychological Review,* 1975, *81(6),* 506-520.

Bem, S.L. Sex role adaptability: One consequence of psychological androgyny. *Journal of Personality & Social Psychology,* 1975, *31,* 634-643.

Bernard, J. Women and new social structures. In M.L. McBee & K.A. Blake (Eds.), *The American woman: Who will she be?* Beverly Hills, Calif.: Glencoe Press, 1974.

Block, Jack. *Lives through time.* Berkeley, Calif.: Bancroft Books, 1971.

Block, Jeanne H. Conceptions of sex role: Some cross-cultural and longitudinal perspectives. *American Psychologist,* 1973, *28,* 512-526.

Botwinick, J. Geropsychology. In P.H. Mussen & M.R. Rosenzweig (Eds.), *Annual Review of Psychology,* 1970, *21,* 239-272.

Bowers, K.S. Situationism in psychology: An analysis and a critique. *Psychological Review*, 1973, *80*, 307-336.

Bronfenbrenner, U. Is 80% of intelligence genetically determined? In U. Bronfenbrenner (Ed.), *Influences on human development*, Hinsdale, Ill.: The Dryden Press, 1972.

Bureau of the Census. Census of Population: 1970: *General Social and Economic Characteristics*, Final Report PC(1)-C-1 United States Summary, Washington, D.C.: U.S. Government Printing Office, 1972.

Bureau of the Census. Births, marriages, divorces, and deaths for 1975. *Monthly Vital Statistics Report*, 1975 (June 25), *24*.

Burgess, E.W. Companionship marriage in the United States. *Studies of the family*, 69-87.

Campbell, A. The American way of mating. *Psychology Today*, 1975 (May), 37-43.

Carlson, R. Where is the person in personality research? *Psychological Bulletin*, 1971, *75*, 203-219.

Carlson, R. Personality. In M.R. Rosenzweig & L.W.Porter (Eds.), *Annual Review of Psychology*, 1975, *26*, 393-414.

Christensen, H.T. Child spacing analysis via record linkage. *Marriage and Family Living*, 1963, *25*, 272-280.

Daniels, A.K. *A survey of research concerns on women's issues.* Washington, D.C.: Association of American Colleges, 1975.

Dixon, R.E. Women's rights and fertility. *Studies in Family Planning*, 1975, *17*, 1-20.

Dohrenwend, B.S. Social status and stressful life events. *Journal of Personality and Social Psychology*, 1973, *28*, 225-235.

Eisdorfer, C., & Lawton, M.P. (Eds.) *The psychology of adult development and aging.* Washington, D.C.: American Psychological Association, 1973.

Ekehammar, B. Interactionism in personality from a historical perspective. *Psychological Bulletin*, 1974, *81*, 1026-1048.

Emmerich, W. Socialization and sex-role development. In P.B. Baltes & K.W. Schaie (Eds.), *Life-span developmental psychology: Personality and socialization.* New York: Academic Press, 1973.

Emmerich, W., Goldman, K.S., & Shore, R.E. Differentiation and development of social norms. *Journal of Personality and Social Psychology*, 1971, *18*, 323-353.

Endler, N.S. The person versus the situation—a pseudoissue? A response to Alker. *Journal of Personality*, 1973, *41*, 287-303.

Erikson, E. *Childhood and society* (2nd ed.). New York: Norton, 1963.

Erikson, E.H. The life cycle: Epigenesis of identity. In H.E. Fitzgerald & J.P. McKinney (Eds.) *Developmental psychology: Studies in human development.* Homewood, Ill.: The Dorsey Press, 1970.

Ginsburg, H., & Opper, S. *Piaget's Theory of Intellectual Development: An introduction.* Englewood Cliffs, N.J.: Prentice-Hall, 1969.

Goffman, I. *The presentation of self in everyday life.* New York: Doubleday, 1959.

Greenberg, M., & Morris, N. Engrossment: The newborn's impact upon the father. *American Journal of Orthopsychiatry,* 1974, *44*(4), 520-531.

Greenberg, M., Rosenberg, I., & Lind, J. First mothers' rooming-in with their newborns: Its impact on the mother. *American Journal of Orthopsychiatry,* 1973, *43,* 783-788.

Griffith, J. Social pressure on family size intentions. *Family Planning Perspectives,* 1973 (Fall), *5*(4), 237-242.

Gurion, R.N. Open a new window: Validities and values in psychological measurements. *American Psychologist,* 1974, *29,* 287-296.

Harper, L.Z. The scope of offspring effects: From care-giver to culture. *Psychological Bulletin,* 1975, *82,* 784-801.

Havighurst, R.J. History of developmental psychology: Socialization and personality development through the life span. In P.B. Baltes & K.W. Schaie (Eds.), *Life-span developmental psychology: Personality and socialization.* New York: Academic Press, 1973.

Heiskenan, V. The myth of the middle-class family in American family sociology. *American Sociologist,* 1971, *6,* 14-18.

Helson, R. The changing image of the career woman. *Journal of Social Issues,* 1972, *28*(2), 33-46.

Henze, L.F., & Hudson, J.W. Personal and family characteristics of cohabiting and noncohabiting college students. *Journal of Marriage and the Family,* 1974, *36,* 722-727.

Hetherington, E.M., & McIntyre, C.M. Developmental psychology. In M.R. Rosenzweig & L.W. Porter (Eds.), *Annual Review of Psychology,* 1975, *26,* 97-136.

Hoffman, L.W., & Nye, F.I. *Working mothers.* San Francisco, Calif.: Jossey-Bass, 1974.

Holzman, P.S. Personality. In M. Rosenzweig & L.W. Porter (Eds.), *Annual Review of Psychology,* 1974, *25,* 247-276.

Jackson, D.W. Advanced aged adults' reflections of middle age. *Gerontologist,* 1974 (June), *14*(3), 255-257.

Jones, M.C., Bayley, N., MacFarlane, J.W., & Honzik, M.P. (Eds.) *The course of human development.* Waltham, Mass.: Xerox College Publishing, 1971.

Kimmel, D.C. *Adulthood and aging: An interdisciplinary, developmental view.* New York: John Wiley, 1974.

Kohlberg, L. Stage and sequence: The cognitive developmental approach to socialization. In D.A. Goslin (Ed.), *Handbook of socialization theory and research*. Chicago: Rand McNall, 1969.

Kotlar, S.L. Middle-class marital role perceptions and marital adjustment. *Sociological Social Research*, 1965, *49*(3), 283-293.

Kramer, R., & Kohlberg, L. Continuities and discontinuities in childhood and adult moral development. *Human Development*, 1969, *12*, 93-120.

Laws, J.L. A feminist review of marital adjustment literature: The rape of the Locke. *Journal of Marriage and the Family*, 1971, *33*, 483-516.

Levitan, T.E. Deviants as active participants in the labeling process: The visibly handicapped. *Social Problems*, 1975, *22*(4), 548-557.

Loevinger, J. The meaning and measurement of ego development. *American Psychologist*, 1966, *21*, 195-206.

Loevinger, J., & Wessler, R. *Measuring ego development* (Vol. 1). San Francisco, Calif.: Jossey-Bass, 1970.

Looft, W.R. Egocentrism and social interaction across the life-span. *Psychological Bulletin*, 1972, *78*(2), 73-92.

Looft, W.R. Socialization and personality throughout the life-span: An examination of contemporary psychological approaches. In P.B. Baltes & K.W. Schaie (Eds.), *Life-span developmental psychology: Personality and socialization*. N.Y.: Academic Press, 1973.

Maccoby, E.E., & Jacklin, C.N. *The psychology of sex differences*. Stanford, Calif.: Stanford University Press, 1974.

Macklin, E.J. Heterosexual cohabitation among unmarried college students. *The Family Coordinator*, 1972, *21*, 463-472.

Mednick, M.S., & Tangri, S.S. New social psychological perspectives on women. *Journal of Social Issues*, 1972, *28*(2), 1-16.

Mednick, M.T.S., & Weissman, H.J. The psychology of women: Selected topics. In M.R. Rosenzweig & L.W. Porter (Eds.), *Annual Review of Psychology*, 1975, *26*, 1-18.

Mischel, W. Toward a cognitive social learning reconceptualization of personality. *Psychological Review*, 1973, *80*, 252-283.

Neugarten, B.L. Adult personality: Toward a psychology of the life cycle. In B.L. Neugarten (Ed.), *Middle age and aging*. Chicago, Ill.: Chicago University Press, 1968.

Neugarten, B.L., & Datan, N. Sociological perspectives on the life cycle. In P.B. Baltes & K.W. Schaie (Eds.), *Life-span developmental psychology: Personality and socialization*. New York: Academic Press, 1973.

Neugarten, B.L., & Gutmann, D.L. Age-sex roles and personality change in middle age: A thematic apperception study. In B.L. Neugarten (Ed.), *Middle age and aging*. Chicago, Ill.: Chicago University Press, 1968.

Neugarten, B.L., & Moore, J.W. The changing age-status system. In B.L. Neugarten (Ed.), *Middle age and aging.* Chicago, Ill.: Chicago University Press, 1968.

Neugarten, B.L., Moore, J.W., & Lowe, J.C. Age norms, age constraints, and adult socialization. In B.L. Neugarten (Ed.), *Middle age and aging.* Chicago, Ill.: Chicago University Press, 1968.

Parsons, T., & Bales, R.S. *Family socialization and interaction process.* Glencoe, Ill.: The Free Press, 1955.

Piaget, J. *The psychology of intelligence.* New York: Harcourt, Brace, 1950.

Presser, H. Early motherhood: Ignorance or bliss? *Family Planning Perspectives,* 1974, *6*, 8-14.

Rollins, B.C., & Cannon, K.L. Marital satisfaction over the family life cycle: A reevaluation. *Journal of Marriage and the Family,* 1974, *36*, 271-282.

Rollins, B.C., & Feldman, H. Marital satisfaction over the family life cycle. *Journal of Marriage and the Family,* 1970, *26*, 20-28.

Rossi, A. Transition to parenthood, *Journal of Marriage and the Family,* 1968, *30*, 26-29.

Sarason, I.G., & Smith, R.E. Personality. In P. Mussen & M. Rosenzweig (Eds.), *Annual Review of Psychology,* 1971, *22*, 393-446.

Sarason, I.G., Smith, R.E., & Diener, E. Personality research: Components of variance attributable to the person and the situation. *Journal of Personality and Social Psychology,* 1975, *32*, 199-204.

Schachter, S. Some extraordinary facts about obese humans and rats. *American Psychologist,* 1971, *26*, 129-144.

Schaie, K.W. Methodological problems in descriptive developmental research on adulthood and aging. In J.R. Nesselroade & H.W. Reese (Eds.), *Life-span developmental psychology: Methodological issues.* New York: Academic Press, 1973.

Schaie, K.W., & Gribbin, K. Adult development and aging. In M.R. Rosenzweig & L.W. Porter (Eds.), *Annual Review of Psychology,* 1975, *26*, 65-96.

Singer, J.L., & Singer, D.G. Personality. In P.H. Mussen & M.R. Rosenzweig (Eds.), *Annual Review of Psychology,* 1972, *23*, 375-412.

Sontag, L.W., Baker, C.T., & Nelson, V.L. Mental growth and personality development: A longitudinal study. *Monograph of the Society for Research in Child Development,* 1958, *23* (Whole No. 68).

Spanier, G.B., Lewis, R.A., & Cole, C.L. Marital adjustment over the family life cycle: The issue of curvilinearity. *Journal of Marriage and the Family,* 1975, *37*(2), 263-275.

Terhune, K.W. *A review of the actual and expected consequences of family size.* Calspan Report No. DP-5333-G-1, July 31, 1974.

Terman, L. The discovery and encouragement of exceptional talent. *American Psychologist,* 1954, *9,* 221-230.

Terman, L.M., & Miles, C.C. *Sex and personality.* New York: McGraw-Hill, 1936.

Vale, J.R. Role of behavior genetics in psychology. *American Psychologist,* 1973, *28*(10), 871-882.

Veevers, J.E. The child-free alternative: Rejection of the motherhood mystique. In M. Stephenson, (Ed.), *Women in Canada.* Toronto: New Press, 1973.

Virginia Slims American Women's Opinion Poll, Vol. 3. A study of the attitudes of women on marriage, divorce, family and Americans' changing sexual morality conducted by the Roper Organization, 1974.

Wolman, C., & Frank, H. The solo woman in a professional peer group. *American Journal of Orthopsychiatry,* 1975, *45,* 164-171.

Women's Bureau. Continuing Education for Women. *Current Developments,* U.S. Department of Labor, Employment Standards Administration, 1974.

Wortis, R.P. The acceptance of the concept of the maternal role by behavioral scientists: Its effects on women. *American Journal of Orthopsychiatry,* 1971, *41*(5), 733-746.

CHAPTER *4*

COMMENTARY: CHAPTERS 2 & 3

MAVIS HETHERINGTON
&
JESSIE BERNARD

COMMENTS BY MAVIS HETHERINGTON

Certain common themes run through Jeanne Block's article on sex differentiation in the socialization behaviors of mothers and fathers, and in Nancy Russo's article on future directions for research on women in the later years. In my discussion I will focus on these common concerns.

The first theme in both chapters deals with difficulties in interpreting the results of studies of the socialization of sex roles because of methodological limitations in the studies. The second theme involves the advocacy of an interactionist perspective focusing on the complex interactions of a multitude of factors in the development of motives, behaviors, attitudes, and values in males and females. The third theme articulated in both chapters is the necessity for a life-span approach to the development of sex-role typing. The fourth theme stresses the need for more studies dealing with processes involved in the socialization of sex roles. Finally, the common theme of the inadequacy and need for reconceptualization of current theories of socialization dealing with sex roles is a pervasive concern of each author.

There are many difficulties in drawing definitive conclusions or building a comprehensive theory of sex typing on the basis of current research findings. Jeanne Block has emphasized the inadequacy of taking a box-score approach to studies of differences in socialization or sex differences in development. Much of the confusion and apparent inconsistency of findings is attributable to the diver-

sity of methods, variations in subject populations, and methodological deficiencies in available studies. Before generalizations can be made, good studies must
be separated from methodologically deficient ones. Block's article, which includes her own study, represents an important step in identifying the effects of
the differential socialization by mothers and fathers of males and females at
different ages.

Russo argues that our thinking about the development of females is limited
by our methodology. Most psychologists have been trained in an analysis of
variance tradition, which is not appropriate for dealing with the multivariate
interactive model Russo proposes as essential in the study of the development of
females. New multivariate methods and designs that control for cohort effects
and age of the subject represent encouraging advances in this area. In addition,
the work of such psychologists as Hugh Lytton and Gerald Patterson in refining
sequential probability analysis, which permits a fine grained examination of the
impact of parent—child interchanges on socialization, is a most important methodological advance in the study of family interaction. It is one of the few
procedures that permits the study of the process rather than just the outcome of
socialization behavior on the development of males and females.

Partly due to methodological limitations and partly because of problems in
the availability of research samples, our knowledge of the development of sex
typing is based on extremely restricted populations. As Jeanne Block points out,
most of our studies of the socialization of sex-related differences have been done
on middle-class, white, pre-school children and their mothers. What is prescribed
by Russo is new directions for research, looking at the interaction of many
variables such as socioeconomic status, ethnicity, sex, and age of the child and
differential socialization practices by both parents at different stages of the
child's development as they shape the development of males and females. The
impact of social agencies and groups such as the family, school, peers, the
church, political forces, and the mass media in defining and maintaining sex roles
also needs further investigation. The only substantial body of research we have
thus far is on the relationship between a limited number of family factors and
sex-role typing. In addition, the relationship between the individual and the
environment needs to be studied.

Socialization and behavior occur in certain situations; the effectiveness of the
socialization and the behaviors exhibited by the individuals involved will vary in
different settings. These factors cannot be understood in isolation; their covari-
ance must be examined. It is unfortunate for many laboratory scientists that

development of behavior is so complex and that it is not a 2-by-2 world. Many laboratory analogue studies of socialization seem to have little ecological validity. Validity seems to have been sacrificed for control. Baldwin said that child psychologists have built a "myth of childhood" based upon children's behavior in the restricted and atypical environment of the laboratory—perhaps in the same way we are building a myth of sex-role typing. Instead of ignoring the complex network of interrelationships involved in the development of males and females in favor of simplistic studies, these interactions should be the focus of our research. I am not advocating sloppy research. The complexities of sex-role development should be examined with the most rigorous available methods, and continuing attempts should be made to evolve new methods to deal with such problems. However, our conceptualization of the development of sex roles should not be constrained by what we can manipulate in the laboratory.

Both Block and Russo emphasize the importance of taking a life-span approach to the study of women. This permits us to view the development of women as a continuous, dynamic, ever-evolving process, rather than focusing almost exclusively on the preschool years as the formative years in sex-role typing, as is done so frequently. It also allows us to examine the interaction between developmental capacities at various times in the life span and the salience of different factors in influencing the development of males and females. In socialization, the socialization agent and the child's capacities, behavior, and expectations change with age. It seems likely that different social input may be more effective in shaping sex typing at different stages of the individual. In addition, there may be different manifestations of the same process at different ages, which can be detected only with a life-span approach. Kagan and Moss, in their analysis of the longitudinal Fels Institute study, report that early aggression and overt rage in girls seems to be transformed into adult achievement motivation.

One strategy in the life-span approach to the study of women would be to examine responses and changes in behavior, attitudes, and self-concept associated with critical developmental events. Some of these critical events would be biological: menstruation, pregnancy, childbirth, nursing, abortion, or menopause. Others would be social: first day at school, loss of a parent, marriage, parenthood, divorce, educational achievements, or advancement or failure in a career. While some events such as pregnancy, menstruation, and abortion are unique to women, most other events are shared by men. Processes and changes associated with these critical events will give us some understanding of how these factors shape the development of women and how women cope with critical events. Investigation of sex-related differences and similarities in the correlates and processes involved in responding to critical events can also serve as a rich avenue to the understanding of women.

I have been discussing processes at such length that it might be thought that a great deal is known about the processes involved in sex-role development. In fact, as both Russo and Block indicate, very little is known about the role of these processes (or, as Russo calls them, mechanisms) outside the laboratory setting. This is partly due to methodological difficulties involved in the study of social processes and partly to the inadequacies of theories dealing with social and cognitive development. Traditional psychoanalytic theory, learning theory, and role theory have all proved deficient as a basis for a psychology of women. Eleanor Maccoby, in a recent paper presented at the Western Psychological Association, argued that cognitive revolution in psychology is leading to more concern about ways in which children process input from the environment and developmental changes associated with such process. Perhaps a theory built around such developmental changes in processes could serve as a foundation for a clearer understanding of female development.

COMMENTS BY JESSIE BERNARD

Ms. Block's critique of sex-role socialization research, and especially her caveat with respect to the Maccoby-Jacklin interpretation of it, are powerful. Having myself fallen into the trap of counting studies summarized in the Maccoby-Jacklin volume without regard for the individual merits of the studies and thus, in effect, giving them all equal weight, I was keenly sensitive to her comments. Fortunately, her critique now becomes available to those who use the research summarized in the Maccoby-Jacklin volume, and are thus forewarned. Both her first and second look at the evidence are productive.

The age bias in so much research on socialization had already struck me, but particularly relevant to my own concerns was the case Block makes against socialization research that does not distinguish between the effect of fathers and mothers. It was illuminating, therefore, to have this difference pointed out and clarified. Table 3.2 is a convincing and impressive contribution. Since I have for some time been advocating more role-sharing by parents, it helps to learn what socialization effects can be expected from fathers vis-a-vis daughters and sons.

I am persuaded that "the critical research studies (on socialization) have not been completed" and that "a more complex model of socialization is required." I sympathize with Ms. Block's desire "to keep open the question of differential socialization" until that critical research has been completed, but I would not assign so high a priority to this research as she does. The political implications of our preoccupation with sex-role socialization deserve some attention. Are we so concerned about sex-role socialization in order to explain away inferiorities attributed to women? As a way to prove that there are no important biologically-determined differences? That if there were no sex-role socialization differences, men and women would be the same? Are we so concerned in order to learn how to socialize children differently? In *Women, Wives, Mothers* I discussed the political implications of the socialization paradigm (pp. 16-18) and will not repeat it here. But I do not think we should ignore them. I predict that as women become liberated and socialized (even as adults) to have better self-concepts, to think more highly of themselves and their sisters, they will be less concerned with sex-role socialization. They won't have to feel apologetic for being just what they are.

With respect to the first of Russo's two-part approach—on strategy, theory, and method—all three of the points she makes strike me as important. The distinction between the static age-psychology and the dynamic-developmental-psychology is useful, especially the emphasis on mechanisms. I would like to see more attention paid to those mechanisms, especially to what Jane O'Reilly has called "the click." I would, in fact, like to see a developmental schema based on the series of "clicks" girls and women experience in the developmental process. With age psychology all we do is report differences in women of different age groupings; with developmental psychology we would try to find out how they got from there to here. I will illustrate when I come to Russo's second or content approach.

I find the emphasis on heritability valuable. In effect, the women's liberation movement has been an attempt to maximize heritability by minimizing the environmental contribution to differences. Easier said than done, I'm sure we all agree.

The third component of Russo's theoretical discussion—emphasis on birth cohort and time of measurement—strikes me as fundamental in developmental psychology. Here she is in an area close to my own heart. In a book published in 1957, I wrote that the older people of the 1960s and 1970s would be quite different from those of the 1930s, 1940s, and 1950s. In still another book, I pointed out that women in their fifties and even sixties, today constituted almost a brand new sex, never known before on land or sea. In a 1974 paper on age and feminist issues I noted that women in their forties differed from both younger and older women. In searching for a possible explanation, I learned from Glen Elder's study, *Children of the Depression,* that women socialized in the 1930s who had lived in deprived families were more familistic in orientation.

The importance of time measurement first struck me forcibly when I noted that, on the basis of research done in the 1950s and 1960s, education was closely tied to family stability—the more education, the greater the likelihood of stable marriages. Today that relation is no longer so true. At least it is in process of attrition; there is a convergence of divorce rates between educated and less educated men.

Having myself played the ages-and-stages game in my most recent book, *Women, Wives, Mothers,* I was especially interested in Russo's content approach to her topic. I want to emphasize especially her statement that "one can only understand a woman's behaviors when they are placed in a larger context." And I go with her all the way when she rejects the self-protective macro versus micro "camps" or "turfs" of psychologists and sociologists. Some of my best friends are psychologists. By the way, I note that Russo's "Women's Lifeline" (Fig. 3.2) includes mastectomy and hysterectomy. There was a time not so long ago when it became almost routine to remove the uterus, as, in my own childhood, the tonsils and adenoids were removed. I have heard radical feminists claim that the removal of the uterus reflected a hatred on the part of the male medics toward so grossly a female organ; hence, sexual revulsion. If menopause no longer destroys femaleness, substitutes for it had to be found. There is now considerable brouhaha as to whether radical mastectomies reflect a similar hatred of femaleness. I am not willing to go to the mat on this issue, but it is worth throwing in as a form of developmental stereotyping.

Returning now to Russo's emphasis on process, I would like to ask for a developmental schema for women in terms of the "clicks" referred to above. When I was in high school, my French teacher once warned us of the shock we would experience when we first heard a railroad conductor say to us, "step lively, lady." We would think he couldn't mean *us!* But he would. We would still feel like children—all right, like girls, *but certainly not ladies.* A great deal of "psychological work" is involved in getting used to the new status being imposed on us from the outside. Without the help of any rite of passage, such sudden changes can be almost traumatic. There is, correspondingly, the opposite situation when the outside world is still dealing with us as children long after we feel grown up.

I would also like to see a developmental scheme which made room for the psychological processes involved when a woman, reared to think of men as her superior, for the first time has to rescue a man—date, husband, whatever. The archetypal case is perhaps the rescue from the shame of failure to have an erection. But there are many others. I would like to know more about the psychological processes when the child, girl, or woman is first disillusioned about her father, when she finds he is not really omnipotent, that he makes mistakes. The boy-father pattern is old hat. And, of course, the "click" that occurs when a woman, all of a sudden, from something said or done in her presence, experiences what is meant by sexism. I am sure dozens of such "moments of truth" will occur to all of you—the moment when a woman has to come to terms with both her own experience and a contradictory outside world.

Common to both men and women is the discovery, as one story has it, that "they're always the same age on Broadway." It was about a star who, playing one day for ter groupies, looked up and said something about one of ter earlier peers. The faces around tem were blank; they did not recognize the name. Of course, tey had to remind temself, how *could* they remember? It was their parents who would have remembered. I have watched so many people, places, and events recede from general memory that it no longer surprises me when even events of the 1960s seem antediluvial to young people. Cohorts, time of measurement. I might add that Bob Hope is a classic case of nondevelopment. He is still making jokes about Bing Crosby, even though a large part of his audience does not remember nor have any interest in Crosby.

One final story. It is about a young woman who entered a convent and never thereafter saw herself in a mirror. Many years later a former pupil returned and took her picture along with a sister nun. When shown the developed picture, her comment was, "I can recognize Sister Mary, but who is that elderly nun with her?" Without feedback from others, what form would development take? The nun was protected in her convent world. But what if we carried forever a self-concept, a self-image of ourselves as we were at 18?

What Research Should Be Done? Some Fragmentary Notes

1. I believe there should be more intrasex research, more about the kinds of people women are. They are as variegated as imaginable, but altogether too much research time and effort is expended on showing how they differ from men. I would propose a moratorium on all research on sex differences.

2. As an example of intrasex differences, I would point to Sandra Bem's paper. I was touched by her "feminine women," who seemed to be almost caricatures of the stereotype of the passive, dependent female. If a dedicated politically oriented feminist like Ms. Bem centrifuges out such personalities in a college population, we ought to study how they got that way. How do they differ in background from masculine women? From androgynous women?

3. Ms. Helsen's work on creative women and the Tangri-Mednick work on achieving women tell us quite a bit about certain kinds of women. But other axes should be explored also.

4. In another place I have called for research on the damaging effect that discrimination has on women. We have a growing body of data on the existence of subtle forms of behavior that—inadvertent or deliberate—hurt women. But now we need laboratory documentation of the damage. I believe some work along these lines is now in process at Harvard. Let's have more. It will be needed if legal action is taken.

5. While we were meeting I read an article in the June, 1975 issue of *McCall's* magazine on "The Books That Teach Wives to Be Submissive." The books are *The Total Woman* and *Fascinating Womanhood,* and they are runaway best sellers. They offer a crass form of the Freudian solution. There is a tremendous amount of pain out there, and it calls for research attention. I have called the mental health of the American housewife "public health problem number 1." Can the researchers tell us how to help?

PART III
WOMEN AND THEIR BODIES

INTRODUCTION

JULIA A. SHERMAN & FLORENCE L. DENMARK

The study of topics related to female bodily functioning is almost totally undeveloped. This appears attributable to the general disinterest of predominantly male researchers, as well as that more general repression of the body, especially the female body, in our culture. On the surface this would seem to contradict the complaint of the Women's Movement that women are regarded too much as sexual objects. In fact, however, of all these topics it is female sexuality that has been most studied, but usually studied from a male point of view and filtered through a male set of perceptions and biases. Women in our society, as well as men, have tended to define their own sexuality by what they have been told it should be and, especially in the case of women, what they have been told has been in a serious conflict with the reality of their own experience. Not until women began to talk with each other about their experiences did they realize the extent of the discrepancy. Topics such as the psychology of pregnancy and menopuase have had little study, and the few studies made were done mostly by women.

At this point there is insufficient information about these topics to permit valid conclusions. The articles in this Part III point to biases and to the emerging bases of knowledge. Perhaps they reflect a hesitance to feed the myth that "Woman is her body." To do research, to draw conclusions about women's psychobiology, is to run the risk of our work being misused. However, if the research remains undone, we run the risk of allowing mythologies to remain unchallenged. This state of affairs could conceivably allow women to remain a mystery, upon whom men can project their fantasies and desires. Even more crucially, women themselves would be deprived of this important knowledge.

Schwartz and Strom's article (chapter 5) ably sets the interpretation of female sexuality more in the realm of female experience. While concluding that it is not now possible to assess the relative strengths of female-male sexual appetites, they point out that the female appetite is strong indeed and that female sexual capacity exceeds that of males. Though more weight could have been given to the importance of time, techniques, and interpersonal and situational factors in their discussion, Schwartz and Strom discuss some topics of more recent interest and concern to women: sexual fantasies, same-sex sexuality, rape, and other forms of sexual abuse. Data have borne out the feminist emphasis on rape as primarily a crime of violence; however, while there are common irrational hostilities which men who rape share with men in general, the evidence does not support the contention that convicted rapists are psychologically no different from other men (Sherman, 1976).

The article by Mary Parlee (chapter 6) is a thorough, scholarly, and thoughtful perusal of literature frequently not admitted as legitimate areas of study in psychology departments. Parlee provides a painstaking critique of the literature on menstruation, childbirth, and menopause, and considers not only a feminist point of view, but also some fundamental methodological and philosophical questions.

Reference Note

Sherman, J.A. *Power in the sexes: Rape.* Paper presented at the American Psychological Association, Washington, D.C., September 1976.

CHAPTER **5**

THE SOCIAL PSYCHOLOGY OF FE-MALE SEXUALITY

PEPPER SCHWARTZ
&
DEANNA STROM

Pepper Schwartz received her Ph.D. degree from Yale University and is currently an Assistant Professor in the Department of Sociology at the University of Washington, Seattle, Washington, with adjunct appointments in Psychiatry and in Women's Studies. She is the coauthor of Women at Yale *(with Janet Lever) and* Sexual Scripts: Social Construct of Female Sexuality *(with Judith Long Laws); also, "Women in the Higher World of Education" (with Janet Lever), "Female Sexuality and Monogamy," Lesbianism and Bisexuality" (with Philip Blumstein), "Bisexuality: Some Social-Psychological Issues (with Philip Blumstein). She is on the National Board of the YWCA and Women's Resource Center, has served on the Sex Roles Council of the American Sociological Association, is a member of the American Sociological Association Committee on the Status of Women, and is a charter member of the International Academy of Sex Research.*

Deanna Strom received a B.A. degree in sociology and history from Indiana University in 1973 and a M.A. in Sociology from the University of Washington. She is presently a graduate student in sociology at the University of Washington. Her research interests are in the areas of the family, female sexuality, gay communities, and deviance.

Female sexual behavior is largely shaped by its cultural context. In this society, women are characterized as sexually passive and less "driven" sexual beings, and it is inferred that this characterization is consonant with women's biological nature. The authors believe, however, that differences in sexual behavior between men and women can be seen as the result of sex-role prescriptions which encourage women to seek sexual satisfaction within the context of a committed relationship, especially marriage, and as a result of a sexual double standard which allows aggressive sexual behavior in men while conferring moral disrepute on women so inclined. Alternative explanations to biological arguments regarding women's sexuality are offered and new research is introduced. Topics for further research are suggested, incorporating a theoretical perspective which locates the causes of differences between female and male sexuality in the sex-role conditioning process.

The Women's Liberation Movement has encouraged the revitalization of sex-role research, which in turn has helped foster a new and emerging literature on the study of human sexuality. The rediscovery of sex-role research has resulted in the questioning of many previously well-accepted theories of sex-role differentiation (such as those of Freud, Fromm, Deutsch, Erickson) as the cultural and methodological biases of these theories became more apparent. Additionally, the study of "women's topics" became more respectable within scholarly circles. Sex-role socialization and stratification by age and sex became the substance of course offerings and research projects in most sociology and psychology departments. Thus, it is understandable that the same process of critical reevaluation of traditional theories of male and female differences would be extended to the area of sexuality.

There are other reasons for the recent interest in research on human sexuality, and on female sexuality in particular. Masters and Johnson's well-received works (1966; 1970) legitimized sex research in a way that even Kinsey had not. Topics that were once considered to be frivolous and unworthy of serious study became compelling and interesting to researchers concerned with the reinterpretation and reevaluation of past research. Additionally, the intellectual and political climate fostered by the Women's Liberation Movement made female sexuality an area of personal concern to many women. The subject had generally been written about by men or by women disciples who accepted the paradigms of their male mentors, reason enough for many feminists to be critical of such work. It also happened that many topics relating to the sexuality of women were uninvestigated. Work on sexual appetite, orgasm, menopause, and sexual assault was either theoretical in nature or primarily concerned with medical complications and consequences. Thus, the process of filling an intellectual deficit began.

This article is an attempt to examine some of the work on female sexuality that has been done up to this point, and to assess its weaknesses, strengths, and effect, paying particular attention to more recent discussions and research. Suggestions will be made, where appropriate, for further research in neglected or poorly researched areas. Since female sexuality is such a broad area, this paper necessarily concentrates on only a few aspects. Thus, we will concentrate on those aspects of female sexuality which we believe have a profound impact on women, and on those areas which are now in the process of being reexamined and reinterpreted. Included are discussions of the sex act itself, sexual fantasy, body image, sexual life-styles, and sexual abuse. Before proceeding, however, we must put our review in the proper context.

THE SOCIAL CONSTRUCTION OF FEMALE SEXUALITY

The common characterization of female sexuality is consistent with a more general model of feminine behavior which has become prevalent within modern Western culture. Just as the female has been generally described as submissive, dependent, passive, and receptive, so has she been characterized as the less aggressive and less needy sexual being. This has not always been the case. Historically, women have also been viewed as tempting, seductive, and sexually insatiable. The duality has been present for a long time, although in this culture the attempts by social scientists to explain female sexuality began during an era in which the passive, almost asexual image of women predominated. In some of the psychoanalytic literature, women have been analyzed as masochistic and narcissistic as well. Feminine fulfillment has also been tied to the wife-mother role in this century, and female sexuality has been typically viewed within the context of love and marriage. Her sexual performance and identity are generally seen as related to marital commitment and "success."

The basis for this view of female sexuality is grounded in psychoanalytic theory, in contemporary psychiatry, and in the marriage and family literature of sociology and psychology (Laws, 1970; Broverman, et al., 1970). Overall, women are presented as less sexual than men. Whether discussions center around topics of sexual drive or interest, arousal, performance during the sex act itself, or sexual fantasies, a woman is seen as slowly arousable, less interested in sex than men, and more likely to suffer from sexual "inadequacies." In other words, she is a less sexual being. Furthermore, the appropriate context for female sexuality is within a committed relationship, especially marriage. The assumption is that a woman's behavior is grounded in biology or "nature" rather than its being a more transitory response to certain cultural prescriptions. In response, our own goal is to demonstrate how much of female sexuality is influenced by the cultural context (in other words, how society constructs and defines female sexuality) and to suggest, where appropriate, alternative explanations for biological arguments concerning the nature of female sexuality.

Before proceeding to the substantive issues, however, it should be noted that much of the literature on female sexuality suffers from methodological problems. The Freudian data were produced from small case-samples of self-selected women who sought treatment in an era of sexual trauma. Volunteers who come to seek treatment or guidance in a clinical situation have often been research subjects. Observations of children have been used, in some instances to make conclusions about adult behavior (Erickson, 1964). Unfortunately, some of the newer research based on survey data did not employ a sampling procedure that would justify their inferences, although many interesting questions were pursued. This body of research must be regarded as suggestive and exploratory. Additionally, the questions asked in much research reflect a cultural bias which is only beginning to be questioned.

Sexual Appetite

The female sexual appetite has been assumed to operate at a lower level than that of males, and to manifest itself within a context of love and marriage. The incidence of sex acts has been reported as almost uniformly lower for women than for men. Researchers have acknowledged a rise in the incidence of premarital female sex acts on college campuses, but the context is still within a traditional framework (i.e., sex with love) according to Reiss (1967). In other words, for college women, it is generally concluded that premarital sexuality is no longer contingent upon their being engaged (Bell & Chaskes, 1970). Permissiveness requiring stable, affectionate relations as a prerequisite for coitus comprises the extent of major change in sexual standards (Reiss, 1967; Bell & Chaskes, 1970). On a more subtle level, what is being said is that women cannot have sex without love, that they do not have the same animalistic needs as men, and that their sexuality is perhaps biologically of a different sort.

There is no evidence for this statement except American custom. If we look at some of the anthropological literature (Marshall, 1974; Ford & Beach, 1951), we note that there are societies where the female is seen as more sexual, more demanding than the male, and as the initiator of sexual activity. She is seen as sexually experienced, sexually voracious, needing two or three orgasms to each orgasm of the male, and critical of male performance. Such dissonant data do not enter the neat model of female sexuality that pervades the literature.

How can the female sex appetite be assessed? Perhaps it would be a good beginning to say that we are unsure of what female sexual capacity is, although there is evidence to suggest that her biological potential may indeed be very strong. We know now that, at least physiologically, the woman is a better sexual "athlete" than the male. Masters and Johnson's (1966) research has shown that all women are potentially multiorgasmic, whereas most men are not, and that each female orgasm gets physiologically more intense. This means that while a woman may not presently prefer to have five orgasms during coitus, she nevertheless is physically able to do so if she desires.

What one desires, however, is based on what one expects and on perceptions of what has a possibility of being given. In Bell's (1974) recent research on marital sexuality, he finds that less educated women know less about what there is to receive, request less, and in fact get less in terms of frequency, number of positions, and different types of sexual practices. More educated women expect more and are more likely to have these expectations fulfilled. Overall, while the educational differences and class differences prevail, still more than a fourth of all women know that they would like to have intercourse more often, were it within their power to control their circumstance (Bell, 1974).

We will not say, then, that the female sexual appetite is stronger than the male's because the mechanism for women is more efficient, but we will say for those who would rely on a biological argument, that evidence suggests that women have a strong sexual potential. Why, then, does the literature remain fixated on the female as a less sexual being?

First of all, it is possible to interpret women's relative disinterest in sex, compared to that of men, as the result of inhibitions existing from several aspects of their differential socialization experiences. The double standard, although recently on the decline, has certainly affected women's propensity to engage in sexual activities. The greater costs incurred by the female for participation in sexual relations has served to make her more reticent. She may be avoiding negative sanctions or, after a period of years, she may be convinced of the naturalness of her own low levels of interest in sex.

Conservative attitudes toward sexual behavior are present in the home. Studies of the attitudes of college women and their mothers toward premarital sex indicate that mothers do not support this behavior (LoPiccolo, 1973; Bell, 1961). In one sample, 83% of the mothers felt that sexual intercourse during engagement was "very wrong," and an additional 15% felt it to be "generally wrong" (Bell & Buerkle, 1961). Of the daughters, 80% fell in these same two response categories. Furthermore, responses did not vary by the educational level, religion, age, or country of birth of the mothers. When negative attitudes toward sexual experimentation are transmitted to children in the home, inhibitions to engage in the behavior is one likely outcome.

Even peer group support for sexual exploration by females is lacking. Females cannot achieve a sexual coming of age in the same way as a young male can. There can be no premier visit to a prostitute, no group induction at a sorority house with the town "loose boy." Her first attempts at sexual exploration are done without peer-group support. Even where supportive norms exist among peers, such as among lower-class black teenagers (Ladner, 1971), the experience is a solitary one, not a group experience.

In addition to the lower levels of interest in sex resulting from socialization experiences, a strong bias in the literature prevents us from seeing women as sexual beyond the confines of love and marriage. Studies of sexually assertive females who do not require an emotional commitment to one man or marriage as a prerequisite for sexual involvement are absent from the literature. Furthermore, researchers predominantly investigate the relationship between sexual behaviors and marital "success" and adjustment.

Women's sexual responsiveness has been shown to be influenced by the quality of their marriage (Clark & Wallin, 1965). Not only did the researchers not consider whether the reverse relationship might be true, but they also sampled couples married at least 20 years, hardly yielding any variation in the "quality of marriage" variable. Whether "successful" marriages can be measured by their duration is not questioned, nor is it questioned whether marriages in which sexual and personal fulfillment are absent should be "adjusted to." To illustrate, it has been maintained that premarital chastity is related to a successful marriage for women (Shope & Broderick, 1967; Reiss, 1966). It has also been found that the greatest proportion of married women experiencing difficulty in achieving orgasm can be found among wives without premarital sexual experience (Burgess & Wallin, 1953). Some concern in studies of marital success should be generated over what conditions women are "adjusting to."

The emphasis on viewing female sexuality in the context of love and marriage has also led to a neglect of the older woman. Topics that bear on the sexual life of the "accomplished" marriage, which has already given its quota of children and survived long enough for some to consider it "successful," are little researched. In particular, the older woman has not drawn much interest because the old are considered unromantic or asexual, and therefore the older woman is primarily seen in terms of problems of isolation or income maintenance and not in terms of her sexuality. The picture engendered by the literature, then, is one of younger women's sexual appetite organized by a concern with committed relationships, followed by a period of near-asexuality in her older years.

The one exception here is the study of menopause, but this has been studied more as a physiological event than as a cultural one. Drug company advertisements picture women going through "middle-age stress," and they attribute it to "the young leaving the nest," boredom, feeling of uselessness, and similar causes. It appears that many women do find compensations in the aging process and are able to adjust to their role changes (Sherman, 1971). Idealizing the role of grandmother may be one mode of adjustment many women experience. All these problems should be researched intelligently and with compassion. There isn't much to read, however, on the management of self-esteem during this period or the reconciliation of one's new asexual placement in the community. It would be interesting to know how some women successfully manage to escape this new image, or how some successfully reconcile themselves to it and still fulfill intimacy needs with men, women, or friends. It would be interesting, for example, to see a comparative sample of older heterosexual women and older homosexual women to see if the same problems of sexual identity exist in both groups. Perhaps a lesbian community has different standards for beauty, and therefore has a different effect on women's self-image as they age. At present, however, studies have not explored this dimension of female sexuality.

Whether the biological component of female sexual appetite can ever be isolated and evaluated is questionable. However, aside from women's strong physiological potential to enjoy their sexuality, it must be asserted that the major component of what appears as a disinterest in sexuality by women may very well be the result of social factors and of an unwillingness to analyze female sexuality among women who have adopted more nontraditional sex-roles.

Sexual Excitation and Arousal

Women have also been reputed to be less arousable than men. Research that investigates sex differences in response to erotic stimuli has produced mixed results. However, there is a body of evidence to suggest that the differences between men and women might not be so great as previously thought. In two experiments, one showing visual sexual materials and one showing written sexual materials, very small differences in male and female response was found (Schmidt, Sigusch, & Schafter, 1973; 1970). These results contradict Kinsey, Pomeroy, Martin, and Gebhard (1953), who felt that female sexuality was dependent on affection and love. Other studies of narrative and pictorial stimuli have found only slightly higher responses for men (Kutchinsky, 1970; Mann, Sidney, & Starr, 1970; Mosher, 1970), and some report equal responses for men and women (Byrne & Lamberth, 1970; Jacobovits, 1965; Griffitt, Veitch, & Littlepage, 1970). Although there is a lack of consensus on this issue, the assumed greater responsiveness for men is unwarranted, given the equally extensive body of literature finding no significant sex differences in responsiveness.

Not only were the women in these studies sexually excited by written and visual materials, but they could also be excited by sexual acts that were unattached to love, affiliation, or affection. While it does seem true that during the sex act, women do enjoy a certain amount of "pleasuring," which refers to nongoal-oriented and nonclimax-oriented sexual play (Masters and Johnson, 1970), it seems that we should not infer from this difference that female sexual response is different from the male's in all circumstances. It may be true that women can manage sexual life-styles that have been traditionally masculine without experiencing any trauma. In fact, nonmonogamous commitments and sexual experience with a variety of partners have always been a part of the sexual repertoire of some women.

What we attribute to biology, such as the response cycles of women to excitation (Masters and Johnson, 1966), are perhaps influenced by socialization experiences. Masters and Johnson (1966) indicated that the male gets sexually excited quickly, peaks to climax, and then recedes to a nonarousal state. The female, on the other hand, arouses slowly, reaches plateau, gets aroused further, reaches plateau, then eventually reaches climax, but does not recede to a state of complete nonarousal, thereby allowing her to be multiorgasmic. The advice that most therapists give is to take a long time "pleasuring" each other, allowing the female to slowly reach the same level of excitement the male has reached, and then, under some conditions, for the male to restrain his orgasm so that he may provide the female with several orgasmic experiences. This is seen as a humanistic, modern, and perhaps even feminist approach to lovemaking, since it is an attempt to give both partners sexual fulfillment.

The difference between male and female response cycles can also be seen as a result of comprehensive adolescent socialization. Adolescent males and adolescent females both learn about sex in a classic double-bind situation, except that the different costs involved produce different sexual styles. The male realizes that sexual experience validates him as a male and provides proof of his masculinity to his peer group. On the other hand, sex is still not sanctioned by his family and certainly not by the majority of young women he meets. Sex is still somewhat unrespectable, and thus must be engaged in a solitary fashion through masturbation or with "bad women." "Bad women" are women who are sexually available before a positively sanctioned time in the age cycle, who have sex with too many people, or who have sex with a partner to whom they are not committed. "Bad women," therefore, are beyond the pale of responsibility and respect, and can be dealt with in a superficial or even brutal manner.

Thus, the typical young male either learns his sexuality with himself or with a woman he may not particularly care for. A combination of inexperience, ignorance of what makes a "good lover," contempt for his partner, and contempt for his own activities produces an act that has aspects of high sexual excitement, but one that the individual would often like to get over with as quickly as possible. During intercourse, the person is out for his own gratification, often ashamed of his acts, and unconcerned with or unknowledgeable about how to treat his partner. In the case of masturbation, the act is also goal-oriented and often tinged with illegitimacy. The result: a quick orgasm and a quick exit.

The female is caught in a similar situation. She, too, is curious about sexuality, and her peer group may give her some credit for being attractive and

alluring to males. On the other hand, she suffers the stigmatization of inappropriate sexual behavior more severely than does her male counterpart. She is
judged by her ability to appear sexual, but to deliver only as much as the
prevailing norms of decency allow. For women, those norms have always been
more restrictive than for males. Therefore, she must be in control, slow to
arouse, slower yet to act, and aware enough of what is at stake so that even at
the height of heavy necking and petting, she can say no. "No" is her responsibility. Should she fail to exercise caution, it is her standing in the community
that will suffer.

Given this training, it is no surprise—indeed, we should be surprised if the
data were otherwise—that the male has a quick sexual response and the female's
is more gradual. Yet this socialization isn't generally taken into account when
sexual response is discussed. We do not have studies, for example, of sexually
liberated women and their pattern of sexual excitation. We know very little, in
fact, of sexually experienced or aggressive women other than prostitutes, whose
professionalization and circumstances of work make them an inadequate group
from which to draw inferences concerning the general population. We do not
know much about what inhibits quick sexual arousal or what facilitates a sexual
pattern that would make the partners more nearly equal in response. In sum, we
know little about what excites different women or what circumstances best
provide for female sexual arousal.

The media, however, are making some guesses about the nature of female
arousal because they feel there is a business market to be tapped. Magazines like
Viva and *Playgirl* offer women the chance to look at male nudes. *Viva* hypothe-
sizes that their readers like tall, lean men, and *Playgirl* assumes that every
red-blooded American woman becomes aroused by undressed football players
and musclemen. Each magazine usually includes a vignette of some fantasy
between the male and female, and publishes light fiction dealing with sex and
romance. The social characteristics of the readership of these publications is
unknown, but there appear to be enough readers, since the magazines are sur-
viving. We are not sure what this says about the sexual tastes of contemporary
women, but it indicates that some research in this area is called for.

The Social Construction of the Sex Act

The images of women as passive, narcissistic, and dependent have been trans-
ported into the bedroom. For a while, the dominant image was of women who

wanted less sex than their husbands (Kinsey et al., 1953), and in the psychiatric literature (Deutsch, 1944; Freud, 1905, 1931), sexual fulfillment was dependent on an orientation to "vaginal" orgasms, which would be achieved through non-aggressive receptiveness to the male. A more oral approach to sexuality was seen as immature and, by some, as unnatural (Bergler, 1951). Even among the more liberal commentators who allowed women different positions or orgasms without intermission, the direction and initiation of the act were to be within the male province.

The very labeling of sexual acts and the weighing of their importance seemed to indicate that the experience was first and foremost oriented by a male perspective. All noncoital sexuality was "*fore*play" (i.e., play as opposed to the "real thing"). There was such a thing as "excessive foreplay." Even the new emphasis on orgasm for women, while seemingly feminist in emphasis, had rather masculine antecedents, since research has indicated that most women can enjoy sexual intercourse without orgasm, but do not generally enjoy it without a certain amount of touching and kissing throughout the experience (Hite, 1974; Kaplan, 1974).

Additionally, women as a group have been viewed as unusually susceptible to problems of sexual dysfunction. We are still stuck with the term "frigidity" even though Masters and Johnson (1970) indicated that it is an inadequate term to describe female sexual dysfunction. Frigidity seems to indicate that the subject has absolutely no sexual feeling, which for the most part is inaccurate. A woman may have trouble reaching orgasm or may have vaginismus or some psycho-physical condition that prevents penetration, but it is rarely without any kind of sexual feeling. Perhaps for a very few who do indeed have this condition, the term might be appropriately used, but this would make the word applicable quite infrequently (O'Neal and Wessen, 1963).

Because of the wide latitude in the usage of the word, it is hard to trust older statistics to identify the rate of real frigidity in the female population. Kinsey et al. (1953) wrote that about 25% to 30% of married women have "impaired orgasmic response to coitus." Another study estimates that for wives without premarital sexual experience, 30% never or only sometimes experience orgasm within marriage, compared with 25% who have had premarital experience with their husbands, and 18% who have had premarital experience with their husbands and with other men before marriage (Burgess & Wallin, 1953). Knowledge of the incidence and causes of frigidity or some lack of sexual pleasure from coitus awaits more precise definitions of the behavior under study.

The research literature on the etiology of this difficulty is inconclusive. The psychoanalytic approach of "immature" development, when failure to transfer the erotic zone from the clitoris to the vagina occurs, has been well dismissed by Sherfy (1966) and by Masters and Johnson (1966). More recent psychological work in this area has put the blame on a repressive society and on childhood socialization (Kinsey et al., 1953; Masters & Johnson, 1970), or on the natural consequence of feminine personality traits (Deutsch, 1944). There are other interpretations. Sometimes, bad marital relations (Terman, 1938) or phobic reactions (Burgess and Wallin, 1953) are identified as the culprit. However, problems with sample representativeness (those who volunteered to be subjects), conceptual clarity (what is frigidity anyhow?), and with specifying relationships (with whom, when, under what conditions) make all previous studies somewhat undependable. A recent review of the subject points out that the findings are inconclusive, were done with inadequate samples, and explain little about female sexuality (Faulk, 1973).

The assumption behind even the most benign treatment of the subject is that the problem necessarily lies with the woman. She is the one who has not "learned correctly" the sexual responses that come naturally for men. However, given the orientation of female socialization in this society, it is probably more accurate to infer that women have correctly learned an appropriate sexual role. There is a blatant neglect in all this literature of men's learning or lack of learning of sexual behaviors that lead to sexual responsiveness in women. In the meantime, a woman's failure to achieve multiple vaginal orgasms represents her own neurotic inadequacy, whereas a man acts upon his impulses. Since research designed to explore female sexual responsiveness in an unbiased fashion is rather recent, it is quite possible that men have not "learned" to meet women's needs, certainly not by instruction from their adolescent male peers or from the young women they meet. Furthermore, women may be hesitant to demand better treatment or to confront a lover with their dissatisfaction. Women who "fake" orgasm may be in this position.

General misunderstanding of women's sexuality may be typical of both sexes. Actually, the complex sequence of events which gets labeled "sexual behavior" is influenced by social factors for both sexes, and it would be best to search for all possible factors to which sexual incompatibility might be related, rather than to assume a priori that an obvious "inadequacy" has resulted from a woman's personality disorder or lack of learning.

Fantasy

The sexual fantasy life of women has been considered less developed than that of men, largely masochistic and neurotic (Gagnon & Simon, 1973; Reich, 1961). Books like *The Story of O* (Reage, 1964) have been viewed as representative of women's masochistic, erotic fantasies. In that book, the main character places herself as an "object" to the wishes of important "others," and is absolved of any responsibility for her behavior. The psychoanalytic view of fantasy, particularly Reich's (1961), is that fantasy is an escape from orgasmic unity with the other person and that fantasy in either sex is neurotic. Indeed, few women would discuss their fantasy life or admit that they had one for fear of exposing their "problem." Fantasy during either masturbation or intercourse seemed to indicate that the person had a dark, threatening netherworld of emotions that tey had not integrated into a "normal" sexual life.

It is hard to know both the content and meaning of women's fantasies. They are certainly richer, more complicated, and more common than previously suspected (Friday, 1974; Hariton, 1974; Hollender, 1970; Hariton, 1973, 1974) reported that 65% of her sample fantasized during intercourse, at least some of the time, and at least 37% had fantasies very often during sexual relations. The two common themes were being with another man other than one's partner and being overpowered and forced to surrender. While Hariton's studies showed that such fantasies were not connected with marital unhappiness or sexual maladjustment, there was no further investigation of the function or meaning of those fantasies in women's lives. She did, however, draw some personality configurations that are interesting. She believes that women who fantasize a great deal are aggressive, impulsive, independent, and nonconforming. Further, high fantasy potential, often exercised during the day in nonsexual moments, seems to be correlated with an actively sexual approach to life. Such persons commonly have premarital relations and extramarital relationships.

Women in Hariton's study who fantasized very little seemed to be less creative and adventuresome. They were generally more traditionally "feminine" (i.e., conciliatory, unassuming, and affiliative). In between, there were women whose fantasies seemed to center around men other than their partners. This was often related to boredom in marriage, but also seemed to be related to some traits found among those who fantasized more regularly, such as creativity and independence. Hariton drew some hypotheses about the woman who primarily focuses on fantasies of sexual force. Such women tend to be passive in bed and generally dependent, controlled, serious, noninquisitive, and conforming.

Hariton concluded that highly independent women can allow themselves extensive fantasy because they are not intimidated by them. She believes that force fantasies are not necessarily masochistic, but may indicate that women want to feel desired and wooed. She points out that these women are not usually rejected in these dreams, and that the fantasies usually lead to orgasm. In cases of easy fantasy for the female, she believes it is the result of positive or non-traumatic sexual experience in childhood or adolescence. Her work is interesting, since it is the first analytic study in this area not guided by psychoanalytic principles. Fantasy is seen as a reflection of sexual strength, rather than of sexual frustration.

Gagnon and Simon (1973, pp. 64-67) feel that men have a more active sexual symbolic life than females, and they trace this back to the more frequent masturbatory experiences of males. They believe that female fantasies are more limited to specific acts in which they are involved in scenarios that depict love, marriage, social attachment, and, in some cases, mild forms of masochism. The men in women's fantasies are either known or are actors who would make appropriate marriage partners. In contrast, the sexual fantasies of men, which can appear to the naive observer to be denuded of social factors, are rich in specifically sexual behavior (Gagnon and Simon, 1973).

Although the Gagnon and Simon hypothesis has not yet been empirically supported, it is interesting to ponder the possible effects of differential masturbatory habits on the content of sexual fantasies. Hariton (1973, 1974) did mention that ability to fantasize is associated with childhood and adolescent sexual experimentation. Perhaps it is true that were we to study masturbation more closely, we would find that it does prepare the individual for a more creative sexual imagination. It does appear that the individual must be innovative in orchestrating an environment that will complement sexual excitation. Indeed, it may be that this preparation for symbolic imagining may affect other dimensions of the personality, and perhaps may be a cause of independence and nonconformity rather than just an outcome of those personality traits. Further, if this were true, we might look less benignly at the lower masturbation rates of females vis-a-vis males. Female sexual independence may be hampered by less access to solitary sexual exploration. Of course these are all hypotheses, but they do suggest that the area of female fantasy is an area of importance which needs far more research.

BODY IMAGE

That the sexuality of women is more closely tied to standards of physical attractiveness than that of men is probably not surprising to anyone. However, its consequent effects on self-image and sexual behavior are not nearly so obvious.

There is little doubt about what is an acceptable female body in our culture. Women know that they should be slim through the hips and buttocks and be adequate of breast (Berscheid, Walster, & Bohrnstedt, 1973). In the 1950s that meant at least a "B" cup or better, but large breasts are no longer so fashionable nor the *sine qua non* of sexuality as they were in the 1950s. Women should have shapely, preferably long legs, and a pretty face. Countless fashion models, the mass media, and hundreds of local, national, and international beauty contests underscore the point. The woman who chooses to disregard these expectations does not do so because she doesn't know what the standards are. She either rejects the standards as a political act because she feels they are demeaning or unflattering to women, or she rejects them because they are impossible for her to achieve; therefore, in order to feel attractive, she cannot pay close attention to the standards.

Most women cannot ignore these guides. Fashion tells them what this year's body should look like—skinny sweaters for lean, active bodies—wide pants legs for tall bodies, and so forth. When they cannot meet the manufacturer's specifications, they are unhappy.

Women are well aware of the rating and ranking of attractiveness in dating situations (Waller, 1937; Lever & Schwartz, 1971). A woman must always be in the process of assessing her chances for securing a particular partner or assessing whether her marketability is equal (Berscheid & Walster, 1972) to that of other women she encounters. Attractiveness for both men and women becomes a major factor in organizing both interpersonal exchanges and the individual's self-esteem.

Since this is such an important area of social life, it is interesting that so little attention has been addressed to it. A recent study has shown that men and women have finely drawn opinions about each part of their bodies (Berscheid et at., 1973). The women in the sample were reported to be generally pleased with their bodies, although less satisfied than the males and increasingly less satisfied with increasing age. Body image was found to be strongly correlated with self-esteem. A woman's self-esteem was related to her feeling pretty and slim; men were concerned with being handsome and with having a muscular chest. Satisfaction with one's face was important for both sexes.

Body image has a definite impact on sexual activity. Men and women who like their bodies have more sexual partners and more sexual activity (Berscheid et al., 1973). Some research indicates that some costs are incurred for women who build their self-esteem around beauty satisfaction in their youths (Berscheid, Walster, & Campbell, cited in Berscheid et al., 1973). The more attractive a woman was in her twenties, judging from college photographs, the less happy and less well-adjusted to her current life she was in her forties. This same relationship was not found for the males in the sample.

The study by Berscheid et al. (1973) pointed out, though, that adolescent beauty is always a plus. At least until middle age, the subjects reported more happiness than those who felt unattractive during the teenage years. At middle age, the differences between the attractive and unattractive adolescents leveled out, even though "fading beauties" were (as we have mentioned) slightly less happy than those who had never been judged attractive by their peers. In fact, an interesting point made by the researchers is that sudden beauty or loss of beauty is somewhat traumatic for the individual. People become so identified with their status that changes in either direction are unsettling.

What does all this mean? It is difficult to tell from these data because the sample was a nonprobability one and somewhat specialized. Furthermore, the subjects in the Berscheid study responded about something so important that they may not have wanted to admit to themselves their self-doubts and inadequacies. This might account for the finding that people are generally satisfied with their bodies. This is not to say that these data are not useful, but the study should be regarded as exploratory. It raised some important questions in which researchers of female sexuality should be interested. For example, since self-image has an important effect on rates of intercourse, those women who feel that they do not meet cultural standards of beauty may be less likely to put themselves in sexual situations where they might be rejected. It is also possible that the quality of sex is different for such women, especially if they are keenly aware that their male partner has been with other possibly more beautiful women than themselves. Since the data indicate that these feelings get crystallized in youth, the peer-group socialization of those years may have a devastating effect for many years afterward.

However, even the "winners" lose, since they have based their self-esteem on their looks, and the aging process causes them to lose their marketability. Unlike men, who retain sexual attractiveness in this culture up to their sixties and sometimes beyond, even the most attractive mature women cannot compete with the cult of youth and beauty in the United States. Perhaps some of the research on menopause should be directed to the stress put upon the female who is no longer regarded as sexual or attractive at age 50, and look at such stress as

antecedent to middle-life crisis, rather than look to hormone imbalance or biological changes to supply a total explanation.

Another dimension of the role of body image on female sexuality, about which we know little, is genital attractiveness. Folk wisdom has described women's genitalia as dirty, particularly when menstruating, odiferous, and unattractive. While breasts are described according to a variety of criteria, including shape and size, genitalia remain undifferentiated in the language. "They all look alike with a paper bag over their head" is an old male street boast. In fact, it would be well for men and women to notice how different vaginas actually are. At some women's health clinics, patients are being given mirrors to see themselves, hopefully to encourage their liking their genitalia. Books like *Our Bodies, Ourselves* (Boston Women's Health Book Collective, 1971) stress the female genitalia's attractiveness and function. But, in general, we believe that women and men are quite ignorant about vaginas and that a good deal of aversion to the vagina remains. We might hypothesize that, since body image is so important to self-esteem, insecurity or unhappiness about the acceptability of the genitalia would have some effects on the individual, perhaps in the rate or quality of lovemaking.

There is some evidence to suggest that these feelings may affect interpretations of bodily changes like menstruation. Paige (1973) did a study of menstruation in 102 women, and her data seem to indicate that the cultural and societal taboos directed toward menstruating women may be more responsible for menstrual cramps and mood changes than are hormonal or biological factors. After centuries of being told that menstruation is unclean, contaminating, and debilitating, many women do indeed believe that they are less sexual and less healthy during their menses. Interestingly, Paige's study showed that these women are more likely to be traditionally "feminine" women rather than career women. Perhaps it is the woman who is most anxious to be wife and mother who would be more likely to react emotionally to the reproductive functions of her body. Of course it has also been necessary for career women to reject the notion of the menstruation period as a less healthy period in order to compete with men equitably for the same occupational positions. However, as Paige pointed out: "It is no mere coincidence that women get the blue meanies along with an event they consider embarrassing, unclean . . . and a curse" (Paige, 1973, p. 46).

SEXUAL LIFE-STYLES: OPTIONS

Atypical life experiences that engender a great deal of social interest are often left undiscussed in the area of female sexuality. Some of these options have traditionally been placed under the study of deviance, but the judgmental aspect of the word "deviance" make us unwilling to use it as a research framework. This is particularly true because much of female sexuality has at moments in our history been seen as deviant by definition. Freud saw sexual hysteria in his patients instead of seeing sexual hysteria in the culture. Medical practitioners have diagnosed many of women's physical problems as psychological problems, without any hard supportive data (Sculley & Bart, 1973). The sparse literature on lesbianism has almost universally condemned same-sex sexuality as a result of character malformation and faulty parental identification (Deutsch, 1944; Reingold, 1964).

New literature is evolving which brings some of these former theories and data into question (Gagnon & Simon, 1973; Money, 1972; Green 1974; Marmor, 1965, 1972; Hooker, 1967, 1968; Sculley & Bart, 1973; Chessler, 1972; Laws, 1970; Seeman, 1972; Oberstone, 1974). These researchers have taken on the medical and psychoanalytic establishment·on questions of female emotional health, the interaction of psychological and biological factors, and the "normality" of same-sex behaviors and identity. We will not attempt to review all the new literature here, but we will address ourselves to two important areas—nonnormative sexual patterns for heterosexual women and same-sex behaviors.

Nonnormative Patterns for Heterosexual Women

In the past five years there has been a great deal of writing on new sexual styles, in particular swinging-comarital sexuality and nonmarital sexuality (Palson & Palson, 1972; Gilmartin, 1975; Walshock, 1971; Libby & Whitehurst, 1973). Many authors have discussed the advantages and disadvantages for the couple and for the community, but very few authors have discussed its effects on the woman. Given that the woman has been socialized to associate love with sexuality and to guard her reputation and "market value" by making her sexuality a scarce resource, we might imagine that nonnormative sexual styles would be likely to result from atypical socialization of the female or from a damaged sense of self. Presently there is little support for either possiblity, although very little research has been directed toward the latter hypothesis. Actually, we know very little about females participating in swinging and comarital sex; other than the fact that they have somewhat more distant relationships with the parents, they are much like nonswingers (Gilmartin, 1975). They are usually not the initiator of swinging in the marriage, and they often wish to continue it longer than do their husbands (Palson & Palson, 1972). Further, it is not unusual for many women to engage in same-sex sexuality, even though they may have never experienced any homosexual fantasies, attraction, or behavior before that time.

What we don't have is an explanation for these findings. Why are women loath to begin but also loath to end nonmarital sexuality? How do they overcome past stigmas about sexuality, both heterosexual and homosexual? How do they relate to their husbands after they have broken this taboo? Some have said that their marriages are happy or happier since swinging, but we do not know the conditions and kinds of intimacy these couples experience once the monogamous contract has been canceled. How does the woman allow the male to persuade her to begin swinging, and what does this do to her sense of sexual adequacy? What does group sex do for a person in terms of making tem feel attractive or less attractive to others? In general, what is the effect on self-esteem and feelings about sexuality and intimacy?

We know even less about the woman who engages in nonmarital sexuality or extramarital sexuality in a negatively sanctioned situation. There have been numerous incidence studies of premarital sexuality which commonly estimate the proportion of women ever having had premarital sexual experiences in the 40% to 50% range (Bell & Chaskes, 1970; Jackson & Potkay, 1973). Some estimates go as high as 80% (Hunt, 1974). Although most researchers believe, however, that the proportions of nonvirgins have been increasing on college campuses, it is unclear whether this should be regarded as a significant change, in comparison to the significant changes in premarital sexual standards of the 1920s (Bell & Chaskes, 1970). Premarital coital rates of 20% to 25% have been reported since the beginning of this century (Bell, 1974).

Researchers have not adequately explained how some women come to be more sexually liberal than others in their age cohorts. Some determinants of permissiveness have been studied, religiosity being the most important explanatory variable (Bell & Chaskes, 1970; Jackson & Potkay, 1973). The attitudes of reference groups appear to have some impact (Trevor, 1972; Mirande, 1968), along with the attractiveness of the female (Berscheid et al., 1973). Young women with a large number of dating partners or those whose first date occurred at a young age also appear to experience greater permissiveness. But social psychological variables are ignored. We know very little about the histories of socialization, general aggressiveness, and measures of conformity that might help explain the behavior of the sexually active woman.

Same-Sex Sexuality: Identity and Behaviors

The recent research into female same-sex behavior and relationship indicates a more profitable pattern of research. In addition to good descriptions of non-clinical populations (Saghir & Robbins, 1973; Gagnon & Simon, 1973; Blumstein & Schwartz, 1974), a new group of subjective journalistic and political accounts of gay life have contributed to our knowledge of same-sex relationships as a life-style and as sexual behavior (Abbot & Love, 1972; Martin & Lyon, 1972; Johnston, 1973). The new literature has pointed out that lesbians are women, and they can best be understood by looking at them in terms of their female socialization and similarity to other women (Gagnon & Simon, 1973). Just as the women's movement has encouraged a rethinking of appropriate standards of sexual behavior for heterosexual women, there appears to be a feminist counterpart within lesbian communities. Some recent research suggests that lesbians with a feminist ideology may be more likely to deviate from the effects of traditional socialization by exploring non-heterosexually-modelled relationships, new standards of female attractiveness, and new standards of femininity (Strom, 1977). Lesbians have interpreted the role playing observed in lesbian relationships as a carry-over from the expectations of heterosexual culture, and many women, especially those with a feminist ideology, seek to disregard those roles (Martin & Lyon, 1972; Strom, 1977).

There is a continuum of behavior and a continuum of commitment to an identity among gay women. Having same-sex behaviors may not cause a person to call temself "gay," nor does a lack of same-sex behavior necessarily result in a heterosexual identity. The question of *what is* a lesbian is now seen as more problematic than previous research would indicate (Blumstein & Schwartz, 1975).

The utility of the framework previously mentioned (of examining lesbian behavior within the context of the more general process of sexual identity among women and within the context of typical female socialization) can be demonstrated here. The finding from the swingers' literature that women seem to be able to engage in homosexual behaviors without previous attraction to women and without trauma is very unlike the responses of heterosexual males who are both offended and frightened of homo-erotic situations. This difference may be attributed to the differential sexual socialization of the sexes. Women are not subject to the same taboos about same-sex relationships that men are. They are not warned about being a "sissy" or about being affectionate in same-sex relationships. They are allowed slumber parties and can be caught cuddling or scratching one another's back without undue concern. Throughout their development, they are encouraged to touch one another, to kiss or embrace people they like, and, in general, to be expressive with family members, close friends, and boyfriends.

Men, on the other hand, have many more body taboos. The taboos can be broken in special circumstances, such as in athletic locker rooms, but the "threat" of homo-eroticism is much more acknowledged and thus guarded against. Since women have not received the same degree of negative information, nor have they experienced the same degree of negative sensitization to cues, they are not as guarded. Further, since they are supposed to be expressive with those they love, physical expressiveness to valued friends seems unremarkable and appropriate.

Thus, women seem to be capable of what we will call, for lack of a better term, "sexual flexibility." We are not sure of all the antecedents of this trait, but it would include a lack of labeling physical responses toward others as a highly stigmatized behavior, and perhaps a lack of defining one's femininity by sex-object choice. Women are trained to be flexible (i.e., to accommodate oneself to another's life plan). Finally, they legitimize sexual expression in love situations and, by extension, in any love situation. Blumstein and Schwartz (1975) found that bisexuals seem to have a general personality characteristic called "tolerance of ambiguity," which allows them to accommodate divergent kinds of information in the same self-identification process without feeling any dissonance. They do not have to apply only one label to themselves, such as homosexual or heterosexual, when both types of sex-object choice are maintained. It would be a creative and important addition to the study of female sexual identity, and to the study of the identity-taking process, to know if women really are more flexible than men and to know what proportions of women have this facility. If we are, as these authors hope, in a period of constructing a new model of female sexuality, we need this kind of information.

SEXUAL ABUSE

The Women's Liberation Movement is particularly responsible for engendering a new concern with the topics of sexual assault, abuse, and mistreatment. Rape, for example, has long been an important problem for women, but only recently has it been presented as a problem for the public conscience. Rape has often been a crime where the victim was as tainted as the offender; as a result, the crime was underreported and underprosecuted. The Women's Movement has supported women who have been raped by assuring them that the rape was not their fault and by counseling them in rape crisis centers and in feminist publications about how to report their assault to the police. As a result, rape statistics have gone up drastically. The volume of rapes increased in 1973 by 12.7% over 1972 and 117% over 1960 (*Crime in the United States,* 1974). Although this may be a result of more rapes, we may assume that some of it can be attributed to a new female perception of the crime. This increase must also be assumed to be less than the real incidence, since it is still hypothesized that only one in four rapes are reported to the police (James, 1976).

The increased awareness of rape has led to new research dimensions. Scholars are interested in learning about why some men find rape an appropriate way of relating to women, what rape says about cultural stereotypes of "good" and "bad" women, and why rape can be internalized by the victim as her fault. Most studies have reported the incidence and have presented the legal approach to the problem (James, 1976). Thus, studies of the male as a sexual psychopath abound. The feminist literature is mostly speculative at this point, but it does encourage looking at rape as an extension of a cultural pattern rather than as an aberration. James (1976) pointed out that convicted rapists show few distinguishable group characteristics. However, they do tend to be young and to fall into the lower end of the occupational and social class scales; minorities are overrepresented among them. Many rapists sometimes commit rape as an afterthought while a burglary is in process. Hopefully, more research work will be done soon in this area.

Incest and child molestation should also be included in this area of sexual abuse. Incest (i.e., sexual intercourse between members of the nuclear family or the close extended family) is far more common among female children than male children (Vincent, 1971). As Vincent's study found when sexual activity is defined broadly so as to include fondling, oral-genital sex, and similar practices, female children are involved ten to one over male children.

Gebhard, Gagnon, Pomeroy, and Christensen (1965) indicated that sometimes the victim is not so innocent. They mentioned the "seductive child" theory that a prepubertal or adolescent child might entice the adult as a way of gaining some power in the relationship. While this does not absolve the adult from responsibility for the situation, research on incest should also examine the child's role in such incidents. Even so, it seems unlikely that the majority of incest cases involve a "seductive child," especially those involving children of four or five years of age.

The most common incest relationship reported is father-daughter, followed by stepfather-daughter, uncle-niece, grandfather-granddaughter, brother-sister, and (only rarely) mother-son. The most common ages are between 7 and 19, and it has been noted that while this is a period where the female is just beginning to develop sexually, the offender is usually in his late thirties or early forties, a period when sexual doubt or masculinity crises may occur. The interaction of the two periods in the sexual-life cycle has not been well researched, but it may be important.

Acts of incest usually continue for a period of years. Wives often do not report the incidents for fear of losing the breadwinner or lover, but they may do so from a sense of outrage or jealousy. The daughter may accede or run away, depending on circumstances. Should the case reach the juvenile authorities, she may be sent to an institution or foster home.

The effects on the female are not precisely known, expecially the long-term effects. James (1976) has hypothesized that such experiences may be a precursor to delinquent activity, prostitution, or other reactions to feeling stigmatized and unworthy. Research on these questions is in progress, but again it is only in the beginning stages.

CONCLUSION

Although research on female sexuality is incomplete and exploratory, it is reassuring to see critical and original thought being applied to the topic in recent publications. There are not enough studies on all stages of women's life cycle (see Laws, 1970), on topics requiring longitudinal research, on minority patterns, on sexual abuse, and on sexual patterns not associated with marital relationships. There is too much preoccupation with the incidence of acts and too little concentration on the social psychological explanation of why and how the acts occur. What they mean to the participants and what they mean for intimate relations and for family life should be investigated. We know little about sexual identity, the role of romanticism, and the construction of the sexual appetite. We have still not adequately addressed ourselves to the interrelationship of the physical and the social, such as the relationship between body image and attractiveness, the aging process, the changing of bodily processes such as menstruation and menopause, and the subjective understanding of orgasm and erotic attraction. The important components of the socialization process, which have only been hinted at in this paper, need comprehensive treatment.

On the other hand, we seem to be more aware of what interesting questions exist. Paradigms that once organized research into female sexuality have been questioned and often dismantled, and new theories have emerged. A great deal of work in many of the areas we have mentioned is excellent, and new research is in progress in many areas. Female sexuality, indeed sexuality in general, is no longer seen as a trivial area of study. We are not sure that this massive area will be adequately investigated in the next 10 years, but the long-range prospects for serious and objective research look promising.

REFERENCES

Abbot, S., & Love, B. *Sappho was a right-on woman.* New York: Stein & Day, 1972.

Bell, R.R. Female sexual satisfaction as related to levels of education. In L. Gross (Ed.), *Sexual behavior.* Flushing, N.Y.: Spectrum Publications, 1974.

Bell, R.R., & Buerkle, J.V. Mother and daughter attitudes to premarital sexual experience behavior. *Journal of Marriage and Family, 23,* 1961, 390-392.

Bergler, E. *Counterfeit sex.* New York: Grune & Stratton, 1951.

Berscheid, E., Walster, E., & Bohrnstedt, G. The happy American body: A survey report. *Psychology Today,* November, 1973, 119-122, 126, 128-131.

Blumstein, P., & Schwartz, P. *The acquisition of sexual identity: The bisexual case.* Unpublished manuscript, 1975.

Blumstein, P.W., & Schwartz, P. Lesbianism and bisexuality. In E. Goode & R.R. Troiden (Eds.), *Sexual deviance and sexual deviants.* New York: William Morrow, 1974.

Boston Women's Health Book Collective. *Our bodies, ourselves.* New York: Simon & Schuster, 1971.

Broverman, I.K., Broverman, D.M., Clarkson, F., Bosenkrantz, P., & Vogel, S.R. Sex-role stereotypes and clinical judgments of mental health. *Journal of Consulting Psychology,* 1970, *34,* 1-7.

Burgess, E.W., & Wallin, P. *Engagement and marriage.* New York: Lippincott, 1953.

Byrne, D., & Lamberth, J. The effect of erotic stimuli on sex arousal, evaluative responses, and subsequent behavior. *Technical Reports of the Commission on Obscenity and Pornography, 8,* Washington, D.C.: U.S. Government Printing Office, 1970.

Chessler, P. *Women and madness.* Garden City, N.Y.: Doubleday, 1972.

Clark, A., & Wallin, P. Women's sexual responsiveness and the duration and quality of their marriages. *American Journal of Sociology, 71*(2), September, 1965, 187-196.

Crime in the United States, Washington, D.C.: U.S. Government Printing Office, 1974.

Deutsch, H. *The psychology of women: A psychoanalytic interpretation.* New York: Grune & Stratton, 1944.

Erickson, E.H. Inner and outer space: Reflections on womanhood. In R.J. Lifton (Ed.), *The women in America.* Boston: Beason Press, 1964.

Faulk, M. Frigidity: A critical review. *Archives of Sexual Behavior, 2,* 1973, 257-266.

Ford, C.S., & Beach, F.A. *Patterns of sexual behavior.* New York: Hoeber, 1951.

Freud, S. *Three essays on the theory of sexuality.* (J. Strackey, Ed. and trans.). New York: Basic Books, 1962. (Originally published, 1905.)

Friday, N. *My secret garden.* New York: Pocketbooks, 1974.

Gagnon, J.H., & Simon, W. *Sexual conduct.* Chicago: Sedine, 1973.

Gebhard, P.H., Gagnon, J.H., Pomeroy, W.B., & Christensen, C.V. *Sex offenders: An analysis of types.* New York: Harper & Row, 1965.

Gilmartin, B.G. *Psychology Today, 8,* 1975, 54 ff.

Green, R. *Sexual identity conflict in children and adults.* New York: Basic Books, 1974.

Griffitt, W., Veitch, R., & Littlepage, G. *Erotic arousal and interpersonal behavior: Influences on interpersonal attraction.* Manhattan: Kansas State University, 1970. (Mimeographed.)

Hariton, E.B. The sexual fantasies of women. *Psychology Today,* March 1973, 39-48.

Hariton, E.B. Women's fantasies during sexual intercourse. *Journal of Consulting and Clinical Psychology, 12,* 1974, 312-32.

Hite, S. *Sexual honesty.* New York: Paperback Library, 1974.

Hollender, M.H. Women's coital fantasies. *Medical Aspects of Human Sexuality, 4*(2), 1970, 63-70.

Hooker, E. The homosexual community. In J. Gagnon & W. Simon (Eds.), *Sexual deviance.* Harper & Row, 1967, 167-183.

Hooker, E. Homosexuality. In D.I. Sills (Ed.), *International encyclopedia of the social sciences, 14,* 1968. New York: Collier & MacMillan, 222-233.

Jackson, E.D., & Potkay, C.R. Precollege influences on sexual experience of coeds. *Journal of Sex Research, 9,* May 1973, 143-149.

Jakobovits, L.A. Evaluational reactions to erotic literature. *Psychological Report, 16,* 1965, 985-994.

James, J. Institutionalized responses to female sexuality. In J.L. Laws & P. Schwartz, *The social construction of female sexuality.* New York: (In press.)

Johnston, J. *Lesbian nation.* New York: Simon & Schuster, 1973.

Kaplan, H.S. *The new sex therapy.* New York: Brunner/Mazel, 1974.

Kinsey, A., Pomeroy, W., Martin, C., & Gebhard, P., *Sexual behavior in the human female.* New York: Simon & Schuster, 1953.

Kutschinsky, B. The effect of pornography—An experiment on perception, attitudes, and behavior. In *Technical reports of the Commission on Obscenity and Pornography* (Vol. 8). Washington, D.C.: U.S. Government Printing Office, 1970.

Ladner, A. *Tomorrow's tomorrow.* Garden City, N.Y.: Doubleday, 1971.

Laws, J.L. Toward a model of female sexual identity. Chicago: *Midway,* 1970.

Lever, J., & Schwartz, P. *Women at Yale.* Indianapolis, Inc.: Bobbs-Merrill, 1971.

Libby, W., & Whitehurst, R.N. *Renovating marriage.* Danville, Calif.: Consensus Publishers, 1973.

LoPiccolo, J. Mothers and daughters: Perceived and real differences in sexual values. *Journal of Sexuality Research, 9*(2), May 1973, 171-177.

Mann, J., Sidman, J., & Starr, S. Effects of erotic films on sexual behaviors of married couples. In *Technical Reports of the Commission on Obscenity and Pornography* (Vol. 8). Washington, D.C.: U.S. Government Printing Office, 1970.

Marmor, J. Notes on some psychodynamic aspects of homosexuality. In *NIMH Task Force on Homosexuality Report,* 1972, 55-57.

Marmor, J. *Sexual inversion: Multiple roots of homosexuality.* New York: Basic Books, 1965.

Marshall, D.S. Too much sex in Mangaia. In E. Goode & R. Troiden (Eds.), *Sexual deviance and sexual deviants.* New York: Morrow, 1974.

Martin, D., & Lyon, P. *Lesbian woman.* San Francisco, Calif.: Glide Publications, 1972.

Masters, W. & Johnson, V. *Human sexual response.* Boston, Mass.: Little, Brown, 1966.

Masters, W., & Johnson, V. *Human sexual inadequacy.* Boston, Mass.: Little, Brown, 1970.

Mirande, A.M. Reference group theory and adolescent sexual behavior. *Journal of Marriage and Family, 30*(4), November 1968, 572-577.

Money, J., & Ehrhardt, A.A. *Man and woman—boy and girl.* Baltimore: The Johns Hopkins University Press, 1972.

Mosher, D.L. Psychological reactions to pornographic films. In *Technical Reports of the Commission on Obscenity and Pornography* (Vol. 8). Washington, D.C.: U.S. Government Printing Office, 1970.

Oberston, A. *A comparative study of psychological adjustment—Aspects of life style in gay and non-gay women.* Unpublished doctoral dissertation. California School of Professional Psychology, 1974.

O'Neal, P., & Wessen, F. Suggested study of human sexual behavior. In Winokur, G. (Ed.), *Determinates in human sexual behavior.* Springfield, Ill.: Charles C. Thomas, 1963.

Springfield, Ill.: Charles C. Thomas, 1963.

Paige, K. E. Women learn to sing the menstrual blues. *Psychology Today,* September, 1973, 41-46.

Palson, C., & Palson, R. Living in wedlock. *Society Magazine, 9* (4) February 1972, 28-38.

Reage, P. *The story of O.* New York: Grove Press, 196. (Originally published 1954.)

Reich, W. *The function of the orgasm.* New York: Farrar, Straus, 1961.

Reingold, J. C. *The fear of being a woman.* New York: Grune & Stratton, 1964, 372-80.

Reiss, I. L. The sexual renaissance: A summary and analysis. *Journal of Social Issues, 22,* 1966, 123-137.

Reiss, I. L. *The social context of pre-marital and sexual permissiveness.* New York: Holt, Rinehart and Winston, 1967.

Saghir, M. T. & Robbins, E. *Male and female homosexuality.* Baltimore: Williams & Wilkins, 1973.

Schmidt, G., & Sigusch, V. Sex differences in responses to psychosexual stimulation by films and slides. *Journal of Sex Research, 6* (4), November 1970, 268-283.

Schmidt, G., & Schafter, S. Responses to reading erotic stories: Male-female differences. *Archives of Sexual Behavior, 2* (3), 1973, 27-45.

Sculley, D., & Bart, P. B. A funny thing happened on the way to the orifice: Women in gynecology textbooks. *American Journal of Sociology, 78* (5), January 1973.

Seeman, B. *Free and female.* Greenwich, Conn.: Fawcett, 1972.

Sherfy, M. J. A theory of female sexuality. *Journal of American Psychoanalytic Association,* 1966.

Sherman, J. A. *On the psychology of women.* Springfield, Ill.: Thomas, 1971.

Shope, F., & Broderick, C. B. Level of sexual experience and predicted adjustment in marriage. *Journal of Marriage and Family 29* (3), August 1967, 424-427.

Strom, Deanna. A lesbian feminist community in a Western city: Its ideological and structural organization. Unpublished master's thesis. University of Washington, 1977.

Terman, L. M. *Psychological factors in marital happiness.* New York: McGraw-Hill, 1938.

Trevor, J. J., Jr. Reference groups and premarital sexual behavior. *Journal of Marriage and Family 34* (2), May 1972, 283-291.

Vincent, D. F. Protecting the child victim of sex crimes committed by adults. *Federal Probation,* September 1971, 15-20.

Waller, W. The rating and dating complex. *American Sociological Review, 2,* 1937.

Walshok, M. L. The emergence of middle class deviant subcultures: The case of swingers. *Social Problems, 18* (4), Spring 1971, 485-495.

CHAPTER *6*

PSYCHOLOGICAL ASPECTS OF MENSTRUATION, CHILDBIRTH, AND MENOPAUSE

MARY BROWN PARLEE

Mary Brown Parlee was born in Oak Park, Illinois, and attended public schools in Illinois and Connecticut. She received her B.A. with honors in biology from Radcliffe College in 1965 and her Ph. D. in general experimental psychology from the Massachusetts Institute of Technology in 1969. She has taught and done research at Wellesley College (1969-1972), the University of South Carolina's Social Problems Research Institute (1972-1974), the Psychiatry Department of the Harvard Medical School (1974-1975), and is currently Associate Professor of Psychology at Barnard. In 1972-1973 she held a Fellowship from the Radcliffe Institute. She is presently a consulting editor for the Psychology of Women Quarterly *and Treasurer of the Association for Women in Science. Her primary research interests and publications are in the areas of psychological concomitants of the female reproductive function, sex differences, and general issues related to psychology and women.*

When Parlee reviewed and verified the foregoing data, she commented: "That's the biographical sketch of my professional life as seen from the traditionally "appropriate" perspective—from the outside. Much is left out of even a professional biography, however, if we don't say something about the way the outside picture articulates with the inner experience of what it means to be female at particular times and places. I would say that one of the most significant things I learned at Harvard and MIT had to do with the role of the professional woman in such institutions: we are invisible. While teaching at Wellesley, I found that there are places where women are taken seriously and where one doesn't have to face daily those little reminders of the sexist assumptions pervading male-dominated institutions.

"When my daughter was born and I left Wellesley to follow my husband into a new phase in his career, it was the Radcliffe Institute, run by and for women, that saved my professional life by giving me a Fellowship. Without that support, I do not think I would have been able to work out any kind of affiliation at the University of South Carolina. As it was, the Psychology Department was supremely indifferent to someone with my training and interests; only one person, the director of the University of South Carolina's Social Problems Research Institute provided the necessary affiliation and research support, and I am very grateful to him. Returning to Boston as a postdoctoral Fellow in the Laboratory of Social Psychiatry at the Harvard Medical School, I found the intellectual atmosphere exciting beyond words, but the attitudes and behavior of the psychiatry residents—all male—toward female Ph.D.'s did little to bolster my sense of professional or personal self-esteem.

Research on psychological concomitants of female reproductive processes has for the most part ignored the social and cultural context within which the biological events occur. Studies of menstruation are needed which explore cycle-related changes in positively valued moods and behaviors as well as negative ones, which include appropriate control groups, and which take seriously the methodological and theoretical implications of the existence of socially shared beliefs about a "premenstrual tension syndrome." Studies of psychological fluctuations associated with the menstrual cycle might be placed in a broader scientific perspective by considering the relationship between these changes and fluctuation related to other biological (e.g., circadian) and social (e.g., weekly) rhythms. Psychological investigations of pregnancy and the postpartum period have likewise focused upon negative features of the experience, rather than positive ones, and, especially in studies of postpartum depression, have not taken into account the psychological implications of the changes in social roles that occur in the transition to parenthood. Research based upon a developmental perspective rather than upon a medical model of birth is needed. Psychological studies of menopause have similarly focused upon biological causes of a presumed "menopausal syndrome," and have failed to consider the psychological implications of role changes experienced by middle-aged women. Biological, psychological, and social processes interact in determining the psychological experiences associated with reproduction; the complexity of this interaction is obscured by research perspectives that consistently emphasize any one of these processes to the exclusion of others.

One of the most obvious differences between women and men, Freudian tradition notwithstanding, is that women are biologically capable of giving birth and men are not. From menarche through menopause, a span of some 40 years, most women menstruate at approximately monthly intervals, and many become

This work was supported by a grant for Research Training in Social Psychiatry to Elliot G. Mishler (NIMH Grant No. 5 TOI MH 08934).

pregnant and give birth to a child. While menarche, menstruation, pregnancy, birth, and menopause can all be defined biologically as aspects of the female reproductive function, it is clear that the physiological events and processes are associated with important psychological phenomena as well.

It is worth noting at the outset that complex conceptual problems arise when scientists try to deal with events-in-time which have both biological and psychological aspects. The mind-body problem, or mind-brain identity theory, has been long and inconclusively debated by philosophers (Borst, 1970), and its implications for psychology are not adequately dealt with by glossing over or ignoring the issues. Words like "psychophysiological" and "psychosomatic" may denote particular kinds of research by psychologists and medical investigators, but they leave unclear the role of physiological constructs in the explanation of psychological phenomena. In research on psychological aspects of female reproductive processes, this lack of clarity has in many cases allowed investigators to perpetrate—without having to state them directly—their implicit assumptions about biology and the nature (and roles) of women and men.

Some investigators studying female reproductive processes do state explicitly, or clearly assume, that psychological phenomena can have direct biological causes (Bardwick, 1971, p. 27; Gottschalk, Kaplan, Gleser, & Winget, 1962, p. 308; Benedek, 1963, p. 315). The quintessential expression of this view appears in the opening sentence of Collins and Newton's chapter in *Biochemistry of Women: Clinical Concepts:* "The female anatomy, mentality, and reproductive biochemistry are initiated, maintained, and controlled by hormones" (Collins & Newton, 1974). Other investigators more subtly imply the primacy of physiological causes by attaching a term with biological meaning to the description of a person who is in a particular psychological state. Describing a woman who exhibits a certain set of symptoms and moods as "menopausal" (or "premenstrual"), for example, might incline one to direct less attention to her present social setting and life circumstances than to the biological status highlighted by the adjective. It seems likely that in many cases a "menopausal woman" is also one whose roles as mother and homemaker are undergoing abrupt transitions (Bart, 1971), and an equally accurate (though differently biased) scientific description might have emphasized the social changes rather than the biological ones.

In addition to allowing scientists to imply that biological factors are of greater importance than personality or social variables, the language used to describe psychological aspects of female reproductive processes has allowed some investigators to insinuate the scientifically unproven notion that the behavior and experience of women are more closely tied to biological functions than are the behavior and experience of men. In discussions of presumed psychological fluctuations occurring throughout the menstrual cycle, for example, it is not uncommon to find phrases like "women *are subject to* cyclic changes . . ." or "the menstrual cycle *imposes upon* the human female a rhythmic variability . . ." (emphasis added)—phrases which imply that females are acted upon by forces outside their control. Similar linguistic constructions seem less likely to be used in descriptions of comparable activities involving males. Sleep/wake cycles, for example, are not "imposed upon" human beings; people are said to wake up or go to sleep.

It may be because of the conceptual and practical difficulties inherent in studying psychological aspects of physiological processes such as menstruation, birth, and menopause that the major psychological journals have until recently contained few reports of research on these topics. Yet, despite the potential complexity, the dearth of research by psychologists on female reproductive functions seems surprising. Not only are such problems of obvious significance to the human race (a criterion which, admittedly, does not always guide selection of topics for psychological research), but they would also seem to lie well within the purview of traditional problem areas and approaches in various subfields of psychology. If physiological psychology, for example, is to be defined by its subject matter rather than by the methodology preferred by those who currently identify themselves as physiological psychologists, then the study of psychological aspects of menstruation, childbirth, and menopause would seem to be as appropriately included in physiological psychology as are psychological studies of such processes as eating, sleeping, and mating. Experimental psychologists, too, might be as interested (on theoretical grounds) in sensory and cognitive changes during pregnancy or the menstrual cycle as much as in those changes occurring, for example, under conditions of sensory deprivation. As developmental problems, the transition to parenthood, or the cessation of fertility, seem as central to the study of the human life cycle as are the psychologist's more traditional concerns with early childhood, adolescence, or aging.

In spite of the apparent relevance of these areas, however, indexes of *Psychological Abstracts*—to say nothing of the contents of introductory textbooks—show that the psychological aspects of female reproductive functions have not been included as significant problem areas in any of the traditional subfields of psychology. Even taken together, the difficulties of formulating and studying the problems, coupled with the force of research tradition, seem inadequate to account completely for psychologists' failure to provide systematic psychological studies of physiological processes unique to females. It is likely that this failure also reflects a more general tendency on the part of psychologists to study females less often than males and to regard the "psychology of women" as something separate from the mainstream of "psychology"—be it social, experimental, or whatever (Parlee, 1975).

One consequence of psychologists' neglect of these problems is that much of the existing psychological research and writing on women and their bodies is to be found in the medical and psychiatric literature. As will perhaps be evident, editorial standards with respect to methodological rigor in these fields differ from those to which psychologists are accustomed. Many of these works, in fact, do not take cognizance of what is (for psychologists) the essential assumption: that human behavior and experience can be studied scientifically (i.e., in such a way that the data can presumably be replicated by others). In the medical and psychiatric literature, one frequently finds that psychological aspects of female reproductive processes are treated as epiphenomena of the physiological functions. Detailed scientific descriptions of the biological processes are followed by generalizations about concomitant psychological events, without any apparent recognition on the investigator's part that these latter assertions are also claims about matters of fact (which may or may not be true) that are subject to scientific examination and testing.

A recent collection of articles on the menopausal syndrome, for example, contains 28 papers on various aspects of the physiology of menopause, all with data and supporting references in the usual manner of scientific reports, and one essay on the psychological aspects, couched in psychoanalytic terms and offering not a single supporting reference or bit of reliable data (Greenblatt, Mahesh, & McDonough, 1974). A similar disregard for the *scientific* study of psychological aspects of physiological processes is evident in the "psychiatric" chapters of obstetrics texts by Eastman and Hellman (1961), by Rovinsky and Guttmacher (1965), and, indeed, in virtually the entire volume on *Psychosomatic Obstetrics, Gynecology, and Endocrinology* edited by Kroger (1962). Those medical and psychiatric studies which do make some attempt to provide replicable data are unfortunately often methodologically flawed and/or distorted (from formulation of the problem through interpretation of the results) by implicit and unexamined assumptions that the investigators hold as to the appropriate social roles for women and men in the United States in the twentieth century.

Rather than focus primarily upon the methodological inadequacies and sexist bias of individual studies in the existing literature, however, an attempt is made in what follows to evaluate and organize existing data in such a way as to identify the strengths and weaknesses of the conceptual frameworks within which research on psychological aspects of female reproductive functions has been conducted. The review will attempt to show that by narrowly construing the range of variables to be studied—in particular by excluding from consideration the effects of socially shared beliefs and expectations about women and their roles—investigators have failed in systematic ways to contribute to a scientific understanding of psychological aspects of women's reproductive processes.

REPRODUCTION AS A BIOLOGICAL PROCESS OCCURRING WITHIN A SOCIAL CONTEXT

Numerous reviews and collections of original papers are available on the biological aspects of female reproductive processes, ranging in readability and detail from pertinent chapters in *Our Bodies, Ourselves* (Boston Women's Health Book Collective, 1973), Sherman (1971), and Bardwick (1971) to Philipp, Barnes, and M. Newton's (1970) collection of papers on the *Scientific Foundations of Obstetrics and Gynecology* and Botella-Llusia's (1973) *Endrocrinology of Woman*. Most obstetrics and basic physiology texts describe the biological aspects of menstruation, pregnancy, and birth at an intermediate level of complexity (e.g., Eastman and Hellman, 1961; Ruch and Fulton, 1960). The chapter by Stoddard (1966) in Danforth's obstetrics text is helpful in that it includes some information on biological changes occurring at puberty and the climacteric; the sections on "emotional changes," however, are fairly typical. For example, in discussing ways in which women respond to the onset of a menstrual period, Stoddard writes that ". . . the unmarried girl who has been indiscreet . . . (is) . . . quite pleased to note the onset of menstruation" (p. 163), a statement so perfectly exemplifying its genre that it needs no further comment. Other researchers (Tanner, 1962; Greenblatt, Mahesh, & McDonough, 1974; Ryan and Gibson, 1971) provide more detailed information on biological aspects of puberty and menopause. Sotham and Gonzaga (1965), and Bell, Christie, and Venables (1975) have reviewed some of the physiological changes associated with the menstrual cycle in ways which seem more suggestive than the usual textbook accounts as to how they might, however indirectly, affect behavior.

In addition to considering the biological aspects of menstruation, birth, and menopause, it seems important to recognize that they are biological processes that occur within a particular social, political, and cultural context. This context, usually taken for granted and left unexamined in psychological research, may well turn out to be as important in determining the kinds of psychological experiences associated with female reproductive functions as are the hormonal fluctuations and other bodily changes. Mean and Newton (1967) suggested the usefulness of a cross-cultural perspective as one way of discovering the taken-for-granted assumptions that form the context for reproductive behavior in our own society.

While a review of the anthropological literature on the social patterning of reproduction is beyond the scope of this article, the following references suggest some of the kinds of cross-cultural research which have been done on different aspects of reproductive behavior. They include: studies of female initiation ceremonies (Young, 1965; Brown, 1963); male initiation ceremonies (Young, 1962; Kluckholn, & Anthony, 1958; menstrual taboos (Stephens, 1961; Young and Bacdayan, 1965); eating habits during pregnancy (Ayres, 1967; Trethowan & Dickens, 1972); couvade (Young, 1965; Ayres, 1961; Trethowan, 1972), and other practices associated with birth (Mead & Newton, 1967; Newton & Newton, 1972; Paige & Paige, 1973; Ortner, 1974). Within a single culture, explicit consideration of the social context of reproduction may also provide a means of assessing the relative significance of biological changes vis-a-vis other factors as determinants of behavior. Alice Rossi's recent work on the relative importance of the hormonal fluctuations of the menstrual cycle compared to the socially defined cycle of the week is suggestive in this regard: she found that women's self-ratings of mood seemed to be more closely related to the day of the week than to the phase of the menstrual cycle (Rossi, Note 1).

Even a brief perusal of studies such as these suggests that the United States may be what anthropologists call an "exotic" (i.e., highly unusual) culture with respect to the social patterning of at least certain aspects of the reproductive function. In some societies, for example, menarche is a time for community celebration (Amarasignham, Note 2; Shostak, Note 3), while in the United States it appears to be accorded little social recognition. (Able and Joffe, 1950, suggested, in fact, that an American girl's first date may be an event of greater social importance and psychological significance than her first menstrual period. See Sherman, 1971.) While menstrual taboos (patterns of behavior designed to isolate the menstruating female) are less obvious and less rigid in the United States now than in many other societies, some indication of the negative feelings surrounding the topic can be inferred from the number and variety of slang expressions used to refer (euphemistically) to menstruation (Ernster, Note 4; Joffe, 1948) and from the general tone of advertisements for tampons and for "feminine hygiene" products. Scattered data also suggest that a "taboo" against (or avoidance of) sexual intercourse during menstruation is still observed by many couples (Paige, 1973; Rossi, Note 1). These negative feelings and the avoidance of intercourse during menstruation are not, however, particularly distinctive of our culture.

At the other end of the reproductive life-span (menopause), there again do not seem to be any social behaviors patterned around the (much less clearly defined) biological event, either in the United States or, it would seem, in other societies. The social significance of a woman's growing older, however, varies greatly from culture to culture, and it is clear that a woman of menopausal age in the United States frequently undergoes role changes of a more negative and psychologically debilitating sort than do women in societies where age and experience are accorded greater respect. (Bart, 1970, 1971; Osofsky & Seidenbert, 1970).

It is perhaps in the area of social practices surrounding birth that the culturally "exotic" nature of the United States is most apparent, Newton and Newton (1972), and Mead and N. Newton (1967) have brought together a variety of cross-cultural data on childbirth practices, and while Newton and Newton are careful to note only that such data "widen . . . the perspective," it is clear from the observations and studies they present that many of the customary procedures surrounding birth in the United States are highly unusual and not necessarily in the best interests of the mother or the baby. More explicit critiques of birth practices in the United States have been offered by others, both from within and outside the obstetrical profession (e.g., Tylden, 1952; Atlee, 1963; Lomas, 1964; Fox, 1964; Shaw, 1972; Haire, 1972; Tennov, 1973; Tennov and Hirsch, 1973; Arms, 1975; Seiden, Note 5), and they merit careful consideration by those concerned with the physical and psychological well-being of parents and newborn infants.

One criticism that recurs throughout this literature, to take a single example, is the routine use of the horizontal position during delivery. In view of a variety of solid data supporting the advantages of an upright position for the woman giving birth (Mitre, 1974; Mengert & Murphy, 1933; Vaughn, 1937), it has been suggested that there seems to be an irrational element underlying "the strongly held cultural attitude that birth is an event experienced lying down" (Newton & Newton, 1972, p. 168). Not only lying down, it should be added, but in many cases strapped down, drugged, shaved, purged, and psychologically isolated to a degree virtually unknown in other parts of the world (Lomas, 1964; Tennov, 1973; Tennov & Hirsch, 1973). Some sense of how really unusual are the routine procedures that surround most hospital births in the United States can be acquired by comparing them with current birth practices in industrialized western-European countries such as England and France, and in the Soviet Union (see chapters by Hopkins & Clyne, Stallworthy, Vellay, and Velvorski in Howells, 1972).

In addition to their negative effects on the mother and child as individuals (Tennov, 1973), customary childbirth practices in the United States may be undergoing another kind of critical scrutiny as a result of studies by Klaus and his coworkers (Klaus, Jeraulk, Kreger, McAlpine, Stefta, & Kennell, 1972; Kennel, Note 6). In a controlled study, Klaus et al. (1972) found that early contact between mother and infant (earlier than is possible under usual hospital routines) was associated with mother-child interactions a month later which were significantly different from those of a control group of mothers who had had only the postpartum contact allowed under usual hospital procedures. A follow-up study suggested that differences between these two groups of mothers in their behavior toward their children were still present two years later (Kennell, Note 6).

Perhaps deliberately invoking connotations of the ethological concepts of "attachment" and "critical period," Klaus and associates suggested that there may be a critical "maternal attachment period" during which important bonds between mother-infant are established (see also Lang, in Tennov & Hirsch, 1973). Fathers were not included in Klaus' study, however, so it is not clear whether the authors demonstrated an exclusively "maternal" phenomenon or whether "parental attachment" in both sexes will occur if allowed to do so. The Greenberg and Morris (1975) description of "paternal engrossment" strongly suggests that it will. Socially organized practices surrounding childbirth in the United States may therefore have the unintended effect of interfering with this early bonding by separating parent and child at the critical interval in the immediate neonatal period.

Lomas (1964) offered one of the most coherent psychological analyses of why this culturally exotic set of childbirth practices might have arisen (see also Atlee, 1963; Barry, 1972, 1973), and why women—to some extent, voluntarily—allow them to be continued. Briefly, he argued that the psychologically damaging practices surrounding birth, although promoted as being for the physical health of the mother, are a reflection of men's hostility toward women and an envy of their procreative function. Lomas believes that women accede to these practices, whose source they accurately perceive, because they see it as a way of appeasing a group more powerful than they; in his terms, women offer themselves in contemporary childbirth as a "ritual sacrifice."

Several other authors have also suggested directly or indirectly that the social patterning of behavior surrounding birth reflects or affects in complex ways certain important aspects of the psychological relationship between women and men. In addition to Lomas' notion of males' envy of females as a motivating dynamic, other suggestions have included the need to assert or defend paternity rights (Paige & Paige, 1973) and a male "fear" of women (Lederer, 1968).

The social and political implications of Klaus' research findings have been the subject of some discussion (Rosen, 1972), with some people apparently feeling that the "attachment" data confirm the necessity of a social arrangement whereby the biological mother serves as the primary care-giver for infants and young children. One, perhaps extreme, view was expressed at a scientific meeting where portions of these data were presented; the author heard one participant urge that women who are "ambivalent" about being mothers should "not be allowed not to have" the extended contact with the infant in the early hours of its life in order to ensure the occurrence of "maternal attachment." Use of the double negative and the passive voice does not entirely obscure the essentially political nature of this judgment about the social application of scientific findings.

It seems equally clear that beliefs about the presumed psychological fluctuations of the menstrual cycle also serve a political purpose when they are used to justify a preferred patterning of social roles for females and males. The headline in the *New York Times* reading "Doctor asserts women unfit for top jobs" (because of the "raging hormonal influences" of the menstrual cycle) is only one example of the social meaning which women's reproductive capability has for some individuals (Berman, Note 7; see also Ramey, 1971). When used in this way—as a last bastion defense of the status quo with regard to political, legal, and economic inequalities between the sexes—the part played by females in reproducing the species takes on something of an aura of a rediscovered wheel. ("Men and women *are* biologically different, after all . . .")

Such rediscoveries are frequently accompanied by an inability or unwillingness to distinguish between the biological capacity to give birth and the social activities involved in child-rearing, and by a failure to recognize that males' biology also seems to be related to socially significant behavior, particularly aggressive behavior (Rose, Holady, & Bernstein, 1971; Rose, Gordon, & Berstein, 1972). Ramey (1973) offered a nice summary and dismissal of the biology-is-destiny argument when it is confined to this clearly political level of rationalizing and justifying the status quo in the executive suite, dean's office, or whatever.

While it is difficult if not impossible to disentangle the interactive effects of social, political, and biological factors, it seems clear that a woman's psychological experience of events in her reproductive life may be as much affected by the social meaning or patterning of the event as by the biological process. The social meaning of the event, furthermore, can perhaps be understood at least partly in terms of the relationship between women and men and their respective social roles, a relationship in which males are usually dominant (Thorne & Henley, 1975). Psychological studies of female reproductive processes that are concerned only with biological factors or with the individual in isolation from the social environment almost surely leave unexplored a set of variables important in understanding the psychological phenomena (Sherman, 1971: Rossi, Note 1). By failing to consider this broader context, investigators may limit themselves to "discovering" only those scientific facts which seem to support existing social institutions rather than facts which might prompt their reexamination. While this may seem politically desirable to some, it is certainly not good science.

PSYCHOLOGICAL CONCOMITANTS OF FEMALE REPRODUCTIVE PROCESSES

The Menstrual Cycle

Several authors have recently reviewed selected portions of the literature on psychological concomitants[1] of the menstrual cycle (Sommer, 1973; Parlee,

---

[1] "Psychological concomitants" here refers to psychological states and processes described, as nearly as possible, without reference to their causal mechanism(s). While the psychological phenomena are temporally associated with the menstrual cycle (and this temporal association is not presumed to be coincidental in some Leibnitzian sense), the extent to which the association is mediated by the specific cultural context is left entirely open.

1973; Koeski, Note 8; Redgrove, 1971; Sherman, 1971; Kane, Kipton, & Ewing, 1969). Until recently (and, perhaps, even now), the majority of investigators studying psychological aspects of menstruation would probably agree that "it is well known that many women have fluctuations of mood, symptoms, and behavior which occur in conjunction with the phases of the menstrual cycle" (Moos, Kopell, Melges, Yalom, Lunde, Clayton, & Hamburg, 1969, p. 37). Some scientists have been considerably more specific about the kinds of "neurotic and antisocial reactions" (Janowsky, Gorney, Castelnuovo-Tedesco, & Stone, 1969, p. 189) the menstrual cycle "imposes on" (Silbergeld, Brast, & Noble, 1971, p. 411) women. In a paper tastefully entitled "The curse; vicissitudes and variations of the female fertility cycle," Janowsky, Gorney, and Kelly (1966) listed "some" (32) of the negative changes ostensibly associated with menstruation. Abramson and Torghele (1961) noted that the menstrual cycle causes women to suffer "at least some inconvenience" and that "women's awareness of her inherent disabilities is thought to create added mental and in turn physical changes in the total body response and thus there result problems that concern the physician who must deal with them" (p. 223).

In considering this literature, it is important to bear in mind that there do exist socially shared beliefs, held by men as well as women, about the kinds of psychological fluctuations in mood and behavior that women experience throughout the cycle (Parlee, 1974). Both men and women believe that women are more irritable, anxious, depressed, tense, and the like during the premenstrual and menstrual phases of the cycle than at other times. These beliefs seem to be held as well by the scientific community, and have repeatedly been expressed as scientific conclusions, although a critical examination of primary sources suggests that supporting evidence for many of these conclusions is less substantial than is generally implied (Parlee, 1973; Sommer, 1973).

Given the existence of shared beliefs about the psychological concomitants of the menstrual cycle, there is an essential ambiguity involved in interpreting the results of any scientific investigation in which questionnaires or self-reports were used and where the subjects were directly asked about menstruation (e.g., Moos, 1968; Coppen & Kessel, 1963; Sutherland & Stewart, 1965). The method involved in such questionnaire studies is, after all, not greatly different from that generally used in social psychological studies of stereotypes or of impression formation: the subject is asked to endorse (or not) certain items as descriptive of a distinct social group. The fact that (in studies of the menstrual cycle) members of the group are asked to provide descriptions about their own group, or about themselves as individual members, does not affect the ambiguity surrounding the validity or scientific meaning of these data.

Part of Bruner and Perlmutter's (1975) study of impression formation, in fact, involved asking individuals to endorse adjectives as characteristic, or not, of someone of their own nationality about whom they had no other information. The subjects' activities in this experiment were characterized as "forming an impression of one's compatriot," not as factually describing the characteristics of that national group. Yet, when women are asked to endorse symptom and mood changes which "women experience" throughout the menstrual cycle, they give the same patterns of responses as do women who are asked to "report" those symptoms and mood changes which "you experience" (Parlee, 1974 or Moos, 1969). These "self-reports" have universally been interpreted as evidence that women do indeed have (experience) these changes. Without external validity data, there would seem on methodological grounds to be no clear way to decide whether a woman's responses on a questionnaire that asks about menstruation represent a fairly accurate report of her own experience or an impression she has formed (by unknown means) of what women experience.

"Self-report" data gathered using the Moos Menstrual Distress Questionnaire (Moos, 1968) tend to support the suggestion that such questionnaires may in fact be tapping stereotyped cultural beliefs or impressions about menstruation as well as (rather than?) biologically determined experiences of the individual. Testing a small sample of women in the United States, Silbergeld et al. (1971) reported that they were able to replicate almost exactly the factor structure which Moos originally derived for his 48-item questionnaire on the basis of responses from a much larger sample of women, also from the United States (Moos, 1969). Culberg (1972), however, reported being unable to replicate this factor structure in an analysis of Swedish women's responses on the Moos Menstrual Distress Questionnaire, and the author was unable to replicate Moos' factors with a sample of women in India (Parlee, Note 9).

While there may be many reasons for failing to replicate the factor structure of a questionnaire when it is administered to a different sample of subjects, a comparison of the Indian and United States sample responses on individual items of the questionnaire suggests that there may be some striking consistencies within the samples and differences between them of "reports" of "changes" in certain symptoms and moods. In a review of cross-cultural data on premenstrual tension symptoms, Janiger, Riffenberg, and Kersh (1972) proposed a similar summary observation: Women in different cultures report different clusters of "symptoms" as the nucleus of a "premenstrual tension syndrome." It remains to be seen whether cross-cultural investigations will reveal a core set of symptoms or moods universally reported to be associated with menstruation. If they do, psychologists would seem then to be faced with what Unger and Siiter (Note 10) have called, in another context, the "kernel of truth problem," that is, how to identify those parts of the stereotype which are accurate descriptions and give a functional account of culture-specific elaboration of the beliefs beyond this "kernel of truth."

Regardless of the ultimate significance of questionnaire data, there are a number of reasons why it is necessary to observe a distinction between beliefs and justified true beliefs, or between verbal statements and verbal statements whose validity can be established in other ways. For example, such a distinction may be important in interpreting data on the positive association found between the reported length of menstrual flow (in days) and "femininity" (Peskin, 1968), or "maternal behavior" (Levy, 1942). Is this sort of relationship, as Levy (1942), Peskin (1968), and Bardwick (1971, p. 28) all imply, a "psychosomatic" phenomenon, a causal relationship between psychological and biological states? Perhaps the duration of menstrual flow is somehow more significant for a stereotypically "feminine" woman (as concern with penis length might perhaps be for a stereotypically "masculine" man); her verbal reports might therefore tend to exaggerate the duration (or adopt different criteria for onset and cessation) of flow. Without more direct evidence as to the duration of menses, it is unclear whether what Peskin and Levy have discovered is a genuine "psychosomatic" phenomenon or an interesting fact about the psychological significance of "duration of menstrual flow" for different women.

While the use of questionnaires involves some fairly obvious problems relating to the external validation of self-report measures, certain other problems that seem to be less often considered in studies of the psychological concomitants of the menstrual cycle should also be noted.

1. Determination of the phase of the cycle (at the time the psychological measures are taken) is extremely difficult. Subject's memories as to the length of their cycles and the date of onset of the last menstrual period have been shown to be unreliable (Frazier, 1959; Matsumoto, Nogami, & Ohkuri, 1962). There is considerable intra- and interindividual variability in cycle length, in the degree and timing of hormone fluctuations, and in the occurrence of anovulatory cycles (Presser, 1974; Whalen, 1975). Taken

together, such data suggest that hormonal assays (or, at a minimum, basal body temperatures) would be necessary to identify precisely the time of ovulation for any given subject.

2. Interindividual variability seems to be marked in psychological as well as hormonal functioning, and the use of averaged data from groups of subjects tends to obscure this variability and result in the loss of potentially valuable scientific information. McCance, Luff, and Widdowson (1937) observed some time ago, for example, that group data and individual records throughout the cycle do not always show the same evidence of rhythmicity. And knowing that symptoms A,B,C, ... are reported by X,Y,Z, ... percent of women in the sample (Coppen & Kessel, 1963; Sutherland & Stewart, 1965; Abramson & Torghele, 1961) does not allow us to discover whether or not some subgroup of women report experiencing all or most of the symptoms while others report only one or two.

3. The domain of behaviors possibly influenced by the menstrual cycle is large, and includes those which carry positive as well as negative connotations. A focus by investigators upon a relatively restricted set of negative behaviors, coupled with the conventional practice in psychology of publishing only statistically significant "results," means that the full range of psychological concomitants of the menstrual cycle remains unexplored and that myths, once established in the literature, die hard.

Few studies, of course, can obviate all these potential problems within the design of a single experiment. But it would be useful if investigators would address them explicitly, and in doing so indicate the nature and extent of the limitations placed upon the generality of the findings by the procedures they use.

Leaving aside problematic data from questionnaires about menstruation, however, and disregarding the many studies of "premenstrual tension," which are difficult to interpret for other methodological reasons (Parlee, 1973), there does seem to be some evidence of fluctuations throughout the menstrual cycle in certain behaviors which seem unlikely to be affected by the existence of socially shared beliefs about menstruation. One category of such fluctuations comprises those that have been demonstrated in basic perceptual or sensorimotor processes. Several of these studies were culled from the literature on sensation and perception, and presented together in a paper by Baker (Note 11) in which they suggested that greater alertness by investigators to the possibility of sex differences in areas where none have traditionally been "expected" might lead to the documentation of many more. Because they were designed as studies in perception, however, with sex differences being a more or less incidental aspect of the results, several of the studies that Baker discussed, as well as some of the additional ones included here, have used relatively small numbers of subjects. It perhaps should be emphasized that such small sample sizes are usual in research on sensory processes (Weintraub, 1975) compared with the larger sample sizes customary in other kinds of research.

According to Baker (Note 11), there are at least three examples of sensory processes that seem to vary in women with the phase of the menstrual cycle: optimal frequency for hearing binaural beats (Tobias, 1972), difference thresholds for perception of cold stimuli (Kenshalo, 1970), and certain kinds of olfactory sensitivity (Elsberg, Brewer, & Levy; 1935). Other perceptual and sensorimotor processes that seem to show similar fluctuations are: reproduction of a particular frequency by someone with perfect pitch (Wynn, 1971); sample reaction time in well-practiced subjects (Wynn, 1973); critical fusion frequency (Kopell, Lunde, Clayton, & Moos, 1969; DiMarchi and Tong, 1972); taste sensitivity (Kaplan, 1968), kinesthetic aftereffect (A.H. Baker, Mishara, Parket, & Kostin, Note 12), and arm-hand steadiness (Zimmerman & Parlee, 1973).

While the causal mechanisms underlying such variations are entirely unknown, one interesting general question about them has been raised by DiMarchi and Tong (1972). Noting that there is a difference between sensory sensitivity and "thresholds" as determined by classical psychophysical procedures (Egan & Clarke, 1966), they use a signal-detection analysis to determine whether it is sensory *sensitivity* that changes throughout the cycle or whether it is fluctuation in placement of the criterion for indicating presence or absence of the stimulus. The results of their study of variations in critical fusion frequency suggested that it is the criterion placement which changes rather than sensory sensitivity.[2] This does not, of course, affect the general point that *some* behavioral change seems

---

[2]Interestingly, DiMarchi and Tong (1972) provided in passing an example of how stereotyped beliefs about menstruation may affect even explanations of fluctuations in *criterion placement*. They noted that criterion placement on the CFF task becomes more "cautious" during the premenstrual phase of the cycle, and they suggested that this represents a strategy adopted by the women to counteract (or compensate for) the "difficulty in concentrating" which, DiMarchi and Tong claimed, women experience during this phase. (They cite only Moos' questionnaire data as evidence for such difficulties in concentrating.) But if concentration difficulties are not, in fact, among the behavioral changes demonstrable in the premenstrual phase of the cycle, DiMarchi and Tong's data on criterion placement might more parsimoniously be interpreted as showing that women exhibit *greater* concentration—as demonstrated by more stringent criterion placement during this phase.

to occur throughout the menstrual cycle which is unlikely to be affected by beliefs or expectations, but it does influence the kinds of causal mechanisms that might be considered by investigators interested in these perceptual processes.

The suggestion that *something* (some psychological state or process reliably measured) seems to change throughout the menstrual cycle is perhaps further supported by studies using the Gottschalk-Gleser technique for content analysis of verbal material (Ivey & Bardwick, 1968; Paige, 1971). Results obtained by using this procedure suggest that negative affect (anxiety and hostility) is higher during the premenstrual and menstrual phases than during the middle portion of the cycle. Since the Gottschalk-Gleser technique involves scoring 5-minute samples of speech gathered in an unstructured setting (Gottschalk & Gleser, 1969), it seems likely that here, too, the results are not influenced by subjects' beliefs about menstruation (Paige, 1971). It is important to note, however, that none of the studies using the Gottschalk-Gleser technique has reported affective fluctuations over time in *individuals,* but rather all have reported differences in the *average* affect scores of *groups* of subjects in (presumptively) the ovulatory and premenstrual phases of the cycle.

Three points can be made about the studies in which changes throughout the menstrual cycle have been demonstrated in behaviors that seem unlikely to be affected by beliefs and expectations about menstruation. One is to repeat the caveat that there is a distinction between statistical significance and psychological significance. A fluctuation or difference from one time to another in a particular psychological process or state may be statistically significant, while at the same time it may be true that the conditions required to demonstrate these fluctuations are so artificially restricted that the experiment has little ecological validity (Brunswick, 1947). A phenomenon may, in other words, be demonstrable in a perception experiment that is either so dependent upon the particular stimulus and conditions or so readily overridden under more "normal" viewing conditions that it has no effects (or existence?) outside the laboratory. Given the rather consistent record of failures to demonstrate intellectual or performance changes throughout the menstrual cycle (see review by Sommer, 1973), it seems reasonable to conclude that small variations in binaural beats, temperature thresholds, and the like have little effect upon psychological activities at more complex levels of analysis.

A second point about behavioral fluctuations throughout the menstrual cycle is that they are not the only type of cyclic changes in behavior to have been demonstrated. Circadian (24-hour) rhythms in human beings, for example, have heen found in a variety of behaviors (Colquhoun, 1971), as have cycles with both longer (Richter, 1968) and shorter (Sanford, 1971) periods. As data accumulate, it seems increasingly likely that rhythmicity may in fact be the norm in biological and psychological phenomena (Halberg, 1969; Luce, 1970). If this is the case, it would seem to be a misleading treatment of a general fact if we were to focus upon 28-day rhythms in adult females without locating them in the context of cyclic phenomena of other sorts.

One study that did attempt to assess the relative magnitude of circadian and menstrual cycle effects (on critical fusion frequency) was that of DiMarchi and Tong (1972), mentioned above. These authors concluded from regression analyses of their data that the menstrual cycle contributed more to the variance of the threshold scores than did the time of day (morning or evening) at which the subjects were tested. (They did not report the results of regression analysis on the criterion placement scores, although both menstrual and diurnal factors had a significant effect.) Their procedure, however, did not allow for an adequate test of the hypothesis expressed in their conclusion. It is well established that subjects are bimodally distributed with regard to whether they reach their peak efficiency in the morning or evening (e.g., Blake, 1971). By using group data in their analysis, DiMarchi and Tong might have allowed the two types of subjects to, in effect, cancel out each other's contributions to the diurnal variability of the data. For each individual subject, the circadian rhythm in performance could have been larger than the menstrual rhythm, but given that subjects may differ in the direction of the circadian effects, the likelihood of finding circadian rhythms more powerful than menstrual rhythms is greatly reduced by using group data. A comparison of variations in reaction time over the menstrual cycle (Wynn, 1973) and over a 24-hour period (Blake, 1971) suggests that the circadian variability may be greater, but these studies can be regarded only as suggestive because they are not comparable in several possibly important respects.

A third point, which needs to be repeated regarding investigations of behavioral fluctuations throughout the menstrual cycle, is that such studies almost without exception have lacked control groups of non-menstruating individuals (Maccoby, 1972; Parlee, 1973). Strictly speaking, if an experiment uses only male or only female subjects, it is not clear whether the results can be generalized to one or both sexes. Richter (1968, 1965) summarized a number of studies which he believed support the existence of monthly or near-monthly cycles, independent of the menstrual cycle, in various biological and behavioral processes. Hersey (1931), using a combination of daily observation and self-report measures, found cycles in adult men of anywhere from 3½ to 9 weeks. Wynn (1973) found cycles, with a period of approximately 20 days, in simple reaction time in a single male subject. Recently, Doering and his colleagues reported finding cyclic variations in plasma testosterone levels in 12 of the 20 subjects they studied; the cycles had an average period of between 20 and 22 days (Doering, Brodie, Kraemer, Becker, & Hamburg, 1974; Doering, Kraemer, Brodie, & Hamburg, 1975). The authors believe they also found cycles, correlated with the testosterone levels, in the subjects' "self-perceived depression" as measured by a multiple affect adjective checklist. Whatever the mechanisms underlying such cycles, it is becoming increasingly clearer that infradian rhythms in female's behavior cannot be attributed to the menstrual cycle without some additional information about the performance of control groups.

None of these three points about behavioral fluctuations throughout the menstrual cycle is intended to "explain away" those that have been demonstrated. They are intended rather to suggest some contexts within which the fluctuations need to be interpreted. Embedded as they sometimes are in rationalizations and justifications of an existing social order, beliefs and expectations about the psychological concomitants of the menstrual cycle seem to have led scientists—members of the society—to emphasize those aspects of their data which support their beliefs, and to ignore or fail to develop a theoretical perspective that might be compatible with other beliefs. A broader theoretical perspective, one that attempts to relate and interrelate the effects of rhythms of many sorts, is more likely to provide a complete and accurate scientific description of the behavior and experience of human beings. Furthermore the "raging hormonal influences" of the menstrual cycle might seem to have less social significance if they were to be considered in the context of the "raging influences" of both circadian and infradian cycles in a variety of biological and psychological processes.[3]

---

[3]It may be the case, however, that feminists and others concerned with the civil rights of groups defined, in effect, as "non-White" and "nonmale" fall into a pernicious trap when they use *scientific* arguments against the supposedly scientific reasons offered as implicit or explicit justification of sexual and racial inequities (e.g., Berman, 1970; Shockley, 1972). On what unspoken grounds would probabilistic statements about groups, which is all any science can hope to provide, justify prejudicial treatment of an individual (i.e., treatment involving prejudgment of the person) without determining the descriptive accuracy of the scientific generalization for the individual case? An implicit "science uber alles" pervades many, if not most, of the scientific/political discussions of race differences in IQ and sex differences in almost anything. (Some have argued, of course, that such discussions are

PREGNANCY, BIRTH, AND THE POSTPARTUM PERIOD

In considering the literature on psychological concomitants of pregnancy, birth, and the postpartum period, a psychologist may be impressed with how little good research is available on these topics, even when compared with the amount and kind of work that has been done on menstruation. This paucity of systematic research may be due in part to the fact that those scientists and practitioners who publish their work in medical journals (and very little is published elsewhere) seem to have noticed only relatively recently that pregnancy and birth have important psychological as well as physical aspects (Boyd, 1942; Cohen, 1943). While such belated recognition may be partly understandable in view of the recency with which most of the physical dangers of childbirth have been brought under control (Cianfrani, 1960), these exhortations from one obstetrician to another to notice the psychological side of pregnancy and birth (Atlee, 1963), is a recent example) have for the most part a strangely innocent ring about them. Whatever the reasons, it is obvious that research on psychological concomitants of pregnancy and birth suffers from a lack of conceptual and methodological rigor which has prevented the development of a scientific understanding of these processes. With the exception of psychoanalytic psychologists, whose work does not usually lack a guiding conceptual framework, much of the psychological research on pregnancy and birth represents the sort of blind empiricism (collection of data without apparent theoretical motivation) that psychology as a whole has largely outgrown.

Since it is somewhat artificial to distinguish pregnancy from birth from the postpartum period—and research investigators rarely focus upon only one aspect of what is in many ways a unitary process—the following discussion will attempt to identify fairly general assumptions implicit in existing research on these topics, and will consider them in light of examples from whatever "problem area(s)" seem most appropriate. General substantive reviews (some with and some conspicuously lacking critiques of specific studies and methods) of portions of the research literature on psychological aspects of pregnancy, birth, and

---

"purely scientific," but there are a good many historical (Kuhn, 1962; Friedrichs, 1970) and psychological (Sherwood and Nataupsky, 1968) reasons to think this is not so.) Feyerabend's suggestion that there ought to be an officially recognized separation between science and the state (analogous to the separation of church and state) arises from other kinds of considerations (Feyerabend, Note 17), but the questions tey raises have some relevance to the relationship between the scientific study of the "psychology of women" and the politically remedial legal, social, and economic discrimination on the basis of sex.

the postpartum period can be found in Shields (Note 13); Kaij and Nilsson (1972); Karacan and Williams (1970); McDonald (1968); Yalom, Lunde, Moos, and Hamburg (1968); Grimm (1967); Jansson (1963); Robin (1962); Thomas and Gordon (1959); White, Prout, Fixen, and Foundeur (1957); Foundeur, Fixen, Triebel and White (1957); and Tetlow (1955). The chapters on pregnancy and motherhood in Sherman (1971) provide an excellent evaluative introduction to research on these topics. Detailed reviews of psychological research on more limited aspects of pregnancy and birth—including cravings during pregnancy, spontaneous abortions, and breast feeding—can be found in volumes edited by Howells (1972) and Morris (1972).

Research Based Upon A "Medical Model"

It seems accurate to say that most of the research discussed in these reviews, as well as that presented in other individual studies, is based upon what might be called a "medical model" of pregnancy and birth. That is, pregnancy and birth have been regarded as a period of increased physical and psychological vulnerability that in some women or under certain stresses can result in severe emotional problems, "psychogenic" physical complications, or even psychotic breakdowns. The opening paragraph of a relatively recent review of the literature on "postpartum syndromes" conveys something of the tenor of this approach.

> From the time of Eve, the experience of childbirth has represented the fulfillment of the gift of womanhood. It is said to be (note the characteristically adroit use of the passive voice) the moment to which all women look forward, sharing the eagerness and anticipation of Sarah, the wife of Abraham. Throughout most of history, the promise of childbearing has also held, paradoxically, a threat of great peril to both mother and child. Modern medicine has eliminated most of this danger, by providing excellent obstetric care and removing most of the risk of infant mortality. Unfortunately, however, the psychoses and less severe emotional problems which characteristically follow the moment of birth continue to bring discomfort to most new mothers and disability to many. (Karacan and Williams, 1970, p. 307.)

Within the medical model there are two views concerning the sort of causal mechanism primarily responsible for the psychological aspects of pregnancy, birth, and the postpartum period. One is that the physiological changes involved in the reproductive process cause, in some complex but fairly direct sense, the psychological changes. The other is that the psychological changes are primarily the result of the intrapsychic processes of the individual as she responds to the biological stages of pregnancy, birth, and the postpartum period. (Tetlow, 1955, and Jansson, 1963, make a somewhat similar distinction.) Very roughly, the difference suggested here is between the view that the psychological states reflect (are closely correlated with) the biological states and the view that the psychological states result from reflection upon (at some level of psychic organization) the biological facts of pregnancy and birth and the personal-interpersonal implications of these facts. While this distinction between different sorts of causal mechanisms is not at this point sufficiently clear to be defended on theoretical grounds, it is at least a commonsense notion which has been used—and seems to be useful—as a way of talking about mechanisms in other areas besides pregnancy and birth (e.g., mental illness, Siegler & Osmund, 1966; menopause, Neugarten, 1967).

Biological theories as to the origin of psychological events in pregnancy, birth, and the postpartum period. Unlike the literature on psychological concomitants of the menstrual cycle, investigators concerned with the psychological aspects of pregnancy and birth are less likely to attribute them to biological causes than to the personal history and personality structure of the individual woman. This may be why (with the exception of some psychoanalytic theorists), one less frequently finds generalizations about what "women" experience in the psychological literature on pregnancy and birth than in the literature on the menstrual cycle. This disparity appears on the face of it somewhat difficult to understand, since the hormonal changes that occur during pregnancy are much greater than those of the menstrual cycle.

There is some agreement among obstetrics texts, however, that mild nausea and vomiting of early pregnancy, and mild, transient "blues" in the first postpartum week may be due to the rapidly changing hormone levels during these periods. The hormonal etiology of these psychological phenomena, in fact, apparently is so taken for granted by many that it is alluded to in passing without reference to good psycho-endocrine studies that would provide support for the hypothesis of physiological causation of clearly defined psychological phenomena. Trethowan and Dickens (1972) cited studies showing changes in the taste thresholds of pregnant women, and suggested that such alterations may play a role in the unusual food cravings or aversions that some women exhibit during pregnancy. They were careful to note, however, that food cravings do not seem to be related to the presence or absence of nausea or vomiting. There is a report in Morris (1972) that mild and transient "blues" are most often found on the fifth postpartum day (in women who breast feed), and it was suggested that the rather fixed timing of onset is a reflection of hormonal changes occurring in a regular sequence after parturition.

Hamilton (1962) believes that acute postpartum psychoses also manifest themselves at a fixed interval after birth and that this is evidence that they, too, are of biological origin. His suggestion that there is a relatively constant interval between parturition and onset of psychosis, however, lacks decisive empirical support (Thomas & Gordon, 1959), and Kaij & Nilsson (1972) noted that Hamilton's experimental study purporting to show that physiological factors underlie postpartum psychoses lacks the control group necessary to interpret the results as he did. Dalton (1971) and Kear-Colwell (1965) also proposed a biological explanation for psychological reactions in the postpartum period, but neither did their data adequately rule out alternative interpretations. It may be, of course, that improvements in obstetrical techniques and the consequent lower rates of infection have in fact reduced the incidence of what were in the past organically based (e.g., septic infections) postpartum psychoses.

These studies of pregnancy and of postpartum depression in which hormonal etiologies were proposed, however, represent a minority viewpoint in the literature on psychological aspects of pregnancy and birth. Lennane and Lennane (1973) briefly reviewed some of the evidence on nausea and vomiting in early pregnancy (and on pain in labor and delivery as well), and concluded that medical investigators have in fact been especially prone to offer or accept an intrapsychic interpretation of these ("psychogenic") phenomena, even when the weight of available scientific evidence suggests that biological causes are more likely. It is certainly true that exclusively "psychogenic" explanations have frequently been offered for psychological and physical phenomena for which a purely physical cause is easily imaginable (e.g., infertility, pain in labor, insomnia in the last trimester, increased activity of salivary glands during pregnancy). But it is also true that a number of investigators and practitioners have assumed or implied the primacy of hormonal determinants. Good scientific data are simply not available to support a simple version of either point of view.

Intrapsychic explanations of the psychological aspects of pregnancy and birth. Many writers have asserted that particular kinds of psychological changes occur in connection with pregnancy, birth, and the postpartum period, and such assertions frequently imply that the changes are (in some unclear sense) a response to (though not directly caused by) the biological processes of pregnancy, birth, and lactation. (The biological event of giving birth to a child, for example, might serve to reawaken a woman's conflicts with her own mother and thus lead to depression.) This kind of thinking is based implicitly or explicitly upon the assumption that the psychological changes are to be understood primarily in terms of the personality dynamics of the individual woman or, occasionally, of Woman.

Many of the pronouncements about psychological aspects of pregnancy and birth are to be found in obstetrics textbooks (e.g., Gardiner, 1966; Asch, 1965; Kanner, 1961). Since they would usually not be regarded by scientists as something other than the textbook author's opinion, they will not be considered here, although their importance in shaping the attitudes and expectations of those who read them should not be underestimated (see Scully and Bart, 1973, for an analysis of the contents of obstetrics and gynecology texts). The general tone, however, may be conveyed by the following excerpt from Leo Kanner's chapter on "psychiatric aspects of pregnancy and childbirth" in the twelfth edition of *Williams' Obstetrics* (Eastman & Hellman, 1961): "For nearly 12 months the obstetrician takes over the guidance of an adult woman, supervises her food intake, regulates her activities, answers her questions, clarifies her puzzlements, advises her about the handling of her baby when it comes, and generally charts her conduct during the 24 hours of the day" (Kanner, 1961, p. 354).

Statements about psychological aspects of pregnancy and birth which are formulated within a psychoanalytic framework, however, appear more often in the research literature than they do in textbook accounts, and they will therefore be considered here. Heiman (1965) represented a rather typical summary of psychoanalytic descriptions of pregnancy (he included references to the classic psychoanalytic work of Deutsch (1944), Benedek (1959), and Bibring (1959), but did not explicitly discuss their contributions to the point of view he expresses).

Briefly, Heiman suggested that "pregnancy represents one of the crucial periods in the life of the woman, a phase which makes her a different person," and that "it (pregnancy) is essentially a phase of both maturation and regression." Although he did not discuss maturation in any detail (or, rather, not at all), many hypotheses were offered concerning the nature and purpose of regression in pregnancy (1965, pp. 480-482). Terming it "regression in the service of reproduction," Heiman suggested that regression allows the pregnant woman to identify with the child in the uterus and to recapitulate with its development her own psychological ontogeny. Because of her regressed state, the pregnant woman is able to respond "as a child" to the therapeutic efforts of her obstetrician or whoever is attempting to deal with the conflicts uncovered as she returns to "earlier stages of her libidinal life." Heiman believes that the concept of regression, which explains why "pregnancy has aptly been called a 'normal illness' " (p. 480), can account for a variety of pregnancy signs and symptoms, including increased activity of the salivary glands, vomiting, and concern about eating. He believes that phenomena such as ambivalence, dependency, orality, phobias, attitudes about sex, and anxiety about childbirth can all be understood as psychological concomitants of pregnancy-related regression.

Heiman's description of pregnancy, and that of others working within a psychoanalytic framework, is presumably based upon his clinical experience and impressions, and the narrative contains numerous examples of case histories that illustrate a point he wishes to make. While an experienced psychoanalyst's observations often seem to capture in some way subtle and important psychological phenomena (e.g., Notman, 1973), they are rarely described in terms that would allow these observations to be replicated or reinterpreted by scientists working within a different conceptual framework. (Kargmen, 1957, briefly discussed and illustrated this problem with examples from research on a different topic.) Even when working within a psychoanalytic framework, an investigator's attempts to clarify a particular finding through usual scientific procedures may have unexpected consequences. Sylvia Marhkan (1961), for example, studied a group of women who had not had postpartum psychotic reactions as a control group for her previous study of women who had had such reactions. She found evidence of depression, oral dependency, hostility to a mother figure, castration feelings, and unresolved masculine strivings in the record of almost every woman in the control group, thus forcing revision of her previous theory that these were the dynamic forces producing postpartum psychoses.

As Marhkan's work suggests, psychoanalytic formations of postpartum depression, like those of pregnancy and birth, also imply that the psychodynamics of the individual woman is the most important determinant of the way she responds to the reproductive process (Zilboorg, 1928, 1931, 1957; Train, 1965). And here, too, the woman's behavior and experience has been described in terms that leave little doubt as to the value judgments the psychoanalyst places upon them.

Not all investigators seeking to explain psychological aspects of pregnancy and birth in intrapsychic terms work, of course, within a psychoanalytic framework. Indeed, it is this nonanalytic and (perhaps) more replicable research that forms the basis for the substantive and critical reviews by Tetlow (1955), Jansson (1963), Grimm (1967), and Kaij and Nilsson (1972). The studies by Shereshefsky and Yarrow (1973); Nilsson (1970); Pitt (1968); Nilsson, Kaij, and Jacobson (1967); Tod (1964); Jansson (1963); Ryle (1961); and Newton (1955) all present fairly large amounts of data collected under presumably reliable conditions. And yet, even this work seems to have produced surprisingly few systematic results. Differences in definition of the psychological phenomena being studied, lack of control groups, inappropriate or nonexistent statistical analyses, inadequate description of subject population and selection procedures, all can be found in a literature that is so lacking in unity of conceptual focus or comparability of measures that even simple empirical generalizations rarely emerge.

The literature on the postpartum period, for example, would be greatly improved by the simple step of adopting and using consistently a set of terms to describe the psychological phenomena being studied. Although the authors have not always used these labels, existing studies can generally be classified as focusing upon one of the following kinds of phenomena:

1. Postpartum "blues," a relatively common, mild, transient experience of "weepiness" that seems inexplicable to the woman (Yalom et al., 1968; Melges, 1968; Hamilton, 1962, chap. 10).
2. Acute psychosis, distinguishable from "ordinary" psychoses only in that it is temporally associated with childbirth (e.g., Paffenbarger, 1964; Pugh, Jerath, Schmidt, & Reed, 1963; Protheroe, 1969).
3. Symptoms of clinical depression or disturbance in the postpartum period. Estimates of frequency and severity, and judgments about etiology, vary; depression seems to be an important feature (Pitt, 1968; Tod, 1964; Ryle, 1961).

In the following discussion, postpartum "-blues," "-psychosis," and "-depression" will be used in accordance with these distinctions.

The lack of agreement about what on the surface are relatively simple matters of empirical fact—a lack that characterizes much of the scientific literature on psychological aspects of pregnancy, birth, and the postpartum period—suggests that a superficial analysis of the phenomena may be inadequate for scientific purposes. In spite of much research on the question, for example, there is little agreement as to whether postpartum psychosis is more frequent with first than with subsequent births (Protheroe, 1969; Paffenbarger, 1964; Jansson, 1963; Pugh et al., 1963; Thomas & Gordon, 1959). But why, after all, should "parity" be an important variable? Kaij and Nilsson (1972) noted that age is correlated with parity and that this "partly explains the conflicting data on this point (whether or not postpartum psychosis is more frequently associated with first births). On the whole (they noted) it seems as if higher age implies a slightly increased risk" (p. 367). Parceling out the effects of age may perhaps account for the conflicting data on the association between "parity" and postpartum psychosis, but age by itself certainly does not seem to be the sort of variable that would be helpful in *explaining* the occurrence or nonoccurrence of the psychoses. Knowing that "higher ages imply a slightly greater risk" (of postpartum psychosis) would simply seem to leave one with the scientific question of why this should be so.

In pursuing the question further, it is reasonable to think that "age" as a variable might drop out of an explanation of why some women have psychotic breakdowns in the postpartum period and others do not. "Age" might, for example, turn out to be imperfectly correlated with certain other psychological or social phenomena of considerable causal importance (e.g., psychological maturity or rigidity, or relatively longstanding performance in a particular set of social roles). Here, apparently, as in other areas of psychology, the selection of variables for study depends upon a more or less well-developed conceptualization of the problem, and research on "postpartum depression" (and on pregnancy and birth as well) would benefit from more explicit attention to the kinds of questions that can legitimately be asked and answered with the variables and measures being employed.

A review of what might be considered the scientific literature on these topics suggests that conceptualization of the psychological problems, including formulation of questions and selection of methods and variables, has been derived in a number of ways, from:

1. Fairly explicit theoretical considerations (Levy & McGee, 1975; Doering & Entwisle, Note 14).

2. Vague hunches based on relatively unstructured (by scientists) accounts of personal experience (e.g., Rubin, 1967).

3. Unexamined acceptance of socially shared beliefs about what constitutes normative behavior (e.g., LeMasters, 1957).

4. Reliance upon such research traditions as exist either in a particular problem area or in an individual investigator's training and scientific habits.

Theoretical considerations, perhaps especially when they are compatible with firsthand accounts of experience (1 and 2 above), apparently offer more desirable criteria for selecting measures to be used in a study than does selecting measures because they are available, convenient, and/or the investigator has used them before. It is accurate to say, however, that the bulk of existing research on pregnancy, birth, and the postpartum period has been formulated in ways suggested in (3) and (4) above.

It is assumed here that more "rigorous" measurement will not solve the problems inherent in flabby conceptualization of the research. Questionnaires and the like can just as efficiently "filter out" potentially significant aspects of a "subject's" experience as can the psychoanalyst's theoretical predisposition to use a relatively limited number of rather elastic concepts. Both the questionnaire and the psychoanalytic framework highlight certain aspects of the experience while ignoring others. Although an investigator can certainly study a phenomenon tey has not experienced, it may be a good research strategy to listen closely, at least at first, to those who have. Perhaps it is true that scientists' failure to select variables that reveal empirical generalizations or to predict acute psychological phenomena in pregnancy, birth, and the postpartum period is due in part to their failure to attend seriously to relatively unstructured firsthand accounts of the experience. Suggesting that investigators might pay attention to what people say about their experiences does not deny the importance of unconscious forces and/or tacit knowledge as determinants of behavior.

Whether scientists have implicitly regarded hormones or intrapsychic conflicts as of primary importance in determining the psychological aspects of pregnancy and birth, one general (implicit) assumption underlying most research based upon the "medical model" is that the potential for acute psychological problems is everpresent and that clinical intervention in such cases can be useful. Much of the research in this tradition, and especially in the literature on postpartum phenomena, has been therefore directed toward discovering those characteristics of the individual woman which will identify her as being one of the population "at risk" with regard to particular psychological problems (e.g., Thomas & Gorgon, 1959). Perhaps because of some of the conceptual and methodological problems referred to above, this effort has not been outstandingly successful.

Noting that "interviews with obstetricians and with psychiatrists dealing with mothers in the childbearing years (having) provided no basis for correlation between the stresses or factors seen in pregnancy and postpartum emotional disturbances." Virginia Larsen (1966) addressed the problem of prediction in what is unfortunately an unusual way. She "therefore ... decided to ask new mothers what they considered to be stresses during pregnancy and after delivery" (p. 32). Although her data, too, failed to provide pre-partum predictors of postpartum distress, her procedure disclosed certain subjectively stressful experiences associated with pregnancy and birth that had not been identified or explored in earlier studies. A large percentage of the stresses women remembered experiencing during labor, delivery, and the hospital stay, for example, arose from hospital routines and physician attitudes, neither of which have received much attention from previous investigators (with the exception of Tylden, 1952; Lomas, 1964; and, indirectly, Newton & Newton, 1972). Darmstadter, Lucatorto, Lupton, and Winnick (1974) provided vivid and moving personal accounts of their experiences of postpartum depression, and suggested—as do the authors of *Our Bodies, Ourselves* (Boston Women's Health Book Collective, 1973)—that psychological studies of the postpartum period have used categories of analysis (conceptualization of the phenomena) so foreign to what is experienced that they are completely irrelevant.

Research Based Upon A "Developmental Model"

In addition to the find-out-who-is-potentially-ill-and-offer-treatment point of view, based on the medical model, another and less coherent clinical research perspective can be identified in the literature. This is based on what might be called a "developmental" view of pregnancy and birth. Starting perhaps with Helene Deutsch (1944), and elaborated by such investigators as Caplan (1975), Bibring, Dwyer, Huntington, and Valenstein (1961), and Benedek (1959), this view regards pregnancy and birth as important stages in the psychological development of every woman. Becoming a parent represents a point of transition in the life cycle, a transition in which, as psychoanalyst Bibring described it, the individual is confronted with new libidinal and adaptive tasks and with the revival of psychological conflicts from earlier developmental periods. This characterization seems to capture some of the psychological features of a sociological definition of an abrupt transition or "crisis" as "any sharp or decisive change (in life situation) for which old patterns are inadequate" (Hill, 1949, p. 51), and it is related, of course, to Benedict's earlier notions of continuities and discontinuities in cultural conditioning (Benedict, 1939). Neugarten (1969) developed these notions in a more comprehensive fashion.

Until recently, it seems that psychoanalytic psychologists and sociologists have directed the most serious attention to the developmental changes that occur as an individual becomes a parent. (Rossi, 1968, reviewed and extended some of the sociological work on the transition to parenthood; Bibring, 1959, Bibring et al., 1961, and Benedek, 1959, represented a psychoanalytic psychological approach.) Psychologists, even developmental psychologists, and medical investigators working within different theoretical perspectives have not in general focused on these changes as a topic of research (Hamburg and Adams, 1967, represent somewhat òf an exception). Most psychological accounts of the postpartum period as a time of development ánd change are therefore formulated in terms of psychoanalytic constructs and processes.

Bibring and colleagues believe that under unfavorable conditions, the tasks and conflicts involved in the transition to parenthood are not successfully resolved but rather lead to neurotic or even psychotic solutions. This belief underlies their designation of pregnancy as a period of "normal crisis," which, in neurotic women, raises psychic problems too overwhelming for the individual to resolve. So, while Bibring et al. (1961) regarded pregnancy and birth from a developmental perspective, apparently they retained an element of the medical model, that is, that the therapeutic goal is still to identify and treat individuals who, primarily because of their psychodynamic makeup, may be unable to cope with the conflicts aroused in the process of becoming a mother.

Caplan's view of pregnancy and birth as a developmental phase appears at first to be only slightly different (Caplan, 1957). Tey interprets the same phenomena that Bibring et al. report (the appearance during pregnancy of a good deal of fantasy material that normally remains suppressed) as a manifestation of relaxed defenses that characterize normal pregnancy. (Bibring's interpretation would be that it is the activation of the particular conflicts unresolved in the individual which causes the loosening of defenses.) Caplan's conceptualization of the psychological phenomena of pregnancy and birth, however, seems to be associated with a set of assumptions, which in effect rejects the diagnose-and-treat-orientation of the medical model. The implication of some of ter work is that "crisis intervention" techniques should be accompanied by the establishment of a supportive and nurturing relationship that will foster the individual's – every individual's—growth as tey masters the developmental tasks posed by a major transition in the life situation.

In some cases, of course, the individual may not have the personal skills or external resources to manage the developmental tasks successfully, and neurotic or psychotic problems may result. But for the majority of women the transition to motherhood may be a phase of significant psychological growth, and this positive aspect can more easily be recognized and facilitated by stepping outside the assumptions of the medical model. The difference in clinical perspective between "support" or "intervention" as a primary aim is very great, although it is no doubt true that in actual practice there is overlap between a medical/intervention approach and a developmental/supportive one.[4]

As a research strategy, what is here rather loosely called a "developmental" approach focuses upon normal or usual patterns of psychological change. Psychotic breakdowns or severe emotional illnesses would be regarded as one possible outcome, a maladaptive variation on the usual patterns. The many positive developmental outcomes of the transition to parenthood, heretofore neglected, would receive considerably more attention. In contrast, research based on the medical model has focused on the unusual outcome at a particular point in time and has sought to identify relatively stable features of the individual's personality that may be associated with the occurrence of severe postpartum depression. Such a strategy emphasizes the static and abnormal, and leaves relatively unexamined the developmental changes that occur in normal individuals. Since these normal developmental changes seem frequently to be associated with mild or moderate depression in the postpartum period in a relatively high proportion of women (Gordon & Gordon, 1959), they are perhaps of clinical as well as theoretical significance.

The "developmental model" as a framework for research on psychological phenomena of the postpartum period.   One persistent theme that runs through existing research on postpartum psychological reactions is that of the mother's

---

[4]Atlee (1963) noted that obstetricians' views on how to manage the physical aspects of pregnancy and birth can similarly be divided according to whether it is seen as a pathological process requiring intervention or as a physiological process that can best be facilitated by patience and support. For a variety of reasons, Atlee suggested, maternity care in contemporary industrialized societies is centered around the concept of birth as an "illness." Mead and Newton (1967) noted that a related dimension seems to emerge from a cross-cultural study of birth practices, with societies differing from what might be described as an attitude of "the faster the better" to one of "let nature take its course." The definition of an obstetrician as "one who sits and waits," Tylden (1952) observed, has largely lost its meaning in contemporary maternity care in the United States and Great Britain, and the management of the physical aspects of normal labor and delivery are focused on intervention rather than on facilitation of a natural process.

fear that some harm will come to the child (Kaij and Nilsson, 1972). Psycho-analysts have generally interpreted this fear as an expression of the mother's unconscious hostility toward the child, and indeed there are sometimes reports of direct expression of hatred of the child. Toward the end of a career largely devoted to the study of postpartum psychosis, Zilborg (cited in Boesky, Cross, & Morley, 1966) apparently believed this hostility might be the single most impor-tant factor in prediction of such psychoses. A milder form of anger, or perhaps ambivalence, might also underlie the fairly frequent reports of normal mothers who feel guilty at not being "better mothers" (LeMasters, 1957) or who seem to express "conflict over mothering" (Melges, 1968).[5] Anger or ambivalence toward the child is usually explained in psychodynamic terms as the result of the mother's psychic history (her relationship with her own mother is often seen as crucial) and of her inadequate "feminine identification" as these affect her relationship to her infant. (A sociological explanation of the same phenome-non—ambivalence toward the child—provides an interesting comparison with a psychoanalytic account; see Green, 1946.)

One early psychological investigator, however, has suggested that expressions (disguised or not) of anger or ambivalence toward the child may not be directed toward the child per se, but toward the child as the nearest social object (Levy-Valensi, 1963/1972). Consistent with this suggestion is the observation of other investigators that anger apparently directed toward the child is frequently asso-ciated with resentment of the husband as well. Perhaps the conflict over mother-ing represents, in part at least, not ambivalence and conflict over being a mother (in which case they would be directed toward the child as an individual in a particular relationship), but over being a "mother" as defined by the prevalent social norm at this time and place (in which case the ambivalence might be directed toward the child as the nearest social object).

It would be conceptually and empirically difficult to try to distinguish be-

---

[5]One feature of Melges' (1968) study deserves notice as an example of how seriously the quest for scientific knowledge can be given priority over other kinds of considerations. As part of an investigation into "postpartum psychiatric syndromes," Melges reported a pros-pective study in which 15 women were subjects. In the "Methods" section he noted that "during delivery and the first 2 days postpartum, all patients received the same drugs, including anasthetic preparations. Drugs were eliminated for at least 24 hours prior to each test period" (Melges, 1968, pp. 96-97). (Notice that tey did *not* say that these women were selected from a much larger population, *because* they had had no drugs during the 24 hours prior to the times tey wished to test). Melges' "controlled" procedure governing the use of medication evidently was adopted more to suit the methodological requirements of the experimenter than to meet the medical and psychological needs of the individual women. To have a momentous experience in one's life and giving birth is surely that— manipulated so that an investigator can reassure ter peers that scientific procedures were followed is outrageous and unconscionable. One wonders how long the "ritual sacri-fice" will continue.

tween those psychological aspects of the mother-child relationship more or less inherent in a biological or adoptive association between mother and child and those maternal qualities and mothering activities that are variable and largely shaped by the culture. Sherman's (1971) chapter on motherhood contains a balanced and sensitive summary/evaluation of empirical studies bearing upon a number of these issues. Wortis (1971) discusses some general problems which have plagued such research in the past. While the notion of a "maternal instinct" as an explanation for "mothering" behavior no longer has much currency, it is reasonable to think that certain behavioral and possibly emotional aspects of an adult-child relationship are essential for the survival of the species, while others—perhaps particularly those that are associated with the sex of the parent—are variable from culture to culture and are in some sense related to other (nonchild-related) features of the society. Some idea of the nature and extent of cultural overlay is suggested by a comparison of the asymmetric meanings of "mother" and "father" as social roles in the United States. If one knows that a woman is a "full-time mother," for example, one can predict with a fair degree of accuracy how she spends much of her time on a day-to-day basis (even when she is not actually interacting with her offspring), whereas knowing that a man is continuously a father does not provide such predictive information (Hartley, 1968).

The medical literature on postpartum depression and the sociological literature on the postpartum period in normal mothers give some evidence that the ambivalence or anger directed toward the child and toward mothering may in fact represent not ambivalence about being a mother but rather a dislike and resentment of certain activities culturally defined as part of the "mother" role. It is difficult to provide support for such a hypothesis, however, because the majority of investigators have described their data in such a way that it is impossible to determine precisely what aspects of "mothering" were troubling to the women in the study. In their framework, "guilt (resentment?)" related to being a mother is unquestioningly regarded as a "symptom" of postpartum psychological disturbance, and such disturbances are indiscriminantly lumped together under the label "postpartum depression." Some investigators, in fact, do not distinguish between childbearing and childrearing, or between those child-rearing activities culturally defined as part of the "mother" role and those that may be more universal features of establishing and maintaining a mother-child relationship. Tetlow (1955), for example, described a patient who had "a delusion that she had 'no maternal instinct'." Citing Bowlby, tey suggested that many patients with postpartum breakdowns lack the "normal instinctive and emotional equipment to set up a home and rear children."

Similarly, Melges (1968) observed that for the majority of women in ter study of "postpartum psychiatric syndromes," "conflict over mothering was the area of greatest difficulty" and tey included it as one aspect of this "difficulty with masculine-feminine identification." One cannot determine from ter report, however, whether "feminine identification" has operational meaning apart from whether the woman does or does not fulfill the social role of "mother." Terms like "conflicts over mothering," "struggle to be or not to be a woman" (Train, 1965), and "feminine identification" may not, in other words, have a meaning that is separable from the woman's response to the culturally contingent features of the social role of "mother." Many of the statements about "femininity" and "motherhood" which appear in the literature on postpartum depression seem uninformed by the cross-cultural perspective advocated by Newton and Newton (1972), or even by an awareness of single examples of societies that pattern femininity and parental care in very different ways from our own (DuBois, 1944; Mead, 1935).

Although they are never explicitly studied, the literature on the postpartum period contains hints that some women do find certain aspects of the social role of "mother" unpleasant. Of Melges' subjects, for example, 64% had major or moderate increases in "entrapment" feelings after birth of their first child, and similar feelings were expressed by Dyer's (1963) subjects. (Here, too, a comparison of a sociological description with a psychoanalytic account of the same phenomenon is interesting: Heinman, 1965, suggested that expressions of a fear of being enclosed are conscious representations of an unconscious fear arising out of identification with the baby.) Many of Larsen's (1966) subjects, as well as those in a number of other studies, found that one stress of the postpartum period was in being awakened for the infant's night feedings and, in general, in providing the large amount of care that newborns require and which mothers are conventionally expected to give. LeMaster's (1957) and Rossi's (1968) sociological studies of the transition to parenthood suggested that women are often unprepared for the sudden assumption of the mothering role and sometimes experience a period of fairly severe crisis while they adjust to its demands.[6]

It hardly seems necessary, however, to master semiscientific documentation for what is by now an often repeated set of arguments. Being a "full-time mother," where the word "mother" indicates a social role in conjunction with a biological or adoptive relationship with a child can be a full-time set of activities, and the literature on the postpartum period corroborates the view that some women find various aspects of this role unsatisfying. The milder forms of postpartum depression which appear to be frequent in normal women (Gordon & Gordon, 1959; LeMasters, 1957) may well reflect the new mother's sudden experience of what it is she is expected to do in her role as mother. The most recent edition of Benson's *Handbook of Obstetrics and Gynecology* (1974) in fact seems to support this view fairly clearly. As tey noted, there may be "a second brief, mild depression . . . about one month after delivery when personal sacrifices and the drudgery of daily duties have taken much of the glamour out of motherhood and resentment toward the child and the husband is often present" (Benson, 1974, p. 450). Boesky, Cross, and Morley (1966) imply that something similar underlies the "5th day blues." The "probable mechanism," according to Morley, is that after birth the attention the woman received during her pregnancy drops off and her responsibilities to herself and her baby increase with resulting "blues" feelings.

Another very common theme in the literature on the postpartum period suggests that it may not be only the assumption of certain aspects of the "full-time mother" role which some women find depressing. A number of investigators have observed that women who suffer from postpartum depression frequently exhibit a rejection of "femininity" and a "decidedly masculine orientation" (Ostwald & Regan, 1957 offer references to this literature). Although these authors do not clarify what this characterization implies in terms of what the women say and do, it is likely that "femininity" here, too, is related to acceptance of the conventional social role of "mother," while "masculine" appears to refer to interests outside the home. Occasionally the equation between "masculine orientation" (or "rejection of femininity") and interests outside the home is made quite explicit. Ostwald and Regan (1957), for example, include "career outside marriage" as a "masculine characteristic," while a "passive-submissive attitude toward others" is viewed as a "feminine" one. Lomas' (1959) description of one woman suffering from postpartum depression is typical of the general tone of this literature. The patient was "an ambitious career girl," tey said, "who had always tried to rival men at their own game."

Dyer (1963), Douglas (1968), Biskind (1958), and Ostwald and Regan (1957) all presented data that, although incidental to the main points of their papers, suggest an association between a previous career outside the home and postpartum depression in women who chose to become "fulltime" mothers. LeMasters (1957) described the reactions of professionally trained and experienced women who remained at home after the birth of their first child as, without exception, "extremely severe." Despite this apparently predictive relationship between strong work commitment "pre-motherhood" and postpartum depression, none of these authors commented extensively upon it or explored it further. LeMasters' data (and also those of Gordon and Gordon, 1959) seem to suggest that postpartum depression is more common among women than scientific reports usually indicate, but controlled studies would be necessary to know whether women with a strong commitment to work outside the home do experience the postpartum period differently from other women.

Rubin (1967) very sensitively described some of the processes that tend to go on as a woman takes on the role of "full-time mother" and "lets go of former occupational status or role." Tey described this latter as "grief work" and suggested its similarity to the process of working through a loss, which was described by Lindemann (1944) in connection with widowhood. Although individuals undoubtedly differ in the extent to which their sense of self is related to their occupational role, Rubin noted that of the women tey studied, "very few relinquished their former identities readily" and that the grief work involved in the loss of this occupational identity was not resolved by the birth of the child nor terminated by taking on the role of "mother" as substitute. There seemed rather to be a "progressive obliteration of former roles and former ideal images," with very gradual changes in self-conception from "I am . . ." to "I used to be

. . ." and "I did . . ." Rubin noted that with increasing numbers of children, ". . . bereavement moved from idealized career . . . (to the) money and interpersonal enrichments of any job." Literature on the psychological impact of retirement (which certainly is not focused exclusively upon women) suggests, too, that "letting go" of an occupational role, be it a professional career or other kinds of work, is rather generally experienced as a loss (Rhee, 1974).

It is reasonable to suggest that, for some women, depression in the postpartum period may be associated with a kind of "mourning" for the loss of an aspect of identity—the occupational—that was important to the individual's sense of self. This is consistent with Clayton, Herjanic, Murphy, and Woodruff's (1974) observation that the symptoms associated with bereavement or grief may be indistinguishable for research purposes from symptoms of depression. Loss of a subjectively important aspect of one's identity might also be expected to lead to lowered self-esteem, and Rossi (1968) in fact argued that there is considerable evidence to support the notion that "for many women the personal (developmental) outcome of experience in the parent role is not a higher level of maturation but the negative outcome of a depressed sense of self-worth." (Rossi, 1958, p. 34.) In fact, Kaij and Malmquist (1971) conducted a study of monozygotic female twins and found that those women who had become mothers had significantly more psychiatric and somatic symptoms than their "control" twin who remained . . . child free. The authors did not, however, emphasize the differences in social *roles* as the operative distinction between the twins. Rather, they said, "Our hypothesis that pregnancy undermines the psychiatric and somatic health of women even in the long term seems to be supported by our investigation" (p. 26).

Masters (1974) suggested that there may be a psychological "gestation period" following some major change or transition in a person's life experience, and that the subjective recognition and acknowledgment of an altered sense of identity may not come until one or two years after the critical event or change. Ter examples include major changes in life experience such as the loss of a spouse, move to another country, entrance into a university—but his analysis might also be extended to the change in subjective identity that occurs in assuming a parental role. The concept of an 18-month "gestation period" may, in fact, account for some of the apparent discrepancy in the sociological literature on the "transition to parenthood." LeMasters' (1957) study involved couples who had apparently been parents for as long as 5 years (the average length of parenthood is not reported), while Hobbs (1968) and Dyer (1963) interviewed couples who were in a much earlier stage of being parents for the first time (24 weeks and 12 months, respectively), LeMasters' data suggested that the transition to parenthood represented an extensive or severe crisis for a large percentage (83%) of normal couples, while Hobbs and Dyer found the proportion of couples experiencing crises of this magnitude to be smaller. It is possible that the parents' understanding and acknowledgment of the extent of crisis, and resulting readjustment, can be achieved only after the one-to-two-year gestation period that Masters suggested is necessary for the identity change to be subjectively assimilated. Rossi (1968) made this point in a slightly different way.

In short, there seems to be scattered evidence to suggest that, for some women, "taking on" the aspects of the social role of mother and "letting go" of a former role that was important to their sense of self can be stressful and depressing experiences. Since the processes that Rubin described as "taking on" and "letting go" in certain ways come to a focus when the child is born, depression caused by stressful changes in social roles could mistakenly be attributed to hormonal or intrapsychic changes which may also occur in the postpartum period. Rather interestingly, Ryle (1961) was concerned with this same problem from the opposite perspective. He suggested that it is "probable that the operation of endogenous (hormonal) factors in depression occurring after childbirth is often unrecognized, the symptoms being attributed to the normal fatigues of caring for small children" (p. 285).

Nuckolls, Cassel, and Kaplan (1972) noted that the extent to which a stressful life event is experienced negatively probably depends in part upon the positive supports ("psychosocial assets") or alternative forms of satisfaction that are available to the individual. Some such view of an interplay between positive and negative environmental pressures, their data suggest, is important in understanding the way a particular woman responds to the biological process of childbirth. This would seem to be true also for understanding the psychological changes in the postpartum period. A woman's subjective experience of the postpartum period may or may not involve depression, depending upon whether her social situation and psychodynamic constitution are such that she receives—and continues to receive—what are for her sufficient satisfactions as if she engages in the processes-in-time of taking on the social role of "mother" and letting go of other roles. It is in no way denying the importance of hormonal and intrapsychic factors or the many positive aspects of the "mother" role to suggest, as the data on postpartum depression do, that some attention ought to be paid as well to the potentially negative psychological consequences of changes in social role.

In fact, however, there is little in the medical or psychological literature to indicate that the social aspects of becoming a mother have been the topic of much research. Investigators have frequently observed in passing that pregnancy and birth is a period of biological, psychological, and social (or "psychosocial") change, but they have rarely if ever considered the psychological implications of the major change or changes in social role which childbirth entails for a large number of women in this society.

It may be that intrapsychic and hormonal theories about the etiology of postpartum phenomena can provide only partial or incomplete explanations, in the same way that intrapsychic and biological theories are believed by many to provide only a partial explanation of mental illness (Scheff, 1974, presented a recent summary of some of this debate). Social labeling theory has been formulated by sociologists as one way to supplement these partial explanations of mental illness (Scheff, 1966; Siegler and Osmond, 1966), and it is possible that a social labeling perspective might prove useful also in the psychological study of postpartum phenomena (Parlee, Note 15). Or it might be that a psychological conceptualization of processes ("transition tasks") similar to those described by Rapoport and Rapoport (1964) in their study of the transition from being engaged to being married might be useful in understanding the transition to parenthood (Rapoport and Rapoport, 1965).

Whatever theoretical orientation or particular way of formulating the questions should eventually prove to be fruitful, it is clear that psychological studies of pregnancy, birth, and the postpartum period will have to include a consideration of the social context within which the biological processes occur. The results of this consideration may appear to be somewhat surprising at first, but upon reflection they may suggest theoretical notions that could serve as guides for further psychological research. In one series of such studies, for example, Rosengren found that the way a woman views pregnancy—as a "sick role" or as a normal biological process—seems to be related to social mobility (and, by inference, to presence or absence of a supportive network of family and friends), to the length of the first stage of labor, and even to her attitudes toward child-rearing (Rosengren, 1961, 1962a, 1962b). The Nuckolls et al. (1972) study mentioned above also suggests an association in certain women between psychosocial assets (many of which involve being part of a cohesive social network) and. *physical* complications of labor and delivery.

The notion of social role—and role changes—may or may not be useful in the long run in explaining the social-psychological-biological interactions, but at present it seems to offer certain advantages over currently used assumptions as a beginning step in the scientific understanding of psychological phenomena of the postpartum period. Among these advantages are the following:

1. It clearly identifies "postpartum depression" and other postpartum experiences as processes in time (the psychological manifestations of a person's continuing interactions with the environment) rather than as an implicitly static psychological state of an individual considered in isolation from a social environment. Time is a problematic dimension that psychologists are going to have to come to grips with fairly soon in contexts other than traditional "developmental psychology," and it is particularly salient in considering psychological consequences of changes in social roles. Bernice Neugarten's perspective and work have gone far beyond this simple enunciation of a human development perspective, and ter formulation may provide the most useful framework for psychological research on pregnancy, birth, and their aftermath (Neugarten, 1968, 1969; Neugarten & Daten, 1974).

2. Considerations of psychological aspects of role change may also broaden the concept of "postpartum depression," at least in a scientifically fruitful way. Scattered data suggest that becoming a father may, for some men, lead to depression or even psychosis in the postpartum period (Lacoursiere, 1972; Bucove, 1964). While psychiatrists' reports of such reactions suggest that they range from psychotic episodes to acute anxiety (and consequent behavior change) over presumed financial responsibility for a family, the sociological literature indicates that the transition to parenthood is experienced in some way as a crisis by a large number of men and women (LeMasters, 1957). Clinical case histories have also been cited as evidence that severe depressions may follow the birth of a child when this event involves role changes for others besides the parents. Becoming a grandparent (Neugarten & Weinstein, 1968), for example, or becoming a sibling rather than an only child may be associated with depressive reactions in some individuals in some situations. Postpartum depression in a woman who becomes a mother may turn out to be related in theoretically important ways to the "postpartum depressions" involved in these other kinds of role changes. Their possibly similar etiologies, however, are not likely to be explored by investigators operating within a medical model and focusing upon hormonal "symptoms" and intrapsychic

causes of depression in women who are biological mothers.

It is difficult to know what to make of reports (and one, at least, a careful study by Trethowan, 1968) of "pregnancy symptoms" in men (Trethowan, 1968; Munroe, 1971).

3. A third advantage to considering the transition to parenthood in light of changes in social roles is that this perspective seems to have clinical usefulness. In an interesting and well-controlled series of studies, Gordon and Gordon (1959) found that moderate postpartum depression in women was associated with certain social variables in their life histories, and in particular with a lack of what Nucholls et al. (1972) would call psychosocial assets. Women with few family and friends whom they could see on a regular basis (often because the women had recently moved to a new neighborhood), and few outside activities and contacts with adults, were more likely to be depressed than were those involved in a more cohesive social network. Gordon and Gordon found that "socially-oriented" prenatal counseling, in which pregnant women were advised to make arrangements for help with child care and to maintain some social activities after the child was born, proved effective in reducing certain manifestations of postpartum depression. In a six-month postpartum interview, women who had had such counseling had fewer problems with their babies (see Carne, 1966) than did a control group of women who had not had the socially oriented "preventive therapy."

It is noteworthy that almost all suggestions made by the Gordons to the pregnant women who received the "socially oriented therapy" involved spending money to make the conventional role of "mother" less isolating and exhausting. They averred that "those (women) with bad present-day situations (presumably including a lack of money) must learn to live with regularly recurring painful experiences. These patients (sic) require more intensive analytical insight-gaining therapy. They need a reorganizing of attitudes and values to permit adjustment despite a chronically unpleasant situation" (Gordon & Gordon, 1959, p. 1081). The Gordons also reported a difference between these two groups of women in a follow-up study four to six years later. They claimed that the counseled women had had fewer physical illness and other serious complaints and were more likely to have had another child (Gordon, Kapostins, & Gordon, 1965).

While Gordon and Gordon's work seems to represent the only controlled study of how modifications in social role may affect depression in the postpartum period, the thrust of their research is compatible with the observations of at least some obstetricians (Youngs, 1974) and organizers of postpartum support groups for women (Turner, Note 16; Rozdilsky & Banet, 1972). This compatibility may be due, at least in part, to the fact that consideration of role changes does touch upon part of what is experientially important to those who are undergoing them.

In sum, there seem to be both theoretical and clinical reasons to suppose that research on pregnancy, birth, and the postpartum period might benefit from explicit consideration (largely absent in existing research) of the psychological aspects of the changes in social role which occur with the birth of a child. It is possible that the reasons why role changes, and particularly negative aspects of parental roles, have not been studied in the past are importantly related to the traditional separation of occupational and family roles (Rapoport & Rapoport, 1965) and to traditional division of work by sex (Thorne & Henley, 1975). By neglecting to attend to the sometimes negative consequences of traditional roles and role changes, and by focusing upon the individual woman in isolation from her social environment, scientists have, as in the study of the menstrual cycle, tended to emphasize those aspects of their data which in the main do not challenge the existing social order. As Friedrichs (1970) and Myrdal (1969) noted, when the data from a social science consistently support and confirm ongoing social practices and institutions, it may be wise to look especially critically at the assumptions, methods, and procedures that produce those data. It may be wise, that is, because the tendency *not* to do so is very strong.

MENOPAUSE

Studies of the psychological aspects of menopause, or more generally, of the climacteric, seem to share many of the features of both the research on the menstrual cycle and that on pregnancy/birth/postpartum. On the one hand, as in the case of the menstrual cycle, there is a fairly widely shared belief that "menopausal women" may experience certain symptoms and moods, including irritability, sleeplessness, anxiety, emotional instability, hot flashes, and night sweats (Achte, 1970). Some questionnaire studies have attempted to determine through self-reports the accuracy of such beliefs (e.g., Thompson, Hart & Durno, 1973; see also references in Sherman, 1971). These are subject to some of the same interpretive difficulties as are questionnaires concerning menstruation.

Several investigators, however, have explicitly formulated their object of study, when questionnaire data are used, as "attitudes toward" menopause (Neugarten, Wood, Kraines, & Loomis, 1963; Maoz, Dowty, Antonovsky & Wijsenbeck, 1970). In the best of the psychological literature, at least, there is the recognition that a woman's experience of menopause is not determined in a simplistic way by any single type of factor, be it hormones, personality characteristics, or changes in social role (Neugarten, 1967). Again, Neugarten's theoretical approach and the data on menopause upon which tey builds are especially interesting and useful (Neugarten & Datan, 1974).

Osofsky and Seidenberg (1970) reviewed some of the less insightful psychological thinking regarding menopause. Their article is noteworthy, both for its content and for the fact that it appears in the medical literature and strongly suggests that physicians' attitudes regarding menopause need "rethinking." (It is a rather uncommon occurrence to find one psychologist asserting in print that ter colleagues are guilty of committing "confused, fuzzy, and prejudicial thinking . . . toward the female" (p. 613)). While the article should be read in its entirety (it contains several excellent passages on the psychoanalytic view of menopause as a time of "mortification and uselessness"), the abstract quoted here conveys what is ordinarily a fairly accurate picture of "menopausal" women vis-a-vis their physicians.

Menopausal depression is an important entity in the lives of many women. The authors review current thinking concerning this condition. In contradistinction to the male, female psychology is seen as being dependent upon biology. Youth, attractiveness, sex, and motherhood are viewed as the important roles for women. Menopause is seen as a time of mortification, with service to the species over. This thinking has influenced the therapy offered for menopausal symptoms. Physiologic symptoms have been treated psychologically, and psychologic symptoms, physiologically. Frequently, psychotherapy has been superficial or designed to gain acceptance of the biologic loss. Mature emotions and cognition have been given little emphasis. The authors suggest that rethinking current notions may aid in treating and preventing menopausal depression. (Osofsky & Seidenberg, 1970, p. 611).

Achte (1970) provided a more extended example of a nonpsychoanalytic psychiatrist's beliefs about menopause. As in the literature on pregnancy and birth, statements are offered about matters of empirical fact ("The libido usually weakens during the postmenopausal period, except in rare cases" (p. 11)) with no acknowledgment of or reference to related scientific work and other viewpoints (e.g., Kaufman, 1971; Daly, 1968).

No attempt will be made here to review substantively the sparse and widely scattered literature on the psychological aspects of the climacteric in women. A search of the literature compiled in *Index Medicus,* however, is suggestive of just how little behavioral research has been done on the climacteric, or the menopause. (There have been fewer than 20 such studies, ranging widely in scientific quality, published in the past four years.) Apart from the work of Neugarten and her colleagues, the psychological concomitants of this portion of the female reproductive process have received considerably less (and less careful) attention than have the physiological aspects (see Greenblatt et al., 1974). The published proceedings of an NIH-sponsored conference on Menopause and Aging (Ryan & Gibson, 1971) exemplify and illustrate in several suggestive ways some of the reasons why this might be so.

In the summary of "Clinical aspects of the menopause" (the only section of the proceedings, apparently, which focuses upon the psychological aspects of the menopause) the following passage appears.

> Psychiatric symptoms are difficult to evaluate in relation to estrogen lack, but Dr. (Howard W.) Jones (Professor of Obstetrics and Gynecology, The Johns Hopkins School of Medicine) characterized menopausal women as being a caricature of their younger selves at their emotional worst. Detailed information on estrogen effects upon mental function is lacking. (Ryan & Gibson, 1971, p. 3)

If Dr. Howard W. Jones was quoted accurately, it is clear that the taxpayers' money could have been used more appropriately than to support his participation in the conference and the public dissemination of his rather revealingly personal opinions. Judging by the published proceedings, this NIH-sponsored conference involved 25 participants, all males. By itself, of course, such an association between the sex of the conference participants and the nature and formulation of the problems addressed is not particularly remarkable, but it is significant in view of the fact that one of the suggestions associated with funding by the NIH of the present Conference on Research Needs of Women was that male participants be included.

IN SUM

It is clear that the psychological aspects of female reproductive processes are embedded in and affected by the social context within which we—men and women—live. Biological, psychological, and social factors, interacting as the individual develops through time, all must play some role in determining how women experience the fact that they are biologically capable of giving birth. Systematic neglect of or emphasis upon any one of these factors, or isolation of the psychological study of women's reproductive processes from other areas of psychology is unlikely to lead to coherent and powerful scientific theories. It is equally clear that the amount and kind of scientific knowledge we have and will have about psychological aspects of female reproductive processes are also importantly related to the social/political context within which science, a social activity, has its being.

REFERENCE NOTES

1. Rossi, A.S. *Physiological and social rhythms; the study of human cyclicity.* Special lecture delivered to the American Psychiatric Association, Detroit, May, 1974.
2. Amarasingham, L.R. Personal communication, October, 1974.
3. Shostack, M. Personal communication, November, 1974.
4. Ernster, V.L. *American menstrual expressions.* Unpublished manuscript, 1974. (Available from the Division of Sociomedical Sciences, Columbia University.)
5. Seiden, A. *The sense of mastery in the childbirth experience.* Paper presented at the Third Annual Conference on Psychosomatic Obstetrics and Gynecology. Philadelphia, 1975.
6. Kennell, K.H. *Early human interaction.* Paper presented at the Third Annual Conference on Psychosomatic Obstetrics and Gynecology, Philadelphia, 1975.
7. Berman, E. Quoted in article headlined "Doctor asserts women unfit for top jobs." *New York Times,* July 26, 1970.
8. Koeski, R.K. *Physiological, social and situational factors in the premenstrual syndrome.* Unpublished manuscript, 1974. (Available from the Department of Psychology, Carnegie-Mellon University, Pittsburgh, Pa.)
9. Parlee, M.B. *Stereotypic beliefs or reports of symptoms?* Responses of Indian women to Moos Menstrual Distress Questionnaire. Manuscript in preparation, 1975. (Available from the Department of Psychology, Barnard College, New York, New York.)

10. Unger, R.K., & Siiter, R. *Sex-role stereotypes: The weight of a "grain of truth."* Paper presented at the Forty-fifth annual meeting of the Eastern Psychological Association, Philadelphia, 1974.

11. Baker, M.A. *Sex bias in perception research.* Paper presented at the Eighty-second annual meeting of the American Psychological Association, New Orleans, 1974.

12. Baker, A.H., Mishara, B.L., Parker, L., & Kostin, I.W. *Menstrual cycle affects a perceptual-cognitive phenomenon: Kinesthetic aftereffects.* Educational Testing Service, Princeton, N.J., Research Bulletin RB-74-6, April, 1974.

13. Shields, S. *Postpartum psychological adjustment.* Unpublished manuscript, 1973. (Available from the Department of Psychology, The Pennsylvania State University, University Park, Pa.)

14. Doering, S.G., & Entwisle, D.R. *Preparation during pregnancy and ability to cope with labor and delivery.* Paper presented at the Third Annual Conference on Psychosomatic Obstetrics and Gynecology, Philadelphia, 1975.

15. Parlee, M.B. *Postpartum depression: A social labeling perspective compared with intrapsychic or hormonal theories.* Paper presented at the Third Annual Conference on Psychosomatic Obstetrics and Gynecology, Philadelphia, 1975.

16. Turner, M.F. Personal communication, February, 1975. (Turner, COPE — Coping with the Overall Pregnancy Experience, 2 Hanston St., Boston, Mass.)

17. Feyerabend, P. *Philosophy of Science: 2001.* Paper presented in the Colloquia Series, Boston University Center for the Philosophy and History of Science, March 25, 1975.

REFERENCES

Abel, T., & Joffe, N.F. Cultural backgrounds of female puberty. *American Journal of Psychotherapy,* 1950, *4,* 90-113.

Abramson, M., & Torghele, J.R. Weight, temperature changes and psychosomatic symptomatology in relation to the menstrual cycle. *American Journal of Obstetrics and Gynecology,* 1961, *81,* 223-232.

Achte, K. Menopause from the psychiatrist's point of view. *Acta Obstetrics and Gynecology Scandinavia (Supplement),* 1970, *1,* 3-17.

Arms, S. *Immaculate deception: A new look at women and childbirth in America.* Boston: Houghton Mifflin, 1975.

Asch, S.S. Psychiatric complications: mental and emotional problems. In J.J. Rovinsky & A.F. Guttmacher (Eds.), *Medical, surgical, and gynecological complications of pregnancy* (2d ed.). Baltimore: Williams and Wilkins, 1965. pp. 461-472

Atlee, H.B. The falling of the Queen of Heaven. *Obstetrics and Gynecology,* 1963, *21,* 514-519.

Ayres, B.C. A cross-cultural study of factors relating to pregnancy taboos. Cited in W.N. Stephens, A cross-cultural study of menstrual taboos. *Genetic Psychology Monographs. 1961,* 64, *385-416. (First published 1954.)*

Ayres, B.C. Pregnancy magic: A study of food taboos and sex avoidances. In C.S. Rod (Ed.), *Cross-cultural approaches: Readings in comparative research.* New Haven, Conn.: Human Relations Area Files, 1967, pp. 111-125.

Bardwick, J.M. *Psychology of women: A study of bio-cultural conflicts.* New York: Harper Row, 1971.

Barry, K. *The cutting edge: A look at male motivation in obstetrics and gynecology.* Pittsburgh, Pa.: KNOW, Inc., 1972.

Barry, K. How they turned the tables on us. In D. Tennov & L. Hirsch (Eds.), *Proceedings of the first international childbirth conference.* Stamford, Conn.: New Moon Publications, 1973.

Bart, P. Mother Portnoy's complaint. *Trans-action,* 1970, *8,* 69-74.

Bart, P. Depression in middle-aged women. In V. Gornick & B. Moran (Eds.), *Women in sexist society: Studies in power and powerlessness.* New York: Basic Books, 1971, pp. 99-117.

Bell, B., Christie, M.J. & Venables, P.H. Psychophysiology of the menstrual cycle. In P.H. Venables & M.J. Christie (Eds.), *Research in psychophysiology.* London: Wiley, 1975.

Benedek, T. Parenthood as a developmental phase. *Journal of the American Psychoanalytic Association,* 1959, *7,* 339-417.

Benedek, T. An investigation of the sexual cycle in women: Methodologic consideration. *Archives of General Psychiatry,* 1963, *8,* 311-322.

Benedict, R. Continuities and discontinuities in cultural conditioning. *Psychiatry,* 1939, 161-167 (May).

Benson, R.G. *Handbook of obstetrics and gynecology* (5th ed.). Los Altos, Calif.: Lange Medical Publications, 1974.

Bibring, G.L. Some considerations of the psychological processes in pregnancy. *Psychoanalytic Study of the Child,* 1959, *14,* 113-121.

Bibring, L.H. Emotional aspects of prenatal care. *Postgraduate Medicine,* 1958, *24,* 633 ff.

Blake, M.J.F. Temperament and time of day. In W.P. Colquhoun (Ed.), *Biological rhythms and human performance*. New York: Academic Press, 1971, pp. 109-148.

Boesky, D., Cross, T.N., & Morley, G.W. Postpartum psychosis. *American Journal of Obstetrics and Gynecology*, 1966, *80*, 1209-1217.

Borst, C.V. (Ed.). *The mind-brain identity theory*. London: MacMillan, 1970.

Boston Women's Health Book Collective. *Our bodies, ourselves: A book by and for women*. New York: Simon and Schuster, 1973.

Botella-Llusia, J. *Endocrinology of woman*. Philadelphia: W.B. Saunders, 1973. (Translated from the Spanish by E.A. Moscovic.)

Boyd, C.A., Jr. Mental disorders associated with childbearing. *American Journal of Obstetrics and Gynecology*, 1942, *43*, 148-163.

Brown, J.K. A cross-cultural study of female initiation rites. *American Anthropologist*, 1963, *65*, 837-853.

Bruner, J.S., & Perlmutter, H.V. Compatriot and foreigner: A study of impression formation in three countries. *Journal of Abnormal and Social Psychology*, 1957, *55*, 253-260.

Brunswick, E. Systematic and representative design of psychological experiments with results in physical and social perception. Berkeley: University of California Press, 1947. (Syllabus series, No. 304.)

Bucove, A. Postpartum psychosis in the male. *Bulletin of the New York Academy of Medicine*, 1964, *40*, 961-971.

Caplan, G. Psychological aspects of maternity care. *American Journal of Public Health*, 1957, *47*, 25-31.

Carne, S. The influence of the mother's health on her child. *Proceedings of the Royal Society of Medicine*, 1966, *59*, 1013-1014.

Cianfrani, T. *A short history of obstetrics and gynecology*. Springfield, Ill.: Charles C. Thomas, 1960.

Clayton, P.J., Herjanic, M., Murphy, G.E., & Woodruff, R., Jr. Mourning and depression: Their similarities and differences. *Canadian Psychiatric Association Journal*, 1974, *19*, 309-312.

Cohen, L.H. Psychiatric aspects of childbearing. *Yale Journal of Biology and Medicine*, 1943, *16*, 71-92.

Collins, W.P., & Newton, J.R. The ovarian cycle. In A.S. Curry and J.F. Hewitt (Eds.), *Biochemistry of women: Clinical concepts*. Cleveland: CRC Press, 1974, pp. 1-22.

Colquhoun, W.P. (Ed.). *Biological rhythms and human performance*. New York: Academic Press, 1971.

Coppen, W.R., & Kessel, N. Menstruation and personality. *British Journal of Psychiatry*, 1963, *109*, 711-721.

Culberg, J. Mood changes and menstrual symptoms with different gestagen/estrogen combination. *Acta Psychiatrica Scandinavia*, Supplement 235, 1972.

Dalton, K. Prospective study into puerperal depression. *British Journal of Psychiatry*, 1971, *118*, 689-692.

Daly, M.J. Sexual attitudes in menopausal and postmenopausal women. *Medical Aspects of Human Sexuality*, 1968, *2*, 48-53.

Darmstadter, R., Lucatorto, K., Lupton, M.J., & Winnick, S. Childbirth and madness. *Women: A Journal of Liberation*, 1974, 3/3, 11-16.

Deutsch, H. *The psychology of women.* New York: Grune and Stratton, 1944.

DiMarchi, G.W., & Tong, J.E. Menstrual, diurnal, and activation effects on the resolution of temporally paired flashes. *Psychophysiology*, 1972, *9*, 362-367.

Doering, C.H., Brodie, H.K.H., Kraemer, H., Becker, H., & Hamburg, D.A. Plasma testosterone levels and psychologic measures in men over a 2-month period. In R.C. Freidman, R.M. Richart, & R.L.V. Weil (Eds.), *Sex Differences in behavior.* New York: Wiley, 1974.

Doering, C.H., Kraemer, H.C., Brodie, H.K.H., & Hamburg, D.A. A Cycle of plasma testosterone in the human male. *Journal of Clinical Endocrinology and Metabolism*, 1975, *40*, 492-500.

Douglas, G. Some disorders of the puerperium. *Journal of Psychosomatic Research*, 1968, *12*, 101-106.

DuBois, C. *The People of Alor.* Minneapolis: University of Minnesota Press, 1944.

Dyer, E.D. Parenthood as crisis: A re-study. *Marriage and Family Living*, 1963, *25*, 196-201.

Eastman, N.J., & Hellman, L.M. *William's obstetrics* (12th ed.). New York: Appleton-Century-Crofts, 1961.

Egan, J.P., & Clarke, F.R. Psychophysics and signal detection. In J.B. Sidowski (Ed.), *Experimental methods and instrumentation in psychology.* New York: McGraw-Hill, 1966, pp. 211-246.

Elsberg, C.A., Bruer, E.D., & Levy, I. Concerning conditions which may temporarily alter normal olfactory acuity. *Bulletin of the Neurological Institute of New York*, 1935, *4*, 31-34.

Foundeur, M., Fixen, C., Triebel, W.A., & White, M.A. Postpartum mental illness: Controlled study. *A.M.A. Archives of Neurology and Psychiatry*, 1957, *77*, 503-512.

Fox, L.P. Antenatal supervision. A review of obstetrical care with suggestions for revision. *California Medicine*, 1964, *101*, 168-173.

Frazier, T.M. Error in reported date of last menstrual period. *American Journal of Obstetrics and Gynecology,* 1959, *27,* 917-918.

Friedrichs, R.W. *A sociology of sociology.* New York: Free Press, 1970.

Gardiner, S.H. Psychosomatic aspects of obstetrics. In N.J. Eastman & L.M. Hellman (Eds.), *William's obstetrics* (X1/8-3/8th ed.). New York: Appleton-Century-Crofts, 1966, pp. 335-355.

Gordon, R.E., & Gordon, K.K. Social factors in the prediction and treatment of emotional disorders in pregnancy. *American Journal of Obstetrics and Gynecology,* 1959, *77,* 1074-1083.

Gordon, R.E., Kapostins, E.E., & Gordon, K.K. Factors in postpartum emotional adjustment. *Obstetrics and Gynecology,* 1965, *25,* 158-166.

Gottschalk, L.A., & Gleser, G.C. *The measurement of psychological states through content analysis of verbal behavior.* Berkeley: University of California Press, 1969.

Gottschalk, L.A.G., Kaplan, S.M., Gleser, C., & Winget, C.M. Variations in magnitude of emotions: A method applied to anxiety and hostility during phases of the menstrual cycle. *Psychosomatic Medicine,* 1962, *24,* 300-311.

Green, A.W. The middle-class male child and neurosis. *American Sociological Review,* 1946, *11,* 31-41.

Greenberg, M., & Morris, N. Engrossment: The newborn's impact upon the father. *American Journal of Orthopsychiatry,* 1974, *44,* 520-531.

Greenblatt, R.B., Mahesh, V.G. B., & McDonough, P.G. *The menopausal syndrome.* New York: Medcom Press, 1974.

Grimm, E.R. Psychological and social factors in pregnancy, delivery, and outcome. In S.A. Richardson & A.F. Guttmacher (Eds.), *Childbearing—Its social and psychological aspects.* Baltimore: Williams & Wilkins, 1967.

Haire, D. The cultural warping of childbirth. *International Childbirth Education Association News,* 1972. (Available from ICEA, P.O. Box 5852, Milwaukee, Wisc. 53220.)

Halberg, F. Chronobiology. *Annual Review of Physiology,* 1969, *31,* 675-725.

Hamburg, D.A., & Adams, J.E. A perspective on coping behavior: Seeking and utilizing information in major transitions. *Archives of General Psychiatry,* 1967, *17,* 277-284.

Hamilton, J. *Postpartum psychiatric problems.* St. Louis: Mosby, 1962.

Hartley, R.E. Sex-roles from a child's point of view. In M.B. Sussman (Ed.), *Sourcebook in marriage and the family* (3rd ed.). Boston: Houghton Mifflin, 1968, pp. 266-275.

Heiman, M.A. A psychoanalytic view of pregnancy. In J. Rovinksy & A.F. Guttmacher (Eds.), *Medical, surgical, and gynecological complications of pregnancy* (2d ed.). Baltimore: Williams & Wilkins, 1965, pp. 473-519.

Hersey, R.B. Emotional cycles in man. *Journal of Mental Science,* 1931, *77,* 151-169.

Hill, R. *Families under stress.* New York: Harper & Row, 1949.

Hobbs, D.F., Jr. Transition to parenthood: A replication and an extension. *Journal of Marriage and the Family,* 1968, *30,* 413-417.

Howells, J.G. (Ed.). *Modern perspectives in psycho-obstetrics.* New York: Brunner/Mazel, 1972.

Ivey, M., & Bardwick, J.M. Patterns of affective fluctuation in the menstrual cycle. *Psychosomatic Medicine,* 1968, *30,* 336-345.

Janiger, O., Riffenburg, R., & Kersh, R. Cross-cultural study of premenstrual symptoms. *Psychosomatics,* 1972, *13,* 226-235.

Janowski, D.S., Gorney, R., Castelnuovo-Tedesco, P., & Stone, C.B. Premenstrual-menstrual increase in psychiatric admission rates. *American Journal of Obstetrics and Gynecology,* 1969, *103,* 189-191.

Janowsky, D.S., Gorney, R., & Kelley, B. "The curse": Vicissitudes and variations of the female fertility cycle: Part I: Psychiatric aspects. *Psychosomatics,* 1966, *7,* 242-247.

Jansson, B. Psychic insufficiencies associated with childbearing. *Acta Psychiatrica Scandinavia,* 1963, *39,* Supplement 172, 1-168.

Joffe, N.F. Vernacular of menstruation. *Word,* 1948, *4,* 181-186.

Kaij, L., & Malmquist, A. Motherhood and childlessness in monozygotic twins, II. *British Journal of Psychiatry,* 1971, *118,* 22-28.

Kaij, L., & Nilsson, A. Emotional and psychotic illness following childbirth. In J.G. Howels (Ed.), *Modern perspectives in psycho-obstetrics.* New York: Brunner/Mazel, 1972, pp. 364-384.

Kane, F.J., Lipton, M.A., & Ewing, J.A. Hormonal influences in female sexual response. *Archives of General Psychiatry,* 1969, *20,* 202-209.

Kanner, L. Psychiatric aspects of pregnancy and childbirth. In N.J. Eastman & L.M. Hellman (Eds.), *William's obstetrics* (12th ed.). New York: Appleton-Century-Crofts, 1961, pp. 354-372.

Kaplan, A.R. Physiological and pathological correlates of differences in taste acuity. In S.G. Vandenberg (Ed.), *Progress in human behavior genetics.* Baltimore: Johns Hopkins Press, 1968, pp. 31-66. (Cited in J.A. Sherman, *On the psychology of women: A survey of empirical studies.* Springfield, Ill.: Charles C. Thomas, 1971.)

Karacan, I., & Williams, R.L. Current advances in theory and practice relating to postpartum syndromes. *Psychiatry in Medicine,* 1970, *1,* 58-64.

Kear-Cowell, J.J. Neuroticism in the early puerperium. *British Journal of Psychiatry,* 1965, *111,* 1189-1192.

Kenshalo, D.R. Psychophysiological studies of temperature sensitivity. In W.D. Neff (Ed.), *Contributions to sensory physiology.* New York: Academic Press, 1970.

Kopell, B.S., Lunde, D.T., Clayton, R.B., & Moos, R.H. Variations in some measures of arousal during the menstrual cycle. *Journal of Nervous and Mental Diseases,* 1969, *148,* 180-187.

Kroger, W.S. (Ed.). *Psychosomatic obstetrics, gynecology, and endocrinology.* Springfield, Ill.: Charles C. Thomas, 1962.

Kuhn, T.S. *The structure of scientific revolutions.* Chicago: University of Chicago Press, 1962.

Lacoursiere, R.B. Fatherhood and mental illness: A review and new material. *Psychiatric Quarterly,* 1972, *46,* 109-124.

Larsen, V.L. Stresses of the childbearing years. *American Journal of Public Health,* 1966, *56,* 32-36.

Lederer, W. *The fear of women.* New York: Grune & Stratoon, 1968.

LeMasters, E.E. Parenthood as crisis. *Marriage and Family Living,* 1957, *19,* 352-355.

Lennane, M.B., & Lennane, R.J. Alleged psychogenic disorders in women—A possible manifestation of sexual prejudice. *New England Journal of Medicine,* 1973, *288,* 288-292.

Levy, D. Psychosomatic studies of some aspects of maternal behavior. *Psychosomatic Medicine,* 1942, *4,* 223-227.

Levy, J.M., & McGee, R.K. Childbirth as crisis: A test of Janis's theory of communication and stress resolution. *Journal of Personality and Social Psychology,* 1975, *31,* 171-179.

Levy-Valensi, J. Psychoses puerperales. *Paris Medicine,* 1921, *21,* 501 ff. (Cited in B. Jansson, Psychic insufficiencies associated with childbearing. *Acta Psychiatrica Scandinavia,* 1963, *39,* Supplement 1972, 1-168, p. 24.)

Lindemann, E. Symptomatology and management of acute grief. *American Journal of Psychiatry,* 1944, *101,* 141-148.

Lomas, P. The husband-wife relationship in cases of puerperal breakdown. *British Journal of Medical Psychology,* 1959, *32,* 117-132.

Lomas, P. Childbirth ritual. *New Society,* 1964, *31* (December).

Luce, G.G. *Biological rhythms in psychiatry and medicine.* U.S. Department of

Health, Education and Welfare, Public Health Service Publication No. 2088, 1970.

Maccoby, E.E. The meaning of being female. *Contemporary Psychology*, 1972, *17*, 369-372.

Maoz, B., Dowty, N., Antonovsky, A., & Wijsenbeck, H. Female attitudes to menopause. *Social Psychiatry*, 1970, *5*, 35-40.

Marhkam, S. A comparative evaluation of psychotic and non-psychotic reactions to childbirth. *American Journal of Orthopsychiatry*, 1961, *31*, 565-578.

Masters, J. The gestation period of identity change. *British Journal of Psychiatry*, 1974, *125*, 472-474.

Matsumoto, S., Nogami, Y., & Ohkuri, S. Statistical studies on menstruation: A criticism on the definition of normal menstruation. *Gunma Journal of Medical Sciences*, 1962, *11*, 294-318.

McCance, R.A., Luff, M.C., & Widdowson, E.E. Physical and emotional periodicity in women. *Journal of Hygiene*, 1937, *37*, 571-605.

McDonald, R.L. The role of emotional factors in obstetric complications: A review. *Psychosomatic Medicine*, 1968, *30*, 222-237.

Mead, M. *Sex and temperament in three primitive societies*. New York: William Morrow, 1935.

Mead, M., & Newton, N. Cultural patterning of perinatal behavior. In S.A. Richardson & A.F. Guttmacher (Eds.), *Childbearing—Its social and psychological aspects*. Baltimore: Williams & Wilkins, 1967, pp. 142-244.

Melges, F. Postpartum psychiatric syndromes. *Psychosomatic Medicine*, 1968, *30*, 95-108.

Mengert, W.F., & Murphy, D.P. Intra-abdominal pressures created by voluntary muscular effort. *Surgical Gynecology and Obstetrics*, 1933, *57*, 745-751.

Mitre, I.N. The influence of maternal position on duration of the active phase of labor. *International Journal of Gynecology and Obstetrics*, 1974, *12*, 181-183.

Moos, R.H. The development of a menstrual distress questionnaire. *Psychosomatic Medicine*, 1968, *30*, 853-867.

Moos, R.H. Typology of menstrual cycle symptoms. *American Journal of Obstetrics and Gynecology*, 1969, *103*, 390-402.

Moos, R.H., Kopell, B.S., Melges, F.T., Yalom, I.D., Lunde, D.T., Clayton, R.B., & Hamburg, D.A. Fluctuations in symptoms and moods during the menstrual cycle. *Journal of Psychosomatic Research*, 1969, *13*, 37-44.

Morris, N. (Ed.) *International Congress of Psychosomatic Medicine in Obstetrics and Gynecology*, (3 ed.). London, 1971. Basel: Karger, 1972.

Munroe, R.L. Male pregnancy symptoms and cross-sex identity in three societies. *Journal of Social Psychology,* 1971, *84,* 11-25.

Myrdal, G. *Objectivity in social research.* New York: Pantheon, 1969.

Neugarten, B.L. (Ed.) *Middle age and aging: A reader in social psychology.* Chicago: University of Chicago Press, 1968.

Neugarten, B.L. Continuities and discontinuities of psychological issues into adult life. *Human Development,* 1969, *12,* 121-130.

Neugarten, B.L., & Datan, N. The middle years. In S. Arieti (Ed.), *American handbook of psychiatry* (2d ed., Vol. 1). *Foundations of Psychiatry.* New York: Basic Books, 1974, pp. 592-608.

Neugarten, B.L., & Weinstein, K.K. The changing American grandparent. In B.L. Neugarten (Ed.), *Middle age and aging.* Chicago: University of Chicago Press, 1968, pp. 280-285.

Neugarten, B.L., Wood, V., Kraines, R.J., & Loomis, B. Women's attitudes toward the menopause. *Vita Humana,* 1963, *6,* 140-151.

Newton, N. Maternal emotions: A study of women's feelings toward menstruation, pregnancy, childbirth, breast-feeding, infant care, and other aspects of the femininity. New York: Hoeber, 1955. (A *Psychosomatic Medicine* monograph.)

Newton, N., & Newton, M. Childbirth in cross-cultural perspective. In J.V. Howells (Ed.), *Modern perspectives in psycho-obstetrics.* New York: Brunner/ Mazel, 1972, pp. 150-174.

Nilsson, A. Para-natal emotional adjustment: A prospective investigation of 165 women. *Acta Psychiatrica Scandinavia* (Supplement), 1970, *220,* 9-61.

Nilsson, A., Kaij, L., & Jacobson, L. Post-partum mental disorders in an unselected sample: The psychiatric history. *Journal of Psychosomatic Research,* 1967, *10,* 327-339.

Notman, M.T. Pregnancy and abortion: Implications for career development of professional women. *Annals of the New York Academy of Science,* 1973.

Nuckolls, K.B., Cassel, J., & Kaplan, B.A. Psychosocial assets, life crises, and the prognosis of pregnancy. *American Journal of Epidemiology,* 1972, *95,* 431-441.

Ortner, S.B Is female to male as nature is to culture? In M.Z. Rosaldo & L. Lamphere (Eds.), *Woman, culture, and society.* Stanford, Calif.: Stanford University Press, 1974, pp. 67-88.

Osofsky, H.J., & Seidenberg, R. Is female menopausal depression inevitable? *Obstetrics and Gynecology,* 1970, *36,* 611-615.

Ostwald, P., & Regan, P. Psychiatric disorders associated with childbirth. *Journal of Nervous and Mental Diseases*, 1957, *125*, 153-165.

Paffenbarger, R.S. Epidemiological aspects of parapartum mental illness. *British Journal of Preventive and Social Medicine*, 1964, *18*, 189-195.

Paige, K.E. Effects of oral contraceptives on affective fluctuations associated with the menstrual cycle. *Psychosomatic Medicine*, 1971, *33*, 515-537.

Paige, L.E. Women learn to sing the menstrual blues. *Psychology Today*, 1973, *7*, 41-46.

Paige, K.E., & Paige, J.M. The politics of birth practices: A strategic analysis. *American Sociological Review*, 1973, *38*, 663-677.

Parlee, M.B. The premenstrual syndrome. *Psychological Bulletin*, 1973, *80*, 454-465.

Parlee, M.B. Stereotypic beliefs about menstruation: A methodological note on the Moos Menstrual Distress Questionnaire and some new data. *Psychosomatic Medicine*, 1974, *36*, 229-240.

Parlee, M.B. Psychology and women. *Signs: Journal of Women in Culture and Society*, 1975, *1*. (In press.)

Peskin, H. Duration of normal menses as a psychosomatic phenomenon. *Psychosomatic Medicine*, 1968, *30*, 378-389.

Philipp, E.E., Barnes, J., & Newton, M. (Eds.). *Scientific foundations of obstetrics and gynecology*. Philadelphia: Davis, 1970.

Pitt, B. "Atypical" depression following childbirth. *British Journal of Psychiatry*, 1968, *114*, 1325-1335.

Presser, H.B. Temporal data relating to the human menstrual cycle. In M. Ferin, F. Halberg, R.M. Richart, & R. Vande Weil (Eds.), *Biorhythms and human reproduction*. New York: Wiley, 1974, pp. 145-160.

Protheroe, C. Puerperal psychosis: A long-term study, 1927-1961. *British Journal of Psychiatry*, 1969, *115*, 9-30.

Pugh, T.F., Jerath, B.K., Schmidt, W.M., & Reed, R.B. Rates of mental disease related to childbearing. *New England Journal of Medicine*, 1963, *268*, 1224-1228.

Ramey, E.R. What did happen at the Bay of Pigs? *McCalls*, 1971 (January).

Ramey, E.R. Sex hormones and executive ability. *Annals of the New York Academy of Science*, 1973, *208*, 237-245.

Rapoport, R., & Rapoport, R. New light on the honeymoon. *Human Relations*, 1964, *17*, 33-56.

Rapoport, R., & Rapoport, R. Work and family in contemporary society. *American Sociological Review*, 1965, *30*, 381-394.

Redgrove, J.A. Menstrual cycles. In W.P. Colquhoun (Ed.), *Biological rhythms and human performance.* New York: Academic Press, 1971, pp. 211-240.

Rhee, H.A. Man's relation to his work and occupation. In H.A. Rhee, *Human aging and retirement,* Geneva: General Secretariat, International Social Security Association, 1974, pp. 207-235.

Richter, C.P. *Biological clocks in psychiatry and medicine.* Springfield, Ill.: Charles C. Thomas, 1965.

Richter, C.P. Periodic phenomena in man and animals: Their relation to neuro-endocrine mechanisms (a monthly or near monthly cycle). In R.P. Michael (Ed.), *Endocrinology and human behavior.* London: Oxford University Press, 1968, pp. 284-309.

Robin, A.A. The psychological changes of normal parturition. *Psychiatric Quarterly,* 1962, *36,* 129-150.

Rose, R.M., Gordon, T.P., & Bernstein, I.S. Plasma testosterone levels in the male rhesus: Influences of sexual and social stimuli. *Science,* 1972, *178,* 643-645.

Rose, R.M., Holoday, J.W., & Bernstein, I.S. Plasma testosterone, dominance rank and aggressive behavior in male rhesus monkeys. *Nature* (London), 1971, *231,* 366-368.

Rosen, R.A. Letter to the Editor. *New England Journal of Medicine,* 1972, *286,* 952.

Rosengren, W.R. Some social psychological aspects of delivery room difficulties. *Journal of Nervous and Mental Diseases,* 1961, *132,* 515-521.

Rosengren, W.R. Social instability and attitudes toward pregnancy as a social role. *Social Problems,* 1962, *9,* 371-378, (a).

Rosengren, W.R. Social status, attitudes toward pregnancy, and childrearing attitudes. *Social Forces,* 1962, *41,* 127-234, (b).

Rossi, A.S. Transition to parenthood. *Journal of Marriage and the Family,* 1968, *30,* 26-39.

Rovinsky, J.J., & Guttmacher, A.F. (Eds.). *Medical, surgical, and gynecological complications of pregnancy* (2d ed.). Baltimore: Williams & Wilkins, 1965.

Rozdilsky, M.L., & Banet, B. *What now? A handbook for couples (especially women) postpartum.* Seattle, Wash.: What now? 3415 N.E. 50th St., Seattle, Wash. 98105, 1972.

Rubin, R. Attainment of the maternal role. *Nursing Research,* 1967, *16,* 237-245, 342-246.

Ruch, T.C., & Fulton, J.F. (Eds.). *Medical physiology and biophysics.* Philadelphia: W.B. Saunders, 1960.

Ryan, K.J., & Gibson, D.C. (Eds.). *Menopause and aging: Summary report and selected papers from a research conference on menopause and aging. May 23-26, Hot Springs, Ark.* U.S. Department of Health, Education, and Welfare, Publication No. (NIH) 73-319, 1971.

Ryle, A. The psychological disturbances associated with 345 pregnancies in 137 women. *Journal of Mental Science,* 1961, *107,* 279-286.

Sanford, A.J. A periodic basis for perception and action. In W.P. Colquhoun (Ed.), *Biological rhythms and human performance.* New York: Academic Press, 1971, pp. 179-210.

Scheff, T.J. *Being mentally ill: A sociological theory.* Chicago: Aldine, 1966.

Scheff, T.J. The labeling theory of mental illness. *American Sociological Review,* 1974, *39,* 444-452.

Scully, D., & Bart, P. A funny thing happened on the way to the orifice: Women in gynecology textbooks. In J. Huber (Ed.), *Changing women in a changing society.* Chicago: University of Chicago Press, 1973, pp. 283-288.

Shaw, N.S. "So you're going to have a baby . . .": Institutional processing of maternity patients (Doctoral dissertation, Brandeis University, 1972). *Dissertation Abstracts International,* 1972, *33,* 3816A. University Microfilms No. 72-32, 121.

Shereshefsky, P.M., & Yarrow, L.J. (Eds.). *Psychological aspects of a first pregnancy and early postnatal adaptation.* New York: Raven Press, 1973.

Sherman, J.A. *On the psychology of women: A survey of empirical studies.* Springfield, Ill.: Charles C. Thomas, 1971.

Sherwood, J.J., & Nataupsky, M. Predicting the conclusions of Negro-White intelligence research from biographical characteristics of the investigator. *Journal of Personality and Social Psychology,* 1968, *8,* 53-58.

Shockley, W. Dysgenics, geneticity, and raceology. *Phi Delta Kappan,* January 1972, pp. 305 ff.

Siegler, M., & Osmund, H. Models of madness. *British Journal of Psychiatry,* 1966, *112,* 1193-1203.

Silbergeld, S., Brast, N., & Nobel, E.P. The menstrual cycle: A double-blind study of symptoms, mood and behavior, and biochemical variables using Enovid and placebo. *Psychosomatic Medicine,* 1971, *33,* 411-428.

Sommer, B. The effect of menstruation on cognitive and perceptual-motor behavior: A review. *Psychosomatic Medicine,* 1973, *35,* 515-534.

Southam, A.L., & Gonzaga, F.P. Systemic changes during the menstrual cycle. *American Journal of Obstetrics and Gynecology*, 1965, *91*, 142-165.

Stephens, W.N. A cross-cultural study of menstrual taboos. *Genetic Psychology Monographs*, 1961, *64*, 385-416.

Stoddard, F.J. Normal adolescence, menstruation, and the climacteric. In D.N. Danforth, *Textbook of obstetrics and gynecology*. New York: Hoeber, 1966, pp. 157-168.

Sutherland, H., & Stewart, I. A critical analysis of the premenstrual syndrome. *Lancet*, 1965, *1*, 1180-1193.

Tanner, J.M. *Growth at adolescence*. Oxford: Blackwell Scientific Publications, 1962.

Tennov, D. The relationship between obstetrical procedures and perinatal anoxia. *Journal of Clinical Child Psychology*, 1973, *2*, 20-22.

Tennov, D., & Hirsch, L.G. (Eds.). *Proceedings of the first international childbirth conference*. Stamford, Conn.: New Moon Publications, 1973.

Tetlow, D. Psychoses of childbearing. *Journal of Mental Science*, 1955, *101*, 629-639.

Thomas, C.L., & Gordon, J.E. Psychosis after childbirth: Ecological aspects of a single impact stress. *American Journal of Medical Science*, 1959, *238*, 363-388.

Thompson, B., Hart, S.A., & Durno, D. Menopausal age and symptomology in a general practice. *Journal of Biosocial Science*, 1973, *5*, 71-82.

Thorne, B., & Henley, N. Difference and dominance: an overview of language, gender and society. In B. Thorne & N. Henley (Eds.), *Language and sex: Difference and dominance*. Rowley, Mass.: Newbury House, 1975.

Tobias, J.V. Curious binaural phenomena. In J.V. Tobias (Ed.), *Foundations of modern auditory theory* (Vol. 2). New York: Academic Press, 1972.

Tod, E.D.M. Puerperal depression: A prospective epidemiological study. *Lancet*, 1964, *2*, 1264-1266.

Train, G.J. Psychodynamics in obstetrics and gynecology. *Psychomatics*, 1965, *6*, 21-25.

Trethowan, W.H. The couvade syndrome: Some further observations. *Journal of Psychosomatic Research*, 1968, *12*, 107-115.

Trethowan, W.H., & Dickens, G. Cravings, aversions and pica of pregnancy. In J.G. Howells (Ed.), *Modern perspectives in psycho-obstetrics*. New York: Brunner/Mazel, 1972, pp. 251-268.

Tylden, E. Psychology and the maternity unit. *Lancet*, 1952, *1*, 231-233.

Vaughn, K.O. *Safe childbirth: The three essentials.* London: Bailliere, Tindall and Cassell, 1937.

Weintraub, D.J. Perception. *Annual Review of Psychology,* 1975, *26,* 263-289.

Whalen, R.E. Cyclic changes in hormones and behavior. *Archives of Sexual Behavior,* 1975, *4,* 313-314.

White, M.A., Prout, C.T., Fixen, C., & Foundeur, M. Obstetricians' role in post-partum mental illness. *Journal of the American Medical Association,* 1975, *165,* 138-143.

Whiting, J.W.M., Kluckholn, R., & Anthony, A. The function of male initiation ceremonies at puberty. In E. Maccoby et al. (Eds.), *Readings in Social Psychology.* New York: Holt, Rinehart and Winston, 1958, pp. 359-370.

Wortis, R. The acceptance of the concept of the maternal role by behavioral scientists: Its effects on women. *American Journal of Orthopsychiatry,* 1971, *41,* 733-746.

Wynn, V.T. "Absolute" pitch—A bimensual rhythm. *Nature* (London), 1971, *230,* 337.

Wynn, V.T. Study of rhythms in auditory perception and simple reaction times. *Journal of Interdisciplinary Cycle Research,* 1973, *4,* 251-260.

Yalom, I., Lunde, D., Moos, R., & Hamburg, D.A. The 'postpartum blues' syndrome: Description and related variables. *Archives of General Psychiatry,* 1968, *18,* 16027.

Young, F.W. The function of male initiation ceremonies: A cross-cultural test of an alternative hypothesis. *American Journal of Sociology,* 1962, *67,* 379-396.

Young, F.W. *Initiation ceremonies: A cross-cultural study of status dramatization.* Indianapolis, Ind.: Bobbs-Merrill, 1965.

Young, F.W., & Bacdayan, A.S. Menstrual taboos and social rigidity. *Ethnology,* 1965, *4,* 225-240.

Youngs, D.D. Exclusive review. *Ob World and Gynecology,* 1974, *3/6,* (November-December).

Zilboorg, G. Post-partum schizophrenics. *Journal of Nervous and Mental Diseases,* 1928, *68,* 370-383.

Zilboorg, G. Depressive reactions related to parenthood. *American Journal of Psychiatry,* 1931, *10,* 927-962.

Zilboorg, G. The clinical issues of postpartum psychological reactions. *American Journal of Obstetrics and Gynecology,* 1957, *73,* 305-312.

Zimmerman, E., & Parlee, M.B. Behavioral changes associated with the menstrual cycle: An experimental investigation. *Journal of Applied Social Psychology,* 1973, *3,* 335-344.

CHAPTER 7

COMMENTARY: CHAPTERS 5 & 6

KAREN ERIKSEN PAIGE & WENDY McKENNA

COMMENTS BY KAREN ERICKSEN PAIGE

Probably no other topics in modern psychology, including the psychology of women, have been so systematically ignored as female sexuality and reproductive behavior. In fact, a substantial proportion of the research and theory devoted to these issues has been produced within disciplines other than academic psychology, most notably psychiatry, with a greater emphasis on developing treatments for what is considered deviant sexual behavior or reproductive "dysfunctions" than on theory construction and theoretically oriented empirical research. Given the obvious significance of female sexuality and reproduction to such subdisciplines as psychophysiology and developmental and social psychology, it is astounding, as Parlee points out, that a greater interest in these fields was not generated decades ago. The quantity and quality of psychological research on human sexuality and reproduction hardly compares to the immense body of research on the sexual and reproductive behavior of lower animals, most notably the rat.

Maccoby and Jacklin's recent review of the sex differences literature, and the numerous handbook articles in both developmental and social psychology, give only passing mention of the potential significance of sexual physiological development, sexual socialization, and reproductive events in the development of sex differences in identity formation and social behavior. These omissions most probably reflect the status, or lack of status, of these critical issues within academic psychology rather than oversights of the reviewers. The two critical review articles in this Part III provide an important first step in demonstrating the serious implications of this ignorance for the analysis of human behavior generally and female psychology in particular. How can psychologists develop a comprehensive framework for understanding human behavior without taking into consideration two of the most fundamental aspects of behavior—sex and reproduction? In my opinion these areas of psychology represent the "underbelly" of personality and social life; just as sex and reproduction are subject to taboos in public life, so are they considered taboo and out of the "mainstream" of serious psychology.

As both articles show, until very recently research on female sexuality and reproductive behavior has been hampered by two serious deficiencies. First, theory and data analysis have too often been based on a simplistic view of human physiology, and second, the research questions most frequently explored have been guided by cultural values about appropriate feminine behavior. Schwartz and Strom make the point, for example, that until recently much of the research on female sexual arousal, sexual cycles, and "appetite" not only was based on a mistaken perception of the magnitude of the sex difference in basic sexual physiology, but also phrased research questions according to the "marital model" of appropriate sexual behavior. While female sexuality within marriage is certainly an important research concern, the assumption that sexual behaviors and motivations that do not conform to cultural expectations are somehow deviant has serious clinical and theoretical consequences. Similarly, within the area of female reproductive behavior, Parlee shows that all too often assumptions are made that have little empirical basis not only about the physiological mechanisms associated with female emotions and activities but also about the social acceptability of responses to reproductive events. While menstrual distress is considered inevitable in women, postpartum depression and ambivalent attitudes about pregnancy and childbirth are perceived as unhealthy.

Both chapters in this Part agree that physiological mechanisms must play some role in sexual and reproductive behavior, just as social beliefs and cultural values influence women's sexual interactions and responses to reproductive events. The nature of the research studies reviewed in each paper indicates clearly that two of the most urgent tasks for psychological researchers at present are to attempt to identify precisely the nature of the linkage between physiology and sexual and reproductive behavior, and to investigate the range of social beliefs about these behaviors and their impact on female sexual and reproductive psychology.

The need for basic psychophysiological research is most evident in Parlee's discussion of menstruation and childbirth. Her review shows that there has been little interest in actually measuring the possible association between variations in biochemical activities associated with reproductive events and variations in affective and behavioral responses to these events among women. Although there is some indirect evidence that certain affective states during the menstrual cycle, such as depression, may be associated with certain cyclic biochemical changes, such as changes in the activities of monoamine oxidase (MAO), all too frequently the biochemical and psychological variables are not measured simultaneously or with equal precision. Medical researchers frequently concentrate on the collection of reliable measures of biochemical activities, but use outdated or unreliable techniques for assessing affective changes. The opposite is often the case among psychological and psychiatric researchers, who measure affect and behavioral changes with some precision but rarely measure biochemical variables directly.

Parlee's comprehensive critique describes in detail some of the major design and measurement problems in much of the published literature to date. Her review suggests that it is premature to dismiss the possibility that female reproductive behavior may be accounted for to some extent by *physiological activity,* since we have very little evidence one way or another about precisely what the extent of the influence of physiological mechanisms on behavior is. Similarly, Schwartz and Strom's discussion of the sexual cycle in men and women suggests that more physiological research is needed. The slower increase in arousability of females as well as the more gradual reduction in arousability after climax may or may not be a consequence of sex differences in physiology. Given that the sexual act takes place within a social context, an analysis of the physiology of sexual excitation of both sexes should control for possible contextual effects.

Research acknowledging the possible *social influences* on sexual and reproductive behavior is often plagued by similar problems. All too frequently, some unspecified cluster of variables—referred to variously as "environment," "society," or "social context"—is assigned the role of accounting for that proportion of the variance not explained by empirical relationships produced by studies of events perceived as biological in nature. Although it is being increasingly accepted that these unspecified or only vaguely defined influences probably do have a substantial effect on reproductive psychology and especially female sexuality, research focused on identifying precisely which aspects of social ideology, which social institutions, and which family experiences are most closely connected with psychological responses to women's bodies has only begun. Identification and measurement of the linkages between social ideology and institutions and psychological processes have always been major foci of social psychological research. The process by which women (and men) internalize social values about sexuality and reproduction, for example, is just as perplexing a problem as the process by which individuals acquire social prejudices and political attitudes. As long as sexual and reproductive behavior was assumed to be somehow "natural," and therefore less interesting to investigate, the causal linkages between behavior, values and institutional policies could not be understood. The increased interest in measuring possible social causes of female sexuality evidenced in the Schwartz and Strom article is encouraging, particularly the increasing rejection of the "marriage model" of sex behavior and the investigation of sexual life styles and sexual abuse.

The negative influence of a culturally biased view of women's bodies limiting the growth of good scientific research on sexual social psychology is just as evident in the research on female reproductive behavior. Parlee shows that while there has been some interest in the social psychology of the childbirth complex, the measurement of social influence on the menstrual cycle and menarche has only begun. There is so little research on menopause that no real theoretical orientation can be identified, although those studies available at present place varying emphases on the social-psychological and biological correlates of menopausal behavioral and emotional changes. Just as sexuality in females has been oriented toward the ideal sexual response in marriage, so has reproductive behavior research emphasized those aspects of the reproductive cycle that are most apparently connected with the traditional values reinforcing the institution of the family and child-rearing motivation in women. The social-psychological emphasis on aspects of birth that Parlee describes should also be considered in research on women's responses to other reproductive events. Women's emotional responses to menarche, menstruation, and menopause are often interpreted in the applied literature as indicators of the psychological health of the female personality rather than consequences of socialization.

Most societies hold well-articulated and rigidly defined conceptions of what is and what is not appropriate female sexual and reproductive behavior; surely, these conceptions influence women's own attitudes about their bodies. It is not enough, however, merely to describe correlations between social attitudes and beliefs and sexual and reproductive psychological variables. Individual attitudes are influenced by a number of different experiences and values, and such attitudes are often part of a complicated network of more general attitudes and belief systems. In order to assess accurately the impact of social beliefs on sexual and reproductive behavior, we must first develop a conceptual scheme for investigating sexual and reproductive attitudes. Schwartz and Strom offer a number of provocative leads concerning the possible connection between sexual behavior and attitudes, body image, and social views about fashion or beauty. If sexual behavior, physical attractiveness, and self-esteem are closely associated among women as some data suggest, then an analysis of the temporal changes in social standards of beauty and fashion could provide some important insights concerning how changes in women's evaluation of their bodies may affect their sexual self-concept and sexual activity over their life cycle.

The impact of historical changes in sexual beliefs among such important opinion leaders as medical doctors on women's sexuality is surely another important research question. Within the area of female reproductive behavior, there exists the same need to describe the system of social beliefs pertaining to reproductive events and to specify how those beliefs play a causal role in determining women's own perceptions about their reproductive capacity and their emotional responses to major reproductive events. Throughout much of Parlee's article, the need to evaluate reproductive behavior in its social context is emphasized. For example, there is little research on the impact both within our own society and in world societies generally of the paradoxical social evaluation of reproductive events as both sacred and abhorrent. Why such beliefs are so widely held is not at all understood, nor is the extent to which such beliefs influence women's own self-image.

By describing the critical substantive issues in the areas of sexuality and reproductive psychology, the major findings that have emerged in the published literature during the past few decades, and the methodological problems of much of the empirical studies that should be avoided in future research designs, the Schwartz and Strom and Parlee articles make the most important contribution to the field to date. The material they present and evaluate clearly suggests which directions of research will be most fruitful in the future. In my view, the development of such a framework can best be accomplished by considering the following research problem areas.

First, *psychologists must continue developing conceptual categories* that are useful in describing and testing empirically the range of behaviors, attitudes, and emotions currently included under the general rubrics of "sexuality" and "reproduction." One of the most important contributions of the Schwartz and Strom and Parlee articles is the discussion of sexuality and reproduction within new conceptual frameworks. Schwartz and Strom, for example, clearly distinguish between the social act of sex, the psychological experience of sex, sexual lifestyles, and sexual abuse, each of which may be best explained by a different theoretical approach. Similarly, Parlee has suggested that the experience of pregnancy, childbirth, and the postpartum could be merged conceptually instead of being treated as distinct events with different causal explanations. In any new science, the process of construct development is continual and the conceptual categories developed during one phase of theoretical development may be modified as new research and theory are produced. Given the lack of vigorous and sophisticated thinking devoted to female sexuality and reproductive behavior until now, the development of a language with which to discuss and begin investigating the variety of complex issues within the field is urgent and should be considered top priority.

A related research issue is the development of a set of constructs that includes what may be called the "exceptions" to the traditional model of female sexuality and reproductive behavior. Just as the traditional model of female sexuality has emphasized marital sexuality and treated exceptions to this behavior as deviant, so has the common description of the reproductive cycle in women implicitly treated such events as miscarriage, physiological infertility, abortion, illegitimate birth, and the manipulation of reproductive physiology through hormonal therapy or surgery as "errors" in the childbearing cycle of women. There are a large number of women whose sexual experiences, sexual identities, and reproductive patterns would be left unexplained if theory construction was devoted entirely to the model pattern.

Second, within this field *there is a particularly urgent need for comparative and historical research.* Like many problem areas within the psychology of women, the development of a comprehensive analytic perspective requires an interdisciplinary approach. Sex and reproduction are not unique to the middle-class American women who are all too often the participants in psychological research. Psychologists will never really be able to make generalizations about the nature of women's sexual and reproductive behavior unless research is carried out among women in different social and historical contexts. Comparative research would be especially useful in evaluating the relative influence of physiological and social psychological mechanisms on sexual and reproductive behaviors. If women living in different social environments with substantially different beliefs about how women should behave during sexual interactions or critical reproductive events share similar psychological responses, the possibility is raised that common physiological processes may help explain those responses. If sexual and reproductive psychology is, however, at least partly caused by social attitudes, cultural values, and institutional policies, then the extent to which historical changes in these attitudes, values, and policies influence women's psychology must be described.

One particularly perplexing problem that has yet to be investigated systematically is the nineteenth-century practice of female genital surgery, purported to modify women's sexual urges and increase their success in childbearing. What were the social forces that produced such a practice and then eventually brought it to an end? What does such a practice indicate about Western attitudes and beliefs about female sexuality and the position of women as childbearers? What was the impact of such a practice on female sexual identity, mental well-being, and physical health? An equally intriguing problem concerns the gradual reduction in the age of menarche. The presence of nubile daughters within the natal family for many years prior to marriage in the present day may lead to socialization practices that were not observed during earlier periods when daughters married soon after menarche occurred. The content, or focus, of female socialization, then, could vary historically depending on changes in the timing of sexual maturity, with such differences in socialization having quite different implications for feminine psychosexual development.

One could list a whole host of interesting questions about the historical processes influencing female sexuality and reproductive psychology which have been almost totally ignored both in psychology and in the other social sciences. The dearth of research on the historical analysis of sexuality and reproductive behavior, however, hardly compares with the lack of systematic analysis of cross-cultural trends. All too often, quotes from the Greeks or Romans, myth, folklore, and personal anecdotes from observers of other societies typify the kind of information presented in popular literature on the extent to which women in other societies share sexual and reproductive experiences similar to those of American women. The absence of systematic cross-cultural research within psychology is surprising, given the availability of both archival and survey data on other cultures and the current interest in the population problems in world societies.

Much of the literature on the reproductive experiences of non-Western women also gives inaccurate impressions, such as the purported lack of pain experienced at childbirth or the absence of concern about menopause and infant and maternal mortality. Each of the issues raised by Schwartz, Strom, and Parlee could be investigated cross-culturally as well as within our own society, including the problems of sexual object choice, sexual responsiveness, rape, menstruation, pregnancy, menopause, and menstrual mood fluctuations.

A third concern of researchers in the field of female sexuality and reproduction should be the *broadening of the range of methodological techniques used both in data gathering and data analysis.* As both the Schwartz and Strom and Parlee articles stress throughout their discussions, one of the problems in much of the past research in the field is not only the lack of concern with methodological problems, but also the inappropriateness of the methodological techniques that are used. Laboratory experiments and the use of analysis of variance may be appropriate for some problems, but certainly not all.

Given the complexity of the issues in the field, the use of a wide variety of different methodological tools and research designs is a basic necessity. The use of household surveys, quasi-experimental designs, archival data, clinical data, and census data is just as applicable as the more familiar experimental or experiential procedures. If the range of data-gathering techniques is broadened, the kinds of statistical procedures used to test hypotheses must be broadened as well. The development of causal models explaining changes in sexual attitudes over time, for example, may require the use of regression and path analytic techniques to sort out the relative effects of competing explanatory variables. Such techniques, however, would not be so appropriate in analyzing ideographic data gathered on a few selected women to measure changes in their sexual identity or affective responses to reproductive events over their life cycles. The strength of both experimental and nonexperimental methods and statistical techniques must be recognized so that solid and sophisticated empirical evidence provides the basis for a new theory of female sexuality and reproductive behavior.

Finally, *both theory and empirical research problems should be phrased so that the recommendations made can be aimed at bringing about sexual equality.* One cannot help but be dismayed that much of the renewed interest in both female sexuality and reproductive events has come about because of an increase in the incidence of reported rape, deaths, and medical difficulties associated with new hormonal methods of contraception, abortion, and reproductive surgery.

Now that both public and scientific interest in women's bodies has increased, however, it is imperative that psychological researchers attempt to influence the nature of public policies that will restructure medical, legal, and other social institutions to benefit women as well as better the quality of life for all individuals.

COMMENTS BY WENDY MCKENNA

One of the most important contributions of Chapters 5 and 6 is that they both underscore a fact which we, as scientists, are finding it more and more difficult to ignore; namely, that what we think of as the ultimate factor differentiating men and women—sexual and reproductive functioning—may be as much of an "arbitrary" social construction as the fact that more men than women are executives in large corporations. The ways in which we, as members of a particular historical, cultural group, give meanings to events (like intercourse and menstruation) and objects (like clitorises and uteruses) exist because they serve as evidence to support more basic beliefs about the way the world is. The meanings are arbitrary only in the sense that they can change and be changed.

If the ways we study and theorize about female sexual and reproductive roles reflect deeply held (and prejudicial) beliefs about the "nature" of women, as both Schwartz and Parlee assert (and with which I agree), then changing our methods and theories will not be enough. We must begin to formulate radically new basic assumptions. Although we may find nineteenth-century theories of female sexuality amusing, they are no more (or less) a reflection of biased thinking than are the most modern, scientific journal articles. It is not very different to assert with a high degree of scientific assurance that using the brain will consume energy needed for the female reproductive organs to function properly (see Bullough, 1975) than it is to "prove," through controlled research, that women tend to be more hostile and anxious premenstrually (Ivey & Bardwick, 1968). Both reflect a need to see female versus male as a critical differentiating category, and both can be interpreted as scientific support for the innate inferiority of individuals with ovaries and a uterus. Perhaps it is time for us to begin thinking of the male/female dichotomy in the same way we think of the short/tall dichotomy. Bem's paper before the APA-NIMH Conference (see Chapter 1) makes this point well.

A second important contribution of Chapters 5 and 6 is that they raise questions that suggest a wealth of new directions for research on women. Pepper Schwartz and Deanna Strom's concept of "sexual flexibility" in women, and their suggestions of possible antecedents of this flexibility, make it clear that good research on the socialization of female sexuality is desperately needed. How do girls and women learn about sexuality? How do sexual fantasies develop over time from childhood? What is the nature of childhood sexuality? What are the ethical and methodological problems involved in answering the preceding question? How do girls learn to label their feelings as sexual? What is the effect of not having an obvious sign of arousal (e.g., an erection) on this labeling process? In terms of peer-group influences, when and how does childhood sexual rehearsal occur? What is the girl's equivalent of the boy's experiences with group masturbation? What "traumatic" events occur in the development of boys which prevent them from developing sexual flexibility? How do those involved in incestuous relationships feel about the experience? In sum, Schwartz and Strom's article points out, with a great deal of insight and creativity, the ways in which our ideas about females construct the kinds of research questions we ask about their sexuality and indicates the direction which new constructions, and therefore, research, can take.

Mary Parlee's critical analysis ought to be required reading for any individual doing research on menstruation, pregnancy, childbirth, or menopause. There is little that one can add to her methodological criticisms. I would underscore several points she makes by encouraging some basic research on the distribution of menstrual cycles in various populations, particularly college students (who are most often subjects in studies of the menstrual cycle and affect or performance). If, as McClintock's (1971) data suggest, the menstrual cycle is not randomly distributed, there are important implications for the types of statistical analyses which are appropriate for analyzing data on the relationship between the menstrual cycle and any type of behavior.

Parlee's article also stimulates many questions amenable to research. How do the ways in which a girl learns about menstruation, pregnancy, and menopause affect her experience of these events? What is the relationship, for example, between what happens when she gets her period for the first time (Whom does she tell? How does she feel about it?) and her future experiences of menstrual discomfort? What are the fantasies, beliefs, and feelings of women about childbirth, pregnancy, and motherhood *before* they become pregnant for the first time, and how are these experiences related to actually experiencing pregnancy and childbirth? Do adoptive mothers suffer from "postpartum" depression? What, if any, are the psychological and behavioral consequences of being born without a uterus for a female? How does the climacteric differ for women who have had children, versus women who have chosen not to, versus women who have not been able to? Are the personal and interpersonal meanings of menstruation, pregnancy, and menopause different for lesbians than for heterosexual and/or bisexual women, and if so, how?

These are only a few of the questions to which we need answers. Some of them seem so obvious that we might wonder what has taken us so long to get to the point where they are asked. Parlee's statement that biological explanations have been used to explain menstrual "disorders," while psychological ones have been used to explain "disorders" of pregnancy, is a point worth noting. What factors in the history, politics, and social psychology of the study of women have contributed to this very interesting conceptualization of the "female problem"?

The areas covered by Schwartz and Strom and Parlee—female reproductive and sexual behavior—are, I believe, the areas in which a new psychology of women can make its most important contribution. We can begin to search for answers to what it means to be a woman, and we can begin to look for indications of how we might proceed to challenge the whole concept of female versus male.

REFERENCES

Bullough, V.L. Sex and the medical model. *Journal of Sex Research*, 1975, *11*, 219-303.

Ivey, M. & Bardwick, J. Patterns of affective fluctuation in the menstrual cycle. *Psychosomatic Medicine*, 1968, *30*, 336-345.

McClintock, N.K. Menstrual synchrony and suppression. *Nature*, 1971, *229*, 244-245.

SECTION II

PART I
WOMEN AND WORK

INTRODUCTION

JULIA A. SHERMAN & FLORENCE L. DENMARK

Women have always worked; they simply have not been paid or paid well for their work, and they have rarely been hired to do work of high status. Hence, paid work has not been considered an important aspect of women's lives. This has now changed and the time has come to examine women's work motivations and how they intersect with her roles. This is important, whether we arc thinking of women aspiring to careers or blue-collar working women, whether they are black or white, whether they have children or not, whether they are young or old.

The article by Helen Astin presents an overview of the movement of women into higher positions in society, with emphasis on the professional and educational aspects of work and career planning.

Judy Long Laws looks behind the facts to develop explanatory concepts about women's work behavior. Her analysis, using expectancy-value theory, illustrates an approach frequently emphasized by conference participants: viewing the woman in the context of her sociocultural milieu.

Janice Gump's article deals with the experience of black women and specifically how, in contrast to white women, paid work has always been a part of their sex-role expectations. Her paper touches upon the raw nerve of the conflict between dependency and independency. It is the "possibility of being dependent" and cherished which has been denied black women. Here, black women and white women seem to be going in opposite directions. If most white women had been cherished through their lifetimes, there would be no Women's Liberation Movement. Which one of us does not know many women who trusted in the magic words "till death do us part," but suddenly found themselves alone, having to cope with totally unexpected problems for which they were not prepared either emotionally or educationally? Many of us see the white woman's Doll House as a snare and a delusion.

CHAPTER *8*

PATTERNS OF WOMEN'S OCCUPA-TIONS

HELEN STAVRIDOU ASTIN

Helen S. Astin is Professor of Higher Education at the Graduate School of Education at UCLA. Between 1971 and 1973, she was Director of Research and Education for the University Research Corporation in Washington, D.C. Previously she was Research Associate for the Bureau of Social Science Research, also in Washington. Previously, between 1965 and 1967, Dr. Astin served as Research Associate for the Commission on Human Resources of the National Academy of Sciences, and from 1967 to 1968 she was associated with the Institute for the Study of Human Problems at Stanford University. She also taught both at Stanford and for four years (1961-1965) at the National College of Education. Her primary research interests are in the fields of educational and career development and higher education, with an emphasis on women.

Helen Astin has been Chairperson of the American Psychological Association's Task Force on the Status of Women in Psychology and President of Division 35 (Division of the Psychology of Women) of the American Psychological Association. Currently, she is serving on the Association's Board for Policy and Planning. She has served as a member of APA's Education and Training Board, is a member of the National Research Council-Board of Human Resource Data and Analysis, and is a Trustee of Hampshire College. Presently, she serves on the Editorial Boards of the Journal of Counseling Psychology, Journal of Vocational Behavior, Psychology of Women Quarterly, Signs, *and* Sage Annuals in Women's Policy Studies.

Among her publications are: Human Resources and Higher Education (with *Folger and Bayer, 1970);* The Woman Doctorate in America; Women: A Bibliography on Their Education and Careers *(with Suniewick and Dweck);* Higher Education and the Disadvantaged Student *(with A.W. Astin, Bisconti, and Frankel);* Open Admissions at CUNY *(with Rossmann, A.W. Astin, and El-Khawas);* Sex Roles: An Annotated Research Bibliography *(with Parelman, and Fisher); and* The Power of Protest *(with A.W. Astin, Bayer, and Bisconti).*

A historical account of women's labor-force participation highlights the growth in numbers of women currently participating in paid employment, describing changes in demographic characteristics from primarily single and low-class women to married women with children. Since higher education institutions play a key part in shaping women for their roles as workers, the focus is on women's development through the college years. During the past decade, changes have occurred in college women's degree aspirations and career plans: More women aspire to postgraduate education and advanced degrees, while their career plans are shifting toward less traditionally female occupations. Theories of occupational development of women have held that women's careers differ from those of men in that they are characterized by discontinuities resulting from marriage and childbearing and child rearing. Empirical studies of career development of women have found that career-oriented women are more autonomous, have high mathematical aptitude, have been supported by important men in their lives, and are more likely to have working mothers. Future research in the occupational development should monitor the trends in choices, preferences, aspirations, and the actual occupational behavior of women. Moreover, it should isolate the personal characteristics of women and determine the early experiences that affect the choice and pursuit of different fields and careers.

In an overview of women and work, it is important to understand women's development for occupational roles thus far, before turning to unresolved issues and questions. An examination of women and work must focus in part on women's labor-force participation—that is, rates of participation, kinds of jobs held, occupational status as reflected in salaries and rank, characteristics of workers, and changes over time. Also, the current scene must be put in historical perspective.

Factors in career choice and development (including the determinants of choice, career patterns, and the barriers and facilitators in women's occupational development) must also be acknowledged. In discussing barriers and facilitators, early socialization and experiences that determine self-perceptions and aptitude development—both of which are important elements in career choice and development—must not be overlooked. Often the barriers include both internalized obstacles that inhibit women from fully actualizing themselves through careers and work, and institutional constraints that hamper them from growing to their fullest potential.

Because educational institutions play a key part in shaping women for their roles as workers, I have chosen to emphasize women's development through the college years. The study of educational institutions and their impact on women also offers information important to formulating policy recommendations, which could change this educational system that so greatly influences women's occupational development.

From a summary of what is known so far about the determinants of occupational choice and development, a framework emerges for future studies of the career development of women.

HISTORY OF WOMEN AND WORK

Before the twentieth century, the lives of low-income women always included work. With the turn of the century, more young and single, and not necessarily low-income, women began to participate actively in the labor force. Over time this pattern shifted as older and married women with children entered the labor market. The World War II years were critical in terms of the kinds of work in women's lives. Society's need for labor facilitated the entry of large numbers of women into the work force, independent of their age and marital status. This movement became an irreversible trend that changed women's attitudes and society's perception of the role of women in the labor market (Chafe, 1972).

The postwar years of the 1950s were characterized by a second trend: Younger married women who lived with their husbands and preschool children chose to participate in paid work outside the home. Economic necessities, lower birth rates, and improved health and homemaking technologies contributed to a continual growth in women's participation in the labor force. By 1970, 31 million women (38% of the labor force) were working. More than 50% of these women were married. Furthermore, the increase occurred not only among married women without children, but also among those with preschool children—an increase

Table 1.1
Distribution of women in selected occupations
1950-1970

Occupation	Women as percentage of total employed in occupation		
	1950	1960	1970
Professions	40	38	40
Dentist	3	2	4
Engineer	1	1	2
Lawyer, judge	4	4	5
Physician, surgeon	7	7	9
College professor	23	24	29
Life and physical scientist	12	10	13
Editor, reporter	38	37	41
Social scientist	n.a.	20	19
Teacher, elementary	91	86	84
Teacher, secondary	57	50	50
Librarian	89	85	82
Social worker	69	63	63
Technician, health	n.a.	68	70
Technician, other	n.a.	8	11
Other occupations			
Manager, administrator	14	15	17
Sales worker	34	36	39
Clerical worker	62	68	74
Craftsman, foreman	3	3	5
Operative (except transport)	n.a.	36	39
Transport equipment operative	n.a.	3	4
Service worker (except private household)	45	52	55
Private household worker	95	96	97
Laborer	4	5	8
Total	28	33	38

Source: Abstracted from a table by V. K. Oppenheimer (Industrial Relations, 1968, 7), using 1960 and 1970 census data.

from 19% in 1960 to 33% in 1973. In essence, the choice between career or marriage in the 1920s has become a choice to combine both in the 1970s.

The distribution of women by occupational classification, however, has remained virtually the same. In 1970, women constituted 40% of all professionals. This 40% was based on 84% of all those in elementary education, men and women, 82% of all those in library work, and 70% of all those technicians in health-related fields; 17% of all managers and administrators; 39% of all sales workers; 74% of all clerical workers; 55% of all those in service occupations; 96.5% of all private household workers; and 8% of all laborers.

Moreover, the differentials in reward, as expressed in salaries, persist. The median wage or salary as a percentage of that received by men in 1970 ranged from a low of 42.8% for sales workers to a high of 66.7% for professional and technical workers. The lower salaries of women are not necessarily attributable to a lower level of skill. Oppenheimer (1968) analyzed the sex labeling of jobs in an attempt to explain these differentials. Tey observed that even in occupations where a relatively high level of skill is required (skill expressed in amount of education necessary), if the occupation is labeled "female," for example, or has a high proportion of women in it, the salaries are relatively low. Even for occupations where schooling is virtually the same for men and women, the income differential still remains. Strong evidence supports discrimination by sex in awarding differential salaries (H. Astin & Bayer, 1972; Bayer & H. Astin, 1975).

Oppenheimer suggested that, in part, sex labeling occurs because certain occupations are characterized by conditions that permit women to enter them readily and to function comfortably while maintaining dual roles as worker and homemaker. For example, in the women's professions of nursing, teaching, and librarianship, training is acquired before employment; jobs exist all over the country, although during the past few years job shortages have existed in teaching; and career continuity is not essential. Thus, women can withdraw and reenter these fields without much difficulty and can follow their husbands to new locations and still find employment. In contrast, men who choose professions of medicine, law, and engineering require lengthy training. Career continuity is essential, especially with an established private practice.

Can this pattern be changed? Can occupations become less sex-typed so that the distribution of men and women within an occupation becomes equal? The promise for such a change lies in part in the educational aspirations and attainment of young women, and in the field and choices they make. It also depends on the elimination of sex discrimination practices. Access to higher education, a critical condition for occupational entry and mobility, must be examined, and policies must be formulated so that internalized and institutionally imposed barriers can be eliminated. Access is determined by choices women do or do not make because of the cumulative effects of socialization and because of institutional barriers, such as ignorance or neglect of women's needs and discrimination in admissions, financial assistance, programs, and services.

Access can be defined in terms of actual participation of women in higher education. The present status of women and the trends over time provide a perspective on where women are now, where they have come from, and where they may go in future decades. It is important to examine women's degree and career aspirations, choices of field, self-concepts, and life goals, since they are all important determinants in access and achievement.

EDUCATION AND EMPLOYMENT OF COLLEGE WOMEN

In spite of the great expansion of postsecondary educational opportunities in recent years, a sizable proportion of young persons who complete high school do not enroll in college. By October 1972, only 49% of all youth who had completed high school in that year had enrolled in college: Of this 49%, men comprised 53%; women, 46%; and non-white youth, 48% (U.S. Department of Labor, 1973). Doubtless, some young persons pursue noncollegiate training, such as on-the-job training or technical and vocational school job preparation. Moreover, a number probably pursue postsecondary education at some later date. Nevertheless, an examination of the figures for different subpopulations reveals that (including those who defer enrollment) women and non-white men continue to attend college in fewer numbers than do white male high-school graduates.

Besides sex and race, family background, as expressed by socioeconomic status, is a key determinant of whether people pursue college, postsecondary training, or go to work. An examination of the proportions of persons from various socioeconomic backgrounds who go on to college reveals that over 90% of those with high ability and high socioeconomic status go to college, while only 66% of men and 50% of women with high ability and low socioeconomic status enroll in college (Folger, Astin, & Bayer, 1970). That socioeconomic status penalizes women more than men can be attributed to stereotypic views of parents, who often expect and hope that their daughters will eventually marry

Table 1.2

Degree aspirations, 1966-1974

Degrees	1966, %		1970, %		1974, %	
	Men	Women	Men	Women	Men	Women
B.A.	33	46	34	44	35	39
M.A.	31	32	32	31	26	28
Ph.D.	14	5	12	7	10	7
Professional	10	2	13	3	16	8

and be supported by someone and that their sons will provide for themselves and their families. These expectations result in inequities between the sexes, as a result of conflict over who receives psychological and financial support from parents to pursue education.

Even though ability and past achievement play important roles in determining who goes to college, it is important to highlight the talent loss that occurs simply because a person happens to be a woman from a relatively poor or uneducated family that lacks sufficient finances or has inadequate information about education—its value, where to obtain it, and how to go about pursuing it.

The sexes also differ in college completion rates and persistence. Women are more likely than men to earn their B.A. degrees within four years, but less likely to persist over longer time periods. Thus, the rate of degree completion over time is often higher among men. In a study of the class of 1970, 49% of the women had completed the B.A. in four years, compared with 45% of the men. However, when persistence was defined as "received a degree, still enrolled, or request transcript to be sent to another institution," 84% of the men and only 78% of the women qualified as persisters (Astin, A.W., 1972).

Trends in Aspirations

A study of the trends in degree and career aspirations of college youth over time indicates changes in the aspirations and plans of young women during the past nine years. In 1966, 7% of all women entering college aspired to doctorates or professional degrees; this proportion had risen to 15% by 1974 (Astin et al., 1966-1974). Even though women's aspirations still do not match those of men, the differentials are becoming smaller (in 1966 the Ph.D. aspiration differential was 9%; in 1974 the difference had shrunk to 3%). Similarly, statistics on Ph.D. completion show a sizable growth for women. In 1968, 12.7% of all doctorates awarded were conferred upon women. By 1973, women were receiving 18% of all doctorates. This change is encouraging when compared with the 1.7% growth in the number of doctorates awarded to women between 1960 and 1968.

In addition to degree aspirations and completion, changes in career choice reflect trends in young women's occupational aspirations and plans. Table 1.4, which presents the trends in the career plans for entering college students since 1966, suggests a shift from occupations traditionally chosen by women to occupations more often chosen by men. Between 1966 and 1974, a large decrease in

Table 1.3

Earned doctorates, 1968-1973

Fields	1968		1970		1972		1973	
	Total No.	Women %	Total No.	Women %	Total No.	Women %	Total No.	Women %
Physical sciences	3,642	5	4,389	6	4,226	6	4,016	6
Mathematics	970	5	1,218	6	1,281	8	1,222	10
Engineering	2,833	.4	3,432	.4	3,475	.6	3,338	1
Biosciences*a*	2,608	17	3,162	16	3,306	19	3,379	21
Life sciences	3,681	14	4,564	13	4,984	15	5,068	17
Psychology	1,452	23	1,883	24	2,262	27	2,444	29
Other social sciences	1,842	12	2,336	12	3,328	13	3,467	15
History	733	13	1,092	13	1,185	15	1,213	15
Arts, humanities	2,411	25	2,834	28	3,516	31	4,151	33
Professional fields*b*	689	4	796	3	1,506	12	1,461	14
Education	4,014	20	5,836	20	7,079	23	7,248	25
Total	22,834	13	29,437	13	33,001	16	33,727	18

*a*Biosciences is subtotal of life sciences.

*b*In 1968 and 1970 this is a less inclusive category than in 1972 and 1973.

Source: Appropriate annual reports of *Summary Report: Doctorate Recipients from United States Universities,* National Research Council, National Academy of Sciences, Washington, D.C.

Table 1.4

Career aspirations of college freshmen, 1966-1974

Careers	1966, % Men	Women	1968, % Men	Women	1970, % Men	Women	1972, % Men	Women	1974, % Men	Women	Gains and Losses, 1966-1974, % Men	Women
Artist (including performer)	5	9	4	8	5	8	5	8	5	7	0	- 2
Businessman	19	3	18	3	17	4	15	5	18	9	-1	+ 6
Clergyman	1	.8	1	.2	1	.2	1	.2	1	.4	0	- .4
College professor	2	2	1	.9	1	.9	.7	.6	.7	.8	-1	- 1
Doctor (M.D.)	7	2	6	1	6	2	8	3	7	4	0	+ 2
Teacher, secondary	11	18	12	18	9	14	5	8	3	5	-8	-12
Teacher, elementary	.8	16	1	19	.9	17	.7	11	.6	7	- .2	- 9
Engineer	16	.2	15	.2	13	.4	10	.3	9	.8	-7	+ .6
Farmer, forester	3	.2	3	.1	3	.4	5	.7	6	1	+3	+ .8
Health (non M.D.)[a]	3	7	3	6	3	6	5	10	6	13	+3	+ 6
Lawyer	7	.7	6	6	6	1	7	2	5	2	-2	+ 1.3
Nurse	.1	5	.1	6	.1	9	.2	10	.3	10	+ .2	+ 5
Research scientist	5	2	4	2	4	2	3	2	3	1	-2	- 1
Other[b]	16	31	17	24	19	25	21	25	25	27	+9	- 4
Undecided	5	4	11	11	12	12	13	14	12	13	+7	+ 9

[a]Includes dietician, home economist, lab technician, optometrist, pharmacist, veterinarian.

[b]Includes architect, business (clerical), psychologist, programmer, housewife, policeman, social worker, skilled other.

Table 1.5

Reasons considered very important
in long-range career plans, class of 1972

Reasons	Men, %	Women, %
Job openings available	23	25
Well-paying career	29	16
Can make important contribution	40	51*
Enjoy helping people	45	68*
Enjoy working with ideas	56	59*
Enjoy working with hands	17	18*
Opportunity for self-expression	43	50*
High prestige	17	8+
Opportunity for independence	53	45+
Rapid advancement	30	10+
Stable future	48	39+

*Intrinsic.
+Extrinsic.

Table 1.6

Reasons considered important in
Long-range career plans, 1974 Freshmen

Reasons	Men, %	Women, %
Job openings available	42	52
Rapid advancement	40	30*
High anticipated earnings	48	35*
Respected occupation	34	31*
Independence	44	38*
Chance for steady progress	52	46*
Contribution to society	41	54+
Avoid pressure	16	18+
Work with ideas	43	45+
Be helpful to others	51	73+
Work with people	50	74+
Intrinsic interest in field	63	72+

*Extrinsic.
+Intrinsic.

the choice of teaching and an increase in the choice of business careers, engineering, law, medicine, and farming and forestry occurred. The non-M.D. health fields showed increases for both sexes.

Even though these shifts suggest that women are beginning to deviate from traditional women's careers, and by the next decade may pursue educational plans and careers similar to those of men, at present some sex differences in the dynamics of career choice remain. Tables 1.5 and 1.6 list college students' reasons for their career choices. Women are as practical as men—or even more so—in choosing their careers in that they select fields in which the likelihood of future job openings is high. Twenty-five percent of the women and 23% of the men in the class of 1972 indicated that "job opening available" was a very important consideration in formulating their long-range career plans. By 1974, 52% of freshmen women, compared with 42% of freshmen men, considered "job opening available" important.

From these data on important job considerations, women appear more motivated by intrinsic than by extrinsic considerations in choosing a career. That is, more women than men indicated as very important to their career choice the following reasons: contribute to society, work with ideas, be helpful to others, intrinsic interest in the field, work with people, and opportunity for self-expression. More men than women checked as their reasons a well-paying career, high prestige, rapid advancement, and stable future. These kinds of findings have been misused and misinterpreted. Women have often been barred from educational experiences and jobs because others see their reasons as "self-actualization" rather than economic interest and need. To date, no research has examined the extent to which self-actualization versus economic reasons affects persistence, achievement, and work commitment.

Turner (1964), in a study on the nature of ambition, found that for women the need for self-actualization is an important determinant in career choice and development. The study was designed to differentiate the ambitions of men and women. Distributions of ambition were examined by levels of aspiration for material goods, education, occupations, and eminence. Educational and occupational ambitions related substantially to material ambitions for men, but not for women. Women's educational ambitions often served intrinsic needs. Women with material ambitions were more likely to expect satisfaction of these ambitions through their husbands; they were also more likely to plan for homemaking. The more recent work of Lipman-Blumen (1972) and Papenek (1973) on vicarious achievement supported this finding. Observing the existence of vicarious achievement in the lives of women, they found that women in Western cultures achieve status through their husbands' career successes. However, Turner found that women who valued intrinsic rewards highly were more likely to seek careers.

College women, who have already made a commitment to education beyond high school, have intrinsic motivations for their educational and occupational aspirations. Are women with intrinsic motivations less likely to exhibit vicarious-achievement tendencies and more likely to be career salient? This question demands further investigation. Also, would changes in the occupational status of women change the nature of their ambition? Would women, as they more often enter the high-status occupations, become less interested in intrinsic rewards, or would the structure of the occupations and the characteristics of persons in those occupations change as a result of a balance of the sexes? That is, do the structure and function of an occupation shape the people in it or do the people shape the occupation?

Self-ratings

Self-concept, as a mediating variable in achievement, has received a great deal of attention in the past few years as efforts have been made to understand why women are not found as often in high-status professional and occupational positions. From recent studies demonstrating the lower valuation of women's traits and products (Broverman et al., 1970; Rosenkrantz et al., 1968; Goldberg, 1968), one can surmise that, as a result of sex-role stereotypes, women are more likely to hold negative values of their worth relative to men.

Measures of self-esteem, as expressed in self-ratings on educational aspirations, achievement, and interpersonal skills, have been of interest to me in research on the educational and career development of students (H. Astin, 1976). Trends in self-ratings are particularly useful in assessing the impact of the Women's Liberation Movement and society's changing views about the appropriate roles of women on young women's sense of self-worth. The extent to which particular college environments and experiences might differentially affect these self-evaluations over time is also an important question, especially for those interested in policy recommendations.

Table 1.7 reports the trends over time and the differences between men and women on ratings of 22 personal traits. A little more than half of both sexes see themselves as above average in academic ability. The sexes also rate themselves alike on "drive to achieve"; there is an increase over time in the proportions of

Table 1.7

Self-ratings of entering college freshmen, 1966-1974

Traits	1966, %		1972, %		1974, %	
	Men	Women	Men	Women	Men	Women
Academic ability	56	59	50	52	53	53
Athletic ability	45	24	46	24	51	26
Artistic ability	16	22	16	20	18	21
Cheerfulness	51	58	48	56	47	58
Defensiveness	28	28	27	27	27	28
Drive to achieve	56	58	51	54	60	60
Leadership ability	41	35	39	30	46	36
Mathematical ability	44	26	38	26	39	27
Mechanical ability	37	11	35	38	37	10
Originality	38	36	35	33	38	36
Political conservatism	18	12	10	7	13	8
Political liberalism	20	18	26	20	22	18
Popularity (general)	35	29	32	26	34	26
Popularity (with opposite sex)	32	25	30	24	33	26
Physical attractiveness[a]	–	–	–	–	28	24
Public speaking ability	24	21	21	17	28	24
Self-confidence (intellectual)	41	31	39	30	46	35
Self-confidence (social)	33	26	30	25	37	31
Sensitivity to criticism	25	30	23	28	23	28
Stubbornness	36	28	35	37	36	28
Understanding of others	55	66	58	67	61	71
Writing ability	26	29	27	29	29	32

Note: Percentages represent self-ratings above average.

[a]Item was not asked in 1966 or 1972.

Table 1.8

Reasons considered very important in
decision to attend college, 1971 Freshmen

Reasons	Men, %	Women, %
My parents wanted me to	22	24
To be able to contribute more to the community	15	23
To be able to get a better job	77	70
To gain a general education and appreciation of ideas	53	69
To improve my reading and study skills	22	23
There was nothing better to do	2	2
To make me a more cultured person	25	34
To be able to make more money	57	42
To learn more about things that interest me	65	74
To meet new and interesting people	36	55
To prepare myself for graduate or professional school	39	29

both women and men who consider themselves above average in this trait. For most traits, no changes over time are noticeable in either direction, which suggests that college populations during the past 10 years have perceived themselves similarly. The only observable change is that both sexes in the recent survey rated themselves higher on "understanding of others," "intellectual self-confidence," and "social self-confidence."

In comparing the 22 ratings of women with those of men, women rate themselves higher on "artistic ability," "cheerfulness," "understanding of others," "writing ability," and "sensitivity to criticism." Men rate themselves higher on traits reflecting academic achievement: "intellectual self-confidence," "originality," "mathematical ability," "public-speaking ability," and "leadership." Even with such traits as "popularity in general," "popularity with the opposite sex," "physical attractiveness," and "social self-confidence," which society ascribes to women more often than to men, and where one might expect women to rate themselves higher, college women rate themselves lower than men. Do women rate themselves lower because they feel less capable or worthy, or because their socialization encourages modesty and suggests that rating themselves high on certain traits—such as "intellectual confidence," "leadership," or "public-speaking ability"—will be inconsistent with their "femininity"? This remains a moot question. The literature on self-esteem is quite confusing and contradictory. However, recent research in attribution theory appears quite promising for understanding women's self-concept and behavior (see Chapter 7).

Some research literature has suggested that women have a lower self-esteem than men. For instance, Berger (1968), in a study of self-esteem, concluded that the self-evaluation of women is partially contingent on their degree of certainty that other people like them. This implies that women's self-esteem is shaped by the messages they receive from important others, rather than by testing their own competencies. Although one would predict an increase in self-esteem as a result of successful competency testing, if the competencies tested are perceived as incongruent with feminine behavior or approval by others, the impact on self-evaluation would tend to be negative.

Maccoby and Jacklin (1974), concerned with an accurate assessment of sex differences in measures of self-esteem, examined 30 studies on self-esteem, but they were unable to discern the existence of any sex differences for this trait. They concluded that "there is no overall difference between the sexes in self-esteem, but there is a 'male cluster' among college students made up of greater self-confidence when undertaking new tasks, and a greater sense of potency, specifically including the feeling that one is in a position to determine the outcomes of sequences of events that one participates in" (p. 158).

My studies and the literature indicate that college women tend to undervalue themselves in contrast to men's self-evaluation on achievement-oriented traits and on social-physical attractiveness. It is important, however, to determine the effect of these self-perceptions on motivation, achievement, persistence, and career development and commitment. The impact of different college environments and experiences on the growth of self-confidence and self-esteem must also be ascertained, since a positive overall self-image, as well as an accurate assessment of intellectual competence and qualities of leadership, are important determinants of success in the world of work.

Employment of College-Educated Women

How do college students view college education? Do they go to college to develop skills and prepare for an occupation? Or do they enroll because they have nothing better to do or because their parents, teachers, and friends expect them to do so? In 1971, one question posed to entering freshmen in the annual survey of the Cooperative Institutional Research Program asked precisely this (A. Astin et al., 1966-1974).

The three most important reasons for attending college, given by both women and men, were: "get a better job," "learn more about things that interest me," and "gain a general education and appreciation of ideas." Both men and women students saw a college education as important not only because it provides opportunities for learning but also because it prepares people for the world of work. However, significantly more men than women perceived the value of education to lie in enabling them to get a better job. More women than men valued the opportunity to learn things that interested them and to gain a general education.

If students begin college expecting to get a better job as a result of a college education, it is important to learn what becomes of college-educated youth. How many pursue postgraduate study? How many enter the labor market? What jobs do they get? Who are their employers? How do they spend their working days, and what salaries do they earn?

In 1971, a large-scale, follow-up study of two college cohorts, the classes of 1965 and 1970, was designed to ascertain the flow of college youth through the college years and into employment (Bisconti & H. Astin, 1973; El-Khawas & Bisconti, 1974; H. Astin, El-Khawas, & Bisconti, 1973). A year after graduation, 70% of the men and 74% of the women of the class of 1970 listed work as a current activity, while 17% of the women and 19% of the men were in post-graduate study. An examination of the activities of the class of 1965 revealed that only 56% of the women but 84% of the men cited work as a primary activity. As time passes after college graduation, women appear to withdraw from the labor market. The 1971 follow-up found these women, then about age 28, busy in the roles of wife and mother. Only 16% of the 1965 women graduates were still single whereas 66% of the 1970 cohort had never married.

Family responsibilities were not the sole cause of the lower labor-force participation among women in the earlier cohort. Differences in degree of career commitment, measured by a self-rating item on preferred combinations of the roles of wife/mother and worker, were also found. One-fourth of the older sample, compared with one-third of the younger group, indicated a preference for combining housewife activities with regular employment. The cohorts also differed in pursuit of advanced study: Among the more recent cohort, 29% of the women had enrolled for advanced study in 1971.

Of the women who entered college in 1961, 19% had enrolled in graduate school in summer 1965. In part, these differentials are due to the lapse of time between matriculation and follow-up; for example, the older cohort was followed up in the summer of 1965, four years after college entry (1961-1965), whereas the younger cohort was followed up approximately five years after college entry (1966-1971). These differences show the interruptions in women's careers during the childbearing and early child-rearing years, as well as some of the changes taking place over time in educational aspirations, career expectations, and preferences.

An examination of the employers and work activities of men and women college graduates of 1965 indicates that, among the women in the labor force, 42% listed occupations in teaching or allied health fields. Among men, 28% listed business; 9%, engineering; and 5%, law. These choices reflect those observed in the general population; that is, a division between the occupations preferred and entered by men and those selected by women. For current employer, 56% of the men listed a private company or self-employed/partnership, compared with 30% of the women, most of whom were in private companies, but not self-employed or in partnership. Moreover, 36% of the women cited elementary and secondary educational institutions as their employers, compared with 15% of the men. The job activities of women reflect, in part, the training they received and the skills they developed in college. Forty-two percent of the women, compared with 19% of the men, reported teaching as their primary activity; 11% of the women, compared with 2% of the men, listed clerical and secretarial activities; 16%, compared with 29%, cited administrative and managerial duties as primary work activities; 16%, compared with 36%, listed sales, promotions, public relations, advertising, and operations. Thus, women are found primarily in teaching, some administrative and managerial, and clerical-secretarial activities.

Salary differentials are not surprising, in view of the employers and work activities of women; for example, educational institutions rather than business and industry, and teaching rather than administration or management. When both men and women were asked about their annual salary, 22% of the women, compared with 16% of the men, estimated their income below $7,000; and 13% of the men, compared with 3% of the women, estimated incomes over $17,000. Moreover, 32% of the women, compared with 2% of the men, indicated no expected salary.

A relatively high proportion of women who received a college education 10 years ago have interrupted their careers. Furthermore, the majority of those in the labor force are in occupations labeled "female" and earn less money than their male counterparts. The employers and work activities of the more recent cohort of graduates remain the same as those of the women college graduates in 1965: 34% in educational institutions and 10% in allied health fields. Job activities in rank order are teaching, service to patients, clerical-secretarial, and administrative-managerial.

Even though women choose to go to college to learn and to prepare for a job, a follow-up in subsequent years indicates that many choose not to work and to engage primarily in the wife-mother role. Moreover, college education does not appear to have opened up options for those interested in work. The majority have limited choices: teaching and health-related work, both occupations of relatively low status compared with those entered by men. Low status here primarily reflects the remunerative aspects of the occupation, not aspects of status such as power, independence in work, flexible scheduling, and so forth.

Whereas education is expected to be an important vehicle in women's preparation and actualization through work, present statistics suggest that college-educated women still have limited occupational options and receive lower salaries than men. In part, this lower status results from women's relatively low aspirations and self-esteem, the result both of socialization and of discrimination by educational institutions and employers.

THEORY OF OCCUPATIONAL DEVELOPMENT

Some of the early vocational theorists (Super, 1957; Ginzberg, Ginsburg, Axelrad, & Herma, 1951), in their treatments of occupational development, incorporated some views on women. However, these early conceptions were primarily descriptive of the usual patterns observed in the career development of women. For example, women's careers differ from those of men in that they are characterized by discontinuities resulting from marriage and childbearing and child-rearing. No efforts were made to identify any of the psychosocial determinants in women's career choice and development.

In the late 1960s, Psathas (1968) and Zytowski (1969) presented theoretical accounts similar in some ways to those presented in the 1950s. Psathas argued for the need to examine the occupational choices of women in the context of sex roles. He focused primarily on variables that affect women's occupational choices differently than those of men; for example, intention to marry, time of marriage, reasons for marriage, and husband's financial status. Zytowski was more concerned with women's vocational patterns and the interactions of women's roles as homemaker and worker. He emphasized such variables as age of entry into the occupational world, and span and degree of labor-force participation.

These four early attempts at theoretical formulations of women and work were all proposed by men whose primary interest and research was the occupational behavior of men. Moreover, all had as their main goal a description of the differences between men and women in occupational choice and development, and placed emphasis on marriage and homemaking as the critical determinants in the career development of women. However, other literature on the subject included research efforts by women social scientists interested in career development of women: Baruch (1967), Tangri (1972), Harmon (1970), Matthews and Tiedeman (1964), Almquist and Angrist (1971), H. Astin and Myint (1971), and H. Astin (1968, 1974). The orientation of their research is quite different: They are interested in isolating factors that differentiate women with certain career choices and commitments from women who are less likely to pursue or persist in careers.

Women scholars in this area have focused on the intragroup variability. They report that career choices, commitments, and patterns for some women parallel those of men, while others choose to be primarily homemakers. The finding from these studies indicate that those who exhibit such characteristics early in their development are differentiated from other women in that they appear to be career-oriented. Those who are not in this group show a weaker career orientation, while still others are primarily oriented toward family and home-making. However, the majority make limited choices. The variables that emerge as significant factors in differentiating women by career choice and commitment are psychological and sociocultural.

These studies on occupational development have been enlightening with respect to personality variables, early experiences, and aptitudes that differentiate career-oriented women, or those choosing nontraditional fields, from women selecting fields most often chosen who are primarily interested in homemaking. Briefly, these studies found that career-oriented women are more autonomous, appear to have been supported or encouraged by a significant man—for example, father, brother, boyfriend, or teacher—and are more likely to have had working mothers. (Often the latter influence has been interpreted to imply the importance of a role model in life choices. I will return to this issue later.) Career-oriented women also tend to value intrinsic rewards, to be less field dependent, and to exhibit more internality. They are quite likely to possess high mathematical aptitude.

With respect to sociocultural variables, the studies found that parental socioeconomic status affects womens' educational attainment and choice of field. Those of high ability but low socioeconomic status are less likely to pursue and persist in college than are men of similar backgrounds. Level of educational attainment is highly related to career orientation and commitment. The higher a woman's educational attainment, the greater her labor-force participation. The higher the spouse's income, the lower the labor-force participation. This finding demonstrates the importance of economic considerations in a woman's decision to pursue an occupational role. It also demonstrates societal norms: It is difficult for a man in a status occupation to accept his wife's work—especially her limited options—since the fact that she works reflects badly on his image as a successful provider.

However, independent of these social and economic constraints, the profile of the career-oriented woman emerges: She is a competent and autonomous woman who is unlikely to attribute her successes to luck or to other persons. She has high mathematical aptitude and has had important men in her life who have encouraged her intellectual and occupational pursuits. Even though the important characteristics of the career-oriented woman can be listed, researchers are not yet able to understand or explain fully which early experiences have enabled her to be different from the majority of women in aptitudes, personal characteristics, and aspirations.

Pursuing demanding careers, in part, presupposes a commitment to higher education. A woman who wants a career has first to make some educational commitments, in that she has to choose to undertake sometimes difficult and lengthy training to prepare for a scientific career or to become a doctor or a lawyer. Such commitments are made only if and when a woman can resolve the marriage and career conflict. A woman can pursue her career goals comfortably if she values herself and is not anxious about being accepted, liked, or loved by men. Women whose educational and occupational aspirations have been "permitted" and supported by important others and those who have developed a sense of self-worth and independence are likely to be able to choose and pursue careers.

How do women develop the necessary autonomy, self-acceptance, and self-regard, as well as the special aptitudes, that predict career commitment? Some indirect evidence suggests that young girls who are permitted to explore their environment at an early age become autonomous and also develop mathematical aptitudes. The development of differential aptitudes in boys and girls appears, in part, to result from the mother-child relationship and interaction. Bing (1963) reported that a marked pattern of help-seeking and help-giving behavior characterized the relationship of the high-verbal child and mother. She concluded that such a pattern interferes with the development of independence and self-reliance required for nonverbal abilities. Mothers tend to use these modes of interaction more often with their daughters than with their sons, perhaps because of the consequences of their own socialization. Moreover, it has been reported that boys in father-absent homes tend to develop higher verbal aptitudes than do boys with both parents present (Carlsmith, 1964). In homes without fathers, the mother often feels compelled to interact with her son to compensate for the father's absence. Close supervision and high verbal interaction with the child might be the important variables in whether a child develops independence, interest in problem-solving, and ultimately high mathematical aptitudes.

Thus, it appears that early experiences are important in predisposing young women, in particular, toward high educational aspirations and careers that are not traditionally feminine.

In view of some of these relationships, one might also reinterpret or elaborate on the role of the working mother in the career development of her daughter. The working-mother factor has been interpreted often in terms of role-modeling theory; that is, young women model themselves after their mothers. Seeing the mother work provides an opportunity for the young girl to observe how a woman handles and performs both roles.

A working mother illustrates by her behavior that many options are available to children later in their lives and in their adult roles. About eight years ago, some of my students and I conducted a small-scale pilot research project with preschoolers in an effort to understand how children develop occupational concepts and work roles. We found that children of working mothers, independent of their own sex, were able to tell us about more activities they would like to engage in than were children of nonworking mothers. The implication is that when both parents perform occupational roles and demonstrate a variety of competencies, children can also aspire to, and perform more, activities of their own. Perhaps later in their lives they will perform a greater variety of roles. However, having a working mother also suggests additional aspects of women's early socialization. A working mother, in addition to providing a role model, is also removed from the growing child for a good part of the day. Consequently, she has fewer hours to engage in help-giving behaviors with her child. These circumstances may permit the child to explore and to solve problems, thereby becoming more independent and self-reliant. In future research it is essential to ascertain the direct and indirect influences of a working mother on the career orientation of her children, especially her daughters.

AREAS OF NEEDED RESEARCH

Three areas of research could expand the understanding of issues in career choice and development of women. This research could also assist in formulating policy recommendations and legislation to permit the fullest development and self-actualization of women.

First, monitoring the trends in choices, preferences, aspirations, and the actual behavior of women must continue now and in the generations to come. This time period is critical to women's social and economic roles. Changes in the behavior, expectations, and preferences of women have already occurred. Perhaps they will become much more homogeneous with respect to career versus homemaking orientations in the near future. College women's attitudes are shifting toward a preference for, and expectation of, performing career and homemaking roles simultaneously. Changes in institutional arrangements, family, education, and work are permitting women to combine these roles more easily and to continue in their careers with only minor interruptions.

Second, variables that characterize women with respect to certain career choices and variables that enhance or inhibit career development must be identified. Their personal characteristics and the early experiences that affect the choice and pursuit of different fields and careers must be determined. Studies can utilize cross-sectional populations; women of different ages, ethnic backgrounds, and socioeconomic status should be examined with respect to plans, choices, preparation, and entry. Those in different fields and with different employers should be studied for their differentiating characteristics, early developmental experiences, and educational experiences. For example, who are the women in the sciences, what were their early experiences, what has given them their sense of independence and self-worth?

Third, intensive longitudinal efforts must be made to identify the critical experiences in the lives of young women which results in differential aptitudes and personality traits, all important determinants in career choice and development. For example, how do young children begin to formulate concepts about work and about themselves? What kinds of home environments and parent-child interactions develop autonomy, high self-esteem, and a sense of competence in a variety of areas? What educational experiences reinforce a sense of self-worth and competence? What role does a liberal arts program, a work-and-study experience, career guidance, or specialized math curricula play in the development of aptitudes and competencies essential to appropriate career choice and development?

These studies should be couched in the context of social institutions. In examining the developmental aspects of women and work, the various institutional practices that affect their full development and utilization must also be examined.

Astin, H.S. Sex differences in mathematical and scientific precocity. In J.C. Stanley, D.P. Keating, & L.H. Fox (Eds.), *Mathematical talent: Discovery, description and development.* Baltimore: Johns Hopkins Press, 1974.

Astin, H.S. The role of continuing education in the development of adult women. *Counseling Psychologist.* (Accepted for publication, January, 1976.)

Astin, H.S., & Bayer, A.E. Sex discrimination in academe. *Educational Record,* 1972, *53,* 101-118.

Astin, H.S., & El-Khawas, E.H., & Bisconti, A.S. *Beyond the college years.* Final Report to National Institute of Health and National Science Foundation, Washington, 1973.

Astin, H.S., & Myint, T. Career development and stability of young women during the post-high-school years. *Journal of Counseling Psychology,* 1971, *19,* 369-394.

Baruch, R. The achievement motive in women: Implications for career development. *Journal of Personality and Social Psychology,* 1967, *5,* 260-267.

Bayer, A.E., & Astin, H.S. Sex differentials in the academic reward system. *Science,* 1975, *188,* 796-802.

Berger, R. Sex differences related to self-esteem factor structure. *Journal of Consulting and Clinical Psychology,* 1968, *32,* 442-446.

Bing, E. Effects of child-rearing practices on development of differential cognitive abilities. *Child Development,* 1963, *34,* 631-643.

Bisconti, A.S., & Astin, H.S. *Undergraduate and graduate study in science fields.* Washington: American Council on Education, 1973.

Broverman, I.K., Broverman, D.M., Clarkson, F.E., Rosenkrantz, P.S. & Vozel, S.R. Sex-role stereotypes and clinical judgments of mental health. *Journal of Consulting and Clinical Psychology,* 1970, *34,* 1-7.

Carlsmith, L. Effect of early father absence on scholastic aptitude. *Harvard Educational Review,* 1964, *34,* 3-21.

Chafe, W.H. *The American woman.* London: Oxford University Press, 1972.

El-Khawas, E.H., & Bisconti, A.S. *Five and ten years after college entry.* Washington: American Council on Education, 1974.

Folger, J.K., Astin, H.S., & Bayer, A.E. *Human resources and higher education.* New York: Russell Sage Foundation, 1970.

Ginzberg, E., Gunsburg, S.W., Axelrad, S., & Herma, J. *Occupational choice.* New York: Columbia University Press, 1951.

Goldberg, P. Are women prejudiced against women? *Transaction,* 1968, *5,* 28-30.

Harmon, L.W. Anatomy of career commitment in women. *Journal of Counseling Psychology,* 1970, *16,* 77-80.

Lipman-Blumen, J. The vicarious achievement ethic and non-traditional roles for women. *Scientific American,* 1972, *226,* 34-42.

Maccoby, E.E., & Jacklin, C.N. *The psychology of sex differences.* Stanford: Stanford University Press, 1974.

Matthews, E., & Tiedeman, D.V. Attitudes toward career and marriage and the development of lifestyle in young women. *Journal of Counseling Psychology,* 1964, *11,* 375-383.

Oppenheimer, V.K. The sex-labeling of jobs. *Industrial Relations,* 1968, *7,* 219-234.

Papanek, H. Men, women, and work: Reflecting on the two-person career. *American Journal of Sociology,* 1973, *78,* 852-872.

Psathas, G. Toward a theory of occupational choice for women. *Sociology and Social Research,* 1968, *52,* 253-268.

Rosenkrantz, P.S., Vozel, S.R., Bee, H., Broverman, F., & Broverman, D. Sex-role stereotypes and self-concepts in college students. *Journal of Consulting and Clinical Psychology,* 1968, *32,* 278-295.

Super, D.E. *The psychology of careers.* New York: Harper & Row, 1957.

Tangri, S.S. Determinants of occupational role innovation among college women. *Journal of Social Issues,* 1972, *28,* 177-199.

Turner, R.H. Some aspects of women's ambition. *American Journal of Sociology,* 1964, *70,* 271-285.

U.S. Department of Labor. *Employment of high-school graduates and dropouts, October 1972: The high-school class of 1972* (Report 155). Washington, D.C.: U.S. Government Printing Office, 1973.

Zytowski, D.G. Toward a theory of career development for women. *Personnel and Guidance Journal,* 1969, *47,* 660-664.

CHAPTER **9**

WORK MOTIVATION AND WORK BEHAVIOR OF WOMEN: New Perspectives

JUDITH LONG LAWS

Judith Long Laws received her B.A. from Radcliffe College and her Ph.D. from the University of Michigan in Social Psychology. She served on the faculty of the University of Chicago from 1967 to 1971, and has served at Cornell from 1971 to the present. Her teaching interests include role theory, formal organizations, feminine psychology, and social psychology. Her research interests focus on female employment and work motivation, female sexuality, and self-identity.

This chapter employs Expectancy Value theory as a framework for examining issues of work motivation. The importance of distinguishing motivation and behavior is stressed, and the complexity of predicting behavior from motivation is noted. Existing research is reviewed, classified with reference to its temporal relation to the individual's work history: prospective, concurrent, or retrospective. It is urged that a dynamic, present-time perspective be taken on incentives and disincentives associated with employment options for women. It is urged that present theories of work incentives and social comparison be extended to women.

A series of influences on women's orientation toward paid employment which stem from sex role are discussed, including the motive to avoid success, role modeling, role partners, and reference groups. In conclusion, a list of proposed future research projects is presented.

Women have for too long appeared only as a footnote in theories of occupational choice, work motivation, work histories or careers, and of achievement motivation. Not only the footnotes but also the theories to which they are appended are inadequate to deal with female employment as a majority (rather than a minority) phenomenon in the United States in the mid-1970s.

Elsewhere (Laws, 1976a) I have summarized the existing theories of women's occupational behavior. These contain distortions and inaccuracies so extensive as to be systematically misleading. In seeking to explore questions of women's work motivation today, therefore, we would do best to start with a review of the empirical research, and then move on to consideration of what the theoretical and research questions might be.

This chapter begins with some necessary conceptual and theoretical points: first, the nature of prospective, concurrent, and retrospective studies of women's work behavior; and second, the important distinction between motivation and behavior.

In the last section of this chapter, I will discuss Expectancy-Value theory as a framework for studying work motivation. In the following sections, existing prospective, retrospective, and concurrent studies of women's work behavior will be reviewed. This will be followed by an analysis of the components of work motivation, and then by a section on sex-role considerations in women's motivation for employment. The final section consists of priority questions for future research.

CONCEPTUAL DISTINCTIONS

In its relation with women's working lives, research may be *prospective, concurrent,* or *retrospective.* Each type of study is capable of telling us rather different things, but only certain things. *Prospective* studies solicit occupational preferences or plans from young persons who have not yet entered the labor force. *Retrospective* studies are used to construct typologies of women's career patterns, or to chart an individual's work history, after the fact. A second type of retrospective study identifies some marked event (e.g., high achievement) and attempts to reconstruct its antecedents. *Concurrent* studies catch the respondent at midstream, and investigate the contemporaneous determinants of her work status. Each type of research asks different questions, and each focuses on a different stage of the work life. Any one corpus is inadequate for understanding the vicissitudes of women's work motivation, as it changes in response to changing life contingencies.

Motivation and Behavior

Existing theory and research on women's labor-force behavior indulges heavily in references to motivational constructs like "choice" and "motivation." Yet, as we will see in reviewing the research literature, virtually all research attempts to measure only *behavior* directly. Rarely do we find any systematic conceptualization of motivation, much less any credible measurement of motivational constructs. The data in most of the research are observations on behavior, which themselves are only items within the complex domain of work behaviors. These behaviors have not been adequately modeled, and the systematic relations among them have as yet been little studied. Motivation is result of multiple influences. Women's employment behavior, in particular, is subject to many extremely powerful external constraints, sex discrimination and family obligations among them. These have been dealt with at length elsewhere (Laws, 1975EE), and will enter this discussion only as they feed back upon motivation.

A distinction between behavior and motivation is fundamental to this review. Behavior is an outcome; motivation, a putative determinant. The relationship is not the simple one of cause and effect, or of the independent and dependent variable. Behaviors (and their consequences) feed back upon motivation in a continuing and dynamic manner. Motivation may be thought of as process rather than an episode.

Motivation, and not behavior, is the primary focus of this paper. Our purpose is to extend and sharpen the conceptualization of work motivation, with an eye to improving the quality of future research. However, in order to deal adequately with issues of work motivation, we will need to improve on the offhand usage common in the literature on working women. Rarely in that literature are any precise definitions of such terms offered. Motivation remains an inferred construct, accessible to the researcher only through verbal behaviors of various sorts. These are affected by many determinants aside from "stable predispositions in the individual." A warranted inference concerning motivation requires a long sequence of theory making and testing, perhaps best exemplified in our time by the tradition of research in the achievement motive. In the absence of such argument and evidence, an inference about motivation is as wildly speculative as an "explanation" of behavior in terms of humor in the blood (or in the ovaries) would be. Authors commonly commit the vulgar error of inferring motivation from behavior. Women are assumed to have "chosen" the situations in which they are found, and the further assumption is made that these outcomes represent women's "first choices," or true preferences. This kind of circular reasoning lends itself to a further error, a neglect (in policy as well as theory) of improving the options of working women. For, if it is assumed that women have chosen their situations, it is assumed (in the absence of organized protest from women) that they are happy with it.

A theoretical framework for motivation.   In this chapter we adopt a humble but workable approach to motivation, which owes something to Lewin (1951), something to McClelland, Atkinson, Clark, and Lowell (1953) and to Vroom (1964). Let us view motivation as a field of forces operating on the individual at a moment in time, within a context of interpersonal influences and material constraints. The irreducible components of motivation are an information term and an incentive term. Vroom's formulation, in its simplest form, specifies that a motivational force that produces behavior is the resultant of the products of expectancies and values associated with a set of possible outcomes known to the individual. This formulation is commonly represented as

$$F i = (E i j \times V j)$$

where E = the subjective probability that act *i* will lead to outcome *j*, and *V* = the anticipated gratification associated with outcome *j*. Presumably by means of this process a motivational force toward each of the possible behaviors considered by the individual is generated, and behavior is determined by the strongest of these.

In Vroom's formulation, cognized instrumentality enters into both the *E* and *V* terms; consequently, informational processes are central to this view of motivation. Vroom's theory is ahistorical; however, in this chapter we are interested in the means by which workers acquire their notions of attractiveness of outcomes, and in the instrumentalities associated with them. We expect that both expectancy and value change over time, reflecting the individual's exposure to a variety of sources of information, including education, the media, and personal experience.

Other extensions of the theoretical framework of the Expectancy x Value theory will be useful in thinking about women's motivation for paid employment. For our purposes, it will be useful to think of the information term as including qualitative information (ε.g., what options are perceived), as well as the subjective probability of success (which constitutes the information term in the Expectancy x Value theory). The much-discussed issue of role modeling is relevant here. If the schoolgirl has not seen a female engineer, does she know that this is a possibility? If not, this option will certainly not appear among the outcomes in her motivational equation, and all questions of instrumentality and valence become moot. Moreover, we should be aware that many different outcomes, each with associated valence, are subsumed in each decision. The motivational complexities of multiple options have received very little empirical study with reference to women. The issue of disincentives, while provided for in the theory, remains unexplored. Similarly, the problem of negative instrumentality of some outcomes, while central to the "sex-role dilemma" discussed later on, has not been researched.

Another useful feature of the Expectancy x Value formulation is that information and incentive(s) interact multiplicatively. The resultant force depends on both, not one, of these terms. Where the incentive value of an option approaches zero, we would predict little effort, or nonchoice. Similarly, however high the incentive value, if expectancy is low, we would make the same prediction.

Motivation, then, is a function of both desire for a goal (its incentive value) and the subjective probability of attaining it. When we use the term "motivation" in this chapter, we presuppose a consideration of both the information term and the incentive term. These vary independently, so it is impossible to characterize an individual's "motivation" or predict ter behavior without a reading on both components. The net motivational tendency (the basis for predicting behavior) may be depressed by a low valuation of the goal or by low expectation of goal attainment.

A good deal of the research based upon the Expectancy x Value theory has been conducted in the laboratory, with all the comforts and conveniences of experimental control and manipulation. The research we review here is both cruder and more complex, permitting only an approximate identification of elements of the motivational theory. The range of outcomes is broad. Behaviors relating to paid employment include occupational aspiration, aspired occupational attainment, entering the work force, changing jobs, continuity or intermittency of labor-force participation (sometimes called "labor-force attachment"), and decisions of various kinds, including those instrumental to a given occupational preference (e.g., kinds of education), or such decisions as working part-time versus full-time. A rough continuity with the experimental research can be maintained, however, if we group together the outcomes having to do with aspiration on the one hand and persistence on the other.

Direct evidence on the motivational antecedents of these behavioral outcomes is even scarcer in the literature to be reviewed. Whenever possible, we will seek to discover the information and incentives operative at the moment in time when behavior is assessed. The lack of such data, however, stimulates many questions for future research.

REVIEW OF EMPIRICAL LITERATURE

Prospective Studies of Women's Occupational "Choice"

In reviewing the empirical literature, we turn first to prospective studies. Research on vocational "choice" is particularly prone to egregious errors in thinking about motivation. All too commonly, occupational aspiration—one of the outcomes that might be predicted on the basis of this motivational model—is interpreted as a measure of "motivation." This reflects a twofold error. On the one hand, such authors are confusing the outcome with one of its predictors. On the other hand, they overlook the expectancy term entirely. They are then in the rather weak position of predicting behavior from pure preference. Moreover, many researchers neglect the social origin of occupational preferences. Another blind spot is the neglect or denial of the effect of material constraints on women's work motivation.

Prospective studies of women's occupational "choice" can give us information on four questions. Certain prospective studies can tell us something about the way women expect to spend their adult years: (a) They can tell us how women expect to distribute themselves over the variety of lifestyles they perceive as options, from "marriage only" to "career only," with various combinations in between; (b) They can inform us as to the extent of life-cycle planning young women are doing at various ages; and (c) They afford us some insight into the incentives that affect preferences among different options. Unfortunately, measurement of value in these studies is crude, at best only a rank-ordering. Little information is gained about the different kinds of incentives perceived and their net effect on motivation. *Expectancy* is rarely measured at all. (d) Other prospective studies focus on expressed preferences among specific occupations.

Unfortunately, there is wide variation in the questions asked of respondents. Some researchers ask the respondent to list all occupations she has ever considered; in Harmon's (1971) study, the mode was 12. Others ask only about current interests, but the wording varies from "interest" or "desire" to "intention." Most studies do not distinguish between the valence of an occupation and the respondent's assessment of how likely she is actually to enter it. That is, the components of motivation for a given occupation (expectancy and value) are not assessed separately. Rarely are respondents presented with an array of occupations representative of the major occupational groupings and queried about their interest and information levels for these. Thus, the existing body of research on occupational intentions provides little information about the processes by which potential careers are selected.

Lifestyle preferences.   Davis (1964), in a study of 925 girls in the seventh to twelfth grades, from blue-collar families, found that 60% believed most women would like to have a job someday. Siegel and Curtis (1963) found that 70% of their sample of college women were oriented toward paid employment sometime in their adult years. Hartley (1960) found, in even younger girls (5-11), an expressed intention to work after marriage, which, however, declined with age.

In the Project TALENT sample, Flanagan, Shaycroft, Richards, and Claudy (1971) found that 90% of the female high-school seniors wanted to work; only 10% preferred "marriage only." In Matthews and Tiedeman's (1964) sample, the majority *expected* to find themselves in the "marriage only" lifestyle 10 years hence. A lower percentage (20%) of female college graduates of 1964 expressed a preference for combining marriage and career. However, we should note that the term "career," as compared with "job" or "employment," has distinctive connotations. For example, Oppenheimer (1972) reported that college women in a study undertaken by the Women's Bureau of the Department of Labor shied away from making the self-attribution "career woman".

Watley and Kaplan (1971) studied the lifestyle preferences of a highly select group of college women (National Merit finalists) and found that 85% intended to have a career. Of these, 46.4% planned an immediate career, plus marriage; 32.8% planned immediate marriage and a deferred career; 6% planned only a career; 8.6% planned marriage only, another 6.2% were undecided with respect to future lifestyle.

In general, studies of college women show "marriage only" to be a minority preference. Of the 1964 graduates, only 8% preferred this option; of Rand and Miller's (1972) college sample, 13% wanted never to work, or to work only until marriage; 35% intended to work most of the time while married and a mother; an additional 20% intended to return to work after children entered school; and an additional 8% would wait until children were grown, and then return to work. Only 2% expressed a preference for "career only."

Rand and Miller (1972) advanced the proposition that the cultural mandate for women now consists of marriage *and* employment; "marriage only" is no longer normative. They compared future plans of junior-high, high-school, and college samples with respect to education, occupation, and marriage. In all samples combined, 95% intended to work after finishing school; no age trend was observed for this variable. The distribution of lifestyle preferences was comparable for the three samples, with college women slightly more inclined to prefer the dual-role lifestyle than were the other two groups. An interesting feature of the research was that respondents were asked to recall what their preferences had been at the age of 12. The comparison shows a marked drop in popularity for both the most traditional lifestyle (marriage only) and the most nontraditional (career only). Various dual-role options emerge as the most preferred, giving strong support to Rand and Miller's thesis.

Table 2.1

Future life plans of 180 women in junior high, high school, and college, at present and recalled from age 12

Life plans	Percentage at present			Percentage at age 12		
	Jr. High	High School	Col-lege	Jr. High	High School	Col-lege
	N=60	N=60	N=60	N=60	N=60	N=60
A. To never work	2	2	3	18	23	25
B. To work until marriage and never work again	7	10	10	15	18	23
C. To work until the birth of children and never work again	18	11	17	11	20	21
D. To work most of the time and remain single	2	–	2	10	20	20
E. To work most of the time, combining a career, marriage and motherhood	28	25	35	22	3	2
F. To return to work after children are in school	20	22	20	8	8	8
G. To return to work after	15	21	8	7	–	–
H. Other	8	8	5	7	7	7

Source: Adapted from Rand and Miller, Journal of Vocational Behavior, 2 (1972), Tables 10 and 11, pp. 326, 327.

Educational and occupational aspirations. In Rand and Miller's (1972) study, a high proportion of the sample intended to go to college, though this percentage declined with age. The respondents' reasons for going to college were overwhelmingly instrumental in nature. Occupational preparation was the modal reason for each age group. Students perceived their parents' reasons for wanting them to attend college as being the same as their own. Occupational choices in the Rand and Miller study were conventional; "teacher" was the modal choice in each sample. Preference for the job of secretary declined with age, but so did preferences for role-innovative occupations.

This accords with Harmon's (1971) finding that occupations which are role-innovative (i.e., nontraditional for women) entered the consideration of young women later than did traditional ones, and were eliminated sooner. Much research remains to be done to uncover the ways in which a broader range of occupational options comes to be perceived as possible for some young women but not for the majority. Existing research indicates that social factors—role models and support from significant others, particularly parents and male peers—are critical.

Many studies have taken as their focus the level of occupational aspiration in women. A number of cross-sectional studies (e.g., Matthews and Tiedeman, 1964) have found that the proportion of "career-committed" women, or women aspiring to professional occupations, is lower among older adolescents than among younger ones. Longitudinal studies (e.g., Schwenn, 1970) confirm the interpretation that women actually lower their occupational aspiration as they proceed toward adulthood. Moreover, this drop is not a "realistic" adjustment of aspiration following failure; rather, a number of studies (Schwenn, 1970; Baird, 1973) show this behavior in women of outstanding academic performance.[1]

Studies demonstrating a drop in measured IQ from seventh to twelfth grade (Campbell, 1973), and the onset of school underachievement in some women at sixth grade (Shaw and McCuen, 1960) seem to reflect the same general phenomenon. Ralph, Goldberg and Passow (1966) found that the ratio of female to male

---

[1] "Career commitment" is another of those ambiguous motivational constructs used with reference to women. In Matthews and Tiedeman's (1964) usage the term approximates intended labor-force attachment (or the proportion of the adult years a woman plans to be in paid employment), a behavioral concept. Tyler's (1972) "career commitment" is a psychological construct. In Tyler's (1972) usage, the term is closer to a sense of motive strength. Tyler implies an invidious comparison between the "weaker" career commitment of women and the (assumed) robust commitment of men. There is some irony here, for psychologists sometimes measure motive strength in terms of *obstacles the organism is willing to overcome* in order to attain the goal state. By this measure, *any* employed woman (not just the "committed" professional) demonstrates motive strength far in excess of most males.

underachievers increases as we go up the educational ladder until the college years, when the number of female underachievers exceeds that of males. Shaw and McCuen found that male underachievers showed this pattern from first grade on, while with females the problem was of late and rather sudden onset. Horner (1972) and her collaborators found that the incidence of motive-to-avoid-success imagery increases with age in the populations studied (seventh graders, high-school seniors, adults). These studies seem to fit in with the picture of adolescence as a time of collision between "femininity" and competence.

School achievement evidently becomes increasingly sex-typed masculine as one moves up through the grades. A discontinuity appears in the instrumental value of school achievement for girls and boys, which perhaps accounts for some of this effect. It is taken for granted that success in school augurs success in an occupation for boys, but marriage is the ultimate success anticipated by most girls, and there is some controversy about how much academic success contributes to this role. Though girls and boys pass through a similar curriculum during these years, the underlying script specifies that boys are preparing for a career, and girls for marriage. In order to be launched on their "career," girls must be acceptable to boys. Sensitivity to the preferences and attitudes of male peers appears as a major factor in research on young women's planning for their futures. In general, we find that young women avoid options that bear the negative incentive of real or imagined disapproval of males who are possible partners (Hawley, 1971; Matthews & Tiedeman, 1964). The cultural script presents marriage as the first priority for women, and in many instances perpetuates the "marriage versus career" polarity. Empey (1958) found that where the future is presented as an either/or choice, women overwhelmingly choose marriage.

This research suggests that marriageability is a very important and desirable goal state for young women planning their future lives. This incentive can be (and is) manipulated, in both positive and negative ways, to shape the behavior of young women toward some, and away from other, cultural options. Policy planning aimed at making better use of womanpower must take into account this powerful factor in the motivational picture.

In research on occupational "choice" among young women, the word "wife" sometimes appears explicitly, and sometimes not. However, the evidence indicates that marriage is part of almost all young women's life planning. In many instances it appears that the occupational options young women consider are contingent upon their assessment of the presumed demands of the invisible option, marriage. There is no evidence that the preparation young women get for marriage is any more realistic or functional than other vocational guidance they receive during the adolescent years.

Studies of occupational "choice." The bulk of prospective studies are concerned with young women's preferences among specific occupations. A large group of these studies can be summarized by saying that they tell us that young women (school age) report the intention, or expectation, or desire to enter a range of occupations that rather accurately reflects the present female labor market. This cognitive map of the female labor market can be reproduced by girls of relatively young age. Harmon (1971) asserted that the map and the preferences have crystallized before the age of 10. Iglitzin (1972) found that fifth graders could sex-type occupations, and that the girls were more traditional than the boys. Looft (1971) traced occupational stereotyping back to second grade, and Papalia and Tennent (1975) to nursery school.

We learn that sex-atypical occupations enter the individual's consideration later than the more typical ones, and drop out of consideration earlier (Harmon, 1971). This appears to be true of at least some of those who end up in role-innovative occupations as well as those who do not (Birnbaum, 1971). Woman-power policy should be concerned with the ways innovative options become known to young girls, and the social support required to keep them under consideration. We conclude from this literature that unselected populations are capable of reporting rather "realistic" occupational expectations. O'Hara (1962), in a study of fourth to sixth graders, found that 66% of girls' choices were teacher, nurse, secretary, or mother. Choices are "realistic" in the sense that they are restricted to the female job ghetto.

Two sorts of "unrealism" may be detected in the occupational preference data. First, the prospective choices do not reflect even the token representation of women in traditionally "masculine" occupations. Second, the "glamour" occupations (ballerina, stewardess, beautician, actress, movie star) are overchosen. These two distortions, though opposite in direction, may be prompted by a common consideration. In prospective studies, information about what a particular job is actually like is minimal, and other factors play a larger role. Preeminent among these may well be the image of the occupation as appropriately feminine.

Table 2.2

Comparison of percent choosing specific occupations: three studies

Occupation	Project TALENT*	Harmon t (1971)	Davis tt (1964)
Housewife	10.4	51	5.5
Elementary-school teacher	9.5	36	13.2
Secretary/clerical/typist	30.3	20	27.4
Actress/entertainer	–	44	1.2
Artist	–	33	1.3
Social worker	–	33	1.2
Nurse	10.1	28	10.9
Interior decorator	–	31	1.1
Model	–	27	1.9
Stewardess	–	27	3.4
Author	–	26	–
Beautician	4.2	–	–
High-school teacher	7.3	25	–
Doctor	–	–	1.9

*Data from Flanagan et al., Project TALENT: *Five Years After High School*, AIR and University of Pittsburgh, 1971.

t Data from L. Harmon, The childhood and adolescent career plans of college women, *Journal of Vocational Behavior* 1,1 (1971).

tt Data from Davis, Careers as concerns of blue collar girls. In *Blue-Collar World*, Shostak and Gomberg (Eds.), New York: Prentice-Hall, 1964.

Table 2.3

Distribution of women workers in major occupational groupings, 1968

Major occupation group	As Percent of total employed women
Professional, technical	14.4
Managers, proprietors	4.3
Clerical	33.3
Sales	6.9
Craftsmen, foremen	1.1
Operatives	14.8
Nonfarm laborers	.4
Private household workers	7.2
Other service workers	15.6
Farmers & farm laborers	2.0
Total employed	100.00 Percent

Source: Adapted from the *1969 Handbook on Women Workers* (Women's Bureau Bulletin No.294), U.S. Dept. of Labor, 1969, Table 40, p. 92.

Occupations typically pursued by men often do not even appear on the (girls') lists (whether by the researcher's oversight or the respondents' is not clear). The range and distribution of choices in three studies may be seen in Table 2.2. A rough comparison with actual labor-force groupings is provided in Table 2.3.

Sex role is a factor in occupational "choice." Some prospective studies provide more information about what young women take into consideration as they form their occupational intentions. In Davis' (1964) study, as we noted earlier, intended occupations were traditional ones. Even so, only 25% expected to achieve their preferred occupation, and 41% saw marriage as the major obstacle to occupational attainment, even of modest degree. Boys in the sample did not expect marriage to affect their careers in this way. The working-class girls in this study perceived a dilemma, but had not discovered any solutions. They are not, however, passive victims; they are not inert with regard to their futures. Rather, they have done more thinking about future occupation than have their male peers. They have incorporated the feedback of academic achievement into their aspirations. Those with higher achievement aspired to higher-level occupations, and those with lower achievement to more traditional "female" occupations. Many of them were already holding part-time jobs while in school.

Work experience is one variable that differentiated the career-oriented women from the traditional in Almquist and Angrist's (1971) study. In terms of the model of motivation employed in that paper, work experience affords an opportunity for learning, which can modify the information or incentive term for a number of occupations. Young women who are not yet in the work force and who have not had summer or part-time jobs are lacking the information that might be so gained. So, too, are the wives who have no history of employment subsequent to completing their education. We might note that it is among this minority that researchers find the most virulent attitudes opposing employment for women—and especially for wives.

The importance of quality and quantity of information about occupational options has probably been underestimated in writing about women's occupational "choice." In Davis' (1964) study, 75% of the respondents reported that they would have liked more information about careers than was made available to them. This is surely an area for policy concern.

The sex-role dilemma emerges as a consideration in Matthews and Tiedeman's (1964) study of "career commitment" in adolescent women. Career commitment dropped from 13% of junior high-school girls to 3% among the high-school girls. Abandoning the intention of a career was associated with the belief that men disapprove of women's using their intelligence.

Almquist and Angrist (1974) conducted a longitudinal study of traditional and career-oriented college women. A number of factors differentiated the two groups. Career-oriented women were more likely to have working mothers, to have more work experience than the traditionals, and to report influence of male peer and of adult role models on their occupational choice. They made their intended career choice earlier, and expressed more certainty that they would actually pursue it. Of the career salients, 80% intended to go to graduate school as compared with 50% of the traditionals.

Traditional women were more likely to be sorority members and to be attached to one partner. Their mothers were active in leisure pursuits, but were not employed. The traditional women reported more influence by *female* peers and family members in their occupational choice. There was some evidence of selectivity in the heterosexual involvements of the career salients. In providing themselves with a partner supportive to their plans, some had broken off a relationship with a partner who was hostile to, and some had intentionally sought a partner who agreed with, their career plans.

Tangri (1972) classified 200 college seniors according to their occupational intention. Role innovators were those choosing occupations with less than 30% females; moderates those choosing occupations with 30-50% women; and traditional those choosing occupations with more than 50% women. All but one of these respondents intended to work after marriage (as compared with 70% of their mothers). A working mother did bear some relation to her daughter's role innovativeness, as did educational level of both parents.

In self-concept, the role-innovative women differed from others in characterizing themselves as less to the feminine extreme on a bipolar scale, not too successful, and concerned with issues of authenticity. Tangri suggested that this last item taps introspectiveness or psychological-mindedness, or sensitivity to others' perception of the career-minded woman as deviant. Tangri also found some evidence for two distinct achievement orientations: vicarious achievement (through husband), which was negatively related to role innovativeness, and direct achievement, which was positively related. Neither the "approach success" nor "avoid success" motive was related to role innovation in this study.

As did Almquist and Angrist, Tangri found that male role models (teaching fellows) and male peers are significantly more important to the role innovators than to the other groups. Tangri analyzed responses of best friends of her respondents, and discovered a strong association between the attitudes of men so named, and the respondent's role innovativeness. Her data suggest that a male's peers must not only approve of a career for his future wife, but appreciate it *for its benefits to her* rather than for other reasons.

Conclusions from the Prospective Studies

The prospective studies give us only an incomplete picture of the processes by which occupational intentions are formed. Young women seem to be low on information with regard to the range of possible occupations, what they entail, and the payoffs associated with them. Most studies are superficial, failing to probe into what women know about potential occupations and the sources of their information. The prospective studies tell us that women are not aiming for occupational futures differentiated realistically by their ability or other factors. Rather, they "choose" stereotypically. The predictive validity of occupational intentions measured in this way is unimpressive (Harmon, 1967). Factors other than those discussed so far are the primary determinants of most working women's occupational histories.

The prospective research does not tell us as much as we would like about women's planned labor-force participation. We have learned that most of today's young women intend both work and marriage, but we do not know whether they plan continuous or intermittent participation, or their degree of planning for their dual roles. In most instances, researchers do not ask what difficulties women anticipate and what solutions they envision.

The existing research does not provide information about incentives associated with any extensive array of options for adult living. Most studies have focused on social factors to the exclusion of others. It is possible that this research gives us an exaggerated idea of the importance of face-to-face personal relationships for women's occupational directions. Moreover, research tends to emphasize the supportive and facilitative relationships; little research has been done on experiences of discouragement or punishment which have been decisive in determining women's occupational and educational directions. Research on male attitudes, women's own beliefs, and projective situations suggest that these may be prevalent and have great impact.

However one-sided this research emphasis may be, it has uncovered strong effects which we must bear in mind in training young women (and men) for adulthood. In reviewing this research, we have found that adequate femininity and marriageability are very important to young women, and that affirmation of these is mediated primarily by male peers. Behaviors that can be interpreted as disconfirming the sense of adequate femininity will be avoided. Conversely, one positive incentive associated with some occupational options is sex-role congruence: As some occupations are seen to enhance "masculinity," so others may be viewed as enhancing or affirming "femininity."

Face-to-face relationships are the mechanism by which cultural norms of femininity are mediated. These norms remain conservative, stressing "femininity" at the expense of competence. The imbalance in emphasis appears to increase as young women approach nubility. Thus, the timing of the discontinuity varies with social position, appearing earlier in noncollege-going populations, and later among women who will attend college before marrying. Komarovsky's (1946) college women reported a rather abrupt discontinuity, as parents who had formerly rewarded academic achievement switched their attention (and reinforcements) to social activity. Other studies show that both females and males evaluate the successful female as a failure and like her less than her unsuccessful counterpart. (Feather & Simon, 1975.)

Subcultural variations in the prescription of what constitutes adequate femininity also appear in the literature. When the employed mother was a rarity, this factor predicted her daughter's occupational aspiration. Now that maternal employment is a majority phenomenon, prediction of a daughter's attitudes and intentions is mediated by other factors as well. Important among these seems to be the daughter's assessment of her mother's success as a model for the dual role lifestyle. This appears to be mediated by the daughter's assessment of the *father's* satisfaction with her partner (G. Baruch, 1972).

Such subcultural variation represents a range of "solutions" to the femininity versus competence dilemma, and merits a closer look. At this point we may summarize by saying that, judging by their expressed intentions, young women extend their competence as far as prevailing definitions of femininity permit, and no further.

Retrospective Studies of Women's Career Patterns

Retrospective studies underscore the limitations of prospective studies by uncovering patterning in women's careers which the prospective studies fail to predict. Sometimes these failures are caused by the respondents, whose systematic distortions of their expectations make them predict their own lives incorrectly.

For example, young women do not appear to have expectations for divorce or bereavement, yet these events are prevalent and have major impact on women's labor-force participation.

Effects of unexpected events.   In a study of 301 Chicago widows, of age 50 and above, Lopata and Steinhart (1971) found that the major life event of being widowed precipitated many entries into the labor force. Although only 10% of these women had never been employed, an additional 26% had not worked since marriage, and 40% had not worked during the time they were living with their husbands. From Lopata's research we get a picture of women who had a capacity to work, although for the most part they had no training for specific jobs. There is no evidence, however, that they planned and prepared for careers; rather, they coped adaptively with the exigencies of marriage and mobility. As their early lives revealed little planning, so Lopata found them not planning for the future at the time of the study.

One virtue of retrospective studies is that they illuminate a greater span of the work history and life cycle than either prospective or concurrent studies. It is then possible to construct empirically based typologies of career patterns. Lopata (1971) suggested a typology of career patterns combining three postures the individual can take toward employment (passive, reactive, or initiating) with three types of work history (inflexible or stable, "changer," and "careerist"). In an intensive study of a subsample (*N* = 20), Lopata illustrated these. The inflexible work history with passive orientation is illustrated by workers who return to the same employer throughout their work and marital history, with interruptions. An externally directed, stable work history was exhibited by the widow of a traveling salesman. When he was alive, she traveled with him, and was consequently not available for employment. Upon her husband's death, a friend found her a job and she stayed in it until retirement. A more self-initiated pattern was exhibited by a woman with professional training (a nurse), a short-lived marriage, and no children. A flexible or "changer" work pattern characterized the respondent who worked a great variety of jobs in response to differing needs and pressures. This pattern may involve high labor-force attachment, but no future orientation, specific training, or identification with the job.

While Lopata's typology is more heuristic than definitive, ter intensive study does indicate the variety of patterns in women's work histories. Inferring motivation from behavior is still risky, however, particularly where we have not carefully distinguished those events over which the individual has control from those over which she has none. As the review of retrospective studies will show, we are still far from having a satisfactory typology of women's work history. An adequate *behavioral* typology would need to incorporate critical life cycle events (e.g., divorce; childbearing), individual resources (e.g., education; age at first marriage), and macrosocial factors (e.g., labor-market demand; sex discrimination).

Mulvey (1963) created a typology of patterns of labor-force participation exhibited by 475 women aged 37-47. The outcomes were distinct and Mulvey tried, appropriately, to distinguish the antecedents of these distinct outcomes. Ter findings underscored the power of material constraints relative to the power of individual preference in determining a woman's work history. In Mulvey's study, no predictive validity was found for personality rating, socioeconomic background, or school achievement as determinants of women's career patterns 20-25 years after high-school graduation. Individual preferences are less of a factor in determining a woman's work history than are material constraints (e.g., husband's domicile, number of children, work opportunities, sex discrimination).

Mulvey's sample was composed of 475 women high-school graduates, surveyed when they were 20-27 years out of school and aged 37-47. Mulvey classified them into 12 career patterns—based upon the temporal ordering of marriage and work roles, and career orientation—dichotomized as work-primary (Career directed)/work secondary (marriage directed). The typology is thus based on a behavioral classification plus a motivational one—and once again "motivation" is inferred from behavior and is neither conceptualized clearly nor measured directly.

Three categories referred to women who had not been employed since marriage (39% of the total). Interrupted work patterns (with return to employment as soon as feasible) accounted for another 20% of the sample. Stable working groups were composed of single women who had worked continuously (17%). Double-track (or dual role) workers comprised 8% of the sample. Another 16% included a group entering employment for the first time after a long period of homemaking, a group with a history of casual and periodic employment, and women who worked for their husbands since marriage.

Mulvey's finding convincingly demonstrated that motivation and behavior are often at odds. In every group there were women whose work behavior and work orientation were at variance. Although 3% had worked uninterruptedly, 25% of this group had work as a secondary orientation. Similarly, 6% of the Conventionals, who had not worked since marriage, characterized themselves as holding work as a primary value. Women in the double-track pattern were evenly divided between work-primary and work-secondary motivation.

Planning for life after 35.   When young women plan for adulthood, it appears that the years beyond age 30 are obscured by a dull gray mist. Life expectancy charts tell us, however, that the woman who marries young and restricts her family size has a second lifetime to look forward to in mid-life. Existing research suggests that this second lifetime is not scripted: Patterns for living this period are not crystallized, and socialization omits the postfamilial decades. Projections from divorce and mortality statistics indicate that most women will spend a third of their adult years alone—a pattern much at variance with their expectations.

Mid-life may be a stage in the life cycle where major changes can be made. Mulvey found that almost all ter respondents anticipated making a change in the near future: changing jobs, taking a job, taking on volunteer activity. Of these, 27% expressed the intention of taking a job—prospective data, to be sure, but a substantial phenomenon if it materialized—and 36% intended no change. The intention to make a change was unaffected by the ages or number of children.

Among Mulvey's sample were a group of women with a substantial period of employment interruption who yet maintained a strong motivation for work achievement. These women had raised their families and, at the period of study, were intensely involved in work. They anticipated expanding their lives at a stage when many of the others anticipated constriction or stagnation. Mulvey characterized them as ambitious and "least feminine" because of their strong career orientation: They are also the group with the highest rated level of psychological adjustment. The female life cycle permits them to launch themselves into a delayed career, although they enacted the cultural mandate first.

Another group, which at mid-life anticipated an expansion in activity, is a dual-role, work-primary group that Mulvey characterized as superwomen. These constitute 13% of Mulvey's sample. The only group that anticipated no change was the group with stable labor-force participation and secondary-work orientation. These women appeared locked into employment by necessity rather than choice, and saw no way out. Even the conventional groups envisioned some change (not necessarily in the direction of paid employment).

R. Baruch's (1967) study of five cohorts of Radcliffe alumnae also suggested an expansion of women's scope as family demands slack off. Baruch grouped respondents according to three stages in the life cycle: before children, child-intensive, and family established. These groups were, respectively, 5, 10, and 15-25 years out of college. Baruch tested need for achievement, finding it highest in the youngest group, lowest among those 10 years out of college, and intermediate in those 15-25 years out of college. Baruch predicted that women whose families were established would be returning to employment. Tey found an association between n-Ach score and a "strong" career pattern in women 21 or more years out of college. Among women 15 years out of college, the need for achievement was high, but material constraints were also high: Of all groups in the study, this cohort had the highest mean and absolute number of children. As these children reach independence, we predict that these mothers, too, will move more actively into paid employment. What is available for them to move into is another question.

Lopata's research on the work histories of older women led ter to question the ways in which paid employment is conventionally structured. Lopata criticized employment policies that assume continuous lifetime employment in one establishment. Tey noted that at every age grouping, for both women and men, opportunities for training and employment are successively reduced. Thus, flexible participation in employment is impeded at the upper age ranges. At the lower age ranges, however, it is much more likely to be women than men who are excluded from consideration.

Both cultural scripts and employer practice define young women out of most career sequences, possibly in a way that precludes later entrance into the sequence. Rossi (1965) argued repeatedly that for careers in the professions, the early years are critical, and the woman who follows the traditional script (early marriage and motherhood) will not be able to catch up or break in. Young women are still being urged away from extensive training early in life, and as the research here reviewed makes plain, they are still accepting that advice.

The retrospective studies reviewed so far afford no basis for characterizing the typical working woman as career-oriented. But is the typical working man career-oriented? And what are the concomitants of having a "career" versus a job history?

Job versus career. In standard sociological sources (Hall, 1969), "occupation" is defined in terms of continuous paid employment of an adult, which defines the individual's social status and constitutes a major focus in the individual's life. The term "career" is usually used with reference to a more or less orderly sequence of jobs over the working span. By implication, all the jobs in a career are part of the same occupation. By implication, too, a career involved a progression from lower 'to higher statuses. Experience or achievement on the job thus cumulates. The assumption is traditionally made by economists that earnings reflect experience and the increased value of the experienced worker. (Conversely, interruptions in employment should adversely affect earnings).

A number of different dimensions thus underlie the concept of career. Each of them is worthy of empirical investigation. In pursuit of this end, a whole set of research projects suggest themselves: (a) Under what conditions does one's occupation determine self-definition in a major way? (b) Among women and men workers, what is the proportion who feel that their occupation is a major part of identity? (c) The temporal dimension implied in the idea of career subsumes several research questions. What is the degree of planning that characterizes workers' employment histories? Are there critical periods when planning must take place, or is planning a continuous process? (d) Continuity and discontinuity also involve a temporal dimension. What are the connections between continuous or discontinuous employment and benefits? Do continuity and discontinuity have different effects on self-identity, and do these differ by sex? (e) The issues involved in the notion of career are multiplex, and the relations among them are so little known that it becomes difficult to evaluate a term like "career commitment." Does this concept refer to direction or strength of intention? Or would we ascertain empirically, after the fact, that some had it and some did not? If commitment means persistence in the face of obstacles, would we be justified in using this term to refer to the majority of males in "careers," for whom obstacles are ordinarily minimal?

By no means are these research questions suggested facetiously. Rather, I have tried to suggest what kinds of information we would need in order to use this term responsibly, and to point out, in the absence of such information, the invidious use to which it is commonly put. Thus, Tyler (1972) characterizes women as lacking "career commitment," a term that is neither defined nor linked, with acceptable evidence, to any other group in the labor force. Empirical data on the suggested dimensions of career would allow us to determine how "career-like" a given work history is. An additional inquiry would inform us how "career-like" a work history *can* be, given the availability of those factors that determine each of the components of a career.

These definitions of occupation and career are much more readily applied to the pattern of work experience that is assumed modal for men than they are to the pattern assumed modal for women. Indeed, they imply the male sex role, and run counter to the female sex role. For the majority of women, tradition-ally, their social status is defined by their husband's occupation rather than their own. Again, while occupation is commonly thought to be the chief component of the adult male sex role, family is thought to be the chief preoccupation of the female.

The unacknowledged intrusion of sex-role ideology into these formulations has the effect—as is so often the case in scholarly work—of deflecting empirical inquiry and making something true by definition. A more appropriate stance would be to treat each of the dimensions as a continuous variable, and ascertain empirically where the two genders distribute themselves. Pursuing these questions will lay the groundwork for more realistic policy, as well as improving the credibility of theory.

Evidence challenging the stereotypes is already available. For the majority of workingmen, the job does not loom as a central life interest (Dubin, 1956). There are many in the work force for whom the job is not a major element in self-definition. Rather, both female and male workers respond adaptively to a range of incentives and disincentives present in the job situation, by no means all of them linked to features of the task itself or to stable self-attributions in the individual (Morse & Weiss, 1955; Centers & Bugental, 1966). Moreover, a num-ber of studies suggest that the role of choice and the value of a theoretical apparatus of decision theories are minimal among parts of the work force (Kries-berg, 1964; Palmer & Brainerd, 1954).

Flexibility in responding to the contemporaneous incentive picture would imply, under certain labor-market conditions, substantial movement from one job to another. Yet, on this question of discontinuities in work history relatively little is known. It is vitally important to know the extent to which women *and* men move, not only in and out of the labor force, but also within it. It is commonly assumed that "intermittency" characterizes women's labor-force par-ticipation, but not men's. Yet, Bayer (1973), in a study of over 42,000 college and university teachers, found that while 20% of the females had interrupted their professional work for a year or more, 25% of the men had done the same.

Current statistics suggest that time out from paid employment will decrease in present and future cohorts of women, closing the assumed gap in labor-force attachment. "Intermittency" has been treated as a "female problem," and has in fact been researched in women. Economists have attempted to attribute wage differentials by sex to a number of factors other than gender. In education (commonly used as a proxy for quality of worker), the female labor force is superior to the male labor force. Absenteeism and job turnover show no reliable sex differences (though myths about this behavior persist.) Intermittency, however, is a negative indicator in which women outdo men. Consequently it is a good candidate for "explaining" wage differentials without recourse to the notion of sex discrimination. Yet, as Sawhill (1973) demonstrated, intermittency does not account for the wage differential. When the earnings of low- or nonintermittent female workers are compared with those of men, the same flat curve is observed as one finds for women who have taken time out from paid employment. Intermittency exists, but it does not account for differences in females' and males' earnings.

Very little research has been done with respect to two related questions: (a) What degree of continuity/discontinuity characterizes the work histories of women and men? (b) What are the consequences for women and men of interruptions or shifts in employment? Answers to these questions have policy implications, and also feed back to the theoretical question: "When" is a career?

Research studies of job versus career.   Miller and Form (1964) divided career into five stages. In the *preparatory phase*, the individual develops attitudes and behaviors that tey takes into the job market. The context for this learning is usually the school and family, rather than actual job experience. As we have seen, most prospective studies of women's occupational preferences tap into this stage of career development while neglecting the others. The second phase is the *initial stage* in which the individual gains actual work experience while still in school. According to the approach to motivation proposed in this article, such employment provides an opportunity to add information to the occupational map. We do not know whether girls and boys are equally likely to get work experience while still in school, or whether such experience has any direct relevance to occupational choice or motivation.

The third stage, or *trial period*, is initiated by the individual's getting her first full-time job. The trial period may involve a series of jobs, but Miller and Form expected that sooner or later the individual would settle down for three or more years in the same job. They dated the *stable period* from this job. In the stable period, the jobholder develops strong ties to the job and the organization. The individual may stay in this stable situation until *retirement*, the final stage in Miller and Form's model. If tey changed jobs, a new trial period would be initiated, which could lead to a stable period and thence to retirement.

Miller and Form's typology is behavioral, not motivational. There is nothing in the model that precludes its application to workers who have other obligations besides the job. The stages occur in a fixed sequence, but these are not limited to specific chronological ages or periods in the life cycle. The model does not preclude interruption. One could apply the model to the woman who completes her education (the preparatory phase) and then marries, entering paid employment (the initial phase) after her children are self-sufficient.

Miller and Form's model does not, however, attempt to deal with individual motivation, with outcomes associated with a given career pattern, or with environmental factors (e.g., characteristics of the employing organization). It gives little consideration to the motivational cycle in which outcomes feed back upon aspiration and persistence.

In Thompson and Carlson's (1962) career model, greater emphasis is given to worker volition. These authors discussed four career strategies that an individual can adopt; conceivably one could adopt different strategies at different stages of the family life cycle. Thompson and Carlson termed a strategy of personal advancement as "heuristic": The heuristically oriented individual will switch organizations in order to advance continuously. In the "occupational" strategy the individual's commitment is to her occupation: She may switch organizations but not professions. The person adopting the "organizational" strategy is loyal to the organization, and will seek to optimize her opportunities within the organization. The person adopting the "stability" strategy is essentially satisfied (or resigned), and is not actively seeking another job.

The "strategies" in Thompson and Carlson's model are ostensibly behavioral concepts, but have a strong (albeit implicit) motivational implication. On the one hand, the strategies are static; they are *initial* strategies an individual may adopt. In this respect they are comparable with the "occupational intentions" surveyed in prospective studies. Like intentions, they are modified by experience. And like all preferences or intentions, they may become operative *if* conditions permit. A female worker may adopt the heuristic strategy *if* she can move upward by changing employers. The facts of occupational segregation, wage discrimination, and employer prejudice put severe limits on most women workers' options. Given these constraints, it would not be surprising to find many women workers following the "stability" strategy. And, as with occupational "choice," it would be a gross error to infer that this is their first preference or that they are satisfied.

Thompson and Carlson suggested that different career strategies fit well with different structural features of the job situation. The authors characterized jobs as having early or late ceilings for advancement and as being defined or controlled by the occupation (as in the case of the professions) or by the employing organization. In the instance of women workers there are, as we have seen, additional constraints. It is not clear to what extent women adopt strategies comparable with those listed by Thompson and Carlson, or whether there are additional strategies more characteristic of women.

Rational career strategy would be informed by consideration of both incentive value and probability. Viewing the caliber of task, the pay rates and the chances for advancement that characterize most occupations in the female labor market (see Table 2.3), we might conclude that both undifferentiated vocational preferences (Tyler, 1972) and movement into, within, and out of the labor force are realistic. Such behavior is what one might predict for any worker confronting these incentives.

There are, however, a body of female workers who do have "careers," even by the restrictive definition. These are the well-researched female professionals. Studies of achieving women, like studies of women with high aspirations, attempt to isolate variables that make them "different from other women." Thus, they adopt a retrospective strategy and are included in the review of retrospective studies.

Birnbaum (1971) adopted a retrospective strategy in attempting to shed light on the differences among three groups of women who were studied 15-25 years after graduation from college. The groups are noncomparable in many ways, but the study did afford a distinctive picture of each. The central sample (the homemaker group) was comprised of women who had never been employed since their first pregnancy, and were living with their first husbands. The other two groups were single professionals and married professionals recruited from a university faculty. These three groups are of major interest to us here.

Women in the *homemaker* group were operating within the context of an extremely restrictive definition of adequate femininity. In this, the homemakers appeared to have re-created their parental homes. Like their parents, they rejected employment for a wife. They devalued personal achievement, believing it incompatible with marriage and motherhood, and recalled their mothers as being the same. In their recollections of themselves as girls, there is the suggestion that Birnbaum's "homemakers" adopted a restrictive role definition early and irreversibly. They were far more likely to characterize themselves as a "little lady," with no admixture of tomboyishness, in recalling childhood. They never recalled themselves as being competitive or intellectual, but as anxious to please.

The sex-role definitions of the "married professional" were much more liberal than those of the homemakers. Although they were as oriented toward marriage and motherhood as the homemakers, they saw no conflict between these commitments and their career commitments. They reported many more pleasures associated with the family component of their life-style than did the full-time homemakers. (They also had fewer children). Their partners shared their enthusiasm for the dual-role life-style, and also shared domestic labor. The wives saw their partners as very rare and superior individuals.

In their recollections of childhood, the married professionals comprised the only group that perceived the relationship between the parents as close. Both parents were highly educated, the father often with a graduate degree, the mother often employed. They recalled themselves as children as being competitive, intellectual, active, and striving to excel. Of this group, 48% characterized themselves as tomboy, and another 44% recalled a combination of tomboy and little lady. Only the parents of these women were recalled as setting high academic standards for their daughters.

The single professionals were distinctive in a number of ways. Their family backgrounds were less affluent than those of either of the other groups. Father's income was often low; yet, the mothers did not work. This group had the highest percent recall of feeling close to the father; yet, there was little commonality of interest or support for their career goals. The experience of upward mobility and, in some cases, a principled rejection of marriage left these respondents without the role models and support that the other two groups enjoyed. An unusual feature of the single professional's childhood was that she played mostly with boys and with mixed groups. They also reported themselves the most tomboyish of the three groups.

Birnbaum (1971) isolated three quite different life-styles in this study. Some background factors appear to provide support for the directions various individuals took in later life; yet, the most careerist group received the least support within the family of origin. Clearly, other influences entered the picture at later, and critical, periods. Interestingly, the three groups showed little difference in the occupations they reported having considered as children. All had considered wife and mother (homemakers most frequently), and all had considered professional careers (the married professionals most). The most career-oriented group (single professionals) had the highest proportion of undecided persons at the early stage, suggesting that their career choices entered their lives later than the age projected on the standard female occupational map.

Birnbaum's data suggest that factors closer in time to the outcome of interest may be better predictors than factors that were operative in childhood. Much retrospective research, however, assumes a direct, linear,.and continuing relationship between early family experiences and occupational behavior of adults. Again, much research seeks prediction on the basis of "personality traits" that are presumably stable over time and situation, discounting the external situation and the vicissitudes of the life cycle. The leap from individual attributes to real-world outcomes often involves a voluntaristic fallacy, as we have seen.

An example of this problem is given in Harmon's (1967) retrospective study of the work histories of women with varying SVIB (Strong Vocational Interest Blank) profiles in college. Harmon assumed that the outcomes observed 25 years later represented the women's choices, and hence expected to find them foreshadowed by intentions they had expressed in college. Most of the women had been homemakers in the intervening years, some with employment. The modal pattern (44.9%) was "early retirement," with no paid employment subsequent to the birth of the first child. Yet, this outcome was not prefigured by high scores on the SVIB housewife scale. Nor did Harmon discover any basis in the SVIB for predicting the occupations pursued by those (27.5%) who worked most of the time since college. In general, the SVIB has been proven to be a fairly good predictor of the occupational choice for men, but has a much poorer record for women. In part, this is due to biases built into the measure, and in part to failure in basic conceptualization. With men, both socialization and material conditions militate toward continuity of occupational intentions. The boy child will be encouraged to express interest in various careers, and to prepare for one; adolescence brings an intensification of these expectations rather than a discontinuity: The male worker does not encounter sex discrimination, and for most the rewards will be sufficient to guarantee continued participation. Finally, marriage and parenthood are not programmed in such a way as to introduce discontinuities into the male occupational history. These conditions and continuity are manifestly lacking for women; consequently, adequate prediction for women would require a different formulation.

Many studies employ a retrospective strategy to seek the determinants of some known, marked outcome. Usually, the outcome is considered remarkable, and the thrust of the research is to discover what makes the individual under study different from others. This difference then becomes the focus of the research endeavor, whether the researcher is pro (e.g., Rossi, 1965) or con (e.g., Douvan & Adelson, 1966). Much of the research on achieving women is of this type. Very commonly, research of this sort does not have a control group;

strictly speaking, the only adequate comparison would be with members of the deviant's cohort who did not exhibit the marked outcome. With respect to achieving women, comparisons with men would also be appropriate.

Sociologists have systematically investigated the effects of "societal reactance," or labeling a deviant. The label affects the way others treat the "deviant," whether the deviant behavior has or has not in fact occurred.

Treatment as a deviant has its effect upon the target person, independent of the effect of deviance itself. To the extent that achievement is considered deviant in women, those effects obtain. A further complication is that the respondent, insofar as she is a well-acculturated member of her society, shares the definition of achievement as deviant, and she, too, is drawn into the game of explaining why she is different. Other informants (family, friends) are also prone to bias their recall in the direction of the event to be explained.

With these shortcomings, the results of research in this mode should be subjected to cross-validation studies. To what extent is the attribute we wish to use as a predictor (e.g., a good relationship with parents) a characteristic not only of college women with high occupational aspirations, but also of women with traditional choices? To what extent is a predictor of occupational success (e.g., birth rank) characteristic of all achievers, and to what extent is it peculiar to women? To what extent can factors identified in retrospective studies be used to predict future outcomes for a present cohort? The findings of a study by Hennig (1973) lend themselves to the asking of these kinds of questions.

Antecedents of career success. Hennig (1973) attempted to isolate childhood factors that distinguished women who were highly successful executives from others who had not risen beyond middle management. The successful executives turned out to be first-born or only children, or members of small, all-girl sib sets. The respondents recalled normal relations with their mothers, and recalled their fathers as more nurturant, emotionally expressive, and sharing than usual. There was an early and emphatic emphasis within the family on the child's achievement and freedom of exploration. Among the elements of family culture were shared pride in the daughter's accomplishments; she learned to set standards for herself and to savor her success. Both parents provided somewhat traditional sex-role models, but accepted and respected the child's androgynous character. The respondents reported some unpleasant surprises with sex stereotyping when they reached school, but the achievement/androgyny pattern was already internalized, and the respondents were backed up by their parents in skirmishes with the school.

Conclusions of Retrospective Studies

The retrospective research leaves us with a number of questions amenable to future research. The question of options for women who have passed the child-intensive phase of the family life cycle needs further study. Reports indicate that, in a time when the demand for higher éducation is shrinking, adult education is expanding. Many adult education students are women. Existing research, however, is unable to tell us whether their goals are vocational, and in what way their contact with educational programs assists them in finding employment.

The questions we have raised about "careers," and about work histories, are not satisfactorily answered by existing data. The habit of viewing women's employment as secondary and episodic rather than as primary and motivated has produced a research corpus in its own image. We have as yet no method for assigning credit for a heterogeneous work history in such a way as not to penalize noncareer workers. Work histories are rarely complete enough to reveal much about triumphs and setbacks in employment, nor do they account for effects of work motivation.

In one respect, retrospective studies confirm what we learned from the prospective studies: Marriage is a powerful determinant of the options a woman can enjoy once married. Husbands' preferences loom large in women's decisions about employment. Some women's husbands "let" them work, but some do not; income needs of the family force some women into employment when they would prefer to stay home. For some women (a decreasing percentage) marriage means "retirement" from paid employment. For some of these, this outcome accords with their preferences; for others, it represents a deprivation. Research has ignored the role conflict of individuals in this situation, while assuming that all working wives (and, sometimes, single workers) suffer role conflict.

Concurrent studies of women in the work force. We rely on concurrent studies to inform us on gross indicators such as women's distribution over employment categories. Some of the most useful of these are large-scale, cross-sectional studies, often undertaken by federal agencies (e.g., the U.S. Census, and the Department of Labor). Such studies afford a look at the factors that vary with various employment outcomes, but do not permit us to draw causal inferences. Ordinarily, these provide some context, but they lack sufficient detail to provide the basis for motivational inferences.

Few concurrent studies investigate the options the worker faced at the time tey entered ter present employment, or the alternatives tey currently entertains. They do not trace the history of occupational decisions or occupational histories. A notable exception is the National Longitudinal Study undertaken by Parnes and his associates. In their research on working women aged 30-45, they employed a panel design, permitting them to follow the same respondents over time. Even these researchers, however, did not elicit a complete work history, querying respondents only concerning first, longest, and current jobs. For the most part, such research makes little effort to enumerate the positive and negative incentives associated with various options.

Positive and negative incentives there are, however. When we compare persons in two employment statuses—in and out of the paid work force—we find evidence for both personal preference and the coercion of material factors. Looking first at women in paid employment, we find strong effects for two variables, which sometimes act in opposite ways. Financial need is the most frequent reason (though not the sole reason) cited by women in explaining their employment (Sweet, 1973, p. 9). The husband's income is often taken as an indicator for the "pull" of women into the work force. As of 1959, the proportion of wives employed ranged from 29.2% to 39.4% when their husbands' incomes were less than $700 annually, dropping to 17.5% when their husbands' incomes exceeded $10,000 (Sweet, 1973, p. 7). The proportion of employed wives among blacks varies much less with a husband's income, remaining stable at 39% at all income levels up to $10,000, and then dropping only to 32.7% (Sweet, 1973). A more complex index of "income adequacy" of the family unit is a function of husband's income and number of dependents. This indicator bears a similar relationship to wife's employment.

Single women and female heads of households, similarly, must work to support themselves. In 1972, 14% of all families with children were supported by women (Ross and Sawhill, 1973); 43% of families below the poverty line were supported by women (Ross, 1973). It is clear that economic necessity pulls into the labor force many who would, by preference, not be there. Nevertheless, the experience exposes them to the operation of incentives, positive as well as negative, which they might not have anticipated. Thus, Mulvey's (1963) retrospective study found two kinds of workers citing as payoffs the characteristics of the work itself (intrinsic incentives). One group was the "career-oriented" group, for whom continuous employment had been their preference. The other was a group with a history of continuous labor-force participation, but without the prior preference. They had discovered rewards in the process of dealing with their task; yet, these rewards were unanticipated and would not have been evident in a prospective study.

Another variable that predicts labor-force participation is education. In 1960, the proportion of college-educated wives currently employed ranged from 27.7% to 56.7% (depending on age), and the proportion of women with greater than college education who were employed ranged from 49.7% to 65.7% (Sweet, 1973). Personal satisfaction looms larger as a reason for working among those with greater educational attainment. Some studies report that college-educated women who are not employed feel "guilty" that they are not putting their training to use outside the family. We may note that those at the higher extreme of the educational distribution often have specialized training that opens up jobs that are more rewarding than those available to the bulk of employed women.

Table 2.3 shows the distribution of employed women in 1968 over the broad occupational categories used in the Census. The reader can infer the nature of the incentives that present themselves to the average woman when she seeks paid employment. Jobs may be examined in terms of extrinsic rewards associated with them as well as the individual needs they satisfy (e.g., a need for achievement). There is an asymmetrical distribution of women across occupational categories. In fact, 85% of all working women are found in low-level white-collar jobs or in service occupations. Secretaries, saleswomen, domestics, and elementary school teachers make up 25% of the total of working women; with the addition of nurses, waitresses, and bookkeepers, a full 33% are accounted for. Only one-seventh are in the high-ranking (and highly paid) technical and professional occupations.

Occupational segregation accounts for this overconcentration of women in only a few occupations. These occupations are "crowded"; the increase in the total female labor force is accounted for by numbers entering traditionally female occupations rather than by expanding into male-dominated fields. One consequence of crowding is to drive down wages, with the economic conseqences we have already seen in today's labor market.

In addition to incentives and disincentives attached to the individual job and to the market for female labor, other factors enter into women's decisions to seek or remain in employment. A sample of women who wanted to work, but were not currently looking for a job, were asked: Why not? The most common reason was "family responsibilities" (29.6%), followed by ill health (16.4%), being in school (14.7%), inability to arrange child care (11.9%), and miscellaneous, less commonly cited reasons (Sweet, 1973, p. 38).

"Family responsibilities" is a pandora's box for the researcher interested in disincentives associated with paid employment. The household of any but the single woman worker is larger and requires more upkeep. The absolute amount of domestic labor to be done increases with the size of the family. How does this work get done in a family where both adults work full time? When a wife pitches in to help the family budget by going out to work, do her husband and children pitch in with household work? Walker (1970) found that husbands contribute 1.6 hours per day to household work; children's contribution is even more negligible. Husbands' contributions did not increase when wives working full-time and part-time were compared. In most families the man gives only token contribution to helping the wife with "her" work. The employed wife, meanwhile, spends from 4 to 7.3 hours a day on domestic labor. The wife who is not employed outside the home spends more time on domestic labor (Hoffman, 1963). For employed women, as for those who do not work outside the home, the work load increases as children come along. Not only does the absolute amount of work increase, but the wife's share also increases disproportionately (Heer, 1958; Geiken, 1964). In a study of couples in the Bay area, Paige (1974) found that all wives spent more than three times as much time in household work as do their husbands. However, both wife's employment status and fertility status made a difference in the ratio of wife's to husband's hours of domestic work. A wife who was neither employed nor a mother put in 11 times as many hours as her husband; a wife with children and no job, almost 4 times as much; an employed mother, almost 3 times as much; and the childless employed women, 1.88 as much.

The evidence then, is, that the employed wife is ordinarily holding down two fulltime jobs, with a predictable sacrifice of leisure and sleep. Her employment may represent a gain to her husband and children, but at a cost to herself.

COMPONENTS OF WORK BEHAVIOR:
INCENTIVES ASSOCIATED WITH THE JOB

The review just completed indicates that existing research cannot tell us much about incentives and information available to the worker at decision points. In both the prospective and the retrospective literature, motivation seems to have a static quality. In both, measures at one period in time are used to predict outcomes at another time. Motivation appears as a statistical relationship between discrete events, rather than as a dynamic process.

The literature in industrial psychology and formal organizations offers evidence of how incentives (and to a lesser extent, information) operate continuously to affect behavioral outcomes. Research in this tradition provides evidence of the multiplicity of incentives associated with paid employment, and their relationship with behavioral outcomes such as persistence of job turnover. Neither the female nor the male worker is adequately described by such simplifications as the notion of "economic man." A variety of incentives is salient for every worker, and their relative priority differs from individual to individual.

Research in work organizations has repeatedly shown that work satisfaction and work productivity are linked. This relationship holds for both quantity of output and quality. Factors that detract from net productivity (e.g., wastage, pilferage, dispensary visits by workers) have also been linked to job satisfaction. Consequently, a great deal of research effort has been expended in the attempt to determine the antecedents of job satisfaction. Factors that individuals find rewarding about their work situation include pay, opportunities for promotion, challenge, interest in the task itself, congenial coworkers, the opportunity to be useful, autonomy or responsibility for one's own work, working conditions, fringe benefits, convenience (e.g., hours; location), opportunity to use or to develop valued skills and self-attributes (or self-actualization). In the literature of industrial psychology, a long tradition distinguishes "intrinsic" from "extrinsic" motivators, often with the invidious implication that the latter are less estimable. Opinion is by no means univocal as to what aspects of work fall into which category. The theoretical distinction holds that intrinsic motivation is characterized by self-reward, whereas extrinsic motivation involves a rewarding agent outside the person. In practice, of course, this distinction is difficult to uphold, especially with events (e.g., recognized achievement) which involve multiple rewards.

Most instances of achievement are in fact a mixture of intrinsic and extrinsic. Although the classic definition involves an "internalized" standard of excellence, this standard is learned in social context and is reinforced by social approval. Moreover, the research on which we base our knowledge of achievement motivation involves a social context with specific features. Arousal is effected by social means, often a reference to interpersonal competition or to the instrumentality of the experimental task for the subject's goals. It may be that, theoretical formulation to the contrary, social comparison processes are integral to achievement motivation in men. This social context is currently of interest in the study of female achievement motivation, but has not yet been subjected to systematic analysis in the case of males.

When task achievement is rewarded on the job, the worker experiences not only the subjective feeling of goal attainment, but also the approval of coworkers or supervisor, and very often a monetary reward or promotion. These contingencies, of course, differ systematically for women and men, and we will return to the question of women's motivation for occupational achievement.

The classification of incentives as intrinsic or extrinsic has no proven utility; rather, it reflects an uncritical class-centrism and sexism. Categorical ascription of intrinsic or extrinsic motivation to one or another group has hampered our understanding of the complex relationships between incentives and work behavior, for men as well as for women. The extension of our knowledge in this area will require that we set aside certain common confusions of thinking. In the current literature, one no longer finds black workers' motivation confused with jobs black people hold, but other categorical characterizations persist. One commonly encounters the assumption that workers higher in the occupational structure are more "intrinsically" motivated than those in less authoritative positions. Some authors have predicted that women are more "intrinsically motivated" in employment than men (presumably because of their privileged position as economic dependents). Others have predicted that women are more "extrinsically motivated," reasoning presumably from the occupational level at which most working women find themselves. In fact, there is no consistent effect of gender. Different jobs offer differing arrays of incentives to the worker. It seems more likely that there are "types" of jobs than that there are "types" of workers.

Ideally, of course, there should be some degree of "fit" between the worker's needs or goals and those of the organization. Many constraints outside the individual's control have an effect on ter freedom to choose so as to optimize work goals. The disproportionate concentration of women workers in occupations offering mediocre levels of incentives should not be taken as a reading on a type of work motivation. Even in prospective studies, women cite a range of outcomes as inducements. Further, it appears that these incentives operate to differentiate various occupational options, and serve as the basis for intended occupational choice. In Rand and Miller's (1972) study, the most prevalent considerations were own interests and abilities. The primary incentives the respondents sought in a job were personal satisfaction and enjoyment of the work (incentives commonly classified "intrinsic"). Convenience (with reference to family demands) appeared in second rank for the junior high school sample, but not in the other groups, whose members placed salary (an extrinsic incentive) second in importance. The college women cited "opportunity for advancement" in third place.

The evidence from this study is at variance with the picture of women workers as reactive or passive with respect to life and work events. Their reasons for attending college were primarily instrumental in nature, occupational preparation being the modal reason for each sample. In these respondents' orientation toward future employment, there was no evidence of a mediocre or indifferent motivation. In ranked preferences for various aspects of work, a majority in each group preferred long-term projects over short-term projects, work requiring maximum training over minimum training, and demanding work over routine work. Only in a preference for "working with people" over "working alone" did the young women in Rank and Miller's study express values consistent with traditional assumptions about working women.

The values individuals seek to actualize in the work situation are, like many other motives, socially learned. It follows that individuals' "work motivation" will reflect the context in which socialization for the world of work took place. Existing research provides evidence of the effect of sex role, social background, and the specialized training of particular occupations. These factors, in varying combinations, affect women workers.

Vocabularies of Motive

"Reasons" for an individual's actions are socially intelligible, and socially accepted, only in recognized contexts. People thus learn to label their experience in line with their social position. Different "vocabularies of motive" (Mills, 1940) can be expected from individuals occupying different positions on major dimensions of stratification: age, sex, class, race. Situated vocabularies of motive are "reasons" which a role partner will accept. They are "situated" in being acceptable reasons for a given audience or within a given setting.

There is some evidence for a vocabulary of motives in the responses of women and men, up and down the occupational hierarchy: Women are more likely to cite opportunity to help others as an incentive associated with a particular job, and men are more likely to cite (lots of) money. The situated context for the expression of these goals is a pair of sex-role prescriptions that designates the males as (the) breadwinner and the female as a "secondary worker." In the traditional sex-role script, the female is oriented primarily toward the care and nurture of living things, and toward a supportive rather than an initiating role. Reality factors aside, there is a hidden payoff in the expression of work goals in line with this script. They are valued-expressive, affirming sex-role respectability or adequacy.

If the cultural mandate holds that women give first priority to their family, then acceptable "reasons" for working will reflect this emphasis. Thus, it should not surprise the reader that women give "financial necessity" as their reason for being employed. It is acceptable for a married woman to see her employment as instrumental to the attainment of family goals (e.g., consumption goals), but not instrumental to personal achievement, self-actualization, self-aggrandizement, or other such "selfish" goals.

Reality factors are also represented. Working women cite bread-and-butter issues as job incentives: (enough) money, opportunities for advancement, etc. We can predict that as women spend an increasing proportion of their adult years in the paid work force, these concerns will loom increasingly larger. There is no contradiction here; rather, these observations reflect the complexity of the dual-role lifestyle that is now the mode in the United States.

The idea of situated vocabularies of motives has important implications for research methodology. When, in collecting data from working women, the work role and work place are made salient, we can expect that the responses of women workers will resemble those of their male peers. When the family role is made salient, women workers' responses will diverge. We should thus expect to obtain more conservative responses from working women when sex-role issues are mentioned or implied.

In past research, salience was probably manipulated unconsciously, with systematic biasing effects upon responses. If working wives are interviewed in their homes, or sampled as part of a family unit rather than part of a work force, the culturally dominant context has already been invoked before the first question is asked. Asking a woman *why* she works (a question not asked of men) instantaneously invokes a traditional sex-role context. In the future, researchers should be sensitive to this unintended source of bias. Work and family roles can be explored as distinct parts of the individual's life, and our understanding of how women integrate dual roles may thereby be extended. However, unthinking confounding of role segments in the researcher's thinking may, when translated into interview questions, serve to arouse role conflict by intimating to the respondent that she should be worrying about her childcare arrangements while she is at work. Future research would do well to explore the mechanisms that working women (like working men) employ to articulate the demands of their multiple roles.

Social background (i.e., the family of origin, with its occupational role models) also provides a vocabulary of motives for formulating work goals. This context provides a script for the goals it is legitimate to seek in the job situation. Professionals typically stress autonomy and the exercise of professional skills when discussing what makes their work desirable; it is somewhat *infra dig* to mention income. This kind of verbal behavior is, of course, what leads to the credulous characterization of professionals as possessing "intrinsic" work motivation. We may note that the effect of this situated context cuts across gender lines, and we find female professionals quite similar to males, college-educated women similar to college-educated men, and unskilled workers of both genders also similar in the way they talk about work.

Blue-collar workers of both genders tend to employ a quite different vocabulary of motives when talking about job satisfactions. Men in blue-collar occupations do not speak of the challenge of their tasks or of their contributions to the total of human knowledge or human welfare. Jobs keep them out of trouble (Morse and Weiss, 1955) and provide social contacts. In their national sample of employed men, Morse and Weiss found that only 12% mentioned the work itself when asked what they would miss if they stopped working. Dubin found that 75% of industrial workers name neither the job nor the work place as a central life interest. Centers and Bugental (1966) found differences in the incentives cited by workers at different strata, but no reliable sex differences.

Effects of Value Differences

Specialized occupational training adds a specific vocabulary of motives regarding one's work. The potency of professional socialization has been repeatedly noted (e.g., Becker, Geer, Hugh, & Strauss, 1961). In addition to training the recruit in specialized skills, such socialization transmits shared definitions of reality, and specific values. The effects of this training override those of social background and gender. Studies have repeatedly shown that females and males in the same professions are more similar in values than they are like others of their own gender who are in different professions (D. David, 1974; White, 1972).

The foregoing remarks suggest some of the social factors that affect the value term of the motivational equation, that is, determinants of what aspects of the work situation are valued, and the incentive values attached to these outcomes. The emphasis here has been on the differential exposure of individuals to certain kinds of socialization with regard to work values, by virtue of their membership in certain broad social categories. However, the motivation thus acquired need not be permanent or static. I have emphasized throughout this chapter that both expectancy and value are modified by experience. An individual with a given sort of socialization history may acquire new values through exposure to the incentives provided in a particular job experience. Equally, outcomes that ter socialization defines as positively valenced may prove not to be so for tem. Although the concept of a situated vocabulary of motives emphasizes the socially shared definition and valuation of reasons for doing things, it would be a mistake to think of it only as a conventionalized response. As with other forms of socialization, a degree of internalization results.

Socialization with respect to work, like other socialization, does not have a uniform effect upon all those who are exposed. In examining between-group differences, we would do well not to overlook within-group differences.

Variation in Work Incentives and Rewards

Although a given job provides only limited satisfaction for many values, there is evidence that most workers seek a variety of incentives in paid employment. From the prospective studies, we can get a reading on aims not yet contaminated by the realities of the work situation. From research on job dissatisfactions and reasons for quitting, similarly, we can derive an inventory of work values that are being frustrated. No worker is responsive only to intrinsic or extrinsic incentives in ter work situation. However, in assessing the bases of work motivation, we encounter a problem similar to that involved in studies of occupational "choice." We must separate questions regarding the worker's preference from questions regarding what rewards the job presently provides.

While workers in professional occupations are more likely than blue-collar workers to report that their jobs provide them with a satisfactory level of autonomy, it does not follow that autonomy is not an incentive for other workers. Indeed, the success of the job enlargement experiments is evidence for the potency of this incentive (e.g., Conant and Kilbridge, 1965). Conversely, while workers in the skilled trades may report satisfaction with wages, relative to levels of other incentives available in their job, it would be an error to conclude that money is a more important incentive to them than to the (well paid) professionals. In fact, the anticipation of high income is a major consideration in the occupational choice of future physicians and attorneys.

The relationship between the worker's felt needs and environmental "supplies" is very complex. While indices of need satisfaction do predict gross outcomes, such as job leaving or staying, many other factors enter in. It will not be possible in this review to explore fully the question of needs the individual brings to the work situation, but it is hoped that this section gives the reader an idea of the range of incentives that workers realize (in varying degrees) in the job setting.

A number of interesting research questions arise from the consideration of job incentives and work satisfaction. A great deal of research needs to be done in the area of assessing the effects of improving incentives offered to working women. Would a promotion (for example) increase a worker's effort or her loyalty to the organization, or both? Will improving incentives enhance recruitment and attract better employees? In what ways will changes in inducements offered in a local labor market alter the movement of women into and out of paid employment?

The discussion thus far has emphasized distinct incentives that are attached more or less closely to the job itself. However, we should not leave this topic without considering another set of concerns, the effects of which has similarly powerful influence on job satisfaction and performance. These concerns involve relations among persons in the work place, particularly among coworkers.

Relative Deprivation and Equity

One of the earliest studies of the psychological determinants of satisfaction and dissatisfaction involved soldiers serving in World War II. Stouffer (1949) and his associates discovered that a feeling of "relative deprivation" resulted when individuals considered that their outcomes were worse than the outcomes of others who were "in the same boat." It was not absolute hardship relative to comparable others. These findings sensitized researchers to issues of social comparison. In general, it appears that when individuals want to make judgments, they seek information. When the judgments concern nonphysical or nonobjective matters, people seek information by comparing with others (Festinger, 1954).

Recent research has demonstrated that such information can be provided the individual in ways other than direct face-to-face interaction with the comparable other, and the processes of social comparison and resulting feelings of fairness or unfairness occur. Industrial psychologists have investigated the relationship among task requirements, rate of pay, and workers' feelings of fairness or equity. Most of the research in the tradition of equity theory is quasi-experimental in design. *Ss* are recruited, not for an experiment, but for a "temporary job."

In studies of equity, *Ss* are simply told what are the qualifications of others working on that task, at a given rate of pay. Researchers have repeatedly found that workers will adjust their task performance in order to bring about a fair balance, or equity. If, according to the experimental induction, they are overpaid, they attempt to produce more. If they are underpaid, they reduce quantity or quality. In this, they employ the standard introduced by the experimenter; they engage in social comparison with a (fictive, as it turns out) peer.

The theories of relative deprivation and equity raise interesting questions about the effect of social comparison on women's work motivation. Women are underpaid, compared with men; and public opinion polls tell us that both women and men accept the principle of equal pay for equal work. Will women make comparisons with men, and become dissatisfied or angry? Will they withdraw their services from the labor market or stage a slowdown?

Sex differences have not been explored in the literature on these two theories. Clearly, research is needed in order to specify the conditions under which women will engage in social comparison with men.

Sex-role consideration in women's motivation for employment.   Much of our concern thus far has been with extending to female workers what is known about workers in general. At a number of points we have noted ways in which women's occupational life is different from men's (e.g., with respect to responsibility for household work). Domestic labor is "added on" to paid employment in the case of women. We might equally say that high income is "subtracted from" employment in the case of women. In such instances, women and men may be characterized by the same formulations, although there are differences between the groups.

There are, however, considerations in female employment which have no ready parallel in the case of men. These relate to sex role—that is, socially scripted ideas about what constitutes appropriate and adequate femininity. Definitions of femininity vary with age and social location, but for the most part notable achievement is thought to be incompatible with, or even subversive to, femininity. Insofar as paid employment has overtones of achievement, sex-role considerations obtain. Work and sex-role adequacy articulate in very different ways for females and males. For the male, occupational identity enhances sex-role adequacy (or masculinity), except in the instances of sex-atypical occupational choice. Since men are spread over a wider range of occupations than women, this atypical event is less likely for the male than for the female. Moreover, as Tresemer and Pleck (1972) pointed out, a male nurse or elementary school teacher may effectively maintain his self-presentation as a male by enacting the occupational role in a *stylistically* masculine manner. The working woman does not have a parallel option. Because the entire world of work is culturally defined as masculine, she is out of place and her role enactment is problematic, whether she opts for a feminine role enactment or presents herself as one of the boys.

All employed women, it appears, must deal with this dilemma in some way. I will now examine some factors that facilitate, and some that impede, the integration of work and sex roles.

I do not mean to imply that sex role is either monolithic or immutable. On the contrary, sex-role expectations are age graded, and therefore "appropriate" sex-role behavior varies over the life cycle. The validation of feminine adequacy requires different behaviors, beliefs, and demeanors at different stages. School achievement is acceptable, even expected, in the prepubertal girl child. The seeming "collision" between femininity and competence results from a clear discontinuity in sex-role expectations. This discontinuity is associated with nubility (not puberty)—that is, perceived marriageability. Thus, Komarovsky (1946) discovered it in college women, but research in nonselected populations has also found it at an earlier age. The "flight into femininity" observed by some authors is a response to the sex-role pressures specific to this stage. It may be that the strictures against female competence are less severe after the stage of nubility, as they are before that stage. Indeed, considerable competence is assumed (if unsung) in the woman who takes responsibility for a household and children. However, sex-role standards restrict the kinds of competence that women may have, and where they may exercise it, if they are not to "lose their femininity."

Femininity and competence.   Passing through the age-specific stages of sex-role socialization exposes the individual to an array of definitions of femininity. Sex-role expectations also differ for girls of distinct socioeconomic and ethnic backgrounds as well. Most individuals get exposure to a variety of sex-role recipes, within situated social contexts. These contexts provide partners and role sets for the enactment of differing productions of femininity. Sex-role pressures communicated by these role partners are powerful, but not necessarily univocal. Moreover, the individual is not the passive target for a one-way flow of influence; she exercises selectivity among role partners, and she engages in a reciprocal process of role bargaining with these partners.

There is a sense in which femininity becomes part of the self; indeed, sexual identity is a central and highly valent component of personal identity. Sex role, however, is an element of social structure rather than a component of personality. The feminine sex role is located in and defined as part of a role system, or network of functionally related roles. Members of this network are those who have a stake in the individual's femininity, in how she enacts her sex role. Their roles are complementary and interlocking. Role-set members share knowledge about their own and the reciprocal roles; they hold expectations for the incumbents of other roles, and communicate their reactions to these role partners. They are thus a source of role pressures, and sometimes sanction specific role performances. However, the existence of the role network itself, with its defined roles, exerts social control independent of discrete sanctions.

Sex roles are made particularly complex by virtue of their diffuseness; many specifics cohere under this broad rubric. Gender constitutes an ascribed status. Being female conditions all social interactions and all achieved roles that an individual enacts. The individual's femaleness may affect the way others interact with her more than it affects her self-definition.

Because gender is one of the major principles of differentiation in a society, there are definitions and images of sex roles which confront the individual, not only in her face-to-face relations but also in the larger world as well. The population is continuously and promiscuously bombarded with images of femininity through symbolic and impersonal presentations in the media. It is notoriously difficult to demonstrate any causal effect on behavior by exposure to the media; sex-role behavior is likely to be no exception. Nevertheless, socialization sensitizes us to the expectations of generalized third parties, and it is possible that presentations in the media affect the information people hold or the valuation they place upon it. For the most part, however, we expect that *effective* role pressure is mediated through face-to-face interaction.

Because gender is a master status, labeling and evaluating the child in terms of sex role is an early and continuous process. Consequently the tendency to approach sex-role congruent items and to avoid sex-role incongruent items is established early. These tendencies can be seen in the school performance of young children. School-age girls set higher performance standards and attainment values in sex-role congruent subject matter areas (Battle, 1966; Stein, 1971). When problems are cast in a feminine form, girls performed better than when they were cast in a neutral (or masculine?) form (Milton, 1959).

These studies seem to show that sex-role congruence is a positive state that facilitates performance. If this is a general tendency, we would expect that items perceived as sex-role congruent (e.g., occupations) would be more attractive to women than to others. The indications of the "cognitive feminization" of their occupational choices by women with sex-atypical aspirations may be interpreted in this light.

Studies of sex-role considerations. Research showing that girls perform better in all-girl schools than in coed schools (Sutherland, 1961; Fahrner & Cronin, 1963) add another dimension to the relationship between femininity and achievement. It remains for further research to tell us whether the beneficial effect is attributable to teachers, female peers, or the *absence* of male peers. Research with college students inclines us to favor the latter interpretation. Horner (1968) found that students high in the "motive to avoid success" performed worst in a situation where they were tested with male peers. Peplau (1973) found that college women were unwilling to compete with their boyfriends. Komarovsky's (1946) study, college women acknowledged that they "played dumb" on dates. The assumption was that men do not like women who appear to be intelligent—the rationale, we recall, for lowering occupational aspirations among Matthews and Tiedeman's (1964) respondents. These studies permit further specification of the sex-role dilemma: Women fear to perform successfully in front of men and/or compete with them.

This dilemma came to light with Horner's (1968) dramatic findings on "motive to avoid success." In the presence of cues defining a particular situation as an achievement situation, the motive to approach success (n-Ach) is aroused, but for many women the motive to avoid success is simultaneously aroused. This motive is related to fears that "success" will result in "failure as a woman," and consequent social rejection. One resolution of this approach-avoidance conflict is to abandon (in fantasy and in fact) the sphere of competition. Another is to lower one's aspiration. Yet another is denial of responsibility for success. Interestingly, recent research on social attribution processes reveals a tendency for the successes of women to be attributed (by themselves and others) to transitory or external causes rather than to stable attributes of the persons. The effect for males is the reverse (Unger, 1975; Dweck, 1975).

Another form of self-attribution common in women is to exhibit lower aspiration, relative to past performance, than is characteristic of males. Girls' expectancy is lower than that of boys, even when their achievement is higher (Crandall, 1969; Baird, 1973). Baird's (1973) study illustrates the dual conservatism of women's aspirations. Ter ETS study of college seniors found that 44.6% of the men but only 29.4% of the women intended to go to graduate school. The discrepancy held up and down the scale of past achievement, so that the proportions of men with C+ averages who planned to go on in school equaled that of women with B+ or A averages. This "confidence gap" is found, as well, among elementary school children.

The "motive to avoid success" has been misinterpreted as a "will to fail." *My analysis would suggest that the goal is not to fail, but simply to produce a performance inferior to that of the male—a particular male or men in general.* The "confidence gap" just cited would have this effect. One wonders, too, about the parallel findings with respect to occupational choice. Far fewer women choose the most demanding (and male-dominated) fields than would be predicted on the basis of their academic potential. The desire to maintain male dominance seems to underlie Weiss' (1962) findings. When women were told that they were squeezing the dynamometer harder than the men, they immediately cut back on performace. Interestingly, they also felt guilty for slacking off, suggesting that (as with the motive to avoid success) the need for achievement was also mobilized.

This brings us to the last time in the sex-role script: The indoctrination of nubile young women. One purpose of the stepped-up sex-role pressures at nubility is to establish the priority of marriage over other options for adulthood. Once this priority is established, the individual is subject to the protocol of courtship. She is encouraged to cast her net wide, construing the pool of eligibles inclusively so as to maximize her chance of being chosen. In order to please all, she must conceal any potentially unpleasing attribute (e.g., competence). This may be a temporary expedient, but where the marital bargain is struck upon the basis of the presented selves of courtship, it may turn out to be binding.

The achievement motive and the motive to avoid success.   Horner's research made an incalculable contribution by establishing the complexity of the phenomena associated with n-Ach in women. For many, as she found, achievement situations arouse an approach-avoidance conflict, making behavioral prediction moot. Both aspiration and task performance seem to be affected by the "motive to avoid success," with fear of sex-role invalidation operating to inhibit striving.

Horner conceived of the motive to avoid success much in the same way as McClelland et al. (1953) conceived the achievement motive; that is, as a stable property of the person, acquired (in the case of M-Succ) in conjunction with sex-role standards. Subsequent researchers have suggested that the expectation of negative outcomes from successful achievement by a woman is part of a cultural script, learned by men as well as women. To the extent that this is so, male Ss should respond to the original Ann/medical school cue with success avoidant imagery, much as female Ss do. Monahan et al. (1974) found that fear of success stories were told by both females and males, and only to the Ann cue. Female Ss (aged 10-16) told few fear-of-success stories in response to a male cue, as did the males. It is not success per se that arouses the avoidance response, but the negative consequences for themselves that females anticipate.

To argue that the motive to avoid success is "merely cultural, existing only as a cognition shared by members of the culture, is to deny its behavioral relevance. The cultural explanation would not predict any alteration in males' behavior of the sorts typically found among females. Males may believe, along with females, that the achieving women runs the risk of social rejection, but this will not inhibit *them* from aspiring high or competing hard. The negative consequences do not apply to them, either in fantasy or in real life.

The discussion of a "motive to avoid success" by Tresemer (1974) and others seems to have been based on a fundamental misunderstanding of the different consequences of success and failure for females and for males. The fear of invalidation in the sex role is central to the motive as defined by Horner, and this meaning is abundantly evident in the response categories scored by Horner (1968). Tresemer is associated with a rather voguish concern with the devaluation of (occupational) success goals by men—quite a different phenomenon. Striving to attain success does not impugn a man's masculinity, whatever the costs to his humanity; and conversely, repudiating such goals does not salvage his masculinity.

The reader would do well to read with care the research purporting to replicate Horner (e.g., Levine & Crumrine, 1975). It is not uncommon to find *any* negative attitudes expressed toward achievement lumped with the scores from Horner's specifically defined categories. The effect is to cancel out sex differences and lend credence (if not credibility) to the claim that the motive to avoid success is as characteristic of males as females.

Another perspective on the motive to avoid success is to treat it as an instance of role conflict, within the context of sex role as defined above. The potential for conflict is ubiquitous, in the complex social world of multiple roles and intersecting role sets. However, the approach-avoidance conflict must be triggered by specific role pressures or signs. One of these might well be the presence of males as witnesses or competitors. It is possible that the single woman would be more affected by this stimulus than the woman who is married or paired, because of the nature of the courtship script. The conflict might also be triggered by the labeling of an activity as masculine.

Further research is necessary to test this thesis that the motive to avoid success, and its behavioral concomitants, is an instance of role conflict. I have suggested here some of the cues that, wittingly or unwittingly, can be used to elicit role conflict. In another section I will discuss the evidence that such situationally induced conflict can be as readily disarmed.

Other scholars interested in women's achievement have gone back into the tradition of achievement research and raised questions about basic conceptualization of the achievement motive. Reconsideration of the unconsciously masculine assumptions of the original work raises new questions. McClelland et al. (1953) defined the achievement motive as a relatively stable disposition to strive for success in any situation where standards of excellence are applicable. Such a definition assumes that "success" means the same thing to all individuals, and assumes that all persons have equal access to opportunities. Standard coding of achievement imagery relies heavily upon an "objective standard of excellence," without taking cognizance of the consensual nature of such standards, or of questions such as who sets standards, and who can and cannot meet them. The issue of an *internalized* standard of excellence then becomes ambiguous as well, for operationally, "success" (socially recognized) and self-approval are triggered by the same event. Moreover, Maccoby and Jacklin (1974) have recently challenged the image of the male achiever persevering in solitude, noting that social arousal seems more essential to the achievement behavior of males than females.

Stein and Bailey (1973) defined achievement motivation as a general pattern of striving for excellence *in self-selected areas.* Their definition preserves the motivational dynamic—striving, and the idea of excellence—without restricting it to arenas in which efforts by women are traditionally discouraged. The implications of this formulation are fundamental. Given what we now know about the disincentives associated with male-oriented success, we are forced to conclude that the existing research literature systematically underestimates women's achievement motivation to an incalculable degree. The idea that the achievement motive may be satisfied in self-selected areas requires us to rethink male-derived ways of defining what "is" and "is not" achievement. Could it be, as Veroff and Feld (1970) said, that parenthood fits the definition of an achievement situation? Could there be something to the claim that some women experience vicarious achievement through their husbands and children? Does the athlete who is not a winner achieve? And what of the solitary craftsperson, working away in her suburban fastness? What scope do the traditional "female" occupations, looked down upon from the perspective of the male professional, provide for the achievement motive?

If we concede that the achievement motive is alive and well in women who are not listed in *American Men of Science,* we must then turn our attention back to the social contexts in which women learn the instrumentalities for achievement and self-actualization motives. Models and modes for enacting work roles always include a conjoint definition of sex role. Most research has focused on the family of origin and male role partners as influences on women's enactment of work roles. The influence of female peers has been neglected, and that of employers and coworkers has been virtually untouched by research. Theoretical writing has grappled gingerly with the issues of role modeling and role conflict.

Role Modeling: A Complex Issue

A conservative bias pervades much of the traditional writing about role modeling. Partially discredited assumptions about frequency of exposure and simple imitation have led to an overemphasis on the same-sex parent. Current research acknowledges that the child is active and selective in modeling, rather than mirroring ter parents. Especially when, as in the case of many young women, they intend a life different from their mothers' traditional lifestyles, models outside the family are of particular importance.

Given young women's expectations for work and family, what they require of role models is different from what their male peers require. In my own research, I have found it useful to distinguish between *occupational role models* and *lifestyle role models.* In the case of young women with high occupational aspirations, neither alone will be an adequate guide. Most occupational role models in the professions are men, and there are limits in the degree to which the initiate can model her life, professional manner, and expectations after them. Lifestyle role models are women, from whom the aspirant learns ways of integrating family relationships and work obligations. The occupations of lifestyle role models, however, are not likely to be those to which the young woman aspires. Hence, they cannot serve as occupational role models. The problem of integrating what is learned from these often distinct sets of role models remains an individual dilemma.

Popular interest in role models for women's careers relates to this point. Role modeling, like motivation, has an information component and an incentive component. If women are to learn how to function in these occupations, there must be women to teach them. One reason is the evidence that men refuse or neglect to teach them, or don't teach them all there is to know. The other is the need of models for lifestyles for which women, and not ordinarily men, are preparing themselves.

The issue of incentive needs more attention in the study of role modeling. One way to conceptualize it is in terms of vicarious learning. It will be helpful to think of it as a two-part process, the first involving information and the second behavior, mediated by anticipated rewards.

Of the thousands of images to which the young girl is exposed in her formative years, which will she take as role models? The research on social learning suggests that perceived similarity between self and model mediates learning. Such learning enters the cognitive structure as information, where it may be stored until it appears instrumental. Research on latent learning tells us that when presented with an incentive, the organism produces a learned behavior never previously exhibited. I suggest that our best bet in analyzing role modeling is to *examine the outcomes that befall the potential model.* The young girl is more likely to adopt the path of a potential model if she observes that it pays off for the model. This proposition applies to the individual's assessment of models presented through the media or secondary sources, as well as her own mother and other adults of her acquaintance.

By this analysis, it is clear, "token" hiring of women will not act as an inducement to young women to choose or persist in a particular option, as long as they can observe that the token does not achieve real success.

Influence of the family of origin.   The family of origin provides the first exposure to sex roles and to work roles. In addition to opportunity for imitative learning, the family provides direct inculcation of values. The relationship between sex-role socialization and socialization for the world of work is by no means simple, and the research reflects this complexity. Two formerly popular theories of nontraditional occupational aspiration in women have fared badly in recent times. Formerly, having the model of a working mother was thought to affect the daughter's aspiration in a simple and direct way. The other "explanation" was that a career-oriented daughter must be "father-identified."

Current thinking about sex-role socialization relies less heavily on simplistic imitation theories, recognizing the complementary nature of sex roles and of cross-sex as well as same-sex parent/child interactions. Moreover, as maternal employment has become a majority phenomenon, we have come to see that mothers have a range of different reasons for working. It seems that young women seek to learn the lesson of their mothers' lives, rather than following their example blindly. We now find that while women with role-innovative occupational choices still tend to have working mothers, the converse does not follow. Many daughters of employed mothers do not exhibit unusual occupational aspirations.

Besides the level of occupational aspiration, two other factors may be influenced by the learning that takes place in the family of origin. First is the relative priority assigned to marriage and to the job: In the nuclear family, sex-role pressures are likely to be greater than pressures for achievement or career planning (Birnbaum, 1971; Matthews & Tiedeman, 1964). Second is a preview of the marital partner a working woman can expect to find. Existing research indicates that the partner who shares responsibility for the home he shares is a rarity. Sex-role learning in the home is likely to legitimize this state of affairs.

The conservatism of men on matters of sex role is relevant to the father-identification hypothesis as well. Tangri (1972) found complex relationships between role innovativeness and a daughter's relationship with her parents. She found no evidence for father-identification among women choosing "masculine" occupations. Indeed, in her data, feeling close to father and agreeing with his values was negatively associated with role innovation. This is not surprising if we assume that these fathers' sex-role attitudes are similar to those of the male population in general. Their role expectations for a daughter will ordinarily not include a "masculine" occupation, and if the relationship is close, the daughters who perceived themselves as *like* their fathers were slightly more likely to be role innovative than were those who *liked* their fathers.

Influence of male peers.   The relative influence of peers over parents begins as soon as children enter school, and is substantial during adolescence. When young people go away to college, the day-to-day, face-to-face influence of parents is substantially attenuated. Moreover, the cultural mandates of courtship and marriage enhance the influence attributed to male peers vis-a-vis nubile females.

The cultural script defines all males as potential mates, and enjoins the unattached female to be as pleasing as possible. The single nubile woman is thus extraordinarily susceptible to the judgments of males. Her success as a female can only be confirmed by making a good match; the role pressures from parents, female peers, and males are all consistent in this. Moreover, the sex-role mandate is given precedence, so there is some pressure to "pay one's dues" by establishing adequate femininity before receiving permission to pursue achievement interests. The courtship script involves a statistical fallacy, which some young women appear to see through immediately. When one has established one's femininity by marriage, the necessity of pleasing men-in-general is abolished, and one can get on with one's career. This early marriage/full-steam-ahead strategy appears to be adopted by some high ability women (Zinberg, 1973; Watley & Kaplan, 1971).

Many achieving women receive vital support and validation from the partners of their private lives. The shortcoming of this solution is that it is particularistic, and that it does not extend into the work place. Although wives in "dual career" marriages feel fortunate, research reveals that these are not relationships of equality and do not confront the central question of competition between the sexes in the labor market.

It is perhaps the fear of competition from women that underlies attitudes of hostility and contempt for women on the part of males. Hartley (1960) found that acquiring misogynist attitudes toward females is part of the socialization of male children when still quite young. There is considerable evidence that many men hold restrictive expectations for wives. Many studies find that working-class men hold more traditional attitudes than do white-collar men (Haavio-Mannila, 1971; Davis, 1964), but some find substantial opposition among male professionals (Kaley, 1971).

Influence of female peers.   In the major agencies of socialization—the family, the schools, and the media—preparation for work roles is subordinated to preparation for marriage. Adequate femininity is defined within a context of heterosexual marriage. Rarely do we find women as models who are not readily perceived as appendages to men—celibates, lesbians, single women.

In my own research on college women, I asked respondents to describe in turn a single woman they felt was successful in both her work and personal life, and a married woman who was successful in both. Some respondents were unable to think of any unmarried woman they thought of as successful.

Social science research mirrors this conservative view. Although the Women's Liberation Movement has been a beam in the media's eye for nearly a decade, it seems to have had no impact discernible by social researchers. Where female peers appear in the literature, they are dismissed as "traditionals," copies of their mothers (e.g., Almquist & Angrist, 1971), while the subjects of interest, the "career-oriented" women, consort with male peers. Female peers appear also as a Greek chorus, reaffirming traditional sex-role priorities. Researchers have not yet identified and studied the phenomena of female solidarity and identification which could have major impact on women's work experience, among many other areas. Women organizing collectively around their work concerns have found repeatedly that shared distress turns out to have common causes, that the causes are objective and not personal deviance, and that shared experience often produces a solution. When it is in the best interest of the dominant group to deny the existence or the seriousness of women's problems, there is no substitute for the validation of that reality by peers, and for the support that peers can offer.

By no means is this kind of peerness—I mean sisterhood, of course—limited to age-mates. There is a sympathy that leaps back and forth between women of all ages, not least between mothers and daughters. Some data from Tangri's (1972) study is relevant in this respect. Tangri found that role-innovative daughters felt close to the mother and shared her values, although they felt she did not understand them. There seemed to be a shared feminine identification, with strong differences in lifestyle.

Support and solidarity among women seems to offer a resolution of the culturally imposed "polarity" between competence and femininity. It seems likely that women will experience greater validation from other women than from men. Though we do not customarily think in these terms, women are the most appropriate persons to validate a female identity. And though there are many factors that make women less appreciative of each other than we might be, there are not the role demands of dominance and superiority which women encounter in men.

Role Conflict: A Dead Herring?

There exists a body of literature which holds that role conflict is endemic in the working wife because of incompatible demands of work and family obligations—and perhaps in the single women as well, since her faulty femininity should cause her some unease. Excavating the underlying premises of this expectation is beyond the scope of this article, but at least one of these should be examined: the notion that role conflict is peculiar to women.

The dominant tradition in role theory has always assumed multiple-role occupancy to be the rule rather than the exception. Role conflict, in the sense of role overload, is thus endemic, as is role strain (Goode, 1960). The possibility that one's roles (or role partners) may demand different behaviors simultaneously haunts us all. A great deal of scholarly effort has gone into mapping the mechanisms by which role conflict can be moderated or prevented (Coser & Rokoff, 1974; Kahn, Wolfe, Quinn & Snoek, 1964). Sieber (1974) devoted a recent paper to the gains inherent in multiple-role occupancy. In particular, organizational roles carry with them certain privileges and protections that may be lacking in other role systems.

The question may be raised whether women are given special treatment; that is, excepted from the protections and privileges of multiple-role occupancy. This is a question for further research; answers to this question will, however, surely lead us back to a consideration of sex role. The critical focus here will be the work setting itself.

Role relationships in the work setting. We have seen that women seek to satisfy certain sex-role constraints while engaging in achievement. They seek to protect an identity of adequate femininity and to avoid competing with, or surpassing, men. One means of satisfying a number of constraints simultaneously is to choose one of the traditional female occupations. These offer a sex-role congruent image, and give some protection from competition with male peers. In many of these jobs, however, women are supervised by men, and in these contacts are vulnerable to invalidation of both their competence and their femininity. Many women have had the experience of repeatedly training replacements for their own boss, without ever being considered for the job. On the other hand, a woman who shows "too much" competence or ambition may be labeled as masculine. Many women have experienced a chill at being complimented for thinking "just like a man." On the reverse side of the coin are the tributes for being "terrific—for a woman." Both serve the identical social control function of reminding the woman worker that males as a category are dominant and superior.

The woman who is a highly visible minority in her work place faces additional problems. Wolman and Frank (1972) inventoried the ways in which the solo woman in a professional group is negated through stereotyping, and her contributions to the tasks undermined. Wahrman and Pugh (1972) documented the way the female participant is made a nonparticipant by ignoring what she says. Laws (1975) described the "gilded" cage of the individual who serves as the token woman in a male organization.

This kind of microanalysis demonstrates the way that role conflict can be elicited in the work situation. If, as we maintain, role conflict is situational, can it be neutralized as well as aroused? The motive to avoid success is the prototype of this kind of conflict. Several existing studies can be viewed as natural experiments in the neutralization of the motive to avoid success. M. Katz (1973), in replicating Horner's study, added one sentence to the *Ann* cue: Tey specified that half of Ann's medical school class was female. The proportion of *Ss* giving avoidant responses was dramatically lower than in other studies. The presence of other women seemed to reaffirm femininity and support the expression of achievement desires. Another reputed "replication" of Horner's study substituted, for the medical context of the original cue, graduate school in child psychology (Hoffman, 1974). Although by this clumsy substitution tey failed to replicate Horner, Hoffman inadvertently helped refine our understanding of what is at stake in the motive to avoid success. By making the context a graduate school, tey retained the implication of excellence, which arouses the success motive. However, by making the occupation sex-role congruent, tey disarmed the motive to avoid success, and found levels of imagery much lower than Horner had found with the medical school cue.

Accommodating sex-role adequacy to occupational ambition.   New research on occupational choice suggests that "cognitive feminization" of traditionally male occupations makes them more sex-role congruent to young women. Keenan (an unpublished study) found that college women concentrating in pre-med characterized the profession in terms that were culturally feminine. By this means, it seems, the students were able to maintain congruence between the valued feminine identity and the attractive profession they had chosen.

Explicit reassurance also has a disinhibiting effect. Farmer and Bohn (1970) collected two measures on the SVIB homemaker and career scales, one under neutral conditions and one in which they assured *Ss* that men liked women who were their equals. The career-scale scores were much increased in the latter condition. One is tempted to infer similar antecedents to explain Hawley's (1971) data. Hawley found a relationship between women's perception of men as egalitarian or traditional and their own choices of innovative or traditional occupations. These choices seem to reflect women's judgments of how ambitious they could afford to be in their careers, given the male attitudes that they were taking into account. It remains for future research to reveal the ways in which feelings of sex-role adequacy and occupational ambition are accommodated in the ongoing relationship.

Compartmentalization is a standard way of sidestepping role conflict, and keeping sexual and business relationships separate is a common pattern. Can the woman whose sexual identity (if not the totality of her sex role) is defined in a relationship that is protected from the work setting "afford" to ignore gambits directed at sex role? This remains a question for future research. However, data on salary and promotion rates of married versus single women professionals strongly suggest that marriage is no protection from sex-role penalties in the labor market. These data should be a reminder that we should be studying the employer and coworker rather than the woman worker.

PRIORITY QUESTIONS FOR FUTURE RESEARCH

1. What must be changed about employers in order for qualified women to succeed in their organizations? We have enough attitudinal data on employers; what we need are data that show us why some can adopt to and profit from the presence of women in formerly male positions and some cannot.

2. We need demonstration projects that focus on the training materials traditionally used with male recruits, compared with materials developed for use with women. What are the comparable success rates?

3. What events in a work history profoundly encourage and discourage women's effort and persistence? Mooney (1968) found that receiving financial support for the second year of graduate study dramatically reduced the attrition rate for female doctoral students. Are there similar signs which women in other occupations take as confirming the rightness of their choice and their capacity to do the work? What are the notable discouragements? Are there particular supervisors or training personnel who ought to be replaced?

4. Research on the options perceived by the young, and their information sources, is needed. Are these unnecessarily restricted? How adequate is the information available to young women?

5. Can we identify the social supports that permit some young women to persevere in demanding occupations and cause others, equally able, to abandon these atypical choices through lack of support?

6. A great deal of experimental work is needed to explore the situational malleability versus stability of the motive to avoid success.

7. We need more research on the female life cycle and its articulation with the work cycle. Are there periods during which absence from the paid work force is more detrimental to women than at other times?

8. It is doubtful that we need to document yet again that the demand for child care far exceeds the supply. We do perhaps need demonstration projects on a *variety* of options tailored to the requirements of different working mothers.

9. We need to develop ways of assigning credit for heterogeneous work histories. Even when intermittency becomes less characteristic of women's work histories, we may continue to find a wider variety of jobs in those histories than in those of men. At present, women are penalized in salary grade and benefits because of this heterogeneity.

10. Basic research on job satisfaction and productivity needs to be extended to women.

11. The implications of equity theory and relative deprivation need to be explored for female workers. What are the effects of occupational segregation, family status, and feminist ideology on female discontent?

12. Research on the attitudes and life planning of young men is needed to complement that of females. To what extent are these potential role partners responsive to the expectations of their female peers?

13. We need to chart the incentive picture for women over the working span. Do most women start with high expectations and seek high levels of gratification from work, as Rand and Miller's (1972) data indicate? If women learn to "settle," by what process is this brought about? Are these changes in expectancies or value, or both?

14. We need more research on older women and the manner in which they find their way among the options available to them. Do they perceive more options than the schoolgirl, or fewer? Who are the major information sources, supports, and role models for them?

15. We need research in which expectancy and value are controlled. Will the value of success (e.g., promotion) increase among women when the probability of promotion increases?

REFERENCES

Almquist, E., & Angrist, S. Role model influences of college women's career aspirations. *Merrill-Palmer Quarterly,* 1971, 17, 3, 273-279.

Almquist, E. & Angrist, S. *Careers and Contingencies.* Kennikat Press, 1974.

Baird, L.L. *The graduates.* Princeton, N.J.: Educational Testing Service, 1973.

Baruch, G.K. Maternal influences upon college women's attitudes toward women and work. *Developmental Psychology,* 1972, 6, 1, 32-37.

Baruch, R. The achievement motive in women: Implications for career development. *Journal of Personality and Social Psychology,* 1967, 5, 260-267.

Battle, E.S. Motivational determinants of academic task persistence. *Journal of Personality and Social Psychology,* 1966, 4, 634-642.

Bayer, A.E. *Teaching faculty in academic, 1972-73.* Washington, D.C.: American Council on Education, Res. Rep. 2, 1973.

Becker, H.S., Geer, B., Hughes, E.C., & Strauss, A.L. *Boys in white: Student culture in medical school.* Chicago: University of Chicago Press, 1961.

Bernard, J., *Women and the public interest.* Chicago: Aldine-Atherton, 1971.

Birnbaum, J.L.A., Life patterns, personality style and self-esteem in gifted family-oriented and career-committed women. Unpublished doctoral dissertation, University of Michigan, 1971.

Campbell, P. Feminine intellectual decline during adolescence. Doctoral dissertation, Syracuse University, 1973.

Centers, R., & Bugental, D.E. Intrinsic and extrinsic job motivations among different segments of the working population. *Journal of Applied Psychology,* 1966, 50, 193-197.

Conant, E.J., & Kilbridge, M.D. An interdisciplinary analysis of job enlargement: Technology, costs, and behavioral implications. *Industrial and Labor Relations Review,* 1965, 18, 377-95.

Coser, R.L., & Rokoff, G. Women in the occupational world: Social disruption and conflict. In R.L. Coser (Ed.), *The family: Its structures and functions* (2nd ed.). New York: St. Martin's Press, 1974.

Crandall, V.C. Sex differences in expectancy of intellectual and academic reinforcement. In C.P. Smith (Ed.), *Achievement-related motives in children.* New York: Russell Sage, 1969.

Crandall, V.C., Katkovsky, W., & Crandall, V.J. Children's beliefs in their own control of reinforcements in intellectual-academic achievement situations. *Child Development,* 1965, 36, 91-109.

David, D. Occupational values and sex: The case of scientists and engineers. Paper presented at the American Sociological Association Meetings, Montreal, 1974.

Davis, E. Careers as concerns of blue collar girls. In A. Shostak & W. Gomberg (Eds.), *Blue collar world: Studies of the American worker.* New York: Prentice-Hall, 1964, pp. 154-164.

Douvan, E., & Adelson, J. *The adolescent experience.* New York: Wiley, 1966.

Dubin, R. Industrial workers' worlds: A study of "central life interests" of industrial workers. *Social Problems,* 1965, *3,* 2, 131-142.

Dweck, C.S. The role of expectations and attributions in the alleviation of learned helplessness. *Journal of Personality and Social Psychology,* 1975, *31,* 674-685.

Empey, L.T. Role expectations of women regarding marriage and a career. *Marriage and Family Living,* 1958, *20,* 152-155.

Erikson, E. Inner and outer space: Reflections on womanhood. In R. Lifton (Ed.), *The Woman in America.* Boston: Beacon Press, 1964.

Fahrner, C.J., & Cronin, J.M. Grouping by sex. *NEA Journal,* 1963, *52,* 16-17.

Farmer, H.S., & Bohn, M.J. Home-career conflict reduction and the level of career interest in women. *Journal of Counseling PsychologySEE MANUSCRIPT.*

Feather, N.T., & Simon, J.G. Reactions to male and female success and failure in relation to the perceived status and sex-typed appropriateness of occupations. *Journal of Personality and Social Psychology,* 1975, *31,* 536-548.

Festinger, L. A theory of social comparison processes. *Human Relations,* 1954, *7,* 117-139.

Flanagan, J.C., Shaycoft, M.F., Richards, J.M., Jr., & Claudy, J.G. *Project TALENT: Five years after high school.* Palo Alto: American Institutes for Research and the University of Pittsburgh, 1971.

Geiken, K.F. Expectations concerning husband-wife responsibilities in the home. *Journal of Marriage and the Family,* 1964, *26,* 3, 3449-3452.

Goode, W.J. A theory of role strain. *American Social Review,* 1960, *25,* 4, 483-496.

Haavio-Mannila, E. Some consequences of women's emancipation. *Journal of Marriage and the Family,* 1971, *31,* 123-124.

Hall, R.H. *Occupations and the social structure.* Englewood Cliffs, N.J.: Prentice-Hall, 1969.

Harmon, L.W. Women's working patterns related to their SVIB housewife and "own" occupational scores. *Journal of Counseling Psychology*, 1967, *14*, 4, 299-301.

Harmon, L.W. The childhood and adolescent career plans of college women. *Journal of Vocational Behavior*, 1971, *1*, 1, 45-56.

Hartley, R. Children's concepts of male and female roles. *Merrill-Palmer Quarterly*, 1960, *6*, 84-91.

Hawley, P. What women think men think: Does it affect their career choice? *Journal of Counseling Psychology*, 1971, *18*, 3, 193-199.

Heer, D.W. Dominance and the working wife. *Social Forces*, 1958, *26*, 342-347.

Hennig, M.M. Fanily dynamics for developing positive achievement motivation in women: The successful woman executive. *Successful women in the sciences: An analysis of determinants.* Annals of the N.Y. Academy of Sciences, *208*, 1973.

Hoffman, L.W. Fear of success in males and females: 1965 and 1972. *Journal of Consulting and Clinical Psychology*, 1974, *42*, 353-358.

Hoffman, L.W. The decision to work. In F.I. Nye & L.W. Hoffman (Eds.), *The employed mother in America.* Chicago: Rand McNally, 1963.

Horner, M.S. Sex differences in achievement motivation and performance. Unpublished doctoral dissertation, Michigan University, 1968.

Horner, M. Toward an understanding of achievement-related conflicts in women. *Journal of Social Issues*, 1972, *28*, 2, 157-175.

Iglitzin, L.B. A child's-eye view of sex roles. *Today's Education*, 1972, *61*, 23-26.

Kahn, R.L., Wolfe, D.M., Quinn, R.D., & Snock, J.D. *Organizational stress: Role conflict and ambiguity.* New York: Wiley, 1964.

Kaley, J. Attitudes toward the dual role of the married professional woman. *American Psychologist*, 1971, *3*, *26*, 301-307.

Katz, M.L. Female motive to avoid success: A psychological barrier or a response to deviancy? Unpublished, Educational Testing Service, 1973.

Komarovsky, M. Cultural contradictions and sex roles. *AJS*, 1946, *52*, 184-189.

Kriesberg, L. Occupational controls among steel distributors. In A.L. Simpson & I.H. Simpson (Eds.), *Social organization and behavior.* New York: Wiley, 1964, pp. 274-281.

Laws, J.L. Work aspiration in women: False leads and new starts. *Signs: Journal of women in culture and society.* Winter, 1976, 33-49.

Laws, J.L. Psychological dimensions of the labor force participation of women. In P.A. Wallace (Ed.), *Equal opportunity and the A.T. & T. Case.* Cambridge: MIT Press, 1975.

Laws, J.L. The psychology of tokenism: An analysis. *Sex Roles,* 1975, *1,* 1, 51-69.

Levin, K. *Field theory in social sciences.* New York: Harper, 1951.

Levine, A., & Crumrine, J. Women and the fear of success: A problem in replication. *American Journal of Sociology,* 1975, *80,* 4, 964-974.

Looft, W.R. Sex differences in the expression of vocational aspirations by elementary school children. *Developmental Psychology,* 1971, *5,* 366.

Lopata, H.Z., & Steinhart, F. Work histories of American urban women. *The Gerontologist,* 1971, *2,* 4, 27-38.

Maccoby, E.E., & Jacklin, C.N. *The psychology of sex differences.* Stanford, Calif.: Stanford University Press, 1974.

Matthews, E., & Tiederman, D.V. Attitudes toward career and marriage and the development of lifestyle in young women. *Journal of Counseling Psychology,* 1964, *11,* 4, 375-383.

McClelland, D.C., Atkinson, J.W., Clark, R.A., & Lowell, E.L. *The achievement motive.* New York: Appleton-Century-Crofts, 1953.

Miller, D., & Form, W. *Industrial sociology.* New York: Harper & Row, 1964.

Mills, C.W. Situated actions and vocabularies of motive. *American Sociological Review,* 1940, 12, *5,* 904-913.

Milton, G.A. Sex differences in problem solving as a function of role appropriateness of the problem content. *Psychological Reports,* 1959, *5,* 705-708.

Mooney, J.D. Attrition among Ph.D. candidates: An analysis of recent Woodrow Wilson Fellows. *Journal of Human Resources,* 1968, *3,* 47-62.

Morse, N.C., & Weiss, R.S. The function and meaning of work and the job. *A.S.R.,* 1965, *20,* 2.

Mulvey, M.C. Psychological and sociological factors in prediction of career patterns of women. *Genetic Psychology Monographs,* 1963, *68,* 309-386.

Oppenheimer, V.K. Testimony before the Federal Commerce Commission, August, 1972.

Paige, K. The effects of sex, children, and dual careers on the uses of time. Paper presented at American Psychological Assn. meeting, August, 1974.

Palmer, G., & Brainerd, C.P. Labor mobility in 6 cities: A report on the survey of patterns and factors in labor mobility, 1950-1960. Committee on Labor Market Research, SSRC, 1954.

Papalia, D.E., & Tennent, S.S. Vocational aspirations in pre-schoolers: A manifestation of early sex role stereotyping. *Sex Roles,* 1975, *1,* 2, 197-201.

Peplau, L.A. Fear of success in dating couples. *Sex Roles,* 2, 3, 249-258.

Rand, L.M., & Miller, A.L. A developmental cross-sectioning of women's careers and marriage attitudes and life plans. *Journal of Vocational Behavior,* 1972, *2,* 317-331.

Raph, Goldberg, & Passon. *Bright underachievers.* New York: Teachers College Press, 1966.

Roderick, R.D. & Davis, J.M. *Years for decision,* Vol. 2. Washington, D.C., 1973.

Roderick, R.D., & Kohen, A.I. *Years for Decision,* Vol. 3. Columbus, Ohio: Center for Human Resource Research, 1973.

Ross, H. Poverty: Women and children last. Washington, D.C.: The Urban Institute, 1973.

Ross, H.L., & Sawhill, I.V. *Time of transition: the growth of families headed by women.* Washington, D.C.: The Urban Institute, 1975.

Rossi, A.S. Barriers to the career choice of engineering, medicine, or science among American women. In Mattfield, J., & Van Aken, C. (Eds.), *Women and the scientific professions.* Cambridge: MIT Press, 1965.

Sawhill, I.V. The economics of discrimination against women: Some new findings. *Journal of Human Resources,* 1973.

Schwenn, M. Arousal of the motive to avoid success. Unpublished junior honors paper, Harvard University, 1970.

Shaw & McCune. The onset of academic underachievement in bright children, *Journal of Educational Psychology,* 1960, *51,* 3, 103-108.

Shea, J.R., Roderick, R.D., Zeller, F.A., Kohen, A.I., & associates. *Years for decision: A longitudinal study of the education and labor market experience of young women.* Washington, D.C.: Manpower Research Monograph No. 24, Vol. 1 (1971).

Sieber, S.D. Toward a theory of role accumulation. *American Sociological Review,* 1974, *39,* 4, 567-579.

Siegel, A., & Curtis. Familial correlates of orientation toward future employment among college women. *Journal of Educational Psychology,* 1963, *54,* 1, 33-37.

Stein, A.H. The effects of sex-role standards for achievement and sex-role preference on three determinants of achievement motivation. *Developmental Psychology,* 1971, 4, 219-231.

Stein, A. H., & Bailey, M. The socialization of achievement orientation in females. *Psychological Bulletin,* 1973, *80,* 5, 345-366.

Stouffer, S.A., Suchman, E.A., DeVinney, L.C., Star, S.A., & Williams, R.M., Jr. *The American soldier: adjustment during army life.* Princeton, N.J.: University of Princeton Press, 1949.

Sutherland, M.B., Coeducation and school attainment. *British Journal of Educational Psychology,* 1961, *31,* 158-169.

Sweet, J.A. *Women in the labor force.* New York: Academic Seminar Press, 1973.

Tangri, S. Determinants of occupational role innovation among college women. *Journal of Social Issues,* 1972, *28,* 2, 177-199.

Thompson, J.D., & Carlson, R. *Occupations, personnel and careers.* Pittsburgh: Administrative Science Center, University of Pittsburgh, 1962.

Tresemer, D. Fear of Success: Popular but unproven. *Psychology Today,* 1974, *7* 82-85.

Tresemer, D., & Pleck, J. Maintaining and changing sex-role boundaries in men (and women). Paper presented at Radcliffe Institute Conference, Women: Resource for a Changing World, Cambridge, April, 1972.

Tyler, L. The antecedents of two varieties of vocational interests. *Genetic Psychology Monographs,* 1964, *70,* 177-277.

Tyler, L. Sex differences in vocational interests and motivation related to occupations. Testimony before the Federal Commerce Commission, August, 1972.

Unger, R. Status, power and gender: An examination of parallelisms. Paper presented at the conference on New Directions for Research on Women, Madison Wisc., May 1975.

U.S. Department of Labor. *1969 Handbook on women workers,* Women's Bureau Bulletin No. 290. Washington: U.S. Government Printing Office, 1969.

Veroff, J., & Feld, *Marriage and work in America: A study of motives and roles.* New York: Van Nostrand Reinhold, 1970.

Vroom, V. *Work and motivation.* New York: Wiley, 1964.

Wahrman, R., & Pugh, M.D. Sex, nonconformity and influence. *Sociometry,* 1972, *35,* 376-386.

Walker, K., Time-use patterns for household work related to homemakers' employment. Paper presented at the 1970 National Agricultural Outlook Conference, Washington, D.C., 1970.

Watley, D.J., & Kaplan, R. Career or marriage? Aspirations and achievements of able young women. *Journal of Vocational Behavior,* 1971, *1,* 1, 29-43.

Weiss, P. Some aspects of femininity. *Dissertation Abstracts,* 1962, 23, 1083.

White, J.J. Women in the law. *Michigan Law Review,* 1972, *65,* 1051-1122.

Wolman, C., & Frank, H. *The solo woman in a professional peer group.* Philadelphia: The Wharton School, University of Pennsylvania, Working paper No. 133, 1972.

Zinberg, D. College: When the future becomes the present. In *Successful women in the sciences: An analysis of determinanats, Annals of the New York Academy of Sciences,* Vol. 208, 1973, pp. 115-124.

Zytowski, D.G. Toward a theory of career development for women. *Journal of Personnel and Guidance,* 1969, *47,* 660-664.

CHAPTER *10*

REALITY AND MYTH: Employment And Sex Role Ideology In Black Women

JANICE PORTER GUMP

Janice Porter Gump was born in 1937 in Chicago, where she received most of her education. She attended the Laboratory School and College of the University of Chicago, receiving the B.A. degree in 1956. From 1957 through 1962 she served on the staff of the National Scholarship Service and Fund for Negro Students. Upon receipt of the Ph.D. in clinical psychology from the University of Rochester, she joined the Children and Family Unit of the Community Mental Health Center at Temple University, where from 1967 through 1970 she served as Clinic Coordinator. Her marriage to Larney R. Gump brought her to the Washington, D.C., area. She has served on the faculty of the Howard University Psychology Department and as Acting Director of its Clinical Psychology Program. Following 1½ years as a staff psychologist in the Counseling Service of Howard University, she entered the private practice of psychotherapy. Dr. Gump has served on the Mental Health Small Grants Committee of NIMH and has acted as Consulting Editor for Professional Psychology, *the* Journal of Consulting and Clinical Psychology, *and the* American Psychologist. *At present, she maintains an active private practice, and is raising a family.*

The traditional role does not exist for the black woman. Historically, the black woman has been prepared to assume a responsibility the white woman has not, and data demonstrating the perpetuation of her economic as well as familial responsibility are presented. The larger participation of the black mother in the labor force is one manifestation of this dual responsibility.

Though expectations, preferences, and actual career patterns indicate a non-traditional orientation among black women, attitudes toward marriage, children, and sex-role appear traditional. Accounting for some of the nontraditional behavior may be an internalization of the necessity to provide for her family, a need that may now exist independent of the external reality. The need may, for instance, be related to the expectations of others. While the black woman's independence is to be treasured, its cost to her—and to her family—has been significant.

We know very little about sex-role norms or ideology for the black woman. An articulated set of expectations, psychological characteristics, and behaviors exist for white women, but whether we speak of affiliative or expressive needs, dependency, nurturance or passivity, we know by and large what the general components of a woman's role have been. Black women have, of course, been exposed to the same norms, but it is unwise to assume that their exposure has resulted in adoption. (It is probably impossible to convey to those who are not black the extent to which race in this country is a characteristic that transcends or modifies all other aspects of identity.) Thus, what may be true for "Miss Ann" may be irrelevant, ridiculed, coveted or idealized, but it is not simply a given. Black women know fairly well what image of womanhood is held for the white woman, since that is the image communicated through the media. It is often admired by the black woman, and is demonstrated in the homes where she works. But *norms* for black women are not equally explicit, and attempts to understand her within the framework of white sex-role ideology may yield no more than a glimpse through the window of another's experience.

The task of formulating sex-role norms for black women is, then, more difficult because of the inadequacies of available conceptual tools. Constructs used so ubiquitously in discussions of sex role (e.g., traditional norms, need achievement, dependency) derive from the dominant culture and are appropriate to it. It is uncertain whether they may be validly applied to a minority group; my attempts to do so have been frustrating because contradictions and questions remain after analysis with the customary yardsticks. Perhaps it is more accurate to say that our assumptions must be questioned. It may be that certain constructs (e.g., dependency) have universal applicability, but we must take care that observation of certain behaviors does not lead us to assume inappropriate meaning of those behaviors for a given cultural group. Turner (1972) found, for instance, entirely different predictors of career expectations for black and white women. White women with high career expectations held equalitarian sex-role attitudes and came from homes in which parents stressed competitive values. Those variables that correlated with high career expectations in black women were related to perceptions of the desires of significant others. Thus, the same event can have different antecedents, and imply different expectations and attitudes.

My attempt to understand something of sex-role expectations, strains, and satisfactions for black women has necessitated a sort of mental stripping. I have had to attempt a kind of anthropological naiveté, to assume I knew nothing of the women I was to discuss. At the same time, I had to be subjective, as my own experience and intuitive understanding were the only guides available to me. I believe it particularly important for psychologists, when attempting to understand molar human behavior, to explore literary, historical, and sociological resources. Our disciplinary strength (i.e., our capacity to validate our hunches) has too often been our disciplinary weakness; our hypotheses about complex behavior are too often prematurely formulated.

Using various kinds of data sources—historical, survey, correlational—I shall attempt in this chapter the kind of understanding I believe must precede formal research. Because this is a first attempt, the effort will lack precision and elegance. Hopefully, however, it will help us begin to formulate those hypotheses that eventually must be put to empirical test.

THE TRADITIONAL ROLE

I doubt that the traditional role, as it is generally understood, exists for the black woman. Certain facts, however, argue against such a position. Though it is questionable that employment should be used as the sole criterion of adherence to the traditional sex-role model, it is perhaps reasonable to examine it as an indication of adherence. Of a representative sample of 1,390 black women, 21.2% had no work experience prior to or following marriage, a figure that exactly parallels similar work experience in white women (Vetter & Stockburger, 1974). Even when the black woman's participation in the labor force is at its highest (61% during the ages between 25 and 34), 39% are not working (Women's Bureau, U.S. Dept. of Labor, 1974). In a study of the career expectations and preferences of 1964 Negro women graduates, Fichter (1967) found 37% desired not to work at all, to work only before the birth of children, or only after children were grown; Kuvlesky and Obordo (1972) found that 45% of their sample of Negro adolescents wanted this pattern.

Clearly, a number of exceptions may be cited to the proposition that black women have not incorporated the traditional role, or at least that aspect of it which calls for nonemployment. It is possible that variations in acceptance of the model may exist according to class membership; Powdermaker (1939) pointed out that differences in the formality of the marriage bond (e.g., common-law, licensed marriage) were correlated with class membership in a group of studied blacks. Expanding upon Powdermaker's observation, Herskovits (1941/1958) discussed differences in acculturation occurring with class, a principle of some inherent reasonableness. Thus, it is conceivable that middle-class and upper-class black women may be more likely to adopt the norms of the majority group. Yet, as family income and education increase, so does the probability of the black woman's employment (see below). Still, my knowledge of older middle-class black women who are traditional in most of their attitudes and behaviors leads me to believe there must be some women within the upper strata who have adopted the conventional pattern.

In fact, fewer poor black women work than do those above the poverty level, leading one to wonder what factors account for this difference. Whether in this instance we are witnessing the effect of poor preparation, number of children, the apathy and despair of poverty, or the holding of more traditional attitudes are questions that remain open to investigation.

Leaving unanswered questions about those black women who may have adopted a more traditional role there remain to be understood the majority of black women who, at least in terms of their work history, would appear to have a different model. By the traditional role I refer to an elaboration of wifely and motherly behaviors (an elaboration which may in truth more accurately describe the middle- rather than the lower-class housewife) which results in a multiplicity of functions. In that I am a black and not a white suburban housewife, I can only describe what this role appears to me to be.

First, there seems to be a concept of meeting the needs of the immediate family in a manner I don't believe is shared by the black woman. This may mean fixing lunch for a husband who works sufficiently close to return home occasionally for the noon meal; it may mean baking bread or repapering a child's room. In addition to such nurturant behaviors for others, the woman and her community may partake of her time and energy. She may take a class in pottery, or paint; she will attend to her nails and her clothes closets; she may run the church bazaar or the clothing sale for the PTA. Whatever may be the activity, the role of housewife is sufficiently differentiated and elaborated that it is a fulltime occupation, *even when* there is household help. Whether these activities are valued by the woman, her children or her husband is not at issue here. Nor am I maintaining that there do not exist great differences among white women as to the degree of creativity, competence, or interest with which such activities are pursued. Rather, I refer to a multiplicity of "motherly," "womanly" behaviors within the boundaries of the traditional role.

Black women appear (and here I again rely on observation and impression) to view the role of the housewife differently. This difference is captured in a comment made by a friend: "I knew they (white mothers with young children in the neighborhood) talked about me, but I just *couldn't* take my kids and go sit on a park bench for two hours. We had a backyard," she continued, "and I saw to it that they got fresh air, but take two hours out to do *nothing* . . . ?" And so, what for a white woman is a proper—and perhaps even important—aspect of her role as mother is viewed by the black woman quoted as a waste of time; it was not within her purview of her role. It will be argued here that the elaboration of the black woman's role includes employment and some striving for advancement (which may or may not include "achievement"—the notion of striving for a sense of excellence). The statement is less simple than it would appear, for it implies that no sex-role violation occurs with employment; rather, it holds that the role of the woman includes within it almost as much expectation of labor-force participation as it does of being a mother and having a home. It is not that the norm is violated out of necessity, but that the norm is *different,* and the notion of violation therefore inappropriate.

It is in attempting to describe this phenomenon that the constructs of the dominant culture seem inadequate. Perhaps some sense of what I refer to can be gleaned from another example of attitude in the black woman previously quoted. My friend holds a Master's degree in psychology. What time she feels she may take from family responsibilities is spent in consulting with day-care centers. (She works six hours a week.) She once asked me if I thought she should go on for the doctorate in psychology. (I should add that she is an extremely competent, articulate, sensitive person whom it would be a pleasure to welcome to the innermost circle of the field.) As we talked and she sensed I was hospitable to her feelings, she told me how Professor X, who had been Chairman of the Psychology Department in which she obtained her M.A., "won't even speak to me," so disappointed was he with her reluctance to pursue the higher degree. Her friends all felt she was crazy, and making a terrible mistake; she could make more money, would have more "clout," etc. No one, in fact, could understand that she liked being home when her children returned from school, that she was so proud and delighted by their competence and mental health (which she attributed to the time and energy she had spent with them) that she simply didn't *want* to pursue the Ph.D. My support of her desire to do what she wanted resulted in an expression of gratitude which revealed as little else could the amount of pressure she had experienced.

In attempting to justify the conclusion of difference in sex-role ideology, I will cite both behavioral and attitudinal characteristics of black and white women. Only as we understand something about what the two groups of women do with respect to work, for instance, and what their attitudes are about self and children, may we begin to make explicit that which has been implicit but determining.

HISTORICAL NOTE

In Africa and Europe as well, when women were essential to the economy of the family, their social and psychological position reflected their importance. Most slaves were brought from West Africa, where women performed important economic tasks. Not only did they serve an agricultural function, but they also held a unique position with respect to the retailing of merchandise. It was they who brought goods to the market, sold them, formed organizations that fixed prices, and retained the profit so acquired. They could, then (and did), become independently wealthy (Herskovits, 1941/1958).

Both the African woman's economic and social position differed from that of the eighteenth-century American white woman. Though most of the tribes from which (it would appear) the American slave originated were patrilineal, some were matrilineal, which meant that consanguinity and descent were traced through the mother, the father forsaking his own family of origin to come live with the wife's family, perhaps bringing a dowry. Wealth was passed through the mother's brother rather than through the father.

But most family structures were probably patrilineal and polygynous. Herskovits (1941/1958) described the physical setting of the typical community from which the "New World Negro" derives:

> The family is typically housed in a compound, which is a group of structures surrounded by a wall or a hedge, to give the total complex a physical unity. The head of the household . . . and all other adult males (such as younger married brothers) have individual huts of their own, to which their wives come in turn to live with them and, for a stated period, to care for their needs. Each wife has her own dwelling, however, where she lives with her children. Once she conceives, she drops out of the routine of visits—a factor in restricting the number of children a woman may bear . . . to resume it only when she has weaned her child. (pp. 64-65.)

This kind of familial organization and the woman's economic role resulted in relative independence for the West African woman. That she and her children maintained separate domiciles, that they shared the husband and father with other wives and their offspring, meant that the woman and her children constituted the elementary family unit. Herskovits was careful to point out that this structure did not result in marginality or nonsignificance for the male, for the husband held a central authoritative position. Nonetheless, such a family structure is clearly distinct from the elementary European family unit made up of husband, wife, and children. Further, West African women were not hampered by any notion of marriage as the ultimate commitment. According to Herskovits (1941/1958), divorce carried with it little social opprobrium either in Africa or in the New World.[1] Thus, ". . . holding their economic destinies in their own hands, [the West African woman was] fully capable of going [her] own way if [her] husband displeased [her]" (p. 180).

In attempting to trace the survival of Africanisms in the New World, Herskovits stated:

> The status of the Negro family at present is . . . to be regarded as the result of the play of various forces in the New World experience of the Negro, projected against a background of aboriginal tradition. Slavery did not cause the "maternal" family; but it tended to continue certain elements in the cultural endowment brought to the New World . . . . The feeling between mother and children was reinforced when the father was sold away from the rest of the family; where he was not, he continued life in a way that tended to consolidate the obligations assumed by him in the integrated societies of Africa as these obligations were reshaped to fit the monogamic, paternalistic pattern of the white masters. That the plantation system did not differentiate between the sexes in exploiting slave labor tended, again, to reinforce the tradition of the part played by women in the tribal economics.
>
> Furthermore, these African sanctions have been encouraged by the position of the Negro since freedom. As underprivileged members of society, it has been necessary for Negroes to continue calling on all the labor resources in their families if the group was to survive; and this strengthened woman's economic independence . . . This convention thus fed back into the tradition of the family organized about and headed by women, continuing and reinforcing it as time went on. And it is for these reasons that those aspects of Negro family life that depart from majority patterns are to be regarded as residues of African custom . . . . For they not only illustrate the tenacity of the traditions of Africa under the changed conditions of the New World life, but also in larger perspective indicate how, in the acculturative situation, elements new to aboriginal custom can reinforce old traditions, while at the same time helping to accommodate a people to a setting far different from that of their original milieu. (pp. 181-182.)

An adequate historical analysis, which the preceding excerpt makes no pretense to be, would also point out the collective nature of the African culture, the absence of individuality, and the concomitant significance of the group (Diop, 1959/1962; Herskovits, 1941/1958; Mbiti, 1969/1970)[1]. The African woman, though in many respects more independent than her European or American counterpart, was not alone, but supported by the collective. Thus, in this way as well may one observe antecedents of the present status of American black women which predisposed them to a different sex role.

LABOR-FORCE PARTICIPATION

Table 3.1 presents employment rates for black[2] and white women for the decades 1890-1970 (excluding 1910), and for 1974. Percentages for the years 1890 through 1940 are not exactly comparable with those for later years because they are derived from decennial rather than annual data. Decennial data differ from annual data in the ways in which they are collected, in time references, and in other ways. In addition, the earlier percentages are based upon women 14 years of age and older, while for 1950, 1960, 1970, and 1974 the data are based upon women 16 years or older. In spite of these differences, however, two conclusions can safely be drawn: Black women have always worked more than white women, and though labor-force participation has increased for both groups, the increment has been dramatic only for white women.

The historical fact of the black woman's labor efforts in this country provides partial explanation of why her sex-role ideology may be different. For the black woman, work has been neither opportunity nor novelty; if one's mother didn't work (and I can't think of *one* childhood friend for whom this was not true), then one's aunt or neighbor did. Work outside the home is not exceptional to the role of wife or mother, but rather is an integral and accepted part of what it may mean to be a black woman.

WORK INTENSITY BY DEVELOPMENTAL MILESTONES

Even more revealing than rates of labor-force participation are the career patterns of black and white women. Vetter and Stockburger (1974) examined

---

[1] According to Mbiti (1970), however, divorce or separation, while common and easy in some communities, was extremely rare in others. "Most peoples [were] between these two positions" (p. 190).

[2] As blacks constitute the majority of all non-white persons in the United States (89% in 1970), it has become customary to consider data reported for minority persons equivalent to data for black persons. In the text, the term black will be used, though the discussion may be based on data for non-whites. Tables, however, will indicate whether data are those of minority or black persons.

Table 3.1

Participation rates of non-white and white women
in the civilian labor force, 1890-1974

Participation rates, %

Year	Non-whites[a]	Whites
1890[b]	37.7.	15.8
1900	41.2	17.3
1920	40.6	20.7
1930	40.5	21.8
1940	37.3	24.5
1950[c]	46.9	32.6
1960	48.2	36.5
1970	49.5	42.6
1974	49.1	45.2

Source: Data for 1890-1940 were derived from *Historical Statistics of the United States: Colonial Times to 1957*, U.S. Bureau of the Census, with the cooperation of the Social Science Research Council, U.S. Dept. of Commerce, Washington, D.C., 1960. Data for 1950-1970 were derived from *Manpower Report of the President*, April, 1974, U.S. Dept. of Labor, Washington, D.C., U.S. Government Printing Office. For 1974, the data were obtained from *Employment and Earnings*, January, 1975, 2|17), U.S. Dept. of Labor, Bureau of Labor Statistics, Washington, D.C.: U.S. Government Printing Office.

a In 1970, blacks constituted 89% of non-white persons.
b Rates are for those 14 years and older, total labor force and total population.
c Rates are for those 16 years and over.

the career-development variables and patterns in a national probability sample drawn by the Bureau of the Census. The sample was composed of 3,606 white and 1,390 black women, aged 30 to 44 at the time data were collected in 1967. An analysis of work intensity during periods between developmental milestones (i.e., leaving school, marriage, and birth of first child) revealed an interesting discrepancy between black and white women. While 68% of the white women sampled had worked after leaving school and prior to marriage, only 50% of the black women were employed (the average time length of this period was three years for both groups); after marriage and before the birth of the first child, the number of women working decreased to 37% among white and 20% among black women. However, from the time of the birth of the first child, up to 1967 (a period averaging 16 years), 39% of white women worked more than 10% of the time, while this was true for 60% of black women. In fact, it was with the arrival of the first child that many black women moved into the labor force, while many whites dropped out. Thus, white women tended to be employed before and not after the birth of children, while the opposite was true of black women.

Though the preceding data may accurately describe the women's participation rates, the data do not necessarily reflect a desired work pattern for either group. Lack of opportunity, differing patterns of marriage, and childbearing suggest that (particularly for black women) the low employment rates during the late adolescent years were imposed and not sought. In 1954, when the youngest women of the studied cohort were in their teens, 18.4% of black and 9.9% of white teen-age girls were unemployed (*Negro Women*, 1967).[3] (Statistics for unemployment are based upon persons who report they sought work but were unable to find it.) That 59% of the black women had less than 12 years of schooling (only 32% of the white women were at this level) may account for some of their unemployment rate (*Dual Careers*, Vol. I, 1970; the sample studied by Vetter and Stockburger is the same sample analyzed in *Dual Careers*).

---

[3]The unemployment rates of minority teen-age girls continue to be higher than those of any other group of teen-agers. In 1972 the rates for minority women and men, 16 to 19 years old, were 39% and 30%, respectively; for white female and male teen-agers, 13% and 14%, respectively (U.S. Dept. of Labor, Women's Bureau, 1974, b). The rates for minority teen-agers continued at the same high level in 1974. The discrepancy between black and white women persists, even though there is no longer an appreciable racial difference in years of education (e.g., white women averaged 12.5 years and black women averaged 12.3 years of schooling).

Secondly, childbearing and marriage depress employment rates for all women. According to *Dual Careers:* "The effect of *one* child on lifetime participation among ever-married women whose one child is either . . . 18 years or no longer living at home is to reduce by 28 percentage points among whites and 20 percentage points among blacks the fraction of years they have been in the labor force" (Vol. I., 1970, p. 74). Further, ". . . one may hypothesize that a woman who marries immediately after leaving school and who has a child during the first year of marriage will have less labor force exposure during her lifetime . . . than a woman for whom there is a several-year interval between school and marriage and/or birth of first child" (*Dual Careers,* p. 22). The average white woman left school at 17, married at 20, and bore the first child approximately two years later. The average black woman, however, left school at 16, married at 19, and gave birth to her first child within a year after marriage. Thus, white women had approximately five years in which to establish themselves as part of the labor force, while black women had three.

The factors of higher unemployment and earlier marriage and childbearing appear to account for at least a part of the early low participation rates of black women. In addition, black women averaged one more child per woman than did whites. (Number of children bore a negative relationship to work-force participation; Vetter & Stockburger, 1974.) Thus, work-force participation of black women, given their unemployment rates, their earlier childbearing, and the likelihood of larger families, makes their work history the more remarkable.

A TAXONOMY OF CAREER PATTERNS

Vetter and Stockburger applied to their data the system proposed by Super for designating women's career patterns, and found six of seven hypothesized patterns appropriate. These categories were (a) *stable homemaking,* composed of women with no significant work experience; (b) *conventional,* which described women who worked prior to marriage and/or birth of first child, and then were fulltime homemakers; (c) *stable working,* composed of single women who worked continuously; (d) *double-track,* women who married and worked full time continuously except for brief periods of childbearing; (e) *interrupted,* comprised of women who resumed working after years of homemaking; and (f) *unstable,* a label applied to women who entered and left the labor market at frequent intervals. (Parenthetically, the negative conceptual labeling of category (f) is curious.)

The conventional and stable homemaking categories describe what may be thought of as traditional patterns of female employment: Women who have no significant work experience or who work prior to marriage and/or the birth of the first child. In fact, 53% of the white women studied were distributed in these two groups. These patterns were typical of only 36% of the black women, however. The largest percentage of black women (30%) were described as unstable in their work-force participation.

As might be anticipated, almost one-quarter (21%) of the black women combined fulltime employment with marriage and childbearing whereas 12% of white women did so. Thus, the career patterns of over 50% of the black women in comparison to 26% of the white women involved either continuous fulltime employment or frequent entry into and exit from the labor force.

What becomes clear from these data is that neither marriage nor childbearing depress the employment rates of black women to the extent that they depress the rates for white women. It is to an examination of some reasons for this difference that we now turn.

ECONOMIC NEED

One of the reasons for the high employment rates of black women is economic necessity. Such need clearly exists in the female-headed household, black or white. Proportionately, there are more female-headed black families than female-headed white families: In 1973, one-third of all minority families and one-tenth of all white families were so constituted (Women's Bureau, U.S. Dept. of Labor, 1974).

Even when a black woman resides with her husband, however, there is a greater need for her financial contribution than there is for her white counterpart's. In 1965, 42% of all minority families would have lived in poverty had they been dependent solely upon the husband's income. (Poverty was defined as an annual income of less than $3,000 per year.) With the wife contributing to the family income, only 19% of black families lived at the poverty level (*Negro Women*, 1967). Another and more current measure of the black wife's contribution to her family was provided by Hill (1971/1972): While in white families with a single provider the median family income was $8,450 in 1969, in black families with both husband and wife employed the median family income was $7,682.

Table 3.2

Labor-force participation rate of wife
in Negro husband-wife families by total family income

Family income, $	Number (in thousands)	distribution, %	Labor-force participation rate of wife, %
v $2,000	478	15.1	25.9
2,000 - 2,999	421	13.3	36.3
3,000 - 4,999	832	26.3	40.9
5,000 - 6,999	614	19.4	52.0
7,000 - 8,999	396	12.5	57.8
9,000 - 9,999	120	3.8	78.3
v 10,000	304	9.6	78.0
Total	3,164	100.0	

Source: Data derived from *Negro Women in the Population and Labor Force*, U.S. Dept. of Labor, Women's Bureau, Washington, D.C.: U.S. Government Printing Office, 1967, p. 27.

Table 3.3

Labor-force participation rates of women,
by educational attainment and race
(women 18 years of age and over)

Years of school completed	White, %	Black, %
Total	38.9	49.5
Elementary school		
None	9.0	15.4
v 8	22.0	40.1
8	28.4	49.6
High School		
1 - 3	36.4	45.6
4	45.3	59.3
College		
1 - 3	41.8	59.5
4	49.8	89.2
5 or more	67.1	86.9

Source: From Women's Bureau, U.S. Dept. of Labor, *Negro Women in the Population and in the Labor Force,* Washington, D.C.: U.S. Government Printing Office, 1967, p. 64.

To view economic need as the only, or even the most important, determinant of the black woman's labor-force participation may be to obscure other explanatory factors, however. Table 3.2 presents employment rates for black women by family-income level. Clearly, the greater the family income, the higher is the probability that the wife will work. Factors other than sheer need would seem to be operative in families with incomes of $10,000 and above, since 78% of the wives were employed, while in families at the $5,000 to $7,000 level only 52% of the wives were working.

Vetter and Stockburger (1974) were able to delineate a number of characteristics of the working and nonworking wife within both racial groups. Their data describe a pattern among black women of increasing contribution to the labor force with increasing family socioeconomic status. The women with the *lowest* labor-force participation rates were those with the *least* amount of education and the *least* desirable incomes. Their husbands were comparable to them in educational and occupational attainment. As both the wife's and husband's education and kind of occupation improved, it became more likely that the wife was also employed. The relationship of family socioeconomic status (SES) to the wife's labor-force participation was not monotonic throughout the range of three categories of work intensity among white women, however. Though women's status, as measured solely by education and occupation, was highest (like that of black women) for women with the greatest participation rates, when the husband's status was taken into account the wife's working was to some extent inversely related to the family's SES. Women with the least work intensity were married to men with most desirable occupations and slightly higher educational levels. Thus, it appears that white women who do not work belong to a higher SES, though in fact this group is probably heterogeneous, with some women not working because of poor preparation, and many not working out of choice. In contrast, the black woman who does not work is the least privileged among her group, while the black woman who does work is the most privileged.

Table 3.3 reveals more clearly the effect of education upon labor-force participation for the two racial groups. With increasing levels of education, higher percentages of both black and white women work, though at each level larger percentages of black than of white women are employed. Interestingly, what brings about a substantial increase in the number of white employed women appears to be the attainment of graduate education; among black women, it is the attainment of the baccalaureate degree.

Table 3.4

Maternal employment of black and white women
by marital status and age of children

Age of Children, Years	Married (Husband Present), %		Widowed, Divorced, or Separated, %	
	Minority	White	Minority	White
6-17	61	49	62	71
v 6	53	31	38	51

Source: Data derived from U.S. Dept. of Labor, Women's Bureau, *Facts on Women Workers of Minority Races*, Washington, D.C.: U.S. Government Printing Office, 1974, p. 5.

Table 3.5

Maternal employment attitudes of black and white women by highest year of school completed

Years of School	Maternal employment attitudes					
Years of school completed	permissive, %		ambivalent, %		opposed, %	
	Black	White	Black	White	Black	White
v 8	28	18	49	61	23	22
9-11	25	19	65	58	10	23
12	29	19	57	54	14	28
13-15	28	19	50	50	22	31
16 or more	43	20	53	54	4	26
Total	28	19	57	54	15	27

Source: U.S. Dept. of Labor, Bureau of Labor Statistics, *Years for Decision*, Vol. 1, Manpower Research Monograph No. 24. Washington, D.C.: U.S. Government Printing Office, 1971, p. 34.
[a] Subjects were nonstudents, 18-24 years of age. The study sample consisted of 1,459 black and 3,638 white women, but exact numbers for the above response categories were not reported.

THE WORKING MOTHER

What clearly distinguishes black from white women in their employment patterns is the participation of the mother in the labor force. Vetter and Stockburger (1974) found that 25% of black women who had not worked regularly prior to marriage and children had *entered* the labor force after the birth of the first child. This was true of only 12% of white women. Statistics from 1973 reveal the propensity of black maternal employment even more clearly (Table 3.4). These data are congruent with data cited earlier; that is, that black women with husbands present had higher participation rates than did white women with husbands present, irrespective of the age of their children. It is of interest to note, however, the relationship of the husband's presence to maternal employment within the two racial groups. White mothers living with their husbands are significantly less likely to work than are white mothers who are divorced, separated, or widowed. Black mothers living with their spouses are no less likely to work than are black mothers who do not live with their husbands: In fact, with children under six years of age, black women are *more* likely to be employed when their husbands are present than when they are not. From 1963 to 1973, the most substantial increase (19%) in the labor-force participation rate of mothers with husbands present occurred among black women with children under the age of 6.

Racial attitudes about maternal employment are congruent with employment rates. Data in Table 3.5 are derived from a five-year study of a representative sample of the civilian population of women aged 14 to 24 years (U.S. Dept. of Labor, 1971). Over 7,000 white and 1,000 black women aged 18-24 were asked the following question:

I'd like for you to think about a family where there is a mother, a father who works full time, and several children under school age. A trusted relative who can care for the children lives nearby. . . . how do you feel about the mother taking a full time job outside the house? (p. 34)

Considerably more black than white women held permissive attitudes toward the mother's working, and twice as many white as black women were opposed (though the similarity of the numbers of those who were ambivalent is striking). It is also of interest that black women with 16 or more years of education were significantly more likely to favor the mother's employment than were black women with less education (43% versus 25-28%), but increasing education did not affect the proportion of white women with permissive attitudes. The authors of the study "... suspect that in addition to reflecting differences in family incomes, these differences between blacks and whites reflect rather deeply rooted variation in the role expectations of young women growing up in the two communities" (p. 34).

OCCUPATIONAL CHOICES

I have suggested that the labor-force participation of black women indicates an inclusion of employment within the definition of appropriate sex-role behavior. In addition to participation rates, however, it would also appear necessary to examine occupational choice as an indicant of nontraditional sex-role prescriptions. I have been unable to resolve some ambiguity with respect to these data, partially, I suspect, because the data themselves are ambiguous.

Until recently it has been clear that black women chose the most traditional of occupations. Their oft-cited overrepresentation in the professions, in comparison to that of white women, has been more apparent than real. Bock (1971) pointed out that black women constituted 60.8% of the black professional class in 1960, whereas white women constituted only 37.2% of white professionals. However, the discrepancy between black and white women derives from the fact that (a) there are so few black males in the professions in comparison to white males, and (b) black women (like white women) contribute so heavily to the professions of teaching, social work, and nursing. Jackson (1971) stated that only when the category of "professional" came to include semiprofessionals in Census Bureau tabulations did the number of black women exceed black men in the professional class. In 1960, according to Bock (1971), 94.8% of black nurses were women, 62.6% of black social workers were women, 84.5% of elementary teachers, and 54.5% of secondary school teachers, were women. However, only 9.7% of black physicians, 9.1% of lawyers and judges, and 33.7% of accountants and auditors were female. Except for the latter category, the proportion of black women in traditionally male professions did not differ substantially from the proportion of white women in such occupations.

Black women's overall representation in the professional category derives, then, from the fact that their numbers in the professions traditional for women are not offset by the numbers of black men in fields traditional for men. From an egalitarian view, *both* black men and black women are underrepresented in the professions. In 1973, 8% of black men in the labor force were professional, while 14% of white men were so categorized; among all black working women, 12% were professional as compared to 15% of white women (U.S. Dept. of Labor, Bureau of Statistics, 1974a). Again, the apparent equality between white men and women and the discrepancy between black men and women are undoubtedly due to the inclusion of traditionally feminine, previously low-status occupations such as nursing and teaching in the professional category. It becomes clear, then, that it is the extent to which black males are excluded from the professions and black (and white) females in lower status occupations are included in the category that accounts for the black woman's apparent overrepresentation.

In fact, within the professional class, black women are concentrated in fewer professions than are black men, or white women or white men. In 1970, 54% of all black women professionals were teachers, while only 39% of white women taught (Sorkin, 1972). If we look at older data, it seems that black women have been at least as constricted as white women in their occupational choices. Fichter (1967) found high similarity between a sample of 1964 women graduating from predominately black colleges and a National Opinion Research Center study of all graduates nationwide (*excluding* black colleges): 65% of the blacks and 61% of whites chose education or social work.

Gurin and Katz (1966), as did Fichter, concluded that the black college women they studied were highly similar to white women generally in their occupational choice. Further, Gurin and Katz identified some attitudinal correlates of occupational choice, which suggested that black college women were (at least in 1966) operating under the same kind of constraints that affected white women. In their study of 2,000 men and 2,000 women attending 10 heterogeneous black colleges, a subsample of same-sexed peers rated the desirability of various occupations. Among black males, the choice of what was desirable occupationally tended to be related (a) to how demanding of ability the occupation was (.64); (b) to how difficult it would be for a black (in comparison to a white) to enter the occupation (.58); and (c) to how nontraditional the occupation was for blacks (.61). However, among the women, occupations that had been deemed desirable were *negatively* related to the same variables. Thus, for girls, a desirable occupation was one that was *not* demanding of ability (-.31), *not* difficult for a black to enter (-.12), and more traditional (-.16).

> If choices that are deemed desirable by like-sexed peers are considered "role-appropriate" choices, the picture emerges that for a girl to have high aspirations, to choose a nontraditional occupation or one demanding a great deal of ability, simultaneously means she is making an "inappropriate" choice for a woman. High aspiration in the occupational area seems to be inconsistent with femininity. (Gurin & Katz, 1966, p. 97.)

Further, the women considered fewer occupations, chose them earlier, and were more certain of their choices than were the men. In several dimensions, then, the women's explorations were more restricted.

The preceding analyses suggest that black women are no less constricted than whites in selection of occupation. Given their stronger work orientation, their constriction of field is paradoxical in that they appear to see marriage and child-rearing as compatible with employment, but apparently think only certain roles are appropriate for them. Such a finding suggests that the sex-role norms of the majority may be operative for black women, though operative at the point of occupational choice rather than at the point of working or not working.

It is possible that the pattern described above is now undergoing some change. The reports of the American Council on Education (ACE) on entering freshmen for the years 1973 and 1974 reveal more nontraditional occupational choices among black women entering Howard University than among a national sample of white women entering other universities. Whereas in 1974, 16% of Howard women chose medicine or dentistry, 6% of white women selected these occupations; law was indicated by 9% of Howard and 4% of white women (ACE, 1974). Similarly, in 1973, 17% of Howard women selected medicine or dentistry, compared with 6% of white women, and 17% black versus 4% white chose law (Gump, in press, a).

These findings do not necessarily contradict the previously stated speculation that sex-role norms may operate in selected areas for black women. It may well be that the Women's Liberation Movement has had impact on black as well as white women. It is also my impression that the urgings several years ago of the black movement for greater passivity on the part of the black woman—a sad testimony to the acceptance that the matriarchy theory received even in the black community—have abated, and less pressure exists for the woman to "walk a step behind."

MYTHS AND REALITIES

It seems clear that, historically, the role of the black woman has been more independent than that of her white counterpart. Not only did she come from a culture that fostered independence—she was also thrust into a culture that necessitated it. She has struggled against poverty, using resources few of us understand, in order to lift herself to a position in which life might hold less despair (Ladner, 1971). She has been denied a mate who could protect and nurture her by a society that has deprived him of his manhood (Cleaver, 1968). There have been available to her fewer men from among whom she might select a husband because many have died prematurely, have been imprisoned or killed (Jackson, 1971). And, should she attain middle-class status, there are even fewer men of equal status available to her. By dint of necessity, she has had to be adequate and independent. But though she has been lonely, embittered, and uncherished, at least she has not had to contend with an image of dependency, passivity, and incompetence. She does not view herself in such a manner, nor, interestingly, does her mate. There exists unusual communality between black men's and women's perceptions of the black woman's role; white women and men exhibit less agreement on the white woman's role (Fichter, 1967; Steinmann & Fox, 1970; *Virginia Slims American Women's Opinion Poll,* Vol. III. 1974).

Several studies suggest that black women see themselves as more competent than white women view themselves. Fichter (1967) noted that for each of eight selected occupations, blacks were less likely than whites to confess they lacked the ability to perform the stated work. White women were also twice as likely to say that they lacked the proper personality for the occupation. Epstein (1972) noted a greater level of self-confidence in her sample of black professional women than in a sample of white professional women.

This attitude of self-sufficiency, of a capacity to go it alone should that become necessary, is also reflected in attitudes toward marriage. Bell (1971) suggested that marriage is of minimal importance for the lower-class black woman in particular, but that even for the middle-class woman it is of less significance than it is for white women. He asked a sample of 75 black mothers with less than nine years of education (low-status group), a sample of 122 black women with 10 to 12 years of schooling (middle-status group), and black and white college graduates the following question: "If you could be only a wife or mother (but not both), which would you choose?" Only 16% of the low-status group and 24% of the middle-group selected the wife role, while 50% of the black college graduates and 74% of the white college graduates selected this option. Similarly, in 1974, 67% of white women strongly believed that a loving husband who could take care of them was more important than making it on their own, while 47% of black women strongly expressed this sentiment (*Virginia Slims American Women's Opinion Poll,* Vol. III, 1974).

When black women desire marriage (Bell suggested that lower-class black women view marriage hostilely because of its threat to the maintenance of the family), their reasons for doing so are more practical and functional: Black women are twice as likely as white women to consider economic security, the better social life of the married couple, and "to have somebody around so you won't feel lonely," as reasons for marriage. More white than black women give love, companionship, and children as reasons for marrying, though the percentages in the survey for being in love were high for both black and white women (83% and 75%, respectively). Similarly, though 44% of black women stated that reasons other than love were more important in a decision to marry, only 29% of white women felt this way (*Virginia Slims American Women's Opinion Poll,* Vol. III, 1974). The two groups of women also differed with respect to the attributes admired in the male sex. Again there is evident a kind of practicality or realism in the qualities selected by black women. They most frequently admired attributes of intelligence, self-control, and leadership ability—in contrast to white women, who also chose intelligence, but who were much more likely to select gentleness, sensitivity to the feelings of others, and a sense of humor as desired characteristics.

Black attitudes toward children indicate a similar kind of "toughness." While black women in the survey placed greater emphasis on discipline and on "letting children have their own way" as influential factors in children's development, white women were more likely than black women to cite examples in morality and ethics, and love and affection, as significant influential factors.

·This image of strength in black women, a sense of adequacy and necessitated independence was most brilliantly captured by Cleaver (1968), who denoted these qualities as those of an "Amazon." Thrust upon her is the "domestic function" of the women in the classes above her; denied to her is her own femininity. The black woman embodies the cast-off force and power inherent in all women. It is this image to which we, as blacks, respond when we reverently speak of our women's courage and strength. But for all her virtues, an Amazon is more amazing than lovely or loved.

Just as the [Amazon's] man has been deprived of his manhood, so has she been deprived of her full womanhood. Society has decreed that the Ultrafeminine, the women of the elite, is the goddess on the pedestal. The Amazon is the personification of the rejected domestic component, the woman on whom "dishpan hands" seem not out of character. ... She envies the pampered, powderpuff existence of the Ultrafeminine and longs to incorporate these elements into her own life. (Cleaver, 1968, p. 197.)

And what is the evidence that this poetic image bears any relationship to reality? It has appeared to me that only as this image is made explicit does it become possible to interpret some puzzling inconsistencies about black women.

The fundamental inconsistency is that while expectations, preferences, and actual career patterns suggest that black women have adopted a nontraditional adaptation, their attitudes toward marriage, children, and sex role are in many respects undeniably conventional or traditional. For example, in a study of 77 black and 40 white college women, I found (Gump, 1975) highly significant differences in their sex-role attitudes. Black women significantly more than white women endorsed the position that identity and happiness would derive from pursuit of the traditional role; that, for instance, "No matter how successful a woman [might] be in utilizing her intelligence and creativity she [could] never know true happiness unless she marri[ed] and [had] a family" (Gump, 1972, p. 83). Though black women disagreed with the notion that a woman should be submissive to a man or that a woman should remain home if she had children, they were not nearly so emphatic in their rejection of such items as were white women. In truth, their responses were closer to uncertainty, a phenomenon I encountered surprisingly often in responses of black women to various sex-role questions.

Moreover, white women were significantly more adoptive of the view that fulfillment for a woman would derive from maximization of her own potential. The scale that measured this attitude (Gump, 1972) presented the view that identity, a sense of self-worth and satisfaction, would result from the woman's pursuit of her own interests and abilities rather than from fostering the interests and abilities of those emotionally close to her. Differences between black and white women were significant at $< .01$ on the nontraditional (Self) scale and $< .001$ on the traditional (Other) scale.

In the Virginia Slims Polls (1970 and 1974), though it appeared that black women were more pragmatic in their attitudes toward marriage, they were also surprisingly more romantic than white women. For instance, only 36% of the black women, in comparison to 57% of white women, believed that sooner or later a married couple stopped being in love, but that the earlier feeling was replaced with a different and deeper sentiment. Black women were more likely (49%) to think that a couple would remain in love throughout their marriage than were white women (37%). Further, 61% of black women, in comparison to 48% of white women, thought that falling out of love was a sufficient reason for considering divorce.

A SENSE OF RESPONSIBILITY

In a study of career antecedents among college women, Turner (1972) found differences between black and white women suggestive of what their respective employment patterns represent. Within each race, a high career expectation and a low career expectation group were identified. From a pool of 78 demographic, attitudinal, and developmental variables that had demonstrated a theoretical relationship to career orientation in women, those variables that discriminated high- from low-career expectation groups were identified through multivariate analyses. These analyses were performed separately for each race. Surprisingly, no overlap of predictors for the two groups of women was found. Variables that discriminated between black women with high or low career expectations were entirely distinct from those that discriminated the two career expectation groups among white women. High expectations among white women appeared to be related to (a) parental stress of competitive values during childhood, with a de-emphasis on correct and obedient behavior; (b) egalitarian attitudes toward male and female roles; and (c) a higher incidence of divorce among the parents.

Exceedingly few measures were identified which discriminated high-career black from low-career black women. Significant relationships were found between high-career expectations and students' perceptions of the expectations and desires of significant others. Students in the high group were more likely than those in the low to say their mothers would expect high work involvement, and that the men they knew would prefer them to have significant work involvement. Yet, even though the item about men's preferences differentiated the two groups, the mean score obtained by the *high* career expectation group was that of homemaker. 'These women expect to work *far* more than they believe men prefer for their wives; yet it seems that (their high career expectation) scores *are* affected by what they think men want" (Turner, 1972, p. 7).

High expectations were also somewhat ($p < .072$) related to an appreciation of parental strictness. Thus, it appears that black subjects' high expectations for work derived not so much from an achievement ethic as from a sense of responsibility. This image of womanhood appears to maintain that the woman should contribute economic support to her husband (even though she thinks he might prefer her at home), and perhaps fulfill some needs of her own mother. Whether the mother's needs relate to her own need for achievement or to a need to be certain that her daughter is capable of self-sufficiency, one can only speculate. But what is missing among these antecedents is any notion that work is viewed as a means of self-fulfillment. This finding is similar to the previously reported data on sex-role attitudes, in which the black woman expressed significantly less interest than did her white counterpart in the achievement ethic or in a need to maintain a private sphere of accomplishment.

I suggest that the sense of responsibility is deeply ingrained in black female sex-role ideology, a responsibility that includes economic provision for the family as well as provision of the more traditional functions. Further, this sense of responsibility has often become detached from economic necessity. There is no question but that most black women who work—and many who do not—need to work in order to ensure the survival of the family. But even when the need in an absolute sense is no longer present, the sense of responsibility, of having to give in this manner, remains. This sense of responsibility has, I believe, become autonomous.

Onus attaches more quickly to the black woman who does not work than to the black woman who does; women "who sit at home" are often described as lazy. Moreover, the better equipped (i.e., better educated) one is to "get a good job," the less excuse there is for "doin' nothin'." But comfort and the good life are determined by no given income level nor specification of goods. It is difficult to know when one has arrived. Given a background of deprivation and the probability that upward mobility is illusory for members of a castelike system, the need to possess the outward trappings of respectability and comfort is great. Such trappings are significant determinants of the middle-class black couple's striving and, thus, of the wife's employment.

Further, it is not only that education and the good job lead to the possession of more goods and status; more importantly they are the avenue to a middle-class husband. The high-career-expectation black woman is significantly more likely than the low to say that a good job will improve her chances of finding a high-status husband (Turner, 1972). Clearly, college and subsequent employment are a direct path to improved status; if one should fail to marry a man who possesses this high status, at least the woman will have acquired the prerequisites of it to give them to her family as well as herself. But the degree and good job are also a means of exposing and making oneself attractive to a man who has them. It is not that going to college to find a husband is peculiar to black women; rather, it is that black women are singularly dependent upon higher education as a resource for obtaining a middle-class mate. "The common pattern for generational mobility among whites has been from manual labor to business, and from business to the professions" (Bock, 1971, p. 120), but most of the middle occupational level has been unavailable to black men. In that managerial and entrepreneurial enterprises have been inaccessible to black men, unlike white men they have tended to move from the lower or lower-middle class into the middle class via higher education, and thus into the professions. While lower middle-class white girls can hope to improve their status by marriage to men in a wide variety of occupations, their black counterparts have been restricted to the kinds of men who could "make it" academically, for this represented one of the few means black men had available for upward mobility.

Parenthetically, though the white woman has been careful to avoid apparent equality with her mate in intelligence or accomplishment, the black woman is made the more attractive by possession of these qualities. To what extent this attractiveness is due to her capacity to be of economic support is unclear, but it is clear that the well-educated and competent black woman is less threatening to the black man than such a white woman has been to a white man.

Familial and group factors have also determined the black woman's striving. The daughter's perception of her mother's expectation has been previously mentioned, as has the uncertainty about what the derivation of such an expectation might be. Another facet of familial and group expectation may also be noted. From lower-and middle-class black men and women I have often received considerable praise for my "accomplishments." That pride is undiminished by my sex. No one has ever wondered how my children or my husband have fared, though interest is often expressed in both. I suspect that the pressures and support for achievement that exist for black children exist for male and female alike. Support for this conclusion is found in a study of parental differences in socialization to achievement according to the sex of the child. As reported by their college-attending offspring, white parents socialized male and female children differently, but black children perceived in their parents no sex differences in socialization to achievement (Turner and Turner, 1971). The girl's greater propensity for better school performance may mean that *more* pressure and support is extended to her than is accorded her brother.

Given the perceived expectations of the family, the prospective mate, and the larger racial group, and given her own internalized sense of how she is to fulfill her responsibility as wife and mother, it is inaccurate to view the black woman's struggle as one for demonstrated competence or independence. That is the white woman's struggle. It might be argued that even if the black woman and man see the black woman as competent and independent, the white man does not. There is reason to believe, however, that white men may not apply to black women the sex-role norms that obtain for his own women. Epstein (1972) suggested that "two statuses in combination create a new status (for example, the hyphenated status of black-woman-lawyer) which may have no established 'price' because it is unique. . . . This pattern may also place the person in the role of a 'stranger' outside the normal exchange system and able to exact a higher than usual price" (p. 914).

Thus, what has been denied black women by the dominant group is not independence, but the possibility of being dependent. Black women can be "taken care of" only when the larger group no longer inhibits the black man's performance of this role. I doubt that, if asked directly, many black women would say they yearn for nurturance and protection: It is suggestive, however, that B.F. Turner (1972) found that her sample of black college women wanted 54% less work involvement than they predicted they would have, while 40% of the white women wanted more.

It may well be, as Fichter (1967) suggested, that black women have learned to prefer what they have learned to expect. None of us would wish to relinquish our sense of competence or self-sufficiency. But whether black women would talk about nurturance or not, my clinical experience leads me unfalteringly to conclude that the deficit of caring has taken its toll, not only upon her but also upon her spouse and their offspring. If one has had very little of something, its absence may not be noted, but this hardly implies it is not needed. Almost all black people have needed more care than they have received, and it is dangerous for us—or for whites—to think that the strength and endurance wrought from necessity were purchased at a small price. I know, from my black childhood and womanhood, something of that cost. One of our tasks as black women may be to specify what deficits have accrued, as well as what benefits, so that we and others may not assume lightly that the dual role in the present cultural and economic structure is one we unquestioningly seek.

REFERENCES

American Council on Education. Report on Howard University freshmen, 1974.

Bell, R.P. The related importance of mother-wife roles among black lower-class women. In R. Staples (Ed.), *The black family: Essays and studies.* Belmont, Calif.: Wadsworth, 1971.

Bock, E.W. Farmer's daughter effect: The case of the Negro female professionals. In A. Theodore (Ed.), *The professional woman.* Cambridge, Mass.: Schenkman, 1971.

Cleaver, E. *Soul on ice.* New York: Dell, 1968.

Diop, C.A. *The cultural unity of Negro Africa.* Paris: Presence Africaine, 1962. (Originally published, 1959.)

Epstein, C.F. Positive effects of the multiple negative: Explaining the success of black professional women. *American Journal of Sociology,* 1972, *78,* 912-935.

Fichter, J.S. Career expectations of Negro women graduates. *Monthly Labor Review,* 1967, *90,* 11, 36-42.

Gump, J.P. Sex-role attitudes and psychological well-being. *Journal of Social Issues,* 1972, *28,* 2, 79-92.

Gump, J.P. A profile of the 1973 freshman class at Howard University. *Journal of Negro Education,* in press. (a)

Gump, J.P. A comparative analysis of black and white women's sex-role attitudes. *Journal of Consulting and Clinical Psychology,* 1975, *43,* 858-863.

Gurin, P., & Katz, D. *Motivation and aspiration in the Negro college* (Final report, U.S. Department of Health, Education and Welfare). Washington, D.C.: U.S. Government Printing Office, 1966.

Herskovits, M.J. *The myth of the Negro past.* Boston: Beacon Press, 1958, (Originally published in 1941.)

Hill, R.B. *The strengths of black families.* New York: Emerson Hall, 1972. (Originally published in 1971.)

Jackson, J.J. But where are the men? *The Black Scholar,* 1971, *3,* 4, 30-41.

Kuvlesky, W.P., & Obordo, A.S. A racial comparison of teen-age girls' projections for marriage and procreation. *Journal of Marriage and the Family,* 1972, *34,* 75-84.

Ladner, J.A. *Tomorrow's tomorrow: The black woman.* Garden City, N.Y.: Doubleday, 1971.

Mbiti, J.S. *African religions and philosophy.* Garden City, N.Y.: Doubleday, 1970. (Originally published in 1969.)

Powdermaker, H. *After freedom.* New York: Russell & Russell, 1939.

Sorkin, A.L. Education, occupation and income on nonwhite women. *Journal of Negro Education,* 1972, *41,* 343-351.

Steinmann, A., & Fox, D.J. Attitudes towards women's family role among black and white undergraduates. *The Family Coordinator,* 1970, *19,* 363-368.

Turner, B.F. Socialization and career orientation among black and white college women. Paper presented at the 80th Convention of the American Psychological Association, Hawaii, 1972.

Turner, C.B., & Turner, B.F. Perception of the occupational opportunity structure, socialization to achievement and career orientation as related to sex and race. Proceedings of the 79th Annual Convention of the American Psychological Association, 1971, 243-244. (Summary)

U.S. Dept. of Labor, Bureau of Labor Statistics. *Dual careers: a longitudinal study of labor market experience of women.* Manpower Research Monograph No. 21, Vol. 1, Washington, D.C.: U.S. Government Printing Office, 1970.

U.S. Dept. Labor, Bureau of Labor Statistics. *Years for decision: A longitudinal study of the educational and labor market experience of young women.* Manpower Research Monograph No. 24, Vol. 1. Washington, D.C.: U.S. Government Printing Office, 1971.

U.S. Dept. of Labor, Bureau of Labor Statistics. *Employment and earnings.* Washington, D.C.: U.S. Government Printing Office, January, 1974, *20,* 7.

U.S. Dept. of Labor, Women's Bureau. *Negro women in the population and in the labor force.* Washington, D.C.: U.S. Government Printing Office, 1967.

U.S. Dept. of Labor, Women's Bureau. *Facts on women workers of minority races.* Washington, D.C.: U.S. Government Printing Office, 1974.

Vetter, L., & Stockburger, D.W. *Career patterns of a national sample of women* (Research and Development Series No. 95). Columbus, Ohio: Technical Education, Ohio State University, 1974.

The Virginia Slims American Women's Opinion Poll. Office of Corporate Relations, Phillip Morris, New York, 1970, 1974.

CHAPTER *11*

COMMENTARY: CHAPTERS 8, 9 & 10

JANET TAYLOR SPENCE

The documentation provided by the authors of the chapters in this Part I gives overwhelming evidence that despite the persistent myth about women's "place," large numbers of women have always worked outside the home and that, in all segments of society, women's participation in the labor force continues to rise. Similarly overwhelming is the evidence that women workers are overrepresented in jobs with low levels of pay and prestige, many of them sex-typed, and that even when women have the same qualifications as men and are assigned the same duties, they are usually paid less and are less likely to be promoted to positions of greater responsibility.

The discrepancy that has historically existed between the vocational attainments of men and women can be attributed in part to rank discrimination—the denial to women of equal access to educational opportunities and to the job market, simply because they *are* women. Although contemporary standards of social justice have led to more even-handed treatment of the sexes, major differences in the achievement of men and women still remain, leading those interested in vocational phenomena to turn their attention to other kinds of causal factors. Astin and Laws explicate some of the more subtle external forces that discourage women (or more particularly, as Gump suggests, white women) from attempting to compete vocationally with men. They also outline the kinds of internal barriers brought about by socialization experiences that "inhibit women," as Astin puts it, "from fully actualizing themselves through careers and work and [by] institutional constraints that hamper them from growing to their fullest potential."

Subtle ideological commitments can creep into discussions of women and work, not always fully recognized or intended. The nature of the internal "obstacles" that one postulates to constrain women's vocational achievements, or indeed one's theoretical model of women's work behavior, is influenced by one's interpretation of the Women's Liberation Movement itself. Among those sympathetic to feminism, a common view is that the current Women's Movement is not only an outgrowth of the Civil Rights Movement of the 1950s and 1960s, but is parallel to the political struggles of oppressed ethnic minorities, particularly blacks, to achieve legal, economic, and social parity with the dominant group. According to this position, women are engaged in a political power struggle with males to escape from a position of inferiority and domination. Women must overcome not only the external forces designed to keep them in a subordinate position, but also the imposition of internal barriers. Women, along with other victimized groups, are deliberately inculcated with attitudes and beliefs about themselves that are designed to justify their inferior status and lead them to accept their position in society as natural and right, rather than to rebel against it. In her essay on women in the 1973 Encyclopedia Britannica, Clare Booth Luce presented an extreme form of this argument with dramatic clarity:

What man now calls woman's natural feminine mentality is the unnatural slave mentality he forced on her, just as he forced it on the blacks. He made her the "house nigger." In the end, man dropped the shackles from woman's body only because he had succeeded in fastening them on her mind. Man did not grant woman the vote until he was reasonably certain that her slave mentality had become second nature and that she would not act to bring about her own emancipation.

Traditional sex-role training, which teaches women that their destiny is to be subordinate to men, and which restricts their permissible forms of activity, is thus seen as a kind of psychological tyrannization.

An implication that may easily be read into this kind of ideological statement is that women who accept traditional sex-role standards are by definition hoodwinked victims who must be rescued, whether they like it or not; women ought not allow themselves to be confined to the home, but to reach their fullest potential, they should go outside it (i.e., be as vocationally and achievement-oriented as men). This is indeed the view of some radical feminists, but it is a position that ought to be taken openly and responsibly rather than (as often seems to be the case) as an implication that can be drawn because of ambiguity of language. Caricatures of feminists' goals are all too easy, and have been used by critics to frighten traditionally oriented women into resisting social and political changes.

Viewing the Women's Liberation Movement solely as a political struggle for greater control of resources misses much of its significance. Sex-role differentiations have all but universally characterized human societies. Abstract considerations of social justice aside, role assignments have been devised in particular societies to be functionally useful, to divide responsibilities between the sexes in a manner that is responsive to the total complex of cultural institutions in that society. They tend to survive only as long as they have adaptive significance; changes in the overall society typically demand realignments of sex-role assignments. What we currently regard as the "traditional" conception of the male and female roles—men as providers and family representatives to the outside world, and women as nurturers of husbands, children, and homes—is itself of relatively recent origin, a product of the Industrial Revolution, and even at that, largely the model for the middle class. But as our society has become increasingly urbanized and technologically advanced, these home-bound roles assigned to women have become less functional or possible to sustain. The most recent emergence of feminism and the widespread societal concern with the status of women, like most social movements, are symptomatic of cultural dislocations that have been taking place over a lengthy period of time, and reflect the pragmatic necessity for redefining sex roles to bring them more in line with contemporary realities.

If one starts from this perspective, then the social changes that are forcing redefinitions of women's roles represent only partially a relief from unwelcome oppression. The major effect of these changes, quite to the contrary, may be one of squeezing women out of traditional roles that have many positive, desirable characteristics and that many would prefer to retain. The discontents of women may reflect less a "rise" in expectations than an uncertainty about expectations and where the possibility of fulfillment lies.

The forces that have put an increasing strain on women's traditional roles have often been documented, but like the facts about women and work, they are worth repeating until we are able to fully admit their existence. Especially for the increasingly large middle class, family size has become progressively smaller. With the growing social acceptance of effective methods of contraception and the reduction of pressures on women to have children, family size may undergo still further shrinkage. Moreover, technological advances that include improved nutritional standards and medical care, have made housework less demanding, have slowed the aging process and have increased the life span. Married women who orient their activities around their home and the care of their family are likely to find themselves technologically underemployed, especially after their children are grown. Married women are entering the job market, not merely for personal fulfillment or to escape boredom (although these motives should not be denigrated), but because their economic contribution to their family's welfare is needed. For many married women, even those with small children, paid labor outside the home has become a more effective mode of contribution than unpaid labor within it. Gump draws our attention to the fact that this has always been true in the typical black family; the working wife, rather than being ignored as though she did not exist, or being downgraded as unimportant, has been fully acknowledged and her role honored.

Reality seems to be catching up with young white women. An overwhelming majority plan to marry, sooner or later. But even among middle-class college students, according to the data cited by Laws, most anticipate that they not only will work at some time during their marriage, but that a combination of marriage and career will also be their preferable lifestyle rather than marriage alone.

Less well known and less pleasant to face is the substantial probability that at some period in her life, a woman will not have a husband. The old tradition that respectable middle-class girls stay at home, supported by their families until they marry, has long since vanished, as has the expectation that the extended family will include the widow or the aging spinster and provide for her maintenance. Unless they are fortunate enough to have ample financial resources under their direct control, able-bodied women without husbands are increasingly expected to support themselves. Divorce is becoming more common and socially acceptable at all age and class levels, and seldom can divorced women count on alimony to provide reasonable support. If divorce does not dissolve the marriage, death may. The average life-span for women is longer than that for men, and social custom continues to dictate that women marry men of the same age or older, thus further increasing the ratio of available (single) women to men. Continuing with this dreary picture, the divorced or widowed woman of middle age or beyond is significantly less likely to remarry than is a man in a similar position. Women wishing to remarry must hope to be sought out by members of a pool of older men whose numbers, relative to their own, continues to shrink with time.

One wonders whether the popularity of *The Total Woman* and other hymns to the subordination of women to their husbands is not in part based upon women's clinging to a version of the just-world hypothesis to ward off their fears. If a wife does just what she is supposed to do to cater to her husband, surely she will be rewarded by his not dying or running off, or treating her unkindly. Propitiation of the gods does not always work, alas. Too many women who, at the urging of their husbands and families, have remained at home, docile and dependent, have learned that the same families or (ex)husbands suddenly expect them to be independent and self-supporting when their husbands are no longer there.

As Laws's critique of the literature on the work behavior of women suggests, it has yet to be fully appreciated that women are not *choosing* to work in increasing numbers; more and more they *have* to work, and for reasons similar to those of men. The implications of this conclusion are many and far-reaching. I will mention only one. One of the harmful consequences of the division of labor between the sexes, which we regard as traditional, is that it has been accompanied by assumptions about the desirable (if not "natural") psychological attributes of men and women. To match what Parsons and Bales characterized as the "expressive" *roles* assigned to women are the "expressive" *characteristics:* unselfishness, the desire to serve others, sensitivity, emotionality, and so forth. Men, in contrast, face the "instrumental" challenges of the outside world and are thus more instrumental in their characteristics: assertive, independent, competent, and so forth. The execution of both masculine and feminine sex roles would seem to benefit from both sets of characteristics, however, and there is no reason to suspect that "masculine" and "feminine" characteristics are, of necessity, mutually exclusive. In fact, the evidence collected by Sandra Bem (see Part I of Volume I), as well as by my colleagues and myself, suggests that they are not. Nonetheless, many believe that a lack of instrumental, "masculine" characteristics is frequently associated with "femininity," and women who have adopted conventional sex roles have too often been encouraged to do so at the expense of their own sense of self. They remain too dependent and passive, too limited in self-confidence, too convinced of women's inferiority. Therefore, they cannot function well in responsible positions if they venture into the job market, whatever their talents and educational attainments, or even be comfortable in running their own lives, should it be necessary for them to do so. Stereotypic "masculinity" simultaneously demands of men that they be superior to women— more competent, more successful, and in a greater position of authority.

If sex roles are to be redefined to adjust to contemporary social conditions, these restrictive conceptions of "masculinity" and "femininity" will have to be modified. Women must become capable of role flexibility, responding adaptively to whatever their present life circumstances permit or demand, while men must become capable of perceiving and accepting women as responsible, self-directing human beings.

This prescription is probably easier for women to adopt than for men. Returning to the theme of Sandra Bem, men are being called upon to restrain and to minimize those self-aggrandizing aspects of their sense of agency (which many consider the essence of their masculinity) that demand that they be superior and more powerful than females. Women, on the other hand, are not being asked to renounce or restrain their sense of communion (the essence of their femininity), but to *strengthen* their sense of agency or instrumentality—in a word, to become more androgynous.

The assumption of responsibility for one's own life, however, is not without cost. We would do well to heed the poignant words of Janice Gump about the black experience:

> Almost all black people have needed more care than they have received, and it is dangerous . . . to think that the strength and endurance wrought from necessity were purchased at a small price . . . One of our tasks as black women may be to specify what deficits have accrued, as well as what benefits, so that we and others may not lightly assume that the dual role [of worker, and of wife and mother]—in the present cultural and economic structure—is one we unquestioningly seek.

PART II
ACHIEVEMENT, STATUS, AND POWER

INTRODUCTION

JULIA A. SHERMAN & FLORENCE L. DENMARK

The papers in this Part II of Volume II pinpoint areas increasingly seen as vital to our understanding of individuals and the collective group. These areas encompass sets of questions. What is achievement? Is having a baby an achievement? Obviously, the latter is not what McClelland et al. (1953) had in mind. The connotations of the traditional achievement literature in psychology refer to achievements in the world of work that have accepted economic value. Having loaded the dice against women in the very definition of achievement or, at best, in the criteria studied in validation studies, the next question often emerging in a tone of anguish has been, "Do women achieve (by this selected definition) as much as men? This question then leads to investigations of possible factors affecting achievement in women (e.g., role conflict, motive to avoid success, achievement based on affiliative needs, external barriers.)

Perception of achievement in women, however, is based not only in the definition of the concept, but also in perception of women's worth and in expectations about what women's achievements will be. The syllogism proceeds as follows:

1. She is a woman.
2. Women do not achieve.
3. She does not achieve. Presupposition 2 guarantees that once 1 is known, deduction 3 will follow.

This train of thinking often proceeds to its logical (given the assumptions) conclusion, even in the face of contradictory empirical evidence. Achievements of women may be evaluated less highly if they are known to be the product of women, and/or achievements by women may be discounted (e.g., attributed to luck, bedroom politics, being a grind) or deliberately ignored.

Unfortunately, the guaranteed nonachievement syllogism is used to justify not hiring women, giving them fewer resources and opportunities for serious, creative intellectual work, and a thousand and one negative and discounting decisions of those in power. Such decisions range from the amount of money parents are likely to spend for scientific toys for their girls, to those subtle decisions in research university settings about whom to ask to be on the "Housekeeping Committee," and about who has the responsibility and access to scarce, expensive scientific equipment. The pervasive, relentless extent of these discrepant conditions is only slowly being appreciated.

Power and achievement are thus reciprocally related. Certain kinds of achievement are only possible with certain kinds of power (money, status, recognition). Achievement itself often facilitates attainment of status and power, at least for men, and at least in theory. These achievements then may appear to legitimate the status: XY has done much brilliant research and deserves ter high status vis-a-vis XX, who has produced paltry and mediocre research (ignoring the fact that XY received $7 million in research funds while XX received only $500).

The contemporary attitude of many women toward power is ambivalent. Having long suffered from the inequitable distribution of power, there is a strong egalitarian attitude within the Women's Liberation Movement. This attitude can be discerned in many women's groups within the Movement, and creates a sort of internal contradiction and/or paradox: The Women's Movement talks of improving the status of women, yet the egalitarian ethos of the Movement may quickly label any woman acquiring status as an elitist. She may well be attacked and/or discredited. In any case she is extremely likely to lose her support and leadership position. This phenomenon is widespread in the Women's Movement. Certain forms of it (e.g., "trashing the leader") are found generally in radical groups.

The article by Denmark, Tangri, and McCandless undertakes the formidable task of summarizing and integrating the theoretical and empirical literatures pertaining to women in the areas of affiliation, achievement, and power. Their presentation is provocative and provides clarification for complex phenomena not before considered in this context.

Unger concentrates on the confounding effects of gender and status in the literature pertaining to status and power. Various types and definitions of power emerge, as well as information about studies relevant to these concepts.

Frieze, Fisher, Hanusa, McHugh, and Valle detail theory and research findings relevant to attributions about women's success and failure, and expectations of others about women's achievements. These important topics begin to explain the dynamics of the sexual politics of achievement.

Helson has long pondered the question of creativity in women. In the contemporary context, ter empirical findings fall into a new and evocative perspective. To what extent does the guaranteed nonachievement syllogism affect creativity in women? Quite plainly, it is very much involved. Ingeniously selecting ter comparison groups, Helson presents us with a set of empirical findings that delineates entrepreneurial and incubative male mathematicians, while the entrepreneurial type is not to be found among female creative mathematicians. The contrasting power and resources of these creative types, and their relationships to their styles of creative approach, are quite striking indeed.

REFERENCE

McClelland, D.C., Atkinson, J.W. Clark, R.A., & Lowell, E.L. *The achievement motive.* New York: Appleton-Century-Crofts, 1953.

CHAPTER *12*

AFFILIATION, ACHIEVEMENT, AND POWER: A New Look

FLORENCE L. DENMARK, SANDRA SCHWARTZ TANGRI & SUSAN McCANDLESS

Florence Denmark is Professor of Psychology at Hunter College, and Executive Officer of the Doctoral Program in psychology at the Graduate School of City University of New York. She was formerly Chair of the Department of Academic Skills at Hunter College.

Denmark's professional activities include: Associate Editor, International Journal of Group Tensions; *editorial board member of* Sex Roles: A Journal of Research *and* The Psychology of Women Quarterly; *Past President of Division 35, American Psychological Association (Psychology of Women); member of the American Psychological Association Board of Directors; Past President of the New York State Psychological Association; and Vice-President of the International Organization for the Study of Group Tensions. She is a Fellow of the American Psychological Association and of The New York Academy of Sciences; and a member of Phi Beta Kappa, Phi Alpha Theta, Psi Chi, Sigma Xi, Who's Who of American Women, and American Men and Women of Science.*

Her numerous publications include: Woman: Dependent or Independent Variable? *Psychological Dimensions, Inc., 1975 (Co-editor with R. Unger);* PROBE: A Program for Planning Ahead Educationally, *Transnational Programs Corporation, 1972;* Women: Vol. I, *Psychological Dimensions, Inc., 1976;* Who Discriminates Against Women? *(Vol. 4, Issue 1,* International Journal of Group Tensions*), Sage Publications, Inc., 1974.*

Susan McCandless received a B.A. in psychology from the University of Connecticut in 1970, and is completing her Ph.D. in Social-Personality Psychology at the Graduate School of the City University of New York. She teaches psychology at Herbert H. Lehman College of the City University of New York.

Sandra Schwartz Tangri received her B.A. at the University of California, Berkeley, with Honors in Psychology, her Master's degree in Psychology from Wayne State University, and her Ph.D. in Social Psychology from the University of Michigan. From the doctorate on, her research has been in the area of women's roles, personality dynamics of achievement in women, population programs and the role of women in them, and the relation of black women to the feminist movement. Earlier research efforts were in juvenile delinquency, anti-Semitism, economic development, and mental hospital commitment procedures. She has taught at Wayne State University, The University of Michigan, Douglass College (Rutgers University), and Richmond College (City University of New York). At present, she is Director of Research for the U.S. Commission on Civil Rights. She is a consulting editor for the Psychology of Women Quarterly, *on the advisory board of Planned Parenthood Association of Washington, D.C., helped plan the conference at which the articles in this volume were first presented, and was on the Task Force on Issues of Sex Bias in Graduate Education in Psychology for the American Psychological Association.*

Achievement, affiliation, and power are very relevant domains for the psychology of women, both as behavior and as motivation. Historically, personality theory and research has focused on motivation considerations. Women are generally presumed to be low in achievement motivation, high in affiliation, and are absent from power-motivation inquiry.

A review of the theory and research in each of these areas leads the authors to conclude that none of them contributes sufficient conceptual clarification and unambiguous empirical data necessary to lead to a more comprehensive and valid theory about the psychology of women. The discussions raise serious issues about methodology and research paradigms. Suggestions for future research are mentioned.

Affiliation, achievement, and power are important areas of investigation for many present-day personality theorists. For explaining certain aspects of behavior—such as intensity, change, and direction—the concept of motive seems to possess intuitive validity, and motivation theory has enjoyed a strong, although ambivalent, relationship within psychology.

Motivational topics have played a central role in thinking about women. Despite the confusion and lack of clarity, which are discussed in detail in this chapter, the theories and literature on achievement, affiliation, and power motivation are important to research on women because of their centrality in sex-role stereotypes. Recent perspectives have yielded greater understanding of achievement concerns in women, but have not yet significantly altered the state of knowledge of the other two topics. Affiliation continues to be seen in stereotypic terms, and power is hardly recognized as a concern of women at all. A critical review of the current literature on these motives may enable us to develop less culture-bound views and a more comprehensive analysis of the inter-actions among all three. This review will provide a framework for a program of needed research.

This chapter is structured into five sections. The first section presents the general framework of expectancy-value theory as the basis for existing research on all three topics. The next three sections consist of reviews of previous work on each of the motivational topics—affiliation, achievement, and power motivation—and the final section is an integrative discussion that proposes a structure for a more heuristic model for motivational questions regarding wom-en.

EXPECTANCY-VALUE THEORY

Expectancy-Value theory has grown out of a number of research traditions. The nearest theoretical parents are the work of Murray (1938), Lewin (1939), and Tolman (1932).

In the 1930s, Murray and his colleagues at Harvard began an intensive study of 50 male Harvard students. From this investigation and from the theories of Freud, McDougall, Jung, Rank, Adler, Lewin, and Allport, Murray's (1938) "personological" theory of personality was formulated. This theory stresses the dynamic (as opposed to structural) forces in personality, particularly those of needs or motives. Murray delineated 20 psychogenic needs. Among these needs were affiliation, achievement, and dominance. The emphases on cognitions such as expectancy and value as important determinants of behavior were taken from Lewin (1938) and Tolman (1932).

In the Atkinson/McClelland (McClelland, Atkinson, Clark, & Lowell, 1953; Atkinson, 1958) version of the Expectancy-Value theory, the terms "motive," "motivation," and "arousal" are important features. They define a motive as a relatively general, latent, and stable personality disposition to derive satisfaction from a particular class of incentives. Motives are thought to be acquired early in childhood and to remain latent until aroused by situational cues. Specifically, motives will be activated in those situations where individuals perceive that the consequences of their actions will lead them to the goal state of the aroused motive. The aroused motive is referred to as "motivation." The tendency to actually perform behaviors leading to the goal state depends on a number of other variables. Resultant or total motivation depends on the combined strength of the motive, the person's subjective probability of being able to attain the goal, and the incentive value of the goal.

In later elaborations of the theory, the possibility of avoidance motives was also taken into account—but only for achievement and power motivation—and in another recent elaboration the functional significance of the immediate task for attaining a future goal has also been incorporated (primarily for achievement motivation; Raynor, 1969). The model for predicting the strength of the tendency to move toward the goal is expressed algebraically as follows:

$$T = (M{+}G \times M{-}G \times IG \times EG)$$

where:

T = resultant tendency to undertake goal-instrumental activity;
$M{+}G$ = strength of the motive to approach the goal;
$M{-}G$ = strength of the motive to avoid the goal;
IG = incentive value of the goal;
EG = expectation of being able to attain the goal.

In achievement and power, the avoidance motives have become increasingly complex. In the achievement domain, there is now the suggestion of a motive to avoid success (M-s, or fear of success), and a distinct motive to avoid failure (M-f). In power, there is the suggestion of a motive to avoid power (M-p, comparable to M-s), to avoid powerlessness (comparable to M-f), and yet a third—to avoid being subject to another's power. In the affiliation domain, there has been no exploration of the possibility of avoidance motives in this theoretical context. Furthermore, not all the other terms of the equation (IG, EG) have received the same intensity of study for each of the motives. However, in all three areas, considerable attention has been devoted to the development of measures for the $M{+}G$ term, or the motive itself. Because of this, it is possible to discuss measurement and other problems common to all three areas.

In the history of the development of all the measures—n-Aff (need Affiliation), n-Ach (need Achievement), and n-Pow (need power)—we find a repeated androcentric bias in the arousal techniques used and the subjects selected, both for standardizing the instrument and for further validation studies. This commonality of androcentric bias, plus other similarities that derive from use of the same measurement approach, lead to the following list of statements:

1. In all three areas, scoring procedures were operationalized on male subjects only (even for affiliation, a stereotypic feminine trait).

2. Scoring categories were selected according to differences in frequency of use between aroused and nonaroused (male) subjects. In each case, the arousal manipulation has an implicitly masculine flavor. For arousal of achievement concerns, reference was made to the task's ability to predict military leadership, among other things, For arousal of power motivation, student candidates for public office were selected. For arousal of affiliation needs, an implied threat to affiliation was used. Less androcentric arousals can be conceived (e.g., referring to acquisition of non-sex-typed skills for achievement, using "crusader" type appeals like voter registration for power, or comparison of cooperatively structured with competitively structured groups for affiliation). 3. In all three areas, subsequent content

3. In all three areas, subsequent content validation was done exclusively or primarily on male students, or without both sexes in the same experiment, making sex comparisons impossible.

4. Androcentric, class, and race biases were exacerbated by exclusive use of college students as subjects.

5. The psychometric properties based on TAT (Murray's projective Thematic Apperception Test) measures have been generally poor.

6. A projective technique calls into question all the problems associated with any projective technique.

7. The terms "affiliation," "achievement," and "power" have sometimes been used to describe both the motive and a specific set of behaviors, the motivation for which has yet to be determined.

8. Different measures of the same motive generally have not been comparable. Correlations between techniques used to assess the same motive are frequently low. A given behavior may relate to one assessment technique, but not to another for the same motive.

9. The relationship between the three motives has not been developed conceptually, and rarely investigated empirically.

10. Some theorists presume a deprivational model (motive level assumed to increase as a function of the lack of something); others do not.

AFFILIATION

In psychological literature there are many uses for the term "affiliation." The usage depends not only upon the theoretical orientation of the author, but also upon the ways in which the concept has been operationalized. These differences in definition make comparisons among various experimental efforts difficult, if not impossible.

The purpose of this section of the chapter is threefold: (a) to investigate the existing theory and empirical work on the motive to affiliate as a general area of research; (b) to see how this body of knowledge relates to women; (c) to reveal those unanswered questions that must be considered and included within any heuristic theoretical undertaking.

Throughout the history of psychology, affiliation has been conceptualized in many diverse ways. Freud (1957) would have considered it within the context of sexual and aggressive instincts, and McDougall (1921) suggested that gregariousness (a tendency to seek out and congregate with other humans) was one of the human instincts. More recently, Zigler and Child (1969), in a review of the literature on dependency, discussed the possibility of both innate and acquired drives for dependency, expressed behaviorally as a desire for nurturance and human proximity. Schaffer and Emerson (1964) and Bowlby (1958) viewed attachment—a concept similar to affiliation, and defined as a tendency of the young to seek the proximity of other members of the species—as having an instinctual basis. It is not difficult to see how early attachment or dependency behavior could be viewed as sources of generalization for later, more diffuse affiliation.

As Zigler and Child (1969) noted, the existence of an innate basis for dependency does not preclude the existence of an acquired drive for dependency as well. And, of course, it is possible that either or both sources of the motivation for human proximity could be utilized by the individual for the satisfaction of the other drives or motives, and be reinforced and perpetuated outside of childhood particularly because they do lead to the satisfaction of other important needs (such as sex, achievement, love, appreciation, comfort, and power/ dominance). Therefore, affiliation, as derived or generalized from early attachment and dependency in childhood, should not be overlooked. Factors that contribute to individual differences in level of dependency (i.e., relation to sex-role standards, parental overprotection, frustration by stringent behavior expectations in childhood, frustration by withdrawal of nurturance, and reinforcement parameters and their effects) could be investigated with fruitful results.

Learning theory suggests that people take on a positive valence through simple association with rewards, or that the actual process of affiliating has been rewarded consistently by important others (e.g., parents approving of "nice" peer-play behavior in young children and society giving a high value to cooperative efforts). Differences in maternal behaviors with neonates by sex of child open intriguing possibilities, such as when Goldberg and Lewis (1972) discovered that mothers touch and vocalize more with their daughters, or that the timing of maternal response is more closely associated with the daughter's need state than with the son's (Moss, 1967). Thus, for the daughter, people may come to be associated more closely with the direct satisfaction of need state.

The most recent work on affiliation has centered on the theory and research of Murray (1938) as expanded by his followers, and Schachter (1959). Their approaches and empirical findings will be reviewed, with special consideration to their implications for a more useful theory about the personality development of women.

Review of Research on Affiliation

Murray and others. According to Murray (1938), the class of needs of which affiliation is a subtheme is one having to do with affection between people—seeking it, exchanging it, giving it, and withholding it. Behaviorally, n-Aff (need affiliation) refers to a need to form friendships and associations with others; to greet, join, and live with others; to cooperate and converse sociably with others; and to love. Three other related needs are n-Rejection, n-Nurturance, and n-Succorance. It would not be surprising if there were important gender-related differences on nurturance and succorance, nor would it be surprising if all three concepts were confounded in many affiliation measurement techniques.

The desires and effects of the affiliation need are said to be

... to draw near and enjoyably cooperate or reciprocate with an allied O; A O who resembles the S or who likes the S. To please and win affection of a cathected O. To adhere and remain loyal to a friend. (Murray, 1938, p. 174.)

Affiliation is considered to have the attendant feelings and emotions of trust, goodwill, affection and love, and empathy. Murray suggested that the chief measurement criteria are (a) friendly feeling; (b) desire to associate, play, and converse; (c) efforts to resolve differences, cooperate, and maintain harmony; (d) readiness to trust and confide; and (e) the number, intensity, and duration of friendships.

Psychologists at the University of Michigan (Shipley & Veroff, 1952; Atkinson, Heyns, & Veroff, 1954; Hayns, Veroff, & Atkinson, 1958) extended Murray's and Lewin's (1938) work by arousing and measuring affiliation needs in the same manner as they had with the achievement motive. They used sociometric rating procedures, ostensibly to arouse concern over affiliation and possible rejection. The procedure seems likely to increase feelings about being seen negatively by others. Since the scoring system stresses concern over establishing, maintaining, or restoring positive relationships with others and feelings of warm companionship, one might suggest that only those who have a strong need to affiliate with others would be likely to become aroused in a possible rejection situation. On the other hand, one might also suggest that they are only one part of the population of those with strong affiliation needs (e.g., the ones who want to affiliate but are not having their affiliative needs met). Conceivably, some people could have affiliative needs that are presently satisfied. These individuals might not be so easily aroused, but when aroused, they may respond with different classes of imagery, or at least with differences in frequency of imagery categories. With this in mind, it is interesting to note that Shipley and Veroff (1952) found that males rejected by a fraternity scored significantly higher in affiliation imagery than did those who had been accepted by a fraternity. In contrast, Mehrabian (1972) developed scales of affiliative tendency and sensitivity to rejection, and found them to be basically unrelated.

It is important to note the following points concerning the affiliation research utilizing a TAT measurement approach as it has thus far been pursued.

1. The scoring procedure was based on the assumption that a threat to affiliation, as in deprivation of affiliation, leads to the same affiliative motivation, for the same reasons, in the same people, as other possible sources of affiliation (i.e., nondeprivational). This particular assumption thus precludes the assessment and understanding of different aspects of affiliation.

2. The scoring procedures were operationalized on male subjects only.

3. The psychometric properties of TAT-based n-Aff are poor; studies have reported very low and, in one case, nonsignificant internal reliabilities (Terhune, 1969).

4. There have been very few studies conducted, and even fewer studies that utilized female subjects. When females are used as subjects, they normally are used without males in the same experiment, thus excluding the possibility of male/female comparisons.

The inferred relationship between n-Aff and other motives is frequently ambiguous. Low n-Aff (as measured by the TAT) was found to be associated with nontraditional (i.e., science) career choices in female college students, while high n-Aff was positively associated with choice of traditional female careers such as elementary education (Sundheim, 1963). Skolnick (1966b) measured n-Aff, n-Ach, and n-Agg (need Aggression) at a 20-year interval and found n-Ach and n-Aff to be positively correlated for both sexes at ages 17 and 37. And finally, Horner (1968) found no relationship between n-Aff and fear-of-success imagery.

One study, which used imagery as well as behavioral indices of affiliation and achievement motivation, was conducted by French (1956) with airmen in groups of four. She varied level of achievement and affiliation motives, plus situational press to determine the individual's choice of a work partner. Experimental subjects in the four-person groups were subjected to manipulations such that three members of the group were made to like each other and dislike the fourth member. It was the fourth member (and not the other three) who was able to solve a concept-formation task. When each of the group was asked which of the other three members tey would like to work with on an additional concept-formation task, those individuals higher in n-Ach than n-Aff chose the successful person significantly more often, while those higher in n-Aff chose a partner who was liked but who was unsuccessful. Again, this study used only male subjects, but the implication is often drawn that women, who are presumed to be higher in *n*-Aff, might sacrifice or subjugate achievement considerations to affiliative concerns. This view implies that women perceive affiliation and achievement satisfaction as contradictory, mutually exclusive activities, regardless of the situation.

The study by French (1956) with male subjects also indicates that level of motivation and type of feedback interact to affect performance. Subjects higher in *n*-Aff than in *n*-Ach performed best at an anagram task when given task feedback stressing affiliation. Those individuals who were higher in *n*-Ach than in *n*-Aff performed best when they were given task-relevant feedback. Clarke (1972) found that twelfth-grade students who were high in both achievement and affiliation motives persisted least, and exhibited the lowest probability of success, at an insoluble figure-tracing task. Such findings suggest a Yerkes-Dodson (1908) interpretation of an optimal level of arousal (in this case, motivation) for any task.

In one of the few studies to examine all three motives simultaneously, McClelland and Watson (1973) investigated the interaction of level of need for achievement, affiliation, and power on risk-taking behavior. They used male and female individuals and found no gender-group differences. The authors suggested that those who are higher in *n*-Pow try to put themselves in the spotlight of attention by taking more extreme risks, while those higher in *n*-Ach take moderate risks, and those higher in *n*-Aff take low risks. The risk-taking behavior examined was gambling. Other areas of risk-taking, such as interpersonal relations, might yield different findings.

In one of the few studies to utilize women as subjects in TAT affiliation research, Exline (1962) found that high *n*-Aff women communicated more personal information and less decision-oriented information to each other in an all-female group working on a task that necessitated cooperation, than did the men in all-male groups.

Schachter's anxiety-reduction model.   The work by Schachter is a major, and currently active, social psychological approach to affiliation. Schachter's (1959) review of anecdotal and clinical evidence suggested to him that people affiliate to reduce fear and anxiety, if for no other motive, because when they are deprived of the opportunity to affiliate, they become anxious and fearful. Schachter's experimental paradigm consisted of having subjects participate in an experiment involving electric shocks, with two or more levels of fear varied by exposure to equipment and the experimenter's comments. The dependent variable was determined by asking subjects to indicate whether they would rather wait alone or with other people while the experiment was being readied. The intensity of this affiliation preference was also assessed. The experiment was thus operationalizing affiliation as a stated verbal preference to wait with strangers before participating in an experiment involving electric shock.

The initial experiments used only females as subjects, and revealed that affiliation was greater under the high-fear condition. The two most common explanations for this finding are that affiliation reduces fear, or that it provides an opportunity for social comparison in a situation of uncertainty about what the individuals are feeling or should be feeling.

For instance, Festinger's (1954) theory of social comparison suggested that the need to evaluate oneself, and thus use information from others, might be greater when one's feelings and emotions are aroused because it is very difficult to find objective criteria to evaluate these states. If the preference to affiliate in the experimental condition was for the purpose of determining what the subject's emotions were, or to determine whether they were appropriate to the situation, then there should be a preference to affiliate with those who are familiar with the situation. Several other experiments supported such an interpretation (Schachter, 1959; Zimbardo & Formica, 1963). Greater uncertainty about what is being experienced also increases the tendency to affiliate (Gerard & Rabbie, 1961; Gerard, 1963). Gerard and Rabbie (1961) varied feedback information about the level of emotionality of the experimental subjects in a paradigm similar to that of Schachter's. Some of the subjects were informed of how emotional they and the other subjects were; some of the subjects were informed only about their emotional level; and some subjects were given no feedback. The amount of affiliation increased in a direct linear relation within the three conditions mentioned. A similar experiment by Mills and Mintz (1972), which varied the nature of the feedback, supported the notion that people affiliate to reduce uncertainty about their feelings. In this experiment, those subjects who were aroused physiologically, but who had knowledge of the cause of the arousal, had the least preference to affiliate with other subjects.

There are some situations wherein people can be a source of discomfort as well as information. Sarnoff and Zimbardo (1961) felt that a distinction should be made between fear and anxiety from a psychoanalytic point of view. In an experiment using all-male college students as subjects, Sarnoff and Zimbardo (1961) used two levels of what they termed "fear" and two levels of "anxiety." Differential fear was aroused by the expectation of high or low levels of electric shock (i.e., what Schachter called "anxiety"). High anxiety was aroused by the anticipation of sucking on oral feeding and sex-related objects; low anxiety was aroused by the anticipation of sucking on more neutral objects. Sarnoff and Zimbardo found that increases in affiliation were directly related to arousal of fear, but that increases in anxiety decreased affiliation behavior. The authors concluded that the decreased affiliation is due to the subject's anticipation that revealing anxiety might be embarrassing. A recent study by Lynch, Watts, Galloway, and Tryphenopulous (1973) suggests that if the anxiety is seen as appropriate for the situation, affiliation increases in men. A study by Firestone, Kaplan, and Russell (1973) supports both Schachter's (1959) finding of greater affiliation of fearful subjects and Sarnoff and Zimbardo's (1961) finding of greater affiliation among fearful than among anxious subjects.

Becker (1967) tested the preference for waiting alone versus waiting with others, with four possible "waiting with other" conditions. The experiment tested 821 undergraduates and found a general tendency to wait with others, but only under certain conditions. Individuals preferred to wait with other(s) when the options were (a) either waiting alone or with others about to undergo the same experiment, or (b) if the other was a physiologist with feedback information about what was happening. There was no preference to wait with others when the choices were (a) waiting with students who had completed the experiment, or (b) waiting with students with no knowledge of the experiment. Becker found a significant tendency for female subjects to affiliate more than males, but only in the first two conditions, where there did exist a stated preference to wait with others rather than alone.

Gerard and Rabbie (1961) modified the Schachter procedure by varying the fear manipulation and extent of feedback about emotionality in self and others, in both male and female subjects. Their results indicated that men choose to remain alone more than women, and that men who wait alone have a higher emotionality index than all those who have chosen to wait with others. This suggests, at least for males, that actual affiliation behavior is not a function of degree of arousal. However, for women, skin-conductance increase was positively associated with a desire to be together. Although implying that women chose to affiliate more, the data suggest that this is true only when comparing first-born and only-child females with first-born and only-child males. There was no gender-related difference in affiliative preference for later-born individuals.

The studies discussed above relate several important areas of research: the distinction between fear and anxiety, the notion that men might not feel it is appropriate to reveal their emotional arousal, and that men are uncomfortable with their state and resolve their problem by staying away from people.

In addition to finding that fear is associated with increases in affiliation, the original Schachter (1959) research with women found that this relationship was particularly strong for first-born subjects. It took a few additional experiments to realize that this birth-order effect was significant only for females.

A study of great ecological validity (but using a small sample, and unsophisticated but understandable sampling technique) is that of Zucker, Manosevitz, and Lanyon (1968) in New York City on the night of the power failure in 1965. They questioned individuals at midnight at a bus terminal and at a hotel about preference to be alone or with others, level of anxiety, and actual affiliation (simple presence/absence). There were significant differences between men and women on preference for affiliation and actual affiliation behaviors, with women higher on both. The two indices were positively correlated for women, but were not correlated for men. First-born women were more likely to be together, but this birth-order effect did not hold true for men. The authors concluded

> It appears that only among women, whose culturally determined sex-role expectations are congruent with the birth-order-affiliation relationship expected from the "early-experience" theory, will the appropriate relationship be manifested. (p. 358.)

In summarizing, this research approach does not conclusively demonstrate that females affiliate more than males, although birth-order effects hold more for the former than the latter. There is also fairly good evidence that the motive-behavior relationship is more clear-cut for females than for males, probably because of sex-typed expectations.

Gender differences.　One cultural belief is that women (and girls), as a class, are more concerned about affiliation than are men and boys. Sex-role stereotype research has documented that this is a prevalent belief in both sexes (Broverman, Vogel, & Broverman, 1972). Hoffman (1972) stated that affiliative needs are stronger in women and conflict with the development and expression of an achievement motive. Bardwick (1971), and Stein and Bailey (1973) made affiliation and sex-role nurturance requirements central factors when discussing how women integrate, channelize, and segment their achievement concerns over their life cycle. Mehrabian (1972) even took this assumption from Anastasi (1958) and used it as indirect proof of the validity of a theoretical postulate. The obvious question arises as to whether this cultural belief about gender differences in affiliation is, in fact, true.

Mehrabian's (1972) work on nonverbal behavior in social interaction does seem to suggest that females evidence relatively greater amounts of *certain* aspects of behavior, which he interpreted as reflecting affiliation. However, on a paper-and-pencil measure of affiliative tendency, a determinant of affiliation behavior, no gender group differences were found.

In Oetzel's (1966) annotated bibliography and classified summary of research on sex differences, only 2 of 14 studies reviewed for sex differences in need for affiliation found that boys or men were higher in affiliation need. In 22 studies concerning interest in and positive feelings for others, 21 studies indicated that girls or women were significantly higher. One study found no difference. The dependent variables differed enormously, from projective techniques and affiliative scales to ratings of sociability by others, to related but more indirect verbal and nonverbal measures such as amount of eye contact, concern with interpersonal relations, and remembrance of names and faces of persons in a memory task.

Developmental studies conducted since 1966 suggest that girls and women stand closer together and face each other more directly when interacting, and that they are more likely to self-report liking for others. On the other hand, girls have a smaller number of friends with whom they enjoy social activities, and there is evidence to suggest that boys may engage in more positive social interaction with their age-mates and that they may be more susceptible to peer influences. The empirical evidence on sensitivity to social cues, or empathy, does not suggest gender differences in this ability or orientation (Maccoby & Jacklin, 1974).

Thus, developmental studies suggest that girls and women may be more directly concerned with social relationships, although this conclusion is certainly not clearly demonstrated by the experimental work of Schachter, or by the researchers using a TAT-based approach.

It is clear, however, that there are shortcomings in the existing approaches to the study of affiliation, and that there is lack of theory and research in many important areas. For example:

1. Studies have used one-gender groups too frequently; in many cases unwarranted conclusions have been drawn about gender-associated differences.

2. Theory and measurement have too often been derived from the exclusive use of male subjects.

3. Affiliation research has used strangers rather than people who know each other.

4. Too little attention has been paid to the function(s) of affiliative behavior.

5. There is little consideration of antecedents and development.

6. There has been no consideration of the possibility that affiliation may be a medium for the satisfaction of other goals.

7. The same term, "affiliation," is used to describe both a motive and a specific set of behaviors for which the motivation has yet to be determined.

8. Different measures of the motive may or may not be comparable. The various dependent measures of affiliation used in these studies add further confusion.

Women are socialized to be dependent on others. They might therefore be more susceptible to the type of dynamic postulated in Festinger's social comparison theory; that is, to rely on others in constructing the meaning of one's experience. Yet, the scarcity of comparable data, the problems of defining motivational constructs such as nurturance versus affiliation, clearly indicates the need for further extensive research in the area of affiliation in women.

ACHIEVEMENT

Achievement is defined in terms of excellence, and achievement motivation is generally assumed to mean a concern for attaining excellence, whatever the behavioral domain.

A great deal has been written in recent years about achievement motivation and behavior, or the lack thereof, in women. The most frequently raised questions have centered around the issues of whether or not women are motivated to achieve to the same extent as men, and whether they are motivated to achieve in the same areas and/or for the same reasons. Within the past few years, the issue of fear of success has entered the literature as an additional factor.

Depending upon the type and breadth of sample that an investigator draws from the literature to review, it is quite possible to come to any one of a number of different interpretations. These interpretations are listed below, and the reader, in comparing them, can see the contradictions in some of them.

1. *Women are not motivated to achieve to the same degree as men.* Possible reasons for this view is that women have too much fear of failure and/or fear of success; that they have had insufficient or inappropriate socialization experiences during childhood and adolescence; and that achievement has not been incorporated into women's sex-role-related self-concept and is therefore not necessary for their self-esteem.

2. *Women are motivated to achieve to a greater degree than men.* They are oversocialized and they respond at a ceiling level to neutral TAT-assessment procedure (i.e., without arousal).

3. *Women are motivated to achieve for different reasons than men.* Women achieve to attain social approval, and men achieve in order to attain power, status, and recognition.

4. *Men and women are motivated to achieve to the same degree—They merely express it in different, "sex appropriate" domains of behavior.*

5. *The TAT measure of n-Ach is valid for men, but invalid for women.* One might come to this conclusion if it is thought that women suppress achievement imagery due to conflict with fear of failure and/or fear of success; or if it is said that achievement instructions stressing intelligence and leadership are not effective in arousing their motives, or arouse conflicting motives.

6. *The n-Ach measure is invalid for both men and women.* It measures stereotypic beliefs, not motivations. The TAT measures achievement imagery only in a state of relative deprivation, or a threat of deprivation. The TAT procedure is invalid because it taps too many other concerns to be a strong predictor of anything.

The most important theoretical and methodological issues will be examined to determine whether new insights can be drawn from this truly complex area of research. Thorough reviews exist elsewhere (Weiner, 1972; Atkinson, 1969; Maccoby & Jacklin, 1974; O'Leary, 1974), and therefore only the most relevant questions are discussed here. A historical framework will be utilized for ease of presentation.

Theory

Although there have been other interpretations of achievement motivation and behavior (Veroff, 1969; V.J. Crandall, 1963; Weiner, 1972; V.C. Crandall, 1969), the work of Atkinson and McClelland (Atkinson, 1964, 1969; Atkinson & Feather, 1966; McClelland et al., 1953) has had the dominant impact in terms of both theory construction and empirical investigation. The Atkinson/McClelland position has evolved gradually over the past 25 years. Early in the investigations, studies began to appear which seemed to indicate that the emerging theory was being confirmed, but for male subjects only. Thereafter, the investigators appeared to decide, with a few notable exceptions, that male subjects would be a more profitable subject universe for sampling purposes. This aspect of the history of achievement motivation research has been known for quite some time. However, the implications of this neglect, in terms of adequacy and completeness of theory, have not been questioned seriously until recently.

The motive to achieve is said to be learned in early childhood as a function of the learning history of the individual in achievement situations, the type and timing of parental training for independence and achievement, and parental and societal imposition of standards of excellence and evaluative criteria. Variables that contribute to whether the motive to achieve will be aroused in a particular situation are belief in personal responsibility for the outcome of the activity, knowledge of results, and the subjective evaluation of the degree of risk involved.

Once aroused, the motive to achieve will result in an active tendency to undertake achievement-oriented activities only if the motive to approach success is greater than the tendency to avoid failure. The motive to avoid failure is also aroused by these achievement situations, and is also learned in early childhood as a function of the individual's history of failure experiences relative to success experiences. Resultant achievement motivation, as distinct from the achievement motive, reflects the joint presence of the tendencies to approach *and* avoid potential success/failure situations.

Assessment of Aroused Motive

Murray's (1938) projective Thematic Apperception Test (or TAT) was modified for use as the assessment technique under the assumption that motives are easily expressed and best measured through fantasy, and that the TAT measure predominantly reflects an individual's fantasy material. A scoring system was derived by McClelland et al. (1953) from the work of Murray (1938) and Lewin (1938). Hours of deprivation of food in male subjects was varied (1, 4, or 16 hours) prior to the administration of the TAT by Atkinson and McClelland

(1948). Within a deficiency-drive model of motivation, it was thought that differential concerns about food, as a function of hours of deprivation, should be reflected in the TAT protocols. These first results did not unequivocally support a need-fantasy relationship, since the scoring category of "food imagery" was not related to amount of deprivation in any systematic fashion. However, deprivation imagery and instrumental activity directed toward removing the source of the deprivation tended to increase with hours of deprivation. Despite these findings, the researchers felt secure enough to move on to achievement needs. The researchers administered the TAT to male subjects who had been experimentally "aroused" by instructions stressing intelligence, organizational ability, and leadership. Comparing the frequency and type of imagery elicited in stories in both neutral and arousal conditions, it was found that most categories evidenced significant increases in imagery under the arousal manipulation. The conclusion was reached that the arousal manipulation had been successful, and that the TAT was sensitive to motivation-determined changes in fantasy imagery.

It should be noted that there were problems, right from the outset, with the application of this approach to women. When female subjects were finally added to this arousal paradigm, most studies were not able to increase the level of achievement imagery (or n-Ach) in these women subjects (Field, 1951; Veroff, 1950, cited in McClelland et al., 1953; Wilcox, 1951; Veroff, Wilcox, & Atkinson, 1953; Lesser, Krawitz, & Packard, 1963). However, McClelland et al. (1953) reported a Brazilian study by Angelini which did get an insignificant increase in college women, and Heckhausen (1967) alluded to German and Japanese studies that were also able to obtain an increase in n-Ach imagery. In addition, Lipinski (1966) was able to obtain an increase in achievement imagery in female college students from neutral to achievement-oriented instructions, although the significance level was not reported. Despite a few scattered studies that evidenced an increase in n-Ach imagery under arousal conditions, the possible reasons for these contradictory findings were not pursued to any great extent by the primary theoreticians.

The early achievement instructions stressed not only intelligence, but also leadership of a particular type by mentioning the TAT's use in predicting military leadership. References to the military, and then to leadership, were gradually dropped. Yet, increases in arousal between neutral and achievement conditions were still not found consistently for female respondents. To our knowledge, testing for an increase in arousal in women ceased about 1966.

Paper-and-pencil measures of need for achievement were developed by Mehrabian (1969), and by Edwards (1959) in the Edwards Personal Preference Scales. These scales appear to be tapping entirely different concerns and have not been utilized extensively in this body of research. However, the French Test of Insight (French, 1958) does relate significantly to TAT imagery, and the test has been used by some researchers. It should be noted, however, that less validation information is available on the French test than on the McClelland measure.

TAT stimuli cues.   Females' achievement imagery from neutral instructions are as high or higher than the males' *n*-Ach scores under either neutral or achievement instructions (Field, 1951; Veroff, 1950, cited in McClelland et al., 1953; Wilcox, 1951; Veroff, Wilcox, & Atkinson, 1953). These results led some researchers to suggest that the achievement-related cues were extremely high for women because of (a) where the experiments took place, and/or (b) greater achievement cues for females than for males when in a competitive situation with the other sex.

Wilcox (1951) tried to reduce the achievement cues in the neutral condition by testing small groups of college women in their own dormitory rooms. The achievement-oriented condition was tested in a classroom with both sexes present. There was no increase in *n*-Ach imagery between conditions. However, having males present only in the achievement-oriented condition could certainly arouse other nonachievement cues. Field (1951, cited in McClelland et al., 1953) gave TAT pictures to both male and female college students under relaxed or failure conditions. The male subjects showed a significant increase in achievement imagery from the relaxed to the failure condition, while the females showed no change. It would have been interesting if a success condition had been included in the experimental paradigm. Veroff et al. (1953) conducted an experiment similar to that of Wilcox (1951) and found almost identical results: no increase in achievement imagery for the females, but a significant main effect for sex of picture cue.

Sex of picture cue has been an important factor in results of all studies, both for men and women. In fact, an alternative explanation for females' failure to increase imagery under achievement conditions is that the achievement cue value for female picture stimuli was too low to engage the subjects' motivation effectively. However, attempts to increase the cue value by changing the picture stimuli have not been successful in raising achievement imagery under achievement-oriented instructions (Wilcox, 1951; Veroff et al., 1953).

Veroff et al. (1953) suggested that both sexes project their achievement motivation to the male pictures because of their stronger achievement-eliciting properties. They found, as have others, that females have higher achievement scores when responding to male pictures (Cowan & Goldberg, 1967; Lipinski, 1966; Lesser et al., 1963; Veroff, 1950; Wellens, 1973; Wilcox, 1951). It has been assumed that individuals will project more of their own motivation to those situations that previously have been associated with achievement cues for them. It is certainly true that males have been associated with achievement to a greater extent than have females, and thus male figures would serve as more potent achievement cues for both women and men.

It has also been assumed that similarity to the TAT figures would facilitate the identification process, although Veroff et al. (1966) argued that too great a similarity between stimulus and subject arouses defensive responses. Support for the "similarity facilitates identification hypothesis" can be drawn from an experiment by Jacobs (1971), which tested white-collar men, blue-collar men, women working outside the house, and housewives. The subjects were allowed to choose four TATs from a sample of 10 TATs, to which they were to respond with a story. The pictures chosen were those that they later reported as being relevant to them. Interestingly, women had significantly higher achievement motivation scores than did the men. Unfortunately, it is not known whether these gender-related differences were due to differences in situations depicted on the selected pictures, or in sex of figures on the TAT pictures, or even perhaps in level of (achievement) deprivation. Along the same lines, Baruch (1967) found a relationship between achievement imagery and paid employment in women, but only to the female picture TAT stimuli. Similarly, Bloom (1972) found a relation between achievement imagery and religion in adolescent females, but only in terms of the female stimuli responses.

At this point it is difficult to state unequivocally whether the relationship between n-Ach imagery and achievement-related dependent variables is stronger for ·TATs using female cues or male cues. It may depend on the nature of the dependent variable, particularly as it interacts with other moderating variables such as sex-role orientation. The issue of whether the TAT assessment procedure taps social-role expectations or individual motivation is unresolved, as the discussion below further illustrates.

Validity issues regarding the TAT. The sex of picture-cue effect and the difficulties in obtaining an increase in arousal from neutral to achievement-oriented instructions have led some to hypothesize that the TAT may be an invalid technique for assessing achievement motivation in women. Wilcox (1951) and de Charms, Morrison, Reitman, and McClelland (1955) discussed this possibility but concluded that it is a valid measure, since it does predict differential performance level on an anagrams task and on a scrambled-word task, as it does with men. However, in contradistinction to the findings of Baruch (1967) and Bloom (1972) discussed above, the relationship between n-Ach scores and performance in women occurred only when the pictures were of men or of women in nonachievement situations. There was no significant motive-performance relation when the motive was inferred from the imagery generated in response to the TAT depicting women in career situations. These results are confusing. Pictures of women in career situations have the strongest achievement-cue values of the female TATs used, and should, theoretically, be the most effective in arousing females' latent motives. These scores then should lead to the strongest relationship with actual achievement behavior.

One might suggest that in the early 1950s when these experiments were run, women in career situations were perceived as women who had been unsuccessful in romance and were working by default, not because they were motivated to do so. This would lower the achievement-cue strength somewhat. Another possible interpretation is that the achievement-cue strength was too high in these pictures and aroused avoidance behavior because career concerns were not considered to be feminine behavior at that time. Such an analysis lends support to the more recent "fear of success" formulation of Horner (1968). In either case, one could say that the subjects were writing stories based on stereotypic beliefs as cued by the stimuli which may or may not lead to avoidance behavior, depending upon other moderating variables. If the stories did not reflect individual motivation, or if they reflected multiple, contradictory aspects of motivation, only a slight relationship or even no relationship with achievement behavior could be obtained. This interpretation lends support to the argument that the TAT is an invalid assessment procedure for achievement motivation in women.

Further support for such a position can be drawn from Scott (1956), who demonstrated that threatening material can lead to avoidance of imagery. Avoiders (defined as people who avoid themes for the highest cued picture) were less likely to give cue-related themes, told shorter stories, were less likely to indicate problem-oriented activity or acceptance of the competitive situation, and were more likely to give up after failure. Another study by Clark (1952) found that males who had been shown pictures of nude females gave less sexual imagery than under neutral conditions using nonsexual TATs. If one were to assume that females have higher motives to avoid success and to avoid failure than do males, it would not be surprising to find that they do not show an increase in achievement imagery under achievement-oriented instructions.

Veroff, Feld, and Crockett (1966) suggested that dissimilarity between occupational setting of TAT pictures and the subject's own background yielded achievement motivation scores with greater predictive validity to the dependent variable. The authors suggested that dissimilar pictures would lead to more valid scores when conflict over the expression of a motive is involved, or when conditions of strong cultural determination of appropriate expression of motivation are present. If this reasoning is followed to its logical conclusion, the implication is that women's TAT stories to male picture cues (strong cultural determinism) and to female-career picture cues (conflict over expression) would be less valid than some other assessment procedure.

McClelland et al. (1953) concluded that women's achievement motivation is related to social acceptability and men's to leadership and intelligence on the basis of the Field (1951, cited in McClelland et al., 1953) study. This study, in addition to standard achievement-oriented instructions stressing leadership and intelligence, had three other conditions; relaxed, success, and failure. For these conditions, the experimental manipulation provided information that the subjects were either thought to be socially acceptable (success) or unacceptable (failure) by a committee of their popular peers. For the females, variations in reported social acceptability increased achievement imagery over those in the neutral condition. This manipulation had no effect on the males' achievement imagery. It would have been interesting to see what differences (sex and condition) would have appeared had need for affiliation been scored as well.

The Field (1951) results and other studies have contributed to conclusions that females' achievement behaviors stem from different motivational dynamics. Females are said to engage in achievement activities because of motivations for social acceptability, approval of others (Veroff, 1969; V.J. Crandall, 1963; V.C. Crandall, 1969), and affiliation needs (Bardwick, 1971; Hoffman, 1972). The empirical evidence for these positions is scanty, and most studies used children as subjects (Veroff, 1969; Hoffman, 1972; V.J. Crandall, 1963; Lansky, Crandall, Kagan, & Baker, 1961). Males are said to be motivated to achieve only, or predominantly, because of their internalized standards of excellence. Although Moss & Kagan (1961) pointed to the close association between achievement motivation and recognition-seeking or status considerations, it has not been suggested that males' achievement behaviors might be partly or solely determined by these other needs.

However, despite the suggestion that females' achievement behavior is determined by motives other than achievement motivation, significant relationships have been found between level of achievement imagery and achievement-related behavior in women. Thus, Moss and Kagan (1961), in a longitudinal study, found a significant positive correlation between adolescent achievement themes and adult achievement behavior in women. Skolnick (1966a) also conducted a longitudinal study with assessment at two ages: 17 and 37. TAT-assessed n-Ach was correlated with behavior, self-ratings, and ratings by others at both time periods. Female adolescent n-Ach was positively correlated with years of education, IQ, strictness of superego, and the CPI subscales achievement via conformity and intellectual efficiency. In adults, female n-ach was associated with grade-point average, years of education, IQ, IQ change, self and husband's social class, social mobility, adolescent achievement-drive rating, strictness of superego, adult interview rating of recognition motivation, and the CPI subscales—capacity for status, achievement via independency, and intellectual efficiency. For the adolescent males, there were no significant correlations between TAT imagery and the behavioral measures.

Sundheim (1963) studied women college students and found that level of n-Ach was unrelated to grades, but that it was related to curriculum major, with high n-Ach women picking more masculine sex-typed fields. Ten years later, Tangri (1972) investigated factors that contribute to or inhibit the choice of non-sex-typical occupational career patterns and found that n-Ach was not related to role innovation in college women. Trigg and Perlman (1975, Note 5) found a significant difference in level of need achievement as measured by the need-for-achievement subscale of the Edwards Personal Preference Scale between women entering traditional versus non-traditional careers. The contradictory findings mentioned above might be explained by the use of vastly different assessment procedures in the investigations.

However, two new measures were developed in the Tangri study (1974), which together predicted role innovation and also related differentially to extrinsic and intrinsic motivational variables. These measures, "Implied Demand Character of the Wife's Future" and "Demand Character of the Future Husband," were derived from projective descriptions of the kind of man the subject would want to marry. This stimulus does not contain cues likely to arouse "fear of success" and provides for unmarried women a suitable ambiguous field on which to project needs and expectations for one's future.

Moderator Variables

Academic values.   The early finding by Angelini (cited in McClelland et al., 1953) that a sample of Brazilian female college students did increase their achievement imagery from neutral to achievement arousal has led some to suggest a sampling hypothesis in that the academically elite nature of Brazilian colleges would mean an "atypical" sample of female college students. Lesser, Krawitz, and Packard (1963) attempted to test this hypothesis by using as subjects a sample of high-school students selected for their academic competence and interests, split into matched groups (by IQ) of achievers and underachievers. The two groups were exposed to neutral and achievement-oriented instructions to both male and female picture cues. No increase in *n*-Ach scores was found for either the achievers or the underachievers. However, achievers increased in achievement imagery in the achievement-oriented condition to female cues but not to male cues, whereas underachievers increased in achievement imagery to the male cues but not to the female cues. A social role model is offered to interpret the findings, but such a model does not explain why achievers do not produce greater achievement imagery to the male cue as well, as achievement is certainly a part of the male social role. Heckhausen (1967) also seemed to prefer a sex-role-based explanation to interpret contradictory cross-cultural studies with women subjects. He stated that non-United States women comprise a select sample whose achievement-related self-concept is closer to that of men.

French and Lesser (1964) investigated a related idea in their study of how values and situational characteristics interact to affect the level of achievement motivation, and how values, situational characteristics, and expressed motivation interact to affect performance. The *n*-Ach scores were higher when the arousal condition matched the subjects' value orientation (intellectual or women's role). However, one's value orientation was not a factor in differentiating when the sex-of-picture stimuli would promote higher *n*-Ach scores. Higher *n*-Ach scores were obtained to the male cue under intellectual arousal and to the female cue under women's role arousal, regardless of individual value orientations. In general, a stronger motivation-performance relation resulted when the arousal cues were related to a valued goal. Presumably, self-concept factors could act to moderate both probability of success and incentive value of success.

Sex-role orientations.   Sex-role considerations have played a major part in deliberations as to the nature and extent of achievement motivation in women.

Stein and Bailey (1973) thought that the traditional definition and arousal procedures for achievement motivation are sex-biased toward white male subjects, and that contrary to theories such as Veroff's and Crandall's, which state that women achieve in the service of other motives, the evidence indicates that women are not invited to achieve in areas appropriate to their female sex-role definition. According to Stein and Bailey, the traditional feminine sex-role is concerned with social skills, and thus it is in this area that the achievement motivation of most females will be revealed. Whether one will show achievement strivings in response to intellectual-competitive cues or social skill cues will be a function, in part, of what activities and goals women have incorporated into their individual concepts of femininity.

Alper (1973, 1974) used a Women's Role Orientation Scale (WROS), which assesses the extent to which an individual ascribes to sex-differentiated personality attributes and behavior patterns on a paper-and-pencil questionnaire. Low sex-typed subjects did not have higher n-Ach scores (McClelland et al. (1953), creative imagination instructions) than the more polarized subjects. Highly traditional subjects had higher n-Ach scores to the male pictures than did the low traditional subjects, and also higher n-Ach scores to the male pictures than to the female pictures. However, the female picture cue did elicit different subthemes as a function of WROS. Low WROS scorers (less sex-typed) do tell more unambivalently successful stories, and high scorers (more sex-typed) tell more stories where success is instrumental to the gratification of love-oriented needs (Alper, 1973).

Other moderating variables that have received insufficient attention are level of ability, social class, racial and ethnic background, and the effects of important cohorts.

Motivation Conflict

With affiliation.   Both Bardwick (1971) and Hoffman (1972) stressed the role of affiliation in their interpretations of the achievement literature. Bardwick (1971) suggested that achievement motivation and affiliation motivation are fused, at least through adolescence, as a function of the internalization of culturally based sex-role prescriptions and sex-typed socialization experiences. Hoffman (1972), in addition to suggesting that achievement needs and affiliative needs conflict in adult females, suggested that females' achievement needs are not as strong as males' because of early childhood sex-typed training and realities. Specifically, Hoffman stressed females' alleged greater dependence, lower self-confidence, and greater problem in attaining some amount of emotional distance from the mother.

Skolnick (1966b) assessed TAT stories for achievement, affiliation, aggression, and power at adolescence and adulthood as part of a 20-year longitudinal study. For both sexes, at both periods of time, achievement and affiliation imagery were positively correlated. In males, at both time periods, aggression and achievement are inversely correlated with one another. In adolescent girls, power and achievement are inversely related, while aggression and affiliation are significantly correlated.

There were no significant differences between adult men and women on group means for any of the four kinds of imagery, nor were there gender-related differences in variability. However, the lack of independence in measuring these motives makes it impossible to draw unambiguous conclusions. The evidence for the hypothesis that achievement motivation conflicts with an affiliation motive has not been tested directly, although Horner's (1968) work on "fear of success" is conceptually similar to this point. Skolnick's (1966) study suggests that n-Ach and n-Aff are positively related, but Veroff and Feld (1970) suggested that one's life requirements and satisfactions may play an important role in determining the relationships among motives. In Veroff and Feld's national cross-sectional study, which is discussed in greater detail in the next section on power, mothers of preschool children had negative relationships between n-Ach and n-Aff. Such differences in relationship of motives within individuals, as a function of age and important life circumstances, suggests the possibility that motivational conflict, if and when it exists, may be a transient phenomenon.

With motive to avoid success.   The concept of motive to avoid success (Horner, 1968; Horner, 1972; Horner & Walsh, 1973, Note 3) has generated a tremendous amount of interest and research in the past ten years. Fear of success is considered to be a motive within Atkinson's expectancy-value theory of motivation, and it was postulated by Horner in an attempt to explain some of the confusing results when female subjects respond to TAT stimuli in achievement situations. It is thought to be a stable personality trait, developed in early childhood and adolescence when a young girl is taught or anticipates that negative consequences will follow her success in achievement situations because of the masculine sex-typed nature of achievement, and because the personality qualities and behavior necessary for such achievement are defined as unfeminine.

In her original research, Horner (1968) found that 65% of the female college students responded with fear of success imagery to the verbal lead "After first term finals, Anne finds herself at the top of her medical school class," compared with 10% incidence for male college students to a male cue in the same stimulus situation. Since 1968, further research has sought to replicate and extend the original findings. The results of such studies have proven to be confusing and/or contradictory with regard to (a) the incidence of the motive to avoid success in both men and women, in adults and developmentally; and (b) its personality and behavioral correlates. At present, it is impossible to state with any degree of confidence exactly what is being assessed by such a projective test. Unfortunately, the same can be said for TAT imagery.

Since the report of the original Horner (1968) study, which was actually conducted in 1965, increases in the percentages of female subjects responding with success-avoidance imagery have been found (Horner, 1972; Alper, 1973, 1974), but the majority of researchers have found no increase (Larsen, 1970; Kresojevich, 1972; Hoffman, 1974), or a small decrease in percentage (Parker, 1972; Alper, 1973; Feather & Simon, 1973; Feather, 1974, Note 1). The results with male subjects are more consistent; they all indicate percentages higher than the 10% originally reported by Horner (Morgan & Mausner, 1973; Alper, 1974; Burghardt, 1973, Note 2; Robbins & Robbins, 1973; Horner, 1972; Monahan, Kuhn, & Shaver, 1974; Hoffman, 1974; Feather & Simon, 1973; and Feather, 1974, Note 1).

The types of "fear of success" stories told by the sexes are equally consistent; females tell stories about affiliative loss as a result of success, whereas males' stories reflect questions about the value of success (Horner, 1972; Hoffman, 1974; Horner & Walsh, Note 3), or have tragic or bizarre consequences follow success (Burghardt, 1973, Note 2, 1974).

Investigators have attempted to clarify the nature of the concept by varying the cue characteristics, samples of subjects used, and congruence between cue characteristics and sample interests (Alper, 1973; 1973, Note 3). For instance, Hoffman (1974) compared the sex-typed nature of the cue (masculine vs. neutral) with disclosure of success (public vs. private), but the frequency of motive to avoid success (M-s) imagery remained constant across conditions, and no sex differences appeared.

Since the motive to avoid success is assumed to arise in childhood and adolescence, developmental studies are most important. While a few cross-sectional studies indicate an increase in M-s imagery with increasing age for both sexes (Horner, 1972; Burghardt, 1973; Note 2), one study found no difference in frequency of such imagery between the sexes (Burghardt, 1973, Note 2), and two studies indicate that female high-school students evidence less imagery than do the males (Morgan & Mausner, 1973; Monahan et al., 1974). The implications of these findings for the motive to avoid success concept have not been dealt with adequately.

Because the original Horner (1968) design was incomplete with regard to sex of cue and sex of respondent variations, subsequent researchers have given the male verbal lead to females and the female lead to males. All such studies have found that both males and females respond with more M-s imagery to the female cue, and that males portray more M-s imagery to the female cue than do females to the same cue (Alper, 1974; Feather, 1974, Note 1; Robbins & Robbins, 1973; Monahan et al., 1974). Are men projecting more of their own M-s to the female cue because the female cue is associated with the avoidance of achievement concerns? Are both genders writing stories that reflect the knowledge of cultural stereotypes, and not necessarily their individual motives?

Of crucial concern to the issue of the validity of the concept is the question of whether it has motivational properties and whether it is a stable trait learned early in life. Originally, Horner (1968) reported that high M-s college females performed better on an anagrams task alone than in a mixed-sex competitive situation. Low M-s females evidenced the reverse pattern, as did the men as a group. She also reported that high M-s women are likely to change their college major and career aspirations to a more traditionally female direction as they progress through college (Horner, 1972).

More recently, the evidence about the relationship between M-s imagery and performance measures is contradictory. Burghardt (1973, Note 2) found that high M-s adolescent girls performed better on a scrambled-word task, whereas level of M-s was unrelated to performance in males. However, Feather and Simon (1973) found no relationship between M-s and performance on an anagrams task in a mixed sex competitive group situation, nor did Parker (1972). However, in this study, the sex-typed label of the task and sex of competitor were important. High M-s women performed better on the "feminine" task and low M-s women performed better on the "masculine" task. High M-s women performed better when competing against a woman, while low M-s women performed better against a man. In contrast, Burghardt (1973, Note 2) found that the experimental condition (sex composition, competitive nature, others vs. alone) did not affect performance levels of high M-s adolescent girls.

McGuiness (1974, Note 4) found that level of task difficulty was an important moderator variable in the relationship between M-s and performance under competitive conditions. In a group of high school juniors and seniors, both sexes improved their performance on an easy task in competition, regardless of how high they scored on the M-s measure. Level of M-s was not related to improved performance on a difficult task, however, female high M-s subjects showed better performance in the same-sex competition than alone, but lower performance in the mixed-sex competition.

Low M-s female subjects did better in both competitive conditions than alone. High M-s males did worse in mixed-sex competition, while low M-s males did better in mixed-sex competition. Thus, the use of task difficulty as a moderator variable may clarify many of the apparently contradictory findings regarding impact of M-s on competitive performance. It is signficant to note that the effect is seen only on moderately difficult tasks. This is also the level of difficulty which was early shown to be the most effective in engaging the achievement motive.

Tangri (1972) found no relationship between role innovation and M-s, and Kresojevich (1972) found a significant and positive correlation between M-s and college grade-point average in women.

A more direct test of the relationship between M-s imagery and achievement behavior occurred in a study by Morgan and Mausner (1973). This study investigated the relationship between the verbal M-s cue and the opportunity to avoid success on a cooperative task venture with a male partner by decreasing her known level of ability. No relationship was found. Perhaps a significant relation would have occurred had the male and female subjects used in this study enjoyed a close, romantic relationship. Schwenn (1970) indicated a trend for high M-s women to lower their aspirations to a more traditional career as they progress through college. Those women who shifted their career aspirations downward were dating men who disapproved of role innovation for women, or were not dating. Women who maintained their non-traditional career choices were dating men who were not opposed to such career choices.

Additional evidence comes from a study by Pleck (1976) wherein dating couples either competed against each other on an anagrams task, or worked together as a team against another couple. Women who were high in M-s, and who adhered to a more traditional conception of the female role, performed at a lower level when competing against their boyfriends than when competing with their boyfriends as a team. Women low in M-s, and those with non-traditional comceptions of women's role, performed equally well in both conditions. The same was true for men in general. However, men who appeared to be threatened by achieving women performed on an independent measure at a higher level against their girlfriends than when competing with their girlfriends against another couple. The emotional relationship with an important male, as well as an understanding of her needs and fears, may very well be the crucial moderating variable in how and under what conditions a woman evidences "fear of success" behavior. Puryear & Mednick (1974) found that "Attachment" to a boyfriend moderated the relationship of M-s to militancy in black college women.

There may be no need to fear the negative consequences of success when competing with individuals whose reactions would be relatively unimportant. Mischel's (1968) criticisms of general, stable personality dimensions are certainly relevant here. It is not inconceivable to suggest that individual subjects are writing stories to the M-s and TAT stimuli in terms of stereotypes. The linkages between stereotype and motive, and motive and behavior, remain unclear.

Impact of Others on Achievement Behavior

The impact of important others in helping to determine achievement behavior in adulthood has not been investigated very thoroughly, although Tangri (1972) and Trigg and Perlman (1975, Note 5) recently shed some light on this topic. In Tangri's investigation of factors related to non-sex-typical occupational choice (role innovation) of college senior women, it was suggested that role innovators may have had male friends, female friends, and fathers who played supportive roles with regard to their career choices. Trigg and Perlman (1975, Note 5) presented evidence which suggests that while both traditional and non-traditional women (in terms of career aspirations) perceived that men in general would prefer a traditional career for women, the perception changes when specific individuals are involved. Non-traditional women perceived mother, father, and male friends as favoring a non-traditional career for women. Traditional women saw their parents as having less favorable attitudes toward any career. Boyfriends were seen as supportive of their girlfriends' career choices, whatever they were. However, non-traditional women's boyfriends were seen as being more supportive in general, and more supportive on non-traditional career choices than were boyfriends of more traditional women.

It is interesting to note that the women in the Trigg and Perlman study diverged in their perception of how women in general feel about non-traditional career choices for women. In contrast to what one might expect, non-traditional females did not perceive that their female friends preferred women to enter nontraditional careers. On the other hand, traditional women perceived that their female friends would prefer to have women enter non-traditional fields. Non-traditional women felt that women in general wanted women to enter non-traditional careers, but traditional women did not think that women in general had a clear preference for women's careers, either way.

Needed Research

Developmental studies would seem to be the most crucial arena for further investigation at this time. A recent study by Rothbart (1971) indicated that mothers of five-year-old children are more demanding of daughters, have higher expectations for their daughters, and use more criticism and anxious intrusive behaviors with daughters in experimental achievement situations than with sons. All the behaviors described above point to different reinforcement histories for boys and girls in evaluative situations, and in ways likely to facilitate fear of failure. This issue has been addressed by some investigators (V.C. Crandall, 1969; Epstein, 1973, Note 6; Hochschild, 1973, Note 7; Hermans, ter Laak, & Maes, 1972; Feld & Lewis, 1969; Atkinson, 1969), but a great deal more needs to be known. Do females have a higher level of fear of failure than males? Is the fear-of-failure situation specific or a generalized personality predisposition, as the Atkinson/McClelland theory postulates?

Fear of failure is but one example of the gaps in our knowledge, in terms of the concepts and processes postulated to occur developmentally by the Atkinson/McClelland model, in terms of their relative stability within the personality, and as determinants for later adult-achievement behaviors.

When it was first discovered that females did not "behave" as nicely as the theory predicted, McClelland et al. (1953) noted the findings with a statement to the effect that achievement was irrelevant to the female sex role in our culture. There has never been an attempt by these authors, or others, to incorporate and explain this gender divergence in terms of their own theory. If the Atkinson/McClelland model of the development and expression of achievement motivation and behavior is correct, then it follows that it should be able to explain the results of female behavior as well as male behavior.

The following queries comprise but one example of the level of analysis required. If one takes the position that females have lower levels of achievement motivation than do males, then one must be able to specify how such an outcome can be derived from the theory.

Do female babies and young children fail to experience positive affective reaction following their task competency or effectance? Do they experience it, yet not attempt to recapture it (re-integration) through further individual mastery? Do differing attributional patterns emerge here through environmental contingencies such that females are oriented away from seeing themselves as the causal agents for their behavior, with the result that the positive affect is not perceived and experienced as a deserved personal consequence? Are female children punished for incompetency and/or ignored when competent, such that their motive to avoid failure is relatively greater than their motive to approach success? Do parents and teachers exhibit different reinforcement contingencies to boys and girls for the same behaviors because of different standards and expectations for them? Boys probably experience more failure situations during childhood and adolescence, in interaction with parents, in school, and in competitive play activities. Does this different exposure remove the "stigma" of failure for the boy, such that instead of looking over his shoulder at possible failure, he is able to orient himself ahead to the goal of success? Is the developmental timing of the imposition of standards of excellence too early or too late for females? Do males and females differ as to the motive-to-avoid-failure and the motive-to-approach-success, or do they differ only on generalized and situation-specific incentive values and subjective probabilities of success? How do these processes affect each other in interaction? The listing of theory-pertinent questions could continue, but the task for the continuing viability of the Atkinson/McClelland expectancy-value theory of achievement behavior, as presently stated, is clear.

An alternative approach would be to question the utility of a theory that places primacy on early learning to the extent that it does not easily allow for the continuing interplay between less static personality factors and experiential interpretation throughout the developmental life cycle (i.e., for change). Perhaps a social-learning approach would be more heuristic at this point.

Whatever one's preference as to theoretical approach, it seems clear that the TAT assessment procedure of n-Ach should give way to a "third generation" attempt to measure motivation. The theoretical derivation and standardization of a way to measure motives through fantasy was a tremendous boon to methodologically sound empirical research in the 1950s, but today it appears to be hopelessly confounded by its defects. It may be that this is a more important issue for research on women than on men, but the influence of theoretically extraneous factors—such as recognition seeking, power, and dominance concerns in males' n-Ach protocols—has not been adequately explored.

An additional important question concerns those personality orientations that are assumed to interact with both motive and behavior: autonomy, self-confidence, and achievement standards (Baumrind & Black, 1967; Feather, 1969; Maimon, 1973). There is growing evidence that the father plays an important role here, and future studies in this area should pay increasing dividends.

Finally, the exciting work in attribution theory should be investigated thoroughly to ascertain its benefits for a fuller understanding of achievement behavior in females (Weiner, 1972; Frieze and co-authors in Chapter 7 of volume). It is known that females have lower expectations for success when faced with a novel cognitive task (V.C. Crandall, 1969; Feather, 1969; Stein & Bailey, 1973, Note 8). There is also some evidence suggesting that females are more likely than males to attribute their successes and failures to external factors such as task difficulty and luck (Frieze et al., this volume; Feather, 1969; Stein & Bailey, 1973, Note 8). These findings could be interpreted as another indication of females' lower expectations for success, as it is a well-documented finding that expected outcomes are attributed to internal dispositions such as knowledge and ability, whereas unexpected outcomes are attributed more to the external factors of luck and task difficulty (Simon & Feather, 1973; Feather & Simon, 1973). Even if it is true that there are differences in attributional patterns between the sexes, it is still unclear as to how these arise (V.C. Crandall, 1969) and how they affect achievement behavior (Stein & Bailey, 1973).

POWER

Power is defined here as the ability to get people to do what one wants, or to influence people in that direction. The greater the number of people one can influence, the greater the power one has. This topic has played a major role in the social psychological literature, although most researchers refer to the concept in terms of control or social influence rather than the explicit term "power." Other related concepts include leadership, authority, Machiavellianism, etc. Traditionally, the emphasis has been on power behavior and power strategies rather than on power motivation. In fact, power motivation has been the least researched of the three topics treated in this chapter. Furthermore, what has been done, as is also true with power behavior, has focused largely on male subjects, male personality development, and masculine spheres of activity. A search of the *Psychological Abstracts,* the *Educational Abstracts,* and *Sociological Abstracts* from 1969 through 1973 yielded no recent references to power motivation in women. A few such references turned up in 1974 publications. Significantly, the studies found that relate to women and power are concerned with their relationships to husbands and children.

None of the theoretical or experimental work on power motivation takes into account, in any systematic way, the special relationship to power that women or any other powerless group—might have. One might think that power is not a relevant or meaningful construct to women if it weren't for the well-documented fact that the pattern of "benign neglect" concerning the psychology of women in psychological theory and research is a generalized phenomenon (Schwabacher, 1972).

However, it is entirely possible that power has less relevancy, at least on some dimensions, to women. If one were to administer a projective test to the phrase "having power and being desirous of power," one would surely elicit responses evoking association and images of masculinity, negativity, and perhaps egotism. Masculinity, by definition, is full of attributes connoting and denoting competency, assertiveness, and the possession of power (Broverman et al., 1972). By association, in myth if not in fact, competency is often equated with power.

The negative responses to a power cue might stem from awareness that the utilization of power can, and frequently does, have negative consequences: dictators, megalomaniacs, driven executives climbing their way up the power hierarchy, and the military. Thus, for women power can be seen as a double negative: masculine and bad. Because of the association of power with masculinity, one might think that females would view power negatively, through expectations that negative social consequences might befall a female who usurped a masculine attribute. This would place it in a similar theoretical position to that of fear of success (Horner, 1968). One could also suggest that the primary negative reaction is reinforced in women by being on the losing end of power plays by dominant others. The end result would then be that women avoid power, both as an agent of power, and if possible, as a subject of another's power tactics. Yet, women accept the submissive role in many situations, and are therefore subjected to the use of power by others.

All of the above discussion is plain conjecture because psychology knows little about power and women. This neglect is interesting in light of the earliest conceptions of power motivation by Adler, Horney, and others. From these first theories to the most recent writings on power motivation, there has persisted the notion that it is a compensatory drive generated by powerlessness, and thus would seem particularly relevant to research on the female personality.

Early Conceptions of Power Motivation

Adler's (1927) concept of striving for power derives from his theory of the inferiority complex, and the consequent striving for superiority. The more the individual's inferiority is focused on interpersonal powerlessness, the greater will be the overcompensatory striving for power in that area. In addition, an individual could compensate for perceived inferiority in some other area by becoming powerful and dominant in interpersonal concerns. As with other large model conceptions of personality, it is difficult to predict in advance in what area the compensatory behavior will occur. Although the inferiority complex is defined as a universal human condition, Adler also recognized both individual and group differences as bases for differential power striving.

Because Adler equated power with masculinity, power strivings in women were defined as "masculine protest" and were more pronounced, in this form, in women than in men. He saw the striving for power as taking either humanitarian or antisocial forms, and although women's roles often served as illustrations of the former, he imputed greater neuroticism to women, based on their greater deprivation of power.

Horney (1950) thought that there are both healthy and unhealthy sources of power motivation. The neurotic quest for power was thought to develop when the individual could not find reassurance for the postulated underlying anxiety through affection. Horney did not develop her model of positive power strivings.

More Recent Theories of Power Motivation

More recently, Veroff (1957), Uleman (1972), and Winter (1973) devoted significant attention to this topic.

Veroff: n-Power. Veroff (1957) was the first to develop and validate a measure for power motivation (*n*-Power). He originally defined the power motive as "that disposition directing behavior toward satisfactions contingent upon the control of the means of influencing another person(s)" (p. 1). This definition, like that of achievement and of affiliation motivation, derives from an expectancy-value theoretical framework in which a relatively stable personality disposition toward attaining a particular kind of goal interacts with the level of expectancy of being able to attain that goal (Ps), and the attractiveness of the goal (Is), to determine the strength of goal-directed (aroused or activated) motivation. The power motive in this framework was therefore conceived as an approach motive, one based on the expectation of satisfaction resulting from the attainment of power.

Veroff's scoring for n-Power was developed in accordance with this theory and used male subjects only. His procedure followed that of the development of the n-Ach measure. He obtained written stories in response to TAT pictures from two groups, an aroused group and a control group. The aroused group contained 34 male Michigan undergraduate volunteers who had been campaigning for student offices and who were, at the time of assessment, waiting for the results of the election. The control group included men only: in dyads, groups, or alone. The scoring theme, like that for n-Ach, hinges on a judgment of whether the relevant imagery is present or absent. "Power Imagery" is scored when a story contains a "reference to the thoughts, feelings or actions of one of the characters which [indicates concern] . . . with the control of the means of influencing a person. Evidence of concern can come from . . . (a) statements of affect; (b) statements of control activity; [or] (c) statements of superior-subordinate role relations" (Veroff, 1957, p. 3). The names and definitions of subcategories were the same or similar to those used for n-Ach.

After dichotomizing the distribution of n-Power scores, Veroff found that high n-Power scorers tended to have lower scores on the Social Value Dimension of the Allport-Vernon Scales of Values, showed significantly stronger interest in the job satisfaction of being leader, were rated significantly higher by their instructors on the frequency of argumentation and the frequency of trying to convince others of their points of view in the classroom, and rated significantly higher the satisfaction of obtaining recognition from their fellows. The high and low scorers did not differ significantly on the value orientations "economic" and "political," on their ratings of the job satisfaction of being boss, and on the number or order of siblings in their families. The correlation between n-Ach and n-Power was +.27. The correlation with n-Aff was not reported.

As a result of subsequent research, Veroff and Veroff (1972) revised the concept of the power motive in a direction more akin to Adler's original compensatory drive notion:

> Many different pieces of evidence support the view that the power incentive defined as "control of influence of others" should not be generally conceived as a *positive* goal in which there is active joy from having impact per se but primarily as a negative goal in which there is, as Adler suggested, an avoidance of feelings of powerlessness as men strive for perfection. (Veroff & Veroff, 1972, p. 280.)

Seen in this way, it becomes the power-relevant equivalent of fear of failure in the achievement domain.

This revision of the concept was based on three kinds of data: (a) demographic distributions of the measure of power motivation in the American social structure; (b) reactions of men and women with high power motivations to being in certain life roles; and (c) relationships to general social adjustment. Veroff and Veroff's (1972) conclusions about high power motivation (or fear of weakness) were as follows:

> (1) It occurs in status groups that are concerned about their weakness; (2) it is correlated with positive social performance and adjustment when the power demands are not publicly salient; (3) it can lead to the avoidance of the power situation, including self-destruction; (4) it can engender conflict if it is the only motivational theme in a persons's life style; (5) it can be associated with a differentiated zestful life in combination with other motives (affiliation and achievement). (p. 200.)

Most of the data available on *n*-Power in women come from the interview study of a representative sample of the American population done in 1957 (Veroff, Atkinson, Feod & Gurin, 1960; Veroff & Feld, 1970). The final sample on which all data were complete consisted of people who, as compared to the general population, were somewhat younger, substantially higher educated, of slightly higher income, and only white adults. The interview schedule consisted of questions tapping satisfactions and frustrations with one's life roles, plus story responses to TATs. Massive as this study of motive-role interaction was, it did not include women's reaction to the work role, nor did the analyses even include the information as to whether a woman worked outside the home. The TAT pictures used for women respondents portrayed female figures (alone, with other females, or with a male), and the protocols of both men and women were scored for *n*-Aff, *n*-Ach, and *n*-Power.

In summarizing the relationships between the three motives, Veroff and Feld (1970) wrote:

> In contrast to the results for men, the significant interrelationships between the motives for women did not form as clear a pattern. A significant positive relationship was found between affiliation and achievement motivation among the grade-school educated wives in our oldest age grouping (50 and older) and the mothers of school age children . . . However, for mothers of preschool-age children, there was significant negative association between affiliation and achievement motivation; for married women with living children, there was a significant negative relationship between affiliation motivation and power motivation. (pp. 57-58)

The last finding, on power versus affiliation motivation, suggests that for a given role set where the norms for behavior permit great variation in style of role enactment, the pursuit or gratification of power and affiliation are antithetical. However, we still do not know whether a high motive score represents greater striving, greater deprivation, or greater gratification.

Married men and women who did not have children had higher power motivation scores than married men and women who did have children. (No consistent relationships were found between parental status and the other two motives.) The authors interpreted this finding as the avoidance of persons with high power needs of a power-threatening situation (i.e., having children who can challenge parental power). This interpretation is based on the assumption that childlessness is voluntary and a result of the motive. However, given the strength of the norms against childlessness, and the prevailing state of contraceptive technology at that time, it is more reasonable to assume that most childlessness among married couples was involuntary. Under this assumption, an alternative interpretation presents itself, namely, that people who are without children are deprived of a major opportunity to exercise significant amounts of power over others. Therefore, their higher *n*-Power scores may reflect greater deprivation of one of the basic and general needs that all people have. This interpretation would also bridge both the finding that the parent-child relationship does not appear to be an appropriate means for gratifying the affiliation motive along with the finding that affiliation and power motivation are negatively related for married women with living children.

Interestingly enough, and contrary to common expectation, the marital role did not appear to be an appropriate means for gratifying affiliation needs. One implication of these findings, taken together, is that married mothers who are not working outside the home may have greater unmet needs for affiliation. In fact, Veroff and Feld's general interpretation of the affiliation-motive-role interaction is that a role which includes obligatory affiliation does not seem to engage n-Aff. However, an alternative interpretation is that such roles not only engage such motivation, but also satisfy it and reduce the level of need or of arousal, thus lowering the n-Aff score. Since the affiliation motive has been satisfied, other motives, like Power, rise in the fantasy hierarchy because the problem of their incompatability with affiliation has been resolved. To what extent similar considerations would apply to other "feminine" occupations, to sex-role expectations in any occupation, and to women in "nonfeminine" occupations is an open and fascinating question.

The authors' general conclusions about power were that the more public a person's power or lack of it in a role, the more likely that the negative features of the motive will be engaged in role behavior.

There have been several thoughtful critiques of these studies and of this measure of power motivation (Winter, 1973; Uleman, 1972). Veroff (1960) and his coauthors have themselves discussed extensively the methodological problems of using Thematic Apperception Tests (TAT) to assess power motives in a large-scale interview study. For instance, the reliability for the scoring of n-Power has always been lower than for the other motives, thus making the interpretation of relationships or their absence very difficult to comment upon.

In addition to the problems discussed above, these data are clearly handicapped in developing a better understanding of female personality by considering motives only in the context of domestic roles. Resolution of some of the uncertainties may in fact hinge on examination of out-of-role behavior, or on how various combinations of roles affect level of motive satisfactions in each role. Even more fundamental is the question of the validity of a measure developed on such a restricted sample of subjects. Since the measure was developed on white male college students, is it so surprising that results for women are harder to interpret and form less clear-cut patterns? We have already referred to the androcentric nature of the arousal condition used to develop the measure.

Veroff and Veroff (1971) have been the only ones to treat the development of power motivation in a systematic fashion. They have treated power motivation as a concern about weakness. Their theory of stages in the development of the motive follows a more general stage theory of development in which a child progresses through the tasks of (a) differentiating the self from others (infancy), (b) differentiating the relationship to another person (childhood), (c) differentiating the relationship to social organizations (adolescence), and (d) differentiating the complex interdependence of the relationships (maturity). Fixation at any stage will prevent the next stage from occurring.

Applying these to power motivation, the first stage requires that the infant learn to want to be near people (proximity or attachment motivation); otherwise, the infant will not become aware of being controlled or of the potential for controlling others. The next stage is to learn to master assertiveness. Fixation will not occur unless the family reacts to the child specifically in power terms. In the two subsequent stages, unsuccessful engagements with power can exacerbate the power motivation residues from partial or unsuccessful mastery of the earlier stages. Some of the situations that have this effect are (a) lack of trust of a colleague, (b) inferior role position, (c) a social position that includes a salient status differential vis-a-vis other people, (d) influence attempts that belittle the person being influenced. All these situations have in common the preemption by another of freedom to choose a social-choice preference.

Veroff and Veroff (1972) are alone in emphasizing the situational bases of power motivation and in recognizing that the success of personal adjustment and beneficence of social outcomes depends on a balance of all the motives discussed here (achievement, affiliation, and power) and on the situational demands in life circumstances. For discussions of the latter issue as it relates specifically to women, see Johnson (1974, Note 9) on social reactions to power use by women, Henley (1973-1974) on power, sex, and nonverbal communication, and Zellman (1974, Note 10) on barriers to the attainment of political power by women. Some of these issues are reviewed by Unger (Chapter 6 in this volume).

It seems apparent that the Veroffs' emphases on situational bases (such as roles) and on the interactions of the three motives are crucial in developing an integrated personality theory that can predict to important social behaviors such as occupation choice, political participation, and preferred familial structure.

We will not attempt an exhaustive cataloguing of results using the Veroff n-Power measure, as they are reviewed elsewhere (Winter, 1973; Veroff & Veroff, 1972). The measure captures some combination of approach and avoidance to power; which of these will appear in behavior seems to depend on how public the outcome of the behavior will be. "Most of the evidence suggests that the negative, defensive, avoidant aspects of the power motive will predominate, unless the target of power is a very easy one" (Winter, 1973, p. 55). Both Winter

(1973) and Uleman (1972) think that these findings were not general to the motive itself, but reflected the kind of arousal used in developing the scoring system. Each of these authors developed alternative measures based on different arousal conditions, which will be described below.

Uleman: n-*Influence.*   Uleman (1972) stated that his concept of need for influence (*n*-Influence) grew directly out of Murray's (1938) and White's (1959) approaches, on three counts. First, he does not consider such a motive to be necessarily compensatory or rooted in feelings of weakness and inferiority (as do Adler and Veroff), but rather that the predominant feeling is one of "confidence." Second, he does not assume that it is good or bad in its social outcomes, but may be either, depending in part on what other motives it combines with. And third, that although "the goal of power or influence frequently operates jointly with other motives," it is analytically distinct from those motives (such as *n*-Aggression, *n*-Exhibition, or *n*-Superiority). Although Uleman (1972) began his work on *n*-Influence intending it to be an improved version of Veroff's *n*-Power, the results from fairly extensive empirical testing and comparison of both measures clearly indicate that they are measuring different things. Uleman (1972) summarized these differences as follows:

> . . . *n*-Influence has to do with social competence and mastery, a kind of interpersonal effectance motive. Success in influencing others is sought as rewarding in its own right, simply as an exercise and expression of one's interpersonal capabilities, or because it generally results in superior payoffs. *N*-Power on the other hand, seems to derive in part from feelings of powerlessness, which can be overcome through gaining power. It is compensatory, and thus more often strained and overbearing. (p. 201)

It should be noted that Uleman used only male subjects in the development of the *n*-Influence measure. In his subsequent discussion of the measure he drew on results from studies that used only male subjects, studies which did not specify sex of subjects; or, in one case he included subjects of both sexes but did not report whether there were gender-related differences.

Uleman (1972) listed the following problems with *n*-Power which motivated him to develop an alternative measure:

1. The fact that less than half of the scoring categories differentiated the criterion groups.

2. Possible confounding effects of self-selection of subjects.

3. Possibility that needs for status and recognition were heavily involved.

4. Appropriateness of competition for student government.

5. Lower interscore reliability (not above .80).

6. Most importantly, the need to avoid arousing fear of powerlessness at the same time.

Neither Uleman, nor Winter after him, nor Veroff's latest contributions consider the exclusion of women from the sample of subjects on whose responses the development of the measure is based as a problem at all.

To create arousal, Uleman's subjects were given the role of experimenter, "giving them the legitimation of Science and the power implicit in the demand characteristics of the psychological experiment" (Uleman, 1972, p. 167). Each experimenter's task was to "frustrate his subject" by beating him at two card games and a match-stick game, ostensibly to study the effects of frustration on imagination. Subjects ($N = 42$) were drawn from two college fraternities in the Boston area. Ten pictures were chosen (for two equivalent forms of five pictures each), on an a priori basis, for their relevance to male college students, for their ambiguity of photographic detail and of the action represented, and for their balanced sampling of types of power situations. All the pictures contained men only, alone or in dyads or in groups, with the exception of one picture of a couple (man and woman).

Comparison of the post-arousal TAT stories of aroused and control subjects yielded nine content categories, each of which differentiated groups at significant levels, and additional "Influence Imagery" category was devised and defined as: "Whenever a party ($P1$) acts toward a second party ($P2$) in such a way that it causes $P2$ to react ... The first *action* must be overt and intentional ... But the *reaction* can be any behavior, overt or covert, caused by $P1$'s action" (Uleman, 1972, p. 171). The other categories, which are scored only if Influence Imagery is present, are Prestige, Organization, Threat, and Separation. One of the important differences between this measure and n-Power is the inclusion of reciprocal, interactive influence in Uleman's measure, rather than the undirectional control of means of influence in Veroff's measure. Intercoder reliability was no better than for n-Power, and test-retest reliability was about .5.

Uleman examined the measures in both his and Veroff's study. In the latter, n-Power was significantly related (or almost so) to theoretical values (Allport-

Vernon Scale of Values), wanting a job where the subject could be a leader, wanting a very interesting job, wanting a job where the subject could be looked upon very highly by ter fellow men, and instructor's rating of argumentativeness and frequency of trying to convince others. The n-Influence was significantly but negatively related only to wanting a very interesting job. In Uleman's study, n-Power was significantly related to running for office, holding office, the California F Scale, and the EPPS Dominance Scale. The n-Influence was significantly related to SPI Dominance, and negatively to Machiavellianism. The n-Influence correlated positively with gambling winnings, but n-Power did not. Uleman summarized his data on n-Influence by characterizing subjects who are high on the measure as being seen as dominant, being open to feedback and influencing others effectively, and reacting to having influence with feelings of confidence.

Winter: Revised n-*Power.*   Winter (1973), also adopting the expectancy-value framework of motivation, defined the power motive as a disposition to strive for certain kinds of goals—those that give one the status and feeling of power and a disposition to be affected by certain kinds of incentives. The goal state of the power motive is to have an effect on the behavior or emotions of another person or persons. Winter assumed that everyone should have some interest in power, with various combinations of approach and avoidance aspects. The avoidance aspect, fear of power, includes fear of the consequences of using one's own power (the power relevant equivalent of fear of success in the achievement domain), and fear of others' power.

A review of Uleman's data did not convince Winter that n-Power and n-Influence were assessing different things, and he believed that the categories used in n-Influence were particularistic, perhaps tied to the particular pictures used. To control for the multiple effects of a natural setting without losing vividness of a real power situation, Winter used for arousal a film of the 1961 inauguration oath and speech of President John F. Kennedy. The research took place after Kennedy's assassination. The control group was shown a film in which a businessman discussed science demonstration equipment. The subjects were 91 male students at The Harvard Business School. Immediately after each film, each group took a six-picture modified TAT and completed some other forms. Two of the pictures contained a couple, one with a man in uniform. The arousal seemed to "take," according to adjectives that subjects checked to describe their mood during the films. The scoring categories evolved from contrasting the stories of the two groups in conjunction with certain a priori notions of expected differences. The outstanding characteristic that differentiated the stories was "vigorous, aggressive, assertive, penetrating actions." Thus, the critical criteria for scoring Power Imagery became "strong vigorous action," "actions that arouse strong affect in others," and "explicit concern about reputation or position."

Ultimately, Winter combined elements from his own and the Uleman and Veroff scoring systems. The subcategories are Prestige, Stated Need for Power, Instrumental Activity, Block in the World, Goal Anticipation, Goal States, and Affect. Further refinements produced separate measures for Hope of Power and Fear of Power, which were uncorrelated. Hope of Power generally predicted the same kinds of actions as overall (revised) n-Power, but with less significant results. Fear of Power is less highly correlated with n-Power than is Hope of Power, and often predicts completely different actions. Winter thought that his total n-Power scores reflected general power saliency because it included both approach and avoidance aspects.

In an effort to utilize more fully the expectancy-value framework, Winter discussed the expectancy and incentive value of power in various situations and suggested that Rotter's (1966) I-E scale might be used to measure expectancy, and that incentive would be a function of domain (number of people over whom one has power) and range (the set of behaviors which one can cause in these people). Thus, the more power potential, the greater the incentive value. Winter does not think that incentive is a function of difficulty level, as in achievement.

Some of the behavioral correlates of high n-Pow and Hope of Power were: (a) being or having been officers in organizations in college, having power positions (resident advisors in dorms), (b) receiving most votes for election to a presidential search committee, (c) working on a newspaper or in radio, (d) participation in individual-against-individual competitive sports (as opposed to individual-against-self sports), (e) urban renewal power politicas (not clubhouse old-guard variety), (f) participation and leadership in small groups, (g) having more prestigious possessions, (h) having smooth relationships with those who make up one's inner circle or power base, but having a competitive, hostile stance toward those of higher status or power who are outside of the immediate group, and (i) being an only or elder son.

Some of Winter's most interesting data concern occupational choice. Students high in Winter's total power motive reported that they would like to be teachers, psychologists, and clergymen. They were not particularly drawn to law, medicine, government, or politics. Furthermore, these relationships between n-Power and occupational aspirations were all confirmed by longitudinal data obtained from another sample of subjects: teachers and business managers were very significantly higher than the average in n-Power, and psychologists and clergymen were also higher than average, although at a lower significance level. Although it may appear odd on the surface that men high on power motivation would choose what could be characterized as more "people-oriented" and therefore stereotypically "feminine" occupations (business excepted), Winter interpreted the attraction of these occupations as being their relatively unstructured character:" . . . the extent to which the situation permits restructuring along the lines of a person's own wishes and the chance to have direct impact on others" (Winter, 1973, p. 112). If this is to be the basis, then women high in power motivation ought to be particularly attracted to the occupation of housewife, since it is probably the most unstructured occupation known. However, it is also relatively unprestigious. Yet, other findings on occupations indicate that high n-Power men tend to occupy positions of formal social power.

The findings reported above, as are all the data presented in Winter's *The Power Motive*, are obtained exclusively from male subjects. Thus, we need studies that indicate whether sex and prestige are linked moderator variables in the relationship between n-Power and occupational choice. Also, since these Ivy-League student subjects were already endowed with status and money, the psychological significance of their occupational choice may be different from similar choices exercised by other classes of students. Thus, class position and possibly race may be other important moderator variables.

Winter also discussed the relationship between symbolic behavior and power motivation, which stimulates some interesting speculation on our part regarding women's fashions. Winter suggested that, since man's power is more fully symbolic than among animals (where symbolic equipment and reputation also make up potential power), man can "more easily create or fake power by the manipulation of symbols and memory" (Winter, 1973, p. 126). Examples might be the use of gestures, personal decorations, and selective histories. If so, it would be interesting to see if there are historical and cross-cultural correlations between women's status, or power, and fashions that suggest power (e.g., historically: high heels, enormous hats, and bouffant hairdos; or currently: military fashions like trench coats, or clothes similar to men's, such as pants and ties). However, the fact that women (with the exception of Chanel) have never been in positions of power and decision regarding the setting and changing of women's fashions may negate this particular relationship.

In his discussion of Fear of Power, Winter listed the following themes which were to be scored: (a) an explicit statement that the power goal is for the benefit of some other person or cause: (b) guilt, anxiety, self-doubt, or uncertainty on the part of the person concerned with power; or (c) irony and skepticism about power as shown by the story writer's style. It is interesting that the first and last themes often turned up in fear-of-success stories written by men. Although Winter recognized and purged the achievement elements in the hope-of-power scoring, there may still be achievement elements in the fear-of-power score. On the other hand, given the present definition of gender and occupational roles, it may not be possible to totally separate the motives empirically. High achievement often leads to more power: failure, to loss of power; and the sex-typing of roles may make this association stronger for men than for women (i.e., because of sex discrimination, achievement in socially valued fields leads more regularly for men than for women to social rewards like prominence, prestige, and power). One of the theoretical benefits from the increasing work on the power motive is the recognition that previous arousal conditions for achievement motivation were "contaminated" with competition and power cues.

As to the developmental origins of power motivation, Winter suggested that women's lack of social power leads them to ambivalence toward their sons and domination of their restricted sphere of interest (home and children). This maternal style creates high power motivation in sons. He did not discuss whether the same or different effects operate for daughters. In his choice of archetype, the Don Juan character, Winter seemed to be saying that power motivation is essentially both a masculine characteristic and compensatory. That is, the clinical interpretation of Don Juan is that he (over)compensates for ambivalence toward a dominating mother.

Winter also found that younger male siblings were higher in his measure of fear of power than eldest or only male siblings, and Hunt (1972) found that youngest children of both sexes were higher in Veroff's *n*-Power, where Uleman's *n*-Influence was higher in eldest children of both sexes. Thus, ordinal position appears to be another determinant of power motivation, and apparently has opposite effects on the approach-and-avoidance aspects. Eldest children presumably experience more successful dominance (vis-á-vis younger siblings) and develop more of the approach motive, whereas younger children are presumably dominated and develop more of the avoidance motive. This approach contrasts with Adler's interpretation that all children, but especially the eldest, feel relatively powerless vis-á-vis the parents, and it is this differential which generates the compensatory need for power.

Similar to McClelland's search for historical consequences of societal achievement concerns, Winter theorized about the societal origins of power motivation and their consequences. McClelland (1971) used various measures of economic expansion, whereas Winter suggested that war and imperialism may be societal

expressions of high power motivation. Since these phenomena often went together (i.e., imperialism and economic expansion), it would be critical, he said,
to examine those occasions when they are independent. Furthermore, one might
ask, if Winter suspects that the subjugation of women and its impact on their
relations to their sons is a primary source for the development of power motivation, why he did not look at the changing fortunes of women within a society as
an historical antecedent of power motivation, rather than at the political and
international activities of men.

In trying to put the psychological power variable back into the social perspective, Winter wrote:

> ... These psychological terms really stand for the constraints and re-
> sources that exist in the objective social situation. We should not permit
> the social variables—class, race, culture—to "disappear" from the final
> description of the results. (p. 206.)

Yet, he omitted gender from the list of variables determining power distribution.
It is almost as if women are only visible in relation to power insofar as they may
create power-motivated sons (that these modern mothers also have daughters,
and what happens to them and their power needs seems beyond his speculation).
For others who are prevented from getting real power in society, there is "aggression, sex, drinking, vicarious participation in sports and sex, gambling and
the quest for prestige" (Winter, 1973, p. 203) as mutually substitutable forms of
power. For women, for whom even these are proscribed by the same sex-role
proscriptions that render them powerless in the first place, there is only ambivalent mothering or belief in shamanism or ecstatic possession left. Thus, as did
Adler, Winter saw no positive outcome for women insofar as power needs are
concerned.

Power Motivation in Women

One of the few recent studies using women subjects was that of Winter and
Stewart (1972, Note 11), who have begun work on the question of sex role as a
moderator variable in power research. They have derived Hope of Power, Fear of
Power, and total n-Power scores for 67 white female undergraduates at a small
women's college, using six TAT pictures (four of which include a male as well as
a female, one shows two women, and one a woman alone). Their moderator

variable, Self-Definition (vs. Social Definition) measures a specific commitment to career (vs. only marriage) and a generalized personality pattern of instrumentality and causal relationships in thought and action (Stewart & Winter, 1972, Note 11). The study also predicts freedom from traditional prescriptions of female norms. They found that Hope of Power predicts holding office in college organizations, and that Fear of Power is negatively related to office-holding. Women who mentioned specific plans for a fulltime career mentioned only teaching and psychology in any appreciable number. They were also significantly higher in Hope of Power than were the others planning fulltime careers. These results are consistent with those obtained from men, and despite the sex-linked connotation of power, the variables Hope of Power, Fear of Power, and total n-Power scores showed the same pattern of intercorrelations for these females as they did for men in other samples. As the significant correlations above with office holding and occupational choice suggest, the motive measures may also correlate to various behaviors similarly for men and women.

Winter and Stewart (1972, Note 11) then created four types of individuals by median-splitting the Self-Definition score against Hope of Power and Fear of Power, and then comparing how these four groups differed in their responses to a questionnaire designed to tap such things as activities, plans, how they perceive their parents, and what things give them pleasure, fears, and secrets. High Fear-of-Power/Socially Defined women are said to evade power and responsibility by absorption in popular trends of an impulsive sort (e.g., demonstrations, liquor and "speed," and freely telling secrets to people). High Fear-of-Power/Self-Defining women are said to seek autonomy in ways more similar to those found among men. While Self-Definition means definition independent of the traditional role, in combination with Fear of Power it leads these women to reject specifically those aspects of the role which makes them the objects of others ascribed power. The high Hope-of-Power/Socially Defined women tend to use a variety of traditional, perhaps even "mystical," strategies for gaining power over men (whether these work in relation to women or mixed groups or even groups of men rather than individual "lovers" is not clear). High Hope-of-Power/Self-Defining women tend to be eldest or only children and to express their power directly in sexual relationships. In light of the host of potentially relevant personality and behavioral variables that might have been investigated in this study of power motivation in women, it is disappointing that the variables chosen were so limited to behavior in the sexual and near-sexual spheres.

As far as the limited empirical research is concerned, it seems that we know little about women and the more positive aspects of power. Confirmation for the negative aspects is provided by Johnson's (1974, Note 9) experiments with male and female subjects' reactions to the use of various sex-typed power strategies by men and women. Tey concluded:

> As power expectations and use exist today, women are guaranteed of maintaining their powerless status. The indirect and helpless power expected of them only reinforces the prejudice against females when used. However, if traditional male power sources are used, the woman is often seen as becoming more aggressive and unfriendly than is considered appropriate for her role. (p. 7)

SUMMARY AND NEW QUESTIONS

Thus, having reviewed the major theoretical contributions, we find the following state of affairs. There is general agreement that there are both approach and avoidance aspects of the power motive, but there is no consensus on which measure is best for assessing either motive. There is general agreement that power-motivated behavior can have either positive or negative social impact, but there is some ambiguity as to whether the determinants of these outcomes are the nature of the motive and which motive leads to which outcome (e.g., approach vs. avoidance), or whether the determinants are situational (i.e., depend on the social context in which the action takes place), or developmental (i.e., depend on the origins of the motive in the individual's history). There is no agreement about whether one expects general gender-related differences in prevalence of the motive, or what the difference ought to be, if any, on theoretical grounds. There is also ambiguity as to whether the measures ought to be considered independent or dependent variables in the way they related to demographic characteristics, behavior in various settings, or occupational roles. Oddly enough, several writers did see relationships between the status of women (either historically or cross-sectionally) and the incidence of power motivation. However, Adler (1927) related it to incidence in women, whereas Winter (1973) referred to its effect for incidence in sons.

According to the compensatory theory of power motivation, women should be higher in power motivation than men. Yet, although they are deprived of power at a societal level, and perhaps often in the marital relationship, it is often not true in a woman's relationship to her children. Parenting is still full of power-related potentials for most women and might represent a stronger power incentive to them. There is no evidence, either conclusive or merely suggestive, that women are lower or higher in power motivation than men (Veroff et al., 1960; Hunt, 1972).

Perhaps conscious awareness is an important moderating variable. Women may not perceive their lack of power because of their interpretation of each situation or interaction in sex-role terms. In the home, they have power; at work, they don't have much power, and they interpret that as dictated by the job role, not by the occupant of the role. Rotter's (1966) work on the perceived locus of control may be heuristic here. Do external women feel less powerful than internal women? Does it bother them? The manner in which one attributes the causes of behavior would also seem to be directly relevant to this topic (see Frieze et al., Chapter 7 in this volume).

All preceding findings lead to the crucial and obvious interaction with sex-role expectations. That is, one must look at values, attitudes, expectations for consequences, previous reinforcement history, personality characteristics covarying with feelings of power, and childhood antecedent conditions, and then project the extent to which they are sex linked.

Are women socialized into personality characteristics related to powerlessness? Since these are interpreted within the framework of appropriate normative female behavior, should they be labeled as negative or unfortunate? Are feminine roles as powerless as we think? On what dimensions of power? Does the male utilize power directly and the female indirectly? Do males and females exercise power in sex-role appropriate activities in a direct fashion and indirectly in sex-role "inappropriate" activities? Jones' (1954) work on ingratiation suggested that females do not utilize power in nonsanctioned ways, but women can and do manipulate people and situations. Perhaps they do it in sex-role appropriate ways as Singer (1964) suggested regarding Machiavellianism and physical attractiveness. In that study, a significant positive correlation existed between the Mach V scale scores and grade-point average for male, but not for female, college students. Singer suggested that because of females' higher social desirability concerns, females would not exercise their attitudes in direct "exploitative" behavior, despite the fact that the males and females did not differ on mean level of Machiavellianism. However, there was a significant positive correlation between first-born females' physical attractiveness and their grade-point average. The evidence cited indicated that first-born females engaged more in behavior that would make them more visible to their instructors, and that they are more conscious of female attractiveness "norms" and their own body attributes in relation to those norms. Later-born females did not show any significant relationships between variables.

Two new developments have begun to address some of the issues raised above. The study by Johnson (1974, Note 9) indicated how others perceive the use of power by women, whether in sex-role appropriate or inappropriate ways. Furthermore, the use of certain kinds of sex-role appropriate power, like helplessness, tends to lower one's own self-esteem and fails to build a power base. These studies of power-use styles in women are very recent. There has not yet been developed a bridge between this work and the research on power motivation. The questions raised here should help direct us toward the continuation of that crucial research.

More recently, Krogh, Landau, Sabini, and Smith (1975, Note 12) have been working on an objective approach to motivation, including power motivation. In this research, 40 statements reflecting diverse situations were rated by 100 undergraduate females on the extent to which these situations have given, or would give, the subjects a feeling of influence over people. When these ratings were factor-analyzed and placed in an orthogonal rotation, four major factors emerged. Although somewhat difficult to interpret, the factors seem to reveal that women possess different orientations toward power potential situations. All the factors can be related to sex-role stereotypes. Factor coefficients were found, and the resultant factor scores were correlated with additional biographical data and other variables derived from scales administered at the same time.

The first factor appears to reflect a fusion of the feeling of influence over people from competency in traditional achievement situations and as a function of satisfying one's affiliative relationships. The factor was significantly correlated with Mehrabian's (1969) fear-of-failure scale and low resultant achievement motivation. The second factor is termed "power as mediated by others" because it appears to relate strongly to the perception of potential influence over others when one is liked. For example, the two highest loading items were (a) being treated with consideration by someone, and (b) being recognized for doing something well. However, the third factor reflects the more traditional conceptions of direct social influence and power, with the highest loading item being "giving orders to people who work under you on your job." This "direct influence" factor was significantly and positively correlated with father's education, occupational level, and his satisfaction with his employment situation. There was a tendency for this factor to correlate negatively with a sex-role stereotype scale. The fourth and last factor was small and it was not interpreted.

Although other powerless groups have also been studied in relation to power, it has most often been conceptualized in political terms, such as alienation. Much more work needs to be done before we understand the similarities and differences between various powerless groups in relation to power motivation.

Although many social correlates of power motivation have been mentioned, only a few appear to have possible causal significance. Being a member of an oppressed group ought to have certain effects on whether approach or avoidance power motivation will predominate, on what forms expression of the motive will take (moderated by other factors such as sex-role standards and one's stance vis-á-vis those expectations); and it may have effects on absolute levels of power motivation. The few studies able to address the latter question did not find significant absolute differences in power motivation between men and women (Winter & Wieckling, 1971; McClelland & Watson, 1973), or did not ask the question (Veroff & Feld, 1960). However, Veroff et al. (1960) did find that blacks scored higher than whites on n-Power. They also found that, of persons in intact homes, females scored slightly higher than males, but the causal direction of this relationship is more ambiguous.

The extensive literature on power needs to be integrated with that on power motivation. Although the use of power and power strategies ought to be related to power motivation, the research on power has not generally considered the question of individual differences in motivation. At most, there have been some inferences about the potential power inherent in certain roles, and how these roles (different occupations, marital partners, or parenthood at different stages) may reflect or affect power motivation. Research concerning women has hardly begun to answer any of these questions. This is certainly a fruitful area for further exploration.

SYNTHESIS

Following the review of three of the most central motives in human personality, as they appear in women, it is much easier to critique the material than to effect a synthesis. The field is quite chaotic, and it is difficult to derive solid conclusions about any of these motives in women, let alone use them as building blocks for a theoretical framework of the relationship among them.

Some of the reasons for confusion are revealed in the words of Murray (1938). Murray noted that needs are frequently experienced only periodically, are commonly fused with other needs (where a single-action pattern satisfies two or more needs at the same time), can be activated in the service of other needs, can conflict with other needs, and can conflict with the "chief aim of the self or with the 'selected personality'." He further stated:

> Introspection and clinical observation reveal that different desires (or trends) may be related in a variety of ways: one form of behavior may satisfy two or more desires, a desire may inhibit another, one trend may finally serve to promote another, a trend may be succeeded by its opposite, etc. (p. 66)

Murray theorized that almost every need could be fused with n-Aff, and that all needs could be subsidiary to the n-Aff needs. He specifically said that n-Aff may conflict with n-Ach, n-Rej, n-Dom, n-Agg, n-Auton, and others.

Regarding achievement and affiliation, women may behave differently depending on the relative strength of their motives and on their reaction to and interpretation of the situational press. For instance, women could

1. Deny achievement needs because affiliation needs are stronger.

2. Deny affiliation needs because achievement needs are stronger.

3. Compartmentalize both needs to different activities.

4. Interpret achievement situations as logically contradictory to affiliation (i.e. competition and the possibility of causing negative feelings in a relationship).

5. Interpret achievement situations as appropriate to the fusing of both needs in that seeking excellence does not require the "doing in" of other people.

6. Use affiliation needs to satisfy achievement needs (to be popular, marry someone successful), and use both to satisfy power needs. Or an affiliation need could be satisfied via achievement activities by a decision to leave an empty house and go to work where one has a better chance of meeting people.

7. Be in conflict because achievement needs are in conflict with an internalized sex-role stereotype of femininity (or "ego Ideal"), which negates achievement as part of the image.

Although Murray did not conceptualize power as a separate need, he said that actions which exemplify ambition, will-to-power, desire for accomplishment, and prestige are in one class, containing n-Sup, n-Ach, and n-Recog. The one subneed most closely aligned with a common idea of power is n-Dom: "To influence or control others. To persuade, prohibit, dictate. To lead and direct. To restrain. To organize the behavior of a group" (Murray, 1938, p. 82).

Subtle versus direct social manifestations of the three motives add additional confusion to the field. Thus, it is often suggested that women are manipulative of people in subtle ways. This may be seen as an indirect way of satisfying power or dominance needs (i.e., getting one's own way). Rosenberg (1972, Note 13) mentioned this as an aspect of femininity of the female role that derives from the status and power distinctions between the two sexes in this culture. As a result, according to Rosenberg, since women have to know the roles of both men and women to survive satisfactorily, women become more adept at role-taking skills and empathy, and become more skilled and subtle in the social use of power, particularly to control the behavior of others.

Such gender differences in behavior may actually reflect differences in motivation, differences in preferred secondary motive but not original motive, or vastly more complicated interactions involving other important psychological variables.

Do some women acquiesce to their prescribed role because it has the secondary gain of allowing them to express their needs for dominance and power by having children and running a household? One should also consider the possibility that affiliating with others may provide an opportunity to affirm oneself—to maintain one's self-esteem: "People like me; therefore, I must be a nice person." Being liked can also be conceived as a means of obtaining power.

Any measurement procedure for motivation should include a realization that motives are not definable only in terms of strength or amplitude, but should potentially consider degree of articulation, complexity, and hierarchical position (Kagan, 1972). There may not be differences in strength of motive to achieve or affiliate between the sexes, but differences in the extent to which that particular motive is ascendant within an individual's hierarchical structure at a particular point in time. Factors that might affect ascendancy are probability of gratification as cued by the situation and previous reinforcement situations, relative deprivation in the sense of when last satisfied, or sex-role considerations indicating that a particular concern is an appropriate or pressing task.

Questions about measurement raise issues about the adequacy of projective measures to assess motivation and to predict behavior. Test-retest reliability is usually low, and the intercorrelations among different measures designed to tap the same motive are also low. Despite the inadequacies and criticisms of the preceding work using the TAT, and despite dissatisfactions with the findings, researchers continue to use either fantasy assessment techniques or derivatives thereof, such as the French Test of Insight. In turn, they usually report still another different set of findings. Sometimes the lack of uniformity in results is based on different scoring methods, sometimes on different validation criteria, sometimes upon a different theoretical base, and sometimes upon a combination of all or any of the above approaches.

Certain needs or objectives for future research can be stated. New assessment techniques or, at least, the use of standardized techniques with standardized scoring and interpretation, are essential. The subject pool for this kind of research, particularly when either standardizing a technique or developing a theory, must be expanded to include women as well as other individuals who cover a range of age, social, and economic levels.

We don't have enough solid information regarding any of the three motives individually, particularly as applied to women, and much less about the relationships among them. Work may have to proceed on each of the three motives separately, including improvement in assessment, before the necessary model-building experiments occur.

Such a model would have to provide us with the means for making some testable predictions, not only about occupational choice, but also about mate choice, child-rearing styles, and perhaps also choice of lifestyles and preference as to the use of leisure time.

For each of the three motives, there is no consensus on the conditions under which avoidance rather than approach will predominate. Indeed, there has been *no* consideration given to an avoidance aspect of the affiliation motive. Sex comparisons could prove both interesting and fruitful here.

Much more research has been carried out and attention given to achievement motivation than to either affiliation or power motivation. Achievement motivation has been considered by psychologists as much more important than the

tainly a wide variation in the extent to which the situation "presses" behavior (such as demands of the task, resources, contributions of individuals, and more institutionalized "presses" such as role and occupational requirements). There is also wide situational variation whereby individual factors appear most clearly. One could structure a continuum of such situations, such that at one extreme we would find situations with very little individual variation, such as mob behavior, to the other extreme of great behavioral differences, such as a marriage. Personality theory must bear these issues in mind.

To date, power personality variables have not dealt adequately with these considerations (McClelland, 1975; Minton, 1972). In contrast, social psychological theories are inadequate in postulating individual variables that would further the understanding, and thus prediction (Schopler, 1965), of power related behaviors. This is particularly true of the more important power-salient behaviors. Within each situation, there is wide variation in actual behavior. Adequate theory would necessarily need to consider the joint interaction of both social and personality contributions. The preceding comment is equally relevant to any behavior that may involve motivational components, and thus would apply to the affiliation and achievement domains as well.

REFERENCE NOTES

1. Feather, N.T. Sex-role stereotypes: Male and female reactions to success and failure. Paper and talk presented at the City University of New York Graduate Center, May 26, 1974.
2. Burghardt, N.R. The development of the motive to avoid success in school-aged males and females. Unpublished manuscript, 1973.
3. Horner, M.S., & Walsh, M.R. Causes and consequences of existing psychological barriers to self-actualization. In R.B. Kundsin (Ed.), Successful women in the sciences: An analysis of determinants. *Annals of the New York Academy of Sciences* (Vol. 208). New York: New York Academy of Sciences, March, 1973.
4. McGuiness, E. Success avoidance and competitive performance. Paper presented at the meeting of the Eastern Psychological Association, Philadelphia, April, 1974.
5. Trigg, L.J., & Perlman, D. Social influences on women's pursuit of a nontraditional career. Paper presented at the meeting of the Western Psychological Association, Sacramento, 1975.

6. Epstein, C.F. Bringing women in: Rewards, punishments, and the structure of achievement. *Annals of the New York Academy of Sciences* (Vol. 208). New York: New York Academy of Sciences, March, 1973.

7. Hochschild, A. Making it: Marginality and obstacles to minority consciousness. In R.B. Kundsin (Ed.), Successful women in the sciences: An analysis of determinants. *Annals of the New York Academy of Sciences* (Vol. 208). New York: New York Academy of Sciences, March, 1973.

8. Stein, A.H., & Bailey, M.M. The socialization of achievement motivation in females. Paper presented at the annual meeting of the American Association for the Advancement of Science. Washington, D.C., December, 1972.

9. Johnson, P. The prejudice of power. Paper presented at the annual meeting of the Eastern Psychological Association, Philadelphia, 1974.

10. Zellman, G.L. Barriers to the attainment of political power by women. Paper presented at the annual meeting of the Eastern Psychological Association, Philadelphia, April, 1974.

11. Winter, D.G., & Stewart, A.J. The power motives and self-definition in women. Unpublished manuscript, Wesleyan University, 1972.

12. Krogh, K., Landau, T., Sabini, J., & Smith, C. Development of an affect-situation inventory. Unpublished research, City University of New York, 1975.

13. Rosenberg, B.G. Sex, sex role, and sex role identity: The built-in paradox. Paper presented at the annual meeting of the American Association for the Advancement of Science, Washington, D.C., December, 1972.

14. McKenna, W.B., & Denmark, F.L. Women and the university. Paper presented at the meeting of the Eastern Psychological Association, New York, April, 1975.

REFERENCES

Adler, A. *Understanding human nature.* Garden City, N.Y.: Garden City Publishing Co., 1927.

Alper, T.G. The relationship between role orientation and achievement motivation in college women. *Journal of Personality,* 1973, *41,* 9-31.

Alper, T.G. Achievement motivation in college women: A now-you-see-it-now-you-don't phenomenon. *American Psychologist,* 1974, *29,* 194-203.

Anastasi, A. *Differential psychology.* New York: Macmillan, 1958.

Atkinson, J.W. (Ed.) *Motives in fantasy, action and society.* New York: Van Nostrand Reinhold, 1958.

Atkinson, J.W. *An introduction to motivation.* Princeton, N.J.: Van Nostrand Reinhold, 1964.

Atkinson, J.W. Change of activity: A new focus for the theory of motivation. In T. Mischel (Ed.), *Human action.* New York: Academic Press, 1969, pp. 105-133.

Atkinson, J.W., & Feather, N.T. *A theory of achievement motivation.* New York: Wiley, 1966, final chapter.

Atkinson, J.W., & McClelland, D.C. The projective expression of needs: II. The effect of different intensities of the hunger drive on thematic apperception. *Journal of Experimental Psychology,* 1948, *33,* 643-658.

Atkinson, J.W., Heyns, R.W., & Veroff, J. The effect of experimental arousal of the affiliation motive on thematic apperception. *Journal of Abnormal and Social Psychology,* 1954, *49,* 405-410.

Bardwick, J. *Psychology of women.* New York: Harper & Row, 1971.

Baruch, R. The achievement motive in women: Implications for career development. *Journal of Personality and Social Psychology,* 1967, *5,* 260-266.

Baumrind, D., & Black, A.E. Socialization practices associated with dimensions of competence in preschool boys and girls. *Child Development,* 1967, *38,* 291-327.

Becker, G. Affiliate perception and the amount of the participation-affiliative motive. *Perceptual and Motor Skills,* 1967, *24,* 991-997.

Bloom, A.R. Achievement motivation and occupational choice: A study of adolescent girls. *Dissertation Abstracts International,* 1972, 33B, p. 417.

Bowlby, J. The nature of the child's tie to his mother. *International Journal of Psychoanalysis,* 1958, *39,* 350-373.

Broverman, I.K., Vogel, S.R., Broverman, D.M., Clarkson, S.E., & Rosenkrantz, P.S. Sex-role stereotypes: A current appraisal. *Journal of Social Issues,* 1972, *28,* 59-78.

Clark, R.A. The projective measurement of experimentally induced levels of sexual motivation. *Journal of Experimental Psychology,* 1952, *44,* 391-399.

Clarke, D.E. The effect of simulated feedback and motivation on persistence at a task. *Organizational Behavior and Human Performance,* 1972, *8,* 340-346.

Cowan, G., & Goldberg, F.J. Need achievement as a function of the race and sex of figures of selected TAT cards. *Journal of Personality and Social Psychology,* 1967, *5,* 245-249.

Crandall, V.C. Sex differences in expectancy of intellectual and academic reinforcement. In C.P. Smith (Ed.), *Achievement-related motives in children.* New York: Russell Sage, 1969.

Crandall, V.J. Achievement. In H.W. Stevenson, J. Kagan, & C. Spiker (Eds.), *Part 1. Child psychology* (The 62nd Yearbook of the National Society for the Study of Education). Chicago: University of Chicago Press, 1963.

deCharms, R., Morrison, H.W., Reitman, W., & McClelland, D.C. Behavioral correlates of directly and indirectly measured achievement motivation. In D.C. McClelland (Ed.), *Studies in motivation.* New York: Appleton-Century-Crofts, 1955.

Denmark, F.L., Baxter, B.K., & Shirk, E.J. The future goals of college women. In F.L. Denmark (Ed.), *Women—Vol. I: A PDI Research Reference Work,* New York: Psychological Dimensions, Inc., 1975.

Edwards, A.L. *Edwards personal preference schedule manual.* New York: Psychological Corporation, 1959.

Escalona, S.K. The effect of success and failure upon the level of aspiration and behavior in manic-depressive psychoses. *University of Iowa Studies in Child Welfare,* 1940, *16,* 199-302.

Exline, R.V. Effects of need for affiliation, sex, and the sight of others upon initial communications in problem-solving groups. *Journal of Personality,* 1962, *30,* 541-556.

Feather, N.T. Attribution of responsibility and valence of success and failure in relation to initial confidence and task performance. *Journal of Personality and Social Psychology,* 1969, *13,* 129-144.

Feather, N.T., & Simon, J.G. Fear of success and causal attribution for outcome. *Journal of Personality,* 1973, *41,* 525-542.

Feld, S., & Lewis, J. The assessment of achievement anxieties in children. In C.P. Smith (Ed.), *Achievement-related motives in children.* New York: Russell Sage, 1969.

Festinger, T. A theory of social comparison processes. *Human Relations,* 1954, *7,* 117-140.

Field, W.F. The effects on thematic apperception of certain experimentally aroused needs. Unpublished doctoral dissertation, University of Maryland, 1951. Cited in McClelland et al., 1953.

Firestone, I.J., Kaplan, K., & Russell, J.C. Anxiety, fear and affiliation with similar state vs. dissimilar state of others: Misery sometimes loves non-miserable company. *Journal of Personality and Social Psychology,* 1973, *26,* 409-414.

French. E. Motivation as a variable in work-partner selection. *Journal of Abnormal and Social Psychology,* 1956, *53,* 96-99.

French, E. Development of a measure of complex motivation. In J.W. Atkinson (Ed.), *Motives in fantasy, action, and society.* Princeton, N.J.: Van Nostrand Reinhold, 1958.

French, E., & Lesser, G.S. Some characteristics of the achievement motive in women. *Journal of Abnormal and Social Psychology,* 1964, *68,* 119-128.

Freud, S. Instincts and their vicissitudes. In *The standard edition of the complete psychological works of Sigmund Freud* (Vol. 14). Hogarth, 1957.

Gerard, H.B. Emotional uncertainty and social comparison. *Journal of Abnormal and Social Psychology,* 1963, *66,* 568-573.

Gerard, H.B., & Rabbie, J.M. Fear and social comparison. *Journal of Abnormal and Social Psychology,* 1961, *62,* 586-592.

Goldberg, S., & Lewis, M. Play behavior in the year old infant: Early sex differences. In J.M. Bardwick (Ed.), *Readings on the psychology of women.* New York: Harper & Row, 1972, pp. 30-34.

Heckhausen, H. *The anatomy of achievement motivation.* New York: Academic Press, 1967.

Henley, N.M. Power, sex, and non-verbal communication. *Berkeley Journal of Sociology,* 1973-1974, *18,* 1-26.

Hermans, H.J.M., ter Laak, J.J.F., & Maes, P.C. Achievement motivation and fear of failure in family and school. *Developmental Psychology,* 1972, *6,* 520-528.

Heyns, R.W., Veroff, J., & Atkinson, J.W. A scoring manual for the affiliation motive. In J.W. Atkinson (Ed.), *Motives in fantasy, action, and society.* Princeton, N.J.: Van Nostrand Reinhold, 1958.

Hoffman, L.W. Early childhood experiences and women's achievement motive. *Journal of Social Issues,* 1972, *28,* 129-155.

Hoffman, L.W. Fear of success in males and females: 1965-1972. *Journal of Consulting and Clinical Psychology,* 1974, *42,* 353-358.

Horner, M.S. Sex differences in achievement motivation and performance in competitive and non-competitive situations. Unpublished doctoral dissertation, University of Michigan, 1968.

Horner, M.S. Toward an understanding of achievement-related conflict in women. *Journal of Social Issues,* 1972, *28,* 157-175.

Horney, K. *Neurosis and human growth.* New York: W.W. Norton, 1950.

Hunt, S.M. A comparison and validation of two thematic apperceptive measures of the need for power. Unpublished doctoral dissertation, University of Michigan, 1972.

Jacobs, S.L. Achievement motivation and relevant achievement contexts: A revised methodology. *Dissertation Abstracts International,* 1971, *32*(5), 2798-A.

Jones, E.E. *Ingratiation: A social psychological analysis.* New York: Appleton-Century-Crofts, 1964.

Kagan, J. Motives and development. *Journal of Personality and Social Psychology,* 1972, *22*, 51-66.

Kresojevich, I.Z. Motivation to avoid success in women as related to year in school, academic achievement and success context. *Dissertation Abstracts International,* 1972, *33*(5), 2348-B.

Lansky, L.M., Crandall, V.J., Kagan, J., & Baker, C.T. Sex differences in aggression and its correlates in middle-class adolescents. *Child Development,* 1961, *32,* 45-58.

Larsen, M.S. Female achievement conflict related to parental sex-typing and identification. *Dissertation Abstracts International,* 1970, *30*(B), 4794-5.

Lesser, G.C., Krawitz, R.H., & Packard, R. Experimental arousal of achievement motivation in adolescent girls. *Journal of Abnormal and Social Psychology,* 1963, 66, 59-66.

Lewin, K. *The conceptual representation and the measurement of psychological forces.* Durham, N.C.: Duke University Press, 1938.

Lipinski, B.G. Sex-role conflict and achievement motivation in college women. *Dissertation Abstracts International,* 1966, *26,* 4066.

Lynch, S., Watts, W.A., Galloway, C., & Tryphenopoulous, S. Appropriateness of anxiety and drive for affiliation. *Journal of Research in Personality,* 1973, *7,* 71-77.

Maccoby, E.E., & Jacklin, C.N. *The psychology of sex differences.* Stanford, Calif.: Stanford University Press, 1974.

Maimon, P.D. The influence of child rearing practices on the development of need for achievement. *Dissertation Abstracts International,* 1973, *33,* 3952B.

McClelland, D.C. *Motivational trends in society.* New York: General Learning Press, 1971.

McClelland, D.C. *Power: The inner experience.* New York: Irvington, 1975.

McClelland, D.C., Atkinson, J.W., Clark, R.A., & Lowell, E.L. *The achievement motive.* New York: Appleton-Century-Crofts, 1953.

McClelland, D.C., & Watson, R.I. Power motivation and risk-taking behavior. *Journal of Personality*, 1973, *41*, 121-139.

McDougall, W. *An introduction to social psychology*. Boston: John Luce, 1921.

Mehrabian, A. Measures of achieving tendency. *Educational and Psychological Measurement*, 1969, *29*, 445-451.

Mehrabian, A. *Nonverbal communication*, Chicago: Aldine-Atherton, 1972.

Mills, J., & Mintz, P.M. Effect of unexplained arousal on affiliation. *Journal of Personality and Social Psychology*, 1972, *24*, 11-13.

Minton, H.L. Power and personality. In J.T. Tedeschi (Ed.), *The social influence processes*. Chicago: Aldine, 1972.

Mischel, W. *Personality and assessment*. New York: Wiley, 1968.

Monahan, L., Kuhn, D., & Shaver, P. Intrapsychic versus cultural explanations of the "fear of success" motive. *Journal of Personality and Social Psychology*, 1974, *29*, 60-64.

Morgan, S.W., & Mausner, B. Behavioral and fantasied indicators of avoidance of success in men and women. *Journal of Personality*, 1973, *41*, 457-470.

Moss, H.A. Sex, age, and state as determinants of mother-infant interaction. *Merrill-Palmer Quarterly*, 1967, *13*, 19-36.

Moss, H.A., & Kagan, J. Stability of achievement and recognition-seeking behaviors from early childhood through adulthood. *Journal of Abnormal and Social Psychology*, 1961, *62*, 504-513.

Murray, H.A. *Explorations in personality*. Cambridge, Massachusetts: Harvard University Press, 1938.

Oetzel, R.M. Annotated bibliography and classified summary of research in sex differences. In E.E. Maccoby (Ed.), *The development of sex differences*, Stanford, Calif.: Stanford University Press, 1966.

O'Leary, V.E. Some attitudinal barriers to occupational aspirations in women. *Psychological Bulletin*, 1974, *81*, 809-826.

Parker, V.J. Fear of success, sex-role orientation of the task, and competition condition as variables affecting women's performance in achievement-oriented situations. *Dissertation Abstracts International*, 1972, *32*, 5495B.

Pleck, J.H. Male threat from female competence. *Journal of Clinical and Consulting Psychology*, 1976, *44*, 608-613.

Puryear, G.R., & Mednick, M.S. Black militancy, affective attachment, and the fear of success in black college women. *Journal of Counseling and Clinical Psychology*, 1974, *42*, 263-266.

Raynor, J.O. Future orientation and motivation of immediate activity: An elaboration of the theory of achievement motivation. *Psychological Review,* 1969, *76,* 606-610.

Robbins, L., & Robbins, E. Comment on: "Toward an understanding of achievement-related conflicts in women," *Journal of Social Issues,* 1973, *29,* 133-137.

Rothbart, M.K. Birth order and mother-child interaction in an achievement situation. *Journal of Personality and Social Psychology,* 1971, *17,* 113-120.

Rotter, J.B. Generalized expectancies for internal versus external control of reinforcement. *Psychological Monographs,* 1966, *80,* 1-28.

Sarnoff, I., & Zimbardo, P.G. Anxiety, fear and social affiliation. *Journal of Abnormal and Social Psychology,* 1961, *62,* 356-363.

Schachter, S. *The psychology of affiliation.* Stanford, Calif.: Stanford University Press, 1959.

Schaeffer, H.R., & Emerson, P.E. The development of social attachments in infancy. *Monograph for the Society for Research on Child Development,* 1964, *29,* Whole No. 94.

Schopler, J. Social power. In L. Berkowitz (Ed.), *Advances in experimental social psychology,* Vol. 2. New York: Academic Press, 1965, Pp. 177-219.

Schwabacher, S. Male vs. female representation in psychological research: An examination of the Journal of Personality and Social Psychology, 1970-1971. *JSAS Catalogue of Selected Documents in Psychology,* 1972, *2,* 20.

Schwenn, M. Arousal of the motive to avoid success. Unpublished Junior Honors thesis, Harvard University, 1970.

Scott, W.A. The avoidance of threatening material in imaginative behavior. *Journal of Abnormal and Social Psychology,* 1956, *52,* 338-346.

Shipley, T.E., & Veroff, J. A projective measure of need for affiliation. *Journal of Experimental Psychology,* 1952, *43,* 349-356.

Simon, J.G., & Feather, N.T. Causal attributions of success and failure at university examinations. *Journal of Educational Psychology,* 1973, *64,* 46-56.

Singer, J.E. The use of manipulative strategies: Machiavellianism and attractiveness. *Sociometry,* 1964, *27,* 128-150.

Skolnick, A. Motivational imagery and behavior over twenty years. *Journal of Consulting Psychology,* 1966, *30,* 463-478. (a)

Skolnick, A. Stability and interrelations of thematic test imagery over twenty years. *Child Development,* 1966, *37,* 389-396. (b)

Stein, A.H., & Bailey, M.M. The socialization of achievement orientation in females. *Psychological Bulletin,* 1973, *80,* 345-366.

Sundheim, B.J.M. The relationship among "n" achievement, "n" affiliation,sex-role concepts, academic grades, and curricular choice. *Dissertation Abstracts International*, 1963, *23*, 3471.

Tangri, S.S. Determinants of occupational role innovation among college women. *Journal of Social Issues*, 1972, *28*, 177-199.

Tangri, S.S. "Implied demand character of the wife's future" and role innovation: Patterns of achievement orientation among women. *JSAS Catalogue of Selected Documents in Psychology*, Winter 1974, *4*, 12.

Terhune, K.W. A note on Thematic Apperception scoring of needs for achievement, affiliation and power. *Journal of Projective Techniques and Personality Assessment*, 1969, *33*, 364-370.

Tolman, E.C. *Purposive behavior in animals and man*. New York: Appleton-Century-Crofts, 1932.

Uleman, J.S. The need for influence: development and validation of a measure, and comparison with the need for power. *Genetic Psychology Monographs*, 1972, *85*, 157-214.

Veroff, J. A projective measure of the achievement motivation of adolescent males and females. Unpublished Honors thesis. Wesleyan University, 1950. Cited in McClelland et al., 1953.

Veroff, J. Development and validation of a projective measure of power motivation. *Journal of Abnormal and Social Psychology*, 1957, *54*, 1-8.

Veroff, J. Social comparison and the development of achievement motivation. In C.P. Smith (Ed.), *Achievement-related motives in children*. New York: Russell Sage Foundation, 1969.

Veroff, J., Atkinson, J.W., Feld, S.C., & Gurin, G. The use of thematic apperception to assess motivation in a nationwide interview study. *Psychological Monographs*, 1960, *74*, 1-32.

Veroff, J., Feld, S.C. *Marriage and work in America*. New York: Van Nostrand-Reinhold Co., 1970.

Veroff, J., Feld, S.C., & Crockett, H.J. Explorations into the effects of picture cues on thematic apperceptive expression of achievement motivation. *Journal of Personality and Social Psychology*, 1966, *3*, 171-181.

Veroff, J., & Veroff, J.B. Theoretical notes on power motivation. *Merill-Palmer Quarterly*, 1971, *17*, 59-69.

Veroff, J., & Veroff, J.B. Reconsideration of a measure of power motivation. *Psychological Bulletin*, 1972, *78*, 279-291.

Veroff, J., Wilcox, S., & Atkinson, J.W. The achievement motive in high-school and college-age women. *Journal of Abnormal and Social Psychology*, 1953, *48*, 108-119.

Weiner, B. *Theories of motivation.* Chicago: Rand McNally, 1972.

Wellens, G.J. The motive to avoid success in high school seniors: N-achievement shifts and psychosocial correlates. *Dissertation Abstracts International,* 1973, *33,* 5529B.

Wilcox, S. A projective measure of the achievement motivation of college women. Unpublished Honors thesis. University of Michigan, 1951. Cited in McClelland et al., 1953.

White, R.W. Motivation reconsidered: The concept of competence. *Psychological Review,* 1959, *66,* 297-233.

Winter, D.G. The need for power in college men: Action correlates and relationship to drinking. In D.C. McClelland, W.N. Davis, R. Klein, and E. Wanner (Eds.), *The drinking man.* New York: The Free Press, 1972, 99-119.

Winter, D. *The power motive.* New York: The Free Press, 1973.

Winter, D., & Wiecking, F.A. The new Puritans: Achievement and power motives of new left radicals. *Behavioral Science,* 1971, *16,* 523-30.

Yerbes, R.M., & Dodson, J.D. The relation of strength of stimulus to rapidity of habit formation. *Journal of Comparative Neurology and Psychology,* 1908, *18,* 459-482.

Zigler, E., & Child, I.L. Socialization. In G. Lindzey & Aronson, E. (Eds.), *The handbook of social psychology,* Vol. 3, (2nd Edition). Reading, Mass.: Addison-Wesley, 1969.

Zimbardo, P.G., & Formica, R. Emotional comparison and self-esteem as determinants of affiliation. *Journal of Personality,* 1963, *31,* 141-162.

Zucker, R.A., Manosevitz, M., & Lanyon, R.I. Birth order, anxiety and affiliation during a crisis. *Journal of Personality and Social Psychology,* 1968, *8,* 354-359.

CHAPTER *13*

THE POLITICS OF GENDER: A Review Of Relevant Literature

RHODA KESLER UNGER

Rhoda Kesler Unger received her B.S. in psychology, from Brooklyn College and her A.M. and Ph.D. in experimental psychology from Harvard University. She is presently in the psychology department of Montclair State College, Upper Montclair, New Jersey. She is coauthor and co-editor (with Florence Denmark) of Woman: Dependent or Independent Variable? *(New York: Psychological Dimensions, Inc., 1975) and author of* Sex-role Stereotypes Revisited *(New York: Harper & Row, Inc., 1975). She has also authored a number of articles for professional journals on interpersonal perception, gender and power, and the development of power differences. Professional activities include Membership Chairperson, APA Division on the Psychology of Women, and representative to the APA Council of Representatives from that division. She has also served as co-chairperson of the committee on the role of women and minorities in psychobiology for the Division of Physiological and Comparative Psychology. She is a member of the Association for Women in Psychology, New York Academy of Sciences, New Jersey Psychological Association, Phi Beta Kappa, Psi Chi, and Sigma Xi.*

This chapter makes the case for the position that much of the behavioral differences between males and females is due to status and power differences rather than sex differences. It is suggested that male gender, in itself, carries with it stimulus value connoting high status and power which is relatively independent of characteristics considered to be appropriately masculine or feminine. Treatment of the gender with low ascribed status (i.e., females) parallels the treatment of other low-status individuals under all conditions examined. Three aspects of the psychological and sociological literature are reviewed in detail with reference to the hypothesis that sex differences can be more parsimoniously viewed as power differences: nonverbal measures of dominance and submissiveness; husband-wife power relationships; and gender differences in small group behavior. Review of the literature in these areas tends to support the hypothesis.

Other points raised by this review suggest that performance differences do not easily eliminate sex-related differences in ascribed status due to differential perception of competent performance on the basis of gender. Assertion of competence and power by a female is likely to define her as a deviant and make her liable to social sanctions. Gender/status identity is institutionalized by our society. It is also suggested that the covert role of physical force and differential size and strength between the sexes may have been underestimated as a source of behavioral differences between them. Lastly, the scientific and social function of reevaluating data in an area such as power, status, and gender is briefly considered.

Although the subject of power relationships between the sexes has been the concern of much rhetoric among those involved in women's liberation, the relationship between various indices of status and power and gender has received surprisingly little attention from serious researchers. The major impetus in the area has come from the theoretical work of Helen Hacker (1951) and the empirical studies of Nancy Henley (1973) on the effects upon women of status inferiority. Their work has led to increased questioning of the principle that sexual equality is the "norm" in the interpersonal transactions between male and female human beings. In fact, male-female relationships may be essentially similar to relationships between individuals varying in other dimensions of ascribed status, such as social class, race, or age.

Sexual equality is actually an exception. In almost every heterosexual behavioral interaction between adults, the male is the more powerful. Male dominance appears to be due to the almost uniform and universal ascription of higher status to maleness than to femaleness. It has been well documented that characteristics supposedly appropriate to males are regarded as more socially desirable and preferable by both sexes than are those considered appropriate to females (Broverman, Vogel, Broverman, Clarkson & Rosenkrantz, 1972). Moreover, male gender, in itself, may carry with a value independent of those characteristics considered to be appropriately masculine. Maleness connotes and confers high status. Many of the behavioral differences between men and women that have been labeled "sex differences" may more accurately and parsimoniously be viewed as "status differences." Since this status asymmetry is based upon ascribed status which is a rather permanent characteristic of individuals, it cannot easily be changed by the performance capabilities of the individuals involved. The effects of status asymmetry upon the power relations of males and females extend throughout the entire behavioral domain, even in areas where relative status does not appear to be relevant. Much of the variance in male-female relationships can be explained by relative status, but because status is so highly correlated with gender, explanations have tended to be based upon sex. This view can be termed a status/gender identity model of sex differences. It will be used as an organizing principle to show that, in many areas, differences between the sexes are essentially similar to differences found among individuals of the same sex who differ in status.

A STATUS/GENDER IDENTITY MODEL: PRELIMINARY CONSIDERATIONS

Definition of Terms

There are many problems in the delimitation and definition of the various terms relating to status and power. Power has been used as both an independent and a dependent variable—to describe the differential behaviors of individuals and to explain what motivates these different behaviors. In a general way, the concept of social power has been used to account for changes that occur in the course of any interaction between two or more individuals. However, any and all relationships contain the potentialities for the exercise of influence and for the induction of change in one or more of the people involved. This review will concentrate on behavioral relationships in which the participants are of both sexes. No attempt will be made to discuss treatments of social power that are based upon viewing it as a personality trait.

For the purposes of this review, various terms relating to power will be defined in a rather general way. *Social power* refers to the ability to influence others. It may be defined as the relative effectiveness of attempts to influence others over time (Sherif & Sherif, 1969), or as the ability to affect the quality of outcomes of others in a mutual interaction (Thibault & Kelly, 1959). Power differs from influence in the sense of implying some source of coercive control. Since, however, it is often difficult to determine what sorts of implicit rewards and punishments are operating within a relationship, power and influence are often used interchangeably by social scientists. Unless otherwise indicated, the two terms will also be used interchangeably within this review.

An extensive definition of terms relating to status is also beyond the scope of this chapter. *Status* may be defined as an individual's position in a hierarchy of power, relations within a social unit as measured by ter relative effectiveness in control of interpersonal behaviors and in group decision making (Sherif & Sherif, 1969). Status refers to potential ability to influence others as opposed to social power which represents actual influence. Sociologists usually recognize two kinds of status—ascribed and achieved. *Achieved status* is based upon performance variables or functions such as the role one performs within an organization or a family. *Ascribed status* is the possession of an individual based upon who tey is. Determinants of ascribed status include age, race, social class, and gender. Other determinants of ascribed status may be physical size, personal attractiveness, and even body build. These latter characteristics are by no means independent of gender and, in fact, may be some of the base on which status/gender confusion is founded.

The area of social power is also complicated by the presence of a large number of terms that have somewhat different implications, but which are often used interchangeably. These terms are *influence, authority, status, dominance,* and *control* when used to describe the characteristics and behavior of the more powerful of the participants in an interaction, and are *compliance, cooperation, conformity, acquiescence, obedience, submission,* and *dependency* when used to describe the characteristics and behavior of the less powerful of those involved in the social transaction. While an extensive definition of each term would consume too much space, you may note that these words have different degrees of connotative loading as well as various implications in terms of sex-role stereotypes. In descriptions of the results of influence attempts, women conform or comply, whereas men cooperate.

An individual may be regarded as a deviant if tey does not respond appropriately to the constraints of the power relationship or if tey aspires to more power and influence than is considered legitimate. Behavior may be labeled *aggressive* if it involves the use of physical force or more constraint of the less powerful individual(s) than is considered appropriate to the situation. *Assertiveness* is a newer term that is being used to describe overt attempts to influence others; however, it is still unclear what relationship it bears to other indices of power. For example, are the identical assertive behaviors perceived and labeled differently when manifested by males and females?

Unresolved Issues in the Study of Social Power

Schopler (1965), in an excellent review article on the theory and empirical findings related to social power, pointed out a number of problems in this area, which should be kept in mind in discussing power relationships.

1. When we study the effect of various kinds of power upon influence processes, we have no guidelines or zero points by which to select or evaluate the effectiveness of the operations. What constitutes zero influence? What constitutes legitimate influence? Hence, various forms of power are always studied relative to each other and often implicitly, relative to societal standards of legitimate control.

2. In most studies of power it is not possible to monitor the recipient all the time. In fact, we are only able to measure the overt results of transactions involving power. Therefore, a recipient who conceals ter responses will appear to have been less affected by the manipulations than one who does not. This problem may be particularly important if one group has more reason (social desirability) to conceal or reveal acquiescence responses than does another, as may be true for males and females.

3. Under what conditions will nonlegitimate access to a power position penalize the occupant? Are these conditions the same for men and women?

Other questions that relate to the use of power by men and women are whether the same factors confer authority, status, and influence upon both sexes and, if so, do they do so to the same degree. We need to know the relationship between gender, the degree of influence attempted or obtained, and other measures of interpersonal evaluation such as liking, attraction, or perception of attitudinal similarity. We also need to know the relationship between evaluative and effectiveness or potency ratings and whether this relationship is the same for both sexes.

A disclaimer. It is not argued that status/gender confusion is the basis for all behavioral differences between males and females, but that it provides an organizing principle within which much disparate information can be interpreted. This review will examine a number of areas where male-female differences in power are known to exist, and will show that these differences are essentially similar to those found among individuals of the same sex who differ in status. Because of limited space in this chapter, a number of related issues will not be explored: (a) the question of whether differences in the need for power exist between men and women; (b) most intrapsychic or personality measures of power; (c) most of the data on developmental aspects of power, or how males and females learn to treat each other; (d) the social reinforcement contingencies that maintain power relationships; (e) the relationship between power and negative attitudes toward women, or misogyny. *Power* is defined as a behavioral construct: a change in the behavior of individuals with reference to controls must be shown. Power is, in general, also used as a global construct, although a number of studies which show that more than one kind of power may exist will be cited.

Difficulties in Researching the Evidence for a Status/Gender Model

It is obvious that in order to investigate the relationship between gender and status, studies on power that repeat the same manipulations for both sexes are required. Surprisingly, a substantial number of studies in this area do not report the sex of the subject at all, and an even more substantial number use different measures when studying behaviors characteristic of power in men and women. A recent investigation by McKenna and Kessler (Note 1) showed that when females were the subjects of investigation, the independent variable manipulation was less likely to involve active treatment or arousal, and the dependent variable was less likely to involve active (as opposed to pen-and-pencil) behavior of the subject.

When interviewed about differential treatment of male and female subjects (Prescott & Foster, Note 2), investigators indicated that they did not believe some manipulations were appropriate for or relevant to women, or that the use of women subjects would only "confuse" their results. Hence, in the investigation of this area, one is hindered by systematic biases in terms of what gets investigated with whom, as well as by what gets published.

In particular, many of the older studies in the area have a number of methodological weaknesses. Especially critical in this regard is the confounding of sex and status. Few studies have performed the same manipulations on men and women. Even fewer studies have used same-sex treatments as a control for the manner in which members of one sex treat the other.

Political Implications of a Status/Gender Identity Model

The relationship between power and gender has until recently been accorded the treatment of "benign neglect," which is so characteristic of many areas of interest to the psychology of women. Some of the reason the area has been relatively neglected may be social proscriptions against the desire for, and use of power in, our society. There exists an "ethic" that power is not exercised in personal relationships, that any influence exerted is due to persuasion and "informed consent." It is especially unthinkable that women should want or use power. The idea of a "norm" of sexual equality in intergender relationships is so all-pervasive that, until recently, it prevented social scientists from investigating whether sexual equality actually exists. All departures from equality were treated as exceptional cases which reflected particular intrapsychic factors rather than the social characteristics of the situation.

It is also possible that the area has been neglected because its very importance necessitates that it be kept invisible. Given power differences lead to outcomes which some males, at least, would like to perpetuate. Not all males are powerful, but most women, certainly, are not. Thus, competition for available resources is reduced. Such an analysis suggests that the stress in social science on sex differences rather than power/status differences may, in part, be a result of implicit political considerations.

Theoretical Implications of a Status/Gender Identity Model

A major problem in examining power relationships between the sexes is that gender is usually confounded with the various variables that denote relative status in a relationship. *Status* is a term more often used by sociologists than psychologists. The term has two separate meanings based on the factors that determine the status. Achieved status is based on performance variables or function such as the role one performs within an organization or a family. Ascribed status is based upon who one "is," and is defined in more or less scalar terms rather than in difference categories, as is usually true of functional status. Status in the scalar sense is often used to predict relationships between individuals in terms of the rewards, benefits, or compliance that they give each other or, in other words, in terms of who has the power in a relationship. If, however, women automatically have a lower ascriptive status than men, sex differences in power must exist. Thus, if women demonstrate less ability than do men to influence others, is this an effect of their gender or their status? When we investigate sex differences in behavior, do we inevitably investigate power differences in behavior?

A STATUS/GENDER IDENTITY MODEL
IN RELATION TO THE PSYCHOLOGICAL LITERATURE

Group Processes

One major area in which male-female differences in power are known to exist, and where these differences can be shown to be similar to those found among individuals who differ in status, is the study of group processes. Although very few studies have examined the relative degree of male-female influence in mixed groups, recently developed data show that women are less likely to influence a group's problem-solving processes than are comparable men (Wahrman & Pugh, 1974). In a naturalistic situation, it has long been known that women are less likely than men to be chosen as foremen during mock jury deliberations (Strodtbeck, James, & Hawkins, 1958). Choices of a jury foreman also vary according to the relative status of the males involved. Males from higher socioeconomic groups are chosen at a rate three and a half times greater than are laborers. Women talk less in a group situation, even in single-sex groups (Alkire, Collum, Kaswan, & Love, 1968), as do low-status individuals. Women conform more within a group, especially as a function of the number of men in the group (Tuddenham, Macbride, & Zahn, 1958), as will low-status males within an all--male group (Allen, 1965). In fact, power structures within groups may create barriers to effective problem solving. Hoffman (1965) cited a study by Torrance on problem solving in Air Force crews which showed that the lowest-ranked member was least likely to influence the group's decision even when tey was correct. Wahrman and Pugh's (1974) data also show that the ability to be correct has little effect upon a woman's influence in a predominantly male group.

Prosocial Behavior

The literature on helping, or prosocial, behavior provides an interesting area in which to examine status/gender effects, for two reasons. First, a social norm about the need to help dependent others appears to exist. Second, helping can be used as a measure by which to estimate attitudes toward those requesting help. Those who are perceived as violating societal norms are less likely to be helped than those who are perceived as upholding these norms. Gender/status confusions may produce results that are related to these two aspects of the relationship between sex and helping.

Although there are many situations where there are no differences between the levels of help offered a male or female, when differences do exist it is the woman who is more likely to be helped (Krebs, 1970). Men are much more likely to help women than women are to help men (Unger, Raymond, & Levine, 1974), especially in naturalistic field situations where some danger or personal inconvenience might be involved (Howard & Crano, 1974). In an interesting experiment contrasting sex, dependency, and helping, Gruder and Cook (1971) showed that the most important determinant of whether or not an individual was helped was the recognition of the dependency of that individual. Dependent females were helped more than nondependent females who received marginally more help than dependent males. Dependency did not appear to be a salient variable in helping men, and there were no effects due to the sex of the potential helper.

Walum (1974) suggested that helping encounters between males and females involve more than empty gestures of courtesy or chivalry. Using door opening as ter behavioral variable, tey investigated by a variety of means what happens when customary norms are violated. When the routine was changed, deference confrontations occurred. Tey compared sex differences in door opening to similar encounters between individuals possessing differing amounts of authority. "The doctor ushers in his patient; the mother, her children; and the Dean, his faculty; the young and able facilitate the old and infirm. Even reference to the 'gate-keepers of knowledge' symbolically acknowledges the role of authority vested in those responsible for the door." Walum suggested that opening a door is a political act, one that reaffirms patriarchal ideology. It is noteworthy that in a recent large-scale field study carried out in various parts of the United States, it was found generally that females receive more help than males and males give more help than females, but that in Atlanta, specifically, these differences are greatly exaggerated (Latane & Dabbs, 1975).

Women are not always helped more than men. An evaluation of the conditions under which women are not helped more than men suggests that this occurs in situations'where they either violate expectations about their dependency or expectations about appropriate "feminine" attire (Harris & Bays, 1973; Unger et al., 1974). Males in deviant dress are also less likely to be helped than those who are dressed conventionally (Raymond & Unger, 1972). It can be argued that relative helping is a U-shaped function of the social status of the individual requesting help. Help is more likely to occur when the helper perceives "temself" to be in a position superior to that of the helpee, but decreases as status asymmetry continues to increase. A number of variables—such as attire, the locale, and the task in which help is being requested—will contribute to the status relationship, and thus to the probability that help will be elicited.

Aggression

Helping and aggression are to some extent inversely related to each other. Hence, one would expect that variables which affect helping behavior might also have some effect upon aggressive behavior. While helping behavior is rather unambiguous, however, there are great problems in the use of the term *aggression*. Aggression may be either overt or covert, and there may be great cultural and familial variation in how much aggression may be expressed and in what way. Maccoby and Jacklin (1974) suggested that girls and women are less often the objects, as well as the agents, of aggressive action. It appears to be true that in a laboratory situation, males are less willing to aggress against females than against other males, but the same constraints do not seem to operate under naturalistic conditions. Deaux (1971), as well as Unger et al. (1974), found that males are less likely to inhibit their aggressive behavior (e.g., horn honking) when the offending driver is a female rather than when he is a male. Such behavior is also directed against other low-status individuals such as hippies. Doob and Gross (1968) found that horn honking was more frequent when the offender was driving a low-status make of automobile.

It has been suggested that insufficient attention has been paid to the role of physical dominance and coercion in relationships between men and women (Barry, 1970). In blue-collar marriages, in particular, physical assault upon wives is not uncommon (Komarovsky, 1964). Considering the social sanctions against assaulting women in a public situation, even when they appear to have behaved in a highly provocative, aggressive manner (Taylor & Epstein, 1967), one would not expect to find such behavior readily accessible to the psychologist.

The issue of rape.   Another area involving male-female differences in aggression, which has been largely left to feminist polemicists, is that of rape. Obviously, more women are raped by men than men are raped by women. It is becoming increasingly clear that rape is primarily a crime of violence and not of sex; that is, the motivation is to hurt, dominate, and degrade women, not to satisfy sexual desire. Although careful empirical studies of the motivations of large numbers of men who rape are lacking, there is some evidence that convicted sex offenders do not constitute a group significantly more disturbed than males who commit other violent crimes (Griffin, 1971). More than 50% of all rapes committed by a single individual are planned and involve individuals who are at least somewhat acquainted with each other (Amir, 1971). The incidence of rape may be determined in part by the ideology a group or individual holds about the nature of human sexuality and the place of women (Sherman, 1975). Whether or not a man rapes may depend more upon his opportunities than upon his motivations. Brownmiller (1975) amply documented the enormous numbers of rapes committed by so-called normal men during periods of warfare. Men are rarely raped, even under conditions of tremendous social upheaval. Janeway (1974), however, did point out that under prison conditions it is the weak, low-status male who is raped.

Modeling, Imitation, and Status/Gender Effects

Subjects of either sex are more likely to comply with a request to sign a peace petition if it is tendered by a male rather than a female (Keasey & Tomlinson-Keasey, Note 3). They are also more likely to sign that petition if a conventionally dressed individual urges them to, as contrasted to one in hippie garb. High-status males in children's camps are more likely to succeed in their influence attempts than are low-status individuals (Lippitt, Polansky, Redl, & Rosen,

1958). Bandura, Ross, and Ross (1963) found that children primarily imitated the model who had the power to reward, regardless of ter sex. They indicated, however, that the sex of the individuals involved did play a role. Despite elaborate experimental manipulations designed to establish differential power and status, a number of children actually attributed rewarding power to the ignored or reward-consuming adult male bystander. Some quotes indicate children's firm conviction that only a male can possess resources and that a female is only an intermediate for the male: "He's the man and it's all his because he's a daddy. Mommy never really has things belong to her . . ."; "He's the man and the man always really has the money and he lets ladies play too . . .". These data indicate that status and power and gender can be confounded even when attempts are made to manipulate them as separate entities.

Gender-Differentiated Determinants of Status/Gender Differences

Still other supporting data are garnered from studies on the role of physical attractiveness as a determinant of status or power. Interestingly enough, investigation of this variable has been almost entirely limited to females. Krebs and Adinolfi (1975) report that there is a positive relationship between physical attractiveness and dating for females, but not for males. Attractive girls are regarded by other children as being less aggressive than others, and are relatively more popular (Dion & Berscheid, 1974). Male subjects reacting to a partner they had met in a laboratory experiment during a two-week interval, thought about her more as a function of her physical attractiveness than of her perceived similarity to them (Kleck & Rubenstein, 1975).

Since Rokeach and Mezei (1966) pointed out that perceived interpersonal similarity is a possible indicant of liking and degree of influence, it would be interesting to study the relationship between physical attractiveness and ability to influence others as a function of gender. Unfortunately, such studies have not been done. Just as attractiveness does not appear to be a salient variable for males, power does not appear to be a salient variable for females. Attractive women, especially, are not expected to need or to use power. A recent intriguing study by Goldberg, Gottesdiener, and Abramson (1975) suggested, in fact, that evidence of a desire for power by a woman may decrease her physical attractiveness to both men and women. Photographs of women supposedly belonging to a women's liberation group were evaluated as being less attractive, even though no differences in ratings of the photographs appeared when no ideological labels were attached. Female status may be largely mediated by appearance and male status by behavior. Attempts to acquire status by means considered appropriate to the opposite sex violate sex-role stereotypes and produce negative sanctions of the aspirant. This effect may not be limited to female pretentions to power, since Farrell's (1974) use of male beauty contests demonstrates that male pretentions to status because of physical attractiveness are also regarded as somewhat absurd.

Occupational Preference, Prestige, and Gender

The disparity in status ratings of "male" and "female" occupations is further evidence of the status discrepancies between sexes. Females simply do not aspire to high-status male professions. Rosalind Barnett, in an unpublished study (Note 4), found that at every age, 9 through 17, correlations for occupational preference and prestige were higher for males than for females. These sex-related differences reached their highest level between ages 15 and 17. In fact, for females, the correlations between occupational prestige and desire to enter that profession were virtually zero. Feather (1975), in a study of university students in Australia, showed that there was a high correlation between masculine dominance of an occupation and its perceived status, which would have probably been higher if one of the occupations used had not been that of janitor. Even more tellingly, Touhey (1974) showed that ratings of occupational prestige and desirability decreased when subjects anticipated increased proportions of women entering them. This decrease in ratings did not differ for male and female subjects. Ratings on adjective pairs taken from the semantic differential indicated that reductions in occupational desirability and prestige were accompanied by attributions of increased passivity, insecurity and uselessness, and decreased success. One wonders if the same results would be found for race, provided one could find experimenters and subjects politically naive enough to participate in such a study.

Sex and Success

Numerous studies document the position that success and competence are male characteristics. Although there are some exceptions, a large number of studies indicate that the productions of males are valued more highly than the same materials attributed to a female (Goldberg, 1968; Pheterson, Kiesler, & Goldberg, 1971; Starer & Denmark, 1974). Similarly, work that has won, rather than being entered in an art contest (Pheterson et al., 1971), or which is attributed to a well-known rather than an unknown artist (Etaugh & Sanders, 1974) will be rated more highly. Some of these data are confusing because sex-role stereotypes appear to play a larger role in cross-sex than in same-sex judgments (Etaugh & Sanders, 1974; Unger & Siiter, 1975). However, it appears that different processes operate in the evaluation of males and females. For example, the highly competent individual who makes a blunder is preferred over one who does not, but only when males are judging other males (Deaux, 1972). Male stimulus persons appear to be evaluated along a broader range, appearing more competent at the positive end of the scale but suffering greater devaluation under conditions of low competence (Deaux and Taynor, 1973).

Data from causal attribution studies also indicate that success and failure in competitive situations are differentially perceived and evaluated according to sex (Frieze, Fisher, McHugh, & Valle, 1977). Whether the authors were evaluating undergraduates or successful physicians on an intellectual task, subjects attributed greater motivation to females (Feldman-Summers & Kiesler, 1974). In addition, males perceived female physicians as being less able than male physicians. Deaux and Emswiller (1974) found that female success was more likely than male success to be attributed to luck, and Feather and Simon (1975) found a pervasive tendency for female subjects to downgrade unsuccessful males as contrasted to successful males, and to downgrade successful females in relation to unsuccessful females. In the latter study, males were evaluated more positively and seen as more powerful if they succeeded; females were evaluated more positively and seen as more powerful if they failed. Fully 70% of the measures of the interaction between sex and outcome were significant, and attributions ranged from global judgments about the individuals to rather trivial assumptions about their behavior following success or failure. Males were rated as more likely to throw a wild party after success; and females, after failure.

Although there are studies showing that competent women are evaluated as positively as competent men (Spence & Helmreich, 1972), some recent studies indicate that this effect is not so clearcut as was first thought. A more recent study by Spence, Helmreich, and Stapp (1975) indicates that interpolating a series of TAT-like questions before the objective questionnaire changes the evaluations of the competent woman with masculine interests. While, in the standard condition, competent individuals of either sex were liked more than incompetent individuals, following the TAT, only profeminist women subjects continued to prefer the masculine competent woman to the competent woman with feminine interests. Spence and her associates suggested that use of the TAT format may force subjects to consider the stimulus persons more actively and elicit less superficial reactions to the objective questionnaire items. In a similar vein, Hagen and Kahn (Note 5) found that men liked a competent woman only when they observed her performance and not when they were involved in interaction with her. Both males and females were more likely to exclude a competent woman from a group than a competent man, and to include an incompetent woman than an incompetent man.

Sex and fear of success.   Since success raises status, data on fear of success can be explained by means of a status/gender model. Success and accomplishment are intrinsic to male status, and a male who fails violates his status and may be regarded as a deviant individual. On the other hand, female success is also a status violation. Failure for females may have a multitude of favorable concomitants, irrespective of the ostensively negative aspects it carries with it. Failure becomes a reaffirmation of female status. Long ago, Margaret Mead observed that whereas men are unsexed by failure, women are unsexed by success. This observation is consistent with the position that fear of success can be a cultural as well as an intrapsychic variable (Monahan, Kuhn & Shaver, 1974). It is also consistent with the position that society legitimizes incompetence or dependence in women—for example, the stranded female motorist or the incompetent woman driver—(Raven, Note 6), and that individual differences in competence are irrelevant to the female role (Bem & Bem, 1970).

If success and (by extension) competition to obtain such success is perceived as a deviant characteristic by most women, likely to make one liable to societal sanctions, we would expect to find denial of competence to be a common behavior. Vaughter, Gubernick, Matossian, & Haslett (Note 7) found that, regardless of ability, individuals predicted their grades in terms of a sex-role definition. Men displayed confidence in their ability to achieve and women displayed verbal modesty. In a study of married couples with known IQs, Perino and Krooth (Note 8) found that wives predicted significantly higher IQs for their husbands than husbands did for their wives, even when actual IQ scores were the same.

Reinforcements for female failure.   Pleck (in press) found that girls who had traditional attitudes about women's roles and feared success, performed less well when competing against their boyfriends than they did when joining them to compete against others. These women may have been taking their cues from the men with whom they were emotionally involved, since Pleck also found that the men who gave "threatened" or hostile responses to stories of achievement by women also increased their performance when competing against their girl-friends, as contrasted to competing with them against others.

The data cited above about preferences for incompetent women would indicate other sources of reinforcement for women's professed lack of ability. Although it is not consistently found at this age, first-grade boys predicted higher scores for themselves than for girls, despite the fact that there was no real difference between boys and girls in task competence (Pollis & Doyle, 1972). The image of female incompetence is fostered by the popular media. Even in the late 1960s, 10% of the humor in the Reader's Digest involved negative female stereotypes and an unfavorable ratio of antifemale to antimale jokes (Zimbardo & Meadow, Note 9). A rank-ordering of the frequency of negative traits attributed to women in this "humor" showed that the stupid, incompetent, and foolish woman was the most frequent category.

NONVERBAL BEHAVIORS, GENDER, AND STATUS

Nonverbal Cues to Status

Females manifest nonverbal behaviors similar to males of low status and are treated by others as though they possessed low status. Females require a smaller envelope of personal space (Lott & Sommer, 1967). Even under naturalistic conditions on a beach, single females or female groups claim considerably less space than do single males or male groups (Edney & Jordan-Edney, 1974). Correspondingly, Sommer (1969) and others have shown that dominant individuals have a larger envelope of inviolability surrounding them. The degree of personal space required may be a function of level of aggression. Kinzel (1970) showed that prisoners convicted of a violent crime required a larger envelope of personal space than did other male prisoners.

Henley and Freeman (1975), in summarizing differences between males and females in nonverbal behaviors, pointed out that females are approached more closely than males. A large number of laboratory and field studies agree that subjects of both sexes are more willing to intrude upon a woman than upon a man (Leibman, 1970; Nesbitt & Steven, 1974; Adler, Note 10). It is also noteworthy that women respond to an intrusion of their personal space by decreasing rather than increasing their motor behaviors (Mahoney, 1974). Spatial invasion appears to affect females more than males, but they do not respond by fleeing the scene of the invasion. Instead, their behavior tends to become more constricted and immobile; hence, they become more easily encroached upon.

Henley's outstanding work on the relationship between status variables and interpersonal touching helped instigate the basic status-gender identity model developed in this chapter. In a large-scale observational study of touching in public, Henley (1973) reported results that support her hypothesis that touch privilege is a correlate of status. She hypothesized that individuals of higher status would initiate touching more frequently and would reciprocate touching more. She argued that the failure to reciprocate touching connotes an acceptance of the legitimacy of the touch and that reciprocation indicates a reassertion of power. She found that males were more likely to touch females than vice versa, and that they would reciprocate a touch initiated by a female more frequently. Data on touching, age, and socioeconomic status as ascriptive variables further indicated that touching is used to communicate asymmetry of power relations. Young people and those of presumed lower economic status (on the basis of attire) were more likely to be the recipients of touching and less likely to reciprocate it.

It has been argued that touching connoted intimacy, but Henley pointed out that there is no necessary contradiction between the same gesture being used to communicate both power and closeness. An analogy is made to the verbal gesture of calling another by ter first name. Used reciprocally, first names connote affiliation; used nonreciprocally, they connote status (Brown & Gilman, 1960). Movement toward greater intimacy is usually initiated by the person with the higher status. Although discussion of psycholinguistic analyses of power relations between sexes is beyond the scope of this chapter, an investigation of sex-related slang vocabulary should be mentioned in this connection. Kutner and Brogan (1974) found 79 expressions equating women with sexual objects among males, compared with only 18 among females. Many fewer slang terms for men were expressed by both males and females, and only five terms equated the man with a sexual object or actor. Women are not necessarily aware of the connotations of these differential uses of gesture and language. Henley and Freeman (1975) pointed out:

> By being continually reminded of their inferior status in their interactions with others, and continually compelled to acknowledge that status in their own patterns of behavior, women learn to internalize society's definition

of them as inferior so thoroughly that they are often unaware of what their status is. (p. 391.)

Eye contact, Status, and Gender

Differences in level and kind of eye contact also exist between males and females. Women engage in mutual visual interaction more than men (Exline, 1963; Exline, Gray, & Schuette, 1965). However, they seem to back down when looking becomes staring (a gesture of dominance). Fromme and Beam (1974) found that males, but not females, reciprocated an increase in eye contact by a confederate. High-dominant females were more likely to reciprocate eye contact than were low-dominant females. Among women, eye contact appears to be positively related to how well liked is the person being looked at (Mehrabian, 1969). Females had the least amount of eye contact with disliked male addressees as compared to liked males, liked females, and disliked females, in that order (Mehrabian & Friar, 1969). In Fromme and Beam's study, low-dominant males associated high levels of eye contact with negative attitudes.

Both males and females have significantly more eye contact with high-status addressees than with low-status addressees (Mehrabian, 1968a). In two additional studies involving status differences, males looked more at, or paid more attention to, high-status men (Efran, 1968; Ellyson, Note 11). In the latter study, the high-status individuals possessed more legitimate power and were also in control of reinforcements for the dyad. Mehrabian (1968b) suggested that eye contact is a parabolic function of attitude toward the addressee. The least amount of eye contact is found toward individuals who arouse intense negative emotions. Eye contact increased toward a maximal amount with relatively neutral individuals and decreases again for individuals who are intensely liked. Weisbrod (1965/1969) found that individuals who were looked at most in a group situation saw themselves, and were seen by others, as being more powerful in a group than those who were looked at less. A status interpretation of male and female gazing behavior would lead to the prediction that females would look more at males than males would look at females unless the situation was perceived as threatening. Henley and Freeman (1975) suggested that gaze aversion may be a way of inhibiting any aggressive or threat behavior. Ethologists have noted this type of response to dominance gestures in many animals, and it has been suggested that autistic children are never attacked by their peers because of this gaze aversion.

In an intriguing, although unfortunately flawed study of the relationship between dominance and sex-related differences in nonverbal responses to different degrees of eye contact, Fromme and Beam (1974) found that high-dominant subjects of both sexes increased their proxemic behavior in response to low levels of direct steady gaze, while low-dominant individuals decreased in proxemic behavior. For males only, high eye contact led to a significantly faster approach rate to the confederate for high-dominant subjects, but a slower (as well as a greater interpersonal distance) rate for low-dominant subjects. They suggest that very high levels of eye contact signal a dominance challenge rather than a request for intimacy. In a nonchallenging situation, there is little sex differentiation in proxemic behavior. In a challenging situation, however, men and women respond differently as a function of dominance level.

Although Fromme and Beam's study represents a rare attempt to separate out status and gender variables, it is flawed by several methodological errors. Both male and female confederates engaged in gazing behavior. However, data for the sex of confederate are not given separately. We do not know if staring by a woman is regarded as a challenge by high-dominant men. Moreover, since subjects were divided into high-and low-dominant groups on the basis of scores above and below the median for their own sex, we do not have data on the comparability of high and low dominance for males and females. High-dominant females may have had scores considerably lower than high-dominant males, and thus may resemble low-dominant males in their levels of dominance.

Posture, Threat and Gender

Males and females appear to differ in their postural attitudes, even under relatively relaxed conditions. Typology studies of male and female postures indicate that males customarily occupy more space than females, even allowing for their larger body size. Women usually hold their limbs closer to the body and their legs crossed or closer than men. Mehrabian (1968b) indicated that a greater degree of body tension and vigilance is characteristic of individuals communicating an intense degree of dislike for another person. Males, however, assume a very relaxed position when addressing an intensely disliked female. Mehrabian interpreted these data to indicate that a disliked person who is perceived as threatening evokes body tension. Females, of course, do not threaten. One could interpret these data also to indicate that females are under a greater stress than males, even under supposedly relaxed conditions. This interpretation is consistent with the hypothesis that females customarily occupy a lower place in the dominance hierarchy than do males.

The Perceptual Response to Status Inferiority

It has been suggested (Argyle, 1969) that nonverbal cues can convey much more information than verbal cues. If nonverbal cues are used to define status in male-female relationships, and if relative status is an extremely important component of these relationships, one would expect that females, by virtue of their position of status inferiority, would be more sensitive to nonverbal cues than would males. After all, as the participants possessing less potential power in a cross-sex interaction, they are more subject to social sanctions if they violate status assumptions.

Heshka and Nelson (1972), using photographs of interacting dyads in natural outdoor settings, found that speaking distance varied according to relationship for females, but not for males. They suggested that since relationship appears to be a more significant determinant of interaction distance for females, females may rely more than males upon nonverbal cues. In a more intensive laboratory investigation of nonverbal cue perception in males and females, Kantor (note 12) found that women were, indeed, more sensitive to facial expression, articles of attire, etc. Tey suggested that this difference in cue perception may be the origin of "feminine intuition." While one does not wish to belabor the resemblance between women and other "oppressed groups," sensitivity to stimuli produced by higher-status others has long been considered a characteristic of minority groups (Hacker, 1951).

POWER IN THE FAMILY

Status among Husbands and Wives

The family considered as a small group becomes a valuable place to examine the hypothesis that status differences are more important than gender differences in the relationships between men and women. There is a vast literature on the family, which is mostly the result of the work of sociologists. One of the earliest theories about husband-wife relationships and one that has had great influence upon the field is that of Talcott Parsons. In one of his numerous papers, Parsons (1942) suggested that the normal man has a "job," which is fundamental to his social status in general. The woman's fundamental status is that of the husband's wife. Women are explicitly excluded from the struggle for power and prestige in the occupational sphere. Although it is sometimes argued that Parsons used status in a functional sense—in terms of differential performance spheres (instrumental or goal-directing for the husband and expressive or affective coordinating for the wife)—it is clear that family status can be translated into scalar terms. The male role, of course, confers higher status than the female role.

A recent study (Felson & Knoke, 1974) indicates that even in the 1970s, husbands and wives appear to pay little attention to the attainment of the wives when evaluating their status. Even though 27% of the wives in the sample had more education than their husbands and 42% had the same amount of education, the wife's position added very little to the variance in social class identification. Other studies (Barry, 1970) have shown that the background and personality factors of husbands, but not of wives, are associated with marital "success." The factors pertaining to the husband which are important to marital success include the happiness of the husband's parents' marriage, his attachment to his father, his level of economic class and education, and the stability of his personality. Lastly, we may look at status factors associated with singlehood in males and females. Spreitzer and Riley (1974) pointed out that higher levels of intelligence, education, and occupation are associated with singlehood among females. Poor interpersonal relations with parents and siblings are associated with singlehood among males. Female scientists and engineers are six times less likely to have married than are their male counterparts.

Marriage, Status, and Mental Health

Bernard's (1972) discussion of the relative value of marriage to men and women is too extensive and too well known to be reviewed here. She documented with considerable data the position that marriage is good for men in terms of better mental health, increased longevity, and economic worth, while marriage is bad for women in terms of decreased mental and physical health. She arrived at her conclusions by a comparison of the relevant statistics for the married and unmarried, male and female.

Dohrenwend (1973) suggested that persons in low social status are disproportionately exposed to stressful life events and that such differential exposure accounts for the link between low social status and individual psychological distress. She found that both hypotheses were supported for sexual status. There was a higher number of life-change scores for women than for men, and this sex-related difference was independent of social class differences. She also found that women's symptom levels were more affected by events they did not control than by all events, suggesting that their psychological distress was associated with the lack of power to control their own lives. In contrast, men's symptom levels were more closely associated with life-change scores based on all events, including some they had probably influenced. Unfortunately, these data do not discriminate between married and single women.

A more recent study by Radloff (1975), however, does discriminate between married and single women, and finds that married women are more depressed than comparable men, although differences in depression are not found between single men and women. Surprisingly, depression scores are not different for those working within or outside the home. Tey suggests that these results are due to the fact that women are more likely to learn to feel helpless than are men. Cross-cultural studies of locus of control (McGinnies, Nordholm, Ward, & Bhanthumnavin, 1974) indicate that women have a higher belief in external control of their lives than do men. It may be that this perceived external control is a reflection of actual differences in the amount of control over their lives, as compared to men, and thus reflects a social reality rather than a personality variable.

Achieved versus ascribed status in the family.   It has been suggested that women's status in the family is due to her lower contribution to the family's economy, which is in turn due to the fact that she is "tied" to the home by the acts of childbearing and child-raising. A number of studies (Blood & Wolfe, 1960; Wolfe, 1959) have shown that husband dominance of the family is associated with high-status occupations, occupational prestige, and income. Wives gain power in the family in proportion to their level of education, the number of years they have worked, and their level of organizational participation (Gillespie, 1971). These data are consistent with the hypothesis that power or status outside the family is correlated with power and status within it. When women have a decreased opportunity to function outside the home, as during their childbearing period, their power in the family decreases.

Cross-culturally, there is no evidence that contribution to the family economy, in itself, accounts for the superiority of the male role. Aronoff and Crano (1975), in an extensive reanalysis of data from 862 societies, found that women contribute appreciably to the family economy; they account for, on the average, 44% of subsistence production. Sanday (1974) analyzed the relationship between the percentage contribution of women to subsistence and a scaled variable of female status in 12 societies and found a curvilinear relationship. When the percentage contributed by women was either very high or very low, female status was low as defined by (a) the woman's ability to allocate property beyond the domestic unit; (b) the demand for female produce beyond the family unit; (c) participation and membership in female solidarity groups devoted to female political or economic interests. When women contribute as much as men, their status is highest. Unfortunately, Sanday was not able to provide much in the way of explanation for this rather puzzling relationship.

Husband and wife power.   Just as the status of the female in the family varies cross-culturally, it also varies as a function of race and socioeconomic status in our own society. It appears that the man's position in the family unit is initially dependent upon his holding some sort of job (Aldous, 1969b). Husband power was greatest among oriental couples and least among black couples (Centers, Raven, & Rodrigues, 1971). There appears to be an interaction between socioeconomic status and race in at least one study (Aldous, 1969a). In a study of working class black and white husbands from the same census tract, tey found that a working wife decreased the husband's decision-making power in black families, but not in white families. The relationship held even when controls for family size, income, and age of the youngest child were made.

An interactive relationship may also exist between race and parity with respect to female powerlessness. Morris and Sison (1974) found that powerlessness was directly correlated with parity in all but black women in the United States, when the authors simultaneously controlled for age, education, husband's occupation, and family income. They found no difference in powerlessness among all users, users of different methods, and nonusers of contraception. Their data did not support the notion that female powerlessness leads to high fertility through the nonuse of contraception, but the data are compatible with the hypothesis that high parity generates female powerlessness. More research is needed to explain why the same dynamics do not appear to work for both black and white families.

In addition to demographic variables, certain personality variables appear to predict relative power in husbands and wives. Both husbands and wives in husband-dominant families have high authoritarianism scores (Centers et al., 1971).

In addition to demographic variables, certain personality variables appear to predict relative power in husbands and wives. Both husbands and wives in husband-dominant families have high authoritarianism scores (Centers et al., 1971). Wolfe (1959) pointed out that wives in husband-dominant families appear to have a greater need for love and affection than those in wife-dominant families. Tey suggested that if the wife is not seeking emotional support from her husband, she may feel freer to exercise power that stems from other need-resource bases. Wolfe did not note whether the wife's exercise of power might lead to a decrease in the love and support she does receive.

There appears to be an implicit assumption in Blood and Wolfe's (1960) analysis of the husband-wife relationship that emotional needs are asymmetrical, with the wife needing far more than the husband. For example, the authors provided a number of tables on the therapeutic utilization of the husband after a bad day, and also included a subchapter on rationales for bothering the husband. Blood and Wolfe's text, which is one of the most widely used in courses on marriage and the family, also contains quotes such as: "The higher the wife's social status, the more apt she is to turn explicitly to her husband for help in trouble, and the less apt she is to turn her negative feelings against him" (p. 187). No comparable discussion with reference to men's emotional needs was given, possibly because men and women believe that emotional or mental illness of men is a cause for social rejection (Phillips, 1964).

Blood and Wolfe analyzed the family power structure in terms of assets contributed by each of the marital partners. These resources include: monetary income that is mostly contributed by the male; personal attractiveness (mostly female); and the quality of performance in various familial roles, such as parent, companion, housekeeper, and sex partner. The greater the gap between the value to the wife of resources contributed by the husband and the value to the husband of the resources contributed by the wife, the greater is the husband's relative power.

The data discussed above about the changes in power as related to husband's and wife's relative educational, occupational, and social status support this notion. Husband power appears to be greatest after the first child is born but is not yet in school. Wife power also varies inversely with the number of children. Since the wife contributes more resources to the marriage in terms of child care during this period, her power ought to increase rather than decrease. Heer (1963) suggested that it is the value placed on the resources contributed by each spouse from outside the marriage that determines relative power. Gillespie (1971) amplified his position and pointed out that the cards are stacked against the woman's acquiring resources outside the marital situation. In the competition with the wife for power, the husband has most of the advantages in terms of (a) differential socialization, which leads to a statistically documented advantage in achievement; (b) differences in the legal rights given the two parties by marriage; (c) differences in occupational income, status, prestige, etc. The author pointed out that suburbanization strengthens the power of the husband by resulting in loss of ties for the wife and her increased isolation and dependence. Who had control of the family car in the suburban family might be an excellent behavioral index of the relative power of husband and wife.

Power in the family: perception and reality. The question of who has the power in the family is not so easily answered as it may appear to be. A number of recent studies question the methodological basis for the evaluation of the relative power of husbands and wives (Safilios-Rothschild, 1969; Olson, 1969; Gillespie, 1971; Bernard, 1972; Larson, 1974). One of the most influential of these studies has been that of Safilios-Rothschild. Tey pointed out that measures of who makes the decisions within families have been mostly based on wives' answers, with the assumption that there is almost perfect agreement between the answers of husbands and wives. Studies done in both Detroit and Athens revealed extensive disagreements between husbands and wives about who controls the decision-making processes in the family. In 55% of the Detroit sample, there was a serious disagreement as to who was the dominant figure in decision-making. Tey found no clear or consistent pattern distinguishing agreeing from disagreeing couples. However, the greatest amount of disagreement seemed to occur in decisions concerning family finances, changes in the husband's job, and changes in the wife's working status (whether or not she should work).

A recent study by Larson (1974) found that perceptions of family reality varied systematically with both age and sex. Although most respondents perceived their families to have egalitarian power structures, fathers and mothers tended to attribute more power to themselves than to their spouses, while sons and daughters assigned more power to fathers than did either parent. Agreement on a global measure of power existed in only 56% of the families and only 24% agreed about their problem-solving processes. Both Safilios-Rothschild and Larson pointed out that there is no necessary reason for assuming that differential perception of family relationships is not an aspect of family reality. Perceptions of reality may be reality to that perceiver.

Not only may differences in the perception of power exist in the family, but measures used to estimate that power may also have serious methodological flaws. The most common device for analyzing global power—and hence for differentiating families into husband-dominant, wife-dominant, or egalitarian—is a questionnaire developed by Blood and Wolfe (1960), which asks who has the final decision in each of eight areas. These areas are:

1. What job the husband should take.

2. What car should be bought.

3. Whether or not to buy life insurance.

4. Where to go on vacation.

5. What house or apartment to rent or buy.

6. Whether the wife should work or quit work.

7. What doctor to have when someone is ill.

8. How much money the family should spend weekly on food.

The rationale for these questions is that they are representative samples of major decision-making areas. Among the criticisms that Safilios-Rothschild (1969) made is that all decisions are given equal weight, even though all may not have equal importance for the family. Also, some decisions occur less often than others, and no note is taken of the amount of work and time that may be required to carry out the consequences of a particular decision. Data from ter United States sample indicate that husbands perceive all "important" decisions to be made either by themselves or equally by themselves and their wives, and perceive as wife-dominant those tasks that are time-consuming, such as purchasing of food and clothing, interactions with relatives, and of course child-rearing. Tey suggested the development of a measuring instrument to evaluate decisions in terms of the importance attached to each, the frequency with which each is made in the family, and the amount of time consumed in carrying out the decision and the tasks associated with it.

An additional reason for difficulties associated with assessing relative family power is that there are discrepancies between "pen and pencil" or attitude measures of power and behavioral measures (Olson, 1969; Mack, 1974). Olson related self-report data taken from a questionnaire with behavioral data from a family discussion session. Tey presented the couples with real, as opposed to contrived, problems by having them discuss areas where differences between the husband's and the wife's responses were revealed by their questionnaires. Behavioral power was measured in terms of the joint decision reached (which had to be contrary to one expressed by one of the spouses). Tey found no relationship between self-report and behavioral measures of power. Tey also found two sources of perceptual bias in the self-report data. Husbands tended to overestimate actual power and wives to underestimate it. Individuals also predicted less power for themselves than their spouse predicted for them. There was more congruence between the actual and predicted power for wives than for husbands, probably because they predicted less power for themselves and actually possessed less. Authority, in terms of who had the legitimate right to make the decision rather than who was predicted to make it, was strongly related to who actually did make it. Olson's data may indicate that social norms and desirability have more influence upon the actual decision-making process than the participants themselves perceive. Larson (1974) noted that the vast majority of respondents indicate an egalitarian relationship that is the social norm in our society.

Several studies (Kolb & Straus, 1974; Tallman & Miller, 1974) stress a relationship among husband dominance, problem-solving ability, and marital happiness. They suggest that the wife gains power only through the husband's ineffectiveness, and that such wife-dominant families experience much strain. Studies of families where power sharing is based upon ideology and the choice of both spouses, rather than upon the relative weakness of one, will be necessary before a conclusion about the necessity of husband-dominance for marital happiness can be drawn. A recent paper by Raven (Note 6) indicates that such a conclusion would ·be much too simplistic. He finds that very satisfied married couples attribute use of referent power, or power based on satisfaction of the goals of the group (in this case, the married pair), as a large component of the decision-making process, while those few respondents who reported themselves very unsatisfied with the marital relationship indicated that coercive power was used.

Love, marriage, and power.   An·analysis of the way in which men and women treat each other in marriage, in terms of power, may appear to be a very materialistic or Marxist analysis. What, one may ask, about romantic love? Until recently, very few studies of romantic love have been found in the psychological literature. Rubin, however, did an extensive analysis of the topic in his book *Liking and Loving* (1973). He tested a large number of "emotionally involved" pairs on measuring instruments that were designed to discriminate "liking" in the sense of friendship from "love" in the sense of emotional involvement. He found that the love scores of men for their girlfriends and women for their boyfriends were almost identical (Rubin, 1970). However, women liked their boyfriends more than they were liked in return. Women attributed higher evaluations to their partners than men did to their partners on such dimensions as intelligence, good judgment, and leadership potential (power?). No differences in these evaluations appeared when these individuals were ranking their same-sex friends.

Sanday (1974) pointed out that, cross-culturally, there is an association between a balanced division of labor by sex and the absence of romantic love as a basis for marriage. We do not know which way, if either does, this relationship works. Does the ideal of romantic love help to impede women from acquiring power and authority in the public domain? Or does equal participation in the household's economy give men the experience and reinforcement necessary for accepting female capability in other domains? Obviously, relative equality in the economic domain leads to more options for women outside the marriage.

The future of marriage

Traditionally in our society, marriage has been more important to the woman because she possesses fewer alternatives for economic support, cannot find sexual satisfaction outside of marriage as easily as a man, and because the rearing of children has remained her responsibility whether or not the marriage contract endures. Hence, since she perceives fewer options outside the marriage, she must bear the burden of maintaining the relationship if at all possible. Thus, one would expect to find most women acknowledging their "inferiority" and at least verbally assenting to the husband's decision-making power. Until recently, the wife has not dominated the family unless the husband has been relatively weak in some way important to our society, and then she does not appear to have been happy about it. She does not appear to be satisfied with the standard pattern of husband-dominant marriages either, as the figures on the relative physical and mental health of single versus married women indicate. As more and more people recognize that the present high divorce rate may very well apply to them, and that they are likely to be "de-married" during some part of their adult lives, power relations within the family may start to shift. If they do, it will be difficult to determine whether the Women's Liberation Movement is a cause or an effect of this shifting balance.

POWER RELATIONS WITHIN SMALL GROUPS

Status and Leadership

Studies of leadership in small adult groups have usually been limited to sexually homogeneous groups and, in fact, mostly all-male groups. Affiliation rather than leadership is the variable more commonly studied in all-female groups. As Maccoby and Jacklin (1974) stated, very few individuals appear to be endowed with a general personal quality of leadership such that they become leaders of different groups having different objectives. Nevertheless, other things being equal, dominance in a group will be asserted by that person whose formal status assigns tem to leadership. Status characteristics such as sex, age, race, and occupational prestige determine the distribution of participation, influence, and prestige among members of groups. This effect is independent of any prior cultural belief in the relevance of the status characteristic to the task at hand (Berger, Cohen, & Zelditch, 1972). Status characteristics become relevant for all situations except when they are explicitly known to be irrelevant.

Achieved versus Ascribed Status in Small Groups

It was suggested by Maccoby and Jacklin that with continued association in informal groups, the "relative competence of the individual group member in skills that are important to the group's objectives should weigh more heavily, so that whenever a woman group member possesses these skills, her dominance should increase if lack of formal status does not prevent it" (p. 262). Even ignoring the evidence that there is differential evaluation of competence based upon sex and that sexual status may always connote formal status differences, the assumption that groups reevaluate dominance hierarchies on the basis of individual performance may not always be true.

Richardson, Dugan, Gray, and Mayhew (1973) studied the effects of individual expertise on the gaining of behavioral social power within a group. Rather than using confederates who evinced different degrees of task competence, they studied the effect upon the group's decision-making process of expertise shown by various subjects who comprised the group. Since they used either all-male or all-female three-person groups, there is no direct information on the effect of sex on influence. However, they found that very little variation (about 20%) in the group's compliance with a particular subject's solution to a problem was related to that individual's degree of success in previous solutions, as measured by the objective number of points gained by that individual. The number of solutions suggested by an individual was a much stronger predictor of ter influence upon the group. In addition, judgments by group members of the demonstrated expertise of each participant were based on differential contributions rather than demonstrable expertise. Perceived participation is not independent of the status of the participants (Hurwitz, Zander, & Hymovitch, 1968). The contribution of high-status members tends to be overrated, compared to that of low-status members.

A much earlier study by Strodtbeck (1951) on decision-making processes in married couples in three subcultures of the United States (Mormon, general American, and Navaho) shows that the spouse who talked most won the majority of the contested decisions. However, who talked most varied according to subcultural attitudes toward husband or wife dominance in terms of economic, religious, and kinship considerations. Hence, Navaho women won more decisions than Navaho men; Texan men and women were essentially similar, with men slightly favored; and Mormon men won considerably more decisions than Mormon women. Wahrman and Pugh (1972; 1974) also showed that influence upon the group is essentially unrelated to competent or incompetent performance of the particular group member.

Parallels between Male and Female Behavior in Groups

There appear to be two methodologically sound techniques for examining parallels between the behaviors of males and females in groups. One technique is to use the same experimental manipulations with equivalent numbers of all-male and all-female groups. This is the technique most often used to examine male and female behavior in competitive games such as the Prisoner's Dilemma. Studies disagree on which sex is the most cooperative and which sex is the most competitive in these games. Most studies report that men are more cooperative and women more competitive (Swensen, 1973). However, the contrary has also been shown. Sex differences also tend to "wash out" after a number of trials in the situation (Tedeschi, Lesnick, & Gahagan, 1968). Three recent studies have indicated that sex-related differences may be a function of differences in other variables that are highly correlated with gender. Vinacke, Cherulnik, and Lichtman (1970) created groups that were high, medium, or low in accomodative characteristics. Highly accomodative groups of either sex were very much alike in their behavior. High exploitative groups differed, with females more accomodative. However, exploitative males were significantly more exploitative than were exploitative females. Pilisuk, Skolnich, and Overstreet (1968) found that friendliness correlated significantly with cooperation on a Prisoner's Dilemma task for females, but not for males. Hrycenko and Minton (1974) found a relationship between internal locus of control and preference for a high-power position for males, but not females. In fact, internal females indicated a preference for low-power positions. These studies indicate that similar manipulations may have different implications for males and females because of differences in the average occurrence of relevant attitudes. There may be a larger number of females with a particular personality characteristic in a typical sample, and similarly, a larger number of males with a different characteristic.

Status and Power Relationships in Mixed Sex Situations

A more valuable technique for analyzing the effect that status variables have upon the behavior of males and females toward each other is observation of mixed-sex groups. An intensive search of the literature revealed very few studies of this nature. Strodtbeck, James, and Hawkins (1958) studied the behaviors of mixed groups in a simulated jury situation. They assumed that jury deliberation requires the presumption of equality. In addition to the finding that fewer women than expected were chosen as jury foremen, they also found that across all occupational groups, males talked more than females. Perception of relative helpfulness, participation, and influence and satisfaction with various members' performances varied with their status level in society. Strodtbeck et al. (1958) did not indicate if, as one might expect, this criterion also varies with sex. Wiley (1973) varied levels of verbal and nonverbal communication as well as the sex of one's partner in a game setting. Tey found no differences between males and females when no verbal communication was allowed. When mixed-sex dyads were allowed to communicate, however, they became much more cooperative in strategy. In all but one case, the male made the first suggestion of a strategy that assured equity. Wiley's results suggested a "chivalrous" attitude on the part of the men. The proportion of individual cooperative choices was almost 17% greater for men in mixed-sex dyads compared with men in same-sex dyads. The comparable increase for women was only 5%. The appearance of sex-related differences only in mixed-sex interaction may suggest cross-sex reinforcement of the traditional role patterns.

The most intriguing studies on power relationships in the behavior of men and women concern the treatment of a single female in an all-male group. Two recent studies, one experimental and one observational, offer surprisingly similar information in this regard. Wahrman and Pugh (1974) investigated the effect upon male subjects of a female confederate who violated procedural rules in a group problem-solving situation early, in the middle, late, or never in a series of trials. The earlier the female violated the procedural rules, the less her influence upon the group, the more disliked, and the less desirable as a co-worker she became. A previous study with male confederates (Wahrman & Pugh, 1972) showed that his early nonconformity led to increased influence and desirability as a co-worker, but also greater dislike. The best liked of all confederates was the conforming female. Competent nonconforming females were preferred less than incompetent nonconforming males.

Wolman and Frank (1975) studied the role of the lone woman in six small groups, three T-groups and three work groups. All participants were presumably of equal status. They were, in fact, peer groups of graduate students or psychiatric residents. In five of the six small groups, the lone woman became a deviant or isolated member of the group. In one group she managed to acquire low-status regular membership. Attempts by a woman to influence the groups were ignored, while similar attempts made subsequently by a man were heeded and credited to him. If trying to influence the group after having been ignored, a woman received either coordinated reaction against her, or no reaction, typical of the way groups react to deviants and isolates, respectively. Geller, Goodstein, Silver, and Sternberg (1974) found that systematic ignoring of female subjects' participation in a conversation greatly reduced their participation. Instead of leaving or getting angry, the subjects reacted by evaluating themselves and the female confederates less favorably than did those controls who had not been ignored. Here, perhaps, is one of the mechanisms that operate to decrease female participation in group processes, and thus limit their degree of social power.

A few field studies have also investigated the behavior of men and women toward one another. Both Deaux (1971) and Unger et al. (1974) found that women drivers in an apparently stalled car were more likely to be honked at faster than comparable male drivers. Both men and women subjects appeared to discriminate against the female driver. Unger et al. (1974) counterbalanced "deviance" (e.g., hippie attire) with sex in two naturalistic behavioral situations. In addition to the stalled car situation, they examined letting someone get ahead in line as a function of the attire and sex of the confederates and the sex of the subjects. Unlike females who were helped more frequently than males, hippies were helped less often in the on-line situation; and, like females, they were honked at more frequently by both male and female subjects. Of particular interest was a significant three-way interaction between the sex of the subject, the sex of the confederate, and ter attire. Individuals were most apt to discriminate against members of their own sex who were attired in an unconventional manner.

The present author and ter associates attempted to analyze the characteristics of the two situations that produced consistent discrimination against hippies and differential treatment on the basis of sex which was similar to the treatment of hippies in one situation and exactly opposite to their treatment in the other situation. They suggested that the two situations varied in terms of the relative power of females vis-a-vis males. In requesting permission to get ahead in a line, the woman is acting in her traditional role as a dependent person. In the stalled-car condition, she is affirming her status as an equal, who is capable of frustrating others. Doob and Gross (1968) showed in the original stalled automobile study that the readiness to honk one's horn at the objectionable driver appeared to be an inverse function of the status of the car being driven. By extension, females and hippies are honked at more readily because they are low-status individuals. It is difficult to attribute the behavior to social stereotypes, since no stereotype about the poor hippie driver appears to exist.

WOMAN AS DEVIANT

Stigma and Status

In many ways, behavior toward women when they "step out of place" is similar to behavior toward stigmatized individuals. Goffman, in his book *Stigma* (1963), stated that a stigma is a characteristic that can create a situation where "an individual who might have been received easily in orderly social intercourse possesses a trait that can obtrude itself upon attention and turn those of us whom he meets away from him, breaking the claim that his other attributes have upon us." For women, that trait is gender, and the most potent attribute that it affects is competence. The finding that women are favored more than men under some conditions does not disprove the notion that they are stigmatized individuals. Raven (Note 6) pointed to the "power of dependence." Some forms of helplessness are legitimized by society. One helps the blind wayfarer, the crippled beggar, and the stranded female motorist.

Status and Competence

Helping a dependent person neither improves likability nor increases appreciation of ter competence. Lerner and Lichtman (1968) found that while subjects would help a partner who had supposedly asked for help, they would also describe ter as relatively unattractive. Berscheid, Boye, and Walster (1968) also showed that when restitution was not possible, harm-doers would seek to restore psychological equity by justifying the victim's suffering. Subjects who had harmed the victim in some way would derogate tem if the person was powerless to retaliate, but they would not derogate one from whom they anticipated retaliation. They would also not derogate one they had not harmed. A considerable amount of literature on the devaluation of female competence may be explained by this finding, since being a female is evidently a stigma for which retaliation and restitution are not possible.

It must be stressed that global derogation of females as females is not to be found. Women are derogated only when they move out of the position that is expected in our society. A clever projective technique devised by Kent (Note 13) serves to illustrate this point. Tey asked students to complete the following stem story of an actual incident involving humiliation and bystander participation:

> As a second year student in medicine, Jane (John) discovered a new method for measuring blood pressure. She (he) demonstrates her (his) technique to one of her (his) classes. Someone comments 'You sure think you're good' . . .

Although tey is still analyzing ter data, Kent has found that the stories did not contain a single instance of someone coming to Jane's rescue, while in stories with a male protagonist, other students and the teacher did intervene on behalf of John.

Deviance and Competence

The concept of women as deviant individuals is by no means original to this article. To cite just a few behavioral scientists who have maintained this position, the list includes: Hacker (1951) (the earliest of the papers taking this position); Anderson (1973); Walstedt, 1974; Henley and Freeman (1975); Unger (1975); and Sherman (Note 14). What is perhaps new about the position is the idea that such deviance cannot easily be eliminated by competent, capable, and independent behavior by women. Berger et al. (1972), in an important article on status characteristics and social interactions, pointed out that, given two equally irrelevant status characteristics, individuals tend to combine all inconsistent status information rather than reduce its inconsistency. Competence is incompatible with inferior female status. Competent, capable, and independent behavior may be labeled as deviant in a woman rather than cause her status to be similar to that of comparable men. Since other women may "identify with the aggressor," they too will label such behavior as deviant. Since joining in group efforts with other women accentuates the gender, and hence the deviance of competent women, fear of being so labeled may account for the phenomenon known as the "Queen Bee syndrome" (Staines, Tavris, & Jayaratne, 1973). This may account for the finding that women who have achieved a considerable amount of stature in the psychological profession are significantly less likely to join a division on the psychology of women than they are to choose one on a more "neutral" topic such as population (McDevitt & Unger, Note 15).

Gender as a label may produce effects independent of any behavior emitted by the stimulus persons. The studies cited above on attributions of causes of success and failure in men and women are examples of the effects of such labels. In a recent study (Henken, Unger, & Aronow, Note 16), we found that, given the same information on potential group leaders (of course, the names were changed for one-half of the profiles), male and female college students slightly preferred male to female group leaders, regardless of any other information about them. More importantly, females figured predominantly in the category of those they wished least to lead them. The potential female leader possessing the largest number of conventional female characteristics was the least preferred candidate, even though a male with the same characteristics was most preferred. For leadership, at least, gender is a more salient characteristic than are the supposedly sex-appropriate characteristics. Leadership and power are the perogatives of males, even when they are unambitious, sensitive, and nurturant.

Deviance and Group Sanctions

Argyle (1969) pointed out that probably the single most important and widely confirmed generalization about social groups is that they form norms. Deviates from the group make norms more explicit and show other members what happens to those who break them. In addition, those who are lowest in the group in terms of perceived value, popularity, and prestige are most likely to leave it. When there is status incongruence—disparity between the individual's performance within the group, ter status, and the rewards which the group is willing to grant that individual—the group will act to reduce the disparity. Because the norms of our society state that women should not have power over men, their assumption of male perogatives is most easily dismissed as deviant. In terms of a cognitive-dissonance type of interpretation, it is easier to dismiss a particular woman as aggressive, castrating, domineering, etc. than to reevaluate our entire attitudes about male-female relationships.

Social deviance is defined as behavior that violates our institutionalized expectations (Bell, 1971). It is not a property inherent in any particular behavior. It is a property conferred upon that behavior by people who are threatened, embarrassed, or made to feel uncomfortable by it. Thus, behaviors in a woman that are identical to those of men in the same situation may produce a label of deviance, and special sanctions may be brought to bear against her.

Wilman and Frank (1975) provided an interesting typology of techniques used by male groups to deal with a woman who has "stepped out of place." They found that when the group members started to interact, women were not allowed to compete freely for status. Men labeled assertiveness as bitchiness or manipulation, and appeared more threatened by competition with women than with each other. Often, they simply ignored assertive behavior from a woman. When a woman showed feelings or advocated their expression, emotionality became identified as feminine behavior. The sexuality of the female was virtually ignored or joked about. When the women tried to escape their role as isolates or deviants by increasing their number of interactions with others, they were increasingly ignored.

> Many coping mechanisms carry sex-role labels in our culture. If she acted friendly, she was thought to be flirting. If she acted weak, the men tried to infantize her, treating her as a "little sister" rather than a peer. If she apologized for alienating the group, she was seen as a submissive woman knowing her place. If she asked for help, she earned a "needy female" label. If she became angry, or tried to point out rationally what the group process was doing to her, she was seen as competitive, in a bitchy unfeminine way. "Feminine" coping mechanisms increased her perceived differences, "masculine" ones threatened the men so that they isolated her more. Any internal ambivalence about her sexual role was rekindled by these labels, and increased her anxiety, which increased her coping behavior, which further increased her deviance! (Wolman & Frank, 1975, p. 168)

Men who affiliated with the single woman in these groups risked being identified with her and sharing her deviance. Since they had been led to expect that the professions were a male sanctuary, the men presumably resented the presence of a woman and acted to prevent her becoming a regular member so that they could have an almost all-male group. The women tended to give up their efforts after a while, becoming depressed instead. One could almost consider them group casualties. Being a woman seemed to be the single salient rationale for these behaviors.

NEGATIVE EVALUATIONS OF POWER USE

Nonconformity, Influence and Being Liked

Assertiveness in both males and females, although it may produce different outcomes in terms of the ability of the individual to influence the group, may produce similar outcomes in terms of the liking of the group for that individual. Wahrman and Pugh (1972) found that nonconformity by a male early in the group's proceedings increased his ability to influence the group, but also increased the group's disapproval of him. They found that influence is an unreliable indicator of approval, and approval is a poor predictor of influence. Nemeth and Wachtler (1974) found that a male confederate who consistently chose a very deviant proposition in discussions was able to influence a group more when he chose the head seat at a table than if he chose a side seat. He was effective in swaying a majority of the group only when he occupied the head seat, even if he had apparently been assigned to it by the experimenter, rather than choosing it himself.

A lack of relationship between liking and influence was also found in this study. The nonconforming confederate was never liked. He was considered unreasonable, unfair, nonperceptive, cold, uncooperative, unliked, and unwanted. He was also seen, however, as independent, consistent, confident, strong, stable, and able to make others think. Nemeth and Wachtler have not yet repeated their experiment with female nonconformists. Wahrman and Pugh (1974) found that early nonconformity in a female confederate decreased both her effectiveness and likability. It is harder for a member of a low-status group to achieve sufficient status to be permitted to innovate or violate procedural rules. Again, in a study apparently involving men (no data on the sex of subjects is given), Alvarez (1968) found that participants in a simulated work organization will allocate more esteem to a deviant in a managerial position than to one in a worker position.

Sex-typing as Power Typing

An extremely interesting study by Johnson (Note 17) attempted to differentiate between various forms of power that may be used. Tey used the French and Raven (1959) typology of bases of social power, for example:

1. Legitimate power that is based upon the possession of some needed skill or competency which is not possessed by another, such as the doctor-patient relationship.

2. Informational power that is based upon possession of some information needed by another, such as the teacher-student relationship.

3. Referent power that is based upon the need to belong to a group and to further its goals, such as the husband-wife relationship or that between various members of a fraternal organization.

4. Helpless power or the power of dependency that is based upon the social norm of helping those who are unable to help themselves.

Ter data on the stereotypes involving these various power bases are somewhat irrelevant here. However, as tey hypothesized, subjects of both sexes tend to characterize legitimate, expert, and informational power as male, and referent and helpless power as female. When given a choice of which form of power to use, male subjects chose legitimate power significantly more often than did female subjects, and female subjects chose helpless power significantly more often than did males. In fact, males almost never chose to use helpless power, and females almost unanimously rejected the use of expert power.

Of particular interest, in terms of the manner in which use of power is evaluated, is Johnson's finding that users of male power are seen as becoming more powerful, aggressive, cold, and competent than are users of female power. When a woman was the user of male power, however, she was not seen as becoming more competent. Even the use of female forms of power, such as helpless power, seems to have been seen as "pushy." Moreover, the use of this form of power did not increase self-esteem as the use of all other forms of power by both sexes appeared to do. Johnson concluded that although women are socialized to view indirect use of power as more appropriate to women, the consequences of the use of indirect power is that no one else recognizes that power has been used. Indirect power may also be a relatively ineffective way of influencing others and may lead to a further decrease in self-image. Collier (1974), in an anthropological paper in the same vein, pointed out that the efforts of women to use power indirectly, by means of the manipulation of others, may result in breaking up domestic units such as those of parent and child or husband and wife. Such conflicts should not be dismissed as mere "domestic tragedies," but should be viewed as the inevitable result of institutionalized limitations upon other forms of power usage by women.

INSTITUTIONALIZATION OF GENDER DIFFERENTIATION

Coser and Rokoff (1971) provided an interesting analysis of the manner in which gender differences have been institutionalized in the occupational world. For example, replaceability on jobs is defined by institutional fiat rather than by a definition based upon actual task requirements. In the below-college educational establishment, absenteeism is institutionalized by the provision of a substitute teacher. Yet, everyone expects that the substitute will be ineffective, that students will be hostile, and that very little learning will take place. In contrast, the normative ethos in hospital internships and residencies is that of irreplaceability, even though all physicians in training are required to be familiar with all patients. The higher the status of the occupation, the less replaceable is the position occupant. The relationship between occupational status and proportion of women has already been discussed.

In addition, higher-status occupations are expected more frequently to make demands upon their occupants that will cause disruptions in their personal lives. Coser and Rokoff pointed out the paradox between the attitude that women are unacceptable in positions where family commitments might cause disruptions, and the attitude that disruptions are to be taken for granted in high-status occupations. In fact, high-status occupants are often congratulated for bringing honor to their organizations by being wanted elsewhere. Our famous colleagues probably cancel their classes more often than our less famous colleagues. Nevertheless, they may be rewarded by their institutions for deviating from a strict adherence to its demands (Coser, 1966). When individuals in insecure status positions (e.g., women) want to be flexible, they are considered to have arrogated for themselves a freedom to which they have no right. Thus, they may be seen to be aggressive when they make a claim for a status they are not readily granted.

POSSIBLE SOURCES OF DIFFERENCES IN ASCRIPTIVE STATUS BETWEEN THE SEXES

Sex Differences in Aggression

It is well accepted even among those who hold an essentially null-hypothesis view of sex differences between males and females (Maccoby & Jacklin, 1974) that, as young children, males are much more aggressive than females. These differences in overt aggression may disappear with age, but definitive studies are unavailable. It is exceedingly difficult (not to speak of unethical) to set up experiments that involve the infliction of bodily harm upon one individual by another. Self-reports of the use of physical force in the implementation of influence attempts are unlikely to come to the attention of any but the psychotherapist, and then to be dismissed as the aberrant case.

It is noteworthy, therefore, that the use of physical power tactics had been reported to vary with sex (Sutton-Smith & Rosenberg, 1968). Beating up, belting and hitting, wrestling and chasing are ascribed to boys. Scratching and pinching and tackling are ascribed to girls. Exertion of direct physical power by older children upon their younger siblings apparently has a strong effect, as these later-born children are the only ones who score higher on anger, shouting, or yelling. Of all possible birth-gender combinations, only a boy with an older sister perceived himself and was perceived by others as not having to seek outside help. Bigner (1974) found that children who have an older male sibling assign more high-power items to older siblings than do those who have a female older sibling. Gender differentiation with respect to power does not change with the increasing age of the subjects tested (5 through 13 years).

The Role of Body Build

Body build is clearly related to the ability to use physical force effectively. Body build is also a determinant of social status in children of both sexes (Felker, 1972; Johnson & Staffieri, 1971; Lerner & Korn, 1972; Staffieri, 1972). From age five through adulthood, males and females associate the mesomorphic body build with "all things good." Both girls and boys would prefer to have mesomorphic body builds, and boys in particular associate the mesomorph with an assertive, aggressive pattern of behavior (Johnson & Staffieri, 1971). At all ages, human males have a larger percentage of fat-free body weight than do females (Garn, 1966). In relative terms, males are mesomorphs and females are endomorphs.

It is not improbable that the physical structure of male children gives them a significant initial advantage. Later, direct physical force is not usually necessary to maintain status; covert manifestations will do as well. Females from age 6 upward possess smaller territorial boundaries than do males (Aiello & Aiello, 1974). Even as adults, females (but not males) decrease their movements upon intrusion into their territories (Mahoney, 1974). And, although we do not have the data on adults, boys with high social power (but not girls) are seen as more threatening (Zander & Van Egmond, 1958). Covert nonverbal behaviors may provide a source of stimuli for, and reinforcement of, masculine dominance without the awareness of any of the participants.

FUTURE ISSUES FOR SOCIAL SCIENTISTS

Political Implications of Looking at Power rather than Sex Differences

A primary requisite is an investigation of the conditions under which gender/ status correspondence is not maintained. Janeway (1974), in a beautifully written chapter on power, suggested that the statement about its being a man's world is misleading: "As always the world belongs to the powerful, and though, almost universally, the powerful are male, we can't reverse that statement. Males are not almost universally powerful" (p. 187). She pointed out that sex typing and limitations of power are not the same thing. The fact that men are interested in sports and women in recipes and fashion is a product of sex differences in socialization, but neither of these activities has anything to do with the exercise of power. She suggested a new phrase: "The weak are the second sex," . . . and said that it is equating weakness with femininity that underlies a great deal of masculine reaction to a redefinition of women's roles. A step up for women may be seen as a step down for men to an inferior level, women's level. The division by sex of the world's population allies both weak and powerful males by means of anatomy. If that alliance is destroyed and the men who stand outside the elite are equated with women, they may fear that they will be treated like women, as objects or "others"; not the doers, but the done-to.

As social scientists, we need to explicate the strong relationship between low status/power, and feminine characteristics and occupations. Does femininity automatically confer low status, or do women exhibit "feminine" characteristics because of their low status? If the former is largely true, as is argued in this article, then changing sex roles will not be enough. A change in the variables that produce and maintain status asymmetry between the sexes will also be necessary.

Reducing Gender/Status Correspondence

If sex relationships are indeed based upon power relationships, one might hypothesize that sex-related differences will decrease if individuals continue to associate with each other. As the group continues to interact, differences in performance now become evident. As yet, there are few data on producing status equality between men and women. Therefore, analogies will have to be made with other groups who are also subject to ascribed status inferiority (e.g., blacks and the young). Freese and Cohen (1973) and Freese (1974), using age as their ascribed variable, found that status inequity will be reduced when group members are exposed to an increasing number of status unequals who possess characteristics that contradict status expectations and whose characteristics are similar to, but not explicitly relevant to those required in group tasks. Cohen and Roper (1973), using race as an ascribed variable, however, pointed out that unless expectations for competence held by both the low- and high-status group are restructured, the high-status group will continue to dominate. Their strongest treatment involved spelling out the relevance of the training task to the criterion game. The results of expectation training, in their study, lowered the task initiation rate of the high-status group as well as increased the rate of members of the low-status group. By analogy, treating the expectations and behaviors of women only, perhaps by assertiveness training, may be ineffective.

What are the assumptions underlying power relationships? Most studies of power have implied a zero-sum situation. Both experimenters and participants have assumed that if one party in a transaction gains influence, the other(s) must lose it. Assumptions that power always involves a zero-sum outcome may generate a self-fulfilling prophecy unless one talks about it explicitly (Laws, Note 18). Situations in which increase in the power of females leads to an increase in access to external resources for both the male and female participant need to be studied. Such a situation would appear to be analogous to a "liberated" marriage.

The Effect of Behavior on the Attribution of Status

Analogies between women and other groups that are subject to low-status ascriptions may .be weakened by the fact that women are the only so-called marginal group that engages in close, daily contact with their "superiors." Presumably, there has been plenty of opportunity for incongruities between performance and status to be observed. Nevertheless, all the data on the relationship between gender and ascriptions of competence, and on the persistence of sex-role stereotyping, would indicate that little change has taken place. Johnson's (Note 17) work on differential use of power by men and women seems to indicate that women engage in behaviors that "feed" attributions about their relative weakness, lack of power, and so forth. However, assertive behavior results in attribution of deviance. Is this another "double bind" situation for women?

One would expect that the choice of behaviors, particularly with reference to behaviors designed to influence others, would be tailored to be most effective in producing the desired effect. Men may continue to choose expert power in order to maintain continued dependent attitudes in women, and women may choose helpless power so as to acquiesce to their dependent status. Women and men may also engage in sex-typed uses of power because they distrust the responses of others if they deviate from them. A vicious cycle ensues in which role expectations produce behaviors that confirm role expectations. It is particularly difficult to break out of this cycle because many of these behaviors are covert and are performed without the awareness of the participants. Many of these behaviors remain to be explicated and their origins and sources of reinforcement explored.

The Effect of Social Norms upon the Attribution of Status

The relatively unexplored role of societal pressure is highlighted by two recent studies. Starer and Denmark (1974) found that the supposed productions of women, as contrasted to those supposedly by men, received lower evaluations by women and equivalent evaluations by men when evaluated in private. In public, however, women evaluated the women's poems more highly and men evaluated them at lesser value. An effect upon gender-related behavior of social expectancies about supposed observers was also found by Borden (1975). Tey found that male subjects observed by a man aggressed more in an experimental situation than did those observed by a woman. These effects of the gender of the observer disappeared when their value system as related to pacificism-aggression was made explicit to the subjects.

Since studies rarely vary the social milieu of the evaluation situation or the effect of its demand characteristics, it is difficult to determine how many put-downs of females are due to the desire to behave according to social expectations rather than intraphsychic attitudes. Unfortunately, it is easier to find subjects who show sexist attitudes than to find those who do not. Studies such as that of Goldberg (1974) indicate that sexism is an almost universal phenomenon that is not particularly related to any other prejudice scales. We need to find out what role misogyny plays in our society and how it is socially mediated. Particularly worthy of investigation are those individuals who do *not* show sexist attitudes. What demographic and/or psychological variables account for these rarities?

The Effect of Violation of Status Assumptions

We need to reconsider our notions about deviance and its consequences. Wahrman and Pugh (1972) pointed out that sociologists tend to take for granted that deviant behavior, regardless of the status of the actor, speaks for itself, the problematic issue being whether or not the group will somehow be prevented from sanctioning the deviant. Psychologists, on the other hand, consider problematic whether high-status nonconformity can be considered deviance, but assume that if behavior is labeled deviant, then overt sanctions will automatically appear. We need systematic study of the operational definition of deviance, especially taking into account the male and female reference groups that differ in achieved and ascribed status. What happens when gender and status information are contradictory? For example, are low-status men treated, and do they behave, like women in group situations? A particularly critical study is the treatment of low-status males in a group of high-status women.

The Social Function of Ascriptive Status

Why is it that social positions are assigned on grounds other than performance capability? Kemper (1974) took the stimulating heuristic position that since power and status are alternative relational modes of obtaining benefits from others, individuals who have the means to obtain benefits by coercive means will attempt to convert a power relationship into a status relationship so that the benefits obtained will be given voluntarily. Tey suggested that the principle for ascriptive differentiation is the distribution of power. When those who have less power accept the legitimacy of receiving lesser rewards for participation in social life, the possibility of performance competition or an out-and-out struggle where there is a victor and a vanquished is decreased. Use of ascriptive categories as opposed to achievement categories has sometimes been described as "cheap." However, it is cheap only for the higher categories on the scale. It is definitely not cheap for the lower categories who pay a large intrapsychic as well as social penalty for the ease with which decisions about differential rewards are made. Assuming Kemper's model is correct for the explication of relationships between males and females in our society, what mechanisms reinforce the conversion of power into status relationships on a personal level? In particular, what mechanisms maintain female sanctions against achieving women?

Social scientists have taken the concept of male authority for granted. Female authority has been regarded as the deviant case due to the inadequacy of the relevant males. Changes in the structure of marriage among some subgroups of the population may make available for study the male-female relationships that involve the voluntary abrogation of power by the male. That they have thus far been regarded of little interest may be another example of social science's inability to separate itself from its culture. So-called liberated marriages have been treated as aberrant, passing phenomena. However, they are worth studying, not only in terms of their effects upon the participants and their children, but also in terms of their effects upon society. An interesting question applied to these cases might be: What are the limits that society will accept in the disruption of the status/gender identity?

New Roles for Social Scientists

It might be helpful to examine ourselves as scientists to see why so little material on status/gender correspondence is available and why so much of the relevant information is of extremely recent origin. We might consider the dearth of empirical studies as a form of cultural inurement. Certain variables, especially those involving the use of explicit or implicit coercion of others, have not been regarded as relevant to women as actors. And, we have even been reluctant to examine the effects upon women as the acted-upon. At the most extreme end of this continuum has been the scarcity of controlled studies upon the phenomenon of rape and its victims.

This author believes that although some of the neglect of these issues has been due to a culturally socialized lack of awareness of them, more of the neglect may be due to the reluctance of "respectable" scientists of either gender to engage in studies that have implications of advocacy. In this area, it is extremely difficult to divorce the consequences of research from the research itself. And, we have been taught that science is objective and unbiased. Examination of the subject of gender, power, and status shows, however, that issues have been ignored because of covert "masculinist" biases. Bias does not necessarily imply the lack of ability to be objective. If others are not unwilling to accept the label of "Skinnerian," "Hullian," or "Piagetian," why should we be unwilling to accept the label of "feminist"—a new way of looking at and reordering the field of psychology? A valuable contribution of feminist psychology is not only the emphasis upon gender as an important stimulus as well as a subject variable in all areas of psychology, but also the delimitation of relationships relevant to both sexes that have been obscured by the limitation of research to just one. The relationships among gender, status, and power are certainly pertinent to productive scientific research and, more importantly, are essential constituents of psychologists' insights into the commonalities as well as the conflicts between the sexes.

CONCLUSION

Since a vast amount of data are compressed into this article, I would like to emphasize the following highlights:

1. Power asymmetries between the sexes are all-pervasive.

2. Such power differences are highly correlated with status differences.

3. Treatment of the gender with low ascribed status, women, parallels the treatment of low-status individuals under all conditions examined.

4. The behavior of males and females toward each other is based upon this difference in relative status. Three areas are investigated in detail: nonverbal behaviors, husband-wife relationships, and small-group behavior.

5. Performance differences do not easily eliminate sex-related differences in ascribed status because of differential perception of competent performance on the basis of gender.

6. Assertion of competence and power by a female is regarded as deviant behavior so that she becomes the recipient of social sanctions.

7. Gender/status identity is institutionalized by our society.

8. Difficulties involved in the change of gender/status identity are examined with particular reference to the role of social scientists in the investigation of this problem.

REFERENCE NOTES

1. McKenna, W., & Kessler, S.J. Experimental design as a source of sex bias in social psychology. Paper presented at the meeting of the American Psychological Association, New Orleans, August, 1974.
2. Prescott, S., & Foster, K. Why researchers don't study women. Paper presented at the meeting of the American Psychological Association, New Orleans, August, 1974.
3. Keasey, C.B., & Tomlinson-Keasey, C.I. Social influence in a high-ego-involvement situation: A field study of petition signing. Paper presented at the meeting of the Eastern Psychological Association, New York City, April, 1971.
4. Barnett, R. The relationship between occupational preference and occupational prestige: A study of sex differences and age trends. Paper presented at the meeting of the Eastern Psychological Association, Washington, D.C., April, 1973.
5. Hagen, R.L., & Kahn, A. Discrimination against competent women. Manuscript submitted for publication, 1974.
6. Raven, B.H. Power relations in home and school. Paper presented at the meeting of the Western Psychological Association, San Francisco, May, 1974.
7. Vaughter, R., Gubernick, D., Matossian, J., & Haslett, B. Sex differences in academic expectations and achievement. Paper presented at the meeting of the American Psychological association, New Orleans, August, 1974.
8. Perino, S., & Krooth, D. Sex-role orientation and perceived IQ as factors in marital adjustment for a selected sample of high intelligence couples. Unpublished manuscript, Hofstra University, 1974.
9. Zimbardo, P.G., & Meadow, W. Sexism springs eternal in the Reader's Digest. Paper presented at the meeting of the Western Psychological Association, San Francisco, May, 1974.

10. Adler, L.L. Interpersonal distance as a function of task difficulty, praise, status orientation, and sex of partner. Paper presented at the meeting of the Eastern Psychological Association, Washington, D.C., April, 1973.
11. Ellyson, S.L. Visual interaction in dyads with legitimate power differences. Paper presented at the meeting of the Eastern Psychological Association, Philadelphia, April, 1974.
12. Kantor, E. Sex differences in cue observations and inferences in person perception. Manuscript submitted for publication, 1976.
13. Kent, M. Higher education and gender role socialization. Paper presented to the American Association of University Women, Washington, D.C., 1974.
14. Sherman, J. Social values, femininity and the development of female competence. Psi Chi invited address, Eastern Psychological Association, Philadelphia, April, 1974.
15. McDevitt, M., & Unger, R.K. Investigation of the Queen Bee phenomenon in a professional population. Presented at the meeting of the Eastern Psychological Association, New York City, April, 1975.
16. Henken, V., Unger, R.K., & Aronow, F. Gender and social deviance: A rose by any other name is not a rose. Manuscript submitted for publication, 1976.
17. Johnson, P. Social power and sex-role stereotypes. Paper presented at the meeting of the Western Psychological Association, San Francisco, May, 1974.
18. Laws, J.L. Personal communication at the conference, "New Directions for Research on Women," Madison, Wisconsin, June 1, 1975.

REFERENCES

Aiello, J.R., & Aiello, T.D. The development of personal space: Proxemic behavior of children six through sixteen. *Human Ecology*, 1974, *2*, 177-189.

Aldous, J. Wives' employment status and lower-class men as husband-fathers: Support for the Moynihan thesis. *Journal of Marriage and the Family*, 1969, *31*, 469-476. (a)

Aldous, J. Occupational characteristics and males' role performance in the family. *Journal of Marriage and the Family*, 1969, *31*, 707-712. (b)

Alkire, A.A., Collum, M.E., Kaswan, J., & Love, L.R. Information exchange and accuracy of verbal communication under social power conditions. *Journal of Personality and Social Psychology*, 1968, *9*, 301-308.

Allen, V.L. Situational factors in conformity. In L. Berkowitz (Ed.), *Advances in experimental social psychology* (Vol. 2). New York: Academic Press, 1965.

Alvarez, R. Informal reactions to deviance in simulated work organizations: A laboratory experiment. *American Sociological Review,* 1968, *33,* 895-912.

Amir, M. *Patterns in forcible rape.* Chicago: University of Chicago Press, 1971.

Anderson, J.V. Psychological determinants. In R.B. Kundsin (Ed.), *Successful women in the sciences: An analysis of determinants.* New York: New York Academy of Sciences, 1973.

Argyle, M. *Social interaction.* New York: Atherton Press, 1969.

Aronoff, J., & Crano, W.D. A re-examination of the cross-cultural principles of task segregation and sex-role differentiation in the family. *American Sociological Review,* 1975, *40,* 12-20.

Bandura, A., Ross, D., & Ross, S.A. A comparative test of the status envy, social power and secondary reinforcement theories of identification learning. *Journal of Abnormal and Social Psychology,* 1963, *67,* 529-534.

Barry, W.A. Marriage research and conflict: An integrative review. *Psychological Bulletin,* 1970, *73,* 41-54.

Bell, R.R. *Social deviance.* Homewood, Ill.: The Dorsey Press, 1971.

Bem, S.L., & Bem, D.J. Training the woman to know her place: The power of a nonconscious ideology. In D.J. Bem (Ed.), *Beliefs, attitudes and human affairs.* Belmont, Calif.: Brooks-Cole Publishing Co., 1970.

Berger, J., Cohen, B.P., & Zelditch, M., Jr. Status characteristics and social interaction. *American Sociological Review,* 1972, *37,* 241-255.

Bernard, J. *The future of marriage.* New York: World Publishing Co., 1972.

Berscheid, E., Boye, D., & Walster, E. Retaliation as a means for restoring equity. *Journal of Personality and Social Psychology,* 1968, *10,* 370-376.

Bigner, J.J. Second-borns' discrimination of sibling role concepts. *Developmental Psychology,* 1974, *10,* 564-573.

Blood, R.O., Jr., & Wolfe, D.M. *Husbands and wives.* New York: The Free Press, 1960.

Borden, R.J. Witnessed aggression: Influence of an observer's sex and values on aggressive responding. *Journal of Personality and Social Psychology,* 1975, *31,* 567-573.

Broverman, J.K., Vogel, S.R., Broverman, D.M., Clarkson, F.E., & Rosenkrantz, P.S. Sex-role stereotypes: A current reappraisal. *Journal of Social Issues,* 1972, *28,* 59-78.

Brown, R., & Gilman, A. The pronouns of power and solidarity. In T.A. Sebeck (Ed.), *Style in language.* Cambridge, Mass.: Technology Press, 1960.

Brownmiller, S. *Against our will: Men, women and rape.* New York: Simon & Schuster, 1975.

Centers, R., Raven, B.H., & Rodrigues, A. Conjugal power structure: A re-examination. *American Sociological Review,* 1971, *36,* 264-278.

Cohen, E.G., & Roper, S.S. Modification of interracial interaction disability: An application of status characteristic theory. *American Sociological Review,* 1973, *37,* 643-657.

Collier, J.F. Women in politics. In M.Z. Rosaldo and L. Lamphere (Eds.), *Woman, culture and society.* Stanford, Calif.: Stanford University Press, 1974.

Coser, R.L. Role distance, sociological ambivalence and transituational status systems. *American Journal of Sociology,* 1966, *72,* 173-187.

Coser, R.L., & Rokoff, G. Women in the occupational world: Social disruption and conflict. *Social Problems,* 1971, *18,* 535-554.

Deaux, K.K. Honking at the intersection: A replication and extension. *Journal of Social Psychology,* 1971, *84,* 159-160.

Deaux, K.K. To err is humanizing, but sex makes a difference. *Representative Research in Social Psychology,* 1972, *3,* 20-28.

Deaux, K.K., & Emswiller, T. Explanations of successful performance on sex-linked tasks: What is skill for the male is luck for the female. *Journal of Personality and Social Psychology,* 1974, *29,* 80-85.

Deaux, K.K., & Taynor, J. Evaluation of male and female ability: Bias works both ways. *Psychological Reports,* 1973, *32,* 261-262.

Dion, K.K., & Berscheid, E. Physical attractiveness and peer perception among children. *Sociometry,* 1974, *37,* 1-12.

Dohrenwend, B.D. Social status and stressful life events. *Journal of Personality and Social Psychology,* 1973, *28,* 225-235.

Doob, A.N., & Gross, A.E. Status of frustrator as an inhibitor of horn-honking responses. *Journal of Social Psychology,* 1968, *76,* 213-218.

Edney, J.J., & Jordan-Edney, N.L. Territorial spacing on a beach. *Sociometry,* 1974, *37,* 92-104.

Efran, J.S. Looking for approval: Effects on visual behavior of approbation from persons differing in importance. *Journal of Personality and Social Psychology,* 1968, *10,* 21-25.

Etaugh, C., & Sanders, S. Evaluation of performance as a function of status and sex variables. *Journal of Social Psychology,* 1974, *94,* 237-241.

Exline, R.V. Explorations in the process of person perception: Visual interaction in relation to competition, sex and need for affiliation. *Journal of Personality,* 1963, *31,* 1-20.

Exline, R.V., Gray, D., & Schuette, D. Visual behavior in a dyad as affected by interview context and sex of respondent. *Journal of Personality and Social Psychology*, 1965, *1*, 201-209.

Farrell, W. *The liberated man*. New York: Random House, 1974.

Feather, N.T. Positive and negative reactions to male and female success and failure in relation to the perceived status and sex-typed appropriateness of occupations. *Journal of Personality and Social Psychology*, 1975, *31*, 536-548.

Feather, N.T., & Simon, J.G. Reactions to male and female success and failure in sex-linked occupations: impressions of personality, causal attributions and perceived likelihood of different consequences. *Journal of Personality and Social Psychology*, 1975, *31*, 20-31.

Feldman-Summers, S., & Kiesler, S.B. Those who are number two try harder: The effect of sex on attributions of causality. *Journal of Personality and Social Psychology*, 1974, *30*, 846-855.

Felker, D.W. Social stereotyping of male and female body types with differing facial expressions by elementary-school-age boys and girls. *Journal of Psychology*, 1972, *82*, 151-154.

Felson, M., & Knoke, D. Social status and the married woman. *Journal of Marriage and the Family*, 1974, *36*, 516-521.

Freese, L.. Conditions for status equality in informal task groups. *Sociometry*, 1974, *37*, 174-188.

Freese, L., & Cohen, B.P. Eliminating status generalization. *Sociometry*, 1973, *36*, 177-193.

French, J.R.P., Jr., & Raven, B. The basis of social power. In D. Cartwright (Ed.), *Studies in social power*. Ann Arbor: Institute for Social Research, 1959.

Frieze, I.H., Fisher, J., McHugh, M.C., & Valle, V.A. Attributing the causes of success and failure: Internal and external barriers to achievement in women. In J. Sherman and F.L. Denmark (Eds.). *Psychology of women: New directions for research*. New York: Psychological Dimensions Inc., 1977.

Fromme, D.K., & Beam, D.C. Dominance and sex difference in nonverbal responses to differential eye contact. *Journal of Research in Personality*, 1974, *8*, 76-87.

Garn, S.M. Body size and its implications. In L.W. Hoffman and M.L. Hoffman (Eds.), *Review of child development research* (Vol. 2). New York: Russell Sage, 1966.

Geller, D.M., Goodstein, L., Silver, M., & Sternberg, W.C. On being ignored: The effects of violations of implicit rules of social interaction. *Sociometry,* 1974, *37,* 541-556.

Gillespie, D. Who has the power?: The marital struggle. *Journal of Marriage and the Family,* 1971, *33,* 445-458.

Goffman, E. *Stigma.* Englewood Cliffs, N.J.: Prentice-Hall, 1963.

Goldberg, P.A. Are women prejudiced against women? *Transaction,* 1968, *5,* 28-30.

Goldberg, P.A. Prejudice toward women: Some personality correlates. *International Journal of Group Tensions,* 1974, *4,* 53-63.

Goldberg, P.A., Gottesdiener, M., & Abramson, P.R. Another put-down of women? Perceived attractiveness as a function of support for the feminist movement. *Journal of Personality and Social Psychology,* 1975, *32,* 113-115.

Griffin, S. Rape: The all-American crime. *Ramparts,* 1971, *10,* 26-35.

Gruder, C.L., & Cook, T.D. Sex, dependency, and helping. *Journal of Personality and Social Psychology,* 1971, *19,* 290-294.

Hacker, H.M. Women as a minority group. *Social Forces,* 1951, *30,* 60-69.

Harris, M.B., & Bays, G. Altruism and sex roles. *Psychological Reports,* 1973, *32,* 1002.

Heer, D.M. Husband and wife perceptions of family power structure. *Marriage and Family Living,* 1962, *24,* 65-67 (a).

Heer, D.M. The measurement and bases of family power: An overview. *Marriage and Family Living,* 1963, *25,* 133-139 (b).

Henley, N.M. Status and sex: Some touching observations. *Bulletin of the Psychonomic Society,* 1973, *2,* 91-93.

Henley, N.M., & Freeman, J. The sexual politics of interpersonal behavior. In J. Freeman (Ed.), *Women: A feminist perspective.* Palo Alto: Mayfield Publishing Co., 1975.

Heshka, S., & Nelson, Y. Interpersonal speaking distance as a function of age, sex, and relationship. *Sociometry,* 1972, *35,* 491-498.

Hoffman, L.R. Group problem-solving. In L. Berkowitz (Ed.), *Advances in experimental social psychology* (Vol. 2). New York: Academic Press, 1965.

Howard, W., & Crano, W.D. Effects of sex, conversation, location, and size of observer group on bystander intervention in a high risk situation. *Sociometry,* 1974, *37,* 491-507.

Hrycenko, I., & Minton, H.L. Internal-external control, power position, and satisfaction in task-oriented groups. *Journal of Personality and Social Psychology,* 1974, *30,* 871-878.

Hurwitz, J.I., Zander, A.F., & Hymovitch, B. Some effects of power on the relations among group members. In D. Cartwright & A. Zander (Eds.), *Group dynamics.* New York: Harper and Row, 1968.

Janeway, E. *Between myth and morning: Women awakening.* New York: Morrow, 1974.

Johnson, P.A., & Staffieri, J.R. Stereotypic affective properties of personal names and somatotypes in children. *Developmental Psychology,* 1971, *5,* 176.

Kemper, T.D. On the nature and purpose of ascription. *American Sociological Review,* 1974, *39,* 844-853.

Kinzel, A.S. Body-buffer zone in violent prisoners. *American Journal of Psychiatry,* 1970, *127,* 59-64.

Kleck, R.E., & Rubenstein, C. Physical attractiveness, perceived attitude similarity, and interpersonal attraction in an opposite-sex encounter. *Journal of Personality and Social Psychology,* 1975, *31,* 107-114.

Kolb, T.M., & Straus, M.A. Marital power and marital happiness in relation to problem-solving ability. *Journal of Marriage and the Family,* 1974, *36,* 756-766.

Komarovsky, M. *Blue-collar marriage.* New York: Random House, 1964.

Krebs, D.L. Altruism: An examination of the concept and a review of the literature. *Psychological Bulletin,* 1970, *73,* 258-302.

Krebs, D.L., & Adinolfi, A.A. Physical attractiveness, social relations, and personality style. *Journal of Personality and Social Psychology,* 1975, *31,* 245-253.

Kutner, N.G., & Brogan, D. An investigation of sex-related slang vocabulary and sex-role orientation among male and female university students. *Journal of Marriage and the Family,* 1974, *36,* 474-484.

Larson, L.E. System and subsystem perception of family roles. *Journal of Marriage and the Family,* 1974, *36,* 123-138.

Latane, B., & Dabbs, J.M., Jr. Sex, group size and helping in three cities. *Sociometry,* 1975, *38,* 180-194.

Leibman, M. The effects of sex and race norms on personal space. *Environment and Behavior,* 1970, *2,* 208-246.

Lerner, M.J., & Lichtman, R.R. Effects of perceived norms on attitudes and altruistic behavior toward a dependent other. *Journal of Personality and Social Psychology,* 1968, *9,* 226-232.

Lerner, R.M., & Korn, S.J. The development of body-build stereotypes in males. *Child Development,* 1972, *43,* 908-920.

Lippitt, R., Polansky, N., Redl, F., & Rosen, S.The dynamics of power: A field study of social influence in groups of children. In E. Maccoby, T. Newcomb, and E. Hartley (Eds.), *Readings in social psychology.* New York: Holt, Reinhart and Winston, 1958.

Lott, D.F., & Sommer, R. Seating arrangements and status. *Journal of Personality and Social Psychology,* 1967, *7,* 90-95.

Maccoby, E.E., & Jacklin, C.N. *The psychology of sex differences.* Stanford: Stanford University Press, 1974.

Mack, D. The power relationship in black families and white families. *Journal of Personality and Social Psychology,* 1974, *30,* 409-413.

Mahoney, E.R. Compensatory reactions to spatial immediacy. *Sociometry,* 1974, *37,* 423-431.

McGinnies, E., Nordholm, L.A., Ward, C.D., & Bhanthumnavin, D.L. Sex and cultural differences in perceived locus of control among students in five countries. *Journal of Consulting and Clinical Psychology*, 1974, *42*, 451-455.

Mehrabian, A. Inference of attitude from the posture, orientation and distance of a communicator. *Journal of Consulting and Clinical Psychology*, 1968, *32*, 296-308. (a)

Mehrabian, A. Relationship of attitude to seated posture, orientation, and distance. *Journal of Personality and Social Psychology*, 1968, *10*, 26-30. (b)

Mehrabian, A. Significance of posture and position in the communication of attitude and status relationships. *Psychological Bulletin*, 1969, *71*, 359-372.

Mehrabian, A., & Friar, J.T. Encoding of attitude by a seated communicator via posture and position cues. *Journal of Clinical and Consulting Psychology*, 1969, *33*, 330-336.

Monahan, L., Kuhn, D., & Shaver, P. Intrapsychic versus cultural explanations of the "fear of success" motive. *Journal of Personality and Social Psychology*, 1974, *29*, 60-64.

Morris, N.M., & Sison, B.S. Correlates of female powerlessness: Parity, methods of birth control, pregnancy. *Journal of Marriage and the Family*, 1974, *36*, 708-712.

Nemeth, C., & Wachtler, J. Creating the perceptions of consistency and confidence: A necessary condition for minority influence. *Sociometry*, 1974, *37*, 529-540.

Nesbitt, P.D., & Steven, G. Personal space and stimulus intensity in a Southern California amusement park. *Sociometry*, 1974, *37*, 105-115.

Olson, D.H. The measurement of family power by self-report and behavioral measures. *Journal of Marriage and the Family*, 1969, *31*, 545-550.

Parsons, T. Age and sex in the social structure of the United States. *American Sociological Review*, 1942, *7*, 604-620.

Pheterson, G.J., Kiesler, S.B., & Goldberg, P.A. Evaluation of the performance of women as a function of their sex, achievement and personal history. *Journal of Personality and Social Psychology*, 1971, *19*, 114-118.

Phillips, D. Rejection of the mentally ill: The influence of behavior and sex. *American Sociological Review*, 1964, *29*, 679-687.

Pilisuk, M., Skolnick, P., & Overstreet, E. Predicting cooperation from the two sexes in a conflict situation. *Journal of Personality and Social Psychology*, 1968, *10*, 35-43.

Pleck, J.H. Male threat from female competence. *Journal of Clinical and Consulting Psychology*. In press.

Pollis, N.P., & Doyle, D.C. Sex role, status, and perceived competence among first-graders. *Perceptual and Motor Skills,* 1972, *34,* 235-238.

Radloff, L. Sex differences in depression: The effects of occupation and marital status. *Sex Roles,* 1975, *1,* 249-265.

Raymond, B.J., & Unger, R.K. The apparel oft proclaims the man: Cooperation with deviant and conventional youths. *Journal of Social Psychology,* 1972, *87,* 75-82.

Richardson, J.T., Dugan, J.R., Gray, L.N., & Mayhew, B.H. Expert power: A behavioral interpretation. *Sociometry,* 1973, *36,* 302-324.

Rokeach, M., & Mezei, L. Race and shared belief as factors in social choice. *Science,* 1966, *151,* 167-172.

Rubin, Z. Measurement of romantic love. *Journal of Personality and Social Psychology,* 1970, *16,* 265-273.

Rubin, Z. *Liking and loving.* New York: Holt, Rinehart and Winston, 1973.

Safilios-Rothschild, C. Family sociology or wives' family sociology? A cross-cultural examination of decision-making. *Journal of Marriage and the Family,* 1969, *31,* 290-301.

Sanday, P.R. Female status in the public domain. In M.Z. Rosaldo and L. Lamphere (Eds.), *Woman, culture and society.* Stanford: Stanford University Press, 1974.

Schopler, J. Social power. In L. Berkowitz (Ed.), *Advances in experimental social psychology* (Vol. 2). New York: Academic Press, 1965.

Sherif, M., & Sherif, C.W. *Social psychology.* New York: Harper & Row, 1969.

Sherman, J. The Coatlicue complex: A source of irrational responses against women. *Transactional Analysis Journal,* 1975, *5,* 188-192.

Sommer, R. *Personal space: The behavioral basis of design.* Englewood Cliffs, N.J.: Prentice-Hall, 1969.

Spence, J.T., & Helmreich, R. Who likes competent women? Competence, sex-role congruence of interests, and subjects' attitudes toward women as determinants of interpersonal attraction. *Journal of Applied Social Psychology,* 1972, *2,* 197-213.

Spence, J.T., Helmreich, R., & Stapp, J. Likability, sex-role congruence of interest and competence: It all depends on how you ask. *Journal of Applied Social Psychology,* 1975, *5.*

Spreitzer, E., & Riley, L.E. Factors associated with singlehood. *Journal of Marriage and the Family,* 1974, *36,* 533-542.

Staffieri, J.R. Body build and behavioral expectancies in young females. *Developmental Psychology,* 1972, *6,* 125-127.

Staines, G., Tavris, C., & Jayaratne, T.E. The Queen Bee syndrome. In C. Tavris (Ed.), *The female experience.* Del Mar, Calif.: CRM Inc., 1973.

Starer, R., & Denmark, F. Discrimination against aspiring women. *International Journal of Group Tensions,* 1974, *4,* 65-70.

Strodtbeck, F.L. Husband-wife interaction over revealed differences. *American Sociological Review,* 1951, *16,* 468-473.

Strodtbeck, F.L., James, R.M., & Hawkins, C. Social status in jury deliberations. In E.E. Maccoby, T. Newcomb, and E. Hartley (Eds.), *Readings in social psychology.* New York: Holt, Rinehart and Winston, 1958.

Sutton-Smith, B., & Rosenberg, B.G. Sibling consensus of power tactics. *Journal of Genetic Psychology,* 1968, *112,* 63-72.

Swensen, C.H., Jr. *Introduction to interpersonal relations.* Glenview, Ill.: Scott, Foresman, 1973.

Tallman, I., & Miller, G. Class differences in family problem solving:The effects of verbal ability, hierarchical structure and role expectations. *Sociometry,* 1974, *37,* 13-37.

Taylor, S.P., & Egstein, S. Aggression as a function of the interaction of the sex of the aggressor and the sex of the victim. *Journal of Personality,* 1967, *35,* 474-486.

Tedeschi, J., Lesnick, S., & Gahagan, J. Feedback and "washout" effects in the prisoner's dilemma game. *Journal of Personality and Social Psychology,* 1968, *10,* 31-34.

Thibault, J.W., & Kelley, H.H. *The social psychology of groups.* New York: Wiley, 1959.

Touhey, J.C. Effects of additional women professionals on ratings of occupational prestige and desirability. *Journal of Personality and Social Psychology,* 1974, *29,* 86-89.

Tuddenham, R.D., Macbride, P., & Zahn, V. The influence of sex composition of the group upon yielding to a distorted norm. *Journal of Psychology,* 1958, *46,* 243-251.

Unger, R.K. *Sex-role stereotypes revisited.* New York: Harper & Row, 1975.

Unger, R.K., Raymond, B.J., & Levine, S.M. Are women a minority group? Sometimes! *International Journal of Group Tensions,* 1974, *4,* 71-81.

Unger, R.K., & Siiter, R. Sex-role stereotypes: The weight of a "grain of truth". In R.K. Unger (Ed.), *Sex Role Stereotypes Revisited.* New York: Harper & Row, 1975.

Vinacke, W.E. Variables in experimental games: Toward a field theory. *Psychological Bulletin,* 1969, *71,* 293-318.

Vinacke, W.E., Cherulnik, P.D., & Lichtman, C.M. Strategy in intratriad and intertriad interaction. *Journal of Social Psychology*, 1970, *81*, 183-198.

Wahrman, R., & Pugh, M.D. Competence and conformity: Another look at Hollander's study. *Sociometry*, 1972, *35*, 376-386.

Wahrman, R., & Pugh, M.D. Sex, nonconformity and influence. *Sociometry*, 1974, *37*, 137-147.

Walstedt, J.J. Women as marginals. *Psychological Reports*, 1974, *34*, 639-646.

Walum, L.R. The changing door ceremony: Notes on the operation of sex-roles in everyday life. *Urban Life and Culture*, 1974, *2*, 506-515.

Weisbrod, R.M. Looking behavior in a discussion group. Unpublished paper, Cornell University, 1965. Cited in M. Argyle, *Social Interaction*. New York: Atherton Press, 1969.

Wiley, M.G. Sex roles in games. *Sociometry*, 1973, *36*, 526-541.

Wolfe, D.M. Power and authority in the family. In D. Cartwright (Ed.), *Studies in social power*. Ann Arbor: Institute for Social Research, 1959.

Wolman, C., & Frank, H. The solo woman in a professional peer group. *American Journal of Orthopsychiatry*, 1975, *45*, 164-171.

Zander, A., & Van Egmond, E. Relationship of intelligence and social power to the interpersonal behavior of children. *Journal of Educational Psychology*, 1958, *49*, 257-268.

CHAPTER *14*

ATTRIBUTIONS OF THE CAUSES OF SUCCESS AND FAILURE AS INTERNAL AND EXTERNAL BARRIERS TO ACHIEVEMENT IN WOMEN

**IRENE HANSON FRIEZE,
JOAN FISHER, BARBARA HANUSA,
MAUREEN C. McHUGH
&
VALERIE A. VALLE**

Irene Frieze is an Assistant Professor of Psychology and Women's Studies at the University of Pittsburgh. Joan Fisher is presently an Urban Policy Specialist for the City of New Orleans. Maureen McHugh is a graduate student in social psychology at the University of Pittsburgh. Barbara Hanusa, after receiving her PhD from Carnegie-Mellon University, is now a research associate at CMU. Valerie Valle is a Research Assistant Professor in the School of Business Administration at the University of Pittsburgh. She received her degree in social psychology from the University of Pittsburgh.

*This chapter was developed from an ongoing research group studying attribu-
tions of success and failure, and reviews the literature on cognitive factors that
inhibit achievement in women. Females in general are shown to have lower
expectancies for success than males and to have beliefs about why they succeed
or fail which limit their pride in achievement and maintain their low expectancies. However, conflicting evidence would suggest that it is difficult to generalize
about sex differences because women have a variety of motives which may lead
to different causal attributions. Causal attributions of others about why women
succeed or fail are also discussed. The literature indicates that these beliefs of
other people are a strong external barrier inhibiting success for women. Possibilities for change are also discussed.*

Success in one's work, sports, college and graduate school, and politics is still
highly valued in the United States. Men, typically, have been socialized to desire
high levels of success in these areas of achievement and to admire such achievements in others. Women have not been so much encouraged to succeed in these
fields, since these pursuits are perceived to be areas of masculine achievement,
and success or failure in them is not considered to be so important to women,
even today, as to men (Feather, 1975). Women are, perhaps understandably, not
as successful as men in sports and politics and appear to be less motivated to
succeed (Epstein, 1971). Even though increasing numbers of women are working
outside the home, they do not typically earn as much money (which is one

The authors would like to acknowledge the many helpful comments of Kay Deaux, Jacque-
lyn Goodchilds, Rita Jackaway, Paula Johnson, Shelley Reno, and Bernard Weiner on earlier
versions of this manuscript.

criterion for success) as men with comparable levels of ability or training. For example, in a national sample of working families taken in 1969, it was found that women received lower salaries than men with equal qualifications and experience (Levitin, Quinn, & Staines, 1971). Numerous other studies document the consistently lower recognition awarded for the achievements of women (e.g., Bernard, 1971; Frieze, Parsons, Johnson, Ruble, and Zellman, in press).

A number of causal explanations for high achievement orientation or desire for success in these "achievement" areas of men and the nonachievement orientation of, or relative lack of, concern with "success" of women have been proposed over the past 20 years. Most of the theoretical and empirical research supporting these explanations has focused on internal psychological factors that inhibit women. Women's relative lack of "achievement" has been attributed by others to deficiencies in their achievement motivation (McClelland, Atkinson, Clark & Lowell, 1953; Veroff, 1969), their high fear of failure (see O'Leary, 1974 for a review of this literature), and their fear of success (e.g., Horner, 1972).

More recently, it has been suggested that women do experience desires to succeed, but that these strivings are directed toward achievement in the home or in traditionally defined feminine tasks (Stein & Bailey, 1973). Tangri (1972) further suggested that some women may desire to achieve vicariously through the accomplishments of their husbands and children. Other researchers cite cognitive factors, such as beliefs about one's own ability and why one succeeds or fails, as of major importance. Although these latter variables are a major focus of this chapter, all this existing research attributes the causes of women's achievement failures to internal factors in the women themselves. Such an emphasis ignores the external factors that are of major importance in determining how people live their lives. Such a bias has important political implications, which women need to consider.

However, rather than being purposefully negative toward women, the research mentioned above may be motivated by a well-known general tendency to attribute the actions of others to dispositional factors within those people (Jones, Kanouse, Kelley, Nisbett, Valins, & Weiner, 1972). McHugh (Note 1) noted this observer bias in much of the sex-difference literature and discussed its similarity to actor-observer differences, which have been well documented in the attribution literature. Research by Jones and Nisbett (1972) demonstrated that a person tends to see ter own behavior as dependent upon the situation, while attributing the behavior of others to their particular personality characteristics.

It is our belief that external barriers to achievement are as important, if not more so, than any internal psychological barriers to achievement in women. However, there is evidence that these internal barriers do exist; since so much of past research has focused upon such variables, the first part of this chapter will analyze one of the major variables: cognitions or beliefs about one's ability and why one succeeds or fails. The second part of the chapter will look at how these cognitive factors affect the judgments that others make about women.

The importance of the cognitive attributional approach for understanding achievement-oriented behavior has been demonstrated by a number of studies, all of which (unless otherwise noted) use white middle-class college students as subjects. Extension of attributional research to other groups is clearly a needed research area. People engaging in achievement behavior have ideas and beliefs about what they are doing. One type of belief is the expectation or the likelihood of being successful. Such expectations influence people's choices of future activities and the level of their subsequent performance (Weiner, 1974). In addition to such expectations, people also make judgments about why particular events occur. A growing body of research concerned with attribution theory has verified that people act as if they were concerned with understanding the causes of events in their environments. The study of this process of assigning causality has enabled researchers to understand many phenomena that previously had not been interpretable within the framework of existing theories (deCharms, 1968; Jones et al., 1972). Within the achievement domain, the causal attributions one makes have implications for one's expectations, degree of pride or shame experienced, and future behavior undertaken (Weiner, 1972, 1974). In addition, internal pride and shame depend upon what one perceives to be the cause of their outcomes (Riemer, 1975; Weiner & Kukla, 1970).

Research oriented toward this cognitive approach to understanding sex differences in achievement behavior has focused on three major areas. First, numerous studies have documented that higher expectancies for personal success are held by men and boys than by women and girls in our society. Second, several studies suggest that men and women habitually make different causal attributions about their successes and failures. Finally, attributions made by other people about why someone else succeeds or fails depend upon the sex of the person being observed.

EXPECTATIONS FOR SUCCESS AND FAILURE

Expectations for success and failure have been shown to affect behavior in achievement situations. Several studies have demonstrated that people with high expectations of success on achievement tasks perform better than those with low expectations (e.g., Battle, 1965; Feather, 1966). While these studies have not eliminated the possibility that these high expectations are based on a history of prior success, other studies (Diggory, 1966; Tyler, 1958) have randomly assigned levels of expectancy. Subjects who were randomly given high expectation levels performed better than those given low expectation levels in these studies, thus demonstrating that expectancy levels directly affect performance.

Differential expectations for success and failure in males and females have been well documented. In a series of studies, V.C. Crandall (1969) demonstrated the generally low expectancies of girls and women in a variety of tasks, ages, and settings. Her samples included: elementary school children who have expectancy estimates for their performance at novel intellectual tasks; eighth-graders who were asked to state how well they expected to do at a digit-symbol matching task; college students estimating grades; and college-aged people from the Fels longitudinal sample, who guessed their performance at a geometric task. The results were consistent; males had higher expectations than females in all situations.

Other researchers have replicated Crandall's findings with a variety of age groups and tasks. Boys expect to do better than girls at marble-dropping games (Montanelli and Hill, 1969), addition problems (McMahan, Note 2), and "sexless" concept-formation tasks (Parsons, Ruble, Hodges, and Small, 1976). These differences appear as early as kindergarten (Parsons, Note 3). Similarly, high-school boys anticipate more favorable performance than that of their female classmates on addition tasks (McMahan, Note 2) and verbal intelligence tests (Brim, Goslin, Glass, and Goldberg, 1969), and college males have higher expectations for anagrams (Bar-Tal and Frieze, 1977; Feather, 1969; Ryckman and Sherman, Note 4) and addition problems (McMahan, Note 2).

A few studies have indicated that sex differences in expectancies are not always clear-cut. In a replication of Feather's (1969) study, Feather and Simon (1973) failed to show expectancy differences between males and females for anagram solutions. McMahan (Note 2) also failed to find sex differences in expectancies for anagram solutions; however, he did find significantly higher expectations for success in males before an addition task.

Specific Versus Generalized Expectancies

In a recent paper, McHugh (Note 2) suggested that some of the discrepancies in the expectancy literature may be the result of the assumption that the expectancy for success is independent of the task. McHugh pointed out that if a subject has had previous experience with a task, the expectancy estimate is based on past experience. However, when giving an expectancy estimate for a novel task, the person must rely upon ter general expectancy level. Rotter (1954) first suggested the importance of this distinction in a general sense, although he did not apply it to sex differences.

House and Perney (1974) demonstrated that this distinction between specific and generalized expectancies is useful when investigating sex differences in expectations. In their experimental situation, expectancies were formed either on the basis of pretest outcomes or on the basis of externally defined levels of success. When expectancies were based on externally based criteria, males had significantly higher expectations. However, when expectancies were based on pretest outcomes, females had significantly higher expectations.

Given the cultural stereotype that males are more intelligent, more achieving, and more competitive than females (Broverman, Vogel, Broverman, Clarkson, & Rosenkrantz, 1972), it is not surprising that males generally report higher expectations than females or that both males and females predict that males will be more successful. However, while this cultural stereotype influences generalized expectancies, it should not have the same effect on specific expectancies. Parsons (Note 3) found this to be the case. She found that while females have lower generalized expectancies than males, they respond to specific success and failure information in a manner similar to males.

When the expectancy literature is considered in light of this distinction of specific and generalized expectancies, some of the inconsistencies in the sex-difference data can be explained. Many studies that demonstrate lower expectancies for females employ novel tasks: digit-symbol matching and geometric tasks (V.C. Crandall, 1969); marble dropping (Montanelli & Hill, 1969), concept identification (Parsons et al., 1976), and identification of hidden objects by small children (Parsons, Note 3). Subjects were presumed to have had little or no experience with these tasks, and therefore these studies may be assumed to have been tapping rather generalized expectancies. Other studies that have not found differential expectancies have tended to use more familiar tasks where expectancies are based on past experience. McHugh, Fisher, and Frieze (Note 5) found additional support for this interpretation of the expectancy results. They introduced a novel ambiguous task (design matching) that involved either abstract intellectual skills, where males would be expected to have higher generalized expectancies, or abstract social skills where females were expected to have higher generalized expectancies. Results indicated that female expectancies were in fact lower than male expectancies for the intellectual tasks, while the reverse was true for the social task.

When cultural stereotypes are made salient by labeling the experimental tasks as masculine or feminine, even specific expectations can be affected: Deaux and Farris (Note 6) manipulated the sex-linkage of anagram tasks. They found that females gave lower expectancy estimates than males when the task was labeled as masculine. However, there were no sex differences in expectancies when the task was labeled as feminine. Similar results were reported by O'Leary and Ridley (Note 7). Existing cultural definitions of sex-linked tasks also affect the expectancies of subjects. McHugh et al., (Note 5) found this to be the case for social versus intellectual tasks. McMahan (Note 2) found that females have lower expectancies on addition-problem tasks, but do not have lower expectancies on anagrams tasks.

While the distinction between specific and generalized expectancies in conjunction with cultural stereotypes explains some of the inconsistent sex differences in expectations, there are results that do not support this explanation. As mentioned earlier, researchers have shown that females have lower expectancies than males at anagrams tasks, although anagrams are not novel nor are they generally considered to be sex-linked. However, Wiegers (1975) did find that high school males reported having significantly more experience with anagrams than did females.

Fisher (Note 8) suggested that differences in the degree of competitiveness, implicit or explicit, in various studies may explain varying results for sex differences in expectancies. For a variety of reasons, females may report lower expectancies in studies with a high degree of competitiveness.

Consequences of Higher Male Expectations

Whether sex differences in expectation levels are explained by generalized versus specific expectancies, cultural stereotypes, experimental manipulations, or other factors, the effects of the higher expectations of males still exist. Higher expectations for success lead to superior performance (Diggory, 1966), and higher evaluations of performances (Shrauger, 1972; Terbovic, Note 9). They may also lead to selection of more difficult tasks (Veroff, 1969). The consequences of these higher expectations are improved opportunities for achievement. Thus, without postulating any ability differences, females with low expectations are at a disadvantage in achievement situations.

Although males have higher expectations than females, females make more accurate estimations of their objective probability of success. When V.C. Crandall (1969) compared subjective expectations with predictions based on objective ability measures, males were found to overestimate their future performances. While the merits of high expectations have been discussed often, the advantages of accurate estimates are usually ignored. If the accuracy of expectations rather than the absolute level of expectation determined performance, females rather than males might fare better. However, the present culture does not punish overstatement of ability for males, while it does applaud absolute levels of performance.

Given the importance of the implications of the level of expectancy on performance, and probably for choice of activities, the generally low expectations for success at achievement tasks held by females is one barrier to achievement in women. While this barrier can be viewed as something that an individual can change, it can also be viewed as an internalization of cultural stereotypes. Each of these views suggests a different method for removing the barrier.

The less complex of the two methods suggested would be to change women's expectations by providing them with success experiences and information about how these experiences should affect their expectations. However, both Dweck (1975) and Jackaway (1974) found that providing subjects with only success experiences does not change generalized expectations for success. Jackaway found that although females performed well in terms of their expectations, they did not increase their expectation for future success to the same extent as males. Dweck (1975) said that although experiencing continued success did not change generalized expectancies, she could increase these expectations if subjects were taught to accept responsibility for their successes and failures.

Another method of eliminating the expectation barrier is to change the cultural stereotypes that affect generalized expectancies. If females were not considered less intelligent, less achieving, and less competitive than males, then generalized expectancies might be based on the summation of past performances rather than upon sex. Further research is needed to determine how this might be done. However, some supporting evidence for this approach is given by a recent study of high-school girls, which shows that nontraditional girls had higher expectancies than those with more traditional sex-role aspirations (Wiegers and Frieze; in press).

ATTRIBUTING THE CAUSES OF SUCCESS AND FAILURE

Weiner and his associates (e.g., Weiner, 1974; Weiner, Frieze, Kukla, Reed, Rest, & Rosenbaum, 1971) have done extensive research demonstrating the importance of attributions or beliefs about why success or failure occurs in understanding achievement-oriented behavior. Most of this research concerns the attributions made by an individual about ter own successes and failures, and how these attributions influence affect, future expectancies, and subsequent achievement strivings. It is assumed that people will be more likely to attempt tasks when they believe they have a high expectancy of doing well, and that they will desire to maximize positive feelings about success and minimize negative feelings about failure. Both affect and expectancy are affected by the type of causal attribution made about why a particular event was a success or failure.

A diagram of the attributional process as conceptualized by Frieze (1975) is shown in Figure 7.1. The attributional process begins with an achievement behavior that is then interpreted as a success or failure. Once the outcome is established, the person utilizes available information—such as his or her expectancy for success at this task, past history of successes and knowledge of how well other people did—to determine the cause of the outcome (Frieze, in press; Frieze and Weiner, 1971). It is hypothesized that in many cases people have well-established patterns of making causal attributions, so that extensive information processing is not necessary. Thus, for example, a highly competent male may see his high abilities as responsible for his successes without having to consider the particular circumstances of any one event (Frieze; in press).

There are many possible reasons why a particular success or failure might occur, and therefore many causal attributions can be made (Heider, 1958). The four most studied causes of achievement outcomes are ability, effort, luck, and task ease or difficulty (Weiner, Frieze, Kukla, Reed, & Rosenbaum, 1971). Thus, a person may succeed at a task because of ter high ability, trying hard, good luck, and/or the fact that the task was relatively easy. Failure may result from low ability, not trying sufficiently hard, bad luck, and/or task difficulty. Most recent work (Elig & Frieze, 1975; Frieze, 1976) has indicated that other causal factors are frequently employed to explain the successes and failures of others as well as of oneself. These include stable effort or a consistent pattern of diligence or laziness, other people who may aid or interfere with performance, mood and fatigue or sickness, having a good or poor personality, and physical appearance (see Elig and Frieze, 1975, for a more complete definition of these causal elements).

These causal attributions can be classified along three dimensions: internal-external; stable-unstable; and intentional-unintentional. This classification system is shown in Table 7.1. Ability, effort, mood, personality, and knowledge are causes originating within or internal to the individual, while task difficulty, other people's help or hurt, and luck are causes within the environment or external to the individual. This internal versus external dimension of causality (the I-E dimension) has been widely investigated, especially in terms of individual differences in stable tendencies to make either internal or external attributions (see reviews by Rotter, 1966; Throop & MacDonald, 1971). This dimension has been shown to be particularly important for affect. More pride or satisfaction is reported by people who attribute their successes internally than if the attribution is made to an external cause (Weiner, Heckhausen, Meyer, & Cook, 1972; Weiner, 1972). These same studies have shown that internally attributed failures lead to more shame or dissatisfaction after failure.

A second dimension along which the various causes may be differentiated is in their stability. Ability, personality diligence, or laziness and task difficulty are relatively stable causes, whereas effort, mood, and luck may be highly changeable. If success at a particular type of activity was due to a person's high ability or the activity's being easy, one would anticipate continued success for that person on the same task. Similarly, if a failure was due to these stable causes, continued failure would be anticipated. Conversely, unstable causes, lead to acknowledging the possibility of change. Failures attributed to bad luck or lack of effort may result in expectations for eventual success, since bad luck might finally change or trying harder might lead to future success.

The stability of the causal attribution has been found to relate to expectancies for the future (e.g., McMahan, 1973; Weiner, Heckhausen, Meyer, & Cook, 1972). Stable attributions lead to expectancies for continued success or failure. Unstable attributions lead to expectations for changes in outcomes.

The two dimensions of internality and stability were developed by Weiner et al. (1971). Rosenbaum (1972) suggested that a third dimension, intentionality,

Table 7.1

A three-dimensional model for classifying causal attributions for success and failure

		Stable	Unstable
Internal			
	Intentional	Stable effort (dilligence or laziness)	Unstable effort (trying or not trying hard)
	Unintentional	Ability Knowledge or background Personality	Fatigue Mood
External			
	Intentional	Others always help or interfere	Others help or interfere with this event
	Unintentional	Task difficulty or ease Personality of others	Task difficulty or ease (task changes) Luck or unique circumstances Others accidentally help or interfere

Source: Modified from Elig and Frieze in *JSAS: Catalog of selected documents in psychology*, 1975, 5.

might be added to the two-dimensional system to differentiate between effort and mood as well as to more fully understand all the various causal attributions. An attribution is considered to be intentional to the degree that the person is perceived to have control of ter actions. Thus, ability and personality are factors within a person over which that person has little control, and events attributed to these factors would be unintentional. However, the actor is perceived to have control over the effort tey exerts so that attributions to effort are intentional (as well as being internal). The intentionality dimension appears to be related to reward and punishment, with most reward given for performances attributed to internal, intentional causes, although further research is needed to clarify these relationships.

Attributional Patterns

Within this attributional framework, certain implications of various causal attributions are clear. Maximum security in success is derived from the perception that the success is due to the internal, stable factor of ability. Pride, on the other hand, is associated with success resulting from trying hard (internal and intentional), but the effort attribution produces little security, since continued effort must be exerted to maintain positive outcomes. Success attributed to external factors produces less pride. If success is perceived as caused by the external, unstable element of luck, there is neither pride nor security that success will reoccur. An opposite pattern of consequences occurs with failure attributions. Maximum shame is associated with failures perceived as caused by low ability or lack of effort. If lack of ability is seen as the primary cause of the failure, not only is there shame (since this is an internal attribution), but there is also an avoidance of the activity in the future, since the person will believe that there will be no way in which future failure could be avoided (except for occasional instances of good luck). On the other hand, failures attributed to bad luck or task difficulty produce less shame. If bad luck is perceived as the primary cause, future successes would be anticipated as luck fluctuates. Lack of effort, although leading to shame, would be changeable and therefore would result in greater expectancy changes than lack of ability attributions.

Although attributions are clearly influenced by situational factors (e.g., Frieze & Weiner, 1971), it is hypothesized that in many cases some people have patterns of making certain causal attributions more than others. Maximum self-esteem would theoretically be associated with a tendency to make internal, stable attributions for success, and external, unstable attributions for failure. Fitch (1970) verified these hypotheses to some degree with data showing that low self-esteem males were more likely to make internal attributions for failure, while high self-esteem males attributed success more to internal causes. Although these patterns of perceiving success and failure may perpetuate self-esteem, other data suggest that maximum achievement striving is associated with slightly different patterns. Kukla (1972) demonstrated that high achievement-motivated men tend to attribute their successes to both high ability and effort, while they perceive their failures as due to lack of effort. Their attribution of failure to lack of effort would lead to greater subsequent trying when they do poorly. This attribution pattern explains the motivating effects of failure for high achievement-motivated males reported by Atkinson (1964) and Weiner (1970). Also, high achievement motivation is generally associated with higher estimates of personal ability (Bar-Tal and Frieze, 1977; Kukla, 1972). Low achievement-motivated male subjects are less likely to see their successes as due to internal causes, but see failures as caused more by their low ability than high achievers do (Weiner & Kukla, 1970; Weiner & Potepan, 1970).

Attributional Patterns of Women

Given the low initial expectancies of women generally, certain overall sex differences in attributional patterns can be predicted from the attribution model discussed above. If a woman expected to do poorly but succeeds, she is likely to attribute the outcome to an unstable cause such as luck. This means she will not change her expectancies, and she feels no pride in her success if the attribution is made to the external element of luck. When a female with low expectancy fails on a task, she expected this, and therefore tends to attribute her failure to lack of ability. This attributional pattern, which Jackaway (1974) referred to as the "low expectation cycle," minimizes the positive effects of success and maximizes the negative effects of failure. These attributions are adopted to maintain cognitive consistency and to justify the initial low expectation. Thus, low expectations are self-perpetuating because they lead to attributions that maintain low performance levels.

A few studies have supported the prediction that women attribute success to luck and failure to lack of ability. Nicholls (1975) found part of this self-derogatory pattern in grade school girls: Failure was attributed to lack of ability to a greater extent than success was attributed to high ability. Crandall, Katkowsky, and Crandall's (1965) work suggested that when feedback is contradictory to expectancies, girls (more than boys) tend to focus on negative feedback as a basis for expectancy formation. Also, McMahan (Note 2) noted that women are more likely than men to attribute failures to lack of ability. This general pattern would seem to be the result of—and serve to maintain— lower expectancies and confidence in women. In addition, one would expect a general avoidance of achievement situations by women having this attributional pattern, since the outcome of achievement tasks, given these attributions, can at most be neutral (for success) and may be negative (for failure).

However, much of the current research does not find these attributional patterns in women. Many studies have instead found a general externality on the part of females (e.g., McArthur, 1976). Some studies have found that females rate tasks as easier than do males in both success and failure conditions (Bar-Tal and Frieze, 1977; Croke, Note 10; McMahan, Note 2). By rating the task as easier after either success or failure, females may have reduced the value of their successes and increased the negative implications of their failures; thus, these task-ease attributions are similar in substance to the self-derogatory pattern discussed above.

A number of studies have found that females make greater use of luck attributions than do males for both success and failure (Bar-Tal and Frieze, 1977; Feather, 1969; Simon and Feather, 1973; Wiegers and Frieze, in press; McMahan, Note 2). This pattern is also characterized by a general externality, but has different implications from task-ease attributions. The pattern of luck attributions implies that, at least within traditionally defined masculine areas such as academic achievement, women take less responsibility for, and feel less pride in, their successes and less shame about their failures. Thus, women employing this attributional pattern would experience relatively little affect in achievement situations.

McHugh (Note 1) noted that this attributional pattern of general externality refers only to the females' greater use of external factors relative to the male subjects. It does not necessarily imply that females using relatively greater levels of external factors believe that these factors are largely responsible for the outcome. In attribution studies using free-response methods (Frieze, 1976) and percentage scales (Luginbuhl, Crowe, & Kahan, 1975), success and failure outcomes were attributed only minimally to external factors by either sexes. In both studies, ability and effort were seen as the major causes of achievement outcomes.

Although it has been found that women's attributions are more external than men's (Bar-Tal & Frieze, 1977; Feather, 1969; Simon & Feather, 1973; Croke,

Note 10; McMahan, Note 2), this pattern of general externality does not seem to be a simple one. As pointed out by Fisher (Note 8), several different mediating variables can be proposed for this pattern. The women who demonstrated this attributional pattern may be doing so for several different reasons. Modesty may be mediating the external attributions of some women, who actually feel pride in their success and raise their ability estimates after doing well, but report low ability estimates or attribute success to luck to avoid appearing boastful. An external locus of control may be producing the external attributions of other women. Women more often than men have an external locus of control (Rotter & Hochreich, Note 11) and, at least during college years, have less of a sense of control over their own fate (Maccoby & Jacklin, 1975).

Individuals with an external locus of control do not see themselves as responsible for outcomes, and might therefore attribute success and failure to external causal factors. The external attributions of other women may be mediated by a fear of social rejection. Horner (1968) proposed that women fear success because of negative social consequences that successful women may receive. While the evidence for a dispositional fear of success in women is conflicting (Tressemer, 1974), Condrey and Dryer (1976) suggested that certain situations do evoke realistic expectancies about negative consequences. By attributing success to luck or task ease, a woman denies responsibility for her performance, thereby eliminating any grounds for social rejection if she performs well. Even within one attributional pattern, then, it can be seen that different variables may be mediating causal attributions.

Considering the many variables that may influence attributions and the number of different patterns of attributions found for women, it appears unlikely that investigators can specify one pattern that differentiates men and women. Women differ from one another greatly, and it may well be that future research will verify that there are a number of distinct attributional patterns for women. Some possible variables which might be relevant are shown in Table 7.2.

Achievement motivation may be an important variable for differentiating groups of women. Women with high achievement motivation appear to have a somewhat different pattern of attributions than traditionally oriented women. For example, observations of professional women indicate that they work very hard and are highly motivated to succeed. In fact, some writers (Bird, 1968; Epstein, 1971) suggested that they must be better at what they do professionally in order to experience any career success. Furthermore, professional women perform at this high level without any of the environmental supports which

Table 7.2

Possible factors influencing expectations and attributions
of women

Factor	Typical Direction of influence
1. Societal expectations	Women expected to do poorly on achievement tasks.
Female success	Success attributed more to luck.
2. Personal expectations for success	Women generally have low expectations for themselves. Attribute success more to luck or the task.
3. Individual differences: Achievement motivation	Highs more internal, believe in effort more.
Fear of success	Denial of responsibility for success through external attributions.
Androgeny	Higher expectations for masculine tasks. More internal attributions for success.
4. Situational factors: Type of task experience	Higher expectancies for tasks with prior history of success.
Type of task sex-role relation	Higher expectancies for female than for male tasks.
Competition	More external for competitive success.

professional men frequently have, such as a supportive wife (Frieze et al., in press). This pattern of continuing hard work as a basis for achievement in these women suggests that they may perceive their successes and failures as being dependent upon effort rather than upon luck or other causal factors. However, data indicating that nearly all women have lower estimates of their own abilities than men would also lead to the hypothesis that even high achievement-motivated women lack the positive belief in their own abilities, which character-izes the high achievement-motivated man.

Preliminary studies have suggested that highly motivated women do employ more effort attributions for both success and failure than low achievement-motivated women (Feldman-Summers & Kiesler, 1974; Frieze, 1973). Bar-Tal and Frieze (1977) also found that high achievement motivation was related to higher estimates of ability for both male and female subjects, although this finding was stronger for men than for women. In one of the few studies using a black sample, Murray and Mednick (1975) found that achievement-motivation levels affected the causal attributions of black women. Also, there appear to be differential attributional patterns for under- and overachieving women and men (Wiegers & Frieze; in press).

These results suggest that achievement motivation is an important variable in predicting attributional patterns for success and failure in achievement-related situations, not only for men but also for women. Another variable that may differentiate people is androgeny. It is often assumed that masculinity and fem-ininity are polar opposites on a single continuum. Recent work by S. Bem (1974) has shown that many individuals have both feminine and masculine characteristics. Bem (1975) found that these psychologically androgynous in-dividuals can adapt to a greater variety of situations than can either masculine or feminine persons; they have characteristics giving them the capacity for effec-tive behavior in both stereotypically masculine and feminine situations. Androg-ynous individuals may have lower expectancies and show general externality on sex-reversed tasks. Specifically, general achievement situations might be more debilitating for highly feminine subjects, since these areas are typically labeled as masculine in our society. This circumstance would lead to a generally lower self-esteem in these highly feminine women. See Bem's Overview in volume I for more discussion of this issue.

Along with individual differences in attributional patterns among women, there are also a number of situational factors that affect attributions. The fact that attribution patterns may vary for an individual across situations is seldom taken into account. It is generally implied that one's pattern of making causal attributions is an enduring disposition. However, the assumption of such consistency is being generally challenged (Bem & Allen, 1974; Mischel, 1973). A relative lack of interest in situational determinants of attribution patterns may be partially responsible for the inconsistencies found in some of the research. That attribution patterns in achievement settings may have important situational determinants is supported by research that varies the type of task (Deaux & Farris, Note 6) and competitiveness (House, 1974; Simon & Feather, 1973).

Fisher (Note 8) suggested that one of the major situational variables that differentially affects men and women is the implicit or explicit competition that exists in many achievement situations. Broverman et al. (1972) found a widespread belief that competitiveness and assertiveness are unfeminine. This norm, by keeping women from competing, may have strong negative impact on their achievement strivings. Women might reduce conflicts over their success in a competitive situation by denying responsibility for it. Therefore, it might be expected that women would make more external attributions for success in a competitive rather than in a noncompetitive setting.

Competition can be explicit or implicit in a situation. Testing subjects in mixed-sex groups should imply a competitive atmosphere (Horner, 1968). Several studies of a mixed-group setting have found that females use more external attributions for success and failure (Feather, 1969; McMahan, Note 2). Bar-Tal and Frieze (1977) had subjects (in mixed-sex groups) announce their success or failure aloud, and found that females made greater use of luck than did males overall. Jackaway (1974) also obtained this result and found that females rated the task as easier after achieving either success or failure in a competitive setting. These results might be interpreted as a denial of competitive success when sex-role conflict is present. In Simon and Feather's (1973) study of attributions for performance on an actual examination, females were more external overall, suggesting that they deny responsibility for success in actual competitive situations.

Few studies have tested subjects individually, so it is more difficult to find support for the prediction that females are not more external than males in a noncompetitive situation. However, Luginbuhl et al. (1975) did test subjects individually and did not find greater externality for females than for males; girls were in fact more internal for failure. In addition, girls felt better about the task when it was described as unimportant (noncompetitive) than when described as an important ability task (competitiveness is implied). Therefore, some suggestive support is found in the literature for the prediction that a competitive, but not a noncompetitive, setting produces more external attributions for females than for males.

Causal attributions are generally considered an internal process that influences the individual's expectancies and affect in a given situation. Attribution therapy (see Frieze, 1975, or Dweck, 1975) has been suggested as a way of altering female attributions to effect a change in their expectancies and resultant achievements. However, attributions are formed on the basis of the individual's experiences in the external world. If fears of social rejection are realistic, and if modesty and/or noncompetitiveness are conditioned into females, then we cannot expect to change attributions without a change in society's values and in the socialization process.

OTHER'S EXPECTATIONS AND ATTRIBUTIONS

Up to this point, this chapter has focused primarily on internal cognitions of the female. However, we will attempt to show that the cognitions of others concerning women in achievement situations are as important, if not more so, than women's internal cognitions. First, the expectations for, and attributions concerning women's achievements by others, such as employers or teachers, can affect hiring, promotion, and other opportunities for achievement. Secondly, as has already been suggested, women's internal cognitive barriers to achievement, such as low expectancies and maladaptive attributional patterns, stem from cultural standards for sex-appropriate behavior.

The available research suggests that women are expected to do more poorly than men at numerous tasks. For example, Feldman-Summers and Kiesler (1974) reported that they were unable to find any occupation in which females were expected to outperform males. For all the professions they chose to canvass, which included those of pediatricians, writers, child psychologists, surgeons, dancers, diagnosticians, clinical psychologists, and biographers of famous women, males were expected to be more successful than females. These lower expectations for women might well affect the original hiring and training of women for these jobs (see Rosen & Jerdee, 1974a; 1974b). These expectations may also directly affect the performance of women. Research has indicated that when people are randomly assigned to high- and low-expectancy groups, the high-expectancy group tends to perform better than the group to which low expectancies were assigned (Tyler, 1958). Similar results were obtained by Rosenthal and Jacobson (1968), who found that teacher expectations had major effects upon student performance, even though the expectations had been based upon randomly assigned information.

Causal attributions for performance also differ according to the sex of the person being evaluated. Deaux and Emswiller (1974) asked both male and female college students to evaluate another's performance at finding hidden objects in a complex design. The task was described as either masculine or feminine; males were expected to do better at the masculine task and females at the female task. When given information that the person had succeeded at the task, males' successes on the masculine task tended to be attributed more to ability, while females' successes were more likely to be attributed to luck. There were no differences on the feminine task.

As has been documented in earlier portions of this chapter, the causal attributions made about a person have important implications, not only for the affect and expectancies of that person but also for the rewards given that person by others. People are constantly being evaluated by others for their achievements, whether being considered for a grade, a job, or a promotion. The kinds of attributions made by the decision makers in these situations have major consequences for those being judged. For example, if a teacher thinks a student passed a test because tey cheated, the reaction of the teacher will be quite different from that tey has if tey believes that the student had studied hard for the exam. Also, a student will probably be more motivated to study in a class where tey thinks the teacher determines grades on the basis of competence and the effort of the student rather than by chance or favoritism. Another example of this process is the reaction of an employer to a poor performance by an employee. If the employer perceives that the poor performance was due to external circumstances over which the employee had no control (such as being given a difficult assignment) or to unstable factors that might be expected to change in the near future (the employee has been sick and is now better), the employer will be more likely to give that employee a second chance. If, however, the employer believes that the poor performance was the result of internal factors such as the employee's being lazy or generally incompetent, the employer might well fire the person.

A pattern of attributing to ability the successes of men to a greater extent than are attributed the successes of women, and attributing the failure of women more to their lack of ability was reported by Feather and Simon (1975) and Etaugh and Brown (1975). Etaugh and Brown also found that female successes were attributed more to effort. Feldman-Summers and Kiesler (1974) also found that male subjects attributed more ability to a male physician than to a female physician. The males attributed the success of the female physician to either her strong motivation or to her having an easier task (i.e., external factors aided her in becoming a doctor). Female subjects in this study also attributed greater motivation to the female physician, but they were more likely to see the male physician as having an easier task.

Although there have not been a great many studies in this area, those that have been done suggest that female successes are more likely to be attributed to unstable factors, such as luck or effort, whereas male successes are more often attributed to the stable internal factor of ability. Such patterns, if they were to be generalized, would imply that even when women do succeed, they would not be expected to continue to be successful, since their successes are attributed more to unstable factors.

Valle (1974) developed a model relating initial expectations and causal attributions that might have important implications for the evaluation of women. Her model suggests that when making a prediction about the future performance of an individual, the perceiver considers both the individual's most recent performance and the expectations that the perceiver had before that performance. Predictions about the future depend upon how much importance is given to this recent performance and how much to the initial expectations. Valle's (Valle & Frieze, 1976) model suggests that the amount of importance given to a previous performance is related to the attributed cause of that performance. If the performance was attributed to stable factors (e.g., ability or task), the previous outcome would be weighted heavily. If, on the other hand, the outcome was attributed to unstable factors (e.g., luck or effort), it should be weighted less heavily. Therefore, the more an outcome is attributed to stable causes, the greater the weight to be given to that outcome in determining predictions for the future, and the closer the expectations for the future will be to the outcome, regardless of initial expectancy. Support for this is seen in correlational studies (McMahan, 1973; Weiner et al., 1971) and in experimental research (Fontaine, 1974, Rosenbaum, 1972; Valle, 1974).

Moreover, the type of attribution ascribed to a performance is dependent upon the situation, and is a function of the difference between the actual outcome and the initial expectancies. The greater the absolute value of this difference, the greater will be the tendency to attribute the outcome to unstable factors such as luck, mood, or effort. The less this absolute difference, the greater will be the tendency to attribute the outcome to stable factors, such as the ability of the actor, or stable effort. For both observer attributions (Feather & Simon, 1971a; Frieze & Weiner, 1971) and self attributions (Feather, 1969; Feather & Simon, 1971a; 1971b; Simon & Feather, 1973), this implication has received wide support: the greater the difference between an outcome and previous expectations (either measured directly or assumed from the information available concerning the actor's past performance), the greater the tendency to attribute the outcome to unstable factors, especially to luck. Correlational data from Valle (1974) provide further support in a direct test of these implications.

To summarize, Valle's model describes a mechanism whereby changes in expectations are minimized by the types of causal attributions that are made. Unexpected outcomes are attributed to unstable causes, and therefore have less weight in determining future predictions; expected outcomes are more attributed to stable causes, and tend to support and reinforce original expectations. Valle and Frieze (1976) found empirical support for these predictions in a number of studies involving judgments made by MBA students about hypothetical life insurance salespersons.

The Valle model has important implications for an employee who is expected to do poorly. If such an employee performs well, the performance will be attributed to unstable factors, which in turn means that the employer will still expect the person to do poorly in the future. This process would be especially detrimental for a minority group member or a woman who is expected to do poorly just because of membership in that group. Because of these initial low expectations on the part of employers, it would be more difficult for such people to establish their competence with their employer. This model for expectancy changes is particularly applicable to the situation of women employed in what are not traditionally considered feminine fields. It is relevant to women only if they are indeed expected to do less well than men.

Research has indicated that the performances of women are usually evaluated lower than those of men. Goldberg (1968) demonstrated that articles supposedly written by women were evaluated lower by female college students than were articles by male authors, even though the authors' names had been randomly assigned. Similar results were found in more recent studies (e.g., Deaux & Emswiller, 1974; Pheterson, Kiesler, & Goldberg, 1971). Other data also support the idea that males are expected to perform better at a variety of tasks. Piacente, Penner, Hawkins, and Cohen (1974) found that males were perceived as more competent than women and that competency in general was perceived to be unfeminine for women. Rosen and Jerdee (1974a) reported that male undergraduate business students rated job applications with female names lower than comparable applications with male names.

Valle's model, then, would predict that in occupations in which women are expected to perform poorly, a successful performance by a woman will tend to be attributed more to unstable factors than would a similar performance by a man. In turn, since this successful performance has been attributed to unstable factors, it will have less impact on the evaluator's predictions for the future success of the woman than would a similar successful performance of a man. In other words, it would be more difficult for a woman to prove her competency by a high-quality performance than it would be for a man. The research that indicated that success by women tends to be attributed more to unstable factors supports this prediction (Deaux and Emswiller, 1974; Feldman-Summers & Kiesler, 1974).

Finally, Valle's model predicts that by manipulating the type of attribution made for a particular outcome, one can lessen or increase the weight given to that performance in making predictions for the future. If employers can be persuaded to attribute the cause of successful performance to stable factors, the vicious circle of low initial and future expectations for women can be reversed by changing the causal attributions.

Although little research has been done to directly test this implication of the model in natural settings, laboratory research by Rosenbaum (1972) and by Valle and Frieze (1976) does lend theoretical support. More extensive research is needed to better understand and document this process. As attempts are made to break the vicious circle, the model also cautions that a woman's performance should not be too deviant from the initially low expectations held for her by others. If a woman is expected to do very poorly, and actually does very well, this will be attributed to unstable factors even more than might be already expected. The model suggests that there is a point of maximum change for any specific situation and that the level of performance should be better than expected, but not too much better (Valle and Frieze, 1976).

On a hopeful note, there is some indication that the attributions made by others about women's performances are changing. In a replication of the Goldberg study, Morris (Note 12) found that, although male subjects rated female authors lower, her female subjects gave high ratings to articles written by females. These data suggest that some women are becoming more supportive of female acchievements and tend to value them more than male achievements, perhaps because of their growing realization of the effort necessary for women to be productive. This supportiveness of women is further seen in a study by Deaux and Taynor (1973). They found, as in earlier studies, that males rated highly competent men higher on intelligence and general competence than comparable women, but that female subjects tended to rate the competent relatively higher on competence. Thus, there may be an increasing trend for clearly competent women to be evaluated more favorably by women, but this trend does not seem to be evident in male perceptions of female competency. Therefore, women must still achieve within the less supportive environment, since most women are evaluated by men rather than by women.

Another possibility for change in the vicious circle described by Valle's model is that as more and more women prove themselves to be capable through a gradual process of changing expectancies, there should be a corresponding decrease in the initial low expectancy for women. In addition, several studies suggest that the availability of role models indirectly affects the expectancies of women themselves. Women whose mothers worked, or who had mothers who reinforced the idea of their working, tend to have higher estimates of female ability and competence in general (e.g., Broverman et al., 1972). One of the stronger predictive factors for high career aspirations for college women is having a working mother to serve as a role model (Almquist & Angrist, 1971; Astin, 1968; Parsons, Frieze, & Ruble, in press).

As was discussed several times in this chapter, the lower expectancies many people have for women in our culture have led to debilitating patterns of attributions by women about their own performances. The studies reviewed in this chapter further suggest that programs that directly affect the causal attributions made by women might be highly beneficial. An example of such an approach is seen in the work of Dweck (1975), but other research is needed in this area. Perhaps the raising of women's expectations and their confidence in their abilities would be a significant step in breaking the low expectancy cycle. This approach, along with the more direct attributional therapy done by Dweck, might help to reduce some of the internal barriers to achievement in women. Once this was done, and women were more successful in areas traditionally defined as masculine achievement areas, the expectations and causal attributions of others about women might then also change.

However, in order for this process of reducing internal barriers to achievement in women to be effective, a number of external barriers to female achievement must also be removed. Successful achievement for women has been not only unexpected for women, but may also be considered unfeminine by others as well as by women themselves (Hoffman, 1972; Piacente et al., 1974). For instance, a man may be threatened by dating or marrying someone who earns more or is more successful in her work than he is. In addition, married women are often responsible for household tasks to a much greater extent than their husbands are, even if both work (Bem & Bem, 1970). Thus, women face external barriers in the attitudes of the people around them if these people are not supportive of their achievements, or worse, actually discourage them. Also, the discriminatory attitudes of employers, both in terms of outright discrimination and in terms of the more subtle attributional processes documented earlier in this chapter, must be changed.

We hope that young girls growing up today are learning attributional patterns different from those dominating previous generations of women. The fact that previously common sex differences are failing to appear in recent studies (Lunneborg & Rosenwood, 1972; Maccoby & Jacklin, 1975) gives us some support that this is happening. Further analyses of cognitive variables such as expectations for success and failure, and of attributions about the causes of successes and failures, will help us to document and understand the processes underlying such changes as they occur. Also, increased understanding and study of these cognitive processes will aid in the planning of specific programs for changing dysfunctional attributional patterns in women and in the people who make important decisions about women's lives.

IMPLICATIONS FOR FUTURE RESEARCH

A great deal of research is still needed to better understand the role of cognitive factors as internal and external barriers to achievement. Many factors affect attributions of women, as described in Table 7.2. More research is needed to outline the specific effects of situational variables upon causal attributions. Also, more attention should be given to group differences. Not all women are alike. How does race, socioeconomic status, or lifestyle affect causal beliefs and expectancies? What types of attributions do children make? adults outside of college? What other personality variables are related to causal attributions? So many of these basic questions are still unanswered.

In addition to more research investigating the types of expectancies and attributions made by women, we clearly need to study how others' expectations and attributions affect the cognitions and behaviors of women. Does having a sexist employer make women perform more poorly than they should, and is a supportive employer going to encourage better performance? What about teachers and their beliefs about women? How can women break out of the vicious cycle described earlier when employers or others have low expectancies for them? All these very practical issues should be addressed.

The particular attributional patterns of successful women should also be studied. Do they have different beliefs about their capabilities, and successes, and failures than do other women? Where did they develop these belief patterns? Such data could provide guides for other, less successful women.

We feel that a greater understanding of cognitive factors will be extremely important in helping researchers and women themselves to achieve at the levels they are capable of, and to gain maximum pride and self-esteem from their successes.

REFERENCE NOTES

1. McHugh, M. Sex differences in causal attributions: A critical review. Paper presented at EPA, New York, 1975.
2. McMahan, I.D. Sex differences in expectancy of success as a function of the task. Paper presented at EPA, New York, 1975.
3. Parsons, J. The development of achievement expectancies in girls and boys. Paper presented at EPA, 1974.
4. Ryckman, R.M., and Sherman, M.F. Interaction effects of locus of control and sex of subject on confidence ratings and performance in achievement-related situations. Paper presented at APA, Hawaii, 1972.
5. McHugh, M.C., Fisher, J.E., and Frieze, I.H. The effects of competitiveness, type of task, sex, and outcome on attributions for one's own performance. Unpublished manuscript, University of Pittsburgh, 1975.
6. Deaux, K., and Farris, E. Attributing causes for one's performance: The effects of sex, norms, and outcome. Unpublished manuscript, Purdue University, 1974.
7. O'Leary, V.E., and Ridley, R. Causal attributions for performance: Sex differences in sensitivity to incongruity between expectancy and outcome. Unpublished manuscript, Oakland University, 1975.
8. Fisher, J.E. Effects of a competitive atmosphere on causal attributions: Theoretical implications. Paper presented at EPA, New York, 1975.
9. Terbovic, M.L. The effects of self-esteem on the perception of one's own and other's performances. Paper presented at EPA, New York, 1975.
10. Croke, J.A. Sex differences in causal attributions and expectancies for success as a function of the sex-role appropriateness of the task. Unpublished manuscript, University of California at Los Angeles, 1973.

11. Rotter, J.B., and Hochreich, D. I-E data from the University of Connecticut. Personal Communication, 1973.
12. Morris, M.B. Anti-feminism: Some discordant data. Paper presented at the Pacific Sociological Association, April, 1970.

REFERENCES

Almquist, E.M., & Angrist, S.S. Role model influences on college women's career aspirations. *Merrill-Palmer Quarterly*, 1971, *17*, 263-279.

Astin, H. Factors associated with the participation of the woman doctorate in the labor force. *Personal Guidance Journal*, 1968, *45*, 240-246.

Atkinson, J.W. *An introduction to motivation.* Princeton, N.J.: Van Nostrand Rinehold, 1964.

Bar-Tal, D., & Frieze, I.H. Achievement motivation for males and females as a determinant of attributions for success and failure. *Sex Roles;* 1977, *3*, 301-313.

Battle, E. Motivational determinants of academic task persistence. *Journal of Personality and Social Psychology*, 1965, *2*, 205-218.

Bem, D.J., & Allen, A. On predicting some of the people some of the time: The search for cross-situational consistencies in behavior. *Psychological Review*, 1974, *81*, 506-520.

Bem, S.L. The measurement of psychological androgyny. *Journal of Consulting and Clinical Psychology*, 1974, *42*, 155-168.

Bem, S.L. Sex-role adaptability: One consequence of psychological androgyny. *Journal of Personality and Social Psychology*, 1975, *31*, 634-661.

Bem, S.L., & Bem, D.J. Training the woman to know her place: The power of a nonconscious ideology. Adapted from D.J. Dem, *Beliefs, attitudes and human affairs.* Belmont, Calif.: Wadsworth, 1970.

Bernard, J. *Women and the public interest.* Chicago: Aldine-Atherton, 1971.

Bird, C. *Born female: The high cost of keeping women down.* New York: David McKay, 1968.

Brim, O.G., Jr., Goslin, D.A., Glass, D.C., & Goldberg, I. *American beliefs and attitudes about intelligence.* New York: Russell Sage, 1969.

Broverman, I.K., Vogel, S.R., Broverman, D.M., Clarkson, F.E., & Rosenkrantz, P.S. Sex-role stereotypes: A current appraisal. *Journal of Social Issues*, 1972, *28*, 59-78.

Condrey, J., & Dyer, S. Fear of success: Attributions of cause to the victim. In D.N. Ruble, I.H. Frieze, and J.E. Parsons (Eds.), *Sex roles: Persistence and change. Journal of Social Issues,* 1976, *32,* 63-84.

Crandall, V.C. Sex differences in expectancy of intellectual and academic reinforcement. In C.P. Smith (Ed.), *Achievement-related motives in children.* New York: Russell Sage, 1969.

Crandall, V.D., Katkovsky, W., & Crandall, V.J. Children's belief in their own control of reinforcement in intellectual-academic achievement situations. *Child Development,* 1965, *36,* 91-109.

Deaux, K., & Taynor, J. Evaluation of male and female ability: Bias works two ways. *Psychological Reports,* 1973, *32,* 261-262.

Deaux, K., & Emswiller, T. Explanations of successful performance on sex-linked tasks: What's skill for the male is luck for the female. *Journal of Personality and Social Psychology,* 1974, *29,* 80-85.

deCharms, R. *Personal causation.* New York: Academic Press, 1968.

Diggory, J. *Self evaluation: Concepts and studies,* New York: Wiley, 1966.

Dweck, C.S. The role of expectations and attributions in the alleviation of learned helplessness. *Journal of Personality and Social Psychology,* 1975, *31,* 674-685.

Elig, T., & Frieze, I.H. A multi-dimensional scheme for coding and interpreting perceived causality for success and failure events: The CSPS. *JSAS: Catalog of Selected Documents in Psychology,* 1975, *5,* 313. MS #1069.

Epstein, C.R. *Woman's place: Options and limits in professional careers.* Berkeley: University of California Press, 1971.

Etaugh, C., & Brown, B. Perceiving the causes of success and failure of male and female performers. *Developmental Psychology,* 1975, *11,* 103.

Feather, N.T. Effects of prior success and failure on expectations of success and subsequent performance. *Journal of Personality and Social Psychology,* 1966, *3,* 287-298.

Feather, N.T. Attribution of responsibility and valence of success and failure in relation to initial confidence and perceived locus of control. *Journal of Personality and Social Psychology,* 1969, *13,* 129-144.

Feather, N.T. Positive and negative reactions to male and female success and failure in relation to the perceived status and sex-typed appropriateness of occupations. *Journal of Personality and Social Psychology,* 1975, *31,* 536-548.

Feather, N.T., & Simon, J.G. Attribution of responsibility and valence of out-come in relation to initial confidence and success and failure of self and other. *Journal of Personality and Social Psychology*, 1971, *18*, 173-188. (a)

Feather, N.T., & Simon, J.G. Causal attributions for success and failure in rela-tion to expectations of success based upon selective or manipulative control. *Journal of Personality*, 1971, *39*, 527-541. (b)

Feather, N.T., & Simon, J.G. Fear of success and causal attributions for out-come. *Journal of Personality*, 1973, *41*, 525-542.

Feather, N.T., & Simon, J.G. Reactions to male and female success and failure in sex-linked occupations: Impressions of personality, causal attributions, and perceived likelihood of different consequences. *Journal of Personality and Social Psychology*, 1975, *31*, 20-31.

Feldman-Summers, S., & Kiesler, S.B. Those who are number two try harder: The effects of sex on attributions of causality. *Journal of Personality and Social Psychology*, 1974, *30*, 846-855.

Fitch, G. Effect of self-esteem, perceived performance and choice on causal attributions. *Journal of Personality and Social Psychology*, 1970, *16*, 311-315.

Fontaine, G. Social comparison and some determinants of expected personal control and expected performance in a novel task situation. *Journal of Per-sonality and Social Psychology*, 1974, *29*, 487-496.

Frieze, I. Studies of information processing and the attributional process in achievement-related contexts. Unpublished doctoral dissertation, University of California at Los Angeles, 1973.

Frieze, I. Women's expectations for causal attributions of success and failure. In N. Mednick, S. Tangri, and L. Hoffman (Eds.), *Women and achievement: Social and motivational analyses.* Washington, D.C.: Hemisphere Publishers, 1975.

Frieze, I.H. Causal attributions and information seeking to explain success and failure. *Journal of Research in Personality*, 1976, *10*, 293-305.

Frieze, I.H. Information processing and causal attributions for success and fail-ure. In J.S. Carroll and J.W. Payne (Eds.), *Cognition and social behavior.* Lawrence Erlbaum, 1976.

Frieze, I.H., & Weiner, B. Cue utilization and attributional judgments for success and failure. *Journal of Personality*, 1971, *39*, 591-606.

Frieze, I.H., Parsons, J., Johnson, P., Ruble, D., & Zellman, G. *Women and sex roles: A social psychological perspective.* New York: Norton. In press.

Goldberg, P. Are women prejudiced against women? *Transaction*, 1968, *5*, 28-30.

Heider, F. *The psychology of interpersonal relations.* New York: Wiley, 1958.

Hoffman, L.W. Early childhood experiences and women's achievement motives. *Journal of Social Issues,* 1972, *28,* 129-156.

Horner, M.S. Sex differences in achievement motivation and performance in competitive and non-competitive situations. Doctoral dissertation, University of Michigan, Ann Arbor, 1968.

Horner, M.S. Toward an understanding of achievement-related conflicts in women. *Journal of Social Issues,* 1972, *28,* 157-175.

House, W.C. Actual and perceived differences in male and female expectancies and minimal goal levels as a function of competition. *Journal of Personality,* 1974, *42,* 493-509.

House, W.C., & Perney, V. Valence of expected and unexpected outcomes as a function of locus of control and type of expectancy. *Journal of Personality and Social Psychology,* 1974, *29,* 454-463.

Jackaway, R. Sex differences in achievement motivation, behavior and attributions about success and failure. Unpublished dissertation, SUNY at Albany, 1974.

Jones, E.E., Kanouse, D.I., Kelley, H.H., Nisbett, R.E., Valins, S., & Weiner, B. (Eds). *Attribution: Perceiving the causes of behavior.* New York: General Learning Press, 1972.

Jones, E.E., & Nesbitt, R.E. The actor and the observer: Divergent perceptions of the causes of behavior. In E.E. Jones, D.I. Kanouse, H.H. Kelley, R.E. Nesbitt, S. Valins, and B. Weiner (Eds.), *Attribution: Perceiving the causes of behavior.* New York: General Learning Press, 1972.

Kukla, A. Attributional determinants of achievement-related behavior. *Journal of Personality and Social Psychology,* 1972, *21,* 166-174.

Levitin, T., Quinn, R.P., & Staines, G.L. Sex discrimination against American working women. *American Behavioral Scientist,* 1971, *15,* 237-254.

Luginbuhl, J.E., Crowe, D.H., & Kahan, J.P. Causal attributions for success and failure. *Journal of Personality and Social Psychology,* 1975, *31,* 86-93.

Lunneborg, P.W., & Rosenwood, L.M. Need affiliation and achievement: Declining sex differences. *Psychological Reports,* 1972, *31,* 795-798.

Maccoby, E.E., & Jacklin, C.N. *The psychology of sex differences.* Stanford: Stanford University Press, 1975.

McArthur, L.Z. Note on sex differences in causal attribution. *Psychological Reports,* 1976.

McClelland, D.C., Atkinson, J.W., Clark, R.W., & Lowell, E.L. *The achievement motive.* New York: Appleton-Century-Crofts, 1953.

McMahan, I.D. Relationships between causal attributions and expectancy of success. *Journal of Personality and Social Psychology*, 1973, *28*, 108-114.

Mischel, W. Continuity and change in personality. In H.N. Mischel and W. Mischel (Eds.), *Readings in personality*. New York: Holt, Rinehart and Winston, 1973.

Montanelli, D.S., & Hill, K.T. Children's expectations and performance as a function of two consecutive reinforcements. *Journal of Personality and Social Psychology*, 1969, *13*, 115-128.

Murray, S.R., & Mednick, M.T.S. Perceiving the causes of success and failure in achievement: Sex, race and motivational comparisons. *Journal of Consulting and Clinical Psychology*, 1975, *43*, 881-885.

Nicholls, J. Causal attributions and other achievement-related cognitions: Effects of task, outcome, attainment value and sex. *Journal of Personality and Social Psychology*, 1975, *31*, 379-389.

O'Leary, V.E. Some attitudinal barriers to occupational aspirations in women. *Psychological Bulletin*, 1974, *81*, 809-826.

Parson, J.E., Frieze, I.H., & Ruble, D.N. Intrapsychic factors influencing career aspirations in college women. *Sex Roles*. In press.

Parsons, J.E., Ruble, D.N., Hodges, K.L., & Small, A.W. Cognitive-developmental factors in emerging sex differences in achievement-related expectancies. In D.N. Ruble, I.H. Frieze, and J.E. Parsons (Eds.), *Sex roles: persistence and change. Journal of Social Issues*, 1976, *32*, 47-62.

Pheterson, G.I., Kiesler, S.B., & Goldberg, P.A. Evaluation of the performance of women as a function of their sex, achievement and personal history. *Journal of Personality and Social Psychology*, 1971, *19*, 114-118.

Piacente, B.S., Penner, L.A., Hawkins, H.L., & Cohen, S.L. Evaluation of the performance of experimenters as a function of their sex and competence. *Journal of Applied Social Psychology*, 1974, *4*, 321-329.

Riemer, B.S. The influence of causal beliefs on affect and expectancy. *Journal of Personality and Social Psychology*, 1975, *31*, 1163-1167.

Rosen, B., & Jerdee, T.H. Effects of applicant's sex and difficulty of job on evaluation of candidates for managerial positions. *Journal of Applied Psychology*, 1974, *59*, 511-512. (a)

Rosen, B., & Jerdee, T.H. Influence of sex-role stereotypes on personal decisions. *Journal of Applied Psychology*, 1974, *59*, 9-14. (b)

Rosenbaum, R.M. A dimensional analysis of the perceived causes of success and failure. Unpublished doctoral dissertation, University of California at Los Angeles, 1972.

Rosenthal, R., & Jacobson, L.R. Teacher expectations of the disadvantaged. *Scientific American,* 1968, *218,* 19-23.

Rotter, J.B. *Social learning and clinical psychology.* Englewood Cliffs, N.J.: Prentice-Hall, 1954.

Rotter, J.B. Generalized expectancies for internal versus external control of reinforcement. *Psychological Monographs,* 1966, *80,* 1 (Whole #609).

Shrauger, J.S. Self-esteem and reactions to being observed by others. *Journal of Personality and Social Psychology,* 1972, *24,* 92-101.

Simon, J.G., & Feather, N.T. Causal attributions for success and failure at university examinations. *Journal of Educational Psychology,* 1973, *64,* 46-56.

Stein, A.H., & Bailey, M.M. The socialization of achievement orientation in females. *Psychological Bulletin,* 1973, *80,* 345-366.

Tangri, S.S. Determinants of occupational role innovation among college women. *Journal of Social Issues,* 1972, *28,* 177-200.

Throop, W.F., & MacDonald, A.P., Jr. Internal-external locus of control: A bibliography. *Psychological Reports,* 1971, Monograph Supplement 1-V28.

Tressemer, D. Fear of success: Popular but unproven. *Psychology Today,* 1974, *7,* 82-85.

Tyler, B.B. Expectancy for eventual success as a factor in problem-solving behavior. *Journal of Educational Psychology,* 1958, *49,* 166-172.

Valle, V.A. Attributions of stability as a mediator in the changing of expectations. Unpublished doctoral dissertation, University of Pittsburgh, 1974.

Valle, V.A., & Frieze, I.H. The stability of causal attributions as a mediator in changing expectations for success. *Journal of Personality and Social Psychology,* 1976, *33,* 579-587.

Veroff, J. Social comparison and the development of achievement motivation. In C.P. Smith (Ed.), *Achievement-related motives in children.* New York: Russell Sage, 1969.

Weiner, B. New conceptions in the study of achievement motivation. In B. Maher (Ed.), *Progress in experimental personality research* (Vol. 5). New York: Academic Press, 1970.

Weiner, B. *Theories of motivation.* Chicago: Markham Press, 1972.

Weiner, B. Achievement motivation as conceptualized by an attribution theorist. In B. Weiner (Ed.), *Achievement motivation and attribution theory.* General Learning Press, 1974.

Weiner, B., & Kukla, A. An attributional analysis of achievement motivation. *Journal of Personality and Social Psychology,* 1970, *15,* 1-20.

Weiner, B., & Potepan, P.A. Personality correlates and affective reactions toward exams of succeeding and failing college students. *Journal of Educational Psychology*, 1970, *61*, 144-151.

Weiner, B., Frieze, I., Kukla, A., Reed, L., Rest, S., & Rosenbaum, R.M. *Perceiving the causes of success and failure.* New York: General Learning Press Module, 1971.

Weiner, B., Heckhausen, H., Meyer, W., & Cook, R.E. Causal ascriptions and achievement behavior: Conceptual analysis of effort and reanalysis of locus of control. *Journal of Personality and Social Psychology*, 1972, *21*, 239-248.

Wieger, R.M. The cognitive mediation of achievement-related behavior. Unpublished doctoral dissertation, University of Pittsburgh, 1975.

Wiegers, R.M., & Frieze, I.H. Gender, female traditionality, achievement level and cognitions of success and failure. *Psychology of Women Quarterly;* in press.

CHAPTER 15

CREATIVITY IN WOMEN

RAVENNA MATHEWS HELSON

Ravenna Mathews Helson received her B.A. at the University of Texas and her Ph.D. at the University of California at Berkeley, where she worked with Brunswik and Krech. Thereafter, she taught at Smith College for three years, after which she returned to Berkeley and engaged in survey research with the California State Department of Health for a period and then became Assistant Research Psychologist at the Institute of Personality Assessment and Research. It was here that she concentrated on studying creativity in women (and men), the childhood background of her Ss and their interest patterns, and the phenomenological research of thought processes. Included in these interests was the study of symbolism and Jungian psychology as applied to literary fantasy, encouraged by Henry Murray through the Frances B. Wickes Foundation.

Ms. Helson is sometimes a visiting lecturer at UCB in the Department of Psychology, having organized and taught special courses on the psychology of women and (with Jeanne Block and others) "research in the making." She is past-President of the Association of Academic Women at the University of California, a Fellow of APA's Division 8, Secretary-Treasurer of APA's Division 10, and a reviewer of articles submitted to The Psychology of Women Quarterly, *the journal of APA's Division 35, along with other journals.*

The study of creativity as it was launched in the 1950's generally neglected women. The Cold War, the anticonformity rebellion, and sex-role conservatism tended to depreciate or divert attention away from creativity in women, though "affluence" had more favorable effects. Ideas about creativity in women were influenced by many latent assumptions, including a "phallocentric" definition of creativity.

Early studies of sex differences in creative thinking abilities concluded that boys were superior, but it became evident that the relative performance of boys and girls on these measures depended upon many specific factors, and the older findings have not been confirmed. However, creative thinking abilities do combine differently with other personality and social variables for boys and girls.

In the 1940s and 1950s it was argued that women could rarely have a creative personality because the masculine assertiveness required would repress feminine receptivity. Nevertheless, empirical work in the 1960s demonstrated a clear creative personality in high-school women, college women, and even in women mathematicians.

A study of sex differences in personality and style in professional mathematicians and writers shows that creative men and women writers are more similar in personality, relative to comparison Ss, than are men and women mathematicians. Creative women have more in common across fields than have creative men. These results are interpreted in terms of both social context and personality organization.

Recent work on masculinity and femininity in relation to creativity suggests that creative individuals do not necessarily have more characteristics of the other sex than their fellows, but that they have characteristics of both sexes in a form that (a) makes difficult a simple identification with either sex role, and (b) facilitates creative expression in a symbolic medium.

The study of subgroups along a continuum of creativity or within a creative sample makes contact with theoretical systems, affords perspective on more general findings about sex differences in creativity, and shows a variety of patterns within each sex that can lead to creative accomplishment.

Creative innovation is facilitated by certain social roles that are not usually available to women. Also, the male judge of creative contributions tends to favor work of those similar to himself, and to recognize innovations that will enhance his own position. Women's contributions do not customarily receive this recognition.

To redress this imbalance, there is an immediate need for studies of creativity that embody the special concerns of women and which help amend such deficiencies in contemporary psychology.

In the Conference of Women's Research Needs in Psychology, creativity in women was assigned to the category of "neglected topics." Why is it a neglected topic? Should it have a lower priority than others? If so, why; and if not, why not? Let us keep these questions in mind. I would like to begin with a survey of the several approaches to creativity that were influential in the 1950s, when research in this area came into prominence. I will suggest that each approach to creativity appealed to, or reflected, an important current of concern in American society during that decade, and I will examine the implications of the various points of view for the study, or neglect, of creativity in women.

IMPLICATIONS FOR RESEARCH ON CREATIVITY IN WOMEN

In 1950, Guilford's article, "Creativity," appeared in the *American Psychologist,* presenting a forceful contrast between convergent and divergent thinking and its seminal ideas for measuring cognitive processes. At that time, creativity had been a long-neglected topic for everyone, men as well as women. Guilford attributed the enormous response which his article evoked to the climate of the Cold War and the interest in space exploration, which were such conspicuous features of the 1950s. Certainly, the impact of his ideas was increased through large grants to investigators who proposed to "spot creative talent" by developing measures of originality for use in grade school and high school, and there was particular concern to spot potential scientists. I will consider some of this work later. Here, I want to suggest that Guilford's admirable program to identify the building blocks of intellect, his cognitive approach to creativity ("creative thinking and problem-solving are one and the same"), and the emphasis on science were not conducive to the demonstration of creativity in women. Later (Guilford, 1967), he wrote:

It is curious that with the less masculine vocations in the arts open to women, the greatest artists have been men. Sex differences on [divergent

production] tests are very small and often not statistically significant . . .
[At the ninth-grade level] there was a tendency for girls to have higher
means on tests of fluency but for boys to have higher means on tests of
flexibility. From this result one might expect the so-called weaker sex to
be a bit long, relatively, on quantity but a bit short on quality of idea
production.

What Guilford found "curious" (we will find this word recurring in connection
with creativity in women) is rendered so because he concentrated on intellectual
skills, with minimal consideration of sex roles, social settings, or even personality
characteristics. This reductionistic approach led to what is almost a stereotypical
joke—based on differences he had already labeled as small and often insignificant
—as an explanation of cultural sex differences in creativity. I admire Guilford's
work and I do not consider him unfriendly to women; I am trying to show how
the subject of creativity in women fared in this most influential, pioneering
approach to the field.

Personality characteristics of creative scientists began to be studied in the
early 1950s. The pioneering work of Roe appeared first in 1951, and Cattell and
Drevdahl published a study of eminent researchers in physics, biology, and
psychology in 1955. Here, the concern with scientists, and especially with the
most prestigious scientists, effectively diverted attention from women.

In these same years, Barron at the Institute of Personality Assessment and
Research (IPAR) began his work on creative personality traits, the first being the
preference for asymmetry versus symmetry, which he investigated in collaboration with Welsh (Barron & Welsh, 1952). Then came the IPAR studies of the
creative personality (MacKinnon, 1961). If the popularity of Guilford's ideas
and the study of scientists were enhanced by the concerns of the Cold War,
perhaps the IPAR studies, dealing with the "softer" concerns of culture, should
be seen in relation to the *affluence* of the 1950s. The Carnegie Corporation was
able then, as it would not have been a decade later, to invest in a pioneering
undertaking that had to be expensive, by the standards of personality research,
to "realize its potential."

Barron was influenced by Kris' (1952) idea of "regression in the service of the
ego." The experience of the creative man in regressing to a feminine identification was often discussed in psychoanalysis and was in fact attributed to Freud
himself (Erikson, 1954). Barron (1957) raised an old question: Is there a division
of labor between the sexes, women creating children (as they certainly were
doing in the 1950s) and men creating ideas? Or is there a creative personality in
women as in men? And if the latter, would creative women be found to have

conspicuous masculine characteristics as creative men seemed to have conspicuous feminine characteristics? MacKinnon (1962) discussed the feminine characteristics of creative men in relation to the Jungian concept of the anima. Thus, there was general interest in feminine characteristics at IPAR, and one of the five main creativity projects was concerned with creativity in women. I will return to it later.

In the 1950s the winds of influence blew strongly around the Cold War, the space program, and Affluence, but there was also another—and that was the anticonformity rebellion. In psychology, one of the main expressions of this current was the attention paid to rebel psychotherapists. Erich Fromm, Rollo May, Abraham Maslow, and Carl Rogers were all represented in the Symposia on Creativity held at Michigan State University (Anderson, 1959). All these authors were apparently friendly toward women. However, they tended to use women for their purpose of protesting against the "system" and against the overvaluation of achievement (i.e., bigness or quantifiable "evidence" of creative effort). Maslow's (1959) concept of self-actualizing creativeness put the emphasis on personality rather than on achievements, considering the latter as epiphenomena emitted by the personality and therefore secondary to it. At the end of his remarks he said that

> [My concept] may help to resolve the dilemma of the "lack" of creativeness in the female, for offhand there seems to be no gender difference in creativeness. If, as I think, there are constitutionally determined self-actualizing differences in interest in production of publications, paintings, symphonies, etc. (women probably are as able to do these things but they are not as interested in doing them), then creativity of the conventional "production" type may be synonymous with a masculine type of productiveness. The old dilemma may then be translated as "Why do women have female interests and not male ones?" Stated so, it resolves itself and disappears. (pp. 94-95.)

Friendly as this may sound, important as it may be, the ears of women with serious creative interests are likely to hear it as a sell-out of their cause. It is a point of view that soon becomes expressed this way: "The really creative women are the housewives who aren't trying to compete with men. Career women just aren't creative." Men who say such things should read Olsen's (1970) account of the human cost of creativity silenced by domestic duties and economic pressures. This kind of "equal but different" position may be comforting to a sensitive male psyche, but it is fatal to the cause of affirmative action at the university or art gallery.

Orthodox psychoanalysis certainly had little to contribute as a starting point for an investigation of creativity in women. Deutsch (1945) said that women were not creative because the intellectuality and assertiveness (masculinity) necessary for achievement killed the spontaneity (femininity) essential to creativity. A few psychoanalysts (mostly Jungian, but they were not widely read) went further into the psychological difficulties of talented women (Harding, 1935; Neumann, 1954a; Greenacre, 1960). Some of their ideas will be considered later. The emphasis on difficulties and disadvantages also pervaded de Beauvoir's *The Second Sex* (1953), but nevertheless that book was a landmark. The creative person, de Beauvoir said, must start from an authentic sense of self, but society has defined woman as the "other."

The force of an interpretation such as de Beauvoir's was impressed upon me when I read *The Potential of Women* (Farber & Wilson, 1963), one of the early manifestations of concern with "the woman problem" in the 1960s. In a chapter entitled "The Roles of Women," a male existentialist philosopher (Peter Koestenbaum) recommended to women that they decide their own lives. "Once [a woman] understands and accepts the nature of her irrefragable subjectivity, she is suddenly relieved to discover a soaring, wraithlike, lissome sense of freedom" (p. 143). She is now an autonomous person, he explained. As a consequence, she makes her decisions intelligently, confidently, with no crippling sense of guilt or regrets. So the author said—but then here are the possibilities he offered: First, as Hera, a woman can assume the noble role of homemaking, her goals being marriage, companionship, security, husband, children, and the satisfying knowledge that she is fulfilling the traditional female role. Or, as Aphrodite, a woman would seek sexual gratification, physical beauty, and the cynosure of power and glory that attend it, the supreme physical and spiritual experience of which her feminine nature is capable. Finally, as Ceres—she can function as a "creator" outside the home. She seeks "worldly excitement; she searches after stature, status, recognition, independence, and aesthetic satisfactions. She is ambitious; she wants strength, influence and money."

What struck me here especially was the strange treatment of Ceres. It seemed impossible for this man, despite obvious poetic gifts, to imagine a woman whose creativity outside the home could be compared to Ceres' greening of the earth each spring, to her bountiful harvests. He was not familiar with Eleusinian mysteries, or did not consider them relevant. It did not occur to him to see possibilities for women in the wise Athene, nor in Artemis, the virgin huntress and guardian of women in the creative agonies of childbirth. For this failure of imagination, one supposes that the blinders of convention were responsible.

Elsewhere in *The Potential of Women* (Farber & Wilson, 1963), several men discussed "What is a Woman?" Karl Pribram made this remark:

> The members of the panel and other speakers today have all touched upon, and then backed away from, as though touching a flame, the subject of why women are not creative. Can you discuss it, or is it a question which cannot be answered? (p. 98.)

Pribram had previously expressed the opinion that cultural differences are exaggerations of biological differences, that actual creative achievements—as contrasted with babies or charm or social atmospheres—are made by men, and that "we cannot take a woman or girl child and make a man of her, a real man in the sense of all that is best about being a man, without an extremely long period of agony." The question that arose in my mind was whether the question of "why women are not creative" might be "flamelike" because it was related to the question of whether women could be *transformed* into men.

I believe that these discussions in *The Potential of Women* probably reflected the sex-role conservatism that was particularly strong in the 1950s. These conservative attitudes made study of creativity in women seem of dubious value.

To summarize this historical overview: The strong interest in creativity which arose in the 1950s showed the influence of the main characteristics of that decade. Most of these influences were not conducive to the study of women as creative artists and scientists, though some of them did make room for women as "self-actualizing persons." By the early 1960s, it was clear that a psychology of creative achievement in women had two important needs: (a) to clarify the unconscious assumptions and biases in thinking about this topic, and (b) to undertake empirical studies of creative women.

ANALYSIS OF IDEAS ABOUT CREATIVITY IN WOMEN

Let us first analyze the idea that women are by nature low in creative potential. The evidence for this statement is, I believe, of two main kinds. First, it is observed that there have been very few eminent women scientists or artists. This fact does not lead logically to the conclusion that women have less creative potential than men. As Nochlin (1972) pointed out, there were almost no great artists from the aristocracy, and yet we do not conclude that men of the aristocracy lacked creative ability, but rather we assume that their duties and way of life precluded dedication to the career of an artist. That has certainly been true of most women. But then the second kind of evidence, which reinforces the first, is the fact that certain traits attributed to the creative person conflict with the traits generally attributed to women. Women have been thought to have less "passion" than men, to have little capacity for abstract thinking, to care little about the future but to be invested in their own homes and families. They are said to be conservers rather than innovators. The fact that the names of few creative women are known to us, plus the fact that we think of women as lacking the daring, the large brain, or the scope and prestige of Michaelangelo or Copernicus or Karl Marx make it seem that the scarcity of creative women has its reasons in women's psychology. We never hear the argument that men are low in creative potential because they do not have the patience for the creative idea to develop, the sharp eye to discriminate critical differences, the access to the life of feeling sufficient to allow the help of the unconscious. These statements would not be very convincing because we know that though they may be true of many men, there are creative men who are different. Ample evidence exists that creative men have these "feminine" characteristics in abundance.

One possible conclusion from the evidence is that where some men have creative feminine traits, if indeed "feminine" is the right label for them, women are not by nature as capable of developing the requisite masculine traits. There is some support for this view in the greater variability often reported for males. Another construction of the evidence would be that women have constituted a caste; that is, a group whose psychological traits are socially perceived to be invariant with their physical characteristics. The characteristics we attribute to women do not explain the paucity of creative women, according to this opinion, but both are to be understood in terms of the effective maintenance of caste boundaries.

It is very easy to show support for the second hypothesis. The familiar mechanisms of social control, propaganda, and prejudiced thinking may be amply illustrated in the way creative women are reduced in number and significance to the point where they seem too rare to justify consideration. There is the familiar network of social roles, which makes it difficult for women to train for or engage in serious creative activity, or to receive rewards for doing so. There is the distortion of history so that creative women are ignored, or their characteristics changed to fit female stereotypes, or (if all else fails) it may be explained that they were essentially male, not women at all! Definitions of creativity are biased so that male values or strengths are highlighted. Here is a humorous example:

> In a study of differences in the creative writings of boys and girls, Colvin (1902) found that the boys were superior to the girls in their general apperception of humor. They were especially superior in the teasing, bullying, and farce comedy type of humor. They were inferior, however, in their apperception of the incongruous, the ridiculous, and the absurd, and of the more subtle and delicate forms of humor.

When the question of creativity in women comes up, it is often said to be a "curious" question, or a "paradox," or like a "flame." Why is it so curious? Nobody says that it is "curious" how few women are in the pulpit or the cabinet, or are governors of their state. People seem to think: "If women like art, why don't they become great artists?" They forget the training, materials, space, courage, confidence, contacts, and freedom from distraction necessary for creative achievement in the arts.

Another factor in the "paradox" seems to be that creativity has come to be associated with a male procreative model. How a woman could be creative does then become a "curious" question. The psychologist's whole language of problem solving—identifying the barrier, the "aha" experience, penetrating to the solution—is adapted to a phallocentric concept of creativity. In different primitive societies, one finds residues of battles between the sexes about who is to get credit for the baby. Some cultures believe it is obviously the hard work of the father that is the important thing, but in other cultures the credit is given to the "growing genius" of the mother. In our society, too, the various "methods" of childbirth have to do, among other things, with the assignment of power roles to male and female. It all seems rather childish, and yet Greenacre (1960) thought that one of the main handicaps of girls with artistic ability was their tendency to identify their talent as phallus, and then to try to hide it or deny it. It would seem that the more emphasis we put on phallocentric models, the more difficult it is to "conceive" creative women.

Evidence that the attribution of creativity to women goes counter to our sex-role stereotypes and to our prevailing power structure does not prove that women would be creative if conditions were different. However, it does put us on our guard that we must consider empirical findings about sex differences in creativity very carefully, and plan our studies of creative women with vigilance.

EMPIRICAL STUDIES

If there were not creative women, that fact would not prove that women might not be creative under different social conditions than those that have prevailed hitherto. Nevertheless, the existence of productive creative women is the best evidence for the possibility of their existence. Therefore, in considering empirical studies, I will emphasize those that are concerned with personality and style in productively creative adults, male and female. First, however, let us survey the literature on the identification of creative cognitive abilities in children and young people.

Sex Differences in Creative Thinking Abilities

The current consensus is that neither boys nor girls show a consistent superiority in creative thinking abilities (Torrance, 1972; Kogan, 1974; Maccoby & Jacklin, 1974). This is, I think, an important beginning statement to be able to make about the subject of creativity in women, even though the concurrent and predictive validities of the measures of creative thinking are not fully established, and even though the conclusion of "no consistent superiority shown by either sex" turns out to be an envelope for the accumulated evidence that many variables affect the way, and the extent to which, boys and girls manifest creative behavior.

Some of the factors that affect the pattern of sex differences on tests of creative thinking abilities are (a) the nature of the specific task, that is, figural stimuli favor boys and verbal stimuli favor girls: (b) the instructions and the way the test is administered, that is, creative boys have an advantage when ideas are spoken out in a group and girls when responses are written down; and (c) the developmental status of the sample, including the saliency of sex-related identification for children of a given grade, as well as the relative proficiency of boys and girls at reading, controlling impulse, and so forth.

Some of the early studies reported that boys are more original than girls, and there was much discussion of these findings. For example, Torrance (1963) found that many girls in the upper grades of elementary school would not even participate in divergent-thinking sessions when the tasks involved science. Furthermore, when girls did offer scientific ideas, their ideas were rated lower than those of boys by the children themselves, though not by adult observers.

Torrance believes that sex differences in measured creative thinking abilities have been diminishing. This opinion would seem to be borne out by a study of Bruce (1974), who repeated some main features of Torrance's earlier study and found sex-related differences neither in the number of science ideas contributed by boys and girls nor in the evaluation of these ideas by the children. However, I would suspect that it is not the "creative thinking abilities" of boys and girls that have changed, but the social pressure to recognize the potential of the girls.

It is still the case that when girls come out better than the boys on these tests, as they often do, the experimenter tends to "tuck away" the findings by implying that the measures are (merely) verbal, or that the results are more equally balanced than they look in the tables, or that it is not the purpose of the study to go into sex differences (Torrance & Aliotti, 1969; Wallach & Wing, 1969). Perhaps the experimenter believes that he cannot eliminate the possibility of sampling biases (maybe some of the more creative boys didn't take the test, etc). It is no doubt shrewd on the experimenter's part to do this: If the discrepancy between expectations about sex-related differences in creativity and the research findings is too great, the reader may conclude that whatever creativity tests measure does not have much to do with real life, or the boys would do better!

Creative Thinking Abilities and Actual Creative Behavior

What do we know, then, about the creativity of boys and girls in real life? When a large group of teachers was asked to reward instances of originality in the classroom, a tally of their reports showed that about two-thirds of the children who had been rewarded were boys. This finding suggests that in "real life" boys are more original than girls, but other plausible explanations are that boys are more exhibitionistic, that teachers "see" originality more readily in boys, or that they use rewards to handle difficult children, who are more often boys. Torrance (1964) suggested that teachers may reward boys for originality, girls for conformity.

However, there is really considerable evidence that both boys and girls who score high on measures of creative thinking engage in more creative activities outside the classroom than do their classmates (Torrance, 1964; Wallach & Wing, 1969). Some studies have used Ss' reports of creative interests and accomplishments as a criterion of creativity or as an important measure in studies of creativity, and have been as successful with girls as with boys in so doing (Holland & Astin, 1962; Drews, 1964; Anastasi & Schaefer, 1969).

There are, of course, large sex-related differences in direction of creative interests. Boys prefer scientific activities; girls prefer writing and art. Attempts to measure intensity of interests in boys and girls are made more difficult both by this difference in direction of interests and by the different relationship of creative achievement to male and female life circumstances. Fox and Denham (1974) reported more fascination with mathematics on the part of high-aptitude junior high-school boys than girls. The boys were much more likely to read ahead, to do extra projects on their own, and to take special courses in mathematics. They enjoyed these classes and benefited from them. The girls were not nearly so interested, but then one pertinent fact was that, even among a group of science contestants, twice as many boys as girls had their strongest interests in the scientific or investigative area. The strongest interest of the largest group of girls was artistic! Astin (1974) visited the homes of these children, and found that parents paid much more attention to the precocity of the boys than to that of the girls. However, interpretation is rendered uncertain by the fact that the parents of the boys were, for some reason, of higher socioeconomic status.

Boys who want to become artists have a battle with their parents preceding the decision to go to art school (Griff, 1970). If they do go to art school, they tend to be strongly committed, much more so than the girls (Barron, 1972). There is not, I believe, a comparable experience in the lives of adolescent girls who go into science, and of course serious interest in creating works of art does not serve the purposes of female identity as interest in science serves the purposes of male identity (Tyler, 1964; McClelland, 1962). We will return to this important question of the strength and origins of creative motivation in men and women.

If the culture supports creative behavior in boys more than in girls, one might expect assessments of it to be more stable in boys. Kogan and Pankove (1972) tested a group first in an individual situation and five years later in a group situation. Reliability was good among the boys, but among the girls a different group emerged as highly fluent when the setting shifted from the personal to the impersonal. Kogan (1974) believes that women's susceptibility to the influence of the social situation, as exemplified in the Kogan & Pankove (1972) study, may be a considerable disadvantage to their creative productivity.

Again, Torrance (1972) reported somewhat better success at predicting creative achievement for boys than for girls. In a follow-up study of high-school students tested 12 years after their first test, number of children was negatively correlated, among women, with quantity as well as quality of creative achievements and creativeness of aspirations. Yet the highly creative women were more likely than the low creative ones to have both career and family (53% for highs, 28% for lows) rather than only family (5% vs. 26%) or only career (29% vs. 36%). Torrance concluded that creative achievement may be more difficult to predict in young women than in young men, not because their choices are more limited, but because there are more options open to them. He means, I think, that women with creative thinking abilities are not under the same pressure as men to express themselves in "achievements." Torrance quoted some women Ss who were certainly not inclined toward achievement, though their day-to-day lives seemed to be filled with self-expressive activity.

Creative Thinking Abilities and Other Personality Traits

Although sex differences in average scores on creative thinking abilities may be negligible, say some investigators, differences in the way these abilities are patterned with other characteristics may be very important (Kogan, 1974). I have anticipated some of this discussion in describing factors affecting the different direction, intensity, and stability of interests in creative boys and girls.

Research on personality traits related to creativity shows recurring concern with the variables of introversion-extraversion; defensiveness or conventionality; ego control; and traits of masculinity and femininity. Let us consider some studies of sex differences in the relation between creativity and these traits.

Introversion. If women are more susceptible to the interpersonal situation than men are, one might expect to find that traits modulating this susceptibility, such as introversion or sociability, would have a different relation to creative behavior in the two sexes. Kurtzman (1967) and Werner and Bachtold (1969) are among those who have found creative or gifted adolescent girls to be less dominant and self-assured than their male counterparts, as compared with peers of the same sex. Rock, Evans, and Klein (1969) reported that "little inclination toward social function" identified individuals whose creative achievement was predictable in a sample of boys, as well as in a sample of girls. However, in the low-sociability group, girls were more predictable than boys.

Defensiveness. There is considerable evidence that creative men are less prone than other men to deny or to avoid recognizing unpleasant aspects of the self, but Kogan (1974) said that defensive strategies used by males are more self-defeating than those used by females. In their researches (Wallach & Kogan, 1965; Kogan & Morgan, 1969), defensive boys were found to clam up, but defensive girls were at least as fluent as the average. The girls would seem to have little real advantage, since Kogan suggests that "fluency in the service of defensiveness may be achieved at the cost of response originality." Also, we will see that creative women, like creative men, are less defensive than comparison Ss. Nevertheless, the point that the *less* creative boys and girls show different *kinds* of defensive behavior is an interesting and important one.

Ego control. Pine and Holt (1960) studied control of primary process thinking, as assessed on the Rorschach, in relation to creativity on a variety of tasks. Ss were male and female college students. They found that men and women seemed to have different response sets, so that creativity was associated with less control—more "regression"—in women than in men. The authors related these findings to the predilection of women for the arts rather than the sciences.

Bowers (1971) found that performance on a variety of creative tasks was related in women (but not in men) to hypnotic susceptibility and to reported experience of unrealistic, trancelike states. In men, creativity was lowest when hypnotic susceptibility was highest. Bowers believed that his results, along with other work on hypnotizability and personal experience, may reflect sex-related differences in the organization of imagination, women's imagination being more "stimulus incited" and that of men more "impulse incited."

Mendelsohn (1976) and Mendelsohn and Covington (1972) demonstrated sex-related differences in the attentional processes of high and low scorers on RAT, the Remote Associates Test (Mednick, 1962), which is sometimes used as a measure of creativity. High-scoring men showed an outstanding ability to maintain several ongoing streams of cognitive activity simultaneously, but the RAT appears not to differentiate among women on the same dimensions. Mendelsohn believes that the RAT does not involve the sort of fluid associational processes generally implicated in creative performance, but taps abilities "useful for creative performance." One possible interpretation is that creativity in women is less likely than creativity in men to rely upon the manipulation of several streams of *cognitive* activity simultaneously.

Masculine and feminine sex-related traits.   Whether creative men are more feminine than other men, and creative women are more masculine than other women, or whether creative individuals are less specialized in sex role or broader in range than the average person, all these have been questions of continuing interest. I postpone this topic to another place because of the longer discussion it requires. Recent empirical studies include those by Urbina, Harrison, Schaefer, and Anastasi (1970); Raychaudhuri (1971); Suter and Domino (1975); and Kanner (1976). Theoretical essays with a psychoanalytic perspective include papers by Besdine (1971) and Martindale (1972).

Summary of Sex Differences in Creative Thinking Abilities

In this section we have seen that girls generally perform as well as boys on measures of creative thinking abilities, and that for both, girls and boys these measures are related to creative interests and accomplishments in real life. However, the direction of interests and the relation of creative achievement to circumstances of life are quite different for the two sexes. Intensity of creative interests and stability of creative behavior across situations may be greater in boys, whether due to stronger cultural support of creative achievement in the male or to this and other cognitive differences. A number of studies show that creative abilities are patterned differently in the sexes, but these studies as yet provide no overall picture.

DEMONSTRATING THE CREATIVE PERSONALITY IN WOMEN

The creative personality is often conceptualized as one in which there is great emotion, sensitivity, or associative fluency in combination with great capacity for ordering, enduring, and achieving. This coupling of "incompatible" traits is recognized as unusual, and authors of reports in the 1940s and 1950s said it would be very difficult indeed for women to combine feminine spontaneity with sustained effort and assertiveness. They dwelt upon the difficulties and said little to acknowledge that there were any creative women at all.

Studies that began to be published in the 1960s took a different tack. For example, the assumptions behind my own work were that there *are* creative women, that they probably resemble creative men in essential respects but might differ in others, and that cultural factors certainly work to their disadvantage. I thought it would be useful to cast off preoccupations about the superiority of the male, and to begin with an attempt to find out what creative women are like, as compared with other women.

The first important finding was that creative women do exist. For example, faculty members in a women's college could identify creative women, and these Ss, when compared with their classmates, were found to possess traits such as originality and flexibility on the one hand, and commitment to sustained endeavor and motivation toward creative achievement on the other (Helson, 1966, 1967a). Such women are not extremely rare. They may constitute 15 or 20% of a college class, as they represented 18% of Drews' (1964) sample of brighter-than-average adolescents.

Nor did it turn out to be very mysterious where these young women had come from. Their parents tended to be independent, intellectual, and artistic, and had emphasized moral integrity rather than sex roles. The daughters were more likely to identify with both parents or with neither parent than with mother or father alone. They generally did well in the "ego building" years of grade school, were less happy in high school, and came into their own again in college. When they married, they tended to marry men whose values were similar to their own and were such as to encourage a creative wife (Helson, 1967a). A study of the brothers and sisters of these college women showed that the siblings of the creatives had higher scores on inventory measures of creative traits than had the siblings of other women, and that the brothers showed more evidence of intellectual achievement than other brothers. As children, the brothers of creative women, in comparison with brothers of other women, felt that their sister had stronger interests than they had and was taken more seriously by their parents (Helson, 1968a).

Even in mathematics, women gave clear evidence of a "creative personality" (Helson, 1961, 1971). That is, creative women, as compared with other women Ph.D.'s in mathematics, combined sensitivity and flexibility with unusual absorption in mathematical research. However, they were usually peripheral members of the mathematical community, often isolated, working in the shadow of a man, or intermittently employed. To find them, it was necessary to design the study in a laborious way that circumvented our conventional reliance on institutional processes of selection. Letters to many mathematicians and mathematics departments solicited nominations for a study of women in mathematics. The criterion of creativity was *quality* of the *S*'s published research, as compared to that of the average research paper in mathematics journals. This meant that ratings had to be obtained onerously from separate groups of specialists in different areas of mathematics. A criterion of number of publications, or of general reputation and influence, though easier to obtain, would have been much less appropriate for the marginal group of women.

Genius, as Albert (1975) argued persuasively, is a label generally awarded to persons whose creative behavior begins early, attracts attention, and is sustained over a long time period. Such a career does not mesh with the life of women. To find creative women, we must look for them where they are trying to survive, not where the spotlight is focused.

CREATIVE PERSONALITY IN MEN AND WOMEN IN TWO FIELDS

In this section I present findings based on samples of men and women engaged in creative work in the same two fields: mathematics and children's literature, literary fantasy in particular. In mathematics, there have been very few women of stature; children's literature, on the other hand, is one of the few fields in which men and women have participated on an equal basis. Whereas mathematics is a field characterized by abstract manipulation of ideas, literary fantasy involves the expression of barely conscious feeling-complexes that assume images of wizards, magical women, or other forms. In the terms of Welsh (1975)—some of whose ideas will be presented in the next section—mathematics is characterized by "intellectence over origence," whereas literary fantasy would seem to be characterized by "origence over intellectence."

Different as the two fields are, they have some common features. One is a certain remoteness from practical reality. The creativity of a mathematician or an author of fantasy can be evaluated with little concern about the influence of team members, opportunity to use expensive equipment, or other factors. There is a second common feature: Few people today doubt that women can be creative interpreters and performers. That a woman can sing or act out a part that the male imagination has created is readily granted (if, indeed, not insisted upon). What is still claimed is that women are deficient in symbolic originality, in manipulating and organizing symbol patterns so that new structures emerge. In both mathematics and literary fantasy, a creative contribution is a work of symbolic originality.

The Samples

Women mathematicians. Names of women who had attended graduate school in mathematics between 1950 and 1960, and had obtained their doctorates, were furnished by the following institutions: Bryn Mawr College, Cornell University, Stanford University, Yale University, the University of California (Berkeley and Los Angeles), University of Oregon, University of Texas, and University of Washington. Mathematicians at these and other institutions also provided additional names, particularly of women they considered creative. Columbia University, the Massachusetts Institute of Technology, New York University, Radcliffe, the University of Chicago, the University of Illinois, and the University of Pennsylvania each produced at least two of these subjects.

A letter sent to Ss inviting them to participate in the study explained the long-term interest of the Institute of Personality Assessment and Research in studying soundness, achievement, creativity, and other forms of high-level functioning, and its present interest in conducting studies of professional women. A small honorarium was offered. Of 53 invitations extended, 44 (83%) were accepted. Ss spent a weekend in a "living-in" type of personality assessment study (Helson, 1971).

The creativity of each S was rated by mathematicians in her field of specialization. A seven-point scale was used, a rating of 4.0 signifying that the S was about as creative as the author of an average research paper in a mathematical journal. The ratings were highly reliable. The distribution of ratings was as follows: 8 Ss received average ratings of 3.0 or below; 8 were rated between 3.0 and 4.0; 12, between 4.0 and 5.0; 8 between 5.0 and 6.0; and 8 above 6.0. Ss rated above 5.0 were classified as "creative," the remaining women as "comparison Ss." The creative group thus consisted of women clearly rated as more creative than the author of an average research contribution in mathematics. We have been advised that there were no important omissions from the creative group.

Male mathematicians. Dr. Richard Crutchfield began a study of creative mathematicians who were Fellows at the Institute of Advanced Study at Princeton. To this group were added other creative and comparison Ss, so selected as to make them comparable in age to the women mathematicians. These Ss were sent tests and a questionnaire by mail (Helson & Crutchfield, 1970).

In each sample, creative Ss had published more papers, submitted their first published paper at a younger age, and received the Ph.D. at a younger age than comparison Ss. Although there were no differences between creative and comparison Ss in quality of the school that had awarded the Ph.D., the creative men were affiliated with more prestigious institutions than all other Ss. Six are now members of the National Academy of Sciences, and four others are regarded as very influential mathematicians. In contrast, one-third of the creative women had no regular position at all, and only two or three had contact with graduate students. Nepotism rules and young children presented common difficulties.

Men and women authors.   A sample of books was first constituted. It consisted of works of fantasy written since 1930 for children aged 8 to 12. The books were mentioned in at least two of six compilations published during the 1950s and 1960s, or they were nominated for inclusion by one of the 15 persons who served in the study as consultants or judges of literary excellence. Invitations were extended to all still-living authors of the books. Personality and life-history data were obtained by mail from 80% of the English-speaking authors (Helson, 1973a, in press).

Thirteen judges rated the overall excellence, defined as "originality, depth, and charm," of the 98 books. An intergroup "agreement" coefficient was .92. Among the highest-rated books were *The Hobbit* (Tolkien), *Charlotte's Web* (E.B. White), *The Little Prince* (St. Exupery), by male authors; and *The Children of Green Knowe* (Boston), *The Borrowers* (Norton), and *Mary Poppins* (Travers), by female authors. Books by men and women did not differ in ratings of excellence.

Personality Characteristics of Creative Women in Assessment Study

As mentioned above, the women mathematicians participated in weekend assessments. The psychological observers did not know which women were classified as creative, and indeed the criterion information has not yet been obtained. The psychologists and the Ss ate together, and the Ss played charades, held group discussions, were interviewed, and took a variety of tests. After the weekend was over, the staff described the Ss by means of the 100-item Clinical Q-sort (Block, 1961) and the Adjective Check List (Gough & Heilbrun, 1965).

The following Q-sort items, since they had the highest average placement for the entire sample, may be taken to describe the women mathematicians as a group: genuinely values intellectual and cognitive matters; appears to have a high degree of intellectual capacity; values own independence and autonomy; is a genuinely dependable and responsible person; and prides self on being objective and rational.

Items that were positively correlated ($p < .01$) with the criterion of creativity were as follows: thinks and associates in unusual ways, has unconventional thought processes; is an interesting, arresting person; tends to be rebellious and nonconforming; genuinely values intellectual and cognitive matters; appears to have a high degree of intellectual capacity; is self-dramatizing; histrionic; has fluctuating moods.

On the Adjective Check List, psychological observers more frequently described the creative Ss as individualistic, original, preoccupied, artistic, complicated, courageous, emotional, imaginative and self-centered ($p < .05$), and they more frequently described the comparison women as cheerful, active, appreciative, considerate, conventional, cooperative, helpful, organized, realistic, reliable, and sympathetic ($p < .05$). The creative women were thus less invested in social roles and interpersonal relationships than were the comparison Ss, and more invested in their own inner life and autonomy. (See also Bachtold & Werner, 1970, and Main, 1973, for evidence of the generality of these findings.)

The writers and most of the male mathematicians were assessed by mail, so that no staff observations of them could be made. However, all writers and mathematicians, male and female, took the CPI, California Psychological Inventory (Gough, 1957), which affords an overall description of personality characteristics.

Effects of Field, Creativity, and Sex on CPI Scales

An analysis of variance for men and women writers and mathematicians shows seven effects attributable to *field,* and many of them are quite large ($p < .0001$). The results support our expectation that mathematicians are more disciplined, objective, and abstract-minded than are writers of fantasy; they score higher on Well-being, Responsibility, Socialization, Self-control, Tolerance and Psychological Mindedness, and lower on Femininity.

Second, across the two fields there are five scales that show significant effects attributable to *creativity:* Well-being, Self-control, and Communality ($p < .05$), and Achievement via Conformance and Flexibility ($p < .002$). Since creative Ss score low on all these scales except Flexibility, one may say that creativity is associated across sex with awareness of unpleasant affect, spontaneity and lack of constriction, absorption in inner life, and dislike of the routine and stereotyped.

Thirdly, there are three scales that show significant effects attributable to *sex*. These are Femininity, of course, and also Social Presence ($p < .01$) and Self-acceptance ($p < .05$). The men score higher on the latter scales, indicating that they are more buoyant and self-assured than the women.

Let us turn now to analyses of variance for four subsamples: all women, all men, all writers, and all mathematicians.

Despite the large differences between mathematicians and writers, the analysis of variance for all women Ss shows significant effects attributable to creativity on six scales (Table 8.1). These are Flexibility and Achievement via Conformance ($p < .001$); Communality ($p < .01$); Dominance ($p < .01$); Sociability, and Self-acceptance ($p < .05$). Creative women score higher on Flexibility and lower on the others. What is important to notice here is the fact that the creative women score lower than comparison women on three measures of extraversion and self-assurance, the last three scales in the preceding list. An interaction between creativity and field on the femininity scale expresses the fact that creative women mathematicians score in a *more* feminine direction than other women mathematicians, but creative women writers score in a *less* feminine direction than other women writers. The two creative groups have almost identical mean scores on Femininity, slightly above the test norm for women.

The creative personality in women, as assessed by the CPI, is similar to the picture given by the staff observation of women mathematicians: Both groups of creative Ss are somewhat stubbornly unconventional and individualistic (low Achievement via Conformance, low Communality, high Flexibility); they tend not to be social leaders or to enjoy group interaction, but to have an original and engrossing inner life. Perhaps the resistance to convention and the avoidance of social commitments serve to nurture and protect the development of symbolic patterns.

However, in the CPI data for all *male* Ss, creativity has a significant main effect on only one scale, Self-control. Except for low scores on Self-control (indicating access to anger and lack of defensive constriction), the creative male writers and mathematicians would appear to have relatively little in common.

For all *writers*, male and female, creativity shows a significant effect on four scales—Well-being, Dominance, Sociability, and Achievement via Conformance—which appear in the analysis of data for all women Ss (Table 8.1). The more creative writers, male and female, scored lower than other writers on these

Table 8.1

Effects of creativity by sex and field on scales of the California Psychological inventory

	All women df = 1,63	All men df = 1,79	All writers df = 1,50	All mathematicians df = 1,92
Main effects[a]	Dominance**	Self-control**	Dominance*	Flexibility**
	Sociability*		Sociability*	
	Self-acceptance*		Well-being*	
	Communality**		Achievement via conformance**	
	Achievement via conformance**			
	Flexibility***			
Interaction effects	Femininity*	Flexibility*	Flexibility*	Sociability*
	(Creativity by field)	(Creativity by field)	(Creativity by field)	Self-acceptance***
				Achievement via Conformance*
				(Creativity by sex)

[a] Creative Ss score higher than comparison Ss on Flexibility and lower on all other scales listed.
* F significant at .05 level.
** F significant at .01 level.
*** F significant at .001 level.

scales. But for all *mathematicians,* male and female, the interactions between sex and creativity are actually more numerous and impressive than the main effects of creativity. Creative men and women mathematicians both score high on Flexibility, but on Sociability and especially on Self-acceptance, the creative women score low and the creative men high, relative to comparison Ss. On Achievement via Conformance, the creative women score low, the comparison women high, and the creative and comparison men do not differ.

This set of findings informs us that the creative male mathematicians differ from the other three creative groups in showing a personality pattern in which there is relatively more social assurance and assertiveness, and less conflict with conventional channels of expression and achievement.

There are two factors that help to explain this pattern of findings. One is the fact that creative male mathematicians, alone of all the groups involved in these analyses, occupy a prestigious institutional status, which rewards them and puts heavy demands on them for competitive exertion and intellectual leadership. The second factor should be stated as an hypothesis: Creative male mathematicians have a *type* of personality in which the ego is relatively more assertive than it is in the personality of creative women mathematicians or creative writers of either sex. This hypothesis was explored in an investigation of work habits and attitudes of the creative Ss. In the next part of the study, I have followed the Jungian analyst, Erich Neumann, in his conceptualization of two types of "consciousness" related to the creative personality. Therefore, it will be useful to present his ideas briefly.

Two Types of Creative Personality

Neumann (1954a) described two types of creative process, which he called "partriarchal" and "matriarchal." They are analogous to male and female pro-creative roles. Briefly, patriarchal consciousness is described as purposeful, assertive, and objective. In matriarchal consciousness, the psyche is filled with an emotional content over which it "broods" until an organic growth is "realized." This type of consciousness reflects unconscious processes, sums them up, and guides itself by them. Matriarchal consciousness does not have the "direct aim of patriarchal consciousness, nor the knife-sharp edge of its analysis. Matriarchal consciousness is more interested in the meaningful than in the facts or dates, and is oriented teleologically to organic growth rather than to mechanical or logical causation."

The creative person, said Neumann, requires both types of ego process. Since matriarchal processes are inconspicuous in most men, this type of feeling-cognition has a particular association with the creative man. However, among creative individuals, the matriarchal type of relationship predominates in some and the patriarchal in others. The matriarchal consciousness is also associated with the feminine, but Neumann said that women are prone to realize their feminine nature concretely, in loving, becoming pregnant, giving birth, and in other outer expression. Men of the matriarchal type, he said, do not suffer the same "danger" to their creative symbolic processes.

Other writers have emphasized a similar dichotomy, which they have referred to as agency versus communion, action-thought versus feeling, fear of dependence versus fear of isolation, bimodal consciousness, and so on. Many of these authors have interesting things to say. Neumann's approach has two features that I would like to call to your attention. Perhaps the most important contribution is his phenomenological description of the organization and positive functioning of a creative person with a low-level ego assertiveness. In Freudian theory, one would tend to think of such a personality as narcissistic or regressive, and the regression would be seen as tolerable if it were temporary and "in the service of the ego." Neumann credited a more positive contribution to the unconscious, and it is probably for this reason that he conceptualized the "matriarchal" consciousness as fruitful and creative.

Secondly, Neumann did not think in terms of isolated traits but rather in terms of complex, enduring gestalten, with roots on the one side in biology and on the other in culture. He was interested in the development of consciousness over the course of human history (1945b). I would argue that matriarchal and patriarchal subcultures are much in evidence today, right in our universities, for example, although it is the value system that identifies them, not the literal masculine or feminine sex of the most powerful figures. Neumann's concepts were explored in an investigation of creative style in several samples (Helson, 1967b, and 1968b), and will now be examined in the mathematicians and writers.

Sex Differences in Creative Style

The Mathematicians Q-Sort and the Writers Q-Sort were developed to study ways of working and attitudes toward work. These instruments consist of 56 items which *S* sorts on a five-point scale according to a forced normal distribution, so as to describe ter own work style. The Mathematicians Q-Sort was developed first, being itself an adaptation of the Research Scientist Q-Sort by Gough and Woodworth (1960). A number of the items were intended to assess "patriarchal" and "matriarchal" styles, but within the context of a wide sampling of characteristics descriptive of work habits and attitudes. In building the Writers Q-Sort, it was possible to use about two-thirds of the items from the Mathematicians Q-Sort with no more than slight rewording.

Cluster analyses of the Mathematicians Q-Sort produced several clusters that differentiated the creative women mathematicians from comparison women (Helson, 1967b). Let us compare creative and comparison women writers on items from the Writers Q-Sort which are parallel to items from the Mathematicians Q-Sort. We will test the hypothesis that the direction of differences between the creative and comparison women writers will correspond to the positive or negative loading of items from these clusters. Such correspondence would indicate an overall resemblance in creative style between the creative women writers and mathematicians.

On four clusters that differentiated creative women mathematicians from comparison women, 22 of the 24 items have equivalents on the Writers Q-Sort. Examples of these items will be given presently. On 16 of the 22 items, the difference between creative and comparison women writers is in the predicted direction, and all substantial differences ($p < .10$) are in the predicted direction. According to the Wilcoxon Signed Ranks Test, which takes both the number and magnitude of the discrepancies into account, the hypothesis of resemblance between creative women writers and mathematicians receives strong support ($T = 41, p < .003$).

Four clusters differentiated creative male mathematicians from comparison men. Of the 27 items comprising these clusters, only 19 have a parallel form on the Writers Q-Sort. Examples of items that *do not* have equivalents are "work tends toward systematization and unification of mathematics" and "Has a good command of basic resources and technical literature in his field." Examples of items that *do* have equivalents are "Work is characterized by inventiveness and ingenuity," "Has a lively sense of mathematical inquiringness and curiosity," and "Has an earnest desire to make a mark in mathematics."

Differences between creative and comparison male writers were in the same direction as the differences between creative and comparison male mathematicians on only 6 of the 19 items. Here is clearly no evidence for overall resemblance between creative male writers and mathematicians. The creative male mathematicians show "patriarchal" characteristics of confidence, initiative, impact on the environment, and intellectual balance and soundness.

Let us finally consider two clusters that differentiated creative women mathematicians not only from comparison women but also from creative men. The items constituting these clusters are shown in Table 8.2. They describe a work style in which the self is totally committed, unconscious as well as conscious processes are involved in the creative effort, and emphasis is directed toward developing what is within rather than exploring or mastering the environment. The ego is not assertive, and social withdrawal is used to protect the creative process. This would seem to be what Neumann had in mind when he spoke of "matriarchal" thought processes.

On the 12 items of these clusters, the Wilcoxon Signed Ranks Test showed the creative women writers to be more "matriarchal" than both the comparison women writers ($T = 10$, $p < .02$) and also the creative male writers ($T = 6$, $p < .01$). However, the latter are themselves more "matriarchal" than comparison writers ($T = 11, p < .053$).

In creative style, then, as in overall personality characteristics, the two groups of creative women show strong similarity. Their style is what Neumann described as matriarchal. The creative male writers are closer to the matriarchal than to the patriarchal, but have features of both.

The one area where creative men differ from creative women in the same way in both fields is that of ambition and dedication to work. Since this is such an important topic, I will go into it in some detail, also drawing on the work of other investigators.

Ambition and Dedication to Work

In the Mathematicians Q-Sort and the Writers Q-Sort, items having to do with ambition and "sense of destiny" are placed higher by creative men than by creative women. It can be argued that this "last infirmity of noble minds" is in fact an essential characteristic of outstandingly creative people, and that its deficiency in women is primarily responsible for their small creative contribution.

Sex-related differences in ambition and self-regard were dramatically recorded by Barron (1972) and his colleagues in interview data from men and women art students. Though the men and women did not differ in the quality of their work as rated by the art school faculty, there were large differences in the way they talked about their work and planned their future careers. For example, to the question, "Do you think of yourself as an artist?", most of the women said no (76%) but most of the men said yes (66%). The men already thought of them-

Table 8.2

Items of clusters from the Mathematicians Q-sort differentiating
creative women mathematicians from comparison women and creative men

Items placed high by creative women

Mathematical insights often come in dreams, upon waking, just before going to sleep or at times other than during a period of concentration.

Feels emotionally tense when a result seems imminent.

Reluctant to strike out in new directions.

Easily distractible; tries to secure optimum conditions for concentration.

Does not enjoy collaboration.

Items placed low by creative women

Has an active, efficient, well-organized mind.

Can imagine enjoying lines of work other than mathematics.

Is flexible in ter thinking; able to shift and restructure easily.

Reacts quickly to research problems, immediately generates ideas.

Desire for a salary increase is an important motivating factor.

Has interests or talents for writing a book or articles for intelligent laymen.

Is neat and orderly in habits and manners of work.

selves as artists, whereas the women viewed themselves as "student artists perhaps—but not artists, not yet."

Of the men, 40% thought their work was superior in comparison to that of others at the art school, and only 14% thought their work was inferior. The percentages were almost reversed for women: only 17% thought their work was superior and almost 40% considered it inferior. The men frequently made statements such as, "If I couldn't paint, I would rather die," and "Painting is my life." Women were much more guarded or tentative, certainly less passionate: "I'm not sure yet, but I like it," "It's half my life, the other half is my future family." These results are all the more striking when one considers that women art students have been described as more adventurous and assertive than other women (Stringer, 1967). These statements convey a strange tentativeness in the area of career commitment.

A factor that needs to be taken into account is that men in art school have been preselected more than the women. A dramatic clash between aspiring male artists and their parents is likely to take place before the decision to go to art school. Thus, the men are already committed, but the women have made no comparable controversial decision—against marriage or children, for example.

But of course, more men than women do have a strong commitment to work. Barron's striking material is registering the effects of different cultural expectations for men and women—that the man should express himself in work and should aim for the highest he can achieve; that the woman should devote herself to her husband and family, and should be modest in her personal aspirations. If she departs from these expectations, she is likely to be self-critical, unsure, and certainly cautious in exposing herself to social censure, ridicule, or retaliation.

The strength of commitment to work is thus understandably a factor that powerfully distinguishes creative women from other women. Among both the mathematicians and writers that I have studied, the single Q-sort item that most strongly differentiated creative from comparison women was this: "Subordinates other things to research (or literary) goals; puts these values before others." Table 8.3 compares creative and comparison men and women on two Q-sort items having to do with ambition and dedication. The creative men have the highest scores on ambition, the creative women on "subordinates other things to (creative) goals." In the study of women mathematicians, there was much evidence that the creative women did restrict their lives to a few things about which they cared a great deal—research, family, and a few leisure activities such as hiking, reading, and music. The comparison Ss spent more time on teaching,

Table 8.3

Placement of Q-sort items about ambition and commitment by men and women mathematicians and writers

Has earnest desire to make mark in mathematics.

(Has keen desire for fame and immortality in literature.)

	Mathematicians (N = 111)			Writers (N = 54)		
	Creative Mean	Comparison Mean	t	Creative Mean	Comparison Mean	t
Women	2.83	3.00	-.56	3.00	2.73	.58
Men	3.94	3.03	4.25***	3.75	2.73	2.43*
t	-4.58***	—		-1.93	—	

Subordinates other things to research (literary) goals; puts these values before others.

	Mathematicians (N = 111)			Writers (N = 54)		
	Creative Mean	Comparison Mean	t	Creative Mean	Comparison Mean	t
Women	3.44	2.43	3.24**	3.67	2.27	3.89***
Men	3.03	2.65	1.28	2.92	2.67	.54
t	1.24	—		1.60	—	

*p v .05
**p v .01
***p v .001

administration, and community or political activities, and expressed interest in a wide variety of leisure activities. Creative women will make sacrifices for their creative work, but they are less likely to think in terms of "dominating the field." Perhaps this is because they have little hope of doing so, perhaps it is because they are hesitant to admit their ambition, perhaps it is because the desire for fame has less place in the matriarchal type of creativity than it has in the patriarchal type of creativity. Certainly, women do not lack motivation. Here is the way one mathematician described her mathematical development in graduate school:

> From the depths of self-doubt came the wonderful dizzying experience of successful research. I proved a theorem. It turned out to be worth publishing, but that was a secondary reward. I learned that for me this is the incomparable experience: to step out alone into the other world which mathematics is, to find structure where first was empty space, to scrutinize this exotic landscape so unknown and so self-willed that one doubts that even God is master there; to lay traps for one new insight, and with intense cunning, patience, and strength penetrate to its very heart of meaning.

Summary Discussion of Creative Personality in Men and Women

There are differences in personality between creative men and women and these seem to manifest themselves in work style. Creative men tend to be more ambitious and assertive; creative women, to work in a more introverted and contemplative way. The differences are more pronounced among mathematicians than among writers, since creative male writers show many features of the inner-oriented, low-assertive style.

The differences among the several creative groups would seem to be attributable, in part, to the different environments in which they work. Virtually all mathematicians are affiliated with institutions, but the differences between the creative men and the other mathematicians—in status, responsibilities, and expectations from the environment—are very great. Most of the writers were not affiliated with institutions but more men than women had responsibilities for supporting a family through their work. For both groups of men, there was more congruence between their work and the demands and rewards of the environment than there was for the women.

In what sense, then, should it be said that there are *sex*-related differences in creative personality? Rather, are there not human beings working under different environmental conditions? These different environments surely produce quite direct effects on style and output. For example, why should one publish a great *many* papers when there is little or no reward for doing so? In these studies, the creative men had published more papers than any other group of mathematicians, but three women who had published at a very high rate all had positions at universities and did not have children.

Besides its direct effects, the environment is influential also in channeling individuals with characteristics that suit or disqualify them for particular ecological niches. One reason that the creative women mathematicians are more introverted than the creative men must be that extroverted women get diverted into other fields, or put emphasis on activities that are more rewarding for them than mathematical research conducted in relative isolation and anonymity.

These effects of the environment are very important. Nevertheless, there may remain broader or deeper sex-related differences in creative personality. That is, more women than men with creative interests and abilities may be low in ego assertiveness or ego control. That was the finding of studies of college students by Pine and Holt (1960) and Bowers (1971), which were described in the section on "Creative Thinking Abilities and Other Personality Traits—Ego Control." The well-known differences in interests and values between men and women would lead one to expect sex-related differences of this sort across the board, but research consistently finds that men and women at different levels of creativity differ from each other in different ways and that, for reasons not yet apparent, it is often the most creative Ss who differ along what would seem to be sex-traditional lines.

The subsequent sections will expand on some of the detail needed to clarify this picture.

MASCULINITY AND FEMININITY IN THE CREATIVE PERSONALITY

Let us assume with Anastasi (1958) that available tests of masculinity-femininity provide "an index of the degree to which the individual's personality resembles the personality of men or women in our culture" (p. 497). What do these tests contribute to an evaluation of the old idea that the creative person is more bisexual, or has more of the characteristics of the opposite sex, than the average person? This hypothesis is sufficiently complicated and the implications sufficiently uncertain that it has afforded a wide variety of results and conclusions.

There is no doubt that artistic and intellectual men score higher on measures of femininity than do average men, but it is not necessarily the case that the more creative among those with artistic and intellectual interests score higher than others in the same field. For example, neither the creative male mathematicians nor writers scored higher on femininity than the comparison men. The fact that the most creative architects in the MacKinnon and Hall study (MacKinnon, 1962) scored higher on femininity than did the least creative is probably related to the fact that the most creative architects had strong esthetic values, whereas the least creative had strong economic values.

Among women, we have seen that the creative Ss sometimes score slightly higher on CPI femininity than do other women, and sometimes slightly lower. The best generalization would be that they do not deviate far from the norm. This was true of the creative college women also (Helson, 1966). The situation thus does not seem to be the same for women as for men, but in neither case is it accurate to say, without qualification, that creative Ss score higher on the other-sex dimension than do comparison Ss.

To this murky discussion, Welsh (1975) recently brought elegant clarification. Welsh presented a two-dimensional approach to personality which was developed for differentiating among gifted Ss. His variables began as intelligence and originality, assessed respectively by the Terman Concept Mastery Test and the Welsh Figure Preference Test. Among gifted Ss, where the range of intelligence is reduced, the Terman Concept Mastery Test becomes a measure of a *tendency* to abstraction, an *interest* in comprehension, and a *motive* to manipulate and express ideas in terms of abstract symbols. Intelligence thus becomes "intellectence." This dimension is conceptualized as opposing the abstract and the concrete. The low-scorer places emphasis on specific or literal events that may be expressed in concrete terms and have practical applications for the usual experiences in life.

The second dimension, "origence," is uncorrelated with intellectence. This is an important point. The dimension distinguishes between those at the high end who find congenial an open and implicit universe which they can structure in their own way, and those at the low end who prefer an explicit and well-defined world that can be grasped by the application of objective rules.

Welsh offered evidence that creative individuals are high on both origence and intellectence. Before we go further into his typology, however, let us stop to compare his two-dimensional approach to personality to some related conceptual structures. Holland (1973) used a "hexogram" of vocational interests (Fig-

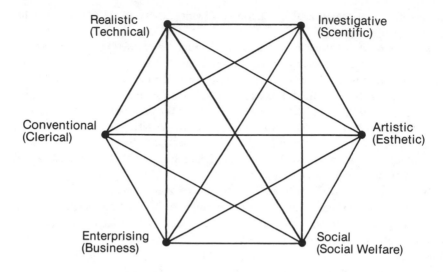

Figure 8.1 The Holland Hexagram of Interests.

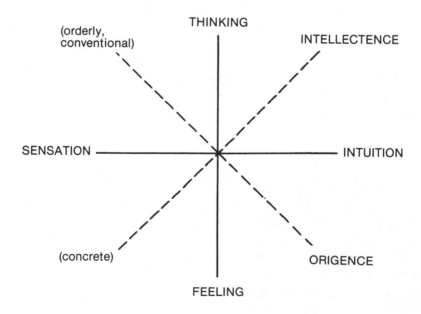

Figure 8.2 Origence and Intellectence in Relation to the Jungian Functions.

ure 8.1) in which the six main types of interests are about the same as those previously identified by Guilford, Christensen, Bond, and Sutton (1954). Creativity, said Holland, is associated with Investigative interests and with Artistic interests. These interests are similar to intellectence and origence. Welsh's dimensions, in fact, may be seen as the top four points of the Holland hexogram, omitting the Enterprising (business) and Social interests that comprise the base. Welsh's dimensions contrast the scientific and the technical, the top two points of the hexogram, which Holland sees as relatively similar, and the artistic and conventional, which both Holland and Welsh put "poles apart." I believe that Welsh's dimensions probably make good sense for the population of talented individuals with which he was concerned, but that comparison of both systems gives a better perspective on each.

In terms of Jung's typological dimensions (Figure 8.2), Welsh seems to have taken as definers of his dimensions measures of intuitive feeling (origence) and intuitive thinking (intellectence), leaving at the low end either sensation mixed with feeling (in the case of intellectence) or sensation mixed with thinking (in the case of origence). His diagonal from right to left then gives the intuition-sensation dimension, with decreasing contributions of thinking and feeling—a very interesting feature! According to Welsh's descriptions, origence is correlated with extraversion, and intellectence with introversion. One may recall that Jung started out by pairing extroversion and feeling, and introversion and thinking. Later, he found it necessary to separate extraversion-introversion as a dimension distinct from thinking-feeling and intuition-sensation. What Welsh did, though, was to allow thinking and feeling to vary independently. This is similar to what Bem (1974), Spence, Helmreich, and Stapp (1975), Kanner (1976) and others have been doing with masculininity and femininity, and it does give some very interesting results, as we will see.

More than a thousand talented adolescents have been assessed on intellectence and origence. Scores are also available for them on several inventory measures of masculinity and femininity, which Welsh regarded as two dimensions rather than one. He composited several measures of masculinity and several measures of femininity, and computed mean scores for Ss showing the nine combinations of three degrees each of intellectence and origence (Table 8.4). He found clear relationships, in the same direction for both sexes, between origence and femininity, and between intellectence and masculinity.

In Table 8.4, positive scores are feminine. Cells at the extreme upper-right represent Ss high on both origence and intellectence; these tend to be the creative Ss. Note that the boys here are not the highest on femininity, nor are the

Table 8.4

Average of z-score means on all M-F scales by Novants

| | Boys | | | |
	Low INT	Medium INT	High INT	Total
High ORIG	+.413	+.394	+.205	+.337
Medium ORIG	+.043	+.005	-.066	.006
Low ORIG	-.277	-.199	-.386	-.288
Total	+.060	+.067	-.082	.000

| | Girls | | | |
	Low INT	Medium INT	High INT	Total
High ORIG	+.203	+.112	-.064	+.084
Medium ORIG	+.144	+.003	-.157	.003
Low ORIG	+.043	-.119	-.215	.097
Total	+.130	-.001	-.145	.000

Source: From Creativity and Intelligence: A Personality Approach by G. S. Welsh. Copyright 1975 by G. S. Welsh. Reprinted by permission

girls the highest on masculinity. Both "creative" groups are intermediate in their scores. Creativity is associated with both origence and intellectence and with a "blending" of masculinity and femininity. An additional finding, which deserves mention, is that boys seem to vary on the measures of femininity more than the girls do on either femininity or masculinity.

Welsh presented an ingenious set of hypotheses about sexual identification as a function of origence and intellectence. Let us consider four combinations of these two variables (Table 8.5). For subjects high in origence and low in intellectence, the feminine end of origence is congruent, he said, with the nonmasculine pole of intellectence, and would lead to salience of femininity in sex-role behaviors. In the family constellation there would be an identification with the mother. The opposite quadrant would also show congruence, but masculinity would be salient and identification would be with the father.

The two diagonally opposite quadrants represent more complicated situations. In the quadrant (III) low on both dimensions, there is compatibility of the nonmasculine pole of intellectence (concrete attitudes) and the nonfeminine pole of origence (orderliness, conventionality). The result is an acceptance of conventional social norms for sex role and overt expression of compatible behaviors. That is, the girl manifests culturally acceptable femininity and represses masculinity; a converse pattern characterizes the boy.

In the quadrant (I) high on both origence and intellectence, where the creative individuals are expected to congregate, the feminine pole of origence is incompatible with the masculine pole of intellectence. This results in rejection of conventional social norms for sex role and in manifestation of mixed masculinity and femininity. Ambivalence and confusion is resolved by identification with the self rather than a parent figure.

This is an interesting and testable set of hypotheses, but it seems too simple to withstand further elaboration. For example, it makes no distinction between the men and women who fall into the high-origence, low-intellectence cell (or between men and women who fall into the low-origence, high-intellectence cell). Surely, their identifications are going to be different in significant ways.

To deal with such problems, psychoanalytic theories have discussed the concept of outer and inner, or "manifest" and "latent," masculinity and femininity (Sanford, 1966; Miller & Swanson, 1960). The creative person is sometimes said to "accept" ter contrasexual characteristics whereas the ordinary person tends to repress them, and thus keeps them in primitive form (MacKinnon, 1962). Welsh made no provision for higher or lower forms of masculinity or femininity, and

Table 8.5

Hypothetical interpretation of sexual identification
as a function of origence and intellectence

FEMININE

I.	HIGH ORIGENCE/ LOW INTELLECTENCE	II.	HIGH ORIGENCE/ HIGH INTELLECTENCE

      Congruence   Incompatibility

salience of feminity   rejection of conventional
in sex role behaviors   social norms for sex role

identification with   mixture of masculinity
mother   and femininity in sex
                                         role behaviors

NONMASCULINE   MASCULINE

III.	LOW ORIGENCE/ LOW INTELLECTENCE	IV.	LOW ORIGENCE/ HIGH INTELLECTENCE

      Compatibility   Congruence

acceptence of   salience of masculinity
   conventional social   in sex role behavior
   expression of socially
   appropriate sex role   identification with
   behavior   father

identification with
others of both sexes

NON FEMININE

Source: From *Creativity and Intelligence: A Personality approach* by G. S. Welsh.
Copyright 1975 by G. S. Welsh. Reprinted by permission.

Table 8.6

Mode of fantasy by degree of creativity
for 98 men and women authors

	Creativity			
	Low	Middle	High	
Pleasant comic	10	5	3	
Countersex-	6	19	15	$X^2 = 28.68$ (df $\mid$ 4)
traditional				$p <$ v .001
Sex-traditional	9	3	28	

his hypotheses are phrased in terms of the acceptance or rejection of sex role rather than in terms of accepting or rejecting other-sex traits. However, his findings, in the format of his schema, seem to support this idea: It is not that creative women are more masculine than other women, or creative men more feminine than other men, but that the contrasexual traits are available in a fluid symbolic form in which they can "blend" more successfully and in which they are available for creative symbolic activity.

(It must be remembered that the findings and hypotheses under discussion take their form around the focus on creativity. If citizenship had been the central concern, or all-around excellence, the results would be different. Different variables would structure the analyses, and different characteristics of the *S*s would be highlighted.)

SUBTYPES OF PERSONALITY IN STUDIES OF CREATIVITY

In earlier discussions of creativity in mathematicians and writers, the creative and comparison *S*s were treated as homogeneous subgroups. Welsh's conceptualization of *two* main variables, with creative *S*s characterized by one particular combination of the two, illustrates a more complex view. A sample may be said to consist of subgroups with quite different characteristics: those high on origence and intellectence; those high on one and low on the other; and those low on both.

Other researchers, of course, have also distinguished subtypes of personality relevant to the study of creativity. Neumann's matriarchal and patriarchal styles were attributed to different types of creative men. One might think of them as men who emphasize origence a bit more than intellectence and those who emphasize intellectence a bit more than origence. Otto Rank described three types of man: the creative, the conflicted, and the adapted. MacKinnon (1965) exposited Rank's ideas and demonstrated their applicability to his sample of architects. Perhaps they are applicable to Welsh's system also. If one turns Welsh's square (Table 8.5) into the position of a diamond or interprets it diagonally, the *S*s high on both origence and intellectence correspond to Rank's creative type, those low on both or high only on the sex-appropriate trait might correspond to the adapted type, and those high only to the contrasex trait: might these be the conflicted?

In a study of 98 works of fantasy, I found an interesting relationship between creativity and mode of story, whether heroic, tender, or comic (Helson, in press). Most of the books rated low on creativity were mildly comic. A few by men were mildly heroic, and a few by women were mildly tender. However, most of the books with middle ratings on creativity were heroic if written by women, and tender if written by men. Of the books rated highest on creativity, those by women were preponderantly tender, but some heroic works were rated equally high; and those by men were predominantly heroic or strongly comic, but with some tender works rated equally high. By classifying the heroic and strongly comic modes as sex-traditional for men and contrasex-traditional for women, and vice versa for the tender mode, it is possible to combine results for men and women into the distribution shown in Table 8.6.

Information about personality and work style, which was obtained from the authors, shows that the least creative group (the authors of what was usually mildly comic fantasy) approximate Rank's idea of "adapted" Ss. Most would fit into Welsh's Low-Low category—externally motivated, pleasant, orderly, and so on. This is equally true of men and women. The authors whose books were rated "middle" on creativity were similar in personality to those whose books were rated highest; both were much less "adapted" than the low-rated group. The authors of heroic and comic fantasy, across sex, were more assertive in work style and less absorbed in "primary process" activity than were the authors of tender fantasy. This was the case for the creative and middle groups combined. The only differences that I have been able to find between the creative and middle authors suggest that the more creative men and women are more consistent in their style, whether heroic-comic or tender. The middle-rated authors showed inconsistencies that one might interpret as indicative of "conflict."

The variables of sex-traditional and contrasex-traditional are of fundamental importance in giving shape to the distribution shown in Table 8.6. Rank would not lead us to expect this, but Jung, I think, does. Jung described the average person as dominated by the persona, or the mask of convention. A more developed person, he said, becomes aware of his anima or her animus, that is, the contrasexual component of the personality. The anima or animus may be "obsessive," or acted out, dominating the personality. When the ego is better attuned to the unconscious, the anima or animus becomes less salient and the self comes into awareness.

The Rankian concepts of adapted, conflicted, and creative types may be parallel, then, to the Jungian stages marked by salience of the persona, animus or anima, and the self. Although these concept-systems are more general and inclusive than empirical typologies such as Welsh's or Holland's or my own, our empiricism helps to explore and clarify these more complex and dynamic sets of ideas.

But what has all of this to do with the psychology of women? Attention to these subgroups is important, in the first place, because of the *perspective* it affords on the differences and similarities between men and women at different creative levels. For example, we see now how the middle group of contrasex-traditional persons contributes to the finding that the creative men are more ambitious and assertive, and creative women more reflective and inner-oriented in their work style than comparison *S*s. Furthermore, if we devote "loving attention" to each part of the spectrum, I think we will find that each has a particular contribution to make. This is easy to see in the case of fantasy because the stories that each group writes have different appeals. Why should we have only hero stories by men? At the present time, I believe that some of the "middle" women may be very effective agents for social change.

In the second place, attention to subgroups is important because it helps us cut down generalizations and study the circumstances under which minority patterns for each sex may be found. Let me give two examples.

Among the women mathematicians, I have constituted subgroups on the basis of high and low scores on two clusters of the Mathematicians Q-Sort (Helson, 1976a). One of these cluster dimensions may be described as disorderly versus orderly (i.e., origence) and the other as inventive and exploratory versus confined, settled, or concrete (i.e., intellectence). The least creative women tend to score low on both dimensions, but here I want to talk about the two groups who score high on the first dimension and who differ on the second dimension. The disorderly and inventive group has the style most common among creative male mathematicians. The study of subgroups enables us to pay attention to the fact that such a group of women exists. As compared with other women, these *S*s were most frequently Protestant, had the least pathogenicity in their backgrounds, had parents the most similar in education, were rated by IPAR observers as the lowest on Femininity, and on the Adjective Check List they had a peak score on the Autonomy scale. In contrast, the women who are high-lows (i.e., disorderly and settled in research style) are the most typical for creative women mathematicians. They were the *least* Protestant, the *highest*-rated on Femininity, had parents the *most* different in education, and their peak score on the ACL was on "Self-Abasement." Another interesting thing about them was that they had the *most* young children.

A follow-up of these women might clarify the extent to which the low-assertive style changes when the mother's life situation changes. In any event, these findings suggest the complexity of relationships between personal history, current life circumstances, and what one may call the "best strategy" for creative work. They indicate, I believe, that women with quite different histories may become creative mathematicians, but that they will go about their work in different ways.

My second example of the usefulness of studying subgroups has to do with the authors of fantasy. Here it is interesting to see how the mode in which an author writes changes with the social climate (Helson, 1973b). There has been a sharp increase in works of heroic fantasy by women authors since the mid-1950s, and recently we have seen a woman author's first serious fantasy with a wizard as central character. It is quite clear that women are *capable* of writing excellent books in the mode that is traditionally male. Why they do so now, but did not do it 20 years ago, presents interesting questions for the study of creativity in the social setting.

STUDIES OF THE SOCIAL CONTEXT OF CREATIVITY

This is such a large and diffuse topic, so important but so little studied by psychologists, that I am simply going to adapt a few propositions from Lasswell (1959) and illustrate them with several empirical studies.

Lasswell defined creativity as the disposition *to make and to recognize* valuable innovations. One might analyze a society, he suggested, in terms of the factors that facilitate or inhibit innovation. Such an analysis would attend to the organization of relevant institutions and subsystems, including the structures we refer to as "roles," and to principles of attribution that affect the process of recognition.

In the making of an innovation, Lasswell said, certain kinds of relationships constitute an important facilitating influence. The *resonator* is a role often played by wives and mistresses who admire and look after the innovator. Innovation is also mightily affected by access to an *intellectual collaborator,* and sometimes a *circle of apostles* is important. The relationships discussed by Levinson, Darrow, Klein, Levinson, and McKee (1974) in their work on personality development in the adult male are similar to some of these, and raise comparable questions about the development and recognition of the female innovator.

Recognition of innovation by a *judge,* said Lasswell, involves norms of expectation and norms of value. The likelihood that an innovation will be recognized may be hypothesized to increase with (a) the belief of the judge that recognition of the innovation will improve ter own position, and (b) the similarity between judge and innovator in values, personality, and social contacts.

Let us illustrate the application of some of these ideas to an understanding of what causes the inhibition of innovation in women. Feldman's (1973) study of women in graduate school shows that both men and women students think the faculty accords women less recognition. His intensive examination of full-time students in the sciences showed that the women rated themselves as less original than the men did, and as less confident and productive. The women were much less likely to have a professor as intellectual collaborator, but women who did have this relationship described themselves as more original and dedicated than other women, and were indeed more productive. Feldman contended that the intellectual collaborator relationship is of crucial importance for the self-concept and confidence of women, but more information is needed to evaluate the alternative interpretation that faculty members choose the few exceptional women as collaborators. Feldman's evidence that married men are the best off in graduate school, whereas divorced men and married women are the worst off, suggests confirmation of the importance of the "resonator" role. Bernard (1971) described vividly the effects on professional women of being seduced into playing the resonator role for their colleagues. Her earlier book, *Academic Women* (1964), has much material relevant to the inhibition of innovation in women in the subsystem of society that is academia. (See also Hochschild, 1975.)

Recognition has been withheld from women artists by art dealers and gallery owners who do not think paintings by women will sell as well as those by men (Rosenberg & Fliegel, 1965). The low opinion of the women held by these middlemen (and middlewomen) is strongly abetted by misogynist attitudes of male artists. The work of Tresemer and Pleck (1974) on male attitudes toward achievement in women is interesting in this connection. Long ago, Jung described the clash between the anima of the man and the animus of the woman. If one thinks of a large proportion of artists as "conflicted" (i.e., tender men and heroic women), one begins to see how these psychological incompatibilities become one-sidedly institutionalized in the art establishment.

A demonstration of the general relationship between male values and recognition of eminence was provided by Smith (1962). She showed that women included in *Who's Who* are bunched in occupations expressive of feminine values, and that both women and these occupations are underrepresented.

How evaluation by judges of the content of an essay is affected by labeling the author as male or female has been investigated by Goldberg (1968) and others. There are many problems in this area of the communication and evaluation of creative work by men and women that should appeal to psychologists, and to which they could bring their knowledge of principles of social perception and judgment.

WHERE DO WE GO FROM HERE?

What are the implications of this survey for those of us who are interested in the study of creativity in women? First, I believe that a reductive approach is ill advised. By "reductive," I mean any approach that conceptualizes creativity in terms of status or abstract intellectual components, and particularly those derived from models based on the academic male. We need an approach to creativity that is emergent and open-ended, one which emphasizes context as much as foci, feeling as much as thinking, art and literature as much as science, life situation as much as performance in the lab, and personal and interpersonal creativity along with creativity of "products." We need not only feminist criticism but also feminist conceptualizations and research design.

Some psychologists feel that such a position isn't quite honorable, that it goes contrary to the objectivity and emotional detachment—to a first concern with the truth—that we cherish as scholars and scientists. My view is that uncritical acceptance of assumptions and conventions perpetuates the society's status quo and stultifies scientific progress. Our whole psychological enterprise has begun to tremble with the realization of its need to reexamine the very floor of the ship (Campbell, 1975; Cronbach, 1975; Jenkins, 1974), and surely those who study the psychology of women have an important contribution to make in this work of renovation (Carlson, 1972).

Furthermore, when it comes to a first concern with the truth, I do not think there is, or is going to be, any one set of truths about who is creative or what creativity is. There are mountains and rivers of the psychosocial landscape that have to be taken into account. As William Empson said, "The heart of standing is, we cannot fly." But beyond these topographical features—still not certainly delineated and perhaps shifting with deep movements of the earth—there is considerable free space, considerable scope for "origence."

A psychology of the creativity of women in this time of transition might well begin with an avowal of the deep longing for validation, meaning, and identity on the part of thousands upon thousands of women. This longing exists because women, like other disadvantaged or minority groups, suffer from *dissociation.* Our problems in attaining identity may be seen as the struggle to put ourselves together, despite cultural definitions that restrict and fragment. Therefore, a conception of creativity as a search for wholeness would afford a powerful center for our investigations. In my own work I have used ideas from Neumann, Rank, and Jung. Others might find a rich source of ideas in the anthropologists who have been concerned with culture and creativity (Mead, 1959) or with the psychological dimensions of ethnic identity (DeVos, 1972). Nor should we deprive ourselves of the fertile mind of Erikson (1954) just because some of us have disagreed with some of his emphases. No work on creativity can go very deep, I believe, if it confines itself to the level of consciousness and social roles. The creative work of the women's movement, it seems to me, is to discover viable articulations for women between personality in its full depth and culture in its full variety. What are troublesome second-order interactions for the methodologists hold out hope to those with minority ways of life.

Study of creativity in women, as I have been saying, needs to begin with an assumption about why women want to engage in creative activity, that is, with a theory or assumption about creative motivation. Secondly, the very idea of creativity in women is itself a creative undertaking, and as such it needs materials to sustain itself. One of the dangers to a brainchild is that the new idea will become dissociated, swallowed up again in the unconscious. Von Franz (1972) said that myths of creation may be regarded as expressions of the creative process itself, and that the long genealogies which accompany some of the major creation myths serve the purpose of fixing the creative idea in time and place, indicating its "relations," and binding it with chains of subsequent associations.

The creations of women in historic times have no genealogy; we have been patrilineal for centuries. Women "creators" have often been neglected because their place could not be ascertained in the "great chain of being." How could one attribute originality to the poetic inventions of Emily Dickinson, said some critics, when she never showed that she was consciously departing from literary conventions? She was left "out of mind." Today, groups trying to establish an ethnic identity are eagerly rereading and rewriting history to find their own part in it. The results often have first-rate intellectual interest. In some areas, the Women's Liberation Movement has already brought about a figure-ground change, the sudden realization of two faces in history, alternating with the great central athletic trophy.

Women interested in psychohistory can give us a most helpful description of the creative activities of women of the past, and how these activities relate to the circumstances of time and place. Douvan's study of women psychotherapists around Freud affords an interesting example (1976). Such studies *root* the creativity of women through periods when it flourished and periods when it was stunted, impoverished, and deviously expressed (Nochlin, 1972; Wood, 1972). We may find useful hypotheses in such investigations for a theory of personality-situation interactions (Block, in press; Helson, 1976b). These studies can clarify the symbolic dimensions of images of men and women, which are taken for granted as attributes of the object but which vary with time and culture (Davis, 1975).

Such longitudinal data are "incomparable," I admit, and the research design is, of necessity, ex post facto (Kerlinger, 1973). Even for those of us whose standards are strictly experimental, however, an awareness of other cultures and the past may help us to see our institutions, arrangements, and personality traits as less inevitable and eternal than they seem when we live only in the present, and in this way free our energy for significant studies. We can then go back to studying the "problems" of creative women, which will no longer have the heavy atmosphere of doom at Marienbad, but will be problems in relationships among men, women, the age-old psyche, and changing institutional forms.

REFERENCES

Albert, R.S. Toward a behavioral definition of genius. *American Psychologist,* 1975, *30,* 140-151.

Anastasi, A. *Differential psychology.* New York: Macmillan, 1958.

Anastasi, A., & Schaefer, C.E. Biographical correlates of artistic and literary creativity in adolescent girls. *Journal of Applied Psychology,* 1969, *53,* 267-273.

Anderson, H.H. (Ed.). *Creativity and its cultivation.* New York: Harper & Row, 1959.

Astin, H. Sex differences in mathematical and scientific precocity. In J.C. Stanley, D.P. Keating, & L.H. Fox (Eds.), *Mathematical talent: Discovery, description, and development.* Baltimore: Johns Hopkins University Press, 1974.

Bachtold, L.M., & Werner, E.E. Personality profiles of gifted women: Psychologists. *American Psychologist,* 1970, *25,* 234-243.

Barron, F.X. Originality in relation to personality and intellect. *Journal of Personality,* 1957, *25,* 730-742.

Barron, F.X. *Artists in the making* (chap. 4). New York: Seminar Press, 1972.

Barron, F.X., & Welsh, G.S. Artistic perception as a possible factor in personality style: Its measurement by a figure preference test. *Journal of Psychology,* 1952, *33,* 199-203.

Beauvoir, Simone de. *The second sex.* New York: Knopf, 1953.

Bem, S.L. The measurement of psychological androgyny. *Journal of Consulting and Clinical Psychology*, 1974, *42*, 155-162.

Bernard, J. *Academic women*. University Park: Pennsylvania University Press, 1964.

Bernard, J. *Women and the public interest*. Chicago: Aldine, 1971.

Besdine, M. The Jocasta complex, mothering, and women geniuses. *Psychoanalytic Review*, 1971, *58*, 51-74.

Block, J. *The Q-sort method in personality measurement and psychiatric research*. Springfield, Ill.: Charles C. Thomas, 1961.

Block, J. Recognizing the coherence of personality. In D. Magnussen and N. Endler (Eds.), *Personality at the crossroads*. Wiley Erlbaum (in press).

Bowers, K.S. Sex and susceptibility as moderator variables in the relationship of creativity and hypnotic susceptibility. *Journal of Abnormal Psychology*, 1971, *78*, 93-100.

Bruce, P. Reactions of preadolescent girls to science tasks. *Journal of Psychology*, 1974, *86*, 303-308.

Campbell, D.T. Qualitative knowing in action research. Unpublished manuscript, 1974.

Carlson, R. Understanding women: Implications for personality theory and research. *Journal of Social Issues*, 1972, *28*, 17-32.

Cattell, R.B., & Drevdahl, J.E. A comparison of the personality profile (16 P.F.) of eminent researchers with that of eminent teachers and administrators, and of the general population. *British Journal of Psychology*, 1955, *46*, 248-261.

Cronbach, L.J. Beyond the two disciplines of scientific psychology. *American Psychologist*, 1975, *30*, 116-127.

Davis, N.Z. *Women on top*. Society and culture in early modern France (chap. 5). Stanford: Stanford University Press, 1975.

Deutsch, H. *The psychology of women* (vol. 2). New York: Grune & Stratton, 1945.

DeVos, G. Social stratification and ethnic pluralism: An overview from the perspective of psychological anthropology. *Race*, 1972, *13*, 435-460.

Douvan, E. The role of models in women's professional development. *Psychology of Women Quarterly*, 1976, *1*, 5-20.

Drews, E.M. *The creative intellectual style in gifted adolescents*. Cooperative Research Program, Project No. E-2. Washington, D.C.: U.S. Office of Education, 1964.

Erikson, E.H. The dream specimen of psychoanalysis. *Journal of the American Psychoanalytic Association*, 1954, *2*, 5-56.

Farber, S.M., & Wilson, R.H.L. (Eds.). *The potential of women*. New York: McGraw-Hill, 1963.

Feldman, S. *Escape from the doll's house: Women in graduate and professional school education*. New York: McGraw-Hill, 1973.

Fox, L.H., & Denham, S.A. Values and career interests of mathematically and scientifically precocious youth. In J.C. Stanley, D.P. Keating, & L.H. Fox (Eds.), *Mathematical talent: Discovery, description, and development*. Baltimore: Johns Hopkins University Press, 1974.

Goldberg, P. Are women prejudiced against women? *Transaction*, 1968, *5*, 28-30.

Gough, H.G. *Manual for the California psychological inventory*. Palo Alto, Calif.: Consulting Psychologists Press, 1957.

Gough, H.G., & Heilbrun, A.B., Jr. *The adjective check list manual*. Palo Alto, Calif.: Consulting Psychologists Press, 1965.

Gough, H.G., & Woodworth, D.G. Stylistic variations among professional research scientists. *Journal of Psychology*, 1960, *49*, 87-98.

Greenacre, P. Woman as artist. *Psychoanalytic Quarterly*, 1960, *29*, 208-227.

Griff, M. The recruitment and socialization of artists. In M.C. Albrecht, J.H. Barnett, & M. Griff (Eds.), *The sociology of art and literature: A reader*. New York: Praeger, 1970.

Guilford, J.P. Creativity. *American Psychologist*, 1950, *5*, 444-454.

Guilford, J.P. Some theoretical views of creativity. In H. Helson & W. Bevan (Eds.), *Contemporary approaches to psychology*. Princeton, N.J.: Van Nostrand Reinhold, 1967.

Guilford, J.P., Christensen, P.R., Bond, N.A., Jr., & Sutton, M.A. A factor analysis study of human interests. *Psychological Monographs*, 1954, *68*, 4, (Whole No. 375).

Harding, M.E. *The way of all women*. New York: Longmans, Green, 1935.

Helson, R. Creativity, sex, and mathematics. In *Proceedings of the conference on "The Creative Person."* Berkeley: Institute of Personality Assessment & Research and University Extension, University of California, 1961.

Helson, R. Personality of women with imaginative and artistic interests: The role of masculinity, originality, and other characteristics in their creativity. *Journal of Personality*, 1966, *34*, 1-25.

Helson, R. Personality characteristics and developmental history of creative college women. *Genetic Psychology Monographs*, 1967, *76*, 205-256. (a)

Helson, R. Sex differences in creative style. *Journal of Personality*, 1967, *35*, 214-233. (b)

Helson, R. Effects of sibling characteristics and parental values on creative interest and achievement. *Journal of Personality, 1968*, 36, *589-607. (a)*

Helson, R. Generality of sex differences in creative style. *Journal of Personality,* 1968, *38,* 33-48. (b)

Helson, R. Women mathematicians and the creative personality. *Journal of Consulting and Clinical Psychology,* 1971, *36,* 210-220.

Helson, R. Heroic and tender modes in women authors of fantasy. *Journal of Personality,* 1973, *41,* 493-512. (a)

Helson, R. Through the pages of children's books and what a psychologist found there. *Psychology Today,* 1973, 7, 107-117. (b)

Helson, R. Subtypes among creative men and women mathematicians. In L.H. Fox (Chair), *Women in mathematics.* Symposium presented at American Association for the Advancement of Science, Boston, 1976a.

Helson, R. Two types of women writers and three periods in time: A psychohistorical analysis. In K.F. Riegel & J.A. Meacham (Eds.), *The developing individual in a changing world* (Vol. 2). Chicago: Aldine, 1976, (b)

Helson, R. The creative spectrum of authors of fantasy. *Journal of Personality.* In press.

Helson, R., & Crutchfield, R.S. Mathematicians: The creative researcher and the average Ph.D. *Journal of Consulting and Clinical Psychology,* 1970, *34,* 250-257.

Hochschild, A. (Ed.). *Women and the potential for change.* New York: McGraw-Hill, 1975.

Holland, J.L. *Making vocational choices: A theory of careers.* Englewood Cliffs, N.J.: Prentice-Hall, 1973.

Holland, J.L., & Astin, A.W. The prediction of the academic, artistic, scientific, and social achievement of undergraduates of superior scholastic aptitude. *Journal of Educational Psychology,* 1962, *53*(3), 132-143.

Jenkins, J.L. Remember that old theory of memory? Well, forget it! *American Psychologist,* 1974, *29,* 785-795.

Kanner, A.D. Femininity and masculinity: Their relationship to creativity in male architects and independence from each other. *Journal of Consulting and Clinical Psychology,* 1976, *44,* 802-805.

Kerlinger, F.N. *Foundations of behavioral research.* New York: Holt, Rinehart & Winston, 1973.

Kogan, N. Creativity and sex differences. *Journal of Creative Behavior,* 1974, *8,* 1-15.

Kogan, N., & Morgan, F.T. Task and motivational influences on the assessment of creative and intellective ability in children. *Genetic Psychology Monographs,* 1969, *80,* 91-127.

Kogan, N., & Pankove, E. Creative ability over a five-year span. *Child Development,* 1972, *43,* 427-442.

Kris, E. *Psychoanalytic explorations in art.* New York: International Universities Press, 1952.

Kurtzman, K.A. A study of school attitudes, peer acceptance, and personality of gifted adolescents. *Exceptional Children,* 1967, *33,* 157-162.

Lasswell, H.D. The social setting of creativity. In H.H. Anderson (Ed.), *Creativity and its cultivation.* New York: Harper & Row, 1959.

Levinson, D.J., Darrow, C.M., Klein, E.B., Levinson, M.H., & McKee, B. The psychosocial development of men in early adulthood and the mid-life transition. In D.F. Ricks, A. Thomas, & M. Roff (Eds.), *Life history research in psychopathology* (Vol. 3). Minneapolis: University of Minnesota Press, 1974.

Maccoby, E.E., & Jacklin, C.N. *The psychology of sex differences.* Stanford, Calif.: Stanford University Press, 1974.

MacKinnon, D.W. (Ed.). *Proceedings of the conference on "The Creative Person."* Berkeley: University of California Extension, 1961.

MacKinnon, D.W. The nature and nurture of creative talent. *American Psychologist,* 1962, *17,* 484-495.

MacKinnon, D.W. Personality and the realization of creative potential. *American Psychologist,* 1965, *20,* 273-281.

Main, C. Characteristics of a group of women science teachers. *School Science and Mathematics,* 1973, *73,* 286-290.

Martindale, C. Femininity, alienation, and arousal in the creative personality. *Psychology,* 1972, *9,* 3-15.

Maslow, A. Creativity in self-actualizing people. In H.H. Anderson (Ed.), *Creativity and its cultivation.* New York: Harper & Row, 1959.

McClelland, D.C. On the psychodynamics of creative physical scientists. In H.E. Gruber, G. Terrell, & M. Wertheimer (Eds.), *Contemporary approaches to creative thinking.* New York: Atherton, 1962.

Mead, M. Creativity in cross-cultural perspective. In H.H. Anderson (Ed.), *Creativity and its cultivation.* New York: Harper & Row, 1959.

Mednick, S.A. The associative basis of the creative process. *Psychological Review,* 1962, *69,* 220-232.

Mendelsohn, G.A., & Covington, M.V. Internal processes and perceptual factors in verbal problem-solving: A study of sex and individual differences in cognition. *Journal of Personality,* 1972, *40,* 451-471.

Mendelsohn, G.A. Associative and attentional processes in creative performance: Research on Mednick's associative interpretation of the creative process. *Journal of Personality,* 1976, *44,* 341-369.

Miller, D.R., & Swanson, G.E. *Inner conflict and defense.* New York: Holt, Rinehart and Winston, 1960.

Neumann. E. On the moon and matriarchal consciousness. *Spring,* 1954, 83-100, (Analytical Psychology Club of New York). (a)

Neumann, E. *The origins and history of consciousness.* New York: Bollingen Foundation, 1954. (b)

Nochlin, L. Why are there no great women artists? In V. Gornick & B.K. Moran (Eds), *Women in sexist society.* New York: Basic Books, 1972.

Olsen, T. Silences: When writers don't write. *Women: A journal of liberation,* Fall, 1970.

Pine, F., & Holt, R.R. Creativity and primary process: a study of adaptive regression. *Journal of Abnormal and Social Psychology,* 1960, *61,* 370-379.

Raychaudhuri, M. Relation of creativity and sex to Rorschach "M" responses. *Journal of Personality Assessment,* 1971, *35,* 27-31.

Rock, D.A., Evans, F.R., & Klein, S.P. Predicting multiple criteria of creative achievements with moderator variables. *Journal of Educational Measurement,* 1969, *6,* 229-235.

Roe, A. A psychological study of eminent physical scientists. *Genetic Psychology Monographs,* 1951, *43,* 121-239.

Rosenberg, B., & Fliegel, N. *The vanguard artist: Portrait and self-portrait.* New York: Quadrangle, 1965.

Sanford, R.N. *Self and society.* New York: Atherton, 1966.

Smith, M.E. The values most highly esteemed by men and women in *Who's Who* suggested as one reason for the great difference in representation of the two sexes in those books. *Journal of Social Psychology,* 1962, *58,* 339-344.

Spence, J.T., Helmreich, R., & Stapp, J. Ratings of self and peers on sex-role attributes and their relation to self-esteem and conceptions of masculinity and femininity. *Journal of Personality and Social Psychology,* 1975, *32,* 29-39.

Stringer, P. Masculinity-femininity as a possible factor underlying the personality responses of male and female art students. *British Journal of Social and Clinical Psychology,* 1967, *6,* 186-194.

Suter, B., & Domino, G. Masculinity-femininity in creative college women. *Journal of Personality Assessment,* 1975, *39,* 414-420.

Torrance, E.P. *Guiding creative talent.* Englewood Cliffs, N.J.: Prentice-Hall, 1962.

Torrance, E.P. Changing reactions of preadolescent girls to tasks requiring creative scientific thinking. *Journal of Genetic Psychology,* 1963, *102,* 217-223.

Torrance, E.P. Role of evaluation in creative thinking. Report on Project Number 725. Washington, D.C.: U.S. Office of Education, 1964.

Torrance, E.P. Creative young women in today's world. *Exceptional Children,* 1972, *38,* 597-603.

Torrance, E.P., & Aliotti, N.C. Sex differences in levels of performance and test-retest reliability on the Torrance tests of creative thinking ability. *Journal of Creative Behavior,* 1969, *3,* 52-57.

Tresemer, D., & Pleck, J. Sex-role boundaries and resistance to sex-role change. *Women's Studies,* 1974, *2,* 61-78.

Tyler, L.E. The antecedents of two varieties of vocational interests. *Genetic Psychological Monographs,* 1964, *70,* 177-227.

Urbina, S., Harrison, J., Schaefer, C., & Anastasi, A. Masculinity-femininity and creativity as measured by the Franck drawing completion test. *Psychological Reports,* 1970, *26,* 799-804.

von Franz, M.L. *Patterns of creativity mirrored in creation myths.* Zurich: Spring Publication, 1972.

Wallach, M.A., & Kogan, N. *Modes of thinking in young children.* New York: Holt, Rinehart and Winston, 1965.

Wallach, M.A., & Wing, C.W., Jr. *The talented student: A validation of the creativity-intelligence distinction.* New York: Holt, Rinehart and Winston, 1969.

Welsh, G.S. *Creativity and intelligence: A personality approach* (Chap. 9). Chapel Hill, N.C.: Institute for Research in Social Science, University of North Carolina, 1975.

Werner, E.E., & Bachtold, L.M. Personality factors of gifted boys and girls in middle childhood and adolescence. *Psychology in the Schools,* 1969, *6,* 177-182.

Wood, A.D. The literature of impoverishment: The women local colorists in America, 1865-1914. *Women's Studies,* 1972, *1,* 3-46.

CHAPTER *16*

COMMENTARY: CHAPTERS 12, 13, 14 & 15

MARTHA TAMARA MEDNICK & SANDRA SCHWARTZ TANGRI

The authors have tried to integrate three areas of research, which have, with minor exceptions, been studied separately. The quest for integration is a worthy venture, and in the light of the origins of this genre of motivational research in Murray's general theory of motivation, it is indeed a surprise that more efforts of this sort have not been forthcoming. It should be noted that an implicit assumption in the discussion is the controversial one that motivation and personality have been useful organizing concepts for psychology and therefore will advance our understanding of the psychology of women. Certainly the data presented here do not lead to an unequivocal acceptance of this assumption. What is clear from this examination of specific motivational concepts in the context of concerns with women's issues is that their applicability is very limited. Thus, as suggested by these authors and others attending the Conference on Women's Research Needs in Psychology, a major reassessment of concepts and measures must be part and parcel of further efforts to study female motivation.

The close tie of concept and measurement fostered by operationalism can be used to advantage when dealing with this problem. By going to original sources we can almost always discover how the concept was measured, and hence what it really means. This is well illustrated in the discussion of power motivation, where we see how the different operations used in developing the various measures can lead to very different conclusions about women and power, and that the contradictions are best understood when the original defining characteristics are made clear. When we forget to do this and focus on a concept with no regard for its operational mooring, we find ourselves lost in a sea of inconsistencies. Thus, we can conclude that women do not want to achieve when we look at TAT protocols, but that they do when we look at achievement indicators such as grade-point average or test scores. This problem, a pervasive one in psychology, is particularly unfortunate for the study of women because, as noted and profusely illustrated throughout the paper, most of these concepts and measures have been defined in the context of masculine values and conceptions. Thus, looking at variables in terms of their measurement anchors must precede or at least go hand in hand with the development of programmatic research on women.

It is also important for such a research program that there be a careful articulation of the behaviors that should be the major foci of explanatory efforts for a psychology of women. The authors note that behavioral and motivational terms and referents are confused. A taxonomy or continuum of outcome (i.e., dependent) variables that serves as a source of behavioral anchors for theoretical equations will go a long way toward untangling the conceptual confusion. Motivational constructs are hypothetical and stand or fall on the extent to which they can guide predictions about what is really interesting, the behavior. An example of such a set of behavioral referents in one area, achievement, would include level of school achievement at all levels and in different subjects, choice of major field, career aspirations, planning for careers, career-related behaviors, career progress, long-term pursuit of goals, career change, and so on. Defining such sets of referents for each area of research on women is fundamental to the development of a psychology of women.

With regard to important predictors, sex-role attitudes, stereotypes, and self-perception are cognitive variables that will refine our understanding of the motivation—behavior question. Attention to sex-role variation has already helped us move from a static perspective that has forced psychology to look at women in contrast to men as though this particular difference tells the whole story. Bem's work (see Chapter I, Vol. 1) shows that sex-role concepts vary and lead to powerful and consistent predictions about behavior. It would be to our advantage to incorporate this variable, with careful attention to mode of measurement, in research on women and motivation.

Turning now to some specific comments on each of the topics, we see that achievement has certainly been and continues to be a central focus of concern. Achievement-related topics were the subjects of several papers at the conference.

This is in itself an interesting phenomenon and deserves some comment. Psychologists have generally found achievement to be an area with great "payoff" for a variety of reasons. We do most of our research in achievement settings; thus these studies are situation-specific, increasing the likelihood of consistent findings. Well-referenced behavioral outcomes are easy to come by. The subjects of the research, usually students, reflect society's preoccupation with attainment, excellence, skill, competence, and competition. Nevertheless, the payoff has been for men and not for women. This has been noted before, and this review further stresses the need for new directions. This will, no doubt, remain an area of great concern for research on women because one of the major issues of our time is woman's failure to achieve at a level commensurate with her potential.

It is intuitively clear that more than one motive is called into play in most situations. Most motivational theorists have recognized this, but it has been practically ignored in research of this genre. Certainly, very little is known about the effects of motive interaction on women's behavior. The one exception is with respect to affiliation and achievement, and the questions asked in this area have been inadequate because they stem from sex-stereotypic thinking. Thus, we hear over and over that women need social approval or have affiliative needs that clash with achievement needs, while most men do not suffer this handicap to their achievement strivings. But men need support from significant figures in their lives, too. The difference, as Stein and Bailey have demonstrated, is that boys and men do get approval (love) for achievement behavior while girls and women do not. Why have we not asked questions about the reaction of non-supportive others in a woman's or girl's environment when she does pursue nonapproved goals, or under what circumstances does she persist (motivational, environmental, etc.), or what are the gains and costs, or how does everyone change in the process? The answers to such questions move us from the pessimistic conclusion that if a woman does not have a supportive lover or husband, she might as well give up. The other point of all this is that the interaction of motives must be studied in a way that would answer appropriate, unbiased questions.

The gaps and inconsistencies in research on affiliation are well articulated in this paper. It must be noted, however, that the laboratory social psychological approach exemplified by the work of Stanley Schachter will not, as Rae Carlson has pointed out, tell us very much about men and women and their desires to be together. Moreover, it is especially uninformative because the paradigm itself, the use of shock and manipulated fear, and the implicit value placed on "going it alone," is masculine in its conception. If such an experiment were done in a hospital recovery room following intensive surgery, I would predict that both men and women would want someone, preferably someone important, to be there when they open their eyes. It is difficult to believe that men and women would show differential affiliative needs or nurturing tendencies under such circumstances. I would also argue that in this situation, a cognitive variable such as "feedback" would be unimportant when compared with affection and caring.

The general case here is that the situation is a variable. Expectation and need for support from significant others will vary with the situation, and degree of social approval or love given by others will also show such variation. This, then, brings us to the repeatedly expressed point that external factors must also be examined very carefully so that we will not be hemmed in by the traditional dead-end, self-blaming, intrapsychic paradigm. This point is well made and elaborated upon by Frieze and her coauthors in the discussion of causal attribution and achievement.

This point is certainly relevant to the case of power motivation as well. Of the three motives, this is the most neglected, but the most provocative. Women are defined as powerless in this world. Harriet Holter, the Norwegian sociologist and student of sex-role change, has pointed out that this principle is so tenacious that as women enter arenas of social power, these arenas decrease in social influence. To illustrate, compare congressional or parliamentary power with that of the presidential advisers or certain cabinet members. And then compare the number of women in each role. It should also be clear that this is a particularly knotty area to untangle when we look at who is in power. These are not mere men, but men who are the most stereotypically "masculine" types imaginable. Remember Haldeman, Ehrlichman, and Mitchell? And, of course, if this is the "ball game," anyone who plays, male or female, must fit the mold. How many androgynous people have survived in these arenas?

The preceding remarks are based on an assumption that those who attain power and influence are highly motivated for it. If we use a need-reduction paradigm, it should follow that those now in power should be willing to step aside and give the powerless a chance (i.e., at some point where one can be satisfied.) This hypothesis has been repudiated over and over again in the "field." The powerful must be pushed aside. A profound research question must now be asked. Assuming women want it, how do they develop the skills needed for pushing for, and maintaining, power while working toward the ultimate goal of an androgynous power model?

This brings us to thoughts about the double bind seemingly inherent in the association of woman and power. If she uses deviant or indirect methods, classic stereotypes are reinforced, but if she uses "male" style and wants to influence and exert strong leadership, she runs the risk of being labeled pushy and aggressive. If this "risk" is accepted by the individual, the question then arises of how this affects her function as a role model. Will other women model someone defined as unwomanly and who is seen as rejected by and rejecting men?

An important aspect of power not mentioned in this chapter is that it is tied in with taking responsibility and being accountable for one's actions, whatever the consequences. This aspect of the power scene must be recognized, and it would be interesting to look at how this varies with sex-role self-concept. In sum, the varieties of power motivation, power behaviors, and power situations, the interrelation of motives, and their functional significance must be defined as an area of prime importance in research on psychology of women.

COMMENTARY ON CHAPTERS 6 THROUGH 8

The list of neglected topics could have been considerably longer. But I am glad that the topics of power, creativity, and attribution were selected for review. On a semantic differential of activities, power and creativity could be placed at opposite ends of a number of dimensions: hard (power), soft (creativity); good (creativity), bad (power); and strong (power), weak (creativity). Unger's and Helson's chapters also diverge considerably in their critique of the literature. Unger finds the subject of women and power subsumable under a more general category of investigation, status relations. Helson argues that creativity in women cannot easily be studied in the present framework of that subject because its very formulation has been male-biased in such a way as to exclude or make very difficult the study of its nonmasculine aspects, whether in men or women. Thus, Unger's paper looks to the well established literature on status relations for an explication of women's powerlessness, whereas Helson's looks to a reconceptualization of the subject of creativity itself.

The suggestion that power relations between the sexes can largely be seen as one case of relations governed by status differentials is useful because it puts these phenomena under the study of more general principles. The parallelisms are certainly abundant enough to warrant this kind of conceptual treatment. However, it does leave unresolved a couple of basic questions, which, when born in mind, should prevent us from slipping into the posture of thinking that there is nothing unique in the power relations between the sexes. Three questions ought to be studied, the first being when and how do norms or habits of chivalry come into play such that they moderate, disguise, or exacerbate the power advantage of men over women? For instance, it is not clear to me how we reconcile the differences among the following: (a) Peplau's finding that men who gave "threatened," or hostile responses to stories of achievement by women also increased their performance when competing with them against others; (b) Unger and associates' finding that women drivers in apparently stalled cars are honked at faster than comparable male drivers; but (c) that women may be let into a line more often than men. No doubt the number of situations over which chivalry rules has been shrinking. What principles govern this retreat?

The second question is: If the power relations are determined by status, and status is based (among other things) on looks, competence, family, and a number of other variables besides sex, why is *sex* the *prevailing* determinant of status? Why is an incompetent (nonconforming) male preferred more (one basis for status) than a competent (nonconforming) female, when competence is otherwise a culturally dominant basis for achieved status? Pursuit of this question would lead us down paths of inquiry into history, economics, and the murky world of men's misogyny. A related question is: Why is status assignment based on gender so resistant to change? This has two senses: (a) Why does being female remain so persistently a low-status category, and (b) why does gender as the basis of status assignment so persistently maintain its preeminence?

The third question is: Why is the status differential between the sexes as universal as it is? Are there somewhat general principles, taking varied cultural forms, which link gender to status, and what are they? If these have to do with average differences in strength, aggressiveness, or with class differences in reproductive function, some of the strategies for changing the status differential might well be aimed at reducing these average differences (e.g., make women stronger and more physically fit; make men less aggressive), and reducing the frequency of reproduction.

In addition, efforts might be directed at changing the social structures and material conditions that favor strength and aggressiveness, and which make childbearing and child-rearing a handicap in the status system.

Finally, one might raise the question of whether our present conception of power is itself adequate. Does the assumption of a general status differential governing a unidirectional flow of influence adequately describe the extent to which the flow of influence is multidirectional or determined by subject matter, duration of interaction, or by size and composition of the decision-making group? None of these questions implies a contradiction with the earlier questions about status and gender. And what of the costs of using "pure" or nonreciprocal power? If power is a resource, its expenditure represents a cost. We need an analysis of these costs, how they are distributed, and how these "debts" are settled. Unger points out, for instance, the costly consequences of the indirect use of power by women in domestic units. I also like her point that changing the status of women must include treating others' expectations as well as women's own expectations.

Frieze also calls for a refocus of attention on the real external barriers to women's achievements, which includes the attributions that others make regarding the causes of women's successes and failures. Thus, we find in an article as "psychological" as Frieze's and as "sociological" as Unger's an increasing concern with the implications for intervention strategy of different research questions. This concern is beautifully articulated in Rosabeth Kanter's paper recently presented at Wellesley (1975).

Other subjects that could have been included in a list of neglected topics are women in sports and the psychology of being "fit"; effects on women of the structure of medical care, of present medical conceptions of pregnancy, nursing, breast cancer, abortion, and other specifically female or reproduction-related conditions, as well as general sexism in medical training; the role of women in, and the effects on them, of changing family structures and new life-styles; and the developmental implications for girls and women of serving as or being expected to be primary child caretakers (some of the interesting questions here are raised by observation of changes taking place in men who assume this role without the anticipatory socialization for it that most women get). This, of course, is only a partial list. That much work remains to be done, and many changes in psychology are to be expected, is abundantly clear and eagerly anticipated. Whether these will have social impact, whether the parameters of our investigation will change as we study them, and how and when was not discussed at all. How to *anticipate* the policy implications of our research, and how to maximize the desired consequences of our work is the most neglected topic of all.

PART III
ATTITUDES TOWARD WOMEN

INTRODUCTION

JULIA A. SHERMAN & FLORENCE L. DENMARK

Inevitably one arrives at a need to evaluate and understand attitudes toward women, since these attitudes permeate and affect every aspect of a woman's existence. Attitudes toward women are obviously more important to women than attitudes toward men are to men because women are a relatively powerless group and thus, for good or ill, are more affected by the attitudes of others toward them. Knowing and understanding attitudes and their development within a sociohistorical framework comprise a logical beginning to the change of negative and restrictive attitudes. However, psychological knowledge has rarely proceeded to this more advanced stage.

The article by Pleck (Chapter 10) reviews the major theories of attitudes toward women. While Pleck's conclusion that men's attitudes toward women are not uniquely different from women's attitudes toward women would, on the surface, appear to be quite sound, there are some questions to be kept in mind before this conclusion is firmly accepted. First of all, Pleck has clearly not sampled the entire universe of items in comparing male and female attitudes toward women. Second, if there were a situation in which the power of males vis-a-vis females were so great that what males thought of females determined the cultural norm also for what females thought of females, then although males and females would usually appear to have similar attitudes toward women, male attitudes would still have been a unique factor in determining those attitudes.

Pleck's further conclusion that "attitudes toward women are not more negative or restrictive than attitudes toward men" also requires some qualification. As he acknowledges in the body of his article, it is not easy to compare the sexes in this regard, for from the point of view of power and status, women are indeed more oppressed than men.

The article by Brannon (Chapter 11) is extremely useful in reviewing the pitfalls in attitudes measurement and in drawing parallels between the literature on prejudice toward blacks and the literature on prejudice toward women. The problem of the behavioral validity of these scales is glaringly apparent.

CHAPTER *17*

MALES' TRADITIONAL ATTITUDES TOWARD WOMEN: Conceptual Issues In Research

JOSEPH H. PLECK

Joseph H. Pleck holds a Ph.D. in clinical psychology from Harvard University and is Associate Director of the Center for the Family, University of Massachusetts at Amherst. Ter research interests are the male sex role and relationships between work and family life. Tey was the editor (with Jack Sawyer) of Men and Masculinity *and is currently preparing a new monograph titled* The Male Role. *Presently, he is Program Director of the Family and Work Program at Wellesley College's Center for Research on Women.*

This chapter first reviews current research on the dynamics of males' traditional attitudes toward females. Five major theoretical approaches to traditional male attitudes are identified in current research: authoritarianism, low self-esteem, masculinity-feminity, the effects of the early mother-child relationship, and inter-group relations. Empirical support for the first four approaches is limited, and the last has been applied only minimally in research. Males' and females' attitudes toward women are then compared, followed by a comparison of attitudes toward women and toward men.

Males' attitudes toward women are not consistently more traditional than women's. A new interpretation of sex-role stereotyping data suggests that attitudes toward women are not more negative than attitudes toward men. Data on responses to sex-role deviance suggest that attitudes toward women are not more restrictive than attitudes toward men, in the sense of not holding women more rigidly to their sex-role norms than men. However, even though role norms may not be more restrictive for women than for men in this sense, it is nonetheless likely that sex-role norms are more oppressive for women, by virtue of the specific content of female-role norms that limit the development of traits that facilitate the attainment of social power.

Because of the similarities in men's and women's attitudes toward women, and of the similarities in attitudes toward women and men, it is argued that males' traditional attitudes are not unique psychological phenomena requiring special explanatory theories to account for them, or having a uniquely powerful and negative impact on women, or having a unique role in accounting for the social oppression of women, as compared to other more social-structural factors. Future research and theory needs to explore further the nature and dynamics of traditional sex-role attitudes so as to determine how large a part they play in maintaining the sexual organization of society.

As women's roles have begun to change in contemporary society, it is commonplace to note that many men continue to hold traditional attitudes toward women. These traditional attitudes have been variously labeled sexism, misogyny, sex-role traditionalism, and the like, and these terms are used interchangeably here. Perhaps the major support for these traditional male attitudes is that they pragmatically benefit men by justifying a social order in which males have relative advantage and privilege. Many men may see adopting more liberal attitudes toward women as being against their self-interest. But in addition, researchers and clinicians have often speculated that men's traditional attitudes toward women also derive from other, purely psychological sources deep within men's personalities. From whatever source, continued traditionalism in men's attitudes toward women inhibit needed change in women's roles.

This chapter considers the psychological sources of men's traditional attitudes toward women in a broader theoretical context than is usually adopted. First, the theoretical perspectives on the sources of male traditionalism used in available literature are isolated and reviewed. Then, male attitudes are subjected to a conceptual "discriminant validity" analysis. In the first part of this analysis, males' attitudes are compared with *females'* attitudes toward women. In the second part of this analysis, attitudes toward women are compared with attitudes toward *men.* While both these comparisons are obvious ones to make for a better understanding of the dynamics of male attitudes toward women, they have not been made systematically before.

Before examining these issues, we should note some limitations in this review and in the available research. This review covers formal research using paper-and-pencil scales for attitudes toward women and toward sex roles, sex-role stereotype measures, and individual survey items on women. Though clinical or case studies are not included, several clinically based theories have been tested in more systematic research and are examined here. In formal research, a great variety of different scales have been used to assess attitudes toward women, many in only a single study. One might easily assume that all these different attitude scales measure much the same thing. However, for those scales for which factor analyses are reported (e.g., Spence & Helmreich, 1972a; Spence, Helmreich, & Stapp, 1973; Ellis & Bentler, 1973; Gump, 1972; Dempewolff, 1974; see also Mason & Bumpass, 1975), factor structures seem different. Different scales appear to reflect different combinations of the possible components of sex-role attitudes and attitudes toward women, and there is little agreement on what the central content dimensions of these attitudes are. There is also variety among available sex-role stereotype measures (Broverman, Vogel, Broverman, Clarkson, & Rosenkrantz, 1972; Ellis & Bentler, 1973; Spence, Helmreich, & Stapp, 1974), and the comparability of studies using different measures cannot be assumed. Since there have been so many different scales and measures, it has been extremely difficult to build a coherent body of findings about their correlates and the constructs they presumably measure in common.

The Attitudes toward Women Scale (AWS) at the present time (Spence & Helmreich, 1972a; Spence, Helmreich, & Stapp, 1973) may become the dominant attitude scale, and the Personal Attributes Questionnaire (PAQ) (Spence, Helmreich, & Stapp, 1974) may become the dominant stereotype measure. Both have to their advantage ease of availability, including short forms, and careful normative data. In the area of individual survey items, Mason, Czajka, and Arber (1974) have identified a group of 16 items used in identical form in at least two of several recent surveys with large samples of known characteristics. Mason et al. suggest that, wherever possible, these items be replicated in future surveys so that change over time can be assessed. Consensual agreement on measures in future sex-role attitude and stereotype research should be a high priority, and will greatly increase the confidence of generalizations and comparisons across studies.

We should also note that the relationship of sex-role attitudes and stereotypes to behavior has not been well established. For example, Spence and Helmreich (1972b) found that AWS scores were unrelated to men's reactions to a competent female stimulus, and both Kenkel (1959) and Hoffman (1962) found that sex-role attitude measures were not related in expected ways to marital power. The only current behavioral validation for a sex-role stereotype measure appears to be that in one study of noncollege-educated Catholic mothers, in which stereotyping was positively associated with family size (Broverman et al., 1972). We might expect, of course, that the link between attitudes (or stereotypes) and behavior is as complicated in the sex-role areas as it is in any other. We should be aware, though, that the attitude-behavior link for sex-role attitudes and stereotypes has scarcely been investigated, let alone confirmed, in available research. Keeping these limitations in mind, let us proceed with review of the hypotheses about the sources of traditional male attitudes which have guided present research.

THEORETICAL PERSPECTIVES ON TRADITIONAL MALE ATTITUDES

Five major psychological hypotheses or theories concerning the sources of males' traditional attitudes toward women can be identified in the literature:

authoritarianism, low self-esteem, masculinity-femininity, the early mother-child relationship, and intergroup relations. Each will be examined briefly.

Authoritarianism

Adorno, Frenkel-Brunswick, Levinson, and Sanford (1964, p. 399) suggested that authoritarians manifest "an ambivalent underlying disrespect for, and resentment against, the opposite sex, often hidden behind an externalized and excessive pseudoadmiration." Consistent with this formulation, a range of studies (Nadler & Morrow, 1959; Centers, 1963; Pincus, 1971; Brannon & Dull, 1971; Worell & Worell, 1971; Goldberg, 1974) found significant relationships between traditional attitudes toward women and measures of authoritarianism in men. Further, Nadler and Morrow's (1959) study distinguished the two superficially paradoxical factors suggested by Adorno's formulation, which they termed "chivalry" and "open subordination of women," and found that F-scale scores correlated with both. Wolman (1974) presented the most recent clinical statement of the authoritarian hypothesis.

There have been two difficulties with the authoritarian hypothesis, however. First, as Goldberg (1974) noted, though the relationship between authoritarianism and misogyny is significant, it is too low to be of much discriminatively predictive value. The proportion of variance in attitudes toward women which authoritarianism accounts for is simply too low. Second, the correlation between authoritarianism and traditional attitudes toward women holds true for women as well. The original formulation of authoritarian personality dynamics, however, specifically predicted negative attitudes only toward the other sex. The rationale was that the authoritarianism represented a maladaptive generalization of defenses against ego-alien and unconscious cross-sex identification. The authoritarian had special psychodynamic reasons for directing negative attitudes specifically toward the other sex because tey needed to defend against ter psychological identification with the other sex.

More recently, of course, the concept of authoritarianism has come to be used in a broader way, referring to rigid cognitive style and attitudes, without the psychodynamics of Adorno's (1964) original formulation. The association between authoritarianism and *women's* traditional attitudes toward women is not a problem in this contemporary broader usage of the construct. But this more modern usage lacks the psychodynamic punch of the original formulations.

By accepting it, we are reduced to saying that individuals (both women and men) who have traditional, rigid attitudes in general have traditional, rigid views of women. In short, we have a simple trait-trait association rather than an explanatory dynamic hypothesis about male attitudes toward women.

Low Self-esteem

Miller (1974), and Vavrik and Jurich (1971), found that males with traditional attitudes toward women have low self-esteem, and Pleck (1973) found that college males who were threatened by competence in women rated themselves less favorably on creativity, intelligence, and satisfaction with themselves. It makes intuitive sense that low self-esteem might lead males to seek security through feeling superior to women and by having other controlling and restricting attitudes toward women. There are disconfirming findings, however. Miller (1974) found that the relationship between traditional attitudes and low self-esteem held true in a sample of males from conservative, church-related colleges, but not in males from more liberal, public colleges. Goldberg (1974), using a sample of high school students, found no relationship between self-esteem and attitudes toward women. Thus, even in the limited number of reported studies, the relationship between low self-esteem and traditional attitudes in males is not always replicated, and holds true only in certain samples.

Further, women also show a relationship between traditional sex-role attitudes and low self-esteem (Gump, 1972). The presence of this relationship in women does not, of course, invalidate the hypothesis about the relationship between the two variables in men, but it does underscore the need for researchers to be explicit about whether they predict the same relationship for both sexes, and why or why not.

Masculinity-feminity

Analysis of a third trait reported in several recent studies relates sex-role attitudes to the psychological trait of masculinity-femininity. These studies have not made theoretical predictions about this relationship, but several are offered here. For women, one coud argue that traditional attitudes should be related to femininity because feminine women should have a psychological investment in the traditional sex-role norms according to which they are highly valued. On the other hand, traditional attitudes might be related to masculinity in women, since traditional attitudes represent male-identified attitudes toward women. For males, one could predict that traditional attitudes toward women are part of traditional male identity, and thus should be positively correlated with masculinity scores.

The data in the three available studies are inconsistent. Spence and Helmreich (1972a) found their Attitudes toward Women Scale nearly entirely uncorrelated with the CPI femininity scale in both males and females. Ellis and Bentler (1973) found that traditional attitudes were related to femininity in women, but found no relationship between traditional attitudes and masculinity-femininity in men. Kando (1972,) in small samples, found a higher association between traditional attitudes and masculinity in males than there was between traditional attitudes and femininity in females. Kando suggested that, as a consequence, women experience more role strain than do men. No studies have yet been published relating sex-role attitudes to androgyny measures, assessing masculinity and femininity as independent dimensions (e.g., Bem, 1974; Spence, Helmreich, & Stapp, 1974). Such analyses may be helpful.

The Early Mother-child Relationship

The theoretical approach to males' traditional attitudes toward women with the longest intellectual history derives from psychoanalytic theory, and concerns the effects of the early mother-child relationship in the male. This approach, presented by Horney (1930) and more recently revived in feminist circles by Chodorow (1972, 1974), develops two central hypotheses. The first, or "domination," hypothesis holds that in the early mother-child relationship, the child experiences the mother as powerful and potentially overwhelming. In psychoanalytic language, the child experiences a "phallic mother" who is aggressively controlling and dominating. Horney interpreted mythology about powerful, evil female forces such as witches and sirens as symbolic expressions of this early experience. For the male child, because he cannot potentially identify or ally himself with these forces, the phallic mother is even more threatening. Thus, according to this view, men seek to control and restrict the fantasied power of women, and seek independence from any situations in which they are potentially subordinate to women. It is these psychological needs that are reflected in males' traditional attitudes.

In the second, or "closeness," hypothesis, more emphasized by Chodorow, the key issue is the male's psychological identification with his mother. In this view, the early attachment to the mother leads to a feminine identification that is problematic for males. Men fear a feminine part of themselves, and seek to control it by restricting and subordinating those who actually are female. In short, males externalize their *intrapsychic* conflict about femininity by making it an *intergroup* conflict. This hypothesis is related to the authoritarianism hypothesis reviewed earlier, namely, that one of Adorno's (1964) central psychodynamic hypotheses was that authoritarianism represented a generalization of defenses against unconscious cross-sex identifications.

Though these two psychodynamic hypotheses have considerable currency in contemporary thinking about men's attitudes toward women, there has been little direct testing of their empirical implications. Testing the domination and closeness hypotheses would require measuring the extent to which males in early childhood are dominated by their mothers, or are closely attached to their mothers (presumably leading to an unconscious feminine identification), and correlating such measures with later adult attitudes toward women. Such an analysis has not been conducted. There are several analyses, however, using males' retrospective perceptions of their relationship to their mothers, which can be examined in light of the theory. Two studies found that males' positive attitudes toward women are associated with reports of *closer* relationships with the mother (Meier, 1972; Rapoport & Rapoport, 1971). A third, assessing perceptions of parental warmth and control separately, found that males' attitudes to women correlate with qualities of the relationship with the *father,* rather than with the mother (Worell & Worell, 1971). Specifically, traditional attitudes were associated with perceived high paternal control.

At first glance, these findings disconfirm the hypotheses that traditional attitudes in males derive from either dominating or close relationships with the mother. It is possible to argue, however, that retrospective ratings of this sort are distorted by the very dynamic processes being studied. That is, if a close or dominating maternal relationship in early life can lead to traditional attitudes toward women, it may also lead to reporting less control or greater distance from the mother. In effect, *reporting* distance or independence from the mother serves the same defensive function as traditional sexist attitudes. It could also be argued that if the relationship with the mother is extremely dominating or close, the male will have pro-female attitudes as a product of that domination or resulting identification. That is, the theory does not specify under what circumstances these characteristics of the mother-child relationship will need to be defended against by anti-female attitudes, and under what circumstances they will be accepted by the male, leading to pro-female attitudes. The Worell and Worell (1971) finding that anti-feminist attitudes are related to qualities of the *paternal* relationship is hard to directly reconcile with the psychoanalytic hypotheses under consideration, although other psychodynamic hypotheses can be devised to account for it. Because of these interpretive ambiguities, these data do not clearly confirm or reject the psychoanalytic view of the male attitudes toward women.

Bowman, Worthy, and Greyser (1965) provided an example of a less direct kind of evidence, which has been used to support the domination hypothesis. In a study of businessmen's attitudes toward women workers, younger men had more negative attitudes toward women than did older men. Bowman, Worthy, and Greyser's (1965) interpretation was that younger men had stronger needs to free themselves from actual or potential domination by women, as postulated in dynamic theories, while older men had worked out this issue. There are several difficulties with this interpretation, however. First, the negative association between age and traditional attitudes toward women appears to be unique to this sample. For example, two recent large studies of representative national samples found, more predictably, that younger men have more favorable attitudes toward women (Roper Organization, 1974, p. 3; Pleck, 1975). (It should be noted that many studies use samples so restricted in age that analysis may not be decisive.) Second, in the study by Bowman and her associates, age was strongly related to rank in one's firm, which was in itself strongly related to attitudes toward women—the higher one's rank, the more favorable one's attitudes. It was not possible to differentiate the effects of age and rank in the analysis. Thus, the effect for age may be an artifact of the relationship of organizational rank to attitudes toward women, which can be interpreted in sociopsychological rather than psychodynamic terms (see "Intergroup Relations," below).

Another way of evaluating the domination and closeness hypotheses is to compare cultures that vary in the degree of closeness or contact between mothers and children. Presumably, cultures with closer, more dominating mother-child relationships should also have more negative male attitudes toward women. In this kind of analysis, we would examine the effects of variations among cultures in mother-child closeness, rather than the effects of variations in mother-child closeness among individuals within one culture. This kind of analysis has not been formally carried out, but it can be applied to recent historical experience. Most would probably agree that the mother-child bond and the significance of mothers in children's lives have become greater over the past several centuries in Western cultures. The strengthening of this bond resulted generally from greater parental investment in the child, as a result of a declining infant mortality and the development of the concept of childhood itself, as well as (and more specifically) from the emergence of a paternal work pattern away from the family and a growing belief in the special psychological importance of the mother-child relationship. One theme in feminist writing, in fact, has been the observation that contemporary Euro-American culture is nearly unique among all cultures of the world in viewing the rearing of children as an exclusive and full-time occupation for adult women. If the mother-child bond has become stronger, then the two psychoanalytic hypotheses would suggest that male attitudes toward women should have become more negative and restrictive over the past several centuries. Most psychologists would say, however, that attitudes toward women have stayed the same or improved slightly over this period.

Thus, in evaluating the usefulness of Horney's (1932) and Chodorow's (1974) hypotheses, extrapolations from available data do not provide much support, either in within-group analyses or in cross-cultural analyses. However, more definitive research directly assessing qualities of the mother-child relationship in early life in relation to later male attitudes toward women has not been conducted at either the individual or cross-cultural levels. It should be emphasized that the psychodynamic hypotheses considered here do not exhaust the possible ways of theorizing how early family experience affects men's attitudes toward women. It may be that early family experiences affects men's attitudes toward women in ways not investigated so far, and it is this broader issue of how family experiences influence men's attitudes, rather than the current psychoanalytic hypotheses, which should be investigated.

Intergroup Relations

One body of research on the social psychology of intergroup relations which has been applied to male-female relations concerns how the terms on which groups interact determine whether that contact will reduce or reinforce stereotypes. As described by Allport (1954), when a subordinate group interacts with a dominant group in roles of equal status, then intergroup contact will reduce the dominant group's negative stereotypes of the subordinate group. If the groups interact on unequal terms, however, then intergroup contact will only reinforce stereotypes. In the one study applying this hypothesis to male-female relations, Bass, Krusell, and Alexander (1971) found that business managers who worked with women in positions of equal status to their own had more positive attitudes toward women workers than did managers who worked with women only as subordinates.

The intergroup relations perspective has not generally been applied to relations between the sexes, beyond this single study (Bass et al., 1971), perhaps because of the oft-noted observation that the male-female case is unique in intergroup relations because women and men have more intimate relations and contact with members of the other group than they do with members of their own. That is, men and women already have a lot of contact, with varying degrees of equality. However, there are many role areas from which women have traditionally been excluded, or in which women have interacted with men only in inferior status—work and professions. Intergroup relations theory has clear application here, and needs to be elaborated in order to deal with the fact that women and men have multiple and varying kinds of contact with each other in different role relationships.

In review, the first three perspectives on males' traditional attitudes toward women (authoritarianism, low self-esteem, and masculinity-femininity) postulate trait-trait relationships that are easy to test. Where relationships have been found, they have been weaker or less consistently replicated than they should be. The fourth and fifth perspectives are more complex and sophisticated as theories. Two hypotheses suggested by psychoanalytic perspective on the effects of the early mother-child relationship on male attitudes do not appear to be supported, but the psychoanalytic hypotheses are sufficiently complex that they are not easily confirmable or rejected. Other possible hypotheses concerning the effect of early family experience on male attitudes toward women have not been developed and tested. The intergroup relations perspective differs from the others in taking a relatively favorable view toward intervention and change in men's attitudes. Rather than viewing male attitude change as requiring alteration in fundamental traits in males' personalities, or as resulting from problems in long-past relationships, the intergroup relations perspective assumes that male attitudes can be changed by manipulating the terms on which women and men relate.

COMPARISON OF MALES' AND FEMALES' ATTITUDES TOWARD WOMEN

Research on male attitudes toward women generally makes the assumption that distinctive psychological processes account for males' attitudes. To gain further insight into male attitudes, it is useful to compare men's attitudes toward women with *women's* attitudes toward women, and then to compare attitudes toward women with attitudes toward *men*. We can think of these two comparisons as parts of a theoretical "discriminant validity" analysis of male attitudes toward women. These comparisons will shed light on the question whether male attitudes toward women are a unique psychological phenomenon in themselves, or whether they are part of a more general set of attitudes (shared by both women and men) concerning both male and female sex roles. We will start by examining similarities and differences in men's and women's attitudes toward women.

Table 10.1 compares males' and females' attitudes toward women, using data drawn from several studies made since 1972. The data include individual items selected from two recent large-scale surveys using representative national samples of males and females, and normative data from the Attitudes toward Women Scale and the Personal Attributes Questionnaire developed by Spence et al. (1974), the attitude and stereotype measures for which the most complete norms on the largest samples are available. Erskine (1971) presented a highly useful summary of male-female comparisons in attitudes toward women in survey data from 1937-1969, which is not reproduced here. The number of studies directly comparing male and female attitudes toward women and sex role stereotypes is surprisingly small.

Several important points emerge from Table 10.1. Using summary measures of attitudes and stereotypes toward women in nonrepresentative but homogeneous samples, men show more traditional views and perceptions than do women. The difference seems to range between about half a standard deviation (for the short form AWS, student sample) and a quarter of a standard deviation (for the AWS short form, parent sample). On the other hand, examining individual survey items from national samples, it appears that men's and women's attitudes are closer together than one might have thought. Further, on a number of items (favoring efforts to change women's role, agreeing women are discriminated against in jobs, more advantages to being a man, approving of women's liberation), men have *more* liberal attitudes than women. These items seem to differ from the other survey items in that they imply a perception of women's status in politicized terms, acknowledging the power differential between the sexes and supporting change. Consistent with this distinction, Erskine's (1971) summary indicated that men now have more favorable attitudes toward a woman President than do women, in contrast to nine other topic areas concerning women's roles in which men are slightly more traditional. In the ratings of qualities admired

Table 10.1

Comparison of men's and women's attitudes from selected recent studies

Item or measure	Men, %	Women, %
1. Favor efforts to change women's role in society	63	57
2. Agree women are discriminated against in obtaining top jobs in the professions	56	54
3. Think more advantages to being a man	42	31
4. Qualities most admired in women:		
(a.) intelligence	55	57
(b.) being sensitive to the feelings of others	38	52
(c.) gentleness	43	37
(d.) being able to express feelings and emotions	24	25
(e.) leadership ability	10	11
(f.) independence	17	24
(g.) sex appeal	26	5
5. Prefer traditional marriage (husband assumes responsibility for providing for family and wife runs house and takes care of children)	50	48
6. Rank "happy marriage" as most wanted for a daughter	77	76
7. Rank "interesting career" as most wanted for a daughter	15	17

8. (Many or most) women don't work as hard on their jobs as men do	22	15
9. (Many or most) women are happiest when they are taking care of a home and children	46	38
10. (Many or most) women are discriminated against in our society	35	36
11. Approve of women's liberation	59	52
12. Attitude toward Women Scale, long form, student sample (high = liberal)	89.26 (SD = 22.5)	98.21 (SD = 23.1)
13. AWS, long form, parent sample	81.36 (SD = 19.3)	86.50 (SD = 17.4)
14. AWS, short form, student sample	44.80 (SD = 12.1)	50.26 (SD = 11.7)
15. AWS, short form, parent sample	39.22 (SD = 10.5)	41.86 (SD = 11.6)
16. Personal Attributes Questionnaire, stereotyped mean score (high = stereotyped)	145.04 (SD = 15.9)	140.85 (SD = 14.8)

Sources:
1-7 Roper Organization (1974), male N = 1000, female N = 3000.
8-11: males, Pleck (1975), N = 801.
8-11: females, Staines (1974), N = 801.
12: Spence and Helmreich (1972a), male N = 713, female N = 769.
13: Spence and Helmreich (1972a), male N = 232, female N = 292.
14: Spence, Helmreich and Stapp (1973), male N = 286, female N = 24 .
15: Spence, Helmreich, and Stapp (1973), male n = 232, female N = 292.
16: Spence, Helmreich, and Stapp (1974), male N = 248, female N = 282.

in women, men show more stereotyped perceptions than women on sex appeal (26 vs. 5%), independence (17 vs. 24%), and gentleness (43 vs. 37%), but less stereotyped perceptions than women on admiration for sensitivity to the feelings of others (38 vs. 52%). Men show slight margins over women in believing that women do not work as hard on their jobs as men do (22 vs. 15%), and that women are happiest when taking care of a home and children (46 vs. 38%), but on preference for traditional marriage and ranking of the importance of a happy marriage and an interesting career for a daughter, men's and women's responses are nearly identical.

It is important to try to put these current data in an historical context, though this is difficult because of the lack of comparability of items and measures over time. Erskine (1971) concluded that the gap between male and female attitudes concerning women has narrowed during the period 1937-1969. On the other hand, it appears that there are greater differences in attitudes toward women in the student samples than in the parent samples administered by the AWS. This comparison may indicate that the gap between male and female attitudes toward women is increasing, at least when comparing older samples with educated younger samples.

Overall, comparing male and female attitudes toward women reveals a differentiated picture of some areas in which men have more traditional attitudes, some in which men have more liberal attitudes, and some in which men's and women's attitudes are quite similar. If attitudes toward women were to be included in Maccoby and Jacklin's (1974) recent review of psychological sex differences, attitudes toward women would probably be classified with those traits in which present literature is inconclusive. Fundamental questions regarding the component structure of sex-role attitudes and stereotypes, as well as cohort and historical changes in attitudes, have to be thought through before a definitive overview can be taken.

The comparison between men's and women's attitudes toward women is theoretically important in at least two ways. First, four of the five major etiological theories attempt to explain traditional attitudes toward women only in terms of men's attitudes. In effect, these theories assume that men have significantly more traditional attitudes than women, which is clearly not the case. Combining this with our earlier review of the correlates of traditional attitudes expressed toward women by both women and men, we conclude that, at the present time, research evidence does not support the hypothesis that men's and women's traditional attitudes toward women differ in either overall level or in their psychological dynamics.

A second way that the similarity of male and female attitudes toward women is theoretically important concerns the processes by which traditional attitudes and stereotypes limit women. One could argue that men's attitudes are the major block to change in women's role because men control resources women need in order to change, and because men are a reference group for women. Alternatively, it could be argued that women's own traditional attitudes constitute the major barrier to change in women. Though these two effects are not incompatible, there do not appear to be any studies that compare or examine their effects in interaction with each other. The fact that women and men have generally similar attitudes toward women makes it more difficult to distinguish the independent effect of each. Further, in couple relationships—an important context in which to examine the influence of male and female attitudes on female behavior-male and female attitudes are highly correlated (Rubin, Peplau, & Hill, 1973), and probably more similar than they are in the general population. That is, sex-role attitudes appear to be one of the variables on which "assortative mating" occurs. Thus, in a male-female couple, a female behavior that is associated with the female's sex-role attitudes is likely to be associated with the male's attitudes as well, making it difficult to distinguish their effects on the female's behavior.

In summary, men do not consistently have more traditional attitudes toward women than do women themselves. These are some areas in which the males' attitudes are more traditional, but others in which male attitudes are less traditional. Further, there is no clear evidence that males' traditional attitudes have a unique or different etiology than females' attitudes, or that males' attitudes have a more restricting effect on women's behavior than women's own attitudes.

COMPARISON OF ATTITUDES TOWARD WOMEN
AND TOWARD MEN

After this comparison of males' and females' attitudes toward women, let us take up the second analytic comparison, the comparison of attitudes toward women with attitudes toward men. Directly comparing attitudes toward women and attitudes toward men is methodologically difficult.

First, there is only one available scale that can be used to assess attitudes about male role performance—Steinmann and Fox's (1974) Inventory of Masculine Values. For a variety of reasons concerning the nature of the scale itself and the way it is reported, it is not usable for our purpose. Second, even if we had a scale to assess prejudiced and restrictive attitudes toward men, it would be hard to compare it with measures of traditional attitudes toward women because we would not have a common metric. Even comparing individual items is ambiguous. If equal proportions of the population say that they would not use a female doctor and not use a male baby sitter, do these reflect equal prejudice or not? If equal proportions say that women are illogical and men are insensitive, are these stereotypes equally negative or not?

For our comparison here, we will first examine the favorability of attitudes toward each sex, and then the restrictiveness of attitudes toward each sex. For the former, we will use data on sex-role stereotyping. For the latter, we will use data from outside the sex-role attitude or stereotype literature entirely—data concerning responses to deviance from sex-role norms in each sex. We will first look at data on sex-role stereotypes.

McKee and Sherriffs (1957) and Broverman et al. (1972), in two major studies, identified sets of adjectives that discriminated ratings made about males and females. The adjectives characterizing men were rated more highly on social desirability than were the adjectives characterizing women. These studies have been widely interpreted as indicating that the male stereotype is more favorable than the female stereotype, and that women are expected and desired to have a variety of negatively valued and dysfunctional personality traits. However, let us take a devil's advocate role and examine some points raised in the stereotype literature which question the validity of this interpretation.

These points derive from the fact that sex stereotypes, either descriptive or prescriptive (i.e., "real" vs. "ideal"), have been defined in the literature in terms of traits that most *differentiate* the sexes, rather than in terms of the traits that most *characterize* each sex, whether sex-differentiating or not. First, Spence et al. (1974) make the obvious but easy-to-overlook observation that for all but a tiny minority of sex-differentiating traits, mean ratings for males and females are on the same side of the midpoint for that trait. For example, men are rated as stronger than women, but women are still rated on the strong side of the strong-weak dimension. Thus, Spence et al. emphasize, the stereotype for women includes masculine as well as feminine traits, in the sense that the mean rating for females is clearly on the masculine side of the midpoint for many traits (though the male rating is higher, of course). The male stereotype is likewise androgynous, including many feminine traits.

Second, Jenkin and Vroegh (1969) also found that male and female ideal stereotypes include many common traits. Their interpretation was that male and female roles were equally socially desirable, and share many traits by virtue of both being considered evaluatively "good." One might reverse the direction of relationship to say that because male and female roles share many common traits, they share equal social desirability.

Sherriffs and McKee (1957, p. 455), in one of the earliest stereotype studies, suggested a third related point. They observed that describing sex stereotypes in terms of traits that discriminate between the sexes can be misleading in that many items seen as highly characteristic of both sexes will be omitted from the stereotype for each because they do not discriminate, whereas other traits will be included if they are of low salience for both sexes, but do discriminate. An example from their study was that a majority of respondents described both men and women as "clever" (using an adjective checklist format), but not in significantly different proportions. On the other hand, though only a tiny fraction described men as "witty," no respondents checked this adjective for women, and the difference was statistically significant. As a result, applying the usual definition of stereotyping, the male stereotype in this study included being witty even though few thought wit was characteristic of men—but not being clever. Further, since wit is a desirable trait, the male stereotype was described as being more favorable than the female stereotype, even though the majorities rated men equally on the desirable trait cleverness.

These points can be applied to some recent stereotype data. Table 10.2 presents a section from the Roper Organization's (1974) Virginia Slims poll on women, concerning traits admired in men and women. Part of these data was used earlier in Table 10.1, comparing women's and men's attitudes toward women. Since these data concern traits *admired* in women and men, they concern prescriptive stereotypes. It would be desirable to have such data on descriptive stereotypes as well, but of the two, prescriptive stereotypes are probably more important.

For samples of the size used here (3,000 women and 1,000 men), most of the traits in Table 10.2 are sex-stereotyped according to the usual criterion of discrimination between ratings made of men and of women. Thus, these data are consistent with other stereotype studies. Some other characteristics of these data are important to note, however. First, for all 13 traits, and for both male and female respondents, the proportions of respondents indicating admiration for each was on the same side of 50% for both sexes. That is, there were no traits admired by a majority for one sex and *not* admired by a majority for the other. Next, the rank orders of the traits admired in each sex are quite similar.

Table 10.2

Qualities admired by men and women

	Qualities most admired in a man		Qualities most admired in a woman	
	Women's Opinions, %	Men's Opinions, %	Women's Opinions, %	Men's Opinions, %
Intelligence	66	66	57	55
Being sensitive to the feelings of others	51	36	52	38
A sense of humor	46	38	42	38
Gentleness	44	16	37	43
Self-control	37	47	41	37
Being able to express feelings and emotions	22	16	25	24
Leadership ability	21	36	11	10
Willingness to compromise	21	18	21	25
Independence	19	20	24	17
Frankness—speaking out on opinions	18	36	21	20
Competence	11	17	12	14
Sex appeal	6	2	5	26
Being competitive	3	7	4	4

Source: Roper Organization, Virginia Slims poll, (1974).

Women's lists of the five most admired traits for men and women include the same items, and the same lists for men include four traits in common (with gentleness being the important exception). It is perhaps important that men's rank-orders of admired traits show less similarity than women's, and that the internal ordering of the five most admired traits vary somewhat. Nonetheless, the traits in the upper part of the distribution of traits admired in one sex are in the upper part of the distribution for the other.

Further, the most admired traits for both sexes include both masculine and feminine elements. The most admired trait for both is intelligence, presumably masculine. "Feminine" sensitivity to the feelings of others, and gentleness (in women's ratings) are also highly valued. Two highly admired traits, self-control and sense of humor, are difficult to classify conceptually. The lowest ranked traits for both sexes include the masculine cluster of competitiveness, competence, frankness, and independence, and the presumably feminine trait of willingness to compromise. While the Roper Organization's selection of these 13 traits is certainly not comprehensive, within this range the most and least admired clusters of traits for both sexes include both masculine and feminine ones, and overall, the feminine traits appear to be slightly preferred for both sexes. Thus, while the traditional analysis of sex stereotyping (comparing ratings *between* the sexes) gives one impression, the alternate analysis presented here (examining trait ratings made *within* each sex) gives a rather different impression. This alternate analysis suggests that male and female stereotypes in content as well as social desirability are not so different as usually thought.

This alternate analysis of sex-role stereotyping is, clearly, a revisionist one. I believe that the revisionism emerging in other areas of sex-role research logically requires a reconsideration of the traditional understanding of sex-role stereotyping. Specifically, I refer to the new analysis of masculinity-femininity, which argues that psychological masculinity and femininity are independent dimensions, not bipolar ends of the same trait (Bem, 1974), and the new perspective that the traditional focus on sex *differences* obscures the fact that women and men are likely similar on most, and the more important, traits. If re-analysis of traditional data and measures shows that women and men have both masculine and feminine traits, and are more similar than different, it should not be a surprise that re-analysis of sex-stereotype data suggests precisely the same points about how the sexes are perceived.

The second part of the comparison of attitudes about men and women to be examined here concerns responses to behavior in each sex which deviates from sex-role norms. Data from several different sources are relevant. First, it has long been speculated that male socialization is more severe than female socialization, in the sense that sex-role deviance is more strongly punished in boys than in girls (Hartley, 1959). Maccoby and Jacklin's (1975, p. 328) review found only two studies directly comparing parental responses to sex-typed behavior in their children (Lansky, 1967; Fling & Manosevitz, 1972), but both supported this conclusion. Feinman's (1974) finding that college students disapproved more of deviant sex-role behavior in boys than in girls provides further support. It is also known that boys show consistent and progressive strengthening of sex-appropriate interests throughout development, while girls go through a developmental phase of exploring masculine interests during latency, departing from the pattern of earlier and later development. Presumably, the different pattern of boys' and girls' development indicates that there is more tolerance for deviant sex-role interests in girls than in boys during this period.

Another source of data is literature on the relationship between masculinity-femininity and adjustment. It is a surprising fact that the classic early studies of this relationship (Gray, 1957; Webb, 1963) predicted (and found) that positive adjustment in females is associated with *low* sex-appropriate interests. This prediction for females was based on still earlier studies going back to the 1940s, which indicated, for example, that popular and well-adjusted girls were rated by their peers as having a variety of "masculine" traits. By contrast, these studies continued to make the traditional prediction that adjustment in boys is associated with *high* sex-appropriate interests (i.e., masculinity). When this prediction for boys was not clearly supported by the data, the lack of confirmation was rationalized away in various ways without calling into question the basic assumption that psychological masculinity leads to good adjustment in males. Now, current reviews such as Bem's (1972) indicate that positive adjustment in both sexes is associated with low sex-typed interests. What is interesting from a sociology-of-knowledge perspective is that it was so relatively easy for academic psychology to discard the assumption that culturally defined sex-appropriate interests lead to good adjustment for females, but so hard to discard the same assumption for males. (It should be noted that in spite of these data, clinicians continued to interpret nontraditional interests in their women patients as signs of maladjustment, however.)

Unfortunately, there is little comparative data in the published literature about reactions to sex-role deviance in adult men and women. There have been a variety of demonstrations of negative attitudes and evaluations of women who deviated from their sex role, but there appears to be some reconsideration under way in this literature. For example, Goldberg (1965) demonstrated an evaluative bias against professional academic writing attributed to females (presumably, such work is deviant for women). Later, however, Deaux and Taynor (1973) found that while there was evaluative bias against women of high competence, there was a corresponding evaluative bias against men of low attributed competence as compared to women. Other studies of evaluative bias and other negative responses to women find difficult-to-interpret complex interactions between sex of stimulus and other variables. Also relevant here is Spence and Helmreich's (1972b) study indicating that men liked competent women with masculine interests, assessing "liking" in terms of potential social and dating relationships as well as work relationships. In general, such data do not support a simple generalization that instrumental behavior in women, or instrumental women themselves, are negatively evaluated by males.

What is lacking are comparable data on responses to sex-inappropriate behavior in males. A few survey items indicate negative attitudes to deviant behavior. For example, Harris (1971, p. 441) found that 58% of men and 69% of women would respect a man less "if he decided to stay home and take care of the children while his wife worked." While attitudes toward married women's working have become more favorable over the past several decades (Erskine, 1971), attitudes toward men who do *not* work are likely to be as negative as ever. Generally, though, it is probable that evaluative ,bias against nontraditional, sex-role-deviant behavior operates against males in as complex a fashion as it does for females. That is, such bias doubltless occurs in some contexts, but there may be other contexts in which deviant behavior in males is highly regarded, just as it is for females. The simple generalization that deviant sex-role behavior is negatively regarded probably applies with equal truth and equal qualification for both sexes.

One important point should be made about this analysis. Negative responses to deviant sex-role behavior in men and women should be differentiated from the social consequences of those negative responses on men and women. Even if there are equally negative attitudes toward deviant behavior in both sexes, the social effects of this common bias are quite different. Since it is "masculine" traits and behaviors that generally lead to social power, ostracizing deviant behavior in females serves to restrict women's power, while ostracizing deviant behaviors in men serves to maintain their power. Thus, looking only at negative attitudes toward deviant sex-role behavior, and the extent to which such attitudes limit the freedom of women and men to express the full range of human potentialities, one would conclude that men's and women's roles are equally limiting (and that men's role may be somewhat more limiting in childhood). However, looking at differences in social power, which derive in part from prejudice against sex-role deviance in females (as well as from other factors), then it is clear that women's role is more limiting. That is, these two ways of defining sex-role oppression are analytically distinct from each other. There is no contradiction in saying that, in one sense, men's and women's roles are equally limiting while, in another sense, women's role is more oppressive.

The general interpretation proposed here is that in some important respects which have been overlooked, attitudes toward women and men are quite similar. The alternate way of looking at sex-role stereotype data suggested by Spence et al. (1974), Jenkin and Vroegh (1969), and McKee and Sherriffs (1957) indicates that male and female stereotypes overlap considerably in content, and that both stereotypes include both masculine and feminine elements. Limited data on responses to deviant sex-role behavior in each sex suggests that sex-role norms are probably applied somewhat more rigidly to boys than to girls in childhood socialization, and that responses to sex-role deviant behavior in adults are complex—negative in some cases, but neutral or positive in others. Thus, considering both stereotypes and responses to deviant behavior, it does not appear that attitudes toward women are uniquely negative or rigid compared to attitudes toward men.

This revisionist interpretation of attitudes toward women needs to be put in the context of other trends in recent research on sex roles. Over the past several years, as feminism re-emerged in our society and sex inequality became re-acknowledged, social scientists generated a number of striking findings that became quickly integrated into the developing feminist analysis. Horner's formulation of "fear of success" in women was perhaps the most notable example, but the stereotype research of Broverman et al. and Goldberg's finding of evaluative bias against females, both cited in this chapter, were also quite significant. What began to happen, however, was that the processes investigated in these studies were interpreted as demonstrating—indeed, as identical with—the unique oppression of women. As in any area of social science research, later studies attempting to replicate and expand these findings suggested the need for clarification and sometimes rejection of the original interpretations of the first studies. It is now much less clear that any of these bodies of research demonstrate the unique oppression of women. This does not mean that women do not have inferior status and power relative to men, or that the processes tapped in these studies are not important enough to study and clarify. It simply means that, contrary to the common interpretation, these particular processes do not constitute the unique oppression of women.

In like fashion, the interpretation offered here of the similarity of stereotypes and responses to deviance in women and men is not incompatible with a feminist analysis. Rather, this interpretation only means that negative or restrictive attitudes in and of themselves are not uniquely applied to women, and that the sources of the special restrictions in women's life-chances in our society must be sought elsewhere. My own intuition is that, in general, the special limits faced by women in our society will be best formulated not in the psychological terms of attitudes, stereotypes, and motivations in or about women, but in terms of the more sociological concepts of social power and access to resources. This interpretation also means that traditional sex-role attitudes are still important phenomena to study, but if we study them as if they were held only by men, and only toward women, we will greatly limit our ability to understand them.

This chapter has reviewed available theories about the etiology of traditional male attitudes toward women, compared men's and women's attitudes toward women, and made a more general comparison of attitudes toward women and attitudes toward men. The overall point of the paper is to suggest a rather different perspective on male's traditional attitudes toward women than is usually taken. There are a variety of theoretical perspectives on the unique dynamic sources of male attitudes, but none are well supported in research. Men's and women's attitudes toward women show a complex pattern of similarities and differences, and data do not support a simple generalization that men have more traditional attitudes toward women than women do. A revisionist analysis of sex-role stereotyping data, and limited data on responses to sex-role deviance in men and women, suggests that attitudes toward women are not necessarily more negative or restricting than attitudes toward men. Each of these points suggests that males' traditional attitudes toward women are not a special, unique phenomenon, requiring special theories and assumptions to account for them. Rather, male attitudes toward women are better viewed as an aspect of a more general sex-role attitudinal process encompassing women's and men's attitudes, and attitudes to both women and men. There is much to learn about the etiology, dynamics, and consequences of this more general sex-role attitudinal process, and about the processes of changing it in men and women for the greater benefit of both.

REFERENCES

Adorno, T.W., Frenkel-Brunswick, E., Levinson, D.J., & Sanford, R.N. *The authoritarian personality* (Part 1). New York: Wiley, 1964.

Allport, G.W. *The nature of prejudice.* New York: Anchor, 1954.

Bass, B.M., Krusell, J., & Alexander, R. Male managers' attitudes toward working women. *American Behavioral Scientist,* 1971, *15,* 221-236.

Bem, S. Psychology looks at sex roles: Where have all the androgynous people gone? Presented at UCLA Symposium on Sex Differences, May, 1972.

Bem, S. The measurement of psychological androgyny. *Journal of Clinical and Consulting Psychology,* 1974, *42,* 155-162.

Bowman, G.W., Worthy, N.B., & Greyser, S.A. Are women executives people? *Harvard Business Review,* 1965, *43,* 4, 14 ff.

Brannon, R., & Dull, C. Racism, sexism, and fascism of white males: Empirical interrelationships. Paper presented at the meeting of the American Psychological Association, Washington, D.C., August, 1971.

Broverman, I.K., Vogel, S.R., Broverman, D.M., Clarkson, F.E., & Rosenkrantz, P.S. Sex-role stereotypes: A current appraisal. *Journal of Social Issues,* 1972, *28,* 2, 59-78.

Centers, R. Authoritarianism and misogyny. *Journal of Social Psychology,* 1963, *61,* 81-85.

Chodorow, N. Being and doing: A cross-cultural examination of the socialization of males and females. In V. Gornick and B.K. Moran(Eds.), *Woman in sexist society.* New York: Basic Books, 1971.

Chodorow, N. Family structure and feminine personality. In M.Z. Rosaldo and L. Lamphere (Eds.), *Woman, culture, and society.* Stanford: Stanford University Press, 1974.

Deaux, K., & Taynor, J. Evaluation of male and female ability: Bias works both ways. *Psychological Reports,* 1973, *32,* 261-262.

Dempewolff, J.A. Development and validation of a feminism scale. *Psychological Reports,* 1974, *34,* 651-657.

Ellis, L.J., & Bentler, P.M. Traditional sex-determined role standards and sex stereotypes. *Journal of Personality and Social Psychology,* 1973, *25,* 28-3?

Erskine, H. The polls: women's roles. *Public Opinion Quarterly,* 1971, *35,* 275-298.

Feinman, S. Approval of cross-sex-role behavior. *Psychological Reports,* 1974, *35,* 643-648.

Fling, S., & Manosevitz, M. Sex typing in nursery school children's play interests. *Developmental Psychology,* 1972, *7,* 146-152.

Goldberg, P. Are women prejudiced against women? *Transaction,* 1965, 5, *5,* 28-30.

Goldberg, P. Prejudice toward women: Some personality correlates. In F. Denmark (Ed.). *Who discriminates against women?* Beverly Hills, Calif.: Sage Publications, 1974.

Gray, S. Masculinity-femininity in relation to anxiety and social acceptance. *Child Development,* 1957, *28,* 203-214.

Gump, J.P. Sex-role attitudes and psychological well-being. *Journal of Social Issues,* 1972, *28,* 2, 79-92.

Harris, L., & Associates. *The Harris survey yearbook of public opinion, 1970.* New York: Louis Harris, 1971.

Hartley, R.L. Sex-role pressures in the socialization of the male child. *Psychological Reports,* 1959, *5, 459-468.*

Hoffman, L.W. Parental power relations and the division of household tasks. *Marriage and Family Living,* 1962, *22,* 27-35.

Horney, K. The dread of women. *International Journal of Psychoanalysis,* 1932, *13,* 348-360.

Jenkin, N., & Vroegh, K. Contemporary concepts of masculinity and femininity. *Psychological Reports,* 1969, *25,* 679-697.

Kando, T.M. Role strain: A comparison of males, females, and transsexuals. *Journal of Marriage and the Family,* 1972, *34,* 459-464.

Kenkel, W.F. Traditional family ideology and spousal role in decision-making. *Marriage and Family Living,* 1959, *21,* 334-339.

Lansky, L.M. The family structure also affects the model: Sex-role attitudes in parents of preschool children. *Merrill-Palmer Quarterly,* 1967, *13,* 139-150.

Maccoby, E.E., & Jacklin, C.N. *The psychology of sex differences.* Stanford: Stanford University Press, 1974.

Mason, K.O., Czajka, J., & Arber, S. Recent change in women's sex-role attitudes. Unpublished paper, Department of Sociology, University of Michigan, 1974.

Mason, K.O., & Bumpass, L.L. U.S. women's sex-role ideology, 1970. *American Journal of Sociology,* 1975, *80,* 1212-1219.

McKee, J.P., & Sherriffs, A.C. The differential evaluation of males and females. *Journal of Personality,* 1957, *25,* 356-371.

Meier, H.C. Mother-centeredness and college youths' attitudes toward social equality for women: Some empirical findings. *Journal of Marriage and the Family,* 1972, *34,* 115-121.

Miller, T.W. Male attitudes toward women's rights as a function of their self-esteem. In F. Denmark (Ed.). *Who discriminates against women?* Beverly Hills, Calif.: Sage Publications, 1974.

Nadler, E.B., & Morrow, W.R. Authoritarian attitudes toward women and their correlates. *Journal of Social Psychology*, 1959, *40*, 112-123.

Pleck, J.H. *Male threat from female competence: An experimental study in college dating couples*. Ann Arbor, Mich.: University Microfilms, 1973, No. 74-11, 721.

Pleck, J.H., & Sawyer, J. *Men and masculinity*. Englewood Cliffs, N.J.: Prentice-Hall, 1974.

Pleck, J.H. Males' traditional attitudes toward women: Correlates of adjustment or maladjustment? Unpublished paper, Institute for Social Research, University of Michigan, 1975.

Pincus, F.L. Relationships between racism, sexism, powerlessness, and antihomosexuality. Paper presented at the meeting of the American Psychological Association, Washington, D.C., August, 1971.

Rapoport, R., & Rapoport, R.N. *Dual-career families*. London: Penguin, 1971.

Roper Organization. *The Virginia Slims American women's opinion poll*, Vol. III. New York: Roper Organization, 1974.

Rubin, Z., Peplau, L.A., & Hill, C.T. Unpublished data, Dating Couples Project, Department of Social Relations, Harvard University, 1973.

Sherriffs, A.C., & McKee, J.P. Qualitative aspects of belief about men and women. *Journal of Personality*, 1957, *25*, 451-464.

Spence, J.T., & Helmreich, R. The Attitudes toward Women Scale: An objective instrument to measure attitudes toward the rights and roles of women in contemporary society. *JSAS Catalog of Selected Documents in Psychology*, 1972, *2*, 66. (a)

Spence, J.T., & Helmreich, R. Who likes competent women? Competence, sex-role congruence of interests, and subjects' attitudes toward women as determinants of interpersonal attraction. *Journal of Applied Social Psychology*, 1972, *2*, 197-213. (b)

Spence, J.T., Helmreich, R., & Stapp, J. A short version of the Attitudes toward Women Scale (AWS). *Bulletin of the Psychonomic Society*, 1973, *2*, 219-220.

Spence, J.T., Helmreich, R., & Stapp, J. The personal attributes questionnaire: A measure of sex-role stereotypes and masculinity-femininity. *JSAS Catalog of Selected Documents in Psychology*, 1974, *4*, 43.

Steinmann, A., & Fox, D.J. *The male dilemma*. New York: Jason Aronson, 1974.

Vavrik, J., & Jurich, A.P. Self-concept and attitude toward females: A note. *Family Coordinator*, 1971, *20*, 151-152.

Webb, A.P. Sex-role preferences and adjustment in early adolescents. *Child Development*, 1963, *34*, 609-618.

Wolman, B. On men who discriminate against women. In F. Denmark (Ed.), *Who discriminates against women?* Beverly Hills, Calif.: Sage Publications, 1974.

Worell, J., & Worell, L. Supporters and opponents of women's liberation: Some personality characteristics. Paper presented at the meeting of the American Psychological Association, Washington, D.C., August 1971.

CHAPTER *18*

MEASURING ATTITUDES TOWARD WOMEN (AND OTHERWISE): A Methodological Critique

ROBERT BRANNON

Robert Brannon attended Harvard University and The University of Michigan. He is currently Assistant Professor of Social Psychology at Brooklyn College of the City University of New York, and is active in The Association for Women in Psychology and The Society for the Psychological Study of Social Issues. His professional interests are in attitude measurement and behavioral prediction, sex-role dynamics, racism, alternate life-syles, and social change. He is co-editor of The Forty-Nine Percent Majority *(Addison-Wesley, 1976), an analysis of the male sex role, with selected readings.*

The concept and techniques of attitude measurement are reviewed, focusing on the evidence of 132 empirical studies of gender-related dispositions, and drawing parallels with the literature of racial prejudice. Attitude is conceived as a generic term, not sharply separable at present from other terms denoting mental constructs associated with response consistencies: thus, the review is concerned with "traits," "beliefs," and other dispositions, as well as those described as "attitudes." Question formats are found to vary widely and with little correspondence to construct labels or content, generating apparent inconsistencies in the literature. The semantic differential seems especially inappropriate for gender-related constructs. Multi-point, one-dimensional rating scales are recommended. "Stereotypes" are viewed as probabalistic generalizations about a social group which are widely held within a given culture, without reference to falsity or psychological process. It remains to be shown that stereotypes are functionally distinguishable from other generalizations. The prevalence of mixed-content scales is reviewed, and an argument is made for structured, multidimensional inventories with homogeneous subscales, developed by a combination of theoretical and empirical procedures. Major emphasis is placed on the lack of concern for behavioral validity, which so plagued the study of prejudice that by the early 1970s many writers were questioning the existence of attitudes. Suggestions are given for devising and scaling indices of behavior toward women.

As a graduate student during the mid-1960s I was a systematic reader of research on racial prejudice, or as we often preferred to call it, "Intergroup relations." It was not an easy task to stay abreast of this huge and constantly growing literature. Full-scale review articles sometimes cited over a thousand articles, studies, and books, while apologizing for their selectivity (Blumer, 1958). The fact is that long before the explosive racial events of the 1960s, social science had effectively adopted racial prejudice as the social problem par excellence; to a rather surprising degree, the history of attitude measurement is coincident with the study and measurement of racial prejudice, with landmarks such as the Likert (1932) item format and the multi-item attitude "scale" (Bogardus, 1925) appearing first as efforts to measure prejudice. Quite literally, mountains of data about prejudice have been collected.

It has never been widely or publicly acknowledged by social scientists, but the net result of all this time and effort seems, to me at least, extremely meager. To demonstrate quite simply what I am referring to, let me suggest a simple exercise. Answer the following questions, either from memory, *or* with the aid of any set of books or articles that you wish!

1. Are males or females more prejudiced, or is there no difference?

2. What is the relationship of prejudice to upward social mobility?

3. What is the relationship of prejudice to age?

4. What is the correlation, *within 30 points,* of prejudice to the California F-scale?[1]

Admittedly these points are not especially important in themselves, but they illustrate precisely the uncertainty, variability, and outright contradictions that the prejudice literature still reveals today, after 50 years of intensive effort and literally thousands of publications. This may seem a harsh or idiosyncratic judgment, but I'm not the only one who thinks so. Blumer (1958), after reviewing hundreds of such studies, concluded that they added up to neither "a body of theoretical knowledge nor, on the practical side, to working procedures needed to change race relations" (p. 40). Clark (1965) was even more caustic about the whole enterprise. The great volume of research on racial prejudice, he noted, "dabbles in reality, but avoids the real arena of action, and reflects among other things both a methodological sterility and theoretical stagnation" (p. 5).

What went wrong? At least one part of the problem I believe was that we were too simple-minded. That vague, all-purpose term "racial prejudice" wasn't just a convenient label to identify the general area of our interest; it was frequently how we actually thought about the complex issues of race relations. Instead of forming questions such as "What levels of expectations are engaged, and by what sets of cues in this instance, to alter perceptions of another person's behavior?", we were asking: *"Where does prejudice come from? How can people be so irrational? How can we eliminate stereotyped thinking?"* If the subtleties and complexities of American racial customs and feelings—so powerfully explored by writers from William Faulkner and Lillian Smith to James Baldwin and Richard Wright—were apparent to social scientists, they certainly weren't reflected in our measurement techniques.

There were other problems as well, for even if our constructs were simplistic, we should have more to show for all that data than we apparently do. Why are there *still* no clear relationships with demographic variables, or even, God help us, with other paper-and-pencil attitude measures? One remarkable fact one notices, when reading through a number of studies of racial prejudice, is that no two studies ever seem to measure prejudice in the same way. There is no standard, accepted scale of racial prejudice, and a surprising number of recent articles use totally new, ad hoc measures. A comparison of various scales that have been used will show striking inconsistencies in both format and content; quite often the items aren't reported at all (De Freize & Ford, 1969; McGrew, 1967; Himmelstein & Moore, 1963; Saenger & Gilbert, 1950). I am not arguing that there should be some single standardized instrument, comparable to the physicists' platinum bar in cold storage; it does seem likely to me, however, that the failure to ever decide on a reasonably consistent approach to measurement has something to do with the chronic record of inconsistent findings. This is especially true of those kinds of measures which psychologists usually consider best: multi-item summative scales. Survey researchers employing carefully worded single questions in probability sample interviews have provided far more durable findings. For a review of data from these sources, see Campbell (1971) and Schuman and Hatchett (1974).

And here we go again!   My reason for beginning with this rather glum assessment of the fruits of five decades of intensive research on race prejudice is that I see strong indications that the same mistakes—both conceptual and methodological—are being made in the rapidly developing area of measuring attitudes and other dispositions toward and about women. As I write these words, I am staring at a stack of xeroxed articles and reprints approximately a foot high, each purportedly dealing with "sex-role stereotyping," "attitudes toward women,"

Table 11.1

Sources reporting paper-and-pencil individual difference measures
of psychological dispositions toward women

1. Arnott (1972)
2. Auerbach & Gackenbach (Note 1)
3. Axelson (1963)
4. Axelson (1970)
5. Baruch (1972)
6. Bass, Krusell, & Alexander (1971)
7. Bayer (1975)
8. Basow & Howe (Note 2)
9. Beckman & Houser (Note 3)
10. Bem (Note 4)
11. Bem (1974)
12. Bem (1975)
13. Bennett & Cohen (1959)
14. Berzins (Note 5)
15. Bledsoe (1973)
16. Bowman, Worthy, & Greyser (1965)
17. Brannon & Dull (Note 6)
18. Brannon (Note 7)
19. Broverman, Broverman, Clarkson, Rosenkrantz, & Vogel (1970)
20. Broverman, Vogel, Broverman, Clarkson, & Rosenkrantz (1972)
21. Centers (1963)
22. Cherulnik & McAndrew (Note 8)
23. Clarkson, Vogel, Broverman, Broverman, & Rosenkrantz (1970)
24. Coffman & Levy (1972)
25. Conyers (1961)
26. Chafetz (1974, pp. 35-39)
27. Dempewolfe (1974a)
28. Dempewolfe (1974b)
29. Ditmar, Mueller & Mitchell (Note 9)
30. Ellis & Bentler (1973)
31. Elman, Press, & Rosenkrantz (1970)
32. Entwistle & Greenberger (1972)
33. Erskine (1970)
34. Etaugh & Gerson (1974)

35. Falbo (1975)
36. Fay (Note 10)
37. Farrell (Note 11)
38. Fernberger (1948)
39. *Fortune* (1946)
40. Frieze (Note 12)
41. Gaudreau (Note 13)
42. Goldberg (1974)
43. Goldberg, Gottesdiener, & Abramson (1975)
44. Gordon & Hall (1974)
44. Greenberg (1973)
45. Gruzen (Note 14)
46. Gump (1972)
47. Gump (Note 15)
48. Haavio-Mannila (1967)
49. Haavio-Mannila (1972)
50. Hawley (1971)
51. Hawley (1972)
52. Herman & Sedlacek (1973)
53. Hill, Adelstein, & Carter (Note 16)
54. Hymer & Atkins (1973)
55. Jacobson (1952)
56. Jenkins & Vroegh (1969)
57. Joesting & Joesting (1974)
58. Kammeyer (1966)
59. Kando (1972)
60. Kaplan & Goldman (1973)
61. Keiffer & Cullen (1974)
62. Kelly & Worell (Note 17)
63. Kenkel (1959)
64. Kitay (1940)
65. Kirkpatrick (1936a)
66. Kirkpatrick (1936b)
67. Kirkpatrick (1936c)

68. Kristal, Sanders, Spence, & Helmreich (1975)
69. Lipman-Blumen (1972)
70. Levinson & Huffman (1955)
71. Lunneborg (Note 18)
72. Mason (1975)
73. Mason, Czajka, & Arber (Note 19)
74. Mason & Bumpass (Note 20)
75. McClelland (1967)
76. McCune (1970)
77. McKee & Sherriffs (1957)
78. McKee & Sherriffs (1959)
79. McMillin (1972)
80. Meier (1972)
81. Miller (1974)
82. Nadler & Morrow (1959)
83. Nash (1975)
84. Neufeld, Langmeyer, & Seeman (1975)
85. Nevill (Note 21)
86. Nielsen & Doyle (1975)
87. Nichols (1962)
88. O'Leary & Harrison (Note 22)
89. Parker (1969)
90. Patrick (1944)
91. Peterson (1975)
92. Pincus (Note 23)
93. Pleck (Note 24)
94. Pleck (Note 25)
95. Reany & Ferguson (1974)
96. Reece (1964)
97. Ricks & Pyke (1973)
98. Ronco (Note 26)
99. Roper (1974)
100. Rosen (1974)
101. Rosenkrantz, Vogel, Bee, Broverman, & Broverman (1968)
102. Ross & Walters (1973)
103. Sanger & Alker (1972)
104. Seward & Larson (1968)
105. Siiter & Unger (Note 27)
106. Shomer & Centers (1970)
107. Sherriffs & Jarrett (1953)
108. Sherriffs & McKee (1957)
109. Spence & Helmreich (1972a)
110. Spence & Helmreich (1972b)
111. Spence, Helmreich, & Stapp (1973)
112. Spence, Helmreich, & Stapp (1974)
113. Spence, Helmreich, & Stapp (1975)
114. Spence, Helmreich, & Stapp (in press)
115. Steinmann & Fox (1966)
116. Steinmann, Levi, & Fox (1964)
117. Stewart & Winter (1974)
118. Turner & Turner (Note 28)
119. Unger & Siiter (Note 29)
120. Vroegh (Note 30)
121. Vavrik & Jurich (1971)
122. Walters & Ojemann (1952)
123. Welling (Note 31)
124. Wetter (Note 32)
125. Woods (Note 33)
126. Worell (Note 34)
127. Worell & Worell (Note 35)
128. Wright & Tuska (1966)
129. Yankelovich (1974)
130. Yorburg & Arafat (1975)
131. Zeldon & Greenberg (1975)
132. Zimmer & Krupat (Note 36)

"sexism," "sex prejudice," "sex-role traditionalism," etc., etc., etc. (A full listing of this collection appears in Table 11.1.) Virtually every conceivable paper-and-pencil method is represented, but what's measured, according to the title of the article, bears no discernible relation to the method used, or even to the exact content of the items. This area of sex and gender roles, attitudes, and beliefs seems to me as complex as that of racial interrelationships, if not more so, and our measurement instruments haven't told us as much as we have deduced through common sense. In fact, the area is already a mess.

In a recent and thoughtful effort to review the substance of this developing literature, Pleck (Chapter 10 in this volume) discussed five theoretical approaches to traditional attitudes toward women: authoritarianism, low self-esteem, masculinity-femininity, early mother-child relationships, and intergroup relations. The reviewer is forced to regard all five approaches as somewhat inconclusive at present, because of the conflicting evidence of the 18 available empirical studies. It seems both relevant—and ominous—that all 18 cited studies used different measures of attitudes toward women.

The purpose of this chapter is to consider the theory and technique of attitude measurement in light of what we presently know, to note briefly where I think the measurement of attitudes toward blacks went wrong, and to show how the measurement of attitudes toward women may avoid these mistakes.

"ATTITUDE": A GENERIC TERM

The term *attitude* appears more often than any other single term in the literature of social science (Berkowitz, 1972). It was once called "the most distinctive and indispensable concept in American social psychology" (Allport, 1935), and today it is still the most popular single category of research and theory (McGuire, 1969). Attitude measurement itself is probably the most extensively studied single research method in social science. One recent review of attitude measurement cites over 1,400 references (Summers, 1970), and the total number of entries cited in this reference literature is clearly beyond counting.

Rather astonishingly, there is no widely accepted definition of what is meant by "attitudes," and there never has been. Nelson (1939) listed 30 separate definitions in use in the literature three decades ago; Allport (1935) spoke of 17 "representative definitions"; Calder and Ross (1973) refer to ten "influential" definitions, and so on. The term's popularity is probably due in part to exactly this ambiguity. Like most useful terms that evolved over many years, the attitude concept has never been the property of any one individual or school of thought. It is happily used by psychologists, sociologists, anthropologists, historians, and economists; it is applied to individuals, groups, and whole cultures, and has often served as the common denominator of interdisciplinary research programs.

Despite its apparent adaptability, the attitude concept does seem to have a core of consistent meaning. Among humans, as with all other organisms, we observe that experience modifies behavior. Some residue of experience is clearly retained and is capable of directing or at least influencing subsequent actions. This universal fact is implicitly accepted by all scientists; it is referred to in many ways and identified by many terms, of which attitude" is but one.

Most theorists agree, furthermore, that the best and most fundamental evidence for these residues of experience is *a pattern of consistency in response to some social object* (Campbell, 1963). Although certain other aspects of responses (e.g., intensity) are tapped by some measurement techniques, consistency is the ultimate evidence for their existence.

The reason that attitude definitions are so abundant, then, is that theorists have almost always sought to *account* for this phenomenon, rather than merely describe it. The reasons for consistency are variously explained in terms of "perceptual equivalence," "action tendencies," "sets," "central nervous-system traces," "symbolic structures," and so forth. Since agreement on these mechanisms has not occurred (and is probably not possible), the definitions have continued to multiply, taking on whatever unique shapes and forms suit the theoretical tastes of their authors.

Distinctions between attitudes and other mental constructs are a matter of controversy. Certain writers use such terms as *attitude, belief, opinion, interest, trait,* and *value* more or less synonymously, while others carefully distinguish them. Unfortunately, these distinctions are almost totally dependent on which theorist one is reading. (Compare, for example, the definitions proposed by Bem, 1970; Berkowitz, 1972; Fishbein & Ajzen, 1972; Harvey, Hunt, & Schroeder, 1961; Osgood, Suci & Tannenbaum, 1957; Scott, 1969; Allport, 1937.) Furthermore, in addition to words borrowed from the natural language, psychologists have added such terms as *tinsits, engrams, neurobiotaxis, canalizations, habs, percepts, schemas, life spaces, valences, apperceptive masses, fixations,* and a host of others.

Dispositions

In an effort to thin out this nomenclature jungle, which often seems to have more to do with pride of authorship than with tangible distinctions, Campbell (1963) proposed that *all* such unobservable mental constructs should be tentatively regarded as equivalent. A general umbrella term (he proposed "acquired behavioral dispositions") could be used to refer to all such mental constructs; more specific terms would then be reintroduced only when empirical evidence had been gathered which showed a distinction to be necessary. The reaction to Campbell's useful suggestion has never been enthusiastic, for most writers simply "know" that an "attitude" is different from a "belief," is different from a "value," is different from an opinion.

The truth is that apart from the variance due to different methods (to be discussed shortly), there is as yet no sizable body of evidence to support the need for separate terms to distinguish different kinds of mental constructs. This is not to say that all such constructs *are* equivalent, only that the most useful distinctions have not yet been empirically established. In the remainder of this chapter, then, Campbell's term "dispositions" will be used in many cases, and where "attitude," "belief," or others are used, no unique properties are implied.

DISPOSITIONS TOWARD WOMEN:
EXPERIMENTAL AND BEHAVIORAL EVIDENCE

When I read those interminable discussions with Otto Rank, Henry Miller, and Lawrence Durrell that Anais Nin reports in her *Diary,* what struck me again and again was the way in which the men took their view of women and the reality of women to be the same thing, without even a chink of difference between them. (p. 28.)

Evaluation Bias

The most convincing evidence of mental dispositions toward women currently comes not from paper-and-pencil attitude scales, but from experimental studies in which sex is a perceptual variable. In the now-classic paradigm introduced by Goldberg (1968), identical performances were attributed either to male or to female authors. Subjects (college women in the original study) evaluated the same performance more favorably when it had a male name attached than when it had a female name. This effect was soon found among male subjects as well (Bem & Bem, 1970; Deaux & Taynor, 1973; Etaugh & Rose, 1975, in press; Feldman-Summers & Kiesler, 1974; Mischel, 1974). It has now been found in a wide variety of evaluation and rating situations (Deaux & Emswiller, 1974; Emswiller, Deaux, & Willits, 1971; Fidell, 1970; Pheterson, Kiesler, & Goldberg, 1971; Rubin, Provenzano, & Luria, 1974; Seavey, Katz, & Zalk, 1975; Starer & Denmark, 1974; Dorros & Follet, Note 37; Will, Self, & Datan, Note 38). Using a variety of situations and evaluation procedures somewhat different from those discussed above, other investigators have now documented biased or distorted evaluations of women in a wide range of settings (Etaugh & Sanders, 1974; Hymer & Atkins, 1973; Koenig, 1972; Landy & Sigall, 1974; Rosen & Jerdee, 1973; Spence & Helmreich, 1972a; Spence, Helmreich, & Stapp, 1975; Touhey, 1974; Bar-Tal & Saxe, Note 39; Brannon & Dull, Note 7; Caplan, Note 40; Kirchner, Note 41; Whitaker, Note 42). There have also been some failures to obtain the effect (e.g., Baruch, 1972), and it is evidently not so powerful that it can overpower all other stimulus factors. In general, however, there now seems little doubt that the attribution of sex as a cognitive label (cf. Grady, Note 43) can substantially change the evaluation of human performance.

Behavioral Observations

There is also considerable evidence of differences in people's expressive and nonverbal behavior toward women and men respectively. Males initiate touching with females far more than females touch males, a pattern of "nonreciprocal touching" which Henley (1973a, 1973b, 1977) has convincingly argued reflects power and status rather than affection or arousal. Men have been systematically observed to force women to move aside when meeting on sidewalks (Silveira, 1972); interrupt women in conversation (Zimmerman & West, 1975); give women smaller envelopes of "personal space" (Willis, 1966); walk slightly ahead while supposedly strolling together (Grady, Miransky, & Mulvey,1976, Note 44); dominate conversation time (Kester, 1972; Argyle, Lalljee, & Cook, 1968; Strodtbeck, James, & Hawkins, 1957); and smile much less often (Bugenthal, Love, & Gianetto, 1971; Silveira, 1972). (For a full discussion of this literature, see Thorne & Henley, 1975.)

Both lines of evidence, evaluation bias and expressive behavior toward women, have certain definite advantages over more abstract evidence. They obviously reveal latent dispositions toward women, they mostly require no interpretation beyond what is obvious, and in some instances they involve outcomes that are clearly important. Fidell's (1970) dependent variable, for example, was actual responses to letters of application for real professional jobs. When we speak of measuring dispositions toward women, however, we are usually referring to measuring individual differences in the extent of such dispositions. The experimental conditions used in these studies are better suited to demonstrating that dispositions exist in a total sample than they are to quantifying individual differences. Theoretically, of course, they *could* be scored for individual differences, especially if a large set of observations was obtained. To my knowledge, only one study (Baruch, 1972) has attempted this. I'll return to this idea later with a suggestion for using the experimental approach in connection with paper-and-pencil methods to quantify individual differences.

METHODS AND METHOD VARIANCE

Virtually every conceivable paper-and-pencil format and scaling method (see reviews by Scott, 1969; Brannon, 1976a) can be found in the rapidly expanding literature on dispositions toward women. If we ignore scaling procedures and consider only individual question formats, the following variations may be distinguished:

1. Adjective or trait check-lists: e.g., Bennett and Cohen (1959).

2. Phrases or statements followed by dichotomous alternatives: agree/disagree, true/false, male/female, etc., e.g., Coffman and Levy (1972).

3. Semantic differentials: A term or "concept" rated between two polar antonymns separated by five or more rating points; e.g., McClelland (1967).

4. Phrases or statements followed by three or more alternatives on a nominally one-dimensional continuum: Agree ... Disagree; True ... Not true of me; always ... rarely; etc.; e.g., Kirkpatrick (1936).

5. Rank-ordering methods (with or without ties or forced distributions); e.g., Unger and Siiter (Note 29).

6. Forced-choice items, with matched pairs of nonmutually-exclusive statements or adjectives; e.g., Reany and Ferguson (1974).

7. Multiple-choice items of all kinds: alternatives unique to each item, not necessarily on a continuum; e.g., Ricks and Pyke (1973).

8. Open-ended items, subsequently coded to yield describable categories; e.g., Conyers (1961).

9. Projective techniques; e.g., Stewart and Winter (1974).

Psychologists discovered more than 30 years ago, not entirely with jubilation, that the variance obtained by any psychological test or instrument is always and inevitably a composite: obtained scores are partly a function of what is being measured and partly a function of the specific instrument, test, or technique being used (Cronbach, 1946; Campbell & Fisk, 1959; Nunnally, 1967). Such venerable nuisances as "halo effects" (Thorndike, 1920), "apparatus factors" (Tyron, 1942), "test-form factors" (Vernon, 1958), and "response sets" (Cronbach, 1946) are simply different ways of referring to the same essential fact: that data invariably include method variance. One consequence of this fact is that at the modest levels of validity common to paper-and-pencil measures, two substantially unrelated measures may appear to be correlated, for no other reason than sharing the same format and method, while instruments that actually measure the same thing may appear uncorrelated due to method differences (see Campbell & Fiske, 1959, for numerous examples).

When we compare the constructs supposedly measured in the disposition literature (judging by an article's title) with the method used, the correspondence is minimal. Something referred to as "sex-role stereotypes" may have actually been measured with the semantic differential (Gordon & Hall, 1974), dichotomous alternatives (Fernberger, 1948), a rank-ordering technique (Unger & Siiter, Note 29), or open-ended questions (Chafetz, 1974). Something called "attitudes" may have been measured with Likert items (Likert, 1932; Spence & Helmreich, 1972), the semantic differential (Herman & Sedlacek, 1973), dichotomous alternatives (Greenberg, 1973), open-ended questions (Patrick, 1944), or projective techniques (Vavrik & Jurich, 1971).

Conversely, data obtained with the same technique (e.g., example 3 in the preceding list) have been variously reported as: *attitudes* (Gump, 1972), *perceptions* (Ross & Walters, 1973), *beliefs* (Kammeyer, 1966), *ideologies* (Kenkel, 1959), *sexism* (Pincus, Note 23), *feminism* (Dempewolfe, 1974), and *misogyny* (Centers, 1963).

Even if we were to assume that all methods are equally valid and advantageous, the current variability is highly undesirable. While it is theoretically useful to have alternate measures of the same construct in order to demonstrate convergent validity (Campbell & Fisk, 1959), this does not mean that constructs should be routinely measured by any method the researcher may find convenient. At the present state of our science, frequent method variations will virtually insure confusion. Consider: Ellis and Bentler (1973) reported "traditional" attitudes to be positively correlated with "femininity," but Spence and Helmreich (1972b) reported the same two constructs to be unrelated. What does such a discrepancy mean? Since all four measures in this case were different in format and/or content, quite probably *nothing*. Until investigators begin to use comparable methods, it is hard to see how the findings of different studies can readily be compared or synthesized.

Choice of Format

It is not actually the case that all question formats are equally desirable. The forced choice between matched pairs, for example, has been found to be difficult for many respondents, time consuming, and difficult to separate from the problem of social desirability of the alternatives (Nunnally, 1967, p. 485). Open-ended questions are excellent in many ways, but they are also time consuming, expensive to code, and hard to compare with other data. Projective techniques are notoriously unreliable (Nunnally, 1967, p. 497).

The semantic differential introduced by Osgood (1962) has been acclaimed as a method that can measure any attitude (Triandis, 1971), but some veterans would add, "but not very well." Because the standard set of semantic differential antonyms can be used with virtually any stimulus, and because much previous research has used this method, young researchers are tempted to choose it without much hesitation. Bem (1974) and Constantinople (1973) have recently raised an important issue that seems to bear directly on the use of the semantic differential. Psychologists in the past usually conceptualized masculinity and femininity as the opposite ends of a single continuum; more importantly, they frequently constructed instruments based so rigidly on this assumption that the data were virtually forced to assume this configuration. Tests on which a high score meant masculinity and a low score meant femininity are the most obvious example; however, even simple rating scales that place a traditionally masculine descriptor (e.g., assertive) at one end of a line, and a traditionally feminine descriptor (e.g., yielding) at the other (or "dominant" on the left and "submissive" on the right, etc.) clearly enforce a preconceived result. A person who can be assertive *or* yielding, dominant *or* submissive, depending on the situation, is thereby forced to choose between stereotypical masculine and feminine descriptions. Recent data have strongly supported this contention. When Bem (1974) allowed subjects to describe themselves on masculinity and femininity scales independently, the two patterns were found to be virtually orthogonal, rather than the poles of a single dimension. Jenkin & Vroegh (1969) analyzed ratings of masculinity and femininity in others and also found patterns that were different, but not opposite ends of a continuum.

The assumption that people and objects can and should be rated on a single continuum between two verbal antonyms is of course precisely what the semantic differential requires. The method thus seems inherently likely to distort any data on human traits in the direction of polar contrasts.

The popular scale introduced by Rosenkrantz et al. (1968) unfortunately contains many items of this type. While some of their items provide neutral "presence vs. absence" dimensions (e.g., Emotional . . . Not emotional), others inexplicably place "masculine" terms at one end and place different but certainly *not* opposite "feminine" terms at the other: dominant/submissive; worldly/home-oriented; active/passive; gentle/rough; tactful/blunt; and so on. Future researchers who wish to use the Rosenkrantz et al. (1968) item pool should *separate* these polar antonyms and use one (or both) with a frequency scale. Even less well advised are the occasional scales in the literature that place the words "characteristic of males" at one end of a line and "characteristic of females" at the other; such a format both assumes and enforces a polarity now empirically shown to be false.

Having noted some questionable methods, and assuming that one still wishes to choose a closed-end paper-and-pencil procedure, what question format is likely to be best? I believe that the weight of current evidence favors the technique that is in fact most common: a complete statement or phrase, followed by a multipoint one-dimensional closed-end rating scale. The familiar "Likert item" (Likert, 1932) with its intensity scale (Strongly Agree . . . Strongly Disagree) is one example of such a format. Bem's (1974) format based on frequency (Never True . . . Always True) is another example, and other one-dimensional ratings are obviously possible. Choice of the rating dimension is, of course, a substantive issue that the investigator must decide.

There are several bases for the preferability of this format. The statement to which the subject responds may be carefully worded to be mild or extreme, abstract or highly specific, and may be organized precisely to deal with the issue or nuance the tester wishes to study. Multipoint rating scales have been found to be more enjoyable for subjects than dichotomous alternatives, equally quick to complete, and considerably more reliable. A number of studies have empirically compared the Likert format to others (reviewed by Seiler & Hough, 1969) and have generally confirmed its superiority. The panic of a decade ago concerning the problem of acquiescent response bias has now proven to be rather exaggerated, especially in the case of college samples (see Samelson & Yates, 1967; Rorer, 1965). For general adult populations in which acquiescence may be an issue, several preventive techniques are available (e.g., item reversals, forced-choice wordings, and open-ended questions).

While the Likert-scale format has been rather widely used, most researchers do not use enough points on their scales to obtain its maximal advantages. Reliability has been shown to increase rapidly up to about seven scale steps, and to continue increasing up to at least 20 steps (Guilford, 1954). Many researchers still use five-point Likert scales, and some use only three-point scales.

Questions followed by simple dichotomous alternatives (true-false, yes-no, checklists, etc.) are acceptable, but require a higher ratio of reading time to information and must be more lengthy to produce reliable scores. Rank-ordering techniques (Unger & Siiter, Note 29) and other Q-methods have certain philosophical and psychometric advantages (Allport, 1961; Nunnally, 1967), but have not been widely used. (It should be noted that rank-ordering 10 attributes is equivalent to rating them on a 10-point scale with the stipulation that each point be used once; so, the methods share certain basic properties.)

Turning from question formats to procedures for combining questions into full-size instruments, we find that a consensus has gradually emerged among practitioners and theorists alike. The simple summative procedure in which the individual item scores are *added* to produce a total score has proven to be equally reliable and far more flexible than the laborious Thurstone and Guttman procedures (Nunnally, 1967, chap. 27). This is now clearly the procedure of choice.

Research Needed

Such situational factors as question ordering (Brannon, Note 7; Cantril, 1947), sex of interviewer or tester (Shomer & Centers, 1970, and physical setting of the questioning (Branno, Cypers, Hesse, Hesselbart, Keane, Schuman, Vicarro, & Wright, 1973) can have significant effects on responses. More disturbing is the report by Shomer and Centers (1970) that sex composition of the group responding to the scale had a dramatic effect on individual responses by males. Shomer and Centers reported that "male chauvinist" answers were frequent when no females were present in the testing room, moderate when an equal number of women were present, and infrequent when a single woman was present. The reported effect in this study was strong (a 30-point difference in mean scale scores), but it was based on rather few subjects. This study should be replicated at an early date.

Twenty years ago there was great ferment and interest in the mundane issues of question format, scale construction, and scoring. Today, research on such modest problems seems to have gone out of style, even though answers are lacking to practical, simple questions such as what difference it will make if an attitude or construct is measured by a ranking, checklist, or rating-scale format. Few investigators have used more than one method or item format in the same reported study (Ellis & Bentler, 1973; Jenkin & Vroegh, 1969; Kammeyer, 1966; Sheriffs & McKee, 1957), and fewer still have made a comparison of methods. I am unable to find a single study that compares data from the same subjects on the same content by using two or more different methods. Nuts-and-bolts research of this type is very much needed.

THE MEANING AND MEASUREMENT OF STEREOTYPES

As soon as I see "all women were ..." or "all men did ..." in word, argument, or inference, part of me withdraws skeptically and wonders, Did they now? Every last one? And I'm lost to the point of being made a hopeless recruit in any marching army (Murray, 1973, p. 26.)

Statements of attitude or preference (how things "should be") and statements of belief (how things "really are") often seem reasonably easy to distinguish, but, as we saw earlier, no sharp empirical line exists. Within the category of "belief," however, the term "stereotype" is used by many writers in a way which suggests that the beliefs described by this label are somehow different than other beliefs, generalities, or dispositions. Like "attitude," however, "stereotype" is a term for which one searches in vain for a clear and widely accepted definition. Theorists have devoted much time to discussing what's *bad* about stereotyping (see Brigham, 1972 p. 142-143) without providing clear criteria for its meaning. In practice, its usage appears more closely tied to a particular question format, the adjective checklist, than to any more general or theoretical distinction.

We say for example, that a person's stated belief that "Blacks are lazy," or that "Jews are cheap," is a *stereotype*. What makes these beliefs stereotypes? Some writers would say: because they're factually invalid (Klineberg, 1951); they're broad generalizations which ignore individual differences (Hayakawa, 1941); they're based on a faulty thought process with inadequate information (Fishman, 1956); they represent a misuse of concepts (Vinacke, 1957).

But suppose that another person believes, with precisely equal generality, rigidity, intensity, and total inadequacy of data, that "Blacks are energetic," and that "Jews are extremely generous." And still another person believes, in similar fashion, that blacks are "shy," "traditional," and "optimistic," and that Jews are "romantic," "punctual," and "conforming." Why do we feel that whatever these beliefs are, they are *not* stereotypes?

Empirical basis of the term. In the study that marked the first empirical reference to the word "stereotype" (borrowed from a popular book by journalist Walter Lippmann), Katz and Braly (1933) showed 100 Princeton undergraduates the names of ten ethnic and national groups, and asked the students to simply check, from a list of 84 trait names, the ones they considered "most typical" of each group. There was considerable consensus as to which traits went with which group. The terms checked most often for blacks were *superstitious, lazy, happy-go-lucky, ignorant,* and *musical;* for Jews, *shrewd, mercenary, industrious, intelligent, ambitious,* etc. Commenting that these designations appeared to be "fixed impressions which correspond very little to the facts," Katz and Braly dubbed them "stereotypes." The term and the method were adopted by other investigators, and over the ensuing years, some interesting properties of these "group reputations" were discovered:

1. They were widely and quite uniformly held throughout the population. One could get essentially the same responses from college students in Maine and retired veterans in Oregon. On crossing national and cultural boundaries, however, differences sometimes appeared. For example, in some European countries, certain traits such as "dirty" were ascribed to

Jews but these were never associated with that group in the United States (Bettelheim & Janowitz, 1964, p. 146).

2. They had no apparent relation to direct contact with or knowledge about the groups in question. Farmers in Iowa who had never met *any* European knew that the French were "romantic," the English "reserved," the Scotch "thrifty," and so forth.

3. Young children appear to confuse the trait assignments, and respond on the basis of "good" versus "bad" groups. Blacks, for example, are less "musical" than whites, less "religious," less "happy-go-lucky," and so on (Blake & Dennis, 1943). By the eleventh grade, however, children conform to the adult stereotypes and reverse these assignments.

4. The number of respondents who seem to endorse these group reputations has gone down over the years, but the lineup of trait assignments by group has appeared remarkably stable. The Katz-Braly (1933) study was replicated at Princeton 19 years later (Gilbert, 1951) and again 18 years after that (Karlins, Coffman & Walters, 1969). While the percentage of students ascribing each trait had gone down dramatically, the configuration by group had changed very little.

5. The qualities ascribed to a given group are also, to a substantial degree, ascribed to that group by members of the group itself when they complete the same kinds of checklist questionnaires (Bayton, 1941; Fink & Cantril, 1937; Saenger & Flowerman, 1954).

Traits ascribed to women.   Numerous studies have found that in response to the stimulus word "women," subjects will check such adjectives as *passive, emotional, sensitive, quiet, tactful, indecisive, talkative, illogical, excitable,* and so on (e.g., Jenkin & Vroegh, 1969, Sherriffs & McKee, 1957). The term "stereotype" has in fact been used to refer to these attributions, though for some reason which is less clear the word "role" is often added, to form "sex-role stereotypes." Perhaps "sex" alone was regarded as connoting sex in the erotic sense; the term "role," however, has specific meanings (Brannon, 1976b; Brown, 1965), which are not referred to in this usage, so a more specific and accurate label such as "gender stereotypes" would have seemed preferable.

The methods used have not always been comparable, but the data that do exist suggest that gender stereotypes have the same properties described previously for ethnic stereotypes. They conform to a consistent pattern within a given country or culture, but tend to vary somewhat across national and cultural lines (Seward & Larson, 1968). In the United States, they appear to have changed very little in total configuration over the past 30 years (Neufeld, Langmeyer, & Seeman, 1975). Furthermore, to the surprise of some investigators, females supply almost exactly the same constellation of responses as do males (see discussion of this by Pleck in chapter 10 of this volume; also Erskine, 1970; Roper Organization, 1974; Rosenkrantz et al., 1968; Seward & Larson, 1968). *But What* Are *Stereotypes?* We have then a considerable body of data which we regard as dealing with "stereotypes," and a widely shared sense of the kinds of beliefs that this term is supposed to include. There is no accepted defintion, however, (cf. Brigham, 1972), and hence no clear statement as to how these differ from any other beliefs and generalizations about groups of people.

The most common feature ascribed to stereotypes in the psychological literature is that they are *false* or *invalid* or (at the very least) *highly exaggerated* generalizations (Katz & Braly, 1933; Klineberg, 1951; Allport, 1958). The question immediately arises as to exactly what stereotypes mean to those who believe in them. If they mean to say that all, or almost all, members of the group in question have the quality alleged by the stereotype, it is easy to show that the allegation is false. Remember, however, that the checklist instructions merely ask what traits are "most typical" of a group, an ambiguous phrase. One study asked respondents, after checking these terms, to state what percentage of people in the specified group actually had that characteristic. The percentages ranged from 10% to 100%, and in many cases respondents said that every trait they had checked for a group actually referred to a minority of its members (Brigham, 1972). If then, as seems likely, people who endorse stereotypes see them as probabilistic generalizations about the group average and not as an infallible guide to individual cases, they become considerably harder to disprove.

There is also the difficulty of definite, though inconclusive, evidence in support of certain stereotypes (evidence of Jews being more "ambitious" and "industrious," for example; see Clark, 1949; Havemann and West, 1952; Terman and Oden, 1947; Seligman, 1950.) While the "grain of truth" contention may have more than one explanation (including self-fulfilling prophesy, and circular effects perpetuated by discrimination), the fact is that at least some group stereotypes do not appear totally invalid. The most fundamental difficulty with this definition, however, is that, for most group stereotypes, there is simply no empirical evidence one way or the other at present (Brown, 1965, p. 179).

There are similar difficulties with most of the other definitions which have been offered. Are they based on hearsay and second-hand information? So are most of the things we believe. We accept that Australia exists and that Venice has canals without actually seeing these things for ourselves. Are they based on little or partial information? So are virtually all our beliefs and generalizations. See Allport's (1958) chapter, "The Normality of Prejudgment."

It has been argued that stereotypes are projections (Ackerman & Jahoda, 1950), products of faulty thought processes (Fishman, 1956), rationalizations for discrimination (Allport, 1958), and distinguished by excessive rigidity and erroneous causal assumptions (D. T. Campbell, 1967; Brown, 1965). While all these arguments are plausible contentions, they remain largely unproven at present. To define a construct in terms of what are as yet essentially hypotheses seems questionable.

Actually, all the data and the findings summarized earlier in this chapter are consistent with a simpler definition that makes no reference to truth or falsity and no presumptions as to internal psychological mechanisms. Working backward from the operations by which the data base was constructed, stereotypes may be defined most parsimoniously as:

Generalizations about the psychological qualities of people in some designated social category, which are [socially learned, and] *widely shared* within a given culture.[2]

The qualifier "socially learned" is placed in brackets because it is an inference that cannot be empirically proven at present. Cauthen, Robinson, and Krauss (1971) stated that "uniformity is by definition determined by cultural factors" (p. 108), but in fact direct evidence about the process of acquiring stereotypes is lacking. Social learning seems strongly implied by the findings on lack of relation to contact, the age pattern of acquisition, and the tendency of the group itself to endorse the majority view. Observational studies suggest that children learn stereotypes from parents, other adults, playmates, mass media, popular fiction, and ethnic and sexual jokes. In the absence of solid data, however, this qualifier of social learning may be held as tentative.

The key to the definition given above is the phrase *widely shared.* Stereotypes are essentially defined as those beliefs about a group which are widely shared within a given culture. This answers the rhetorical question with which we began this section. "Blacks are lazy," for example, is a belief that some individuals have; we can say that it is also a stereotype because it is widely shared within our culture. The belief that "Blacks are energetic" might be held by another individual in exactly the same way, but this is not a stereotype because it is not a widely shared belief. Thus, stereotypes are technically cultural rather than individual variables. At the individual level, they are simply beliefs about the characteristics of a group; to ascertain if such a belief is also a cultural stereotype, the psychologist must have data from many other individuals as well (or rely on such data from previous studies). Phenòmenologically, this argument corresponds to the fact that people almost never tend to view or describe their *own* beliefs about groups as "stereotypes."

Some Empirical Issues

How wide is "widely"?   Although studies in this area have invariably had some criterion for selecting stereotypes, there is nothing very compelling about the exact procedures usually reported. Katz and Braly (1933) arbitrarily used only the first five adjectives checked by each subject, and reported the 12 adjectives checked most often for each group, regardless of frequency. In addition to including as "stereotypes" some adjectives checked by only 11% of the sample, this prejudgment of numbers would seem to preclude some interesting comparison among group stereotype patterns.

A criterion based on absolute frequency, such as "characteristics cited by 70% or more of the population" (or 60%, or 80%, etc.), would seem to be more neutral, and closer in meaning to the definition of stereotypes as widely shared beliefs. But where should one draw the line? It is easy to assign an arbitrary cut-off point, but this is simply to avoid an interesting substantive question. One can imagine a continuum of endorsement for all possible beliefs, ranging from 0% to 100% of the population that shares any particular belief. Is there some quality of "stereotype-ness" that increases, as one looks from 0% to 100% endorsement? In the Katz-Braly (1933) data blacks are described as "superstitious" by 84% of the sample and as "naive" by only 14%. The authors reported them both as "stereotypes," but isn't there some meaningful difference in their psychological properties, correlates, or influence on other kinds of thoughts or judgments? This raises the issue of the empirical status of stereotypes, to which I'll return shortly.

Whatever criterion is used—and even if the choice is essentially arbitrary—researchers should reach a consensus, since study-to-study variations serve no purpose except to make comparison impossible. Rosenkrantz et al. (1968) reported a total of 41 gender stereotypes, based on the arbitrary criterion of 75% subject agreement. Clarkson, Vogel, Broverman, and Broverman (1970) used the same instrument, but switched to a new criterion (the .001 level of significance); they found 57 gender stereotypes. Spence, Helmreich, and Stapp (1974) used essentially the same instrument, but switched to the .05 level of significance, which resulted in 112 gender stereotypes. The similarity in instruments should have allowed some interesting comparisons among these studies, but no comparisons are possible because the criteria were varied for no apparent reason

Should stereotypes be comparisons? It may be argued that the perceived qualities of any group amount to an implicit comparison with all other groups. If we say that the Scotch are "thrifty," this presumably means in comparison with everyone else; if everyone on earth were Scotch, the statement would have little meaning. Still, traditional stereotype measures do not force subjects to compare the different ethnic and nationality groups while making ratings, and do not assume a zero-sum division of qualities. The English need not be viewed as "spendthrifts" because the Scotch appear more thrifty. Subjects who rate blacks as "religious" are not compelled by the scoring method to describe whites as "irreligious."

For some reason, however, researchers have usually allowed subjects to state what is "female" only in comparison to what is "male," and vice versa. Virtually all published accounts of gender stereotypes are based on some form of male-female comparison, either within the individual item format or in the process of choosing the stereotypes (Broverman, Broverman, Clarkson, & Rosenkrantz, 1970; Rosenkrantz et al., 1968; Spence et al., 1974; also Fernberger, 1948; Neufeld et al., 1975; Sherriffs & Jarrett, 1953).

It may be argued that since there are only two sexes, a comparison is implicit under any procedure. Methodologically, it is worth noting that a criterion based on direct comparison will generate a different list of stereotypes than one based on independent grounds. Testing for statistically significant differences between ratings of males and females guarantees a very large number of findings, since small differences are significant with large samples. The few studies that have judged stereotypes independently for each sex have obtained much smaller lists (Jenkin & Vroegh, 1969; McKee & Sherriffs, 1957; Sherriffs & McKee, 1957). Also, qualities considered rare in either sex (e.g., noisy, witty, vindictive) appear as "stereotypes" in comparison data when they are ascribed to one sex slightly more often than to the other (cf. Sherriffs & McKee, 1957).

The stereotype versus belief in the stereotype.   If stereotypes are cultural variables that can be defined only in terms of the culture as a whole, it makes little sense to go through the process of discovering and describing them each time new data are collected. This is especially true when working with small or specialized samples, which is often the case in psychological studies. One may posit, of course, stereotypes within population subgroups (e.g., college students' stereotypes of women, urban-dwellers' stereotypes of blacks). This seems likely to needlessly proliferate constructs, however, and is not supported by most empirical evidence now available. A striking feature of stereotypes is their uniformity across age, class, and other demographic lines.

Granted that the cultural patterns must be determined empirically, studies using small and atypical samples should utilize the substantive descriptions of stereotype content reported by large-sample studies. What should and in fact *must* be determined separately for each subject in each study is not the overall lineup of qualities generally associated with the group but some more individualized measure of "stereotype acceptance," or intensity, or certainty, or trans-situationality of stereotype holding by the individual. Here as always, the investigator must make decisions as to precisely what to measure.

The study by Rosenkrantz et al. (1968) may be used to illustrate such a two-step process. The authors first determined a list of gender stereotypes, on the basis of the extent of agreement in their sample as a whole. This provided the instrument for which their study is rather well known. They then could have, and should have, used individual scores in stereotype acceptance to investigate the connections with self-concept and social desirability explored in the remainder of the study. (Instead they appear to have correlated stereotype *means* in one sample ($n = 154$) with percentage scores obtained in a different group of individuals ($n = 121$). (See Rosenkrantz et al., 1968, pp.288, 291-292.))

A study by Ellis and Bentler (1973) illustrates another kind of confusion about stereotype acceptance. These authors started with the list of stereotypes used by Rosenkrantz and his associates, but noticed during analysis that a few subjects had happened to rate women closer to the ostensibly male pole than they rated men. They therefore reversed the designation of the stereotypic pole for these subjects on these items, to make the score "more meaningful." While such a procedure may be justified for certain purposes or uses, the resultant data should *not* have been reported as "sex stereotypes."

Why tie the stereotype construct to one method? Apparently as an almost incidental consequence of the absence of a conceptual definition, reviewers have tended to identify "stereotype research" primarily by reference to the question format. The Katz-Braly (1933) study which introduced the word "stereotype" had used a simple adjective checklist. In the absence of any conceptual or other guideline, the implicit definition seems to have been that "stereotypes are the things produced by an adjective checklist." (By a similar unwritten law, anything measured with Likert-type items is usually described as an attitude.)

But as we saw earlier, the checklist is not the most efficient, reliable, or flexible format for measuring psychological constructs. Within the stereotype literature itself, there is evidence of drawbacks in this method. Ehrlich and Rinehart (1965) compared responses on a checklist to free-response statements about the characteristics of ethnic and nationality groups; the checklist data contained three times as many terms as the free responses, but was less substantively cohesive, and included more negative and undesirable qualities. The checklist also provides different data when one group is rated at a sitting than when many groups are rated (Diab, 1963).

A more mechanical aspect of the checklist format is that it tends to encourage the study of only one type of belief about the characteristics of a group: beliefs about the general, trans-situational qualities which can be conveniently summarized in a single word or short phrase. Some longer clause, such as "Most women are . . .", is of course implicit in the list of trait words, but since this is constant it need not be stated.

The definition of stereotypes as widely shared beliefs about a group does not tie the stereotype concept to the checklist or to any other particular format, and it does not limit stereotypes to beliefs about general behavior traits. The following statements are examples of beliefs that might be found to be widely shared and to qualify as stereotypes:

A woman's place is in the home.

Children need full-time mothers.

No woman can have a full, happy life without marrying.

A real man never cries.

The exclusive use of paper-and-pencil materials would raise the possibility that stereotypes are elicited solely or primarily by the verbal stimulus of the group's name ("women," "Jew," "Negroes"), and do not appear as responses to unlabeled individuals. (It is known, for example, that subjects who respond quite negatively to ideas labeled as "Fascist principles" may respond favorably to the same ideas when unlabeled (Stagner, 1936a, 1936b.)) There is some evidence, however, that unlabeled photographs do elicit stereotyped evaluations of ethnic minorities (Lindzey & Rogolsky, 1950; Martin, 1964). Secord (1956) and Secord, Bevin, and Katz (1959) have further shown that on a sequence of photographs ranging from clearly black ancestry to clearly white ancestry, stereotyped evaluations appear at whatever point the subject first identifies the individuals as black. Only one recent unpublished study (Cherulnik & McAndrew, Note 8) reported significantly stereotyped responses to male and female stimulus persons presented (on videotape) without verbal labels.

Do we need the stereotype concept? The most interesting (and trenchant) question has not yet been asked. It is essentially this: Do we actually need, and can we justify, a separate term to designate those particular beliefs about social groups which are widely shared within our culture? The fact that such a term exists, and is widely used, and designates a supposedly distinctive body of literature does not necessarily mean that we should continue to use it. As D.T. Campbell (1963) has so cogently argued, distinctions in nomenclature should be supported by some kind of empirical evidence that the distinction is real and is needed, that "*X*" actually differs in some nontrivial way from "non-*X*." Are the widely-shared generalizations about women in our culture different in any functional way from generalizations that an individual might hold that are not at all widely-shared? If not, we need only talk about "generalizations" and forget the whole issue of cultural stereotypes. And in that case, we might as well throw away all that stereotype data, which was arbitrarily restricted in a way which had no functional significance.

I've stated this point a bit too sharply, merely to underscore its ultimate importance and the total lack of attention it has received. If a defined construct cannot be shown to have any special properties, other than those that define it, there is no more reason to prefer its use rather than any other division of the world (such as, say, alphabetical categories). Yet, the tendency is strong in social science to perpetuate words as if they had some reality apart from empirical evidence. We speak and write as though "stereotypes" had some special relevance to or influence on the way people think about the members of social groups. This could easily be the case if, for example, the cultural consensus were to give these beliefs a special saliency, certainty, potency, or resistance to change. (Remember Asch's finding about the effects of unanimous versus non-unanimous group reports?) But what is the evidence?

A very large number of studies (e.g., Broverman et al., 1970; Goldberg, Gottesdiener, & Abramson, 1975; and many of the studies of evaluation bias reviewed earlier) may be interpreted as showing a correspondence between cultural stereotypes of women and the way in which women are evaluated. Such findings are obviously subject to more than one interpretation. More to the point would be evidence that individual differences in stereotype acceptance are related to thinking, perception, or judgment about individuals in the stereotyped group. Only two studies have investigated this in the case of ethnic stereotypes, both with largely negative results (Brigham, 1969; Mann, 1967). In the realm of gender stereotypes, only one study comes close: Spence et al. (1974, see Table 3 therein) reported that individual differences in stereotyping were slightly correlated (.25) with *self*-evaluations in a stereotyped direction, and only for male subjects on male-valued stereotype characteristics.

But as to the issue raised here, the difference between stereotypes and other beliefs as an influence on thinking or acting, there is simply no evidence at all. With imagination, or over a stiff cocktail, a pattern of mean scores found in the data of Rosenkrantz et al. (1968, see tables 1 and 3 therein) might be interpreted as suggesting that stereotypes exert a greater pressure on self-evaluations than do "nondifferentiating" or non-stereotype beliefs; since these are sample means rather than individual scores, however, the interpretation of the pattern is uncertain.

At present, then, we must conclude that there is no empirical evidence for a distinction between cultural stereotypes and other beliefs about women, or indeed about other social groups. There is certainly no evidence to justify a separate methodology or division of the literature devoted to stereotypes.

IS SEXISM ONE THING, OR MANY?

The early scales of racial prejudice sought the respondent's reaction to a heterogeneous melange of cultural stereotypes, policy recommendations, perceptions, and practical personal issues. The following items, for example, are found on the original Likert "Attitudes Toward the Negro" scale (1932):

- If you heard of a Negro who had bought a home or a farm, would you be glad?

- In a community of 1,000 whites and 50 Negroes, a drunken Negro shoots and kills an officer who is trying to arrest him. The white population immediately drives all Negroes out of town. (approve— disapprove)

- Would you shake hands with a Negro?

- Would most Negroes, if not held in their place, become officious, overbearing, and disagreeable?

- Negro homes should be segregated from those of white people.

- If the same preparation is required, the Negro teacher should receive the same salary as the white.

This everything-but-the-kitchen-sink philosophy of measurement reflected a conception of "racial prejudice" as a basic aversion to, and antagonism against, blacks, prejudice which was revealed in greater or lesser degree by different kinds of questions. The years have not been kind to this rather simplistic view of race relations (Allport, 1958; Banton, 1967; Saenger, 1953), but scale builders and users, in their quest for that "ole Debil" prejudice, were never overly concerned with the exact substantive contents of the items on their scales. The well-known Hinckley (1932) scale, for example, was provided in two alternate forms for use as alternate or repeated measures; the scale had been in use for some years before someone noticed that Form A was primarily concerned with economic and legal issues, while Form B was focused more on social contacts between the races (Bolton, 1937).

A remarkably similar range of contents can be seen in almost all scales currently purported to measure "attitudes toward women," "sexism," "sex prejudice," and the like. The very first popular scale in this category, published by Kirkpatrick (1936), included the following statements:

- Women have as much right to sow wild oats as do men.

- Women are too nervous and high-strung to make good surgeons.

- A husband has the right to expect that his wife be obliging and dutiful at all times.

- One should never trust a woman's account of another woman.

- Women should not be permitted to hold political offices that involve great responsibility.

Several more recent and well-known instruments were developed by taking the Kirkpatrick scale as a starting point (Spence & Helmreich, 1972; Dempewolfe, 1974; Arnott, 1972). While these researchers revised, updated, and added to the Kirkpatrick item pool, they did not question the suitability of a mixed content, all-purpose instrument. The same is true in varying degrees of most other recent scales for measuring attitudes toward women (Centers, 1963; Greenberg, 1973; Ross & Walters, 1973; Steinmann & Fox, 1966).

What is the result of substantive diversity in the contents of scale items? The most obvious effect is that any functional differences associated with content are obscured when the data from different items are summed into a single total score. Standard item-analysis procedures typically require that each item have at least a moderate correlation with most other items or with the scale total. While this provides some limit to heterogeneity, experience has shown that it is not a very stringent limitation. More importantly, if a variety of different scales with the same title (e.g. "attitudes toward women") and assumed to measure approximately the same thing happen to emerge with appreciably different substantive contents, the stage has been set for exactly the kind of inconsistency and contradictory results that plagued the study of racial prejudice.

Instruments with heterogeneous contents may be defended on the grounds of content validity; i.e., that they accurately represent a predefined heterogeneous domain of content (Messick, 1975; American Psychological Association, 1966) Whether sexism and related constructs are best defined as heterogeneous domains is, of course, a matter of judgment for the investigator. If our longer-term aim is to understand rather than simply to measure, instruments that are effectively homogeneous in response qualities have been argued to be essential (e.g.,

Loevinger, 1957, p. 645). In the final section of this paper dealing with empirical predictions, another reason for content-homogeneous measures will be described.

The optimal solution, and one to which investigators of aptitudes, interests, and abilities turned some years ago, is the development of what are sometimes called "structured" inventories, composed of a set of smaller homogeneous sub-scales that may be used separately or in combination to provide an overall index (Meehl, 1945; Anastasi, 1961, p. 15; Nunnally, 1967, p. 254). Multidimensional attitude inventories of this type have been advocated for many years (e.g., Abelson, 1954), but are still rare in practice.

THEORY-INSPIRED TYPOLOGIES

Given the desirability of a dimensional instrument, how should the categories best be determined? One approach, which is decidedly not recommended, is the imposing of abstract, theory-inspired typologies upon the measuring instrument. Efforts to build empirical scales around such lofty abstractions as Parsons and Shils' (1951) theory of action have proven to be so invariably disastrous (e.g., Tarter, 1969) that no other comment seems necessary—except that no one has been known to attempt it twice.

There is one typology, however, that seems as immortal as the superhero of a Marvel comic book: the ancient notion reportedly dating back at least as far as Plato that attitudes have *cognitive, conative,* and *affective* components. This three-fold formulation has been touted for so long by theorists who should know better (D.J. Bem, 1970; Chein, 1951; Ehrlich, 1973; Harding, Proshansky, Kutner, & Chein, 1969; Kramer, 1949; Smith, 1947; Triandis, 1971), that it is now dutifully memorized by most introductory students as a concrete fact about attitudes.[3]

Yet, on the numerous occasions when empirical scales have been tailor-made to correspond to these three components of attitudes (Kahn, 1951; MacKenzie, 1948; Mann, 1959; Merz & Pearlin, 1957; Ostrum, 1969; Weiss, 1961; Wrightsman, 1962; D.T. Campbell, Note 45), the resulting data have seldom even vaguely supported the model—despite the distinctly Procrustean efforts of a few researchers to somehow bend their data to fit the model. More damaging still is the fact that empirical studies beginning with a large pool of statements about a given subject have never isolated anything remotely resembling these three components (Gardner, Wonnacott, & Taylor, 1968; Ferguson, 1939; Spence & Helmreich, 1972b; Woodmansee & Cook, 1967; Collins & Haupt, Note 46). Like some intellectual chain letter that can't be stopped or called back, this discredited notion has acquired a life of its own and now proliferates unhindered by the need for confirming data.

Empirically Derived Subscales

A sounder approach is some type of empirical procedure for discovering functional divisions, an idea sometimes referred to as "carving nature at the joints." Unfortunately, by far the best-known method of this general type—the procedure known as factor analysis—does not seem to be well suited to the task of sorting attitude items into meaningful substantive clusters. Most psychometrics texts still recommend factor analysis for this purpose, (Guilford, 1954, p. 462; Nunnally, 1967, p. 534), so some explanation of this statement seems necessary.

Both I and other researchers with whom I've discussed this procedure have considerable experience in factor-analyzing a pool of heterogeneous attitude items, usually in the hope of discovering some meaningful dimensions inherent in the data. The results have generally been disappointing in two respects. As Allport (1961, p. 329) once noted, one of the major challenges of factor analysis is in even naming, much less making psychological sense of, the curious hodgepodge of item loadings that frequently result. This, by itself, would be easily tolerable, however, if once they were discovered, the factors remained consistent from one dataset to the next. Yet, even under what seem to be ideal conditions (cf. Guilford, 1964), it has been rare for two analyses of the same domain to turn up easily comparable results.

Since these frustrations might naturally be attributed to incompetence on the part of the investigator, it seems worthwhile to examine the published results of other efforts to factor-analyze attitude item pools. Robinson, Rusk, and Head (1968, p. 17) note that one subscale, which had been carefully constructed to represent a single personality dimension, yielded no less than eight separate factors. The set of items comprising the California F-Scale have been factor-analyzed numerous times over the past two decades (Eysenck, 1954; Fruchter, Rokeach, & Novak, 1958; Hofstaetter, 1952; Kerlinger & Rokeach, 1966; Krug, 1961; O'Neil & Levinson, 1954; Prothro & Keehn, 1956; Rokeach & Fruchter, 1956; Rubenowitz, 1963; Struening & Richardson, 1965). Remarkable as it may seem, no two published studies in this series have ever reported the same factor structure. There are doubtlessly valid reasons for these discrepancies, but the overall record can hardly inspire confidence in the average researcher who is seeking a method.

Factor analyses of attitudes toward women.   What is the evidence provided by factor analyses of items concerning women and sex-role issues? I am aware of seven such studies conducted in recent years, all with orthogonal factor-rotation methods. There are a great many discrepancies in reporting, but the basic outcomes may be summarized as follows:

1.   Dempewolf (1974) factored 80 items, drawn primarily from Kirkpatrick (1936b), and reported on major factor with 40% of the total variance, one much smaller minor factor, and several very peripheral factors. Sempewolfe concluded that 80 items were "relatively homogenous."

2.   Gump (1972) factored 39 items, drawn primarily from Fand (1955), and reported seven factors, the largest accounting for 14% of the variance. Factor labels were as follows (consult Gump's report for actual item loadings):

     I   Identity Derived Through Traditional Roles
     II   Woman's Role Is Submissive
     IIII Need for Individualistic Achievement and Satisfaction
     IV   Home-Oriented, Duty to Children Stressed
     V   Traditional Role Implies Some Relinquishing of Needs for Personal Fulfillment
     VI   Sense of Autonomy and Heightened Independence
     VII Family Inadequate to Completely Fulfill Needs

3.   Ellis and Bentler (1973) factored 71 items. largely composed by themselves, and reported two factors: "Since the two factors did not clearly differ in content, the best items of each were selected to form one . . . factor" (p. 31).

4.   Turner and Turner (Note 28) factored 15 semantic differential items paired with the following stimulus: "Most women are . . ." They reported five factors:

     I   Supportive, Giving Female—53% variance
     II   Physically and Mentally Robust Female—16% variance
     III Warm Female—11% variance
          Effective, Efficient Female—11% variance
     IV   Active, Expressive Female—10% variance

5. Hawley (1971) factored 80 new items concerning women, and reported five factors "conceptually related" in some (unspecified) way to constructs labeled as follows:

    I   Woman as Partner: Division of responsibility, power, and labor between the sexes in work and the conjugal relationship.
    II Woman as Ingenue: Woman in her most dependent state, as a possession, a decorative item, and a sex symbol.
    III Woman as Homemaker: Emphasis on the traditional role as a keeper of the house.
    IV Woman as Competitor: Woman's right to compete with implications for the man-woman relationship.
    V   Woman as Knower: Appropriate ways of knowing, for instance, the assumption that women are naturally intuitive and men naturally rational.

6. Spence and Helmreich (1972b) factored 78 items, drawn primarily from Kirkpatrick (1936b). They performed the analysis separately for each of four samples:

    a. College females (2 groups); 2 factors obtained
    b. College males (2 groups); 3 factors obtained
    c. Mothers of college students; 3 factors obtained
    d. Fathers of college students; 4 factors obtained

The factors are difficult to describe briefly, but consult Spence and Helmreich (1972b) for excellent descriptions. Comparisons across the four samples show some definite consistencies, but there are also complex shifts in item assignments. The authors devoted four pages to description of the factors, but offer no conclusions. It is difficult to resist noting that despite this unprecedented wealth of factorial data, the authors preferred to present the items "informally categorized into *six* more or less independent groups according to their content" (p. 5; emphasis added). The six ad hoc groups seem quite reasonable on visual inspection, but bear little relation to the reported factors.

7.   Spence, Helmreich, and Stapp (1973) factored 25 items comprising a short form of the scale developed in time 6, above, which correlated .97 with the longer version. This short form was determined to be "essentially unifactorial," with the first factor accounting for 67% to 69% of the total variance.

Better empirical techniques.   It would obviously be imprudent to conclude on the basis of these cases that factor analysis cannot (or will not) yet identify meaningful dimensions of attitudes toward women. Still, the variability seen here accords with my own experience in factor-analyzing item pools. There are several technical reasons, and one substantive one, why I think factor analysis does not usually produce meaningful groupings in item data. The correlations among single items are often rather small, as are the standard deviations of such correlations; factor analysis works best when the *range* of correlations in the matrix is reasonably large (Nunnally, 1967, p. 255). More importantly, the variance obtained from single items is relatively high in specific and stylistic factors tied to item wording (Cronbach, 1951), plus proximity and order effects related to item position. These features, which are largely irrelevant to substantive content, often seem to influence factor resolutions very substantially (see Jackson, 1971, p. 244).

The substantive reason is that virtually all popular computerized rotational programs extract *orthogonal* (uncorrelated) factors. This is mathematically and conceptually elegant, but makes little psychological sense for most conceivable social attitude domains. Do we really believe that the most useful dimensions of attitudes toward women will be, or should be, uncorrelated with each other? By insisting on orthogonal factors, the program forces an outcome that may have little to do with the strongest communalities that actually exist in the data.

Non-orthogonal factor rotations do, of course, exist, but a better course is to bypass the splendors of factor analysis altogether in favor of simpler methods of item analysis. Loevinger, Gleser, and Dubois (1953) developed one simple procedure that is well suited to developing homogeneous subscales from large pools of diverse items. With this and other simple correlational procedure, the investigator remains much "closer" to the data, and is able to exercise judgments and notice substantive patterns that computerized solutions will invariably miss. In this way, the investigator may also discover logical gaps in the item pool, which can lead to reformulation of the construct or writing of new items.

One study in the gender area (Haavio-Mannila, 1967) hints at this approach and focuses on attitudes toward married women's employment and social participation in Finland. Inspecting the matrix of item correlations, the investigator composed subscales and changed the item assignments until a reliable and interpretable pattern was found, a promising step in the right direction.

The best current example of empirical subscale construction is the monumental study of racial attitudes reported by Woodmansee and Cook (1967). In a research program involving more than 2,000 subjects over a three-year period, the investigators started with orthogonal factor analysis, but later switched to Tyron's key cluster analysis, a procedure that permits correlated empirical factors (Tyron & Bailey, 1966). Woodmansee & Cook eventually isolated 11 consistent attitude dimensions, some rather closely related to each other and others rather isolated (average $r = .36$). While not a definitive study, this is an excellent model for researchers in the area of gender attitudes.

Balancing subjectivity and empiricism. The definite merits of empirical scale construction have led some researchers to virtually ignore manifest item content, seemingly a matter of "subjective" judgment, as being too "unscientific" for the hard-nosed scientist. By simply analyzing a large pool of existing items, one should be able to discover the most meaningful dimensions in the domain.

In a recent paper, Jackson (Note 47) demonstrated the fallacy of this assumption, and outlined a procedure for scale development which combines subjective and empirical contributions. In brief, Jackson advocated the following five steps:

1. Start with a set of well-thought-out constructs (i.e., the dimension or variable that each subscale will attempt to measure). Define each as precisely as possible.

2. Think of all areas and applications in which each such construct might be manifested. ("Judgment plays a very important role here. In fact it has no equal." See Jackson, 1971, p. 237).

3. Compose a substantial pool of new items to represent each construct. Interestingly, this need not be done by expert item-writers or even professional psychologists. Jackson provided evidence that undergraduate classes can do this task quite well.

4. Screen, edit, and refine the items, simplifying wording and structure, and balancing for agreement and other technical considerations. Item content should always have some *apparent* and theoretically defensible relation to the construct (Loevinger, 1957), though the connection may be subtle. For example, the item "I think newborn babies look very much like little monkeys" is acceptable as a negatively worded item for the construct of "nurturance." The connection is apparent to the informed reader, if not necessarily to the eventual respondent.

5. Now gather data from an appropriate subject population. If using a simple correlational approach, correlate each item with scale totals for all constructs, including a social desirability scale. Discard items that correlate too highly with desirability or with any construct other than their own. Each item retained should be associated with only one scale. The more elaborate selection procedures described by Loevinger et al. (1953), Tyron and Bailey (1966); Neill and Jackson (1970), and others may also be used for this purpose.

Empirical selection of items from content pools constructed in this manner is enormously more efficient than starting with existing or unselected item pools. Items borrowed from past scales and multipurpose inventories often cut across several constructs and cannot be firmly associated with any one subscale. In one illustrative study that tested this method (Jackson, 1971), 99.9% of the items that survived empirical selection were drawn from a pool which was newly composed for that construct. More importantly, Jackson provided rather impressive evidence for convergent and discriminant validity of scales constructed in this way, using the multitrait, multimethod procedure suggested by D.T. Campbell and Fiske (1959).

Rather than starting with the Kirkpatrick scale, the Rosenkrantz scale, or some other old favorite, new researchers in the gender area should generate item pools to represent specific constructs that make sense to the investigator. The constructs should then be subjected to empirical scrutiny, consisting at least of checks on homogeneity as described above.

Where to start. The factor-analysis studies cited previously provide some possible suggestions for gender attitude dimensions; other studies have suggested dimensions derived on more intuitive grounds. Nadler and Morrow (1959) rather insightfully examined the positive and negative duality in traditional views of women. On frankly a priori grounds, they constructed two measures:

1. Open Subordination of Women Scale (20 items)
   (a) Support of traditional restrictive policies
   (b) Beliefs in natural inferiority
   (c) Beliefs in women's narrowness of interest
   (d) Views of women as nagging, exploitative, and offensive
2. Chivalry Scale (18 items)
   (a) Advocating chivalrous gestures of assistance and protectiveness
   (b) Support of stylized gestures of deference and politeness
   (c) Idealization of women as pure and honorable

Nadler and Morrow argued that, while seeming to be opposites, Chivalry and Open Subordination were merely two sides of the same social bargain. They showed that the two scales correlated with each other (.35) and with the California F-scale (.60 and .66), but unfortunately failed to explore the subscale constructs empirically. A related scale, also built around hypothesized constructs, was the Traditional Family Ideology scale by Levinson and Huffman (1955).

An extensive and valuable compendium of more than 600 gender-related attitude items has recently been developed by Mason (1975), consisting of items used in surveys, scales, interviews, and national polls over many years. The items are organized into sections according to the apparent substantive contents, insofar as they relate to the institutions of the family, the labor force, the educational system, politics and leadership roles, and the military. Within each category except the family and where the number of items permits, Mason used a classification that reduces roughly to the following:

- How women and men should behave

- How women and men do behave

- How women and men are treated

- How women and men should be treated

This typology raises a general question about the wording of verbal items, which, so far as I know, has never really been answered, namely: How much difference does the verb make? Common sense tells us that people often do distinguish between "what is" and "what should be." Certain theorists (e.g., Fishbein & Ajzen, 1972) also postulate very different outcomes from such psychological constructs as factual beliefs, attitudes, behavioral intentions, reports of past behavior, and the like. One can hardly help noticing, however, what slight changes in sentence wording are required to switch among categories such as these: "I believe," "I feel," "I should," "I will," "I have." *Logically* the meanings may be quite different, but it's not entirely clear that respondents always appreciate or respond to such differences. Is the item "Women are the fair and gentle sex" a statement of "what is," or "what should be," or both? For many traditional people, one suspects that the line between what is and what should be is less obvious than in the perceptions of reformers and social scientists.

The distinction between one's own behavior and treatment by others is also not always clear. "Politics is too dirty a business for women" may seem like advice to women to voluntarily stay out of politics but it may also be an inclination to vote against women candidates ("for their own good").

Obviously these are empirical questions, but virtually no evidence on question wording versus content is available at present. In order to form "constructs" upon which to build scales, the investigator must make some initial decisions. Should "factual" wordings be distinguished from evaluative wordings? Should the constructs be large, such as "independence," "autonomy" and "needs;" or should they be small, such as "responsibility for birth control"? Only time and empirical evidence will tell, and the answers will come quickly if different alternatives are tried.

As a possible stimulus to multidimensional scale building, since it's easier to see what is wrong with someone else's formulation than to start from scratch, I have compiled Table 11.2, a rather fine-grained taxonomy of constructs concerning women. It should be obvious that the categories defined are no more than guesses about what aspects of issues will "go together" in the minds of most respondents. The number of divisions is totally arbitrary. One might easily sub-

Table 11.2

POSSIBLE TAXONOMY OF CONSTRUCTS CONCERNING WOMEN
A STARTING POINT FOR DIMENSIONAL SCALE CONSTRUCTION[a]

I. GENERAL

1. *What most women are like: personal traitlike qualities seen as
   general and nonsituational.*
   Note: Most of the data usually referred to as "stereotypes"
   will fall in this category. Many kinds of qualities may be
   ascribed in this way, and as stated, this construct is probably
   too broad to be useful; the subdivisions should ideally be
   chosen, however, on empirical grounds. Some obvious distinctions are desirable versus undesirable qualities and "instrumental" versus "expressive" qualities, but there are many
   other possibilities.

2. *What women should be like: general nonsituational qualities
   of the "ideal woman."*
   Note: The kinds of ratings obtained by Broverman et al.
   (1970) fit into this category, as do all ratings of the "ideal
   woman" (Bennett & Cohen, 1959; McKee & Sherriffs, 1959;
   Reece, 1964; Seward & Larson, 1968; Spence et al., 1974).
   The note concerning subdivisions under (1) above applies here
   as well.

3. *What I am like: women's ratings of their own trait qualities,
   when seen as general, nonsituational characteristics.*
   Note: Self-evaluations by individual women do not quite
   logically belong in this taxonomy and are not mentioned
   hereafter; in the case of general traitlike qualities, however,
   the implicit comparison with (1) and (2) above is obvious and
   interesting. Also, the current measures of androgyny by Bem
   (1974) and Spence et al. (1975) are of this type and are
   attracting considerable interest and use. The note concerning
   empirical subdivisions applies here as well.

II. SOCIAL-INTERPERSONAL RESPONSES TO WOMEN

4. *Reaction to conventional unladylike behavior on the part of
   women.*
   Drinking, smoking, using profanity, etc. (but not including
   sexual immodesty).

5. *Support for chivalry and etiquette.*

    A. Rituals and ideology suggesting a Gentleman's responsibility to defend, shelter, and protect all Ladies (pseudopractical issues).

    B. Rituals and ideology suggesting that a Gentleman honor, respect, and defer to all Ladies (symbolic deference, e.g., avoiding profanity).

6. *Relative importance of women's physical attractiveness.*
Importance of beauty, relative to other qualities, desirability of cosmetics, fashions, and coiffures versus comfort and naturalness.

7. *Sexuality*

    A. The valuing of virginity, innocence, and lack of sexual experience.

    B. Belief that women do not like sex or feel sexual urges as strongly as do men; hence, that not "going too far" is up to women.

    C. Double standard of sexual exclusivity; faithfulness in impulse and deed, more natural and more desirable for women than for men.

    D. Belief that a sexually passive style (e.g., not initiating, not responding aggressively) is characteristic and natural for women.
Note: C and D do not separate beliefs about what is natural from views of how women "should" behave; it should be determined empirically whether these co-vary or should be distinguished.

E. Rape: beliefs that women want to be raped, enjoy being raped, tacitly encourage men to rape them. Also, beliefs about subsequent effects: "trauma" versus "no big deal" and beliefs about rapists: perverted monster versus innocent victim.

8. *Reactions to women who otherwise deviate from strongly stereotyped norms.*

A. Reactions to extremely intelligent and/or competent women.

B. Reactions to agressive, domineering women.

C. Reactions to women who don't like children.

D. Reactions to physically powerful and/or athletic women.

III. WOMEN AND MARRIAGE

9. *General desirability and naturalness of marriage to one member of the other sex; being single an unhappy and unnatural state.*
Note: As stated, this is a general ideology apart from wanting children or opting against a career; it may not be separable from these, however.

10. *View of marriage as complementary division of labor and power versus an essentially practical equal partnership with some specialization*

A. Beliefs that women's and men's basically different "natures" underlie and require role separation.

B. Approval of husband being the "Boss," head of family, final decision maker; appropriateness of "personal service," wife waiting on husband.

C. Wife's sexual duties to husband (never say "no," etc.).

D. Money; husband controls it versus equal sharing and responsibility.

E. Cooking and housework; totally wife's role versus work to be done by someone, depending on time and other duties.

F. The home as wife's special domain and responsibility; decorating, etc.

11. *Divorce: a reasonable response to unhappiness, or a selfish and foolish decision for women?*
Views on alimony and division of property: approval of heavy benefits to wife versus pragmatic or equal division of resources.

IV. HAVING AND RAISING CHILDREN

12. *Belief in natural desire of all women to have children, greatest experience of any woman's life, etc.*

13. *Belief in special relationship of mother to children, natural emotional bonds with children, maternal instinct.*
Belief that work and responsibility of raising children primarily the mother's.

14. *Valuing of personal self-fulfillment in life versus sacrificing for children*
Belief that mother in particular should sacrifice ter own needs to those of ter children in all cases.

15. *Approval of differential treatment for sons and daughters; encouraging sex-appropriate choices versus individual fulfillment.*

    A. Encouraging independence versus obedience and conformity.

    B. Differential encouragement to continue education.

    C. Differential encouragement toward types of careers corresponding to sex-typical norms.

    D. Differential restrictiveness and protectiveness concerning sex.

16. *Divorce and children*

    A. Belief that mother should always take custody versus case-by-case mutual decisions on individual or pragmatic grounds.

    B. Beliefs about divorced father's financial responsibility to children.

    C. Divorced father's emotional and companionship rights and responsibilities to children.

V. CONFLICT OF CAREER AND FAMILY

17. *Ideological disapproval of careers for wives*

    A. Unnatural for wife to work away from home unless financially required.

    B. Difficult to retain "femininity" as a career employee.

C. Career women take jobs away from male breadwinners.

18. *Conflicts with needs of husband*

A. Wife's career detracts from ter fulfillment of husband's practical, companionship, emotional, and sexual needs.

B. Wife's career a status threat unless tey earns far less than ter and is less visibly successful.

19. *Conflicts with needs of children*

A. Practically and emotionally best for small children to be with their mothers; children of working mothers suffer.

B. Beliefs about effects of day-care centers and nursery schools on children.

20. *Beliefs in the greater suitability of some careers than others for women*

A. Part-time work more suitable for women than full time.

B. Women should choose among careers traditional for women: teacher, nurse, secretary, librarian, social worker.

C. Women are better at "people" than "technical" jobs.

D. Women's jobs shouldn't be too dirty, tiring or dangerous.

VI. DISCRIMINATION AGAINST WOMEN

21. *Women's performance in paid employment. Are women as competent, hardworking, and productive as men who do the same work?*

A. Motives for working: beliefs that women work for diversion, "extra" income, or frivolous reasons.

B. Reliability: beliefs that women are absent more often and always likely to quit to quit married or have children.

C. Ambition and responsibility: beliefs that women have little desire to advance in their careers.

22. *Approval of strict equality in the hiring, compensation, and advancement of women versus discrimination based on arguments in (17), (18), (19), (21).*

23. *Women in positions of power or leadership.*

A. Belief that people don't like to work for women.

B. Belief that women lack the special qualities to be leaders or executives.

C. Belief that women executives and leaders lose their femininity and become tough, hard and unattractive.

D. Belief that women who get to be important outside the home are neglecting their husbands and children.

E. Personal willingness to work for a woman, vote for a woman, follow the leadership of a woman.

24. *Does unfair discrimination against women exist in fact?*

A. In life in general.

B. In hiring, salaries, and opportunity for promotion.

C. In gaining leadership positions and political offices.

D. In social and marriage relationships.

25. *If discrimination exists, should one expect and accept this or strongly oppose and condemn it?*

A. Support for compensatory discrimination-in-reverse.

VII. THE WOMEN'S MOVEMENT

26. *Basic sympathy or hostility to perceived aims and goals of the movement.*

A. Quarrels with specific issues, styles, or strategies of the movement.

27. *Beliefs about negative personal qualities of women's-libbers (sic.): aggressive, unfeminine, cold, humorless, unhappy, unattractive, etc.*

28. *(women's) Personal sense of identification with, or separateness from, the women's movement: "us" versus "them."*

Note. Except where otherwise specified the constructs in this table are assumed to refer to all women or women-in-general. An investigator may of course define constructs limited to smaller classes of women, e.g. college women, black women, etc. It is also assumed here that respondents are always reporting their own views or beliefs. Each construct above might be paralleled by how the respondent believes various others feel ("most men," "most people," etc.)

a All entries in this table refer to substantive content, with no implication as to question format. All constructs operationalized in a multi-dimensional instrument however should employ a consistent format. A phrase or complete statement followed by a multiple-point one-dimensional rating scale is recommended for reasons discussed earlier.

divide these into even smaller units, or combine them into larger constructs. There is also a tendency to conceive of issues in terms of what seems logical, but the "psychologic" of respondents (Abelson, 1958) may be entirely different. In short, this or any other taxonomy is a starting point for empirical scale construction, and no more.

In defining a set of constructs, one must make a number of judgments. The constructs in Table 11.2 are purposely designed to refer to women per se as often as possible, in contrast to constructs or items based primarily on comparisons of the two sexes. As discussed earlier, it is arguable that most people see human beings as specifically male or female so that any evaluation of women is an inherent comparison with men.[4] Since research has shown that the sexes are not perceived as mirror images (S.L. Bem, 1974; Jenkin & Vroegh, 1969), the practice of asking only about contrasts is likely to provide a distorted image.

For some gender constructs, on the other hand, a reference to men is unavoidable, since complementary behavior patterns are involved. The taxonomy seen here, however, has women as its central focus. Sets of constructs concerning "sex roles" or "men" would overlap with those in Table 11.2, and would also introduce issues not applicable at all. (For some recent discussions of male sex-role issues, see Brannon, 1976b; David & Brannon, 1976; Pleck & Sawyer, 1974; Fasteau, 1974.)

Beyond nomothetic constructs.   Implicit in the preceding discussion of which items "go together" was an implication of strictly nomothetic solutions. In other words, we were assuming that it is reasonable to look for and measure a given attitude in every member of the population. Naturally we expect individual differences, but these will be reflected in the intensity or consistency with which each person manifests the attitude in question.

As early as 1937, Gordon Allport was arguing that this assumption was unrealistic and naive. Strictly speaking, he said, no two people ever have exactly the same attitude or trait; true, constructs can be found that are descriptive of many people but even then it's a mistake to apply them to all individuals. For some people, our preconceived attitude or trait may be irrelevant and inapplicable; to classify them as "medium" on the scale simply adds error variance and unreliability to the data.

The problem with this insight is that it seems at first to rule out psychological measurement. As one psychologist explained, "Of course it's true but it's one of those truths that can't be accepted." Thus, for decades, psychology has devoted itself to the search for nomothetic constructs and laws: things that are relatively true of people-in-general, terms, and explanations that account for as much variance as possible without seeking to capture the exact essence and dynamic of any one individual. To most of us, this *is* scientific psychology. The nomothetic assumption has taken us a long way, and there remains vast potential for improvement. Since real people do not actually have generalized nomothetic attitudes, however, it stands to reason that we could understand them better if we could work with the dispositions they really do have.

A purely individualized idiographic psychology isn't feasible at present. It would allow subjects to somehow describe their own unique attitudes and traits, with every quirk and peculiarity, as well as situations and objects for which each such attitude is psychologically relevant. It is not necessary to go this far, however. Suppose that for whatever reason an investigator wishes to study a particular attitude, such as "opposition to hiring mothers of young children." Recognizing that not all people will have a coherent attitude that fits this definition, the investigator could first set out to find those who do. Recognizing that the attitude may not be relevant to certain cases for all people, the investigator could locate those for whom it is. Psychology would thus deal with "some of the people, some of the time" . . . but in those cases might not its explanatory power rise dramatically?

After lying neglected for nearly 40 years, Allport's insight has been rediscovered and applied to psychological measurement. D.J. Bem and Allen (1974), using a technique based on the variance of responses to items measuring the same construct across many situations, looked for subjects who did and did not appear to have the cross-situational traits of *friendliness* and *conscientiousness.* Next, they measured a series of overt behaviors relevant to these traits, quite independently of the scale responses. The standard nomothetic trait measures, using all subjects, could predict friendly behavior at only $r = -.06$, and conscientious behavior at only $r = -.12$. As usual, paper-and-pencil measures seemed to have no relation to behavior. For those 50% of the subjects who had seemed to have the cross-situational traits defined by the scales, the same correlations were $+.61$ and $+.43$!

Much more work remains to be done with this new approach, but it seems clear that we should not forever assume that each attitude we measure has to be meaningful for every individual. Without going all the way toward personalized measurement for every subject, we can easily move in that direction, with substantial gains in explanatory power in prospect. Scales may be developed to apply only to some people, together with empirical decision rules for applicability. With a large number of such scales, considerable tailoring to the individual will be possible with no special effort. This is another powerful argument for multidimensional inventories.

Measuring Attitudes about Women: Why Bother?

Why measure attitudes? The earliest empirical use of this term was tied to the fact that certain "mental sets" seemed to affect behavior (specifically, reaction time: Lange, 1888). The basic rationale for studying attitudes has in fact always been that these mental constructs must have quite a bit to do with overt, real-life behaviors. "Words are actions in miniature," stated one early author. "Hence, by the use of questions and answers we can obtain information about a vast number of actions in a short time" (quoted in Hyman, Cobb, and Feldman, 1954). "The actions of the individual," an introductory textbook noted, "are governed to a large extent by his [sic] attitudes" (Krech, Crutchfield, & Ballackey, 1962).

This seemingly reasonable assumption began to unravel in the 1960s; and by the early 1970s, it was on the verge of abandonment in many quarters. The measurement of *racial prejudice,* in particular, the focus of so many attitude studies, had proven to be such a disaster that it gradually brought the entire concept of attitude into disrepute. In brief, what happened was that efforts to predict race-related behavior, on the basis of prejudice measures met such repeated and dramatic failures that the issue of behavior prediction could no longer be avoided. The first such study, by LaPiere (1934), discovered that responses to a mailed questionnaire about accepting Chinese customers were totally at variance with the real behaviors directly observed in the same establishments. There followed a gradually accelerating number of such studies (Saenger & Gilbert, 1950; Bray, 1950; DeFleur & Westie, 1958; Linn, 1965; Berg, 1966; Fendrich, 1967; McGrew, 1967; Warner & DeFleur, 1969; DeFriese & Ford, 1969; and others), which almost invariably found low or zero correlations between prejudice measures and independently observed racial behaviors. In each case, the investigators had persuasive explanations for what had gone wrong; yet the next study produced no better results. With the passage of years and accumulations of failures, reviews began to draw increasingly ominous and general conclusions:

- Studies on the relation of attitudes and behavior almost consistently resulted in the conclusion that attitudes are a poor predictor of behavior (Ehrlich, 1969).

- Most researchers had little success in predicting behavior from attitudes toward ethnic groups (Brigham, 1972).

- The stipulation of a direct attitude-behavior relationship . . . became increasingly untenable (Azjen, 1971).

- Numerous studies, especially in race relations, were devoted to this issue, ending almost invariably in negative or ambiguous results (Weitz, 1972).

- There was a growing awareness among investigators that attitudes tend to be unrelated to overt behaviors (Fishbein & Azjen, 1972).

- Although attitude is frequently considered as a predisposition to behavior, periodic reviews noted the failure of attitude measures to predict behavior (Sample & Warland, 1973).

- Again and again it was demonstrated that there is little relationship between attitudes and overt behavior (Brislin & Olmstead, 1973).

Developments in experimental social psychology were meanwhile establishing the relative *ease* and *power* with which external social and situational forces could influence behavior: The studies of conformity by Asch (1951), compliance by Milgram (1963), subject passivity by Orne (1962), and bystander nonintervention by Latane and Darley (1968) were only some of the many contributions to this literature. When it was discovered that forced behavioral change could actually change attitudes (Cohen, 1964; Insko, 1968)—that instead of standing up for what they believed, subjects appeared to believe whatever they'd been paid to stand up for—the humiliation was complete. The behavioral tail had begun to wag the attitudinal dog.

The stage was thus set for the radical, but seemingly defensible, view that attitudes were largely irrelevant to a psychology of behavior; they existed, if at all, as a sort of epiphenomenological scum on the surface of mental life. In an influential review, Wicker (1969) concluded that there was "little evidence to support the postulated existence of stable, underlying attitudes within the individual." This was followed by Tarter's (1970) review, in which tey concluded that "attitudes are just another of the many hypothetical and largely unproduc-

tive mental states that behavioral scientists have tried to measure and use in prediction of overt behavior." As to the value of careful attitude measurement, Tarter said: "Since (attitudes) play no real role in behavior, an intense nothing contributes no more than a moderate nothing" (pp. 276-277).

The outright dismissal of the attitude concept appears to have been a case of premature burial. Some recent empirical studies have been able to identify a relationship between attitude measures and overt behavior, ranging up to 80% predictability over three months time (Goodmonson & Glaudin, 1971; Wicker, 1971; Brannon, Cyphers, Hesse, Hesselbart, Kean, Schuman, Vicarro & Wright, 1973; review by Brannon, 1976a). These encouraging results can be attributed to several conceptual and methodological refinements, to be discussed shortly. In the process of attacking the attitude concept, however, the new behaviorist challenge dramatically exposed a fundamental weakness of the attitude theory and measurement literature, a weakness that is still apparent in virtually every-thing one reads about attitudes. I am referring to the almost universal absence of any more than perfunctory interest in the *validity* of psychological measure-ment.

Attitude Scale Validity

Validity refers generally, of course, to any meaningful evidence that an instru-ment is in fact measuring the construct it was intended to measure. Prediction of relevant behaviors toward the attitude object is not the only acceptable evidence of validity, but it is certainly the best. Recall that the basic evidence that theorists usually cite for the existence of attitudes is "a pattern of consistency in a person's responses to a social object." Nonetheless, as McNemar noted bluntly over 30 years ago,

Although complex and "high sounding" definitions of attitudes are pro-posed, practically all attitude research is on the verbal level. The validity of attitude measures, i.e., the degree of the relationship between overt non-verbal and verbal behavior, is not known, and apparently is of little inter-est to most investigators. Some investigators have sidestepped the problem of validity by denying that anything exists beyond the verbal expressions,

hence there is no problem of validity. Others have adopted the idea that scales or questions test whatever they test, so why worry (McNemar, 1946; quoted by Wicker, 1969, p. 45).

It is only necessary to brouse through any collection of current attitude scales (Robinson & Shaver, 1973; Robinson, Rush & Head, 1968; Bonjean, Hill, & McLemore, 1967; Shaw & Wright, 1967; Miller, 1964) to note the astonishing degree to which McNemar's trenchant observation remains true today. Frequently, there is no discussion whatsoever concerning validity; where evidence is cited, it is more often than not of the three types listed below, all next-to-irrelevant to the hard issues of validity.

1. *Self-reports and other dubious indices of behavior.*   Studies that have compared self-reports of behavior with independent observations of the same behavior have long shown that substantial minorities of subjects give inaccurate reports. Even on such simple matters as having voted in the last election, owning a driver's license, purchasing a brand of cereal, or attending a particular meeting, from 10% to 30% of all respondents give factually invalid reports (Dean, 1958; Jenkins & Corbin, 1938; Parry & Crossley, 1950). On behaviors more strongly tied to social desirability, the percentages giving false reports are even higher. Nonetheless, some investigators have "validated" attitude scales by relating them to self-reports of church attendance, cheating on exams, use of birth control, financial contributions, or participating in civic activities.

2. *"Known-group validation."*   Members of two overtly opposing-value groups (ministerial students and atheists; radical feminists and "Total Woman" graduates) are given an attitude scale patently applicable to the dimension separating them. If they obtain significantly different scores, the scale is said to be "validated." One must virtually kneel in awe at the triviality of such a demonstration. To my knowledge, no scale has ever failed the test of known-group validation. Part of the reason for this is that the exercise is largely circular: The groups' values are "known" mainly on the basis of their verbal pronouncements and public positions, therefore the demonstration amounts to showing that they *say* the same things on attitude scales that they usually say in other ways.

3. *Correlations with other paper-and-pencil instruments.*   While substantively interesting, at best, such findings have modest standing as evidence of validity. Communalities of method variance can easily inflate such correlations, and it is not uncommon to see new measures "validated" by moderate (.40-.50) correlations with older measures for which claims to validity are made sparingly. The result is a closed system of interrelated paper-and-pencil measures, the relationship of which to behavior in the real world is unknown.

Some writers (e.g., Messick, 1975) slightly disparage predictions of behavior as being narrowly tied to a particular criterion. Stress is laid instead on the broader process of "construct validation," involving multiple checks on the relation between a measure and the theory underlying it. Since for most interesting psychological constructs (anxiety, submissiveness, etc.), there is no one perfect behavioral criterion, and the construct subsumes a great many activities and situations, the investigator must look at a variety of lines of evidence. I have no quarrel at all with the strategy of construct validity, but believe that most of its proponents have seriously understated, or underestimated, the importance of relating verbal measures to behaviors. The multitrait-multimethod matrix introduced by Campbell and Fisk (1959), for example, has been widely admired; it ostensibly provides both convergent and discriminant evidence of validity in one convenient table. The convergent evidence, however, amounts to no more than a finding of "substantial" correlations between measures of the same construct while using "different" methods. In many favorably cited examples, *all such methods consisted of paper-and-pencil rating scales.* I believe that convergent evidence confined to paper-and-pencil measures has relatively little value. In fairness, Campbell and Fisk called for "maximally different" methods, including direct observations of behavior. But, in the wave of admiration for the logic of their matrix, the much more basic need to validate psychological measures by reference to overt behaviors received little emphasis and was widely overlooked.

Current Evidence for Validity of Gender-Attitude Measures

Validational evidence of any kind is generally lacking for current gender-attitude measures. A few scales have been validated by the "known groups" method (Dempewolfe, 1974a; Kando, 1972; Kirkpatrick, 1936a). Correlations with other paper-and-pencil construct measures have been reported often (Centers, 1963; Dempewolfe, 1974b; Ellis & Bentler, 1973; Goldberg, 1974; Gump, 1972; Nadler & Morrow, 1959; Brannon & Dull, Note 6). Spence and Helmreich (1972a) reported some interesting second-order relations between attitudes toward women and reactions to video-taped female stimuli; the dependent variable was also a paper-and-pencil measure, however. Hymer and Atkins (1973) reported a relation between women's feminist attitudes and the tendency to "respond to aggression" with verbal *retaliation,* again measured with a paper-and-pencil instrument.

A few studies have attempted to relate attitude measures to independently measured overt behavior. Ditmar, Mueller, and Mitchell (Note 9) predicted and found a negative relation between feminist attitudes and conformity in heterosexual groups for 24 high-school women; feminism, as measured by the Dempewolfe (1974a) scale, was correlated -.35 with experimental conformity to unanimous group pressure.

Kenkel (1959) failed, however, to find a consistent relationship between the "traditional family ideology" scale (Levinson & Huffman, 1955) and laboratory bargaining behavior in married couples as coded by the Bales (1951) interaction scheme. Hoffman (1960) reported another study with similar negative results. These artificial bargaining situations may elicit unnatural behaviors; moreover, the hypothesized relationships among present attitudes, observed bargaining patterns, and prior experience with the spouse are not made sufficiently clear in either case.

Baruch (1972) found no relation ($r = .12$, n.s.) between an (unreported) attitudes-toward-dual-role scale and individual differences in evaluation bias derived from a Goldberg (1968) type of paradigm. Unfortunately, however, no evaluation bias toward females was found in this sample overall, one of the few failures to replicate the Goldberg effect, and so the meaning of individual differences on the measure is not entirely clear.

Auerbach and Geckenbach (Note 1) found that "sexist females," defined as those above the median on the Ellis and Bentler (1973) scale of sex-role traditionalism, required more trials to learn a pairing of photographs with nonsense syllables than did less sexist females. There was no such effect for males.

An unpublished study by Brannon (Note 7) found a small but significant behavioral effect following a successful attitude-change manipulation. An experimental interview-procedure with Brooklyn housewives produced a significant change toward modest agreement with feminist objectives and perceptions. A subsequent and ostensibly unconnected mailing offering subscriptions to a women's newsletter, received more affirmative replies from women in the experimental interview condition than in the control interview conditions.

The preceding studies concerned attitudes toward "women," "feminism," or "sex roles" in general; what about measures of personality that call for self-evaluation on items scored for gender stereotyped content? Clarkson et al. (1970) reported the interesting, if ambiguous, finding that Catholic mothers who described themselves as high on instrumental/competence traits had significantly fewer children (3.1) than mothers who rated themselves lower on these factors

(3.9). The interpretation is unclear, since the sense of competency might be adversely affected by family size as readily as vice versa! There is separate evidence, however, that unmarried Catholic college women who are high in competency also plan to have fewer children than those lower in competency (Broverman, Vogel, Broverman, Clarkson, & Rosenkrantz, 1972, p. 73). The difference reported by Clarkson et al. (1970) is not large, but considering the sample's limitation to families with two or more children, and the many obvious influences on family size other than mother's personality, it is interesting evidence.

The most extensive and sophisticated evidence relating gender-aspects of self-evaluations to overt behavior is seen in a recent series of studies by Bem (1974) and her associates, using the Bem Sex-Role Inventory (BSRI). This research is reviewed by Bem in Chapter 1 of Volume 1, so no effort will be made to summarize it here. It does, however, include a number of overt behaviors—conformity, playing with a kitten, responding to a human baby, comforting a lonely transfer student, and others—each measured independently and quite objectively. The reported relationships are not all especially strong, but taken together, they provide ample behavioral evidence for the construct validity of the BSRI—the only gender-related instrument for which this statement can currently be made.

To summarize this brief review, behavioral validation evidence for gender-attitude measures is rare, inconsistent, and weak. A few measures have generated significant relationships in the predicted direction, but speaking in terms of predictive power rather than mere significance, not one of them could be remotely considered "behaviorally validated." The truly meaningful question of validity is not whether an instrument measures a construct *at all*, but how well it measures it. Viewed from this simple and realistic perspective, the current status of gender-attitude measures is totally unvalidated. (In fairness, much the same thing must be said of virtually every category of attitude measure employed by psychology today.)

Lessons Learned from Predicting Behavior

For years, virtually all "improvements" in attitude-measuring instruments and scaling methods have been based primarily on showing increments in *reliability* (the Likert-scale format, summative scoring procedure, number of scale-points, etc.). Since validity was a pipe-dream anyway, the relative merits of different procedures for improving validity were hardly a matter of interest. In recent years, an increasing volume of research has dealt with the prediction of behavior, and the obtained correlations have begun to reach more respectable levels. Some of the techniques for achieving this are essentially trivial and offer no new insights into the measurement process: choose behaviors that are ritualized, and highly stable, or behaviors that are utterly trivial to the individual; narrow the time interval to a few seconds, and ask the subjects *precisely* what they plan to do next (Ajzen & Fishbein, 1970). Other developments are more generally promising because they point to specific improvements that can be made in the quantification of psychological constructs (For a more extensive review of these issues see Brannon, 1976a.):

Congruence. One of many studies that failed to find a relation between prejudice and social behavior was reported by Bray in 1950. Bray's attitude measure was the antiquated Likert scale (1932) with its particular emphasis on lynching and mob violence against blacks. The behavior to be predicted was whether white undergraduates at Yale, in 1950, could be influenced by the performance of a well-dressed black confederate on a test of visual perception. Bray obviously thought that "a prejudice scale" should predict the extent of this influence; a close look at the individual times shows how ludicrous this hypothesized relationship actually was.

Brannon (1976, p. 152) distinguished three aspects of *congruence,* or the "fit" between attitudinal and behavioral indices: (a) substantive facts about issues and the connections that are implicit in the common-sense knowledge based on experience in a given culture; (b) level of generality, or the implicit reference to many objects and situations versus a single unique case; and (c) multi-item indices versus single questions.

In general, the more congruent an attitude measure is with a behavioral index, the more successful it is in predicting the behavior. Wicker (1969, p. 64) found, for example, that students' attitudes about *scientific research* had no relation to volunteering for a psychology experiment; attitudes about *psychological research* had a slightly higher relationship, and attitudes about *participating as a subject in psychological research* had a significant positive relationship. Recent studies that have proved most effective in predicting behavior (Goodmonson & Glaudin, 1971; Brannon et al., 1973) have invariably featured high congruence between measures.

One consequence of the congruence requirement is to strengthen the argument made earlier for content-homogeneous attitude scales. A measure with diverse-item contents cannot be highly congruent with any individual behavior of the kinds that are practical to observe and measure at present.

Conflict–questions.   Wicker (1971) was interested in predicting two kinds of objective behaviors: physical attendance at a Protestant midwestern church over a 10-month period, and financial contributions to the church during the same time. Both behaviors were carefully and objectively recorded without the awareness of the church members. Wicker then devised four different styles of paper-and-pencil attitude measures for predicting each behavior. A style that he called "influence of extraneous events" turned out to predict both attendance (.42) and contributions (.45) better than any other style. In this procedure, a series of hypothetical conflicts and distractions were described, and the respondent was asked to judge how such a conflict would affect ter behavior. "Would you attend church if you had weekend guests who didn't want to go?" "Would you still contribute money if the congregation voted to spend funds on a project you disapproved of?"

Brannon et al. (1973) predicted public petition-signing for or against "open housing legislation" over a three-month interval in a probability sample of all metropolitan Detroit, using a single interview question that was highly congruent with the content of the petitions. The question was based on the principle of making salient the basic value-conflict underlying most attitudes about open-housing legislation; that is, the unfairness of refusing to sell to a qualified buyer because of race versus the individual rights of homeowners to dispose of their private property as they choose. The single question posing this value-conflict was able to correctly predict 80% of all responses to petitions circulated three months later.

It is still premature to judge the merits of conflict questions, versus conventional questions (such as "How strongly do you feel about this belief?"), but there are theoretical reasons to believe that conflicts may be especially revealing. Schuman (1972) perceptively argued that while most white Americans now believe that racial discrimination is wrong, they also believe in *group harmony, economic success, paying attention to the opinions of one's neighbors, a good education for the children, keeping law and order,* and many other values:

Only to a true believer will any of these values win out in all situations, regardless of other values with which it competes. A few people will go to the stake for a single value, but history and common sense tell us that most people work out compromises, depending on the exact balance of positions (p. 352.)

The relative strengths of different values and attitudes may be more important than the absolute intensity of any one. While there are different ways to assess this, it may be that the individual question is the best place to pose a conflict to the subject.

Combining several attitude measures.   There is some evidence that better behavioral predictions are possible with a set of attitude measures than with a single index. In studies of voting in the 1956 Presidential election, attitudes toward Dwight D. Eisenhower were the best single predictor of votes ($r = .52$). However, a combination of this and five other political attitudes permitted even better prediction of final voting choice ($r = .71$; Campbell, Converse, Miller, & Stokes, 1964, p. 38). Brannon et al. (1973) significantly increased predictions of behavior by combining the effects of two different interview questions on different aspects of housing integration. DeYoung, Cattell, Gaborit, and Barton (1973) found that frequency of lovemaking (self-reported in daily logs) correlated no better than .27 with each of five separate personality measures. However, when the five were considered jointly, the relationship rose to .54.

Multivariate predictions are still rare in attitude research, but they seem to be an effective way to improve predictions of behavior, and they should increase with the development of multidimensional inventories. Since most techniques tend to capitalize somewhat on chance factors, cross-validation designs are very much in order.

Matching individuals with constructs.   In a previous section I discussed the development of procedures for going beyond nomothetic assumptions by isolating the individuals who have coherent and stable dispositions matching the hypothesized construct. This technique was derived from efforts to predict overt behavior with paper-and-pencil measures. It is doubtful that it would have been discovered, or would have demonstrated its empirical advantage, in a context limited to comparisons of paper-and-pencil measures.

Measuring Behaviors Toward Women

This is the crux of the matter, the bullet that psychologists must bite if the scientific study of attitudes, personality traits, and other dispositions is to advance beyond a parlor game of verbal interrelationships largely unrelated to the real world. Psychology is occasionally described as "the science of behavior," but the timidity with which attitude researchers have approached the step of actually measuring behavior is sometimes amazing. For example, no less an authority than Herbert Hyman (1969) wrote: "I do not think it would be too farfetched to obtain independent measures on the behavior of very small numbers of . . . contrasted types of respondents, thereby validating the procedure" (p. 23). Good Grief! Is it actually so difficult as all that? Not really, and as soon as researchers begin to recognize the necessity of measuring behavior directly, I think we may see an explosion of new studies along this line. After briefly clarifying what I mean by behavior, I will close with some suggestions for behavioral studies.

What is behavior?   Everybody has a sense of what is meant by "overt behavior," as opposed to purely verbal expressions of sentiment, but when we look clearly at the issue it is not so clear exactly what is and what isn't behavior, or *why*. Obviously, in a narrow and technical sense, checking an answer on an anonymous attitude questionnaire *is* an action. Why then does the phrase "overt behavior" connote something entirely different? Beyond occasionally noting this paradox (e.g., Kiesler, Collins, & Miller, 1969, p. 23), psychologists have offered surprisingly little guidance as to what exactly they mean by "behavior." The first distinctions one thinks of—language versus nonlanguage, symbolic versus direct, physical presence versus absence of the target object—do not hold up under close analysis. Without developing the argument fully here, I believe that the most important criterion is the *perceived consequence* of an action to the individual. Consequences may take many forms, but any action—verbal or physical—which people see as likely to have important consequences to them personally, or to others they care about, is generally viewed and treated as "behavior" by everyone concerned. (For a more detailed discussion of this argument, see Brannon, 1976a, pp. 148-151.)

The most important aspect of this model is that "behavioralness" is not a yes-or-no proposition, but a relative attributional quality that varies roughly in proportion to the perceived consequences of a given action. One may conceive of a continuum along which various behavioral measures vary. Those that people invariably see as having high consequence (joining the army, signing a contract, donating $1,000 to a cause) are emphatically "overt behavior." Even those that have lower consequences (attending a meeting, signing a controversial petition, donating $1.00 to a cause) partake in part of this behavioral quality, and should be influenced in proportion by the same factors that influence more consequential actions.

Viewed in this way, there is a wide range of useful behavioral measures available to the psychologist. There is still a significant gap, however, between virtually any index of overt behavior and the kinds of responses elicited by a typical verbal attitude measure, of the kinds discussed earlier in this chapter. Standard procedures of attitude measurement (anonymity, explanations of purely scientific interest, interviewer neutrality, etc.) go to considerable lengths to assure respondents that what they say will have *no* personal consequences whatsoever, so that they may answer without regard to utilitarian calculations. This then is the long-sought attitude-behavior gap; or perhaps we might say "validity gulch." It may seem but a small leap across it, from one form of measure to another, but the bleached bones of all those early attitude scales should be ample warning that there is no automatic link between unconstrained sentiments and actions with consequences.

Generic Behavioral Measures

There are several forms of behavior, as defined above, that are applicable to a variety of different contents and issues:

Signing one's name to a document.   In American society, signing "on the dotted line" is widely viewed as a significant commitment—for example, contracts, checks, and agreements. DeFleur & Westie (1958) used signatures on a legal-looking document as a behavioral measure and found that subjects perceived the request as extremely realistic and stress-producing. Signing a controversial public petition has been used as a behavioral commitment by several investigators (DeFriese & Ford, 1969; Kamenetzky, Burgess, & Rowan, 1956; Silverman & Cochrane, 1971), and a considerable amount is now known about the factors influencing petition signing (Blake, Mouton, & Hain, 1956; Helson, Blake, & Mouton, 1958). The implicit consequences of signing may also be made

more salient to the respondent; Brannon et al. (1973) found that while 85% of
one group signed a public petition, only 59% would agree to let their signatures
appear in a newspaper advertisement presenting the same petition to the general
public.

Petitions concerning abortion, sex discrimination, salaries, day care, marriage
laws, responsibilities for children, divorce, rape, and many other issues relevant
to women offer a rich and largely untouched source of behavioral data.

Donating money to a cause. This hasn't been used to my knowledge, but it
could and should be. (Isn't "put your money where your mouth is" the street-
corner method of demanding behavioral validity?) Money is nicely quantitative:
the more one gives, the greater the behavioral commitment—assuming equal
resources to start with. One way around that might be to give each subject an
equal amount to "distribute" among various charities and causes (the Heart
Fund, the Boy Scouts, pro-ERA, anti-ERA, etc.), with the funds to be provided
by a fictitious, benevolent foundation. Or subjects might simply vote on how to
divide a class charity fund among competing organizations and causes.

Buying cause-related materials. The business world has always regarded pur-
chases as the ultimate criterion of popularity. Again there's the problem of unequal resources, but if the price is low enough, and every member of the sample
is equally solicited, a good case can be made for the meaningfulness of purchasing decisions. Brannon and Safran (Note 48) offered a trial issue of a new
"women's news digest" for the sum of 50c. No money was actually collected in
this case, but women were asked to sign order cards pledging them to pay if the
trial issue was successfully published. (It wasn't, and apologies were sent to all
concerned.) There is no reason, however, why real subscriptions to *Ms.* magazine, *Majority Reports, Off Our Backs, Rough Times, Bread and Roses,
K.N.O.W. News,* and my own favorite, the *A.W.P. Newsletter,* can't be legitimately hawked to a selected audience in the service of behavioral data.

Volunteering time to causes. One's time is obviously a valuable resource to
contribute, but the usual problem of equal initial resources is a serious one. It
might be possible to adapt a subject-pool or class-project requirement to permit
activities related to different issues: preparing statistics on sex discrimination,
researching rape laws, designing a display against or for the ERA, traffic safety,
Bicentennial activities, and so on. Choice of what-to-work-on could be

strengthened as an index by varying the "estimated" number of hours allotted to each project on the sign-up sheets.

Observation of routine interactional behavior. This, of course, is a traditional measurement technique (outside the attitude area) for which a huge literature is available. The only problem, and not a major one, is thinking of observable behavior that can have a clearly hypothesized relationship to some particular mental construct toward women. Some possibilities would include interrupting women in conversation (Zimmerman & West, 1975), dominating conversations with women (Kester, 1972), power-assertive touching (Henley, 1973), not responding to women's points in group discussions, and many others. Such issues as habit strength and situational factors will pose interpretational complexities, but this is a promising, accessible, and interesting source of behavioral data.

Specifically Contrived Behavioral Measures

Not every issue concerning women can be approached with one of the all-purpose behavioral measures mentioned above, but it is usually (always?) possible to design a feasible behavioral measure relevant to the concept of interest. The book by Webb, Campbell, Schwartz, and Sechrest (1966) is one source of ideas for imagining and then quantifying relevant behaviors. The authors' examples deal not at all with women's issues, but the procedures are often ingenious. Some more relevant proposals are discussed below.

Game or negotiation outcomes. Dominance in rats is measured by starting two rats from each end of a narrow tube at the same time. Among humans, we may give each person a (private) goal, and equal (or different) financial contingencies, and let them negotiate to a mutually accepted outcome. The outcomes themselves may be taken as the behavioral data, but the technique can be richened by behavioral observations of the process of arriving at the final outcome. This general procedure has been used to study wife-husband power relationships (e.g., Kenkel, 1959), but it is obviously applicable to any mixed-sex or same-sex pairs, triads, or small groups.

Child socialization. Observing adults with children—their own or someone else's—is a rich source of behavioral data. There is actually a large literature of this type, but almost none of it has approached the data from the validational perspective I am proposing. Serbin, O'Leary, Kent, and Tonick (1973) observed, for example, that nursery school teachers responded differently on the average to similar aggressive misbehaviors by boys and girls: "soft" reprimands to girls; loud, extended, and "directive" instructions to boys. In this, as in most such studies, behavior variations among teachers were not examined, and no effort was made to relate behavior differences to attitudinal or other individual differences. There is no good reason why such studies cannot be done. Observations of parents' individual tendencies to treat sons and daughters differently would, of course, be especially interesting from this perspective.

Chivalry. If this attitude construct should be of interest, why not directly observe whether a man rises when a woman enters the room? Helps put on coats? Opens doors? Lights cigarettes? With a little effort, numerous situations can be contrived to give the chivalrous impulse its full opportunity to emerge.

Relative importance of physical attractiveness. Attractiveness is an easy variable to manipulate with the simple use of photographs, pretested and rated by subjects from the same population as the behavioral sample. Behavioral responses to people one hasn't actually met are easy to obtain in several ways: choosing whom to include in a proposed discussion group, by means of comparing "application forms"; assigning cash prizes to people for various creative or objective accomplishments; and so on. (As long as respondents can be made to believe that their ratings aren't merely personal opinions, but will have some degree of influence on rewards given to the people they're evaluating, the ratings have meaning as behavioral responses.) By combining photographs of varying attractiveness with lists of accomplishments, pretested without the photographs, a nice quantitative calibration of the effects of attractiveness could be made.

Evaluation bias against women per se. To me, one of the most fascinating and significant phenomena documented by feminist psychology is still the evaluation bias effect first reported by Goldberg (1968). The *identical* intellectual or creative performance is perceived as better when accomplished by a man than by a woman. This is a simple but basic phenomenon, seen in both sexes, which has some interesting implications for social policy (such, for example, as supporting *quotas* for women rather than trusting case-by-case evaluations of merit across sex lines). Evaluation bias—as an individual behavioral difference—has received virtually no attention, and we know nothing about its relationship to person-ality and attitudinal variables. All studies to date, with the exception of Baruch (1972), have focused on merely showing that sex bias exists in a total sample.

Evaluation bias might plausibly be linked with several dimensions of attitudes concerning women in general, women's task performance, and other conceptual factors. Conversely, a verbal measure or battery successfully validated against behavioral sex bias would have interesting practical and research applications. One program of research directed toward achieving this, with respect to bias against women in employment decisions, is now being developed by the author with Esther Juni, Kathy Grady, Arthur Kurtz, Marilyn Rall, Sharon Klinebergy, Glen Hass, Terry Landau, and students at Brooklyn College, CUNY. Many more such efforts will clearly be needed before the conceptual bases of sex bias are understood.

Scaling Behaviors

The mystique of behavior has been such in the past that virtually any nonver-bal observation, no matter how crude, was happily accepted as a criterion of "real-world overt behavior." (Even unconfirmed *self-reports,* obviously and demonstrably biased, often constitute the "behaviors" referred to in titles of recent articles.) An investigator with a single observation of a single dichotomous behavior (the student did or did not *vote;* the manager did or did not show the *apartment* to a black couple) could point with pride to having measured behav-ior at all, rather than feeling apologetic for the stark simplicity of the measure. Yet, behavioral measures (like any others) are logically subject to error, mislabel-ing, and overgenerality. A second, third, and fourth observation of the same behavior choice might yield a different conclusion than a single observation. At a bare minimum, repeated observations would provide reliability estimates and increased test variance.

If what one really wants to assess is "unprejudiced behavior," however, or chivalrous inclinations, or ignoring women, or supporting the feminist move-ment, the reliance on any one behavioral criterion should be questioned. A variety of related actions, all apparently exemplifying the behavioral construct as defined, should be measured and combined to form a behavioral index. As with attitude-scale construction, furthermore, there is no necessity to retain each of the measures determined in advance. A process analogous to item analysis can determine which measures fail to covary with the others, suggesting deletion of these measures or reformulation of the behavioral construct.

As LaPiere (1934) observed when the general surge of paper-and-pencil attitude measures was just getting under way:

> The questionnaire is cheap, easy and mechanical. The study of human *behavior* is time consuming, intellectually fatiguing, and depends for its success on the ability of the investigator. Yet it would seem far more worthwhile to make a shrewd guess regarding that which is essential than to accurately measure that which is likely to prove quite irrelevant. (p. 237.)

The contention of this paper is a bit more optimistic. By carefully operationalizing both behavior responses (i.e., those with perceived consequences) and expressions of verbal sentiments, we can discover the detailed relation of the latter to the former, contingent on all the complexities and situational constraints we know to be true of human behavior. Put simply, there is ultimately no point in measuring attitudes at all unless they are relevant to events in the real world about us. No one who introspects about the origins of their own behavior can doubt that this is the case, but it is time for psychology to go cold turkey and break its long addiction to armchair typologies and unverified abstractions.

REFERENCE NOTES

1. Auerback, S.M., & Gackenbach, J.I. The effects of individual differences in sexism and sex on learning of nonsense syllables paired with pictured situations differing in sex-role appropriateness. Unpublished manuscript, Virginia Commonwealth University, 1975.
2. Basow, S.A., & Howe, K.G. Sex and sex-role attitudes of college students as factors affecting the influence of role models. Paper presented at the meeting of the Eastern Psychological Association, Chicago, August, 1975.
3. Beckman, L.J., & Houser, B.B. Employed women's attitudes toward women's liberation, family decision-making and tasks. Paper presented at the meeting of the American Psychological Association, Chicago, August, 1975.

4. Bem, S.L. Psychology looks at sex roles: Where have all the androgynous people gone? Paper presented at the U.C.L.A. Symposium on Women, Los Angeles, May, 1972.

5. Berzins, J.I. New perspectives on sex roles and personality dimensions. Paper presented at the meeting of the American Psychological Association, Chicago, September, 1975.

6. Brannon, R., & Dull, C.Y. Racism, sexism, and fascism of a military sample of white males: Empirical interrelationships. Paper presented at the meeting of the American Psychological Association, Washington, September, 1971.

7. Brannon, R. Attitude change in the context of an interview. Paper presented at the meeting of the Eastern Psychological Association, New York, April, 1975.

8. Cherulnik, P.D., & McAndrew, F.T. Sex-role stereotype and favorability of impressions of men and women. Paper presented at the meeting of the Eastern Psychological Association, New York, April, 1975.

9. Ditmar, F., Mueller, N., & Mitchell, J. Females' attitudes toward feminism and their conformity in heterosexual groups. Paper presented at the meeting of the American Psychological Association, Chicago, Septermber, 1975.

10. Fay, T.L. Ideal and typical males and females: Stereotypes in three cultures. Paper presented at the meeting of the American Psychological Association, Chicago, September, 1975.

11. Farrell, W.T. The political potential of the women's liberation movement as indicated by its effectiveness in changing man's attitudes. Unpublished doctoral dissertation, New York University, 1974.

12. Frieze, I.H. Changing self images and sex-role stereotypes in college women. Paper presented at the meeting of the American Psychological Association, New Orleans, September, 1974.

13. Gaudreau, P. Bem sex-role inventory validation study. Paper presented at the meeting of the American Psychological Association, Chicago, September, 1975.

14. Gruzen, J. The relationship of attitudes toward women to political orientation and sexual sophistication. Paper presented at the meeting of the American Psychological Association, San Francisco, August, 1970.

15. Gump, J.P. A comparative analysis of black and white female sex-role attitudes. Paper presented at the meeting of the American Psychological Association, San Francisco, 1970.

16. Hill, C.E., Adelstein, D., & Carter, J. Similarity of friends on the androgyny scale. Paper presented at the meeting of the American Psychological Association, Chicago, September, 1975.

17. Kelly, J.A., & Worell, L. The relation of sex-role categories to dimensions of parental behavior. Paper presented at the meeting of American Psychological Association, Chicago, September, 1975.

18. Lunneborg, P.W. Trying to take sex role out of self-concept. Paper presented at the meeting of the American Psychological Association, Chicago, September, 1975.

19. Mason, K.O., Czajka, J., & Arber, S. Recent change in women's sex-role attitudes. Unpublished manuscript, University of Michigan, Population Studies Center, 1225 S. University Avenue, Ann Arbor, Michigan 48104, 1974.

20. Mason, K.O., & Bumpass, L.L. Women's sex-role attitudes in the United States, 1970. Paper presented at the meeting of the American Sociological Association, New York, August, 1973.

21. Nevill, D.D. Sex roles and personality correlates. Paper presented at the meeting of the American Psychological Association, Chicago, September, 1975.

22. O'Leary, V.E., & Harrison, A.O. Sex-role stereotypes as a function of race and sex. Paper presented at the meeting of the American Psychological Association, Chicago, September, 1975.

23. Pincus, F.L. The relationship between racism, sexism, authoritarianism, powerlessness and anti-homosexuality. Paper presented at the meeting of the American Psychological Association, Washington, September, 1971.

24. Pleck, J.H. Male threat from female competence: An experimental study in college dating couples. Doctoral dissertation, Harvard University, University Microfilms No. 74-11,721, Ann Arbor, Michigan, 1974.

25. Pleck, J.H. Males' traditional attitudes toward women: Correlates of adjustment or maladjustment? Unpublished manuscript, Institute for Social Research, University of Michigan, Ann Arbor, Michigan, 1975.

26. Ronco, W. Public opinion about women and the family: Has anything really changed? Unpublished manuscript, Center for the Study of Public Policy, Cambridge, Mass., 1973.

27. Siiter, R., & Unger, R.K. Ethnic differences in sex-role stereotypes. Paper presented at the meeting of the American Psychological Association, Chicago, September, 1975.

28. Turner, B.F., & Turner, C.B. Race and sex differences in evaluating women. Paper presented at the meeting of the American Psychological Association, New Orleans, September, 1974.
29. Unger, R.K., & Siiter, R. Sex-role stereotypes: The weight of a "grain of truth." Paper presented at the meeting of the Eastern Psychological Association, Philadelphia, April, 1974.
30. Vroegh, K. Young children's sex role and knowledge of sex stereotypes. Paper presented at the meeting of the American Psychological Association, Chicago, September, 1975.
31. Welling, M.A. A new androgyny measure derived from the personality research form. Paper presented at the meeting of the American Psychological Association, Chicago, September, 1975.
32. Wetter, R.E. Levels of self-esteem associated with four sex role categories. Paper presented at the meeting of the American Psychological Association, Chicago, September, 1975.
33. Woods, M.M. The relation of sex-role categories to autobiographical factors. Paper presented at the meeting of the American Psychological Association, Chicago, September, 1975.
34. Worell, J. Issues in the measurement and development of sex-role styles. Paper presented at the meeting of the American Psychological Association, Chicago, September, 1975.
35. Worell, J., & Worell, L. Supporters and opposers of women's liberation: Some personality correlates. Paper presented at the meeting of the American Psychological Association, Washington, September, 1971.
36. Zimmer, M., & Krupat, E. Sex-role stereotypes and the effect of labeling upon person perception. Paper presented at the meeting of the Eastern Psychological Association, New York, April, 1975.
37. Dorros, K., & Follet, J. Prejudice towards women as revealed by male college students. Unpublished manuscript, 1969.
38. Will, J.Z., Self, P., & Datan, N. Maternal behavior and sex of infant. Unpublished manuscript, West Virginia University, 1975.
39. Bar-Tal, D., & Saxe, L. Effects of physical attractiveness on the perception of couples. Paper presented at the meeting of the American Psychological Association, New Orleans, August, 1974.
40. Caplan, P.J. Sex and other factors as determinants of report of learning problems. Paper presented at the meeting of the American Psychological Association, New Orleans, August, 1974.

41. Kirchner, E.P. Subject and examiner sex: Effects on the actual and judged test performance of preschool children. Paper presented at the meeting of the Eastern Psychological Association, New York, April, 1975.

42. Whitaker, S.L. Sex differences in self-esteem as a function of assigned masculine and feminine characteristics. Unpublished manuscript, Governors State University, Park Forest South, Ill., 1974.

43. Grady, K. Androgyny reconsidered. Paper presented at the meeting of the Eastern Psychological Association, New York, April, 1975.

44. Grady K., Miransky, J.L., & Mulvey, M.A. A nonverbal measure of social dominance. Paper presented at the meeting of the American Psychological Association, Washington, September, 1976.

45. Campbell, D.T. The generality of social attitudes. Doctoral dissertation, University of California, Berkeley, 1947.

46. Collins, M.E., & Haupt, E.J. Factor analysis of prejudice items. Unpublished report, Research Center for Human Relations, New York University, 1965.

47. Jackson, D.N. Discriminantly valid personality measures: Some propositions. Paper presented at the meeting of the American Psychological Association, Chicago, August, 1975.

48. Brannon, R., & Safran, P. Persistence of attitude change following a field experiment. Unpublished study, 1973.

REFERENCES

Abelson, R.P. A technique and a model for multi-dimensional attitude scaling. *Public Opinion Quarterly*, 1954, *18*, 405-418.

Abelson, R.P., & Rosenberg, M.J. Symbolic psycho-logic: a model of attitudinal cognition. *Behavioral Science*, 1958, *3*, 1-13.

Ackerman, N.W. & Jahoda, M. Anti-semitism and emotional disorder. *New York:* Harper & Row, 1950.

Ajzen, I. Attitudinal vs. normative messages: An investigation of the differential effects of persuasive communications on behavior. *Sociometry*, 1971, *24*, 263-280.

Ajzen, I., & Fishbein, M. The prediction of behavior from attitudinal and normative variables. *Journal of Personality and Social Psychology*, 1970, *6*, 466-487.

Allport, G.W. Attitudes. In C. Murchison (Ed.), *A handbook of social psychology*. Clark University Press, 1935.

Allport, G.W. *Personality: A psychological interpretation.* New York: Holt, Rinehart and Winston, 1937.

Allport, G.W. *The nature of prejudice* (abridged). New York: Doubleday-Anchor, 1958. (Originally published, 1954.)

Allport, G.W. *Pattern and growth in personality.* New York: Holt, Rinehart & Winston, 1961.

American Psychological Association. *Standards for education and psychological tests and manuals.* Washington, D.C.: American Psychological Association, 1966.

Anastasi, A. *Psychological testing* (2d. ed.). New York: Macmillan, 1961.

Argyle, M., Lalljee, M., & Cook, M. The effects of visibility on interaction in a dyad. *Human Relations,* 1968, *21,* 3-17.

Arnott, C.C. Husbands' attitude and wives' commitment to employment. *Journal of Marriage and the Family,* 1972, *34,* 673-684.

Asch, S.E. Effects of group pressure upon the modification and distortion of judgments. In H. Guetzkov (Ed.), *Groups, leadership and men.* Pittsburgh: Carnegie Press, 1951.

Axelson, L.J. The marital adjustment and marital role definitions of husbands of working and nonworking wives. *Marriage and Family Living,* 1963, *25,* 189-195.

Axelson, L.J. The working wife: Differences in perception among Negro and white males. *Journal of Marriage and the Family,* 1970, *32,* 457-463.

Bales, R.F. Interaction process analysis. Cambridge, Mass.: Addison-Wesley, 1951.

Banton, M. *Race relations.* New York: Basic Books, 1967.

Baruch, G.K. Maternal influences upon college women's attitudes toward women and work. *Developmental Psychology,* 1972, *6,* 32-37.

Bass, B.M., Krusell, J., & Alexander, R.A. Male manager attitudes toward working women. *American Behavioral Scientist,* 1971, *15,* 221-236.

Bayer, A.E. Sexist students in American colleges: A descriptive note. *Journal of Marriage and the Family,* 1975, *37,* 391-397.

Bayton, J.A. The racial stereotype of Negro college students. *Journal of Abnormal and Social Psychology,* 1941, *36,* 97-102.

Bem, D.J. *Beliefs, attitudes and human affairs.* Belmont, Calif.: Brooks/Cole, 1970.

Bem, D.J., & Allen, A. On predicting some of the people some of the time: The search for cross-situational consistencies in behavior. *Psychological Review,* 1974, *81,* 506-520.

Bem, S.L. The measurement of psychological androgyny. *Journal of Clinical and Consulting Psychology,* 1974, *42,* 155-162.

Bem, S.L. Sex-role adaptability: One consequence of psychological androgyny. *Journal of Personality and Social Psychology*, 1975, *31*, 634-643.

Bem, S., & Bem, D.J. Case study of a nonconscious ideology: Training the woman to know her place. In D. Bem, *Beliefs, attitudes, and human affairs.* Belmont, Calif.: Brooks/Cole, 1970.

Bennett, E.M., & Cohen, L.R. Men and women: Personality patterns and contrasts. *Genetics Psychology Monographs*, 1959, *59*, 101-155.

Berg, K.E. Ethnic attitudes and agreement with a Negro person. *Journal of Personality and Social Psychology*, 1966, *4*, 215-220.

Berkowitz, L. *Social psychology*. Glenview, Ill.: Scott, Foresman, 1972.

Berkowitz, L. *A survey of social psychology*. Hinsdale, Ill.: Dryden, 1975.

Bettelheim, B., & Janowitz, M. *Social change and prejudice*. New York: Free Press, 1964, p. 146.

Blake, R., & Dennis, W. Development of stereotypes concerning the Negro. *Journal of Abnormal and Social Psychology*, 1943, *38*, 525-531.

Blake, R.R., Mouton, J.S., & Hain, J.D. Social forces in petition-signing. *Southeastern Social Science Quarterly*, 1956, *36*, 385-390.

Bledsoe, J.C. Sex differences in self-concept: Fact or artifact? *Psychological Reports*, 1973, *32*, 1253-1254.

Blumer, H. United States of America: Research on racial relations. *International Social Science Bulletin*, 1958, *10*, 403.

Bogardus, E.S. Measuring social distance. *Journal of Applied Sociology*, 1925, *9*, 299-308.

Bolton, E.B. Measuring specific attitudes toward the social rights of the Negro. *Journal of Abnormal and Social Psychology*, 1937, *31*, 384-397.

Bonjean, C.M., Hill, R.J., & McLemore, S.O. *Sociological measurement: An inventory of scales and incites.* San Francisco: Chandler, 1967.

Bowman, G.W., Worthy, N.B., & Greyser, S.A. Are women executives people? *Harvard Business Review*, 1965, *43*, 14 ff.

Brannon, R. Attitudes and the prediction of behavior. In Seidenberg, B., & Snadowsky, A. (Eds.), *Social psychology: An introduction.* New York: Free Press, 1976 (a).

Brannon, R. The male sex role: Our culture's blueprint for masculinity, and what it's done for us lately. In D. David and R. Brannon (Eds.), *The forty-nine percent majority: The male sex role.* Reading, Mass.: Addison-Wesley, 1967 (b).

Brannon, R., Cyphers, G., Hesse, S., Hesselbart, S., Keane, R., Schuman, H., Vicarro, T., & Wright, D. Attitude and action: A field experiment joined to a general population survey. *American Sociological Review,* 1973, *38,* 625-636.

Bray, D.W. The prediction of behavior from two attitude scales. *Journal of Abnormal and Social Psychology,* 1950, *45,* 64-84.

Brigham, J.C. Ethnic stereotypes. In J.C. Brigham and T.A. Weissbach (Eds.), *Racial attitudes in America.* New York: Harper & Row, 1972, pp. 109, 141-143.

Brislin, R.W., & Olmstead, K.H. An examination of two models designed to predict behavior from attitude and other verbal measures. *Proceedings of the 81st Convention of The American Psychological Association,* 1973.

Broverman, I., Broverman, D., Clarkson, F., Rosenkrantz, P., & Vogel, S. Sex-role stereotypes and clinical judgments of mental health. *Journal of Consulting and Clinical Psychology,* 1970, *34,* 1-7.

Broverman, I., Vogel, S., Broverman, D., Clarkson, F., & Rosenkrantz, P. Sex-role stereotypes: A current appraisal. *Journal of Social Issues,* 1972, *28,* 59-78.

Brown, R. *Social psychology.* New York: Free Press, 1965.

Bugental, D.E., Love, L.R., & Gianetto, R.M. Perfidious feminine faces. *Journal of Personality and Social Psychology,* 1971, *17,* 314-318.

Calder, B.J. & Ross, M. *Attitudes and behavior.* Morristown, N.J.: General Learning Press, 1973.

Campbell, A. *White attitudes toward black people.* Ann Arbor, Michigan: Institute for Social Research, University of Michigan, 1971.

Campbell, A., Converse, P.E., Miller, W.E., & Stokes, D.E. *The American voter* (abridged). New York: Wiley, 1964.

Campbell, D.T. Social attitudes and other acquired behavioral dispositions. In S. Koch (Ed.), *Psychology: A study of a science* (Vol. 6), *Investigations of man as socius: Their place in psychology and the social sciences.* New York: McGraw-Hill, 1963.

Campbell, D.T. Stereotypes and the perception of group differences. *American Psychologist,* 1967, *22,* 817-829.

Campbell, D.T., & Fiske, D.W. Convergent and discriminant validation by the multitrait-multimethod matrix. *Psychological Bulletin,* 1959, *56,* 81-105.

Cantril, H. *Gauging public opinion.* Princeton: Princeton University Press, 1947.

Cauthen, N.R., Robinson, I.E., & Krauss, H.H. Stereotypes: A review of the literature 1926-1968. *Journal of Social Psychology,* 1971, *84,* 103-125.

Centers, R. Authoritarianism and misogyny. *Journal of Social Psychology*, 1963, *61*, 81-85.

Chafetz, J.S. *Masculine/feminine or human?* Itasa, Ill.: Peacock, 1974.

Chein, I. Notes of a framework for the measurement of discrimination and prejudice. In M. Jahoda, M. Deutsch, & S.W. Cook, *Research methods in social relations*. New York: Dryden, 1951.

Clark, E.L. Motivation of Jewish students. *Journal of Social Psychology*, 1949, *39*, 113-117.

Clark, K.B. Problems of power and social change: Toward a relevant social psychology. *Journal of Social Issues*, 1965, *21*, No. 3, 5.

Clarkson, F., Vogel, S., Broverman, I., Broverman, D., & Rosenkrantz, P. *Science*, 1970, *167*, 390-392.

Coffman, R.N., & Levy, B.I. The dimensions implicit in psychological masculinity-femininity. *Educational and Psychological Measurement*, 1972, *32*, 975-985.

Cohen, A.R. *Attitude change and social influence*. New York: Basic Books, 1964.

Constantinople, A. Masculinity-femininity: An exception to a famous dictum. *Psychological Bulletin*, 1973, *80*, 389-407.

Conyers, J.W. An exploratory study of employers' attitudes toward working mothers. *Sociology and Social Research*, 1961, *45*, 145-156.

Cronbach, L.J. Response sets and test validity. *Educational and Psychological Measurement*, 1946, *6*, 475-494.

Cronbach, L.J. Coefficient alpha and the internal structure of tests. *Psychometrica*, 1951, *16*, 297-334.

David, D., & Brannon, R. (Eds.). *The forty-nine percent majority: The male sex role*. Reading, Mass.: Addison-Wesley, 1976.

Dean, L.R. Interactions reported and observed: The case of one local union. *Human Organization*, 1958, *17*, 36-44.

Deaux, K., & Emswiller, T. Explanations of successful performance on sex-linked tasks: What is skill for the male is luck for the female. *Journal of Personality and Social Psychology*, 1974, *29*, 80-85.

Deaux, K., & Taynor, J. Evaluation of male and female ability: Bias works two ways. *Psychological Reports*, 1973, *32*, 261-262.

DeFleur, M.L., & Westie, F.R. Verbal attitude and overt acts: An experiment on the salience of attitudes. *American Sociological Review*, 1958, *23*, 667-673.

DeFriese, G.H., & Ford, W.S. Verbal attitudes, overt acts, and the influence of social constraint in interracial behavior. *Social Problems,* 1969, *16,* 493-504.

Dempewolfe, J.A. Development and validation of a feminism scale. *Psychological Reports,* 1974, *34,* 651-657.(a)

Dempewolfe, J.A. Some correlates of feminism. *Psychological Reports,* 1974, *34,* 671-676.(b)

DeYoung, G.E., Cattell, R.B., Gaborit, M., & Barton, K. A causal model of effects of personality and marital role factors upon diary-reported sexual behavior. *Proceedings of the 81st Annual Convention of the American Psychological Association,* 1973, *8,* 355-356. (Summary)

Diab, L.N. Factors determining group stereotypes. *Journal of Social Psychology,* 1963, *61,* 3-10.

Ehrlich, H.J. Attitudes, behavior, and the intervening variables. *American Sociologist,* 1969, *4,* 29-34.

Ehrlich, H.J. *The social psychology of prejudice.* New York: Wiley, 1973.

Ehrlich, H.J., & Rinehart, J.W. A brief report on the methodology of stereotype research. *Social Forces,* 1965, *43,* 564-575.

Ellis, L.J., & Bentler, P.M. Traditional sex-determined role standards and sex stereotypes. *Journal of Personality and Social Psychology,* 1973, *25,* 28-34.

Elman, J., Press, A., & Rosenkrantz, P. Sex roles and self-concepts: Real and ideal. *Proceedings of the 78th Annual Convention of the American Psychological Association,* 1970, 455-456. (Summary)

Emswiller, T., Deaux, K., & Willits, J.E. Similarity, sex, and requests for small favors. *Journal of Applied Social Psychology,* 1971, *1,* 284-491.

Entwistle, D.R., & Greenberger, E. Adolescents' views of women's work role. *American Journal of Orthopsychiatry,* 1972, *42,* 648-656.

Erskine, H. The polls: Women's role. *Public Opinion Quarterly,* 1970, *34,* 275-90.

Etaugh, C., & Gerson, A. Attitudes toward women: Some biographical correlates. *Psychological Reports,* 1974, *35,* 701-702.

Etaugh, C., & Rose, S. Adolescents' sex bias in the evaluation of performance. *Developmental Psychology. In press.*

Etaugh, C., & Sanders, S. *Evaluation of performance as a function of status and sex variables. Journal of Social Psychology,* 1974, *94,* 237-241.

Eysenck, H.J. *The psychology of politics.* London: Routledge & Kegan Paul, 1954.

Falbo, T. The effects of sex and "masculinity" on person- and space-related perception. *Sex Roles,* 1975, *1,* 283-295.

Fand, A.B. Sex-role and self-concept: A study of the feminine sex-role as perceived by 85 college women for themselves, their ideal woman, the average woman and man's ideal woman. Doctoral dissertation, Cornell University. Ann Arbor, Mich.: University Microfilm, 1955. (No. 55-11, 901.)

Fasteau, M.F. *The male machine.* New York: McGraw-Hill, 1974.

Feldman-Summers, S., & Diesler, S.B. Those who are number two try harder: The effect of sex on attributions of causality. *Journal of Personality and Social Psychology,* 1974, *30,* 846-855.

Fendrich, J.M. A study of the association among verbal attitudes, commitment, and overt behavior in different experimental situations. *Social Forces,* 1967, *45,* 347-355.

Ferguson, L.W. Primary social attitudes. *Journal of Psychology,* 1939, *8,* 217-223.

Fernberger, S.W. Persistence of stereotypes concerning sex differences. *Journal of Abnormal and Social Psychology,* 1948, *43,* 97-101.

Fidell, L.S. Empirical verification of sex discrimination in hiring practices in psychology. *American Psychologist,* 1970, *25,* 1094-1098.

Fink, K., & Cantril, H. The collegiate stereotype as a frame of reference. *Journal of Abnormal and Social Psychology,* 1937, *32,* 352-356.

Fishbein, M., & Ajzen, I. Attitudes and opinions. *Annual Review of Psychology,* 1972, *23,* 487-544.

Fishman, J.A. An examination of the process and function of social stereotyping. *Journal of Social Psychology,* 1956, *43,* 27-64.

Fortune Magazine. The Fortune survey: Women in America, Part 1. *Fortune,* 1946, *34,* 5-12.

Fowler, M., Fowler, R., & Van de Riet, H. Feminism and political radicalism. *Journal of Psychology,* 1973, *83,* 237-242(a).

Freedman, J.L., Carlsmith, J.M., & Sears, D.O. *Social psychology* (2d. ed.) Englewood Cliffs, N.J.: Prentice-Hall, 1974.

Fruchter, B., Rokeach, M., & Novak, E.G. A factorial study of dogmatism, opinionation, and related scales. *Psychological Reports,* 1958, *4,* 19-22.

Gardner, R.C., Wonnacott, E.J., & Taylor, D.M. Ethnic stereotypes: A factor-analytic investigation. *Canadian Journal of Psychology,* 1968, *22,* 35-44.

Gilbert, G.M. Stereotype persistence and change among college students. *Journal of Abnormal and Social Psychology,* 1951, *46,* 245-254.

Goldberg, P. Are women prejudiced against women? *Trans-action,* 1968, April, 28-30.

Goldberg, P. Prejudice toward women: Some personality correlates. In F. Denmark (Ed.), *Who discriminates against women?* Beverly Hills: Sage, 1974. (Revised version of paper presented at APA convention, Honolulu, September, 1972).

Goldberg, P.A., Gottesdiener, M., & Abramson, P.R. Another put-down of women? Perceived attractiveness as a function of support for the feminist movement. *Journal of Personality and Social Psychology*, 1975, *32*, 113-115.

Goodmonson, C., & Glaudin, V. The relationship of commitment-free behavior and commitment behavior: A study of attitude toward organ transplantation. *Journal of Social Issues*, 1971, *27*, 171-183.

Gordon, F.F., & Hall, D.T. Self-image and stereotypes of femininity: Their relationships to women's role conflicts and coping. *Journal of Applied Psychology*, 1974, *59*, 241-243.

Greenberg, S.B. Attitudes of elementary and secondary students toward increased social, economic, and political participation by women. *The Journal of Educational Research*, 1973, *67*, 147-148.

Guilford, J.P. *Psychometric methods.* New York: McGraw-Hill, 1954.

Guilford, J.P. When not to factor analyze. *Psychological Bulletin*, 1964, *61*, 270-276.

Gump, J.P. Sex-role attitudes and psychological well-being. *Journal of Social Issues*, 1972, *28*, 79-92.

Haavio-Mannila, E. Sex differentiation in role expectations and performance. *Journal of Marriage and the Family*, 1967, *29*, 568-578.

Haavio-Mannila, E. Sex-role attitudes in Finland, 1966-1970. *Journal of Social Issues*, 1972, *28*, 93-110.

Harding, J., Proshansky, H., Kutner, B., & Chein, I. Prejudice and ethnic relations. In G. Lindzey and E. Aronson (Eds.), *The handbook of social psychology* (Vol. 5). Reading, Mass.: Addison-Wesley, 1969.

Harvey, O.J., Hunt, D.E., & Schroder, H.M. *Conceptual systems and personality organization.* New York: Wiley, 1961.

Haverman, E., & West, P.S. *They went to college.* New York: Harcourt, Brace, 1952.

Hawley, P. What women think men think: Does it affect their career choice? *Journal of Counseling Psychology*, 1971, *18*, 193-199.

Hawley, P. Perceptions of male models of femininity related to career choice. *Journal of Counseling Psychology*, 1972, *19*, 308-313.

Hayakawa, S.I. *Language in action.* New York: Harcourt, Brace, 1941.

Helson, H., Blake, R.B., & Mouton, J.S. Petition-signing as adjustment to situational and personal factors. *Journal of Social Psychology*, 1958, *48*, 3-10.

Henley, N. The politics of touch. In P. Brown (Ed.), *Radical psychology*. New York: Harper & Row, 1973. (a)

Henley, N. Status and sex: Some touching observations. *Bulletin of the Psychonomic Society*, 1973, *2*, 91-93.(b)

Henley, N. *Body politics*. New Jersey: Prentice-Hall, 1977.

Herman, M.H., & Sedlacek, W.E. Measuring sexist attitudes of males. *Proceedings of the 81st Annual Convention of the American Psychological Association*, 1973, *8*, 341-342.(a)

Herman, M.H., & Sedlacek, W.E. Sexist attitudes among male university students. Research Report 3-73. Counseling Center, University of Maryland, College Park, Maryland, 1973.(b)

Himmelstein, P., & Moore, J.C. Racial attitudes and the action of Negro- and white-background figures as factors in petition-signing. *Journal of Social Psychology*, 1963, *61*, 267-272.

Hinckley, E.D. The influence of individual opinion on construction of an attitude scale. *Journal of Social Psychology*, 1932, *3*, 283-296.

Hoffman, L.W. Parental power relations and the division of household tasks. *Marriage and Family Living*, 1960, *22*, 27-35.

Hofstaetter, P.R. A factorial study of prejudice. *Journal of Personality*, 1952, *21*, 228-239.

Hyman, H. Social psychology and race relations. In I. Katz and P. Gurin (Eds.), *Race and the social sciences*. New York: Basic Books, 1969.

Hyman, H.H., Cobb, W.J., Feldman, J.J., Hart, C.W., & Stember, C.H. *Interviewing in social research*. Chicago: University of Chicago Press, 1954.

Hymer, S., & Atkins, A. Relationship between attitudes toward women's liberation movement and mode of aggressive expression in women. *Proceedings of the 81st Annual Convention of the American Psychological Association*, 1973, *8*, 173-174. (Summary)

Insko, C.A. *Theories of attitude change*. New York: Appleton-Century-Crofts, 1968.

Jackson, D.N. The dynamics of structural personality tests. *Psychological Review*, 1971, *78*, 229-248.

Jacobson, A.H. Conflict of attitudes toward the roles of the husband and wife in marriage. *American Sociological Review*, 1952, *17*, 146-156.

Jenkin, N. & Vroegh, K. Contemporary concepts of masculinity and femininity. *Psychological Reports*, 1969, *25*, 679-697.

Jenkins, J.C., & Corbin, H.H. Dependability of psychological brand barometers: II: The problem of validity. *Journal of Applied Psychology*, 1938, *22*, 252-260.

Joesting, J., & Joesting, R. Attitudes about sex roles, sex, and marital status of anti-Nixon demonstrators, comparison of three studies. *Psychological Reports*, 1974, *35*, 1049-1050.

Kahn, L.A. The organization of attitudes toward the Negro as a function of education. *Psychological Monographs*, 1951, *65*, 13, (Whole No. 330).

Kamenetsky, J., Burgess, G.G., & Rowan, T. The relative effectiveness of four attitude assessment techniques in predicting a criterion. *Educational and Psychological Measurement*, 1056, *16*, 187-194.

Kammeyer, K. Birth order and the feminine sex role among college women. *American Sociological Review*, 1966, *4*, 508-515.

Kando, T.M. Role strain: A comparison of males, females, and transsexuals. *Journal of Marriage and the Family*, 1972, *34*, 459-464.

Kaplan, R.M., & Goldman, R.D. Stereotypes of college students toward the average man's and woman's attitudes toward women. *Journal of Counseling Psychology*, 1973, *20*, 450-462.

Karlins, M., Coffman, T.L., & Walters, G. On the fading of social stereotypes: Studies in three generations of college students. *Journal of Personality and Social Psychology*, 1969, *13*, 1-16.

Katz, D., & Braly, K. Racial stereotypes of one hundred college students. *Journal of Abnormal and Social Psychology*, 1933, *28*, 280-290.

Keiffer, M.G., & Cullen, D.M. Women who discriminate against other women: The process of denial. In F. Denmark, (Ed.), *Who discriminates against women?* Beverly Hills: Sage, 1974.

Kenkel, W.F. Traditional family ideology and spousal roles in decision-making. *Marriage and Family Living*, 1959, *21*, 334-339.

Kerlinger, F., & Rokeach, M. The factorial nature of the F and D scales. *Journal of Personality and Social Psychology*, 1966, *4*, 391-399.

Kester, J. Report. *Parade Magazine*, May 7, 1972.

Kiesler, C.A., Collins, B.E., & Miller, N. *Attitude change: A critical analysis of theoretical approaches.* New York: Wiley, 1969.

Kirkpatrick, C. The construction of a belief-pattern scale for measuring attitudes toward feminism. *Journal of Social Psychology*, 1936, *7*, 421-437. (a)

Kirkpatrick, C. An experimental study of the modification of social attitudes. *American Journal of Sociology*, 1936, *41*, 649-656. (b)

Kirkpatrick, C. A comparison of the generations in regard to attitudes toward feminism. *Journal of Genetic Psychology*, 1936, *49*, 343-361. (c)

Kitay, P.M. A comparison of the sexes in their attitudes and beliefs about women: A study of prestige groups. *Sociometry*, 1940, *3*, 399-407.

Klineberg, O. The scientific study of national stereotypes. *International Social Science Bulletin*, 1951, *3*, 505-515.

Koenig, F. Sex attribution to hypothetical persons described by adjective trait lists. *Perceptual and Motor Skills*, 1972, *35*, 15-18.

Kramer, B.M. Dimensions of prejudice. *Journal of Psychology*, 1949, *27*, 389-451.

Krech, D., Crutchfield, R., & Ballachey, E. *Individual in society*. New York: McGraw-Hill, 1962.

Kristal, J., Sanders, D., Spence, J.T., & Helmreich, R. Inferences about the femininity of competent women and their implications for likability. *Sex Roles*, 1975, *1*, 33-40.

Krug, R.E. An analysis of the F scale: Item factor analysis. *Journal of Social Psychology*, 1961, *53*, 285-291.

Landy, D., & Sigall, H. Beauty is talent: Task evaluation as a function of the performer's physical attractiveness. *Journal of Personality and Social Psychology*, 1974, *29*, 299-304.

Lange, L. Neue Experimente uber den Vorgang der einfachen Reaktion auf Sinnescindrucke. *Philosophical Studies*, 1888, *4*, 479-510.

LaPiere, R.T. Attitudes versus actions. *Social Forces*, 1934, *13*, 230-237.

Latane, B., & Darley, J.M. Bystander intervention in emergencies: Diffusion of responsibility. *Journal of Personality and Social Psychology*, 1968, *8*, 377-383.

Levinson, D.J., & Huffman, P.E. Traditional family ideology and its relation to personality. *Journal of Personality and Social Psychology*, 1955, *23*, 251-273.

Likert, R. A technique for the measurement of attitude. *Archives of Psychology*, 1932, No. 140, 44-53.

Lindzey, G., & Rogolsky, S. Prejudice and identification of minority group membership. *Journal of Abnormal and Social Psychology*, 1950, *45*, 37-53.

Linn, L.S. Verbal attitudes and overt behavior: A study of racial discrimination. *Social Forces*, 1965, *44*, 353-364.

Lipman-Blumen, J. How ideology shapes women's lives. *Scientific American*, 1972, *226*, 34-42.

Loevinger, J. Objective tests as instruments of psychological theory. *Psychological Reports*, 1957, *3*, 635-694.

Loevinger, J., Gleser, G.C., & DuBois, P.H. Maximizing the discriminating power of a multiple-score test. *Psychometrica*, 1953, *18*, 309-317.

MacKenzie, B.K. The importance of contact in determining attitudes toward Negroes. *Journal of Abnormal and Social Psychology*, 1948, *43*, 417-441.

Mann, J.H. The relationship between cognitive, affective, and behavioral aspects of racial prejudice. *Journal of Social Psychology,* 1959, *49,* 223-228.

Mann, J.W. Inconsistent thinking about group and individual. *Journal of Social Psychology,* 1967, *71,* 235-245.

Martin, J.G. Racial ethnocentrism and judgment of beauty. *Journal of Social Psychology,* 1964, *63,* 59-63.

Mason, K.O. *Sex-role attitude items and scales from U.S. sample surveys.* DHEW Publication No. (ADM) 75-248, 1975. U.S. Department of Health, Education, and Welfare: Alcohol, Drug Abuse, and Mental Health Administration, 5600 Fishers Lane, Rockville, Md. 20852.

McClelland, D.C. Wanted: A new self-image for women. In R.J. Kifton (Ed.), *The women in America.* Boston: Beacon, 1967.

McCune, S. Thousands reply to opinionnaire; many document cases of sex discrimination. *American Association of University Women Journal,* 1970 (January), 73-74; (May), 203-206.

McGrew, J.M. How "open" are multiple-dwelling units? *Journal of Social Psychology,* 1967, *72,* 223-226.

McGuire, W.J. The nature of attitudes and attitude change. In G. Lindzey and E. Aronson (Eds.), *The handbook of social psychology* (Vol. 3). Reading, Mass.: Addison-Wesley, 1969.

McKee, J.P., & Sherriffs, A.C. The differential evaluation of males and females. *Journal of Personality,* 1957, *25,* 356-371.

McKee, J.P., & Sherriffs, A.C. Men's and women's beliefs, ideals and self-concepts. *American Journal of Sociology,* 1959, *64,* 356-363.

McMillin, M.R. Attitudes of college men toward career involvement of married women. *Vocational Guidance Quarterly,* 1972, *21,* 8-11.

McNemar, Q. Opinion-attitude methodology. *Psychological Bulletin,* 1946, *43,* 289-374.

Meehl, P.E. The dynamics of "structured" personality tests. *Journal of Clinical Psychology,* 1945, *1,* 296-303.

Meier, H.C. Mother-centeredness and college youths' attitudes toward social equality for women: Some empirical research. *Journal of Marriage and the Family,* 1972, *34,* 115-121.

Merz, L.E., & Pearlin, L.I. The influence of information on three dimensions of prejudice toward Negroes. *Social Forces,* 1957, *35,* 344-351.

Messick, S. The standard problem: Meaning and values in measurement and evaluation. *American Psychologist,* 1975, *30,* 955-966.

Michel, H.N. Sex bias in the evaluation of professional achievements. *Journal of Educational Psychology*, 1974, *66*, 157-66.

Middlebrook, P.N. *Social psychology and modern life.* New York: Knopf, 1974.

Milgram, S. Behavioral study of obedience. *Journal of Abnormal and Social Psychology*, 1963, *67*, 371-378.

Miller, D. *Handbook of research design and social measurement.* New York: David McKay, 1964.

Miller, T.W. Male attitudes toward women's rights as a function of their level of self-esteem. In F. Denmark (Ed.), *Who discriminates against women?* Beverly Hills: Sage, 1974.

Murray, M. *A house of good proportion: Images of women in literature.* New York: Simon & Schuster, 1973.

Nadler, E.B., & Morrow, W.R. Authoritarian attitudes toward women, and their correlates. *The Journal of Social Psychology*, 1959, *49*, 113-123.

Nash, S.C. The relationship among sex-role stereotyping, sex-role preference, and the sex difference in spatial visualization. *Sex Roles*, 1975, *1*, 15-32.

Neill, J.A., & Jackson, D.N. An evaluation of item selection strategies in personality scale construction. *Educational and Psychological Measurement*, 1970, *30*, 64, 7-661.

Nelson, E. Attitudes: Their nature and development. *The Journal of General Psychology*, 1939, *21*, 367-399.

Neufeld, E., Langmeyer, D., & Seeman, W. Some sex-role stereotypes and personal preferences, 1950 and 1970. *Journal of Personality Assessment*, 1975, *39*, 110-113.

Nichols, R.C. Subtle, obvious, and stereotype measures of masculinity-femininity. *Educational and Psychological Measurement*, 1962, *22*, 449-461.

Nielsen, J.M., & Doyle, P.T. Sex-role stereotypes of feminists and nonfeminists. *Sex Roles, 1975, 1,* 83-95.

Nunnually, J.C. *Psychometric theory.* New York: McGraw-Hill, 1967.

O'Neil, W.M., & Levinson, O.J. A factorial exploration of authoritarianism and some of its ideological concomitants. *Journal of Personality and Social Psychology*, 1954, *22*, 449-463.

Orne, M.T. On the social psychology of the psychological experiment: With particular reference to demand characteristics and their implications. *American Psychologist*, 1962, *17*, 776-783.

Osgood, C.E. Studies on the generality of affective meaning systems. *American Psychologist*, 1962, *17*, 10-28.

Osgood, C.E., Suci, G.J., & Tannenbaum, P.H. *The measurement of meaning.* The University of Illinois Press, 1957.

Ostrom, T.M. The relationship between the affective, behavioral, and cognitive components of attitude. *Journal of Experimental Social Psychology,* 1969, *5,* 12-30.

Parker, G.V.C. Sex differences in self-description on the adjective check list. *Educational and Psychological Measurement,* 1969, *29,* 99-113.

Parry, H., & Crossley, H. Validity of responses to survey questions. *Public Opinion Quarterly,* 1950, *14,* 61-80.

Parsons, T., & Shils, E.A. *Toward a general theory of action.* Cambridge, Mass.: Harvard University Press, 1951.

Patrick, C. Attitudes about women executives in government positions. *Journal of Social Psychology,* 1944, *19,* 3-34.

Peterson, M.J. The asymmetry of sex-role perceptions. *Sex Roles,* 1975, *1,* 267-282.

Pheterson, G.I., Kiesler, S.B., & Goldberg, P.A. Evaluation of the performance of women as a function of their sex, achievement, and personal history. *Journal of Personality and Social Psychology,* 1971, *19,* 114-118.

Pleck, J.H., & Sawyer, J. *Men and masculinity.* Englewood Cliffs, N.J.: Prentice-Hall, 1974.

Prothro, E.T., & Keehn, J.D. The structure of social attitudes in Lebanon. *Journal of Abnormal and Social Psychology,* 1956, *53,* 157-160.

Reany, M., & Ferguson, L.W. Forced-choice adjectival masculinity-femininity scale. *Psychological Reports,* 1974, *34,* 595-602.

Reece, M.M. Masculinity and femininity: A factor-analytic study. *Psychological Reports,* 1964, *14,* 123-139.

Ricks, F.A., & Pyke, S.W. Teacher perceptions and attitudes that foster or maintain sex-role differences. *Interchange,* 1973, *4,* 26-33.

Robinson, J.P., Rusk, J.G., & Head, K.B. *Measures of political attitudes.* Ann Arbor, Mich.: Institute for Social Research, University of Michigan, 1968.

Robinson, J.P., & Shaver, P.R. *Measures of social psychological attitudes.* Institute for Social Research, University of Michigan, 1973.

Rokeach, M., & Fruchter, B. A factorial study of dogmatism and related concepts. *Journal of Abnormal and Social Psychology,* 1956, *53,* 356-360.

Roper Organization. *The Virginia Slims American Women's Opinion Poll* (Vol. III). New York: Roper Organization, Inc., 1974.

Rorer, L.G. The great response-style myth. *Psychological Bulletin,* 1965, *63,* 129-156.

Rosen, B., & Jerdee, T.H. The influence of sex-role stereotypes on evaluations of male and female supervisory behavior. *Journal of Applied Psychology*, 1973, *57*, 44-48.

Rosen, R.A. Occupational role innovations and sex-role attitudes. *Journal of Medical Education*, 1974, *49*, 554-561.

Rosenkrantz, P., Vogel, S., Bee, W., Broverman, I., & Broverman, D. Sex-role stereotypes and self-concepts in college students. *Journal of Consulting and Clinical Psychology*, 1968, *32*, 287-295.

Ross, S., & Walters, J. Perceptions of a sample of university men concerning women. *The Journal of Genetic Psychology*, 1973, *122*, 329-336.

Rubenowitz, S. *Emotional flexibility-rigidity as a comprehensive dimension of mind.* Stockholm: Almquist & Wiksell, 1963.

Rubin, J.Z., Provenzano, F.J., & Luria, Z. The eye of the beholder: Parents' views on sex of newborns. *American Journal of Orthopsychiatry*, 1974, *44*, 512-519.

Saenger, G. *The social psychology of prejudice.* New York: Harper & Row, 1953.

Saenger, G., & Flowerman, S. Stereotyping and prejudiced attitudes. *Human Relations*, 1954, *7*, 217-238.

Saenger, G., & Golbert, E. Customer reactions to the integration of the Negro sales personnel. *International Journal of Opinion and Attitude Research*, 1950, *4*, 57-76.

Samelson, F., & Yates, J.F. Acquiescence and the F scale: Old assumptions and new data. *Psychological Bulletin*, 1967, *68*, 91-103.

Sample, J., & Warland, R. Attitude and prediction of behavior. *Social Forces*, 1973, *51*, 292-304.

Sanger, S.P., & Alker, H.A. Dimensions of internal-external locus of control and the women's liberation movement. *Journal of Social Issues*, 1972, *28*, 115-129.

Schuman, H. Attitudes vs. actions versus attitudes vs. attitudes. *Public Opinion Quarterly*, 1972, *36*, 347-354.

Schuman, H., & Hatchett, S. *Black racial attitudes: Trends and complexities.* Ann Arbor, Mich.: Institute for Social Research, University of Michigan, 1974.

Scott, W.A. Attitude measurement. In G. Lindzey and E. Aronson (Eds.), *The Handbook of Social Psychology* (Vol. II). Reading, Mass.: Addison-Wesley, 1969.

Seavey, C.A., Katz, P.A., & Zalk, S.R. Baby X: The effect of gender labels on adult responses to infants. *Sex Roles*, 1975, *1*, 103-109.

Secord, P.F. Stereotyping and favorableness in the perception of Negro faces. *Journal of Abnormal and Social Psychology*, 1956, *53*, 78-83.

Secord, P.F., Bevan, W., & Katz, B. Perceptual accentuation and the Negro stereotype. *Journal of Abnormal and Social Psychology*, 1956, *53*, 78-83.

Seidenberg, B., & Snadowsky, A. *Social psychology: an introduction.* New York: Free Press, 1976.

Seiler, L.H., & Hough, R.L. Empirical comparisons of the Thurstone and Likert techniques. In G.F. Summers, (Ed.), *Attitude measurement.* Chicago: Rand McNally, 1970.

Seligmann, B.B. The American Jew: Some demographic features. In *American Jewish Yearbook,* 1950, *51,* 3-52.

Serbin, L.A., O'Leary, K.D., Kent, R.N., & Tonick, I.J. A comparison of teacher response to the pre-academic and problem behavior of boys and girls. *Child Development,* 1973, *44,* 796-804.

Seward, G.H., & Larson, W.R. Adolescent concepts of social sex roles in the United States and the two Germanies. *Human Development,* 1968, *11,* 217-248.

Shaw, M.E., & Wright, J.M. *Scales for the measurement of attitudes.* New York: McGraw-Hill, 1967.

Sherriffs, A.C., & Jarrett, R.F. Sex differences in attitudes about sex differences. *The Journal of Psychology,* 1953, *35,* 161-168.

Sherriffs, A.C., & McKee, J.P. Qualitative aspects of beliefs about men and women. *Journal of Personality and Social Psychology,* 1957, *25,* 451-464.

Shomer, R.W., & Centers, R. Differences in attitudinal responses under conditions of implicitly manipulated group salience. *Journal of Personality and Social Psychology,* 1970, *15,* 125-132.

Silveira, J. Thoughts on the politics of touch. Eugene, Oregon: *Women's Press,* February 1972, *1,* 13.

Silverman, B.I., & Cochrane, R. The relationship between verbal expressions of behavioral intention and overt behavior. *Journal of Social Psychology,* 1971, *84,* 51-56.

Smith, M.B. The personal setting of public opinions: A study of attitudes toward Russia. *Public Opinion Quarterly,* 1947, *11,* 507-523.

Spence, J.T., & Helmreich, R. Who likes competent women? Competence, sex-role congruence of interests, and subjects' attitudes towards women as determinants of interpersonal attraction. *Journal of Applied Social Psychology,* 1972, *2,* 197-213. (a)

Spence, J.T., & Helmreich, R. The Attitudes toward Women Scale: An objective instrument to measure attitudes toward the rights and roles of women in contemporary society. JSAS *Catalog of Selected Documents in Psychology,* 1972, *2,* 2, 66. (b)

Spence, J.T., Helmreich, R., & Stapp, J. A short version of the Attitudes to Women Scale (AWS). *Bulletin of the Psychonomic Society,* 1973, *2,* 219-220.

Spence, J.T., Helmreich, R., & Stapp, J. The personal attributes questionnaire: A measure of sex-role stereotypes and masculinity-femininity. JSAS *Catalog of Selected Documents in Psychology,* 1974, *4,* 43. (Ms. No. 617)

Spence, J.T., Helmreich, R., & Stapp, J. Ratings of self and peers on sex-role attributes and their relation to self-esteem and conceptions of masculinity and femininity. *Journal of Personality and Social Psychology,* 1975, *32,* 29-39.

Spence, J.T., Helmreich, R., & Stapp, J. Likability, sex-role congruence of interest, and competence: It depends on how you ask. *Journal of Applied Social Psychology.* In press.

Stagner, R. Fascist attitudes: An exploratory study. *Journal of Social Psychology,* 1936, *7,* 309-319. (a)

Stagner, R. Fascist attitudes: Their determining conditions. *Journal of Social Psychology,* 1936, *7,* 438-454. (b)

Starer, R., & Denmark, F. Discrimination against aspiring women. In F. Denmark, (Ed.), *Who discriminates against women?* Beverly Hills: Sage, 1974.

Steinmann, A., & Fox, D.J. Male-female perceptions of the female role in the United States. *The Journal of Psychology,* 1966, *64,* 265-276.

Steinmann, A., Levi, J., & Fox, D.J. Self-concept of college women compared with their concept of ideal woman and men's ideal woman. *Journal of Counseling Psychology,* 1964, *2,* 370-374.

Stewart, A.J., & Winter, D.G. Self-definition and social definition in women. *Journal of Personality,* 1974, *42,* 238-259.

Strodtbeck, F.L., James, R.M., & Hawkins, C. Social status in jury deliberations. *American Sociological Review,* 1957, *22,* 713-719.

Struening, E.L., & Richardson, A.H. A factor-analytic exploration of the alienation, anomia, and authoritarianism domain. *American Sociological Review,* 1965, *30,* 768-776.

Summers, G.F. *Attitude measurement.* Chicago: Rand McNally, 1970.

Tarter, D.E. Toward prediction of attitude-action discrepancy. *Social Forces,* 1969, *47,* 398-405.

Tarter, D.E. Attitude: The mental myth. *American Sociologist,* 1970, *5,* 276-278.

Terman, L.M., & Oden, M.H. *The gifted child grows up.* Stanford: Stanford University Press, 1947.

Thorndike, E.L. A constant error in psychological ratings. *Journal of Applied Psychology,* 1920, *4,* 25-29.

Thorne, B., & Henley, N. (Eds.). *Language and sex.* Rowley, Mass.: Newbury, 1975.

Touhey, J.C. Effects of additional women professionals on ratings of occupational prestige and desirability. *Journal of Personality and Social Psychology,* 1974, *29,* 86-89.

Tyron, R.C. Individual differences. In F.A. Moss (Ed.), *Comparative psychology* (2d ed.). New York: Prentice-Hall, 1942.

Tyron, R.C., & Bailey, D.E. The BCTRY computer system of cluster and factor analysis. *Multivariate Behavior Research,* 1966, *1,* 95-111.

Triandis, H.C. *Attitude and attitude change.* New York: Wiley, 1971.

Vavrik, J., & Jurich, A.P. Self-concept and attitude toward acceptance of females: A note. *Family Coordinator,* 1971, *20,* 151-152.

Vernon, P.T. *Educational testing and test-form factors* (Res. Bull. RB - 58-3). Princeton, N.J.: Educational Testing Service, 1958.

Vinacke, W.E. Stereotypes as social concepts. *Journal of Social Psychology,* 1957, *46,* 229-243.

Walters, J., & Ojemann, R.H. A study of the components of adolescent attitudes concerning the role of women. *Journal of Social Psychology,* 1952, *35,* 101-110.

Warner, L.G., & DeFleur, M.L. Attitude as an interactional concept: Social constraint and social distance as intervening variables between attitudes and action. *American Sociological Review,* 1969, *34,* 153-169.

Webb, E.J., Campbell, D.T., Schwartz, R.D., & Sechrest, L. *Unobtrusive measures: Nonreactive research in the social sciences.* Chicago: Rand McNally, 1966.

Weiss, W. An examination of attitude toward Negroes. *Journal of Social Psychology,* 1961, *55,* 3-21.

Weitz, S. Attitude, voice, and behavior: A repressed affect model of interracial interaction. *Journal of Personality and Social Psychology,* 1972, *24,* 14-21.

Wicker, A.W. Attitudes vs. actions: The relationship of verbal to overt behavioral responses to assitude objects. *Journal of Social Issues,* 1969, *25,* 41-78.

Wicker, A.W. An examination of the "other variables" explanation of attitude—behavior inconsistency. *Journal of Personality and Social Psychology,* 1971, *19,* 18-31.

Willis, F.N. Initial speaking distance as a function of the speaker's relationship. *Psychonomic Science,* 1966, *5,* 221-222.

Woodmansee, J.J., & Cook, S.W. Dimensions of verbal racial attitude: Their identification and measurement. *Journal of Personality and Social Psychology,* 1967, *7,* 240-250.

Wright, B., & Tuska, S. The nature and origin of feeling feminine. *British Journal of Social and Clinical Psychology,* 1966, *5,* 140-149.

Wrightsman, L.S. Dimensionalization of attitudes toward the Negro. *Psychological Reports,* 1962, *11,* 439-448.

Wrightsman, L.S. *Social psychology in the seventies.* Belmont, Calif.: Brooks/Cole, 1972.

Yankelovich, D. *The new morality: A profile of American youth in the 70's.* New York: McGraw-Hill, 1974.

Yorburg, B., & Arafat, I. Current sex role conceptions and conflict. *Sex Roles,* 1975, *1,* 135-146.

Zeldon, P.B., & Greenberg, R.P. The process of sex attribution: Methodology and first findings. *Sex Roles,* 1975, *1,* 111-120.

Zimmerman, D.H., & West, C. Conversational order and sexism: A convergence of theoretical and substantive problems. In B. Thorne and N. Hanley (Eds.), *Language and sex.* Rowley, Mass.: Newbury, 1975.

CHAPTER *19*

COMMENTARY: CHAPTERS 17 & 18

ELI A. RUBINSTEIN

The chapters by Brannon and Pleck, perhaps more than most of the other papers of this conference, are themselves critical examinations of areas of investigation in the development of new directions in research on women. It would seem, therefore, more important to look at the implications of these two chapters than to attempt any substantive critique or evaluation of their interpretations. The latter approach would be less fruitful because both papers are competent and hard to find fault with, and each chapter sets itself a somewhat different task.

Brannon is primarily concerned with the misdirections being taken in research on measurement of attitudes toward women. He correctly subsumes this misdirection under the general weakness of attitude-measurement research, insofar as the goal of such research is to develop predictors of behavior. In general, attitudes do not predict behavior, especially when that attitude does not have a clear identity with the expected behavior. To use Brannon's own words, "a measure with diverse item-contents cannot be highly congruent with any individual behavior of the kinds that are practical to observe and measure at present."

The fact that almost all psychological measurement suffers from the same weakness in predicting individual behavior does not detract from Brannon's criticism. Aptitude scales similarly function poorly if the predicted behavior is markedly different from what is being measured.

Brannon's solution is to eschew measuring attitudes in the traditional fashion and to focus on the validity of attitude measures rather than on their reliability. As he points out, this approach quickly gets to the point of measuring behavior directly, as the ultimate in achieving validity in the measurement. His main point, which is eminently practical, is that there is no value in measuring attitudes unless they tell us something about what people actually do.

Pleck takes a somewhat different theoretical approach, but ends up equally critical of what the published research tells us about how attitudes predict behavior. He neatly points out that as artificial as stereotypes may be, too much has been made of the differences that emerge from ratings of traits identifying male versus female characteristics. In fact, the male and female stereotypes are more alike than different. (This theme of much more similarity than difference between male and female was one of the most repeated points at this conference and deserves continuing attention.)

Pleck's most important argument supporting the similarity thesis is in his comparison of male and female attitudes toward women. It is fairly clear from his analysis that there is no sharp demarcation of male versus female attitudes toward women on any clear dimension. Certainly, men are not clearly more traditional, or more conservative, in their attitudes toward women than women are themselves. And, as he points out, in couple relationships, where differences in attitudes could make a behavioral difference, the data suggest that male and female attitudes are highly correlated.

The important implication in both papers is the effort not just to make future research more effective as a scientific inquiry, but to do so in terms of using the new understanding to influence women and men, as Pleck puts it in his closing comment, "for the greater benefit of both."

It is this hope and expectation—which is also voiced in some of the other papers—that deserves some independent comment. It has become all too evident in recent years that scientific information, in and of itself, does not change behavior, even though it may to some extent modify attitudes. The most visible recent example of this discrepancy between knowledge and action has been the widespread dissemination of the finding that "cigarette smoking is dangerous to your health" and the absence of any marked decrease in smoking. And there are numerous examples from national commissions on violence, and on obscenity and pornography, that scientific evidence does not lead directly to changes in social policy.

Drawing attention to these examples of the chasm between social science research and social policy to the present situation may seem premature. It could be argued that much needs to be done to make the research on women more meaningful, more relevant, and more action-oriented before worrying about the problem of translating that knowledge into action. And yet, it is interesting that Brannon quotes Kenneth Clark in the latter's criticism of most research on racial prejudices, about which Clark said: ". . . dabbles in reality, but avoids the real arena of action, and reflects among other things both a methodological sterility and theoretical stagnation."

Brannon, I believe, falls into error by assuming that Clark was primarily criticizing the *quality* of the research. I think Clark was more concerned with *direction* and wanted research whose findings would both demand and illuminate courses of action.

It is at this point, I believe, that both Brannon and Pleck fail to make just this distinction between improving the quality of research and making that research more directly a basis for action and social policy. Doing better research, with improved methodologies, using more valid measuring instruments, and even using behavioral predictors that show significant power does not automatically lead to new and more effective social policy.

Take a hypothetical leap into the future and assume that a body of literature has been developed which clearly affirms the general finding so often stressed at the conference and highlighted in Pleck's article (chapter 10) by "the traditional focus on sex differences obscures the fact that women and men are likely similar on most, and the more important, traits." Assume in fact that a general finding has been established as follows: For some women in some ways, some sex differences are significant to behavior. For most men and most women, most so-called sex differences are not significant to behavior.

The issue, so far as social policy is concerned, then becomes what should be done in the light of such a finding? The smoking and health illustration, mentioned earlier, suggests that even a widespread dissemination of this finding would probably not change many attitudes, let alone behaviors.

Let me borrow from another example of the separation between social science knowledge and consequent social policy. In 1972, the Surgeon General's Scientific Advisory Committee on Television and Social Behavior concluded, on the basis of a large body of specially commissioned research, that there was evidence of a causal relationship between TV violence and later aggressive behavior in children. Despite that finding, no major change has occurred since then in television programming. The reason is that no clear social policy, *translatable into effective behavior*, derives from that scientific finding. What is still needed is a careful examination of the available options in making appropriate changes in television programming and/or modifying public attitudes so that effective influence can be brought to bear on the television industry to make such changes.

How these changes are to be accomplished is far from self-evident. More than likely, some second-order effect is now becoming apparent in the smoking and health situation. Ten years of public education have done little to decrease the level of smoking directly. Indeed, teen-age girls are now smoking more than they were ten years ago. That development may be related to an intriguing interaction between changing attitudes by women about women and smoking behavior. In any case, the massive public education program has not reduced the overall number of smokers.

However, that public education program has made the "nonsmokers" more aware of and more zealous of their rights as nonsmokers. Thus, local ordinances establishing nonsmoking areas in public conveyances and in airplanes have sensitized nonsmokers to their identity as nonsmokers. It is now common practice at various meetings (including this very conference) to establish rules about nonsmoking from the beginning. And smokers are gradually and grudgingly complying with such demands. If and when nonsmokers are able to supply sufficient pressure, there may be a marked overall decrease in smoking because of this group pressure.

Unfortunately, the specific nature of second-order effects is rarely predictable. For example, it is hardly apparent what may develop as both information and social pressure increase to improve the status of women in society. It is a too simplistic expectation to predict that sex-typed interests will decrease, or that "masculine" and "feminine" traits will disappear; or that androgynous behavior will prevail.

These second-order effects are at least two steps removed from the research developments proposed by Pleck and Brannon. Learning more "about the etiology, dynamics, and consequences of a more general sex role attitudinal process," as Pleck proposes, and improving attitude measurement so that we are examining behaviorally relevant attitudes, as Brannon proposes, are both worthy research goals and should be vigorously pursued. But the real world is already moving too fast to assume that the findings of such improved research will immediately make an important contribution to behavior change. It is much more likely that such research will tell us where our attitudes and behaviors have been than where they are going. But even that would be no small contribution in this complex area where mythologies about sex roles and attitudes toward women are still so prevalent. Once the research really begins to look at what has actually been happening in *changes* in attitudes—a point that neither Pleck nor Brannon stresses—we will be moving in the right direction. At that time, the research will come closer to having relevance for new social policy. And that will be the time to convene another conference dedicated to examining the issues of translating those research findings into social policy.

CONCLUDING REMARKS ABOUT NEW DIRECTIONS

JULIA A. SHERMAN & FLORENCE L. DENMARK

This conference on Women's Research Needs was originated and funded with many purposes in mind. The APA Committee on Women in Psychology envisioned a gathering of psychologists and other social scientists interested in theory and research about women. This was the first such conference on the psychology of women. It is hoped that it will *not* be the last. One purpose was the sharing of knowledge and insights, as well as confusions, with other individuals interested in the same topic and similar issues. For most participants, the conference was also a time to meet other colleagues, a time to find out who the other interested professionals were, and to hear their views. That aspect of the conference was a resounding success.

An additional purpose, and one that was of particular concern to the funding agencies, can be variously described as delineating the research needs of women, indicating new directions for research on women, and/or establishing research priorities. Each of these goals is somewhat different.

One might suppose that women's *research needs* might be more accurately determined by a survey of women. What would they want to know? What would they consider important? We do not know. Perhaps they would not consider research an important priority at all, but perhaps they should be asked.

The conference participants were clearly more suitable to address the questions of new research directions and research priorities. Even so, there were perceivable difficulties in the definition of new directions in research, and the establishment of research priorities. There are undoubtedly many reasons for this. This is a new field, and hence relatively unstructured and undefined. One is hesitant to derive simple, unidimensional, conceptual frameworks for an inherently complex reality—the reality of women. There are, however, at least two other sources of hesitation. One is the problem of values; the other is the related issue of methodological and conceptual errors and ambiguities, which when unrecognized and unanalyzed distort data collection and subsequent interpretation.

THE PROBLEM OF VALUES

There has been much philosophical debate on the existence of values in science, and on sociology of knowledge issues. As Theodore Sarbin said in the preface of Braginsky & Braginsky's *Mainstream Psychology: A Critique:*

> the Doctors Braginsky have extended the lessons so well taught in their earlier books: what implicit extra-scientific commitments guide much of the activity of the practitioners of the normal science of psychology, that research and practice in psychology are directed by implicit principles and premises that have their origins in politics, in morality, and in bureaucracy. (1974, p. vii.)

While the debate continues, perhaps we should be explicit about both our values and our assumptions (Campbell, 1975). For example, let us assume that the sex-role transcendent personality embodies an ideal, in terms of mental health. Such a person, combining the valued competency characteristics of the male stereotypic role and the valued expressive characteristics of the stereotypic female sex role, would represent a new ideal for both genders. How can we rear our children to be transcendent personalities? What techniques enhance development of competencies and expressive characteristics in boys and girls, and in women and men? Once deciding upon the value of the transcendent personality, certain other questions become irrelevant (e.g., measuring "masculinity" and "femininity," correlates of "sex-role adjustment" in boys and girls).

When one values the sex-role transcendent personality, questions associated with "sex differences" research also align themselves in a different manner. There is less interest in the question of what are the differences between the sexes and the determinants of these differences. Rather, interest focuses on behaviors considered especially important for a variety of reasons. For example, what relates to assertive, rather than passive or aggressive, behavior in boys and girls? Perhaps ways of reaching the valued end point may be somewhat different for the two sexes. The need is not to treat the sexes the same, but to treat them equitably in the sense of effective care to achieve a valued result.

There seemed to be a basically shared humanist valuing among conference participants. There was, however, no generally agreed-upon vision of the ideal humanist world. Since the psychology of women is an intensely value-laden area, new research directions and priorities are more than commonly mixed with value issues. Greater collective value-clarity would thus facilitate research directions. Humanism and empiricism are not mutually exclusive, however. Perhaps it would be wise to distance oneself, as a researcher, from past psychological theories and fields of literature. If past research about women is seen as largely damaging and/or irrelevant, then it might be a good idea to pose the most obvious, basic questions.

At some point, *not* conducting important research, because one cannot readily identify or recognize the theoretical "vehicle," becomes self-defeating and unnecessarily conservative in orientation and effects. Additional questions, and questions not without their imbued values, might start with: What variables, both static and dynamic, seem to facilitate and inhibit both those valued *and* devalued characteristics and behaviors of our society? Such questions assume that our behavior in the present situation reflects the conjoint and interacting contribution of multiple "dimensions." The term "dimensions" can and is used metaphorically. Perhaps not all contributing factors should be conceptualized along dimensional lines. This is but another example of the complex questions confronting researchers in this area.

Research should not be delayed unnecessarily because of recognized deficiencies and uncertainties of methodology, or because of concern about the validity and utility of the scientific experiment.

METHODOLOGY AND CONCEPTUAL PROBLEMS

The psychology of women opens every can of worms in the field of psychology. Predictions for males do not hold true for females, thus revealing the weakness of the theories involved. Sloppy methodology and conceptualization, which would have little social impact in other areas of psychology, become of acute importance to the social risk of females as a group. These errors and confusions constitute a long list of research abuses. One can only hope that reiterating them will serve to alert scholars, editors, and readers to possible trouble spots.

Inferences from Inappropriate Samples

Inferences are drawn about adult human females on the basis of infra-human, male, or childhood and adolescent female results. Is animal research being followed by empirical examination of the evidence in regard to humans? In many cases, the parallel research could be done with humans, but has not been. Clearly, we also cannot conclude that results that hold true for males will hold for females. Some experimenters would like to ignore the sex variable altogether, whereas others consider the introduction of sex of subject into the experimental design as a rather reactionary move that will serve to exaggerate the differences between the sexes. There is no easy answer to these questions. Theoretical and practical use of data is obscured when the sex of the subject is not reported or separately analyzed. On the other hand, many "sex differences" reported in such circumstances will certainly not be attributable to "sex" per se. Unfortunately, researchers often do not go beyond a mere reporting of sex-related differences. This failure to think about the factors involved in producing the obtained differences could leave the impression with the reader that it is not important, or that the differences reflect "error," or that the differences derive from chromosomes and hormones.

Generalizing from results of subjects of one age to those of another age is clearly important. One must look for the ages of the subjects studied, and then at the nature of the conclusions drawn. "Sex differences" found at early ages are not necessarily lifetime differences. Nor, for example, is it true that "sex differences" that emerge later are necessarily not biologically based. It is true that they are *less* likely to be biologically based than are those "sex differences" occurring at birth, but since many behaviors emerge in a biologically timed sequence that extends throughout the lifetime, the assumption cannot be made.

Assumption of unmodifiability

The assumption is frequently made, without a firm factual basis and without explicit statement, that certain behaviors are innate and/or cannot be modified (e.g., skill in spatial perception). A variation of this is the assumption that behaviors cannot be significantly modified after early childhood. Although the evidence for this viewpoint is weak, this assumption lies behind much research, much reporting of research, and much funding of research. The political consequences for such an implicit assumption could be enormous.

Statistical Errors

A woeful lack of sophistication is often evident in the use of statistical analyses. For example, some persons remain impressed with findings of significant "sex differences" after comparing 1,000 males and 1,000 females. They are unaware that the larger the number of subjects, the smaller the difference needed to be statistically significant. The difference may be of no practical importance. Or, readers may be so mesmerized by the apparent scientific value of such a large sample, that they fail to inquire if other relevant factors are controlled. For example, studies have been reported showing "sex differences" in mathematics performance without controlling for background in mathematics training.

Inferences are sometimes drawn from comparison of the sexes on the basis of statistical tests conducted only *within* sex. For example, a statistically significant difference could be found on a variable for males, but not for females. Some experimenters mistakenly inferred that this variable makes *more* of a difference for males than females, although a statistical test of interaction was never run.

The most fundamental and common error of design, however, has to do with control of conditions. A seed company that accepted the results of studies so poorly controlled as those purporting to investigate "sex differences" would doubtless go bankrupt. The old elementary statistics books carefully spelled out that Seed A and Seed B should be sown at the same time on random plots and thereafter given the same water, fertilizer, insecticide, cultivation, and the like. They would be harvested at the same time and their yield measured, and then the merits of Seed A would be compared with Seed B. Such conditions are, of course, impossible to meet in comparing the two human sexes, but unless these studies explicitly deny that their results cannot permit inferences about sex differences, they allow these misinterpretations.

Language

The lack of precision in the English language contributes to the distortion of research findings. For scientific purposes, using male pronouns to refer to both sexes is simply inadequate. If it occurs nowhere else, at least the neuter, single pronouns should be used in scientific writing. *Tey, ter* and *tem* have the advantages of providing a neuter, single pronoun for each grammatical case.

Interpretive Distortions

Additional problems occur in the manner in which concepts may be labeled. Some labels carry a freight of excess meaning that may be damaging or distorting to women (e.g., "analytical cognitive style," "frigid"). In some instances, results that fit stereotypes are accepted readily. Results, however, that do not fit stereotypes are often ignored or interpreted in a seriously distorted manner. Helson, for example, pointed out that the finding of girls being more creative than boys tends to be ignored. In other instances, findings themselves are interpreted in light of the stereotype. For example, researchers (Sherman, 1971) were surprised to find that, compared to young men, young women rated a variety of acts as more severe transgressions of morality. They concluded that, since "we all know" that females are more emotional, females can be seen as more petty than males (e.g., not more severely sensitive).

The Absence of a Critical Mass

No one knows what the field of psychology would look like if women participated in it equally, at all levels and in all fields. The psychology of women would probably become a recognized area of specialty. It would encompass a variety of topics associated with XX sex: their genetics, anatomy, hormones, and the gender role usually associated with XX persons; their status, the sanctions for noncompliance, the limits of noncompliance, the strategies for moving to a transcendent personality, the psychology of biological and social life events, preparation and planning strategies for young women, psychosomatic and bio-behavioral topics, practical topics related to health, legal status, and child care; attitudes toward women, reactions to women, rape, relations between the sexes, and sexuality. Human psychology would doubtless receive more emphasis.

When it comes to praising and the reporting of research questions, one can suppose that the sexes might differentially attend to certain facets. It seems likely that if studies of achievement behavior for females yield different results than for males, rather than dropping females as subjects for achievement motivation studies, inquiry might be focused on the determinants of female achievement behavior. It seems likely that the continual damaging confusion of motivation and behavior would no longer be so likely to occur. For example, if women do not apply for managerial jobs, it is inferred that they do not want to do so.

Many phenomena are transient, but this part remains unrecognized. Many cross-sectional, longitudinal studies are flawed by cohort effects that render comparisons erroneous. Inferences about women today are drawn from data of another time. Date of collection is often not given.

If traits, universal biologically based stages, and invariant universal principles are not to be found, perhaps more complex, multiplicatively determined models of situation and person variables will yield more powerful results.

Researchers attempting reconceptualization, however, are often handicapped considerably more than persons working in more established fields, since attempting to locate relevant variables and devising ways to measure them does not permit the quick manufacture of technically elegant empirical research with statistically significant findings. Such research is the criterion for professional competence in many departments of psychology. This can be the source of a subtle sexism in disguise, which passes for high standards.

One would hope that the presence of large numbers of women at all levels in psychology would prevent some of the more pompous and egregiously erroneous statements about women (e.g., the cervix is insensitive to pain). Likewise, researchers would be more likely to consider effects on women in various biological phases (e.g., drug effects or even Vitamin C effects may be very different, depending upon whether a woman is menstruating, pregnant, or menopausal).

One suspects that many questions about sexuality would be refocused (e.g., a shift from "frigidity" to duration of intercourse). In actuality, when women became popular as part of the sexual treatment team, the shift went to "whatever each couple finds satisfying." Who would wish to quarrel with such a conciliatory view? However, the point is that the more than token presence of women is necessary to avoid bias. Male researchers, professors, and funding agencies should continue to intensify their efforts to facilitate the professional participation of women at all levels and in all ways.

CONFERENCE CONCLUSIONS

The conference arrived at a general consensus on the need to focus research attention in late childhood and thereafter, rather than concentrating so heavily on the early years. There was considerable recognition of the need for more sophisticated research, the need for less bias in framing questions and interpreting answers, and the need for reconceptualizing whole areas to identify variables and then devising ways to control and measure them. These steps were seen as necessary preconditions to achieving a more accurate understanding of female

In order to provide some further indication of the breadth of ideas produced, some listing of thoughts might be illuminating. Other topics for research included:

- The limits of nonconformity

- Misogyny: the factors influencing it; its benefits and the social contexts that do and do not support it
- Ways of dealing with mental simplicities that incline people to think in dualities and bipolarities, and make them reluctant to tolerate ambiguity

- Status attainment and power tactics among feminist professionals

- Effect on observers of outcomes for models (e.g., the lesson of mother's life)

- Content analysis of literature, television, and fairy tales

- Emotional costs for career-successful women

- Study of effects of specific attitudes (not traits) of women's bodily functioning

- Study of the psychological and social context of "sex differences" in sexual and bodily functioning

- Study of the meaning and value of works

- Positive and negative incentives for work

- Influence of employers and co-workers as situational factors affecting women's work

- Women's critical life events within a developmental perspective

After the conference, Martha Mednick summarized her assessment of research needs as follows:

There is a continuing need, within each of the areas, for a forum for exchanging ideas. Bringing investigators together who are working in similar areas will decrease unnecessary duplication of efforts, avoid some of the methodological and conceptual pitfalls we raised, and most important, move research forward. It may be argued that this is not exclusively a need for those in the psychology of women, but our area is more full of young and less well-heeled investigators than is true of traditional fields and there are as yet no large centers or institutes which might serve such a function. Therefore, in all of our efforts we must push for any and all supports for such exchange. This will also provide a model of collaboration which will enhance accumulation and organization of knowledge in the field and perhaps in psychology as a whole. Senior investigators should be encouraged to support and encourage younger women to be involved, and this might well be one of the criteria to be used in awarding grants and contracts.

In each of the areas we delineate as important, we should stress the need for a taxonomy of behavioral referents. That is, we should always be asking, what are the *outcome* variables that are more important? Stress should be placed on programmatic and theory-based research. When descriptive work is done, it should be based in a broad context that has spelled out the value of such a data collection.

Those of us at the conference have indeed some sense of our own direction and what is needed. It is to be hoped that women with research interests in the psychology of women will be hired and promoted in our colleges and universities. It is to be hoped that their research will be funded and their results published. If not, our talking will have been in vain and the intellectual castration of the female caste may be expected to continue.

Although not a purpose of this conference, meetings such as this one can have the effect of laying bare the lie that there are no good data about women, and that there are no qualified female professionals engaged in meaningful theorizing and research on women. The message is clear to policy planners and funding agencies. Hopefully, a renaissance has begun.

REFERENCES

Braginsky, B.M. & Braginsky, D.D. *Mainstream psychology: A critique.* New York: Holt, Rinehart and Winston, Inc., 1974.

Campbell, D.T. On the conflicts between biological and social evolution and between psychology and more tradition. *American Psychologist,* December, 1975, *30* (12), 1103-1126.

Sherman, J.A. *On the psychology of women.* Springfield: Charles C. Thomas, 1971.

INDEX